国际会议现场 1

国际会议现场 2

韦钰院士主持会议讨论

授予小泉英明教授东南大学“名誉教授”仪式

授予奈森·福克斯教授“客座教授”仪式

International Symposium on cutting-Edge Research of Early Child Development

2014.5.18th -21st Nanjing China

国际会议合照

International Symposium on Cutting-edge Research of Early Child Development

儿童早期发展前沿研究
国际会议论文集

柏 毅 主编

东南大学出版社
SOUTHEAST UNIVERSITY PRESS
·南 京·
NANJING

内 容 简 介

当前，儿童早期发展得到了前所未有的重视。世界各国都相继调整了儿童早期发展的政策。我国也面临着改革儿童早期发展的大好机遇。在《国家中长期教育改革和发展规划纲要(2010—2020年)》中，儿童早期发展成为一个新的亮点，得到各级政府、社会和家庭的高度重视。“学前教育三年行动计划”执行效果明显，下一步的发展计划即将启动。同时，儿童早期发展的研究与实践发展迅速，国际上启动了一系列研究和实践项目，特别是在脑科学研究的指导下，取得了许多重要进展。总结近年来的实践经验，借鉴国内外研究成果，有效规划未来儿童早期发展势在必行。本次国际会议邀请了国内外儿童早期发展研究领域的重要专家，共同交流探讨脑科学的最新进展对儿童早期发展的影响，有效促进我国儿童早期发展的研究与实践。

图书在版编目(CIP)数据

儿童早期发展前沿研究国际会议论文集 / 柏毅主编. —南京:东南大学出版社,2014.9

ISBN 978-7-5641-5185-0

Ⅰ.①儿… Ⅱ.①柏… Ⅲ.①儿童教育—早期教育—国际学术会议—文集 Ⅳ.①G61-53

中国版本图书馆CIP数据核字(2014)第208868号

儿童早期发展前沿研究国际会议论文集

主　　编	柏　毅
出版发行	东南大学出版社
出 版 人	江建中
社　　址	南京市四牌楼2号
邮　　编	210096
经　　销	全国新华书店
印　　刷	虎彩印艺股份有限公司
开　　本	700 mm×1000 mm　1/16
印　　张	32
字　　数	612千字
版　　次	2014年9月第1版
印　　次	2014年9月第1次印刷
书　　号	ISBN 978-7-5641-5185-0
定　　价	80.00元

(本社图书若有印装质量问题，请直接与营销部联系。电话:025-83791830)

序　言

由于近几十年来科学和技术的发展，特别是无损伤脑成像技术和分子生物学的发展，使得人类对自我的认知产生了质的飞跃。在哲学研究的主流领域，认为人的心智和脑的生物存在并无关联的两元论被摒弃了，从而在许多相关领域中出现了颠覆性的创新。教育在塑造着人的灵魂，必然是与此变革相关的重要领域。教育发展和改革迎来了一个绝好的机遇，一个新的重要的教育学发展方向——神经教育学诞生了。

在神经教育学的领域中，最早产生重大影响的成果就是指出了早期儿童发展的重要性。来自发育心理学、认知科学、神经科学、人类学和经济学不同的研究结果汇集在一起，得出了十分一致和重要的结论：儿童早期的经历对人的感知、语言、认知能力、社会情绪能力、健康具有独特而强大的影响；早期儿童脑的可塑性最好，存在某些功能发展的最佳发展期，同时也是容易受到伤害的敏感时期，特别是对处于不利状况的儿童更需要及早进行支持和帮助。儿童的早期发展状况会影响到一个国家未来劳动者的素质健康和工作效率、国民的生活质量以及社会的公平、稳定与发展。

基于来自实证性科学研究的结果，在世纪之交，许多国家，包括发达国家和发展中国家，都相继调整了他们早期儿童发展的国家政策。联合国教科文、联合国儿童基金会（UNICEF）、世界卫生组织（WHO）、经济合作与发展组织（OECD）和世界银行（WB）相继发表了明确的对国家政策制定的指导意见。在中国2010年公布的《国家中长期教育改革和发展规划纲要(2010—2020年)》(以下简称《纲要》)中,儿童早期发展成为了新的亮点。《纲要》中对早期儿童教育和发展的重视,正确地反映了近三十年来科学研究的新成就,以及早期儿童发展的国际趋势。《纲要》的制定为我国早期儿童发展和教育提供了重要的历史机遇,随后教育部又成功地实施了早期教育三年行动计划。

当前,当务之急是要普及有关的科学知识,培训养育者,包括家长和教师。要做好培训,首先相当部分的教育专家们要更新观念,认真学习新的知识。这些新的科学研究成果是近二三十年中新出现的,是十分重要的,但是也是很多人不熟悉的,这些知识更新很快。必须清醒地认识到,两元论已经被颠覆了,不依靠科学研究,而只靠直觉和经验来指导儿童发展不仅低效,还会对儿童的发展造成伤害,今天仍然不考虑脑科学的心理学是落伍的学科。

2002年,东南大学正式成立了研究神经教育学的学习科学研究中心(以下简称中心),继而在教育部的支持下,成立了儿童发展与学习科学教育部重点实验室。中心致力于实证性的转化教育学研究,特别是神经教育学的研究。在诸多的研究方向中,中心一直把对儿童早期发展的研究作为重点研究方向。中心的研究具有两个很鲜明的特点:一是努力站在国际研究的前沿,进行转化研究;二是紧密围绕我国教育改革和发展的需要,包括国家宏观政策制定的需要来进行。

2007年11月,全国政协教科文卫体委员会会同国务院妇女儿童工作委员会、教育部、卫生部、全国妇联、中国科协共同举办了“儿童早期发展高层论坛”,中心是主要的协办单位。会议上,全国人大副委员长顾秀莲同志,以及国务院妇女儿童工作委员会副主任黄晴宜同志都作了重要发言,会议主要汇集了国内外早期儿童发展的专家,包括专程前来参加会议的世界银行专家 Mary E. young 和 J. Fraser Mustard。会议的成功举办,有力地推动了我国早期儿童发展国家政策的制定和研究工作的开展。

在上述会议的前后,中心相继举办过多次有关早期儿童发展的国际会议,包括在2005年4月、2006年6月和2009年6月举办的三次有关儿童社会情绪能力培养的国际会议,以及在2008年10月举办的神经教育学的国际会议。这些会议都对我国儿童早期发展的研究起到了重要的带领作用。

近期的科学研究揭示,早期发展不等同于幼儿园教育,更不是要把小学的课程提前教给幼儿。盲目地提出所谓“不要输在起跑线上”的说法是错误的。在许多方面,0

到3岁的幼儿发展比4到6岁的幼儿园教育更为重要。在我国当前的早期发展中必须关注近期科学研究的新成果。为此中心经过一年多的认真筹备，于2014年5月在南京召开了"儿童早期发展前沿研究国际会议"。会议邀请到来自美国、加拿大、英国、日本4国及联合国教科文组织和联合国儿童基金会的共10位著名专家，专家们在会上作了重要的发言，介绍了他们在这个领域中最新的研究进展和教育实践经验。我国主要专家学者也出席了会议，和国际同行交流了我们的研究和实践经验。会议对于指导和推动我国当前的儿童早期发展的研究和政策制定具有十分重要的意义。

会议上专家报告的内容十分重要，例如美国科学院院士Fox教授介绍了他们国际专家团队在罗马尼亚孤儿院近十年的研究结果，指出0到3岁存在着关键期；美国哈佛大学研究生院院长Fischer教授介绍了基于脑的不间断和不均匀发展的动态理论；英国剑桥大学Leong教授介绍了关于儿童语言发展的研究；日本小泉英明教授介绍了关于日本早期发展计划和评测仪器的发展。此外还有加拿大魁北克省儿童早期发展实践项目，美国华盛顿州在哈佛大学支持下的关于儿童执行功能的早期发展项目，联合国儿童基金会专家和国际脑、心智、教育学会主席发言，等等，都具有十分重要的指导意义。国内专家的报告也反映了我们在这方面研究工作的快速进展。

感谢中心的同志在柏毅教授的组织下，完成了会议论文集的编辑任务，使这次会议的成果能够惠及更多的人群，这正是此次会议的目的。

韦钰

2014年12月31日

CONTENTS

目录

议题1　儿童早期发展的内容和教育标准的制定及其科学依据

…… 001

Are There Sensitive Periods for the Effects of Early Experience on Cognitive and Social Competence?
Lessons from the Bucharest Early Intervention Project
Nathan A. Fox

…… 002

Driving Science-Based Innovation to Reduce Intergenerational Disparities in Learning, Behavior, and Health: Creating a New Era in Policy and Practice
Jason Gortney

…… 003

Learning and Development Guide for Children Ages 3—6: Finding Foothold in China's Native Culture and Reality
Xiaoxia Feng

…… 004

Perception of Parental Raring and Adolescents' Self-esteem, Depression and Autonomy of Academic Motivation: A Mediation Model
Ping Zhong, Zongbao Liang, Huihua Deng, Zuhong Lu

…… 005

Association between Parental Attachment and Parenting Styles
Yinping Zhang, Yapeng Liu, Yin Zhu, Guangzhen Zhang, Zongbao Liang, Zuhong Lu, Huihua Deng

…… 014

The Influence of Experiential Learning on Pupils' Creative Personality Development
Canming Wang, Zhiyan Gu, Yifeng Yan, Zhiquan Zhang
…… 020

Research Progress in the Relations between Parental Marital Conflict and Problem Behaviors in Children
Xueli Yang
…… 033

The Effects of Positive Emotions on Children "Learning by Doing"
Di Wu, Xiaolin Lai
…… 040

Effects of Growing-class on the Development of the Remote Association Ability Among Elementary Students
Jie Zhao, Zhu Deng, Qing Yan
…… 045

Association between Adolescents Friendship Quality and Social Anxiety: Maternal Psychological Adjustment as a Moderator
Ping Zhong, Zongbao Liang, Huihua Deng, Zuhong Lu
…… 048

议题 2　儿童早期发展的前沿研究成果和关键问题
…… 057

The Science of the Individual
Kurt W. Fischer
…… 058

The Impact of Neuroeducation on "Learning by Doing" Project
Yu Wei
…… 059

The Illusion of Understanding: In the Classrooms and Beyond
Marc Schwartz
…… 063

iECD: From Research to Implementation
Robert W. Scherpbier
…… 064

The Dynamic Brain: Measuring Growth and Learning
Kurt W. Fischer
…… 065

Parents' Control and Children's Adjustment and Their Relations in Migrant and Nonmigrant Children
Guangzhen Zhang, Zongbao Liang, Ning Jiang, Huihua Deng
…… 066

Problems and Solutions in K-2 STEM Education: A Chinese Case
Zhaoning Ye, Yan Ye, Yu Chen
…… 073

The Importance and Social Policies of Early Environment and Experience for Children: A Review of Brain Based Researches
Yanwei Li, Dongchuan Yu
…… 080

The Intervention and Assessment of High-Risk Infants: A Review
Chen Li, Xuejun Kang, Yuan Song
…… 089

Association of Hair Cortisol with Somatic Complaints and Schizoid Behavior among Autistic Children
Xinliang Qi, Qiaozhen Xie, Wei Gao, Hengzu Pan, Xiaoyan Ke, Huihua Deng, Zuhong Lu
…… 094

The Antecedents and Consequence of Perceived discrimination among Chinese Migrant Children
Ning Jiang, Guangzhen Zhang
…… 099

Progress in Research of Non-invasive Biomarkersin Autism Children
Kangwei Shen, Dongchuan Yu, Chen Li
…… 110

Guardian Role Weakening Restriction and Auxiliary Measures of Left-behind Children's Social Development
Xiaorong Wang
…… 116

A Study on Teaching of Using Conflict Strategy to Promote Preschool Children's Conceptual Change: Taking the "Sinking and Floating" Concept as an Example
Fang Wang
...... 122

The Role of Stigma Experience and Perception in Chinese Migrant Children's School Adjustment
Guangzhen Zhang, Ning Jiang, Zongbao Liang, Huihua Deng
...... 134

Analysis on Preschoolers' Fine Motor Skills for Self-caring
Yibin Zhang, Jiabin Li, Chao Xue, Jinliang Qin
...... 140

Interventions of Children's Executive Function: A Review
Lei Zhao, Yuankui Yang
...... 146

Literature Review on the Relationship between Internet Addiction and Family Factors among Adolescents
Shuang Ji
...... 157

Developmental Cognitive Neuroscience of Arithmetic Ability: Implication for Math Training
Yolanda Binglei Zhao
...... 164

Association of chronic stress and the ratio of cortisol to cortisone for mothers with children in developmental disorders
Xingliang Qi, Jing Zhang, Yapeng Liu, Zheng Chen, Huihua Deng
...... 172

A Case Study on Primary Problem Student in Yemen
Alhashedi Sena Abdulkarem Noman
...... 178

Design and Algorithm Implementation of Children's Arm Motion Detection System
Liang Sheng, Yangtao Li, Dongchuan Yu
...... 184

The Mediation Effect of Adolescents' Study and Interpersonal Stress on the Relationship between Positive School Climate and Depression
Youyun Xu, Huihua Deng
...... 192

议题3　神经科学视野下儿童社会情绪能力发展的研究

…………………………………………………………………………………… 199

What Can We Learn from the Longitudinal and Genetically Informed Study of Birth Cohorts? Findings from Two Quebec Cohorts
Michel Boivin
…………………………………………………………………………………… 200

The Behavioral Features and Brain Mechanisms of Emotional Cognition in Infants
Yuejia Luo
…………………………………………………………………………………… 201

Early Experience, Brain Development, and Early Childhood Education
Nathan A. Fox
…………………………………………………………………………………… 202

Development and Social-Cultural Learning of Cooperation: Sharing Behaviors in China's Only Children and Children with Siblings
Liqi Zhu
…………………………………………………………………………………… 203

Maternal Depression Moderates Effects of Early Child Emotionality on Parenting Styles
Ying Zhu, Yapeng Liu, Yinping Zhang, Guangzhen Zhang, Zongbao Liang, Huihua Deng
…………………………………………………………………………………… 204

Study on Clinical Efficacy of Early Development in High-risk Infants by Health and Education Partnership
Xinglian Liu, Qiong Dai, Haiqing Xu
…………………………………………………………………………………… 211

Predictive Models of Autism Spectrum Disorder(ASD) of Children Based on Neuroimaging Technology
Kun Bi, Chu Liu, Qing Lu, Zhijian Yao
…………………………………………………………………………………… 220

Association of Paternal Mental Health and Preschoolers' Behavioral Problems: The Moderating Role of Child Negative Emotionality
Yapeng Liu, Guangzhen Zhang, Zongbao Liang, Zuhong Lu, Huihua Deng
…………………………………………………………………………………… 233

A Quantitative Analysis on the International Literatures about Emotional Development in Early Childhood Base on WOS Database
Yufei Yang, Lin Ye, Yangyang Liu
…… 240

Behavioral and Event-related Potential Studies of Preschoolers' Expression Cognition of Cartoon Face and Real Face
Jingmei Wang, Xian Zheng, Xiaoqun Zhang, Xiaoya Zheng, Yingjun Lu, Jinliang Qin
…… 252

The Impact of Internet on Youth Socialization
Liu Yang, Xuesong Li
…… 271

Advances in Brain Mechanism of Social Exclusion
Jili Zhang, Yue Leng
…… 276

议题 4　神经科学视野下儿童语言发展的研究
…… 289

Neuroimaging Studies of Early Language Development, Reading and Reading Disability: An Update on Recent Findings
Kenneth R. Pugh
…… 290

Deficits of Visual Magnocellular Stream in Chinese Children with Developmental Dyslexia
Hongyan Bi
…… 291

The Child as a "Naive Engineer": How the Brain Extracts Phonology from the Speech Signal and Implications for Dyslexia
Vicky Leong
…… 292

Development of Reading in Adults with Atypical Hemispheric Dominance for Speech and in Young Children
Qing Cai
…… 293

The Emotional Processing in Chinese Sentence Comprehension: A Near-infrared Spectroscopy Study
Shengnan Guo, Xuesong Li, Xiaoxiang Chen
·· 294
Human Identity Verification Based on Heart Sounds
Jinzhou Cai, Lanyi Liu, Jun Xu, Duyang Li, Zhuoqian Li
·· 301
Classification of Emotion in Chinese Words Based on EEG
Minmin Cheng, Haixian Wang, Zuhong Lu
·· 312
Plasticity, Sensitive Period and Language Development
Wei Song, Hongli Xue
·· 317

议题 5　儿童早期发展的评测方法与工具

·· 327
Optical Topography Noninvasive brain imaging method for early child development studies
Hideaki Koizumi
·· 328
Affective Computing and Social-Emotional Competence Assessment
Wenming Zheng
·· 331
Assessment and Training of Children's Social Emotion Competency
Renlai Zhou
·· 332
Development and Education of Academically Supernormal Children in Mainland China in the Last 35 Years
Jiannong Shi
·· 334
A Study of K-12 STEM Education in America: A Trend of Integrated STEM Education
Xuan Zeng, Yi Bai
·· 335

Synchronization Likelihood of Whole-brain Functional Connectivity on Resting-state：A MEG Study of Depression
Chu Liu, Qing Lu, Kun Bi, Zhijian Yao
…… 342

An Overview of Technology and Design Education Development in England
Jing Xu, Yi Bai
…… 352

A Novel Method for Psychological Assessment Based on the Analysis of VOCs in Exhaled Breath
Shibing Yu, Xuejun Kang, Yan Yan, Siwei Deng, Xiaoxiao Wu
…… 359

The Research of Technology and Engineering Literacy Assessment and Test Paper Based on Computers for the 2014 National Assessment of Educational Progress in the United States
Yan Xu, Yi Bai
…… 364

Study on Selection Operator in Feature Selection of Physiological Signals Based on Genetic Algorithms
Yun Liu
…… 375

A Pilot Investigations of the Effects of Gender, Diurnal Variation, and Age in Children Salivary Imidazole Compounds Profiles
Zhao Zhang, Xuejun Kang, Lei Ma, Yu Wang, Xiaoxiao Wu
…… 384

The Study on Development Situation of Information and Communication Technology Education in China, Singapore, Korea and Japan—Base on PISA2012 ICT Questionnaire Data
Zhishan Liu, Yi Bai
…… 389

Rapid and Automated Determination of Salivary α-amylase by Flow Injection Analysis for Children Exercise Stress Response Research
Lei Ma, Yu Wang, Yuan Ying, Biao Sun, Xiaobo Cai, Xuejun Kang
…… 400

In Exploring on Science Teacher Training Model in England—A Case Study of York University
Yingsi Qi, Yi Bai
…… 408
Development of a Parenting Assessment Tool for Chinese Parents of Infants/Toddlers
Lijun Wang, Zonghan Zhu, Yaohua Dai, Xiaohua Xie, Aihua Liu, Ni Jia
…… 415
The Revelation of Primary Science Curriculum Evaluation from PISA and TIMSS
Jia Liu, Yi Bai
…… 427
Influence of Sensory Integration Level on Children's Breaststroke Learning Outcomes
Yang Liu, Lei Ma, Chao Du
…… 433
A Comparative Study of Elementary School Science Curriculum and TIMSS Test Objective
Yexin Zhang, Yi Bai
…… 444
Online Science Education Evaluation System Research Based on iOS systems
Ruoyun Xu, Xiaojun Xia
…… 450
Histidine in Saliva of Child Response to Stress Task and Impact of Age
Xiaoxiao Wu, Xuejun Kang, Lei Ma, Yu Wang, Zhao Zhang, Shibing Yu
…… 457
Gender and Age Differences of Steroids in Human Hair
Shifei Li, Jing Zhang, Youyun Xu, Yijiang Chen, Zheng Chen, Wei Gao, Huihua Deng
…… 463
The Development of Chinese Early Childhood Environment Rating Scale (CECERS) and Its Initial Validation
Kejian Li, Biying Hu, Jiayi Chen, Xuejiao Qin, Jinliang Qin
…… 470

议 题

儿童早期发展的内容和教育标准的制定及其科学依据

Are There Sensitive Periods for the Effects of Early Experience on Cognitive and Social Competence? Lessons from the Bucharest Early Intervention Project

Nathan A. Fox

Distinguished University Professor

University of Maryland

Developmental psychologists and educators assume that early experiences shape the brain and neural circuitry for emerging cognitive and social behaviors over the first years of life. Most of the evidence for these assumptions is based on rodent and non human primate animal research. Far less has been published on the effects of early experience that is not correlational in nature. The Bucharest Early Intervention Project (BEIP) is the first randomized trial of a family intervention for children who experienced significant psychosocial neglect early in their lives. A group of infants living in institutions in Romania were recruited and randomized to be taken out of the institution and placed into family/foster care homes or to remain in the institution. Follow up of these children occurred at 42 and 54 months of age and at 8 years of age. Multiple domains, including cognitive, socio-emotional, psychiatric, and brain imaging were assessed at each age. Three questions are posed in this study and this talk: first, are there lasting effects of early psychosocial deprivation as children develop over the school years? Second, is intervention successful in ameliorating deficits as a result of institutionalization? And third, are there sensitive periods in delivering the intervention that explain both success and failure to improve cognitive and socio-emotional behavior?

Driving Science-Based Innovation to Reduce Intergenerational Disparities in Learning, Behavior, and Health: Creating a New Era in Policy and Practice

Jason Gortney

community manager at Children's Home Society of Washington

Launched in May 2011 by the Center on the Developing Child of Harvard University, the Frontiers of Innovation (FOI) initiative focuses on the work of a community of researchers, practitioners, policymakers, philanthropists, and experts in systems change from across North America.

The goal of FOI is to bring about substantially improved outcomes for vulnerable young children whose needs (or whose caregivers' needs) are not being fully met by existing policies and programs. To do that, FOI seeks to spur change in the field by forging cross-sector collaborations that prompt creativity, support experimentation, and foster learning from experience.

Washington State represents the cutting edge of the FOI work, with multiple collaborative efforts currently being tested in a variety of settings, exploring new ways to support child development and build caregivers' capacity to provide developmentally supportive environments for young children free from toxic stress. The efforts in Washington State have had a particular focus on strengthening the executive function and self-regulation skills of both children and their caregivers.

This presentation will focus on the framework of innovation used by FOI, providing several real world examples of the process of co-creating and testing new strategies and with a look forward to next steps in the developing initiative.

Learning and Development Guide for Children Ages 3—6: Finding Foothold in China's Native Culture and Reality

Xiaoxia Feng

Professor at Beijing Normal University

In order to provide young children with a suitable, supportive environment, we have to start from raising public awareness about the scientific knowledge on early child development. As a result, the Ministry of Education decides to learn from international experience and develop China's Learning and Development Standard for Children Ages 3—6 (Hereinafter referred to as The Guide) to increase public knowledge about child development, "help kindergarten teachers and parents understand the basic patterns and characteristics of the learning and development of young children ages 3 to 6, establish reasonable goals for child development, and implement scientific child care and education". Development of The Guide (originally called The Standard) took over 6 years, from its formal launching in 2006 till its formal publication in October 2012. While the development group learned from experience and practices from other countries throughout its development work, it pondered ways to adjust the text to suit the cultural psychology and thinking habits of the Chinese public, facilitate understanding and resolve prominent issues in current preschool education, as well as to avoid and alleviate the problems of misreading and misapplication, endeavoring to reflect these thoughts in The Guide. We believe that with the increasing prevalence of The Guide, the quality of Chinese preschool education will improve significantly and life of Chinese children will be happier and healthier!

Perception of Parental Raring and Adolescents' Self-esteem, Depression and Autonomy of Academic Motivation: A Mediation Model

Ping Zhong[1,a], Zongbao Liang[1,b], Huihua Deng[1,c,*], Zuhong Lu[1,d]

[1]Key Laboratory of Child Development and Learning Science of Ministry of Education, Research Center for Learning Science, Southeast University, Nanjing, 210096, China

[a]xiaoxinzp@163.com, [b]liangzongbao225@163.com,

[c]dengrcls@seu.edu.cn, [d]luzuhong@gmail.com

[*] Corresponding author

Keywords: parental raring practice; depression; autonomy of academia motivation; self-esteem; self-determination theory

Abstract: In this study, we examined the effects of perceived maternal and paternal raring practice for adolescents' needs for autonomy and relatedness on the psychological adjustment of young adolescents ($N = 355$) in urban China. Particularly, we examined the mediating effect of self-esteem between the link of parenting and adolescents' depression as well as autonomy of academic motivation. Results showed that both maternal and paternal supports for autonomy indirectly and directly predicted the depression and motivation of adolescents. Particularly, path analysis indicated that adolescents' self-esteem mediated the link between maternal support for autonomy and adolescents' depression, extrinsic and intrinsic academic motivations. Though paternal support for autonomy did not predict the self-esteem of adolescents, the control and punishment from fathers predicted the depression of adolescents.

青少年感知父母教养与抑郁、学习自主性的关系：自尊的中介作用

钟萍[1,a]，梁宗保[1,b,*]，邓慧华[1,c]，陆祖宏[1,d]
[1]儿童发展与学习教育部重点实验室，东南大学学习科学研究中心，南京，210096，中国
[a]xiaoxinzp@163.com，[b]liangzongbao225@163.com，
[c]dengrcls@seu.edu.cn，[d]luzuhong@gmail.com
*通讯作者

关键词：父母教养方式；抑郁；学习自主性；自尊；自我决定理论

中文摘要：青春期是个体寻求自我认同和实现的重要阶段。本研究探讨了父母教养方式对青少年心理适应性的影响路径。研究选取南京市三所初中的355名学生，考察青少年感知到的母亲和父亲的温暖教导、控制惩罚和自主鼓励分别对其自尊、抑郁和学习自主性水平的影响及青少年自尊在父母教养和抑郁、学习自主性水平之间的中介作用。结果表明，母亲的自主鼓励通过青少年自尊的完全中介效应分别间接负向预测其抑郁水平和外在学习动机，间接正向预测内在学习动机；父亲的自主鼓励直接正向预测青少年的内在学习动机，控制惩罚直接正向预测抑郁水平。母亲的温暖教导直接正向预测青少年的外在学习动机，以及母亲和父亲的控制惩罚都直接正向预测内在学习动机。

1 引言

青春期是个体寻求自我认同和实现的重要阶段[1]。面对学业、生活和自我发展的压力，很多青少年开始出现低自尊、抑郁、学业不良以及攻击等心理和行为问题。父母对青少年健康发展有着重要的影响[2]。大量研究表明，父母对青少年的无条件接纳和理解，对其自主活动的支持，可以正向预测青少年稳定的高自尊水平[3,4]。父母对孩子的无条件温暖、指导和鼓励会促使他们逐渐内化和认同学习活动的价值，在学习过程形成稳定的高自尊，从而学习成为具有较自主水平的非工具性活动或任务卷入活动[5]。反之，父母对孩子的条件性控制，既将关爱和认同作为控制手段要求孩子按照自己要求行动，孩子无法达到时就批评、冷漠和指责，可以正向预测青少年的内疚感、羞愧感和条件性自尊[6]。例如，研究发现父母的条件性控制虽然可以令青少年完成父母对其学业成绩的要求，但同时会形成不稳定的自尊水平以及对父母的怨恨和反感，学习成为具有较低自主水平的工具性活动或是自我卷入活动[7,8]。可见，父母的控制与指责对青少年的自尊心水平有显著影响。自尊对青少年心理适应性的各个方面也有重要影响。例如，跨文化研究表明父母的温暖通过青少年的自尊影响其抑郁症

状[9]。然而,现有父母养育方式和青少年心理适应性的影响的研究中,大多考察养育方式的直接作用,对自尊的中介作用研究较少。因此本文重点探讨青少年自尊在父母养育方式对其抑郁和学习自主性的中介作用。

此外,在现有父母教养方式的研究中,大多数考察的是母亲或父母总体的教养方式,父亲和母亲的教养方式分别探讨的研究相对较少[10],对于母亲与父亲教养方式与青少年心理适应性关系的研究结论尚需探讨。

基于上述问题,本研究重点考察以下问题:第一,青少年感知到的父母教养方式对自尊、抑郁和学习自主性的影响以及教养方式是否通过青少年自尊水平的中介作用间接影响抑郁和学习自主性;第二,青少年感知到的父亲和母亲不同教养方式的影响机制的差异。针对研究问题,提出以下假设:第一,青少年可以感知到的父母温暖教导和自主鼓励正向预测自尊水平和内在学习动机,负向预测抑郁水平和外在学习动机,惩罚控制负向预测自尊水平和内在学习动机,正向预测抑郁水平和外在学习动机,自尊水平在教养方式各维度与抑郁、学习自主性的关系之间起到中介作用;第二,青少年感知到的母亲教养方式对其心理适应性和学习动机的影响机制与父亲的影响机制不同。

2 研究方法

2.1 被试

本研究采用分层随机抽样法,选取南京市教学水平为高、中、低的三所初级中学初一年级的355名学生(平均年龄为12.25岁,$SD=0.56$)为被试,其中女生204名(57.5%),男生151名(42.5%)。

2.2 数据收集

数据收集于2006年秋季。分析数据和量表复合效化数据,选取自习时间进行施测,学生问卷完成时间约为40分钟。

2.3 研究工具

采用简版《儿童抑郁量表》(Children's Depression Inventory: Short Version)[11]测量青少年的抑郁状况。量表共10题,每题由三个程度不同的陈述组成,被试根据自己两周内的状况选择最符合自己的陈述。CDI在中国有较好的信效度[12]。本研究中该量表的内部一致性信度为$\alpha=0.75$。

研究采用《Rosenberg自尊量表》(Rosenberg Self-Esteem Scale)[13]测量青少年的自尊状况。量表共10题,被试根据个人情况选择选项,其中五道题反向计分。SES在中国有较好的信效度[14]。本研究中该量表的内部一致性信度为$\alpha=0.79$。

研究采用《儿童教养方式问卷》(The Children Rearing Practice Report)[15]测量儿

童青少年的父母养育方式。本研究选取其中20道题采用5点计分编制为青少年父母教养方式问卷(如:在很多事情上,我妈妈/爸爸让我自己作决定),分为温暖教导(6题)、惩罚控制(7题)和自主鼓励(7题)三个维度;采用5点计分(1=完全不符合,2=不太符合,3=有点符合,4=比较符合,5=完全符合)。被试根据自己感知到的父亲或母亲的教养方式分别填写父亲版CRPR和母亲版CRPR。运用SEM进行验证性因素分析检验量表结构,结果表明将量表题目分为三个维度是合适的。温暖教导、惩罚控制和自主鼓励三个维度的内部一致性系数α分别为0.87(0.85)、0.81(0.80)、0.78(0.81)。其中,括号外为父亲版CRPR统计数据,括号内为母亲版CRPR统计数据。复合效度检验指标良好。

2.4 《学习动机问卷》

研究采用自编的《学习动机问卷》(Academic Motivation Questionnaire)测量青少年的学习自主性水平。AMQ为4点量表,分为内在动机和外在动机两个维度,每个维度包含4个题(如:我认为学习是件有趣的事情,1=完全不符合;2=不太符合;3=比较符合;4=完全符合)。运用SEM进行验证性因素分析检验量表结构,结果表明将量表题目分为两个维度是合理的。本研究中,内在动机和外在动机两个维度的内部一致性系数α分别为0.66、0.67。复合效度检验指标良好。

3 数据分析与结果

3.1 统计方法

研究采用SPSS16.0对研究变量进行相关分析。采用LISREL8.70[16]进行路径分析。中介效应采用联合显著性检验[17]和PRODCLIN2程序检验[18]。

3.2 结果

3.2.1 变量之间的相关系数

如表1所列,父亲和母亲的温暖教导和自主鼓励分别与青少年的自尊水平和内在学习动机呈显著正相关,与抑郁水平呈显著负相关;父亲和母亲的控制惩罚分别与自尊水平呈显著负相关,与青少年的抑郁水平和外在学习动机呈显著正相关;母亲的控制惩罚与青少年的学习内在动机呈显著负相关。青少年自尊水平与抑郁水平、外在学习动机呈显著负相关,与内在学习动机呈显著正相关。

表1 研究变量相关分析

	抑郁水平	自尊水平	母亲温暖教导	母亲控制惩罚	母亲自主鼓励	父亲温暖教导	父亲控制惩罚	父亲自主鼓励	学习外在动机	学习内在动机
抑郁水平	1.00									
自尊水平	−0.54**	1.00								
母亲温暖教导	−0.37**	0.24**	1.00							
母亲控制惩罚	0.34**	−0.21**	−0.59**	1.00						
母亲自主鼓励	−0.37**	0.32**	0.69**	−0.48**	1.00					
父亲温暖教导	−0.33**	0.29**	0.52**	−0.27**	0.50**	1.00				
父亲控制惩罚	0.28**	−0.21**	−0.20**	0.46**	−0.20**	−0.45**	1.00			
父亲自主鼓励	−0.26**	0.24**	0.40**	−0.22**	0.60**	0.71**	−0.36**	1.00		
学习外在动机	0.19**	−0.22**	−0.07	0.14**	−0.07	−0.03	0.15**	−0.01	1.00	
学习内在动机	−0.31**	0.32**	0.36**	−0.14**	0.37**	0.30**	−0.06	0.32**	0.14**	1.00

$N=355$ * $p<0.05$(双尾检验) ** $p<0.01$(双尾检验)

3.2.2 母亲教养方式对青少年抑郁和学习动机的影响:自尊的中介作用

建立包括测量变量和潜在变量在内的全模型,即以母亲教养方式的温暖教导、控制惩罚和自主鼓励为预测变量,青少年的自尊为中介变量,以抑郁、内在学习动机和外在学习动机为结果变量。该模型拟合指数为:WLSχ^2 = 1 706.83,df = 1 062,WLSχ^2/df = 1.61,RMSEA = 0.041,CFI = 0.96,NNFI = 0.96,表明该模型拟合良好。显著的标准化路径系数如图1所示。

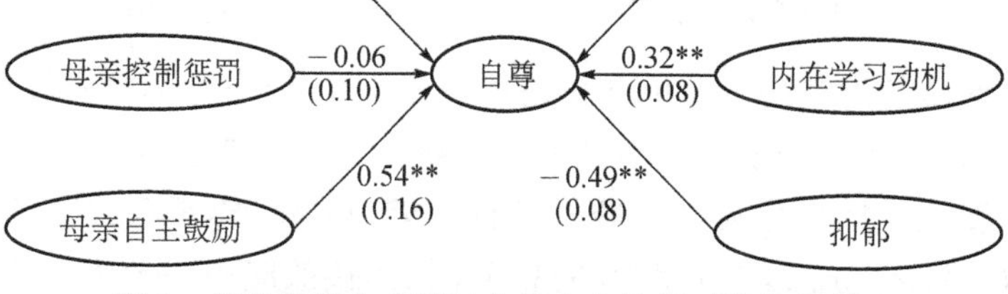

图1 母亲教养方式通过自尊中介作用对抑郁和学习自主性水平影响的非标准化路径结构(* $p<0.05$ ** $p<0.01$)

根据图 1 所示的潜在变量非标准化路径的显著性，对自尊的中介效应进行联合显著性检验，分析只有在自主鼓励—自尊路径中 $\hat{\alpha}$ 显著，三条路径中 $\hat{\beta}$ 全都显著，因此只有在自主鼓励—自尊—外在学习动机、自主鼓励—自尊—内在学习动机、自主鼓励—自尊—抑郁三条路径中，自尊的完全中介效应显著。根据潜在变量非标准化路径系数及其标准差，输入图 1 标出的 $\hat{\alpha}$ 值、$\hat{\beta}$ 值、$\hat{\sigma}_\alpha$、$\hat{\sigma}_\beta$ 以及 $\hat{\alpha}$ 和 $\hat{\beta}$ 的相关（在间接效应中一般为 0）以及 Ⅰ 型错误率（$\alpha = 0.05$），应用 PRODCLIN2 程序直接检验中介效应，结果与联合显著性检验一致，见表 2。

表 2　PRODCLIN2 程序中介作用路径检验结果

中介作用路径	非对称置信区间	显著性
自主鼓励—自尊—外在学习动机	[−0.311，−0.014]	$p < 0.001$
自主鼓励—自尊—内在学习动机	[0.034 2，0.378]	$p < 0.001$
自主鼓励—自尊—抑郁	[−0.526，−0.061]	$p < 0.001$

3.2.3　父亲教养方式对抑郁和学习动机的影响：自尊的中介作用

建立包括测量变量和潜在变量在内的全模型，即以父亲教养方式的温暖教导、控制惩罚和自主鼓励为预测变量，青少年自尊为中介变量，以抑郁、内在学习动机和外在学习动机为结果变量。该模型拟合指数为：$WLS\chi^2 = 1\ 684.38$，$df = 1\ 062$，$WLS\chi^2/df = 1.59$，$RMSEA = 0.041$，$CFI = 0.96$，$NNFI = 0.96$，表明该模型拟合良好。显著的变量标准化路径系数如图 2 所示。

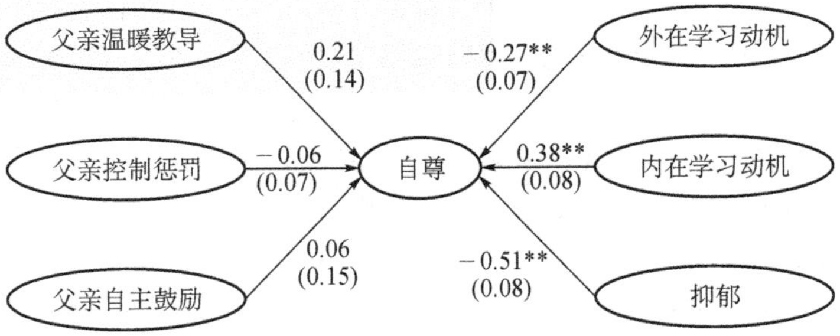

图 2　父亲教养方式通过自尊中介作用对抑郁和学习自主性水平影响的非标准化路径结构 * $p < 0.05$　** $p < 0.01$

根据图 2 所示的潜在变量非标准化路径的显著性，对自尊的中介效应进行联合显著性检验，发现在三条路径中 $\hat{\alpha}$ 全不显著，三条路径中 $\hat{\beta}$ 全都显著，因此中介作用不显著。根据潜在变量非标准化路径系数及其标准差，应用 PRODCLIN2 程序，输入图 2 标出的 $\hat{\alpha}$ 值、$\hat{\beta}$ 值、$\hat{\sigma}_\alpha$、$\hat{\sigma}_\beta$ 以及 $\hat{\alpha}$ 和 $\hat{\beta}$ 的相关（在间接效应中一般为 0）以及一型错误率（$\alpha = 0.05$），直接检验自尊中介效应，结果与联合显著性检验一致。

4 讨论

与以往研究一致[19-21]，本研究证明母亲对孩子的自主支持对于青少年形成高水平的自尊具有重要预测作用。研究表明[22,23]，当青少年的父亲与母亲都更多采取自主鼓励的教养方式时，孩子的自尊将达到最高水平。高自尊会促使青少年对于自我和学业充满信心，避免对成绩和竞争产生过多忧虑以及将学习成绩作为衡量自我价值的工具。

研究结果表明父亲的温暖教导、控制惩罚和自主鼓励对于青少年的自尊没有直接效应，虽然这与我们的研究假设不符，但与很多研究的结论相似[24-25]。我们认为这可能是由于父亲是家庭经济收入的主要来源，他们会将更多的时间投入到工作和应酬中，与孩子相处时间较少，因此不能显著影响孩子的自尊水平。特别是处于青春早期的孩子自尊水平本身就不稳定，父亲的影响作用就更难以体现。从而，自尊在父亲自主鼓励与青少年抑郁、学习自主性关系中的完全中介作用不显著。

本文研究尚有不足需要完善。首先，本研究为横断研究设计，需要长期追踪父母教养方式才可以更为有力深入的探讨其影响作用。其次，本文的数据来源都为青少年，需要来自父母和老师等多方数据来源，数据会更为客观和全面。

综上所述，本文研究结果显示父母教养方式对青少年自尊、抑郁和学习自主性有着中央的影响作用，在母亲的自主鼓励维度的影响路径中，青少年的自尊具有完全中介作用，父母的影响路径有着显著差异。

致谢

本文为教育部科技创新工程重大项目培育资金项目资助（项目批准号 704025），教育部人文社会科学基金（项目批准号 11YJAZH019），江苏省社会科学重大项目（项目批准号 09JYA002）阶段性研究结果之一。

References

[1] E Erikson. Identity: Youth and Crises. New York: Jeffrey Norton Publishers, 1968.

[2] W S Grolnick, C O Kurowski, K G Dunlap. Parental resources and the transition to junior high. Journal of Research on Adolescence, 2000, 10: 465 - 488.

[3] R M Ryan, K Brown. Why we don't need self-esteem: On fundamental needs, contingent love, and mindfulness. Psychological Inquiry, 2003, 14(1): 71 - 76.

[4] R W Tafarodi, N Wild, C Ho. Parental authority, nurturance, and two-dimensional self-esteem. Scandinavian Journal of Psychology, 2010, 51: 294 - 303.

[5] K M Sheldon, A J Elliot. Not all personal goals are personal: Comparing autonomous and

controlled reasons for goals as predictors of effort and attainment. Personality and Social Psychology Bulletin, 1998, 24: 546 - 557.

[6] R M Ryan, K Brown. Why we don't need self-esteem: On fundamental needs, contingent love, and mindfulness. Psychological Inquiry, 2003, 14(1): 71 - 76.

[7] A Assor, G Roth, E L Deci. The emotional costs of parents' conditional regard: A self-determination theory analysis. Journal of Personality, 2004, 72: 47 - 88.

[8] R M Ryan. Control and information in the intrapersonal sphere: An extension of cognitive evaluation theory. Journal of Personality and Social Psychology, 1982, 43: 450 - 461.

[9] P F Susan, C S Chen, E Greenberger. Adolescent self-esteem in cross-cultural perspective: Testing measurement equivalence and a mediation model. Journal of Cross-culture Psychology, 2004, 35: 719 - 733.

[10] V Phares, S Fields, D Kamboukos. Still looking for Poppa. American Psychologist, 2005, 60: 735 - 736.

[11] M Kovacs. The Children's Depression Inventory (CDI) Manual. Toronto: Mult-Health System Inc. 1992.

[12] D Yu, X Li. Preliminary use of the children's depression inventory in China. Chinese Mental Health Journal, 2000, 14: 225 - 227.

[13] M Rosenberg. Society and the Adolescent Self-image. Princeton: Princeton University Press, 1965.

[14] X Q Li, H Zou, R M Wang. The developmental characteristics of temporary migrant children's self-Esteem and its relation to learning behavior and teacher-student relationship in Beijing. Psychological Science, 2008, 31: 909 - 913.

[15] J Block. The Child-Rearing Practices Report (CRPR): A set of Q items for the description of parental socialization attitudes and values. Unpublished manuscript, Institute of Human Development, University of California, Berkeley, 1981.

[16] K Jöreskog, D Sörbom. LISREL 8.70. Chicago: Scientific Software International Inc., 2004.

[17] J Cohen. Applied Multiple Regression/Correlation Analysis for the Behavioral Sciences. New Jersey: Lawrence Erlbaum, 2003.

[18] D P Mackinnon, S M Fritz, J Williams. Distribution of the product confidence limits for the indirect effect: Program PRODCLIN. Behavior Research Methods, 2007, 39: 384 - 389.

[19] V I Chirkov, R M Ryan. Parent and teacher autonomy-support in Russian and U. S. adolescents: Common effects on well-being and academic motivation. Journal of Cross-Cultural Psychology, 2001, 32: 618 - 635.

[20] M F Lynch, J G La Guardia, R M Ryan. On being yourself in different cultures: Ideal and actual self-concept, autonomy support, and well-being in China, Russia, and the United States. The Journal of Positive Psychology, 2009, 4: 290 - 304.

[21] D Rudy, K M Sheldon, T Awong. Autonomy, culture, and well-being: The benefits of inclusive autonomy. Journal of Research in Personality, 2007, 41: 983 - 1007.

[22] R Bulanda, D Majumdar. Perceived parent—child relations and adolescent self-esteem. Journal of Child and Family Studies, 2009, 18(2): 203 - 212.

[23] L G Simons, R D Conger. Linking mother-father differences in parenting to a typology of family parenting styles and adolescent outcomes. Journal of Family Issues, 2007, 28: 212 - 241.

[24] A Milevsky, M Schlechter, S Netter. Maternal and paternal parenting styles in adolescents: Associations with self-esteem, depression and life-satisfaction. Journal of Child and Family Studies, 2007, 16: 39 - 47.

[25] D Laible, G Carlo. The differential relations of maternal and paternal support and control to adolescent social competence, self-worth, and sympathy. Journal of Adolescent Research, 2004, 19: 759 - 782.

Association between Parental Attachment and Parenting Styles

Yinping Zhang, Yapeng Liu, Yin Zhu, Guangzhen Zhang, Zongbao Liang, Zuhong Lu, Huihua Deng[a,*]

Key Laboratory of Child Development and Learning Science of Ministry of Education, Southeast University, Research Center for Learning Science, Southeast University, Nanjing, 210096, China

[a]dengrcls@seu.edu.cn

[*] Corresponding author

Keywords: parental attachment; protection/concern; harsh parenting; acceptance

Abstract: This study aimed to examine association between early parental attachment and parenting styles among 269 children. Parents reported their respective parental attachment relationships at 14 months of age and parenting styles at 24 months of age. Results revealed that mother-child attachment positively predicted maternal acceptance, and did negatively maternal protection/concern and harsh parenting. Father-child attachment positively predicted paternal acceptance and did negatively paternal harsh parenting, but could not predict paternal protection/concern.

Introduction

Family ecosystem suggested that factors concerning parents have important influence on children's psychological development, especially parenting styles[1]. Thus, psychological researchers have focused much attention on factors influencing parenting styles.

There are many factors impacting parenting styles, among which family ecosystem is a significant proximal factor[2]. A great number of past studies had examined parents and child individual characteristics and family environment as predictors. To date, there was lack of research on the prediction of interaction between parents and children (e. g., parental attachment), which may constitute an independent family subsystem[3]. Parental attachment is a special emotional connection between individuality and parents, which is intimate and lasting and provide emotional supports, sense of security and confidence[4,5]. Theoretically, there may be a bidirectional effect between them[1,2] because parental attachment and parenting styles are two different family subsystems[3,6].

However, a plenty of previous empirical studies had focused on the unidirectional influence of parenting styles to parental attachment[7-10]. There are few empirical studies concerning the influence of parental attachment to parenting styles. To our knowledge, only two studies had attempted to examine the influence of parental attachment to parenting. They found that secure attachment in early childhood could increase parental sensitivity[11,12]. Therefore, it needs more empirical research to explore how parental attachment in early childhood impact future parenting styles.

Because mother is primary caregiver in early childhood, lots of previous studies focused principally on maternal parenting and few on paternal parenting. Father shows marked different parenting styles and plays different role and unique effect in children's daily life compared to mother[13-16]. Furthermore, father-child attachment is moderately related to mother-child attachment although they are similar in nature[17,18]. In addition, they have different effects on child development[18,19]. Therefore, it is essential to explore whether the direct effects of parental attachment on parenting styles vary with parents.

The present study aimed to examine the effects of the early parental attachment at child age of 14 months on parenting styles (acceptance, protection/concern, harsh parenting) at child age of 24 months. We hypothesized that parental attachment would have direct effects on parenting styles and that the direct effects of parental attachment on parenting styles would vary with parents.

Materials and Method

Participants

Participants were obtained from a longitudinal international study, Nanjing Metroteen Project. They consisted of 269 children (132 boys and 137 girls) and their parents recruited from a maternal and child service center in Nanjing.

Procedure

Data were collected at two assessment time points. When children were 14 months old, parents reported demographic information and respective parental attachment. When children were 24 months old, parents reported parenting styles, respectively.

Measures

Parental Attachment adapted from Attachment Q-Sort[20], a rating scale (consisting of 18 items), was used to assess mother-child attachment and father-child attachment[21].

Parents were asked to rate how well each item described the child on a 5-point scale (1 = very undescriptive, 5 = very descriptive). A global score of parental ratings of attachment relationship was computed by summing the item scores. It showed good reliability and validity in Chinese sample (Chen et al., 2000). In this study, the internal consistency of the scale was 0.78 for mother-child attachment and 0.83 for father-child attachment, respectively.

Parenting Styles adapted from Child-Rearing Practices Report Q-Sort, a rating scale (on a 5-point scale), was used to assess maternal and paternal parenting[22]. This study focused three dimensions: protection/concern, harsh parenting and acceptance. The internal consistencies for the three dimensions of maternal questionnaire and paternal questionnaire were 0.69, 0.71, 0.78, 0.66, 0.74 and 0.76, respectively.

Statistical methods

Hierarchical multiple linear regression where child gender and education degree were entered as control variables on the first step and parental attachment on the second step was done separately for examining the hypothesis.

Results

As listed in Table 1, mother-child attachment positively predicted maternal acceptance and negatively predicted maternal protection/concern and harsh parenting. As listed in Table 2, father-child attachment positively predicted maternal acceptance and negatively predicted paternal harsh parenting, but did not predict paternal protection/concern.

Table 1 Summary of hierarchical regressions: attachment to mother predicting dimensions of maternal parenting style (n = 269)

	Protection/concern		Harsh parenting		Acceptance	
	ΔR^2	β	ΔR^2	β	ΔR^2	β
Step 1	0.00		0.01		0.00	
child gender		0.05		−0.03		−0.05
education degree		−0.02		0.08		−0.02
Step 2	0.02*		0.04**		0.11***	
mother-child attachment		−0.13*		−0.20**		0.34***

Table 2 Summary of hierarchical regressions: attachment to father predicting dimensions of paternal parenting style ($n = 269$)

	Protection/concern		Harsh parenting		Acceptance	
	ΔR^2	β	ΔR^2	β	ΔR^2	β
Step 1	0.02*		0.00		0.01	
child gender		0.12*		−0.04		−0.04
education degree		0.06		0.03		0.11
Step 2	0.01		0.04***		0.07***	
father-child attachment		−0.09		−0.20***		0.27***

Discussion

Parental attachment in early childhood had expected direct effects on parental parenting styles. It was found that both mother-child and father-child attachments significantly increased maternal acceptance and decreased maternal harsh parenting. These results are consistent with previous findings in past studies. Previous studies found that the mother who had a securely attached child showed significantly higher acceptance score than the mother who had an insecurely attached child[23] and that secure attachment negatively predicted maternal negative parenting[24]. High quality attachment relationship could enhance parents' self-confidence as parents, thereby they may experience more positive emotion and adopt more positive parenting (e. g., warm, support)[25,26]. On the contrary, parents may show more negative parenting in low quality attachment relationship because parents may experience more negative emotion[25,26].

In this study, mothers with high quality of mother-child attachment tended to have less protection/concern. If the quality of mother-child attachment was high, the trust between the child and mother could become stronger. Thus, mother permitted the child to take activities autonomously and then showed less protection/concern[27]. In contrary, mother showed more protection/concern. However, father-child attachment could not predict paternal protection/concern. Attachment to fathers is more associated to children's external world, while attachment to mothers is more associated with children's internal world[17]. Thus, fathers may have high expectation and requirement in children's social development and make children more independent.

The present study demonstrated that parental attachment as an independent subsystem could impact parent's subsystem in family ecosystem. This study also extended the past unidirectional effect of parent's subsystem to child development to the bidirectional influence between parent's subsystem and child subsystem.

Acknowledgement

This study is supported by the Cultivation Fund of the Key Scientific and Technical Innovation Project, Ministry of Education of China *The Longitudinal Study on Child Social-Emotional Development in China: from Gene to Behavior*(704025), the Research Innovation Project in Universities Graduate Students of Jiangsu Province *The Effect of MAOA Genotypes and Parenting on Child Behavioral Problems*(CXLX13_115) and the Special Funds of Basic Scientific Research Operating Expenses in the Central University.

References

[1] B Sang, J Z Xi. A study on the effect mechanism of family ecosystems on development of children's mental health. Psychological Development and Education, 2005, 21: 80 - 86.

[2] U Bronfenbrenner. Ecology of the family as a context for human development: Research perspectives. Developmental Psychology, 1986, 22: 723.

[3] J Byng-Hall. The crucial roles of attachment in family therapy. Journal of Family Therapy, 2008, 30: 129 - 146.

[4] M D S Ainsworth. Attachments beyond infancy. American Psychologist, 1989, 44: 709 - 716.

[5] J Bowlby. Attachment and Loss: Vol. 1, Attachment. 2nd. New York: Basic Books, 1982.

[6] M J Cox, B Paley. Families as systems. Annual Review of Psychology, 1997, 48: 243 - 267.

[7] M S De Wolff, M H van IJzendoorn. Sensitivity and attachment: A meta-analysis on parental antecedents of infant attachment. Child Development, 1997, 68(4): 571 - 591.

[8] L Karavasilis, A B Doyle, D Markiewicz. Associations between parenting style and attachment to mother in middle childhood and adolescence. International Journal of Behavioral Development, 2003, 27: 153 - 164.

[9] N Lucassen, A Tharner, M H Van IJzendoorn, et al. The association between paternal sensitivity and infant-father attachment security: A meta-analysis of three decades of research. Journal of Family Psychology, 2011, 25: 986 - 992.

[10] M A Nievar, B J Becker. Sensitivity as a privileged predictor of attachment: A second perspective on De Wolff and Van IJzendoorns Meta-analysis. Social Development, 2008, 17: 102 - 114.

[11] G L Brown, S C Mangelsdorf, C Neff. Father involvement, paternal sensitivity, and father- child attachment security in the first 3 years. Journal of Family Psychology, 2012, 26: 421 - 430.

[12] M A Easterbrooks, G Biesecker, K Lyons-Ruth. Infancy predictors of emotional availability in middle childhood: The roles of attachment security and maternal depressive symptomatology. Attachment and Human Development, 2000, 2: 170 - 187.

[13] K Adamsons, C Buehler. Mothering versus fathering versus parenting: Measurement equivalence in parenting measures. Parenting: Science and Practice, 2007, 7: 271 - 303.

[14] M A Barnett, M Deng, W R Mills-Koonce, et al. Interdependence of parenting of mothers and

fathers of infants. Journal of Family Psychology, 2008, 22: 561 - 573.

[15]C McKinney, K Renk. Differential parenting between mothers and fathers implications for late adolescents. Journal of Family Issues,2008, 29: 806 - 827.

[16]J Roopnarine, H N Fouts, M E Lamb, et al. Mothers' and fathers' behaviors toward their 3-to 4-month-old infants in lower, middle, and upper socioeconomic African American families. Developmental Psychology, 2005, 41: 723 - 732.

[17]H Steele, M Steele, P Fonagy. Associations among attachments classifications of mothers, fathers and their infants. Child Development, 1996, 67: 541 - 555.

[18]M Veríssimoa, A J Santosa, B E Vaughnb, et al. Quality of attachment to father and mother and number of reciprocal friends. Early Child Development and Care, 2011, 18: 27 - 38.

[19]Y L Liu. An examination of three models of the relationships between parental attachments and adolescents' social functioning and depressive symptoms. Journal Youth Adolescence, 2008, 37: 941 - 952.

[20] E Waters. The Attachment Q-sort. Monographs of the Society for Research in Child Development, 1995, 60: 234 - 246.

[21]X Y Chen, M W Liu, B S Li, et al. Maternal authoritative and authoritarian attitudes and mother-child interactions and relationships in urban China. International Journal of Behavioral Development,2000, 24: 119 - 126.

[22]X Y Chen, P D Hastings, K H Rubin, et al. Childrearing attitudes and behavioral inhibition in Chinese and Canadian toddlers: A cross-cultural study. Developmental Psychology, 1998, 34: 677 - 686.

[23] S K Rosen, F Rothbaut. Quality of parental caregiving and security of attachment. Developmental Psychology, 1993, 29: 358 - 367.

[24]Bates, J E Olson, S L Pettit, et al. Dimensions of individuality in the mother-infant relationship at six months of age. Child Development, 1982, 53(2): 446 - 461.

[25]E K Adam, M R Gunnar, A Tanaka. Adult attachment, parent emotion, and observed parenting behavior: Mediator and moderator models. Child Development, 2004, 75: 110 - 122.

[26]S Y Rueger, R L Katz, H J Risser, et al. Relations between parental affect and parenting behaviors: A meta-analytic review. Parenting: Science and Practice,2011, 11: 1 - 33.

[27]D Laible, T Panfile, D Makariev. The quality and frequency of mother—toddler conflict: Links with attachment and temperament. Child Development, 2008, 79: 426 - 443.

The Influence of Experiential Learning on Pupils' Creative Personality Development

Canming Wang[1,a,*], Zhiyan Gu[2,b], Yifeng Yan[3,c], Zhiquan Zhang[1,d]

[1]Institute of creativity education, Nantong University, Nantong, China

[2]Tongan center elementary school, Suzhou high-tech zone, Suzhou, China

[3]School of Education, Shanghai Normal University, Shanghai, China

[a]china.wcm@126.com, [b]gzy1224@126.com,

[c]yanyifeng@126.com, [d]zzhq110@sina.com

[*]Corresponding author

Keywords: experiential learning; the experiential learning cycle; localized reconstruction; creative personality

Abstract: Under the attacts of instrumental rationalism education mode and examination system, chinese pupils' creative personality come to serious a distortion edge. This study introduced the theory of the most prominent experiential learning expert David A. Kolb's experiential learning theory and reconstruct it locally. Reduce the risk of activity through the simulated situation. carefully designed intresting games, activities and problem solving situation. Using class or spare time to carry out a series of theme activity. The experiment results show that pupils' creative personality is significantly increased whether on overall or on the four dimensions of imagination, challenging, adventure or curiosity. This will open a new way for the cultivating of China's early creative talents.

体验学习对小学生创造性人格发展的影响

王灿明[1,a,*],顾志燕[2,b],严奕峰[3,c],张志泉[1,d]
[1]南通大学创造教育研究所,南通,江苏,中国
[2]苏州市高新区通安中心小学,苏州,江苏,中国
[3]上海师范大学教育学院,上海,中国
[a]china.wcm@126.com,[b]gzy1224@126.com,
[c]yanyifeng@126.com,[d]zzhq110@sina.com
*通讯作者

关键词:体验学习;体验学习圈;本土化重构;创造性人格

中文摘要:在工具理性主义的教育模式与考试制度的夹击之下,我国小学生的创造性人格产生了严重的畸变现象。本研究引进当代世界最杰出的体验学习专家大卫·库伯的体验学习理论并进行本土化重构,通过情境的合理创设降低活动的冒险性,精心设计趣味盎然的游戏、活动和问题解决的情境,利用班会或课余时间开展系列主题活动。实验结果表明,小学生的创造性人格无论是整体水平,还是想象力、挑战性、冒险性、好奇性四个维度都得到显著提升,这也为我国创新人才的早期培养开启出一条新的路径。

1 引言

随着新课程改革的不断深入,建构主义、人本主义和后现代主义对基础教育的影响越来越大,如何创设宽松愉悦、民主和谐的教学情境,实现学生的同化与顺应、认知与情意、个性自由和团队精神的平衡发展,已成为中小学教师普遍关注的话题。在此背景下,风靡全球的体验学习也被引入我国并日益引起研究者的重视。[1-4]

体验学习(Experiential Learning),也译为“体验式学习”“体验性学习”,其思想可以追溯到美国著名哲学家、教育家杜威(John Dewey)的“从经验中学习”。在他看来,“经验是一种主动的尝试和被动的承受的事件,而不是一种认识的事件”[5]。他举例说,一个小孩仅仅把手指伸进火焰,这还不是经验,只有当这个行为和他感受到的剧烈疼痛联结起来时,才构成经验。从此以后,他就知道手指伸进火焰可能被灼伤。因而,学习是一种结果,更是一种过程;是一种体验,更是一种反思。然而,真正把体验学习作为一种崭新的学习方式进行研发的却是德国教育家哈恩(Kurt Hahn),他创建了外展教育学校(Outward Bound School,简称 OBS),利用高山、沙漠、海洋、湖泊、小溪等自然环境,通过精心设计的野外探险活动,为青少年提供挑战自我、磨炼意志、熔炼团队的机会,以激发他们对大自然的热情,增强他们的野外生存能力,“由于这种培训形

式新颖、效果良好,体验学习很快就风靡了整个欧洲的教育培训领域"[6]。20 世纪 60 年代以后,外展教育学校在美国遍地开花,几乎所有的名川大山都能见到 OBS 的踪影,特别是主题式冒险训练(Project Adventure,简称 PA)取得美国联邦教育部的支持以后,体验学习更是在校园里盛行开来。在体验学习领域最具里程碑意义的理论成果是著名学者大卫·库伯(David A. Kolb)的专著《体验学习:让体验成为学习和发展的源泉》。这部开创性的著作用去了库伯教授整整 17 年时间,在美国国家教育研究所和斯宾塞基金的资助下,他不仅系统地探讨了体验学习的概念、过程与结构模型,而且立足于认识论、心理学和生理学研究的最新成果,阐述了体验学习的知识观、发展观和评价观。该书出版后轰动全球,已成为当今世界引用最多、影响最大的体验学习研究的经典名著[7]。在华东师范大学熊川武教授的指导下,笔者将它译为中文出版后,已就其本土化重构展开一系列研究,并取得了初步进展。[8-11]

创造性人格是美国著名心理学家吉尔福德(Joy Paul Guilford)提出的一个新概念,用来代表创造性人物的行为特性的组织方式[12]。通过对创造性天才成长的研究,他认为创造力并不能保障创造成果的产生,真正保障这种成果产生的是创造性人格。中国科学院心理研究所施建农教授认为,创造性人格影响创造力的主要机制是其智力导流量[13]。创造性人格强的人在创造活动中有更多的智力导流量,他们花在创造性活动中的时间更多、注意力更集中,也更执著,所以更容易取得高水平的创造成果;反之,创造性人格弱的人,即使有非凡的智力,因为在创造性活动中缺乏足够的智力导流量,他们也未必会取得很高的创造性成果。北京师范大学林崇德教授通过对三十年来西方创造力研究的审视,也鲜明地提出"创造性人才 = 创造性思维 + 创造性人格",认为:"培养和造就创造性人才,不仅要重视培养创造性思维,而且要特别关注创造性人格的训练[14]。"近年来,我国学者在儿童创造性人格发展领域取得了颇为丰硕的研究成果,对创造性人格的培养也日益引起教育工作者的关注,人们纷纷从课堂教学、课外科技活动、学校德育和美育等多种途径探讨儿童创造性人格的培养问题,但关于体验学习促进儿童创造性人格发展的相关研究还没有新的进展。

基于以上分析,本研究选择东部沿海某省属大学附属小学进行体验学习实验,获取较为全面的实证资料,以期为推进我国创新人才的早期培养、更好地实现十八大提出的"创新人才培养水平明显提高"的奋斗目标探索一条新路径。

2 实验方法

本实验的理论假设是引进体验学习进行实验干预,能够有效地促进儿童创造性人格的发展。研究主要采用教育实验和心理测量相结合的方法,其中教育实验采用等组前后测实验设计,心理测量采用《威廉姆斯创造倾向量表》进行。

2.1 实验对象

经过课题组和实验学校的校长、教导主任的认真讨论,选取六(A)班为实验班,六

(B)班为对照班。两班均为普通班级、普通学生，班主任和任课教师亦为普通教师。之所以选取普通班开展实验，主要是为了提高实验结论的真实性和有效性。前测中的两班人数均为 56 人，但实验期间两班都有人数变化，为严格保证实验的对等性，最终剔除插进和调出的学生，因而实际统计人数均为 53 人，均不存在躯体或精神疾病。

2.2 实验变量

2.2.1 自变量：体验学习

体验学习迥异于常态化的课堂教学，“真正的体验学习并非以知识为本位的课堂学习，而是指在某种特定的场景中，通过学生的亲身经历和反思内省，不断提升自我概念，形成积极的情感、态度和价值观，促进人格升华的户外团队活动”[15]。为了贯彻执行教育部、公安部等十部委联合颁发的《中小学幼儿园安全管理办法》和教育部制定的《中小学公共安全教育指导纲要》，确保学生上学期间的人身安全，本实验将它从野外转入校内，从户外转入室内，开发出适应小学生主题班会或课外活动使用的情境性主题活动。

实验流程主要基于库伯提出的“体验学习圈”(The Experiential Learning Cycle，见图 1)，旨在搭建小学生亲历体验、头脑风暴和自我突破的成长平台。

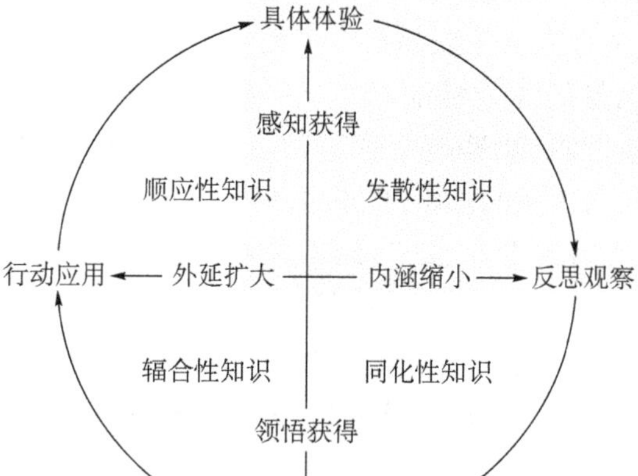

图 1　体验学习圈

资料来源：[美]大卫·库伯. 体验学习：让体验成为学习和发展的源泉[M]. 王灿明，朱水萍，等，译. 上海：华东师范大学出版社，2008：37.

具体地说，体验学习过程分为四个环节：

① 具体体验。开展体验学习，首先必须引导、激励学生积极投入到主题活动之中，全方位地调动学生的多感官参与，使他们尽情享受游戏、活动和问题解决所带来的快乐。此阶段特别强调学生的团队组建，应建立团队的共同愿景，并通过团队成员之间的信任与合作来应对挑战，创造性地解决他们共同应对的难题。

② 反思观察。既要对自己的体验过程进行及时的反思，又要从团队及其成员的行为观察中得到启示，通过自己和别人的比较发现自己的优势和不足。可以说，没有反思和比较，我们的学生就无法从体验中学习，因而这一阶段的关键是透过反思内省，提高体验的丰富性，从而形成一些新感悟、新观点和新发现。

③ 抽象概括。学习者将反思观察的各种结果加以整合，归纳出解决问题的主要策略，并优选出最佳策略。体验学习历来倡导“修正过去，激活现在，改写未来”，该阶段的关键是将观察到的成功体验进行概括，进而产生自我突破的强烈动机。

④ 行动应用。鼓励学生将抽象概括的结论主动运用到新的情境中，从中获得自我肯定和成就感。此阶段是对概括化经验的迁移，“让学习回归到现实生活中去，通过体验生活、体验学习，使知识不只浅存于记忆之中，而是深藏于心灵之中，让知识成为学习个体心灵的一部分”。[16]

2.2.2 因变量：创造性人格

创造性人格有广义和狭义之分，广义的创造性人格是所有创造活动赖以进行的必要条件，它并不仅仅局限于高水平的创造活动，每个人都有自己的创造性人格；狭义的创造性人格是指那些与高水平的创造活动、表现出高度创造性的问题解决活动相联系的人格特征，它仅为少数从事高创造性劳动、生产具有高度社会价值的产品的创新人才所独有。儿童的创造性人格主要是指广义的创造性人格，其操作性定义为《威廉姆斯创造倾向量表》所测量的四个维度，其中想象力包括视觉化和建立心像、幻想尚未发生过的事情、直觉地推测、能够超越感官和现实的界限；挑战性包括寻找各种可能性、了解事情的可能及与现实的差距、能够从杂乱中理出秩序、愿意探究复杂的问题；冒险性包括勇于面对失败或批评、敢于猜测、能在杂乱的情境下完成任务、勇于为自己的观点辩护；好奇性包括富有追根究底的精神、主意多、乐于接触模糊和不确定性的情境、肯深入思考事物的奥妙、能把握特殊现象并观察结果。四个维度单独计分，各个维度的分数累加后得出量表的总分，得分越高，表明创造性人格越强。

2.2.3 干扰变量的控制

干扰变量的控制是教育实验的本质特征和精髓。为了控制无关及额外变量的干扰，尽可能减少实验误差，本研究采取了多种技术处理方式：① 实验班和对照班学生的人数、性别比例、学业成就和家庭背景大致平衡；② 实验班和对照班任课教师的教学水平及使用的教材、教学进度、教学时间、课外活动大致相等；③ 为了避免实验中可能产生的新奇效应、霍桑效应和约翰·亨利效应，按“盲法控制”原则建立保密制度，对实验班学生实行严格保密，使他们不知道自己在进行实验；同时，跟对照班的师生也严格保密，以维护正常的教学秩序，避免形成人为竞争的氛围。

2.3 实验进程

本实验历时一年，主要包括前期准备、实验研究和总结推广三个阶段。

2.3.1 前期准备阶段

该阶段有三项主要任务。一是召开课题论证会。邀请有关高校和教育科研机构的七位专家进行开题论证,与会专家认真审阅相关材料,听取课题组的开题报告,并经过质询、讨论,一致认为选题新颖独特,既有开阔的国际视野,也有本土化的诉求,具有鲜明的时代性、前瞻性和应用推广价值,希望课题组认真落实研究方案,抓好实验过程的管理和指导,确保预期目标能够如期实现。二是进行实验前测。采用《威廉姆斯创造倾向量表》进行前测,对实验班与对照班的平均分进行独立样本 T 检验,结果显示:想象力、挑战性、冒险性和好奇性四个维度的得分不存在显著差异($p>0.05$),两班学生前测的总分也没有显著差异($p>0.05$),说明选取它们作为实验班和对照班是切实可行的。三是教师培训。包括理论和技能培训,其中理论培训采取个人自学、辅导讲座和专题讨论相结合的形式,内容涵盖大卫·库伯的《体验学习:让体验成为学习和发展的源泉》,英国谢菲尔德哈莱姆大学柯林·比尔德和牛津大学约翰·威尔逊合著的《体验式学习的力量》,华东师范大学叶斌的《青少年户外体验式学习实用手册》以及著名儿童教育家、情境教育创始人李吉林的《李吉林文集》(共8卷);技能训练以工作坊形式进行,包括暖身游戏、角色扮演、情境创设、头脑风暴、案例分析等内容。此外,还到生存训练营进行了为期两天的野外拓展训练,以自己的亲身感受加深对体验学习的理解。

2.3.2 实验研究阶段

借鉴李吉林的情境教育理论,本研究对欧美国家的体验学习过于强调"野外活动"和"冒险刺激"进行了适当的"扬弃",通过实体情境、模拟情境、语表情境、想象情境、推理情境等多重情境来降低活动的风险性,运用多媒体技术为儿童提供生动逼真的教学情境,呈现丰富多彩的教学资源,并将以美为境界、以思为核心、以情为纽带、以儿童活动为途径、以周围世界为源泉作为情境性主题活动的操作要义。[17]在台湾省外展教育基金会副执行长廖炳权、台湾省冒险世界户外学校执行长简浩炀的指导下,我们设计出29次既有情境性和互动性,又有启发性和挑战性的主题活动,具体包括亲情感恩、信任背摔、通天塔、盲人方阵、插上想象的翅膀、未来的汽车、填笔画、三角形个数不同变、比力气看新意、创意救人、比坚固、点子大比拼、穿越电网、创意外星人、盲人与拐杖、走格子、向规则挑战、比比谁高、谁动了我的奶酪、雨伞变变变、纸飞机大比拼、原型启发、加一加、组合出新招、跳出你的思维、孤岛求生、巧变、隐藏的正方形、思维大爆炸,利用班会或课余时间进行,每周聚焦一个主题,每次40分钟。按照课题的《实验手册》,每次主题活动都要经历从"具体体验",经"反思观察""抽象概括"与"行动应用",再回到"具体体验"的完整过程,每个学生都全身心、全方位地参与到多维情境体验活动之中,有效地促进了他们知情意行的和谐发展。

2.3.3 总结推广阶段

该阶段重点完成了两项任务。一是实验后测。使用《威廉姆斯创造倾向量表》对实验班与对照班进行后测，共发放问卷112份，回收110份，有效问卷106份，回收率98.21%，有效率96.36%。二是结题鉴定。基于实验数据的统计分析，完成研究报告的撰写，并通过了江苏省教育科学规划办组织的结题鉴定。专家组一致认为："课题选取实验学校进行体验学习理论的本土化实验，标志着课题研究取得了具有突破意义的进展，这也是国内首次通过实验方法验证体验学习成效的教育科研项目。"课题主持人先后应邀在中国创造学会全国代表大会暨创造创新研讨会、教育部重点课题"情境教育与儿童学习的实验与研究"推进会、创造学与创造教育前沿论坛、学习科学与教育创新国际论坛上发布和推广该实验报告，得到中国教育学会副会长李吉林、中国创造学会副理事长唐殿强、中国发明协会高校创造教育分会副理事长李嘉曾等专家的高度评价。

2.4 测量工具

采用美国创造力研究专家威廉姆斯（F. E. Williams）编制的《威廉姆斯创造倾向量表》（CMQ，台湾师范大学林幸台、王木荣主持修订），测量时间为25分钟，实行团体测验，施测前主试详细解释指导语，等学生明白后开始答题。该量表有四个分量表，共50道题目，其中40道为正向记分题，10道为反向记分题。本量表为李克特3点量表，"很适合"记3分，"部分适合"记2分，"很不适合"记1分，反向题的记分方式与此相反。本次使用中，该量表的内部一致性系数为0.746；各分量表之间均呈显著相关，相关系数在0.317—0.845之间，说明该测验有较好的信度、效度。研究采用SPSS12.0进行所有统计分析。

3 实验结果

将实验班与对照班创造性人格的前后测结果进行比较，表明体验学习对促进小学生创造性人格的发展具有极其显著的功效。

3.1 实验班与对照班后测结果的比较

对实验班与对照班学生创造性人格后测的得分进行了独立样本T检验，结果见表1。

表1显示，实验班与对照班学生创造性人格后测总分之间的差异极其显著（$p < 0.001$），其中"挑战性""好奇性"两个维度后测得分之间的差异也极其显著（$p < 0.001$），说明经过体验学习训练以后，实验班学生的创造性人格无论是整体水平，还是"挑战性"和"好奇性"都明显领先于对照班，体验学习实验的结果是非常显著的。

表1 实验班与对照班学生创造性人格后测结果的比较

维度	实验班		对照班		t
	M	SD	M	SD	
想象力	28.77	4.48	27.11	4.77	1.847
挑战性	30.36	3.43	26.75	3.17	5.627***
冒险性	25.72	3.28	25.00	2.66	1.241
好奇性	34.62	4.26	30.89	3.70	4.813***
总分	119.47	13.21	109.57	11.14	4.171***

注:* $p<0.05$,** $p<0.01$,*** $p<0.001$,下同。

3.2 实验班前测与后测结果的比较

实验班前测与后测结果的配对样本 T 检验结果见表2。

表2 实验班前测与后测结果的比较

维度	实验班前测		实验班后测		t
	M	SD	M	SD	
想象力	27.15	3.85	28.77	4.48	2.766**
挑战性	28.32	3.59	30.36	3.43	3.976***
冒险性	23.72	2.86	25.72	3.28	4.552***
好奇性	32.62	4.05	34.62	4.26	3.364***
总分	111.85	11.89	119.47	13.21	4.946***

表2显示,从总分上看,实验班学生前后测总分之间差异极其显著($p<0.001$),其中“想象力”的前后测均分之间差异比较显著($p<0.01$),而“挑战性”“冒险性”和“好奇性”的前后测得分之间差异极其显著($p<0.001$)。说明通过体验学习训练,实验班学生的创造性人格无论是整体水平,还是“想象力”“挑战性”“冒险性”和“好奇性”四个维度都得到了非常显著的提高。

3.3 对照班前测与后测结果的比较

对照班前测与后测结果的配对样本 T 检验结果见表3。

表3 对照班前测与后测结果的比较

维度	对照班前测		对照班后测		t
	M	SD	M	SD	
想象力	27.66	4.29	27.11	4.77	-0.801
挑战性	28.21	3.05	26.75	3.17	-2.476*
冒险性	24.34	2.72	25.00	2.66	1.529
好奇性	32.94	3.71	30.89	3.70	-3.701***
总分	113.53	10.53	109.57	11.14	-2.417*

表3显示，对照班学生的“想象力”“冒险性”的前后测得分之间没有呈现出显著差异($p>0.05$)，但“挑战性”“好奇性”后测得分较前测却分别下降了1.46分、2.05分，并产生了比较显著的差异($p<0.01$)；从总分上看，后测得分也较前测降低了3.96分，两者之间具有显著差异($p<0.05$)。这就表明，在常规教学条件下对照班学生的创造性人格发展水平非但没有得到提高，反而明显下降了。

4　结论与思考

根据以上分析，体验学习实验促进了小学生创造性人格的显著发展，对“想象力”“挑战性”“冒险性”和“好奇性”四个维度都有积极的提升效应，而常规教学却明显降低了小学生的创造性人格水平，尤其对“挑战性”和“好奇性”两个维度更有压抑作用。这就以客观数据反击了一些保守者的怀疑观望和旁观者的冷言冷语，证明了实验的理论假设。课题组成员在欣慰之余，也展开了更广泛的分析和更深入的探讨。

4.1　对小学生创造性人格发展的畸变现象必须加大干预力度

不少研究者认为，人格是最稳定、最持久的，它不仅能够说明现时和过去的行为，还能预测其未来。也有学者基于国内外创造性人格研究成果的深入分析，得出这样一个结论：创造性个体的行为在时间和空间上具有一致性。[18]与此相呼应的还有两种流传甚广的理论：一是遗传论。有学者认为创造性人格特征与其神经系统和大脑皮质的觉醒水平有关，也有学者认为与个体的大脑皮质神经细胞群配置及细胞结构的特点有关，还有学者认为主要是由有机体的生理状态及遗传机制决定的，较少受社会文化背景和特定情境因素的影响。二是早期经验论。其中最具代表性的是弗洛伊德，他特别强调早期经验对创造性发展的重要作用，认为创造性的核心部分在五六岁时就已完全形成，进入学校以后其行为表现会有所不同，但人格结构并不会发生太大的变化。不管是遗传论，还是早期经验论，我们都能从中得到一条启示：创造性人格很难改变，亦无需培养。而本研究恰恰得出与此不同的结论，表1、表2、表3的分析结果都说明，小学生的创造性人格培养不仅是可能的，而且是必要的，培养了创造性人格就能得到显著发展，不培养还会出现停滞甚至衰退的现象。这也从一个侧面说明，长期存在的工具理性主义的教育模式与考试制度的夹击，已经使我国小学生的创造性人格发展产生了严重的畸变现象，学校和家庭必须加大干预力度，决不可掉以轻心。

4.2　体验学习可以扩展小学生的积极情绪，对好奇心和挑战性具有激活效应

通过前后测数据的分析，我们发现对照班学生的创造性人格总分较前测有较大程度的下降，尤其是在“挑战性”“好奇性”上有更大幅度的下降。究其原因，毕业班所有的学生都面临着复习和升学的双重压力，他们成天趴在课桌上听课、看书、做习题，过

重的课业负担挤掉了那些本属于他们的娱乐、游戏和运动的时间，分数至上的价值取向以各种规训乃至强制的方式扼杀了他们的好奇心和想象力，他们无心也无力怀疑课本的科学性、挑战教师的权威性，这就意味着批判精神和创造能力的丧失。尽管实验班也有升学的压力，但每周一次的情境性主题活动却行之有效地激发出小学生的积极情绪，透过游戏、活动和问题解决课程，在富有挑战而快乐高效的情境中，同学之间相互了解，彼此信任，建立开放的心胸，他们在开怀大笑中放松身心，在问题解决中体验成功，在头脑风暴中提高自我，在巅峰体验中重组经验。将对照班和实验班相比较，我们不难发现，体验学习之所以能够促进小学生创造性人格的发展，其中一个原因就是体验学习所伴随的积极情绪（如快乐、感恩、自豪、幸福等）起到了非常重要的作用。美国著名心理学家芭芭拉·弗雷德里克森（Barbara Fredrickson）提出著名的“扩展和建构”理论，认为积极情绪具有一种扩展和建构的功能，给人生带来更多的可能性和开放性。[19]它就像那春天里的一缕明媚的阳光，不断释放和扩展着自己的正能量，扩大自己的意识与注意范围，增加智力导流量和自我效能感，激发更高的情绪生产力，进而影响小学生的心智成长和人格发展。从消极方面分析，它有利于调节复习和备考所带来的学习倦怠、考试焦虑和精神紧张，增强他们的心理韧性和弹性；从积极方面分析，它可以给儿童带来乐观向上的信心和希望，鼓舞他们去挑战和创新。

4.3 “体验学习圈”促进了自我与情境、感性与理性的交互作用，彰显出体验学习影响的深刻性

其实，体验学习之所以能够产生上述显著成效，还有一个更为重要的原因，那就是实验自始至终遵循了库伯的“体验学习圈”。这里以“亲情感恩”主题活动为例，具体分析“体验学习圈”影响小学生创造性人格发展的心理机制。首先，“具体体验”有助于培养小学生的冒险性。在本环节，教师用眼罩蒙住孩子的眼睛，先请家长牵着孩子的手走进报告厅的小舞台，再让孩子猜猜自己是谁领进来的。结果，大多数同学认出了自己的家长，但也有个别同学没有辨认出来，比如把妈妈当成了班主任。该环节能够诱发儿童置身于不确定情境中的情绪冲突，让他们细心体验和大胆猜测，培养他们敢于面对失败的心理素质。其次，“反思观察”有益于培养小学生的好奇性。盲行与牵手活动结束后，教师及时引导同学们陈述自己辨识的理由。有的孩子说：“是爸爸牵我手的，因为我爸爸手上有个伤疤，我感觉到了。”也有孩子说：“是我的妈妈，因为我闻到了妈妈身上熟悉的气味。”那个将妈妈错认为老师的同学却说：“我认为是朱老师，因为我感觉那是朱老师软软的手。”该环节引导儿童对那些不确定性的情境推本溯源，在日常生活体验和当下情境之间寻找有机联系，实现了儿童与情境之间连续不断的交互作用，提高了他们对亲情和细节的感受性。再次，“抽象概括”有利于培养小学生的想象力。在本环节，教师引导同学们和他们的家长将体验活动与其旧有经验链接并触及可能的新经验，并通过比较和提炼，揭示出体验活动所具有的当下或未来的

意义。一些家长对孩子能够辨认出自己感到非常自豪,那个被错认的妈妈紧抱着自己的女儿,泣不成声地说:“都怪我平时对你关心不够。”她对自己疏于照应女儿忏悔不已,提议所有家长都要抽出时间来陪伴自己的宝贝。通过对话与分享,全班同学和他们的家长形成一条共识:“父母和子女只有多沟通、多交流,才能达到心与心的交融,形成良好的亲子关系。”正是反思内省,实现了个体知识与社会知识之间的转换,使他们感受到蕴含在亲情感恩活动背后更为深刻的生命意义、更加积极的生活态度和更高境界的生存智慧。最后,“行动应用”有助于培养小学生的挑战性。在本环节,教师为每位同学准备了一张贺卡,要求孩子在贺卡上写上祝福送给自己的家长,并承诺永远这样做下去,直至长大成人。当着老师和全体同学的面,毕恭毕敬地向父母鞠躬,大声朗读满怀深情的贺卡,这需要勇气,更需要真诚。该环节将具体体验后形成的概括化经验又回归到现实生活之中,以爱心滋养儿童的成长,使他们的内心变得越来越纯净、越来越强大。诚如库伯教授所言,体验学习就是体验的转换并创造知识的过程,是“连续不断的创造与再创造”。[20] 从“具体体验”,经“反思观察”“抽象概括”到“行动应用”,同学们从“亲情感恩”主题活动中增进了理解,体验着亲情,感受到成长,促进了自我与情境、感性与理性的交互作用,这种交互作用最终提升了他们的自我意识、自我价值感以及自我挑战能力。因而,体验学习对儿童创造性人格发展的影响是深刻而持久的。

4.4 从情境课程中汲取丰富营养,对西方的体验学习进行本土化重构

反思西方体验学习的核心价值,无论是早期的 OBS,还是后来的 PA,都十分强调冒险刺激,学员往往置身于无法预测、神秘性和戏剧性的情境之中[21]。有近 20 年外展教育经验的华东师范大学心理咨询中心主任叶斌也提醒我们:“体验式团队学习,尤其是户外拓展训练活动,由于存在实际的身体活动(甚至是高度风险性和身心挑战性的活动),所以多少会存在风险”[22]。在“安全重于泰山”的我国中小学,唯有对源自西方的体验学习进行科学合理的技术改进和可行性论证,才能将它引进校园。课题组多次访问江苏情境教育研究所所长李吉林,并在系统学习和借鉴她的情境教育理论基础上,设计编制了完备的《实验手册》,试图通过教学情境的合理创设来降低活动的冒险性,精心设计了趣味盎然的游戏、活动和问题解决的情境,利用班会或课余时间开展系列主题活动。体验学习的改进是全方位的,既有目标的改进,又有方法的改进,既有形式的改进,又有内容的改进。实验结果表明,实验班学生的创造性人格有了显著的提高。最耐人寻味的是,在前测中,实验班学生的创造性人格低于对照班 1.68 分,而实验结束后实验班学生的创造性人格却高于对照班 9.9 分。这一进一退,充分说明改进后的体验学习对儿童创造性人格的发展起到了很好的促进作用,也让我们清醒地认识到,体验学习植根于西方的文化土壤,必然带有西方文化的深刻烙印,我们不能简单地抵制它,也不能机械地移植它,而应该结合我国的具体国情和现实选择,在移植中

改进，在改进中完善，最终实现本土化重构的美好愿景。这就需要我们有志存高远的心气，更需要有脚踏实地的行动。

致谢

本文为国家社会科学基金项目教育学一般项目《情境教育与儿童创造力发展的实验与研究》（BHA120051）和江苏省教育科学规划重点资助课题《中小学体验学习的研究与实验》（B-a/2006/01/030）的阶段性成果之一。本研究得到了中国教育学会原副会长李吉林、全国教学论专业委员会副主任熊川武、台湾省外展教育基金会副执行长廖炳权、台湾省冒险世界户外学校执行长简浩炀的亲切关怀和指导，特此谢忱！

References

[1] Colin Beard, John P Wilson. The Power of Experiential Learning. Translated by Ronghua Huang. Guangzhou: Zhongshan University Press, 2003.

[2] David A kolb. Experiential Learning: Experience as the Source of Learning and Development. Translated by Canming Wang and Shuiping Zhu. Shanghai: East China Normal University Press, 2008.

[3] Jiayi Wang, Zhihou Li. On experiential learning. Theory and Practice of Education, 2004, 24: 44 - 47.

[4] Weiguo Pang. On experiential learning. Global Education Outlook, 2011, 40: 9 - 15.

[5] John Dewey. Democracy, Education. Translated by Zhengmei Peng. Shang Hai: Shanghai People's Publishing House, 2009.

[6] Mei li. The basic idea and strategy of learning experience. Guang Dong Education, 2003, 21: 4 - 7.

[7] Alice Y Kolb, David A Kolb. Learning styles and learning spaces: Enhancing experiential learning in higher education. Academy of Management Learning & Education, 2005, 4: 193 - 212.

[8] Leishan Shi, Canming Wang. David Kolb's experiential learning. Theory and Practice of Education, 2009, 10: 49 - 50.

[9] Canming Wang, Zhaoyang Li. Experience and experimental research of mental health education model. Theory and Practice of Education, 2008, 9: 40 - 45.

[10] Yifeng Yan. Experiential learning cycle: Process mechanism of experiential learning. Shang Hai Research on Education, 2009, 4: 59 - 61.

[11] Yifeng Yan, Limin Xie. Experience teaching how to conduct—based on the experiential learning cycle perspective. Curriculum. Teaching Material and Method, 2012, 32: 21 - 25.

[12] Joy Paul Guilford. Creative Talents: Their Nature Uses and Development. Translated by Liangfang Shi. Beijing: People's Education Press, 2006: 6 - 7.

[13] Jiannong Shi. System model of creativity. Journal of Developments in Psychology, 1995, 3: 1 - 5.

[14] Chongde Lin. Education and Development: A Study of Psychological Integration of Innovative Talents. Beijing: Beijing Normal University Press,2004.

[15] Canming Wang. Interpretation of experiential learning. Global Education Outlook, 2005, 34: 14 – 17.

[16] Erli Zhang, Danning Zhang. The philosophical thinking of Experiential learning. China Educational Technology, 2013, 26: 19 – 23.

[17] Jilin Li. Talk about the classroom operating point situational education. Educational Research, 2002, 24: 68 – 73.

[18] Qinglin Zhang. Psychology of Creativity. Beijing: Higher Education Press, 2004.

[19] Barbara Fredrickson. Positivity: Groundbreaking Research Reveals How to Embrace the Hidden Strength of Positive Emotions, Overcome Negativity, and Thrive. Translated by Jun Wang. ShangHai: China Renmin University Press, 2010.

[20] David A kolb. Experiential Learning: Experience as the Source of Learning and Development. Translated by Canming Wang and Shuiping Zhu. Shanghai: East China Normal University Press, 2008.

[21] Juze Cai, Binghuang Liao. Creative Design and Implementation of Education. Tao Yuan (Tai Wan): The Exploration Education Development Association, 2008.

[22] Bin Ye. Teenagers Outdoor Experiential Learning Practical Handbook. ShangHai: East China Normal University Press, 2006.

Research Progress in the Relations between Parental Marital Conflict and Problem Behaviors in Children

Xueli Yang[1,a,*]

[1]Key Laboratory of Child Development and Learning Science of Ministry of Education, Research Center for Learning Science, Southeast University, Nanjing 210096, China

[a]yangxueli227@ outlook. com

[*]Corresponding author

Keywords: marital conflict; problem behavior

Abstract: Family is always viewed as the most important socialization places for early childhood, harmonious family is conducive to form a positive relationship and children development. If parents are rapport with each other, that will be helpful to form a safe environment for children. In secure environment, children are more likely to form a secure attachment with parents, that will be conducive to the children's healthy growth. Parents who are experienced long-term marital conflict, if not properly solved, children will think the family is not safe, and parents can not rely on, which may affect the parent-child relationship, parent-child attachment is able to accommodate the impact of family conflict on children's mental adaptation. Parents who are experienced unfavorable marriage may bring the negative experience to children, caused children more likely to have behavioral problems.

父母婚姻冲突对儿童问题行为影响的研究进展

杨雪莉[1,a,*]
[1]东南大学学习科学研究中心，南京，210096
[a]yangxueli227@ outlook. com
[*]通讯作者

关键词：婚姻关系；儿童；问题行为

中文摘要：家庭是儿童早期最主要的社会化场所，良好的家庭氛围更有利于形成积极的良性的夫妻关系。如果父母关系融洽，那么就有利于形成安全的环境和氛围。儿童在安全的环境中更容易对父母形成安全型依恋，有利于儿童健康成长。父母长期的婚姻冲突如得不到妥善解决，儿童会认为家庭是不安全的，父母是不能依靠的，会影响到亲子关系的健康发展，亲子依恋能够调节家庭冲突对儿童心理适应的影响。婚姻关系不良的父母所养育的孩子也更容易出现行为问题。

1 婚姻冲突和儿童问题行为

良好婚姻关系是家庭和谐的重要内容。父母之间的良好关系对子女健康成长的重要作用越来越受到社会各界的广泛关注。父母关系不良对儿童发展尤其是心理发展的破坏性是不可估量的。另外，这与儿童自身的人格特征、认知方式、心理承受能力等都是密切相关的。如今越来越多的研究者开始关注家庭内部关系对儿童身心发展的重要作用。

问题行为指违反社会公认的正常儿童青少年行为规范和道德标准以及在情绪或社会适应方面不成熟的行为[1]。父母间的冲突即婚姻冲突，主要指夫妻由于意见分歧而引起的言语或身体的攻击与争执，它可由冲突发生的频率、强度、内容、风格（公开的/隐蔽的）及冲突是否得到解决等特性来描述[2]。许多研究表明，经常发生的公开婚姻冲突与儿童的多种问题行为（如攻击性、不服从、反社会行为、抑郁、退缩及自我概念发展障碍等）有关。研究者发现，儿童问题行为不仅受到社会环境、父母因素还有儿童自身等社会心理等因素的影响，还和亲子关系、父母婚姻关系等因素密切相关。

几乎所有的婚姻中都会存在一定程度的冲突，但是并不是所有的冲突都会给儿童的身心带来伤害，只有长期的恶性的婚姻关系不良才会对造成儿童社会适应困难。事实上，有些冲突作为家庭成员之间沟通的方式，对婚姻、家庭是必要的，如果父母能够理性地、有效地处理婚姻中的矛盾，儿童也可以通过观察父母在处理矛盾中使用的有效应对策略学会处理自己生活中的问题。然而，从不同领域、不同样本得到的结论都表明婚姻冲突与儿童问题行为之间存在着显著的相关。Emery 等人的研究发现男孩对婚姻冲突频率的感知与其外部问题、行为问题之间存在正相关[3]。Kelly 等研究结果表明儿童家庭环境的冲突性与儿童的社会适应能力、学校表现等都存在显著相关性[4]。此外，还有研究发现父母婚姻状况与教师所报告儿童的问题行为和学业成就相关(Archie, 1988)[5]。

如果夫妻关系和谐，那么他们便能相互扶持，儿童同样能从父母和谐的关系中获益，得到更多的身体上和情感上的支持与照料。研究发现，父母婚姻关系与儿童的攻击行为存在显著正相关。如果夫妻关系融洽，彼此能够相互提供支持，那么他们在养育孩子的时候会更加投入，育儿能力更强，对孩子的需求更加敏感，并且亲子关系会更加密切。父母恩爱的儿童同样表现出更好的适应性和积极的态度。而那些婚姻关系中充满矛盾、敌意等负性情绪的父母会造成儿童的问题行为。当这些问题发生在儿童年幼的时候，儿童就不太可能形成对父母的安全型依恋(Frosh 等, 2001)[6]。当矛盾发生在儿童长大以后，儿童就可能变得具有攻击性或者抑郁。

回顾现有研究，研究者们一方面力图从理论角度构建理论模型来解释婚姻关系与儿童适应问题之间的关系，较著名的理论有社会学习理论(the theory of social learning)、间接作用观点(the ideas of conflict as family system disruption)、认知—背景理论(the cognitive-contextual framework)和情感安全假设(the emotional security hypothesis)。另一方面研究者也着手从实证研究的方向考察婚姻关系对儿童适应问题的影响及二者间的数量关系。本文试图从理论和实证两方面梳理婚姻关系与儿童问题行为的关系。

2 父母婚姻关系对儿童问题行为影响的研究进展

2.1 儿童问题行为的相关研究

从发展的视角来看，很多研究表明儿童时期的问题行为都会影响到其后的发展，成人期的问题行为很可能起源于儿童时期的易感性。先前关于儿童问题行为的研究主要集中在儿童身上已经出现的问题行为上，但实际上，在正常儿童群体当中也会出现适应问题和问题行为。如 Richman 等人在对伦敦郊外地区学前儿童进行的一项大型追踪研究结果表明：62% 的儿童在 3—8 岁之间的问题行为是稳定的[7]。Robins 等人进行的一项追踪研究结果也表明儿童期出现的问题行为可持续到成年期，具有相当程度的稳定性[8]。

攻击性行为、反社会行为具有发展的特质，它始于童年时期，有可能持续到青春期和成年期。有的学者认为攻击是一种相当稳定的特性，儿童期攻击性的稳定性系数可与 IQ 的稳定性系数相比。Huesman 等对 600 多名被试进行的历时 22 年的追踪研究发现，无论是男性还是女性，8 岁时的攻击性记录都能够很好地预示他们成年以后的攻击性行为[9]。有人在韩国首尔地区的一项研究说明儿童期的问题行为，包括外化问题行为和内化问题行为都与成人期的行为问题显著相关（Shin, Sung, Lim, Park & Cho, 2012）[10]。所以攻击性是一种比较稳定的特质。

儿童问题行为不仅具有稳定性，而且在性别及其他方面上也存在着显著差异。比如对于男孩和女孩来说，儿童期的外化问题行为都和成人期的外化问题显著相关，但是对于女孩来说，童年期的内化问题行为与成人期的内化行为存在显著负相关，但在男孩身上没有看到这种关联性（Shin 等, 2012）[10]。Leve 等人在 5—17 岁儿童为研究对象的研究中发现，男孩和女孩的外显问题都呈现出随年龄逐渐下降的趋势，但是只有女孩的内隐问题行为会随着年龄的增长逐渐减少。在他们的研究中发现害羞/害怕和母亲抑郁可以预测儿童 17 岁时的内化问题行为，也就是说，严厉的约束可以单独预测男孩 17 岁时的内隐行为，而母亲的抑郁和家庭低收入可以显著地预测女孩内隐问题行为的增长（Leve, Kim & Pears, 2005）[11]。

2.2 夫妻关系对儿童问题行为的影响

1994 年，Davies 和 Cummings 提出"情绪安全假设"，强调儿童的情绪在感知、解决婚姻冲突中的核心作用。该理论以依恋理论和认知—背景理论为基础，提出婚姻冲突可能通过直接和间接两种途径威胁儿童情绪安全导致问题行为，其引发机制集中在儿童的情绪上[12]。目前研究证实的受婚姻冲突影响的儿童外显问题行为包括攻击行为、同伴关系不良、敌对、不服从、撒谎等，内隐心理问题包括抑郁、焦虑、羞耻、退缩、低自尊等。

很多研究表明有行为问题或者学习障碍的儿童，其家庭功能通常也存在问题，如果父母关系不良，父母在家庭中表达的消极信息等可以通过语言、手势等影响家庭气氛，都会给儿童的发展造成消极影响。如梁宗保、张光珍等人的一项关于婚姻关系和亲子关系的研究表明拥有较高婚姻关系质量的父亲和母亲在家庭中更多表达积极情绪，更少表达消极情绪，从而增加了父子和母子关系的亲密性[13]。他们在以前的一项研究中发现父母的积极情绪表达对儿童的社会能力有促进作用，消极情绪表达则有负向作用。父母的情绪教导、情绪紊乱除了对儿童社会能力具有直接作用外，还通过其情绪表达对儿童的社会能力具有间接影响[14]。

过去关于儿童在对父母离婚适应性上的研究发现，许多从破碎家庭中走出的儿童会报告更多的外化问题，一般来说，相较于女孩，男孩会出现更多的适应困难问题。在已经离婚的父母报告中发现，父母会在离婚之前报告更多的养育困难[15]。Cummings 等人考察了儿童对亲生父母冲突的反应，研究表明，儿童感受到的痛苦水平随着父母争吵强度和破坏性程度的上升而上升。那些目睹了父母激烈、破坏性冲突的儿童会遭受不安全感、抑郁、焦虑、行为问题、人际关系困难、情绪调节能力差等问题的困扰，这些影响可能会持续数年之久[16]。在某些情况下，儿童应对压力的生理能力也会遭受损害。相反,如果父母能建设性地处理双方的分歧,表现出对对方意见的尊重,彼此表达温暖和支持,建立有效的冲突谈判策略,就能减轻对儿童的负面影响。目睹建设性的争端解决甚至能教会儿童进行冲突谈判,并在其他场合解决与他人的争论。如果父母频繁、激烈,甚至通过身体冲突发泄愤怒,而且争端最终没能得到解决,在这种情况下儿童最有可能出现问题。

2.3 夫妻关系与儿童问题行为的相互作用

持有间接作用观点的心理学家认为婚姻关系是通过作用于亲子关系间接作用于儿童的行为的。这些研究者深受系统论的影响,他们将家庭看作是一个系统,认为一个子系统得到优化或者破坏,那么其他子系统也将受到影响。如,婚姻关系子系统受到破坏后,亲子子系统也将受到破坏,那么整个家庭功能将得不到正常发挥,从而诱发儿童问题行为的产生。儿童出现问题行为必然会影响父母的行为和情绪反应。张晓、陈会昌等人的研究表明家长与儿童交往时,不同行为特征的儿童会影响到家长的教育态度和情绪表达方式的选择。如他们在研究中发现,父母婚姻关系的好坏与儿童退缩、攻击性等行为问题的双向作用影响显著,对儿童社会化和人格的形成有着重要作用[1]。儿童问题行为的出现,如果父母未能很好地处理,那么儿童的问题反过来会成为父母的问题,影响到家庭氛围,造成或加剧婚姻关系的紧张。

尽管父母关系不良会对儿童发展产生不利影响是不争的事实,但必须承认的是,一些儿童无论在较差的环境中还是在较好的环境中,都能很好地适应,并不会产生诸如焦虑、退缩、攻击等严重的社会适应问题。这与儿童自身的气质等个体素质是密不可分的。以往研究多将儿童视为一个被动受家庭环境、养育方式、父母冲突影响的个体,而忽略了儿童作为一个正在发展中的认知个体的反作用,即父母不仅通过教养方式和养育态度等来影响儿童的发展,儿童也会通过自身的气质特征和个体能动性对家长产生影响。这种观点也得到了实证研究的支持。比如,Stevens 等人发现父母对惩罚方式的选择会受到儿童活动水平的影响。当活动量很大的孩子和安静的或中等活动水平的孩子都表现出同样的不良行为时,活动水平高的儿童可能会引发父母更加严厉的惩罚措施,当然惩罚方式也与儿童的性别有关。

3 婚姻关系与儿童行为关系研究的启示

家庭是儿童早期最重要的社会化场所,其重要性自不待言。父母作为儿童最初的也是最好的老师,倘若父母关系不良,必然会在家庭生活中表达出更多的负性情绪,进而影响到整个家庭的气氛。长期经历父母冲突的儿童会对家庭系统中的微妙变化非常敏感,若再加上先天的气质易感性,会大大增加他们出现问题行为的概率。此外,如果父母长期面临婚姻矛盾,他们往往会忽视儿童的需要或者通过溺爱孩子来填补婚姻中的缺憾,儿童会认为自己是不值得被爱的,是自己的原因造成父母的冲突,但是无论忽视还是溺爱，对儿童的健康成长都是极为不利的。

班杜拉的社会学习理论是最早被用来解释婚姻冲突和儿童问题行为关系的理论。该理论指出，儿童可以通过观察和模仿他人的行为习得重要的社会技能，比如与他人交往的模式、亲社会行为和反社会行为等。此外，儿童通过观察父母的行为来学习如何与他人交流并解决冲突。如果父母吵架，儿童会学会攻击性的互动策略，在与他人交往的过程中也会采用通过模仿习得的父母之间的交往方式对待同伴。赵梅总结了婚姻冲突中对儿童的一些保护性因素，如亲子关系、父母监管、同辈关系等（赵梅，2005）[17]。如果亲子关系密切，就有可能缓解父母关系不良对儿童造成的压力，同样，如果父母监管功能正常、同伴关系良好，就有可能弥补父母冲突给儿童带来的伤害。

总之，来自各领域、不同年龄的样本都表明，父母婚姻关系的好坏与儿童的健康发展息息相关。良好的夫妻关系有利于营造和谐的家庭环境，促进父母在教养方式上的一致性，不仅能够促进儿童的健康发展，也有可能使儿童已出现的问题行为得到改善。当然任何问题都不是单方面的因素造成的，儿童问题行为也与生物因素、社会因素、自身等因素密切联系。所以在面对儿童已出现的问题行为时，应综合考虑各方面的因素，结合实际情况，妥善处理矛盾，解决困扰。

References

[1] Zhang X, Chen H. A longitudinal study of parent-child relationships and problem behaviors in early childhood: Transactional models. Acta Psychologica Sinica, 2008, 40(5): 571 - 582.

[2] Yu Guoliang, Xin Ziqiang. Social Development Psychology. Hefei: Anhui Education Publishing House, 2004.

[3] R E Emery. Interparental conflict and the children of discord and divorce. Psychological Bulletin, 1982, 92: 310 - 330.

[4] J B Kelly. Children's adjustment in conflicted marriage and divorce: A decade review of research. Journal of the American Academy of Child and Adolescent Psychiatry, 2000, 39: 963 - 973.

[5] J Archie. The relationship of early hypertension folio wing carotid endarterectomy to intraoperative cerebral ischemia. Annals of Vascular Surgery, 1988, 2: 108 - 113.

[6] C A Frosch, S C Mangelsdorf. Marital behavior, parenting behavior, and multipe reports of preschoolers' behavior problems: Mediation or moderation? Developmental Psychology, 2001, 37: 502 - 519.

[7] N Richman, J Stevenson. Pre-school to School: A Behavior Study. London: Academic Press, 1982.

[8] R K Robins. Adult disorders predicted by childhood conduct problems: Results from NIMH epidemiologic catchment area project. Psychiatry, 1991, 54: 116 - 132.

[9] L R Huesman, L D Eron. Stability of aggression over time and generations. Developmental

Psychology, 1984, 20: 1120 - 1134.

[10] Y M Shin, M J Sung, K Y Lim. The pathway of internalizing and externalizing problems from childhood to adolescence: A prospective study from age 7 to 14—16 in Korea. Community Mental Health Journal, 2012, 48: 384 - 391.

[11] L Leve, H Kim, K Pears. Childhood temperament and family environment as predictors of internalizing and externalizing trajectories from ages 5 to 17. Journal of Abnormal Child Psychology, 2005, 33(5): 505 - 520.

[12] CHI L, Wang Y. Theoretical advance on the relations between marital conflict and problem behaviors in children. Advances in Psychological Science, 2002, 10(4): 411 - 417.

[13] Liang Z, Zhang G, Deng H. Links between marital relationship and child-parent relationship: Mediating effects of parents' emotional expressiveness. Acta Psychologica Sinica, 2013, 45(12): 1355 - 1367.

[14] Liang Z, Zhang G, Chen H. Relations among parental meta-emotion philosophy, parental emotion expressivity, and children's social competence. Acta Psychologica Sinica, 2013, 44(2): 199 - 210.

[15] D Shaw, R Emery, M Tuer. Parental functioning and children's adjustment in families of divorce: A prospective study. Journal of Abnormal Child Psychology, 1993, 21: 119 - 134.

[16] E M Cummings, R J Iannotti, C Zahn-Waxler. Influence of conflict between adults on the emotions and aggression of young children. Developmental Psychology, 1985, 21: 495 - 507.

[17] Zhao M. Marital conflict and its influence on teenagers. Beijing: Beijing Normal University, 2005.

The Effects of Positive Emotions on Children "Learning by Doing"

Di Wu[1,a], Xiaolin Lai[2,b,*]

[1]Shantou university institute of higher education, Shantou, Guangdong, China

[2]Shantou university medical college "learning by doing" center, Shantou, Guangdong, China

[a]12dwu@stu.edu.cn, [b]xllai@stu.edu.cn

[*]Corresponding author

Keywords: positive emotions; "learning by doing"; innovative; inquiry learning

Abstract: This document first explains the concept of positive emotions, functions, and the relationship of "learning by doing" quality to cultivate children's creative thinking. Then introduces the theory support and research results of children's creative performance under different emotional states by predecessors, as well as the importance of emotion on child development. Positive emotions are reviewed for children in the activities of "learning by doing" influence and enlightenment. This document also focus on the effect mechanism of how positive emotions affect the children during the inquiry learning. Finally, this paper points out the problems of activities from the "learning by doing" combined with positive emotions in the future, and give some suggestions and prospects.

积极情绪对儿童“做中学”的影响

吴迪[1,a], 赖小林[2,b,*]

[1]汕头大学高等教育研究所,汕头,广东,中国

[2]汕头大学医学院“做中学”中心,汕头,广东,中国

[a]12dwu@stu.edu.cn, [b]xllai@stu.edu.cn

[*]通讯作者

关键词:积极情绪;做中学;创新性;探究学习

中文摘要:本文首先介绍了积极情绪的概念与功能,以及“做中学”与儿童创新性思维品质培养的关系。再介绍了前人对儿童创造性在不同情绪状态下的表现的理论支持和研究成果,以及情绪对儿童发展的重要性;综述了积极情绪对儿童在“做中学”活动中的影响和启示;探究了积极情绪对儿童在探究学习中的影响机制。最后,指出未来“做中学”活动中与积极情绪结合可能会遇到的问题,并给以一定的建议和展望。

1 积极情绪

1.1 积极情绪的概念

积极情绪是指个体由于体内外刺激、事件满足个体需要而产生的伴有愉悦感受的情绪。积极情绪能够激活一般的行动倾向,对于认知具有启动和扩展效应,能够建设个体的资源,撤销消极情绪产生的激活水平,能够促进组织绩效。积极情绪是心理健康的重要组成部分,同时对身体健康具有促进作用。积极情绪对于个体的适应具有广泛的功能与意义。[1]

1.2 积极情绪的功能

研究认为情绪是有机体在进化过程中由于适应环境而被赋予或设置的,尤其是消极情绪(负性情绪),是在应对具有生存威胁的环境中逐渐进化而来。在进化的阶梯上,消极情绪与特定行动趋势密切联系,例如,愤怒生成攻击欲求,恐惧产生逃离欲求,厌恶引发驱逐欲求等。这种特定行动的趋势对于应对危险和生存挑战是必需的和关键的。但对于积极情绪,一般研究认为并不伴随特定行动趋势,只伴有一般性激活,如高兴、愉快伴随无目的激活;兴趣与注意定向相联系,兴趣引起个体一种希望研究、探索或卷入的感受以及通过整合新的信息到自我中和获得对于客体和他人新的经验;而满意与放松的状态相联系。

2 积极情绪与“做中学”的联系

2.1 什么是“做中学”

“做中学”科学教育改革计划是在了解国外科学教育的发展动态和趋势，总结我国中、小、幼科学教育已取得的成就、丰富经验和分析存在的问题，吸收和借鉴国际科学教育的先进观念和教育方法的基础上提出的。该计划由热心于提高基础教育阶段科学教育水平的科学家、致力于科学教育研究和改革的教育研究工作者和生气勃勃、勇于进取的一线教师共同参与、联合推进和实施。“做中学”科学教育的目标是：让所有学前和小学阶段的儿童有机会亲历探究自然奥秘的过程，使他们在观察、提问、设想、动手实验、表达、交流的探究活动中，体验科学探究的过程，建构基础性的科学知识，获得初步的科学探究能力，为促进儿童的全面发展，成长为具有良好科学素养的未来公民打下必要的基础。

“做中学”的精神告诉我们，不能轻易对孩子说“你错了”，“你这样不行”，等等[2]。这样，教师会把我们未来的小科学家摧毁在萌芽中，扼杀在摇篮里。教师应该是积极地给予鼓励。从这一点，也同样可以看出在孩子“做中学”的过程中引入积极情绪的具体行为，比如鼓励、关怀、包容等，对于孩子创新力以及“做中学”能力的培养是十分重要的。

从20世纪五六十年代探究作为课程走进校园以来，关于探究教学的研究大多从概念转变、概念理解等知识掌握以及提出问题、科学猜想、科学假设、解释现象等探究能力方面进行。对于探究式科学教育中儿童在社会情感能力方面的研究还不很成熟。学者王星娜通过研究[3]发现：探究科学课堂上学生人数不多，每个人都会受到关注，也就是被倾听，从而有一种被尊重的感觉。这种情绪状态对于学习的探究是有益的。并且，探究科学更注重学生情感体验。学生可以充分发挥想象力，表达思想与情感而无所顾忌。这对充分发挥学生的创新性思维是有好处的，促进了学生发散创新的积极性。

2.2 “做中学”的意义

而学者王婷婷在其研究中也提到[4]，在国外课堂上，学习是每一个学生都在主动进行的，而不是在老师的强迫下进行的。在学生主动学习的过程中，老师运用各种方法在促进和推动。其中之一便是创造舒适安全的环境。孩子们随意地坐在教室前面的地毯上进行学习、记录，甚至他们可以趴在地上听老师讲课。关键在于，这种看似随意的坐姿，却能在一定程度上给学生创造一个很舒适很安全的环境，就跟在家里一样。在这种舒适安全的环境里，每一个人都愿意自由地、尽情地表达自己的观点，愿意和其他人分享自己的想法，因为大家知道在这样的情境下更多的是一种观点的交流活动，不会被批评，更不会被嘲笑，都不害怕说错。在做一些探究性的活动时，不会太担心失败，而是大胆地放开去尝试，这种营造轻松环境，将积极情绪与探究学习相结合的做法也符合了“做中学”中提到的自由地发现学习，从探索中发现学习的规律与方法，从而有效率地内化为自身的经验的一部分。

2.3 积极情绪与“做中学”

积极情绪原则是教学心理卫生的基本原则。这一原则要求教师在教学过程中应尽可能满足学生在安全、归属、求知、审美、自尊和受到尊重等方面的基本需求，使他们在学习过程中能够表现出饱满的热情、专注的神情，同时还要让他们经常感受到各种积极的情绪情感体验，如新奇感、趣味感、轻松感、兴奋感，被教师关注、关心和关爱的满足感等。这一原则是使学生能够对学习形成积极态度的重要基础和保障。因此，教师在课堂教学中，应该努力营造出轻松的学习环境。这不仅在一般的课堂教学中要重视带入积极的情绪情感重要性，在强调儿童探究性学习的“做中学”教学中一样要努力多营造积极轻松的教学环境。

当然，轻松的学习环境并不意味着懈怠。积极的情绪状态强调的是让学生有愉悦感。一般而言，教师的情绪状态会直接影响学生的学习情绪。作为教师的“严”，要表现在要求上和管理上，而不是表露在威严上、面部表情上。否则，会使学生的心理负担加重，课堂上很难出现大胆举手、积极发言的效果，这样便会在很大程度上束缚学生的创造力和探索欲望，限制学生在“做中学”教学中的学习效果。环境也是影响创造力的一个重要因素，具有自由、鼓励、认同、时间充裕、资源充足、压力适当、具有挑战性、人际关系良好等特征的环境能够促进人的创造力发展，而限制较多、资源不足、评价不当、缺乏热忱、时间紧张、人际关系不良以及过分强调现状等特征的环境阻碍人的创造力发展。[5]

3 积极情绪对儿童“做中学”的影响与启示

“做中学”科学教育实验非常重视教师的作用，强调教师的首要任务是为儿童创设一种情境，使儿童能在这种情境中发现问题和思考问题；当问题提出后，教师要引导儿童探索，帮助儿童建构新知识。在整个教学过程中，教师是儿童探究的合作者、联络者、组织者、帮助者和引领者，而不是控制者、策划者和主导者。我国中小学科学教育长期存在重知识轻能力、重结果轻过程、重教师传授轻学生探究、重实用价值轻科学精神等弊端。21世纪初，我国基础教育课程改革开始全面启动，力求借鉴西方发达国家教育改革的经验，加强儿童科学教育，改变传统的“说科学、听科学”教学方式。实施“做中学”科学教育实验，是科学教育改革国际化和本土化的共同诉求。“做中学”科学教育实验的目标是让所有学前和小学阶段的儿童有机会亲历探究自然奥秘的过程，建构基础性的科学知识，获得初步的科学探究能力，为其成长为具有良好科学素质的公民打下基础。同时，该实验希冀从科学教育改革入手，探出一条实施素质教育的具体途径。

如果教师能渲染积极的情绪氛围，会使学生消除紧张的心理，保持开朗、轻松、愉快的心情，学习情绪就会高涨，课堂气氛就会活跃，最终提高了学生的学习效率和探索学习的积极性。因此我们可以看出，培养积极的情绪状态对于在学生中开展以探索性学习为主的“做中学”教学具有重要的影响意义。

在“做中学”活动中，学生作为学习的主体，其情感直接影响着学习的效果与质量。鼓励学生在积极参与“做中学”的同时，保持良好积极的情绪状态，产生好奇心和求知欲，在学习活动中获得成功的体验，锻炼克服困难的意志，建立自信心，形成实事求是的态度以及质疑和独立思考的习惯等，正是全日制义务教育《新课程标准》明确提出的发展学生“情感与态度”的目标。情感教学的最大特色是“知情并行”，也就是在学生获取知识的同时，其情感品质也能得到升华和提高。教师应该充分挖掘并刺激学生的心理源泉，通过恰当的途径和方法，激起学生健康、积极的情绪体验，以高尚的情感去感染学生，促使学生自觉地进行学习活动。

致谢

本研究系通讯作者主持的2010年度教育部人文社会科学研究规划基金项目“做中学”儿童探究式科学教育中积极心理培养的研究（10YJA880051）和汕头市科技计划项目“未成年人探究式科学教育中创新思维培养的研究”（E200900191）的部分成果。

References

[1] Guo Xiaoyan, Wang Zhenhong. Concept, function and meaning of positive emotion. Advances in Psychological Science, 2007, 15(5): 810 - 815.

[2] LaiXiaolin, LiuLei, LinJin, et al. Effects of the “Learning by Doing” Program on Children's Emotional Expression. Psychological science, 2005, 28(6): 1483 - 1486.

[3] Wang Xingna. Problem students' differences in the inquiry learning and conventional learning research. Guilin: Journal of guangxi normal university, 2011.

[4] Wang Tingting. Learning the foreign advanced experience to promote students' active learning. Science Lesson, 2013 (2): 110 - 111.

[5] Amabile T M. A model of creativity and innovation in organizations. Research in Organization Behavior, 1988, 10: 123 - 167.

Effects of Growing-class on the Development of the Remote Association Ability Among Elementary Students

Jie Zhao[1], Zhu Deng[1,a,*], Qing Yan[2]

[1]The Department of Psychology, Nanjing Normal University, Nanjing, China, 210097

[2]The Primary School Attached to Nanjing Normal University, Nanjing, China, 210018

[a]zdeng_psy@163.com

[*]Corresponding author

Keywords: growing class, instructional experiment, creative thinking, Remote Association Test

Abstract: The development of adolescent's personality and intelligence is closely related to teaching methods of basic education. Taking creative thinking as an example, it will be explored if growing class promotes the development of student's characteristics through the contrast of the development of the ability of remote association between experimental growing class and non-experimental class. A 3 ×4 mixed factorial design was adopted to assess the ability of remote association of all subjects with the task of "Pupils' Remote Associates Test" which was Well-prepared. There were 919 pupils, from Nanjing Normal University Preparatory School (309 from experimental growing class, 310 from non-experimental class) and Lang Yak Lu primary school (300 from non-experimental class). Students from different kinds of class were all from second grade to fifth grade. The dependent variable is score of the task of "Pupils' Remote Associates Test".

Results showed that: (1) in total, Class property affected testing score significantly. Students' scores of experimental growing class are significantly higher than non-experimental class of Nanjing Normal University Preparatory School and the control classes of Lang Yak Lu primary school. (2) Students' scores of experimental growing class are significantly higher than non-experimental class of Nanjing Normal University Preparatory School and the control classes of Lang Yak Lu primary school among each grade. (3) The interaction of class property and grade are significantly. The degree of difference is different with the change of grade. Specifically, testing scores of the control classes of Lang Yak Lu primary school are higher than non-experimental class of Nanjing Normal University Preparatory School for second grade while testing scores of the control classes of Lang Yak Lu primary school are lower than non-experimental class of Nanjing Normal University Preparatory

School for fifth grade.

Conclusions: (1) Remote Association ability of growing class students is better than non-experimental class of the same school and the control classes of Lang Yak Lu primary school. It reflects that the teaching method of growing class promote creative thinking of pupils effectively. (2) The superiority degree was different with the change of grade. The extent of educational training and the degree of task difficulty will be factors.

“生本课堂”对小学生远距离联想能力发展的影响

赵洁[1]，邓铸[1,a,*]，闫勤[2]
[1]南京师范大学心理学院，南京，210097
[2]南京师范大学附属实验小学，南京，210018
[a]zdeng_psy@163.com
*通讯作者

关键词:生长课堂;教学实验;创造性思维;远距离联想测验

中文摘要:基础教育教学方式与青少年智能及人格发展关系密切。为了探索“生本课堂”教学是否能有效促进学生生长特质的发展，拟以创造性思维发展为取样，对“生本课堂”教学实验班与对照班学生的远距离联想能力进行比较。在精心编制“小学生远距离联想测验”作业单之后，采用3×4因素型实验设计，对所有被试进行了远距离联想能力的测试。其中，被试来源于南师附小“生本课堂”实验班、南师附小对照班、对比学校琅琊路小学的对照班，均包括二年级、三年级、四年级、五年级，共计919名小学生。因变量为“小学生远距离联想测验”作业单成绩。结果显示:(1)被试班级性质变量主效应显著。平均而言，南师附小“生本课堂”实验班学生远距离联想成绩显著高于南师附小和琅琊路小学对照班学生的成绩;(2)分别对各年级的实验班、对照班学生的测试成绩进行比较，则均显示出“生本课堂”实验班学生的远距离联想成绩显著高于对照班学生的测试成绩;(3)被试所在班级性质与所在年级两个变量存在显著的交互效应。显示出在不同年级、不同班级间的差异程度有所不同。具体表现为:二年级时对比学校对照班级学生的成绩高于南师附小对照班，且差异显著;五年级时南师附小非生本班学生成绩高于对比学校对等班级，差异边缘显著。

研究结论:(1)“生本课堂”实验班学生的远距离联想能力整体优于同学校的对照班和对比学校的对照班，反映了“生本课堂”的教学方式能够有效地促进学生创造性思维能力的发展;(2)在不同年级，“生本课堂”带来的学生远距离联想测验成绩的优势有所不同，这与教育训练程度及测试作业的难度有关。

Association between Adolescents Friendship Quality and Social Anxiety: Maternal Psycho-logical Adjustment as a Moderator

Ping Zhong[1,a], Zongbao Liang[1,b], Huihua Deng[1,c,*], Zuhong Lu[1,d]

[1]Key Laboratory of Child Development and Learning Science of Ministry of Education, Research Center for Learning Science, Southeast University, Nanjing, 210096, China

[a]xiaoxinzp@163.com, [b]liangzongbao225@163.com,

[c]dengrcls@seu.edu.cn, [d]luzuhong@gmail.com

[*]Corresponding author

Keywords: adolescents' social anxiety; friendship quality; maternal psychological adjustment; moderating effect

Abstract: This two-year longitudinal study aimed to explore how maternal psychological adjustment and adolescents' friendship quality affect adolescents' social anxiety. Participants were 310 adolescents and their mothers. The results revealed that the adolescents' affection/satisfaction in friendship negatively predicted their social anxiety at the second year. The maternal depression and anxiety moderated the association between adolescents' friendship quality and their social anxiety. Specifically with lower maternal negative adjustment, adolescents are more sensitive to the friendship quality.

1 Introduction

Social anxiety is characterized by intense fear of negative evaluation that may lead to the avoidance of fear-eliciting stimuli and events such as performance demands and potentially embarrassing social situations[1]. It is generally characterized along two dimensions: 1) behavioral (e.g., social avoidance and distress in both novel and general situations) and 2) cognitive-affective (e.g., fear of negative evaluation)[2]. By early adolescence, adolescents experience huge changes psychologically and environmentally, such as independent seeking, expanding peer circle and complicating social structure. They become more sensitive to their self-images, identities and self-worth in peer relationship and close friendship. For social anxious individuals, early adolescence is much more a vulnerable period because of their anxiety about the evaluation from important others and the lack of social skill needed in interpersonal process. Previous studies have shown that social anxious individuals have lower social skills than non-anxious sample[3], which impair their peer relationship such as the peer acceptance, validation and affection[4,5]. Furthermore, the close mutual friendship is also damaged by their interpretation of friendship and negative behavioral style[6,7]. Although there are a great amount of studies discussing the social anxiety influence the quality of peer relationship and mutual friendship, there is a few studies examine the effect of interpersonal relationship quality on the development of social anxiety. La Greca and her colleagues[8] found that peer crowd affiliations, positive qualities in best friendships, and the presence of a dating relationship protected adolescents against feelings of social anxiety, whereas relational victimization and negative interactions in best friendships predicted high social anxiety. However, one limitation of the above mentioned studies is that they mainly investigated the cross-sectional association between social anxiety and friendship quality. Another limitation is that previous studies typically explored the overall quality of friendship such as negative and positive instead of various facets of interpersonal processes. Indeed, friendship quality is multidimensional, with intimacy, satisfaction, affection, companionship and conflict all making potential contributions to the experience of emotional and social affiliations and validation. Hence, since an understanding of the various factors that serve to exacerbate and/or maintain social anxiety is of invaluable importance in prevention and intervention, it is imperative to study this developmental phenomenon longitudinally.

Though developmentally, friendship plays a more important role in early adolescents' life, the parents remain their influence on adolescents' psychological adjustment[9–11]. For social anxious adolescents, high levels of parental anxiety, parental overcontrol/overprotection, and parental rejection have been specifically noted as being associated with high levels of social anxiety symptoms and disorders. The link between parental and offspring anxiety has been established through twin and family studies[12–15]. For instance, Lieb[16] found that adolescent offspring of parents with anxiety disorders had higher rates of social phobia than offspring of parents without an anxiety disorder. Candice and colleagues's research[17] showed that the strongest predictors of social anxiety symptoms were parental anxiety and friendship quality. The mentioned-above studies have focused primarily on the direct association between parental risk factors and offspring's anxiety, no study consider about the effect of the interaction between friendship quality and parental psychological adjustments. Although friendship shapes, perpetuates and alleviates individuals anxiety level, it is possible that their parents' anxiety and depression will moderate this process, especially, on different time points of adolescents' development.

Thus, this two years longitudinal study was designed to explore the effects of adolescents' friendship quality on their social anxiety, and the moderating effects of maternal psychological adjustment on the association between adolescents' friendship quality and social anxiety development. We measured the three dimensions of friendship quality, affection/satisfaction, companionship/intimacy, and conflicts. Based on the mentioned-above studies, it is hypothesized that higher levels of affection/satisfaction and companionship/intimacy will be associated with lower levels of adolescents social anxiety. Higher levels of conflict will be associated with higher levels of adolescents social anxiety. Maternal anxiety and depression will moderate the association between adolescents friendship quality and social anxiety development, such that the adolescents with conflict friendship plus negative adjustment mothers will have the highest level of social anxiety.

2 Method

2.1 Participants

Participants were 310 mother-youth dyads (136 boys and 174 girls), part of a larger study of Nanjing Metro Teen Longitudinal Program. The adolescents (M = 12.25 years, SD = 0.56 years) from three different junior high schools in Nanjing city were initially recruited when they were in grade 7. Of their mothers (M = 38.6 years, SD = 2.83 years), 23.0% had graduated from junior high school and below, 42.7% from senior high school, and 34.3% from college and above. We had our second data collection next year.

2.2 Measures

2.2.1 Social Anxiety

The adolescents' social anxiety was measured with 9-item Cheek and Buss Shyness Scale (CBSS)[18]. Each item is answered on a 5-point Likert type scale ranging from 1 = strongly disagree to 5 = strongly agree. The CBSS has good reliability and validity and the Cronbach's alpha coefficient was 0.79[18]. In this study, we modified 2 items in CBSS and added one item according the characters of adolescents' social life. In this study, the Cronbach's alpha coefficients were 0.72 for the first year and 0.76 for the second year.

2.2.2 Friendship Quality

The quality of friendship was assessed with the Network of Relationships Inventory (NRI)[19]. The NRI consists of 30 questions assessing the quality in 10 dimensions. This study focused on 5 dimensions, companionship, affection, intimacy, satisfaction and conflict from the original NRI. This study emerged affection and satisfaction as affection/satisfaction, and companionship and intimacy as companionship/intimacy. The 3 dimensions showed the Cronbach's alpha coefficients at 0.91, 0.79 and 0.78 for the first year and at 0.94, 0.81 and 0.84 for the second year.

2.2.3 Maternal psychological adjustment

Maternal psychological adjustment was assessed with the Symptom Checklist (SCL-90)[20]. The SCL-90 is comprised of 90 items each measured on a 5-point scale of distress from "not at all" (0) to "extremely" (4). The SCL-90 quantifies psychopathology in terms of nine primary symptom constructs. This study used 6 items from anxiety and depression dimensions: (a) Feeling tense or keyed up, (b) Feeling so restless you couldn't get still, (c) Feeling no interest in things, (d) Feeling hopeless about the future, (e) Feeling everything is an effort, and (f) Feelings of worthlessness. The Cronbach's alpha coefficients were 0.83 for the first year and 0.89 for the second year in our study.

3 Results

3.1 Preliminary Analyses

As shown in Table 1, adolescents' social anxieties at T1 and T2 were significantly and negatively correlated with adolescents' affection/satisfaction, and companionship/intimacy at T1 and positively with conflict at T1. Adolescents' social anxiety at T1 was significantly and negatively with maternal psychological adjustment at T1.

Table 1 Descriptive statistics of variables and bivariate correlations between variables ($N=310$)

	M	SD	1	2	3	4	5	6
1. T1 Adolescent Social Anxiety	2.47	0.73	1.00					
2. T2 Adolescent Social Anxiety	2.40	0.66	0.57**	1.00				
3. T1 Affection/Satisfaction	4.28	0.61	−0.22*	−0.26**	1.00			
4. T1 Companionship/Intimacy	3.72	0.80	−0.13*	−0.13*	0.56**	1.00		
5. T1 Conflict	2.07	0.74	0.13*	0.15*	−0.16**	−0.11	1.00	
6. T1 Maternal psychological adjustment	2.33	0.63	−0.11*	−0.01	0.10	0.03	0.04	1.00

Note: T1 = the first year, T2 = the second year. $^{*}p<0.05$; $^{**}p<0.01$.

3.2 Regression Analysis

A series of hierarchical multiple regression analyses were conducted to examine the effect of the first-year adolescents' friendship qualities (affection/satisfaction, companionship/intimacy, and conflict) in predicting adolescents social anxiety at the first and second years, and the moderating effect of the first year maternal psychological adjustment. For predicting adolescents' social anxiety at the first year, adolescents' gender was entered as control on the first step as listed in Table 2. Then, affection/satisfaction, companionship/intimacy, conflict were entered on the second step. On the third step, maternal psychological adjustment was entered. On the final step, the products of maternal psychological adjustment and each friendship quality were entered. For the second-year analysis as listed in Table 2, we controlled the gender and the first year adolescents social anxiety on the first step, and the following steps were as the same as the above steps. At last, we conducted simple slope analysis to further analyze the moderation effect of maternal psychological adjustment on each friendship quality.

Table 2 T1 friendship qualities and maternal moderating effect predict T1/T2 adolescents' social anxiety

	T1 Adolescents Social Anxiety		T2 Adolescents Social Anxiety	
	ΔR^2	Beta	ΔR^2	Beta
Step 1	0.001		0.332	
Gender		−0.039		0.128*
T1 Adolescents Social Anxiety		—		0.524**
Step 2	0.064**		0.019	
T1 Affection/Satisfaction		−0.252**		−0.151*
T1 Companionship/Intimacy		−0.020		0.034
T1 Conflict		0.090		0.052
Step 3	0.008			
T1 Maternal Depression and Anxiety		0.098		0.060
Step 4	0.021		0.014	
T1 AS × MDA		0.161		0.217*
T1 CI × MDA		−0.131		−0.127
T1 Conflict × MDA		−0.176*		0.062

*$p<0.05$; **$p<0.01$; Note: T1 = the first year, T2 = the second year, AS = Affection/Satisfaction, CI = Companionship/Intimacy, MDA = Maternal Depression and Anxiety.

3.2.1 Maternal psychological adjustment at T1 as a moderator of relationship between T1 friendship qualities and T1 adolescents' social anxiety

The first year affection/satisfaction in adolescents' friendship was associated with lower social anxiety, Beta = −0.252, $p<0.01$. Maternal psychological adjustment moderated the association between conflict and social anxiety, Beta = −0.176, $p<0.05$ (see Table 2). To examine the moderation effect, the effect of conflict on social anxiety was examined when maternal depression and anxiety was low (−1 *SD*) and high (+1 *SD*)[21]. Follow-up analyses revealed that conflict was strongly associated with social anxiety only when maternal depression and anxiety at a lower level (slope = 0.205, $t=2.781$, $p<0.01$) (See Figure 1).

3.2.2 Maternal psychological adjustment at T1 as a moderator of relationship between T1 friendship qualities and T2 adolescents' social anxiety

The first year affection/satisfaction in adolescents' friendship was associated with higher

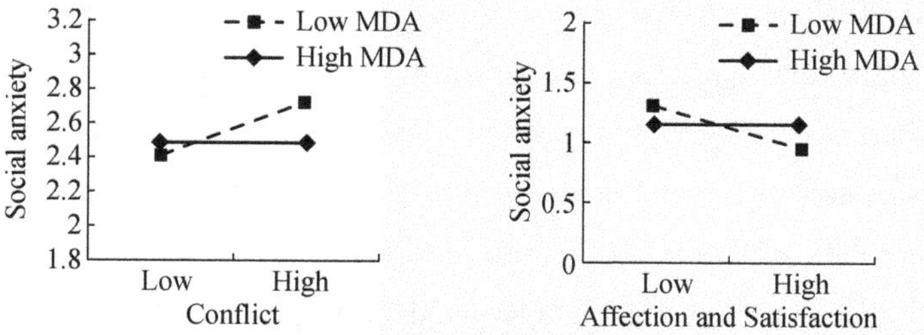

Figure 1　Left: Associations between T1 conflict and T1 social anxiety at higher and lower level of T1 maternal depression and anxiety. Right: Associations between T1 affection/satisfaction and T2 social anxiety at higher and lower level of T1 maternal depression and anxiety

second year social anxiety, Beta = -0.151, $p < 0.05$. First year maternal psychological adjustment moderated the association between affection/satisfaction and social anxiety, Beta $=0.217$, $p<0.05$ (see Table 2). To examine the moderation effect, the effect of affection/satisfaction on social anxiety was examined when maternal depression and anxiety was low (-1 *SD*) and high ($+1$ *SD*)[21]. Follow-up analyses revealed that affection/satisfaction was strongly associated with social anxiety only when maternal depression and anxiety at a lower level (slope = -0.256, $t = -2.928$, $p<0.01$) (See Figure 2).

4　Discussion

This longitudinal study extended the friendship quality into its sub-dimensions for prospectively examining the specific influence of sub-dimensions of friendship quality on adolescents social anxiety, and examining the moderating role of maternal psychological adjustment on the association between adolescents friendship quality and social anxiety. The results supported our hypothesis. The affection/satisfaction in adolescents' friendship quality at the first year was negatively associated with social anxiety at the first and second year. Maternal psychological adjustment would moderate the association between the adolescents friendship quality and social anxiety. When the maternal depression and anxiety was in a lower level, adolescents are more sensitive to friendship quality.

Our results were consistent with prior researches suggesting that adolescents friendship quality has important influence on social anxiety[17]. Especially, the affection/satisfaction was a significant protect factor to decrease the possibility of social anxiety. Plenty of studies showed that friendship could support the emotional and social development of adolescents. For example, Pontari's study[22] found that while introducing themselves to another person via video, participants high in social anxiety appeared more socially competent with a friend present than when alone. Being with a friend also provided valuable opportunities for adolescent to learn and practice social skills, such as effective communication and perspective taking. As for friendship's companionship and intimacy, conflict, they were not significantly associated with social anxiety. One of the explanations is that we collected the friendship quality data when the adolescents just came to a new school and the friendship was quite new, there were not enough time for them to play together and disclose intimacy secrets. And for the freshness of the friendship, there were not many conflicts could happen between our participants.

Furthermore, we focused on the moderating effect of maternal anxiety and depression in current study, which are important indicators of psychological adjustment and had been shown in several well-designed, controlled studies finding that children of parents with anxiety disorders are at increased risk of developing anxiety disorders compared to children of normal control parents or children of parents with other psychiatric disorders[12,23]. Interestingly, our results showed that adolescents are more sensitive to friendship quality when maternal depression and anxiety at a lower level. Specifically, at the first year of junior high school, adolescents of lower level maternal depression and anxiety are more vulnerable to friendship conflict. It is possible that early adolescents are becoming independent from the family, especially with parents in a healthy psychological condition would have more freedom to construct interpersonal relationships with peers. However, it also provides more potential risk for them to get hurt in the relatively immature relationship, because they still need plenty of social skills to support and maintain their friendship. As our results indicated, when mother has lower level negative emotion symptoms, adolescents are more sensitive to conflicts with their friends, which are more obvious when the conflict are intense. Moreover, the two-year longitudinal result indicated the same pattern in the effect of friendship quality on social anxiety, but the affection/satisfaction in friendship quality is a more significant factor to buffer adolescents social anxiety at the second year when maternal depression and anxiety in lower level. These results showed the time-dependent maternal moderating effect depends on the developmental period of adolescents.

There are several limitations to this study. First, only six items for examine maternal depression and anxiety maybe not enough to reflect the psychological adjustment status of mothers. Next, we only assess the subjective perception of adolescents friendship quality. Although several studies have showed that subjective feelings have stronger association with psychological outcome[24], the friends' perception are more valuable because some study indicated that social anxiety adolescents have more immature and negative perspective about friendship than the normal peers[25].

In conclusion, the current study confirmed the specific effects of sub-dimensions of adolescents friendship quality on their social anxiety, especially the affection/satisfaction in friendship negatively predict the second year social anxiety. Moreover, we found that the maternal depression and anxiety moderate the association between adolescents friendship quality and social anxiety. Specifically with lower maternal negative adjustment, adolescents are more sensitive to the friendship quality.

Acknowledgment

This study was supported by the Cultivation Fund of the Key Scientific and Technical Innovation Project (704025), and the Humanities and Social Science Foundation (11YJAZH019), Ministry of Education; and Jiangsu Provincial Social Sciences Key Project (09JYA002), China.

References

[1] D C Beidel, T L Morris. Social phobia//J S March. Anxiety Disorders in Children and Adolescents. New York: Guilford, 1995.

[2] A M La Greca, W L Stone. Social anxiety scale for children-revised: Factor structure and concurrent validity. Journal of Clinical Child and Adolescent Psychology, 1993, 22: 17 - 27.

[3] L A Greco, T L Morris. Factors influencing the link between social anxiety and peer acceptance: Contributions of social skills and close friendships during middle childhood. Behaviour Therapy, 2005, 36: 197 - 205.

[4] A M La Greca, N Lopez. Social anxiety among adolescents: Linkages with peer relations and friendships. Journal of Abnormal Child Psychology, 1998, 26: 83 - 94.

[5] E M Vernberg, D A Abwender, K K Ewell. Social anxiety and peer relationships in early adolescence: A prospective analysis. Journal of Clinical Child Psychology, 1992, 21: 189 - 196.

[6] B H Schneider. An observational study of the interactions of socially withdrawn/anxious early adolescents and their friends. Journal of Child Psychology and Psychiatry, 2009, 50: 799 - 806.

[7] A M Crawford, K Manassis. Anxiety, social skills, friendship quality, and peer victimization: An integrated model. Journal of Anxiety Disorders, 2011, 25: 924 - 931.

[8] A M La Greca, H M Harrison. Adolescent peer relations, friendships, and relationships: Do they predict social anxiety and depression? Journal of Clinical Child and Adolescent Psychology, 2005, 34: 49 - 56.

[9] K B Ehrlich, J Cassidy, M J Dykas. Reporter discrepancies among parents, adolescents, and

peers: Adolescent attachment and informant depressive symptoms as explanatory factors child development. Child Development, 2011, 82: 999 - 1012.

[10] D R Nelson, C Hammen, P A Brennan. The impact of maternal depression on adolescent adjustment: The role of expressed emotion. Journal of Consulting and Clinical Psychology, 2003, 71: 935 - 944.

[11] A G Michael, E R Watkins, J G Simmons. Maternal parenting behaviors and adolescent depression: The mediating role of rumination. Journal of Clinical Child & Adolescent Psychology, 2013, 42: 348 - 357.

[12] D C Beidel, S M Turner. At risk for anxiety: Psychopathology in the offspring of anxious parents. Journal of the American Academy of Child & Adolescent Psychiatry, 1997, 36: 918 - 924.

[13] T C Eley, A M Gregory. Behavioral Genetics//T L Morris, J S March. Anxiety Disorders in Children and Adolescents. 2nd ed. New York: Guilford, 2004: 71 - 97.

[14] K S Kendler, M Neale, R C Kessler. Major depression and phobias: The genetic and environmental sources of comorbidity. Psychological Medicine, 1993, 23: 361 - 371.

[15] A Schrier, H-U Wittchen, M Hofler. Anxiety disorders in mothers and their children: Prospective longitudinal community study. The British Journal of Psychiatry, 2008, 192: 308 - 309.

[16] R Lieb, H-U Wittchen, M Hofler. Parental psychopathology, parenting styles, and the risk of social phobia in offspring: A prospective longitudinal community study. Archives of General Psychiatry, 2000, 57: 859 - 866.

[17] C C Festa, G S Ginsburg. Parental and peer predictors of social anxiety in youth. Child Psychiatry Human Development, 2011, 42: 291 - 306.

[18] J M Cheek, A H Buss. Shyness and sociability. Journal of Personality and Social Psychology, 1981, 41: 330 - 339.

[19] W Furman, D Buhrmester. NRI, children's perceptions of the personal relationships in their social networks. Developmental Psychology, 1985, 21: 1016 - 1024.

[20] L R Derogais. The SCL-90 Manual Ⅰ: Scoring, Administration and Procedures for the SCL-90. Baltimore: Johns Hopkins University School of Medicine, Clinical Psychometrics Unit, 1977.

[21] L S Aiken, G M West. Multiple Regression: Testing and Interpreting Interactions. Newbury Park: Sage Publishing, 1991.

[22] B A Pontari. Appearing socially competent: The effects of a friend's presence on the socially anxious. Personality and Social Psychology Bulletin, 2009, 35: 283 - 294.

[23] S Knappe, K Beesdo, L Fehm. Do parental psychopathology and unfavorable family environment predict the persistence of social phobia? Journal of Anxiety Disorders, 2009, 23: 986 - 994.

[24] N A Gonzales, A M Cauce, C A Mason. Interobserver agreement in the assessment of parental behavior and parent-adolescent conflict: African-American mothers, daughters, and independent observers. Child Development, 1996, 67: 1483 - 1498.

[25] B H Schneider, N G Tessier. Close friendship as understood by socially withdrawn, anxious early adolescents. Child Psychiatry Human Development, 2007, 38: 339 - 351.

议 题

儿童早期发展的前沿研究成果和关键问题

The Science of the Individual

Kurt W. Fischer
Charles Bigelow Professor at the Harvard Graduate School of Education

Our goal is to establish a science of the individual, grounded in analysis of individual patterns of growth. We start with a focus on how individuals grow, based on models of pathways and contexts that shape development. Our argument is that individuals grow in distinctive ways, showing patterns of variability that are not captured by models of average or mean growth. The average does not represent normal growth. Instead individuals show distinctive growth patterns, often unique. Different people grow along distinct pathways, which typically show extensive variability. Both pathways for learning and patterns of cellular growth in cancer document this variability. To find consistent patterns of growth, scientists need to focus on consistent individual pathways and differences, not averages or means. Concepts from dynamic systems can be used to model individual pathways and patterns.

The Impact of Neuroeducation on "Learning by Doing" Project

Yu Wei

Research Center for Learning Science, Southeast University, China

In 1993 ICSU has set up CCBS (Committee on Capacity Building in Science) in order to initiate a joint effort of scientists and educators on IBSE (Inquiry Based Science Education) world widely. Later IAP-IBSE committee (Inter-Academy Panel) continually takes the same responsibility even more actively. As a successful result of international collaboration, the Pilot Project "Learning By Doing" (LBD) has been co-initiated by Ministry of Education of P. R. China and China Association for Science and Technology in August 2001, aimed at promoting the children's science education as well as their holistic development and wellbeing. LDB is an Inquiry Based Science Education and Learning in Kindergartens and Primary Schools (5—12 years). Over 10 years' practice, LBD reach out to 22 provinces and benefiting over 200,000 students and thousands of teachers. LBD has become a sound foundation for revising the National Standard of Science Education in Primary Schools and facilitated the national policy changing on early child development. LBD has got Purkwa Price in 2006 and the First Class Award of Education Research from MOE, China in 2010[1].

In the last decade or so, the accumulated knowledge of human brain has exceeded that acquired during thousands of years' civilization. Therefore a trans-disciplinary field—Neuroeducation has been emerging and developing during the last decade. It provides a wonderful opportunity for education research innovation that will change the education policies as well as the classroom practices. Neuroeducation as a trans-disciplinary field could be drafted below, as shown in Figure 1[2].

In 2002, Research Center for Learning Science (RCLS) has been founded at Southeast University. The unique character of LBD is to apply the research of Neuroeducation to the practices of LBD. LBD project has been advanced by the new research way in following aspects:

1 Deepening the pedagogy of IBSE by empirical studies

The development of IBSE has faced a lot of new challenges in the pedagogy, such as preconception, concept construction, the role of interaction between teachers and students, choosing of key concepts and building learning progressions in science, and

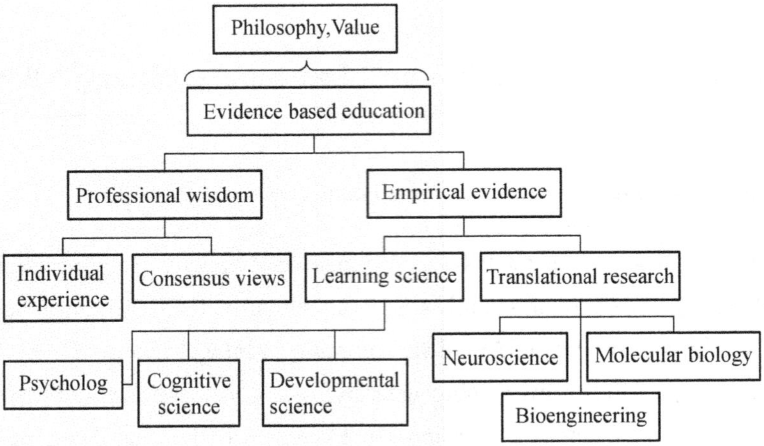

Figure 1 Scheme of Neuroeducation

more importance of the creativity cultivating of students, etc. Conducting scientific research on mind, brain and education can get more reliable and clearer arguments that come from the process of the implementation of LBD.

2 Supporting the policy decision of early child development

In the turning point of this new century, many countries have changed their early child development policies based on brain research. Chinese government also studied the new policies and made the important initiative of early child development in The Outline of China's National Plan for Medium and Long-term Education Reform and Development (2010—2020).

3 Making breakthrough in cultivating social emotion competency

It is drawn a framework of human competencies and skills as Figure 2.

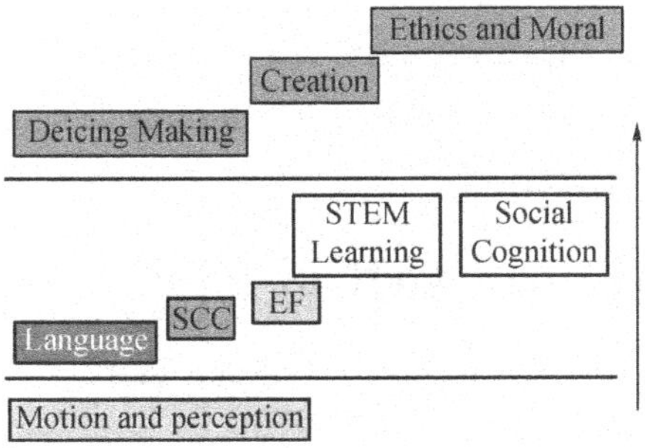

Figure 2 A Framework of Human Competencies and Skills

Although it is realized that the socio-emotional competence is the best prediction for the future success and happiness of our children, the present education curricula focus more on children's academic development than on cultivating children's socio-emotional competence. Based on our knowledge of emotional influences on learning and development, we have included the socio-emotional learning standard for the first time in the content standard of LBD science education[3]. Socio-emotional competence consists of five aspects as follows: (1) Self-awareness: Assess oneself in a proper way. (2) Self-management: Regulate one's own emotions, inspire oneself. Children are supposed to overcome their own self-complacence and hesitation, learning to manipulate their emotions to attain their goals with persistence. (3) Social awareness: Children ought to be sensitive to and know well the emotions, interests and viewpoints of others, learning to appreciate different opinions and emotions on different matters from different people. (4) Relationship skills: Cope efficiently with interpersonal relationship. (5) Responsible decision making.

Considering the special status quo of one-child policy in China, priority is given to children's empathy of emotional competencies and self-esteem of personal characteristics. The requirements and learning stages are also proposed in the standard. Research has shown that IBSE has effectively promoted the social emotion competency of students, particularly the empathy and cooperation behaviors.

4 Creating scientific tools applying to measuring learning outcome in classroom practices

The trans-disciplinary research on Neuroeducation can not only support the pedagogy of IBSE but also create scientific tools applying to measuring learning outcome in classroom practices. Four series of instruments and softwares are being developed in our RCLS center: (1) Multiuser On-line Assessment and Record System for Inquiry-Based Education. (2) Social Emotional Competence Assessment System, in which the recent research will be focused on empathy and communication. In addition to the traditional questionnaire, this system will also utilize the physiological signal analysis, behavior analysis and the facial expression recognition, such that the assessment of empathy as well as the related social emotional competence becomes more reliable.[4] (3) Estimating key concept proficiency system. Virtual reality created by computers and the EEG/ERP technology are combined together[5].

The above are only some of the examples which go to illustrate the great importance of conducting scientific research in the process of science education. Doing education research in a scientific way does not only help us reduce mistakes to a minimum, but also make it possible for us to pursue a path with our own unique features, and possibly make breakthroughs in education reform.

References

[1] Wei Yu. What 10 Year's Practices of LBD Tell Us? Beijing: China Science and Technology Press, 2012.

[2] Wei Yu. The impacts of neuroeducation (Translational Education) on inquiry based science education. Peking University Education Review, 2011, 36(4): 15-17.

[3] Wei Yu. Contents Standard of "Learning by Doing" Science Education Program. Beijing: People's Education Press, 2006.

[4] Yang Y k, Ye Zn. The effect of "learning by doing" on the development of pupil's empathy. Curriculum, Teaching Material and Method, 2011, 31(5): 82-86.

[5] Zhu Y, Qian X, Yang Y, et al. The influence of explicit conceptual knowledge on perception of physical motions: An ERP study. Neuroscience Letters, 2013, 541: 253-257.

The Illusion of Understanding: In the Classrooms and Beyond

Marc Schwartz

University of Texas

This presentation explores the ongoing challenge of defining what learning and understanding mean from the perspective of the learning sciences. These observations provide a framework for understanding the learning process (and resulting studies), and when applied to different learning environments reveal what I call the illusion of understanding. I replace that view with a more authentic understanding of the learning process and the means to achieve it especially as it unfolds in all children from the very young to those seeking advanced studies.

iECD: From Research to Implementation

Robert W. Scherpbier

Chief of Health, Nutrition, Water, Environment & Sanitation at the United Nations Children's Fund (UNICEF) in Beijing

Environment & Sanitation at the United Nations Children's Fund (UNICEF) in Beijing International experience has shown that early interventions—from pre-pregnancy to the first six years in life—can be a highly effective way to break the intergenerational transmission of poverty, address social exclusion, and enhance school readiness. These early interventions include nutritional supplementation, health care, protection, child stimulation, and pre-school education. Research has also clearly demonstrated that to achieve the best results for poor children, an integrated set of service interventions is needed. The integrated Early Childhood Development (iECD) project aims to demonstrate the importance of a holistic approach and its enhanced effectiveness relative to single-issue programming approaches, to promote childhood development in the remote and poor rural areas in China. The presentation will provide an overview of the iECD project, outlining how research has contributed to design and implementation, and raises some questions to guide the potential of research in the project's further development.

The Dynamic Brain: Measuring Growth and Learning

Kurt W. Fischer

Abstract: Dynamic growth models specify the ways that brain growth, cognitive development, and learning all fit together. Brain development shows not a ladder of stages but instead a network of interaction, including attractors, nested cycles, progressions, regressions, groups of discontinuities, and stable performance levels. Cognitive activity and cortical development turn out to be closely related, especially when the system is functioning optimally, as when a teacher or textbook supports optimal performance. We look forward to the time when teachers join us in cognitive neuroscience research, helping to discover the important challenges of connecting education to research on learning.

Parents' Control and Children's Adjustment and Their Relations in Migrant and Nonmigrant Children

Guangzhen Zhang[1,a,*], Zongbao Liang[1,b], Ning Jiang[1,c], Huihua Deng[1,d]

[1]Key Laboratory of Child Development and Learning Science of Ministry of Education, Southeast University, Nanijng, 210096, China

[a]zhangguangzhen@ seu. edu. cn, [b]liangzongbao225@ 163. com,

[c]jiangning199243@ 163. com, [d]dengrcls@ seu. edu. cn

[*]Corresponding author

Keywords: behavioral control; psychological control; school adaptation; longitudinal study

Abstract: The aim of the present study is to investigate the role of parents' control in children's adjustment in Chinese children. Four hundred and seventy adolescents (254 boys and 216 girls) and their teachers participated in the present study when children were in grade 7 (Mage = 12.95, *SD* = 0.91) initiatively (T1). One year (T2) and two year (T3) later, respectively, data collections were conducted again. Children were asked to report parents' behavioral control and psychological control. Teachers were asked to rated children's school adaptive competence and problems. Results of ANOVA indicated that parents exerted more behavioral control towards girls than boys, whereas no gender difference was found in psychological control. Girls were higher in school competence and lower in externalizing problems and learning problems than boys. Results of structural equation modeling indicated that parental behavioral control at T1 positively predicted children's school competence at T2 and negatively predicted children's externalizing problems, internalizing problems and learning problems at T2, after controlling the continuity of outcome variables from T1 to T2. Parental behavioral control at T2 positively predicted children's school competence and negatively predicted children's learning problems at T3. Parental psychological control at T2 positively predicted children's learning problems at T3. Children's school competence at T1 positively predicted parental psychological control at T2, and children's externalizing problems at T2 positively predicted parental psychological control at T3, and children's school competence at T2 positively predicted parental behavioral control at T3. The results indicate that parental behavioral control is beneficial to children's development, whereas the role of parental psychological control in children's school adjustment is not substantial.

流动与非流动儿童的父母教养行为与其社会适应之间的关系

张光珍[1,a,*],梁宗保[1,b],姜宁[1,c],邓慧华[1,d]
[1]东南大学儿童发展与学习科学教育部重点实验室,南京,210096
[a]zhangguangzhen@seu.edu.cn, [b]liangzongbao225@163.com,
[c]jiangning199243@163.com, [d]dengrcls@seu.edu.cn
[*]通讯作者

关键词:行为控制; 心理控制; 学校适应; 追踪研究

中文摘要:本研究采用追踪研究设计,考察了父母的行为控制和心理控制对儿童的学校适应的影响。共 470 名初中生(254 名男孩,216 名女孩)及其班主任老师参与了本研究。在初一上学期期中考试结束两周之后,我们让儿童(M 年龄 = 12.95 岁, SD = 0.91)报告了父母的行为控制和心理控制,让其班主任老师报告了儿童的学校适应能力和学校适应问题。在初二和初三的时候,我们再次邀请儿童及其班主任老师分别报告了父母养育行为和儿童的学校适应。方差分析的结果表明,父母对女孩的行为控制一直都高于对男孩的行为控制,但在心理控制上性别差异不显著。女孩在学校适应能力上的得分一直高于男孩,而在外显问题和学习问题上低于男孩,在内隐问题上性别差异不显著。结构方程模型的结果表明,在控制了儿童学校适应各变量自身的连续性之后,第一年的父母行为控制能够正向预测第二年的学校适应能力,负向预测第二年的外显问题、内隐问题和学习问题;第二年的父母行为控制能够正向预测第三年的学校适应能力,负向预测第三年的学习问题。而父母的心理控制对儿童的学校适应的影响整体上不明显,唯一例外的是第二年的父母心理控制可以正向预测第三年的儿童学习问题。儿童第一年的适应能力正向预测第二年的心理控制,第二年的适应能力正向预测第三年的行为控制,第二年的外显问题正向预测第三年的心理控制。本研究的结果表明,在中国,父母的行为控制对儿童的发展较为有利,而心理控制对儿童的影响不明显。

1 引言

随着我国市场经济的快速发展,越来越多的人口从农村迁移到城市,或从小城镇向大城市迁移。随之而来的一个问题就是大量流动儿童的出现。已有的大量研究发现,流动儿童在行为、心理和社会适应方面都面临诸多困难[1-3]。流动儿童面临的这些困难,一方面是由于不公平的教育安置引起的,这方面已有大量的讨论。另一方面,流动儿童面临的这些困难,也可能是由于家庭内部的因素引起的。例如,流动儿童的父母大多受教育程度比较低,他们从事的工作大多劳动时间长、工作强度大、收入水平低。家庭经济压力往往会导致流动儿童的父母表现出不恰当的养育方式,从而影响流动儿童的适应。但以往的研究较少从家庭内部来探讨流动儿童社会适应的不利因素。

在影响流动儿童社会适应的因素当中,最重要的可能就是父母的养育方式。许多研究者从温暖和控制两个纬度来考察养育方式,最近十多年来,有一些研究者进一步区分了父母控制这一纬度,将父母控制细分为行为控制和心理控制。行为控制指父母对子女日常活动和行踪的监控与管理[4]。心理控制指父母通过干涉和侵犯儿童的独立性和自主性发展,从而使个体对父母产生情感依赖,进而达到控制儿童的目的[5]。研究表明,父母对儿童的行为控制可以有效地抑制外化问题及反社会行为的发生[5],是儿童发展的保护因素;而父母的心理控制会阻碍青少年心理自主的发展,并且导致儿童青少年内化问题的发生[5],对儿童发展具有消极影响。另外也有研究者发现,父母的行为控制和心理控制会受到儿童行为的反作用。但这些研究大多是在西方国家进行的,在中国文化中还较少进行验证。

本研究关注的问题是流动儿童的父母与城市非流动儿童的父母在对儿童的行为控制和心理控制上是否存在差异,父母的行为控制和心理控制对儿童的行为和心理适应有何影响。本研究采用追踪研究设计,对 281 名流动儿童和 189 名非流动儿童从初一追踪到了初三,以此来揭示父母教养行为与儿童适应之间的准因果关系。

2 方法

2.1 研究被试和研究程序

被试来自于苏州的三所初中,其中一所初中全部是流动儿童,另外一所初中全部为非流动儿童,还有一所初中的流动儿童和非流动儿童各占一半。采用整群取样的方法,从三所初中各抽取一些班级的学生参加本次研究。在第一次测查中,共 470 名儿童(254 名男孩,216 名女孩,281 名流动儿童,189 名非流动儿童)参与了研究,平均年龄为 12.95 岁($SD=0.91$)。在流动儿童群体中,父亲和母亲的教育水平为小学以下、初中、高中、大学以上的分别为 14.5% 和 35.5%,63.8% 和 51.8%,17% 和 8%,5% 和 5%。在非流动儿童中,父亲和母亲的教育水平为小学以下、初中、高中、大学以上的分别为 3.8% 和 1.6%,21.7% 和 31.9%,41.3% 和 34.6%,33% 和 32%。

在儿童初一上学期期中考试结束两个星期之后开始第一次数据收集。儿童的数据收集由受过培训的主试以班级为单位展开,让儿童报告父母的养育行为,然后让儿童的班主任和父母分别填写问卷,报告了儿童在学校的适应情况。一年之后(初二上学期)、两年之后(初三上学期),分别再次进行数据收集工作。三次数据收集中,有效的儿童问卷分别是 442 份、432 份和 395 份;有效的教师问卷分别是 447 份、442 份和 398 份,有效的父母问卷分别是 417 份、406 份和 343 份。所以在后面的数据分析中,被试的数目不一致。数据收集之前,我们征得了儿童、家长及教师的同意。

2.2 研究工具

2.2.1 父母行为控制

采用 Kerr 和 Stattin[4]编制的父母监控问卷,该问卷共24道题目,5点评分,包括四个方面:父母监控、父母控制、父母问询、儿童表露。第一个方面测量父母对儿童活动和行踪的了解程度,后三个方面考察父母从哪些渠道获得这些信息。本研究中,我们计算四个纬度分的平均分作为父母行为监控的指标。分数越高,表明父母的行为控制越高。该问卷三年的信度在0.90—0.92间,信度很好。

2.2.2 父母心理控制

采用 Wang 等人[6]编制的心理控制问卷,该问卷总共18道题目,5点评分,分为三个方面:诱导内疚(guilt induction)、爱的撤回(love withdrawal)、强调权威(authority assertion)。本研究中,我们计算各个题目的平均分。分数越高,表明父母的心理控制越高。该问卷三年的信度在0.90—0.94间,信度很好。

2.2.3 儿童社会适应

采用 Hightower 等人[7]的教师—儿童评价量表,该问卷分为儿童学校适应能力和儿童学校适应问题两大部分,其中学校适应能力又包括挫折耐受、任务定向、果敢社交、自我控制等纬度,学校适应问题又包括内隐问题、外显问题、学习问题几方面。分别让教师和家长填写该问卷,其中家长版问卷在表述上作了细微改动。由于学校适应能力的各个子纬度具有较高相关,在本研究中,我们将其作为一个大的纬度。学校适应能力、内隐问题、外显问题、学习问题三年的信度在0.71—0.95间,信度良好。

3 研究结果

父母行为控制、心理控制和儿童学校适应各变量的平均值和标准差见表1。方差分析结果表明,在三次测查期间,流动儿童的父母在行为控制上要低于城市父母,在心理控制上与城市父母差异不显著。此外,流动儿童比城市儿童表现出更多的外显行为问题,但在内隐行为问题和学习问题上与城市儿童差异不显著。在前两次测查中,流动儿童与城市儿童在学校适应能力上差异不显著,但在第三次测查中,流动儿童在学校适应能力上的得分要高于城市儿童。父母对女孩的行为控制要显著高于男孩,在心理控制上的性别差异不显著。女孩的学校适应能力高于男孩,外显问题和学习问题要少于男孩。

表1 父母养育行为和儿童社会适应各变量的平均值和标准差

变量	流动男孩		流动女孩		城市男孩		城市女孩		F（性别）	F（流动）
	M	SD	M	SD	M	SD	M	SD		
行为控制1	3.71	0.77	3.92	0.69	3.34	0.73	3.49	0.74	6.42*	31.78***
心理控制1	2.70	0.89	2.63	0.99	2.73	0.77	2.69	0.87	0.62	0.36
适应能力1	3.11	0.74	3.29	0.78	3.20	0.75	3.32	0.70	4.58*	0.55
外显问题1	1.98	0.90	1.34	0.50	2.03	0.85	1.60	0.55	52.85***	4.74*
内隐问题1	1.98	0.82	1.83	0.67	1.92	0.62	2.01	0.64	0.19	0.66
学习问题1	2.55	0.91	2.07	0.74	2.45	0.89	2.16	0.82	20.64***	0.01
行为控制2	3.70	0.80	3.94	0.70	3.32	0.73	3.58	0.76	11.77***	25.59***
心理控制2	2.86	0.92	2.73	1.05	2.82	0.84	2.65	0.92	2.76	0.53
适应能力2	2.93	0.76	3.41	0.64	3.01	0.64	3.27	0.71	31.30***	0.16
外显问题2	2.03	0.83	1.46	0.51	2.14	0.88	1.68	0.56	53.31***	5.71*
内隐问题2	1.90	0.64	1.80	0.64	1.86	0.61	1.83	0.63	1.24	0
学习问题2	2.59	0.93	2.04	0.70	2.71	0.97	2.17	0.72	44.54***	2.09
行为控制3	3.57	0.83	4.00	0.71	3.24	0.66	3.58	0.68	27.84***	26.17***
心理控制3	2.88	1.07	2.74	1.11	2.96	0.79	2.73	0.84	4.18*	0.27
适应能力3	3.17	0.73	3.68	0.86	2.99	0.61	3.23	0.66	27.16***	18.71***
外显问题3	2.07	0.80	1.48	0.56	2.13	0.69	1.73	0.61	52.65***	5.08*
内隐问题3	1.96	0.66	1.77	0.64	2.00	0.59	1.88	0.66	6.22*	1.42
学习问题3	2.57	0.89	2.06	0.79	2.72	0.91	2.25	0.72	33.11***	3.84

注:1＝第一年,2＝第二年,3＝第三年;*** 表示 $p<0.001$,** 表示 $p<0.01$,* 表示 $p<0.05$。

在 Mplus7.0 软件中用结构方程模型分别对父母的行为控制、心理控制与儿童的社会适应之间的关系进行分析,控制各个变量自身的连续性之后,考察父母教养行为与儿童社会适应之间纵向预测关系。各变量之间的未标准化的路径系数见表2。从表2可以看出,第一年的父母行为监控可以正向预测第二年的学校适应能力,负向预测第二年的外显问题、内隐问题和学习问题,第二年的父母行为监控可以正向预测第三年的学校适应能力,负向预测第三年的学习问题,第二年的父母心理控制正向预测第三年的学习问题。第二年儿童的学校适应能力可以正向预测第三年的父母行为监控,第二年的外显问题正向预测第三年的心理控制。

表2　父母养育行为和儿童社会适应的路径分析结果

	第一年→第二年			第二年→第三年		
	B	*SE*	*t*	*B*	*SE*	*t*
行为控制→适应能力	0.12	0.04	2.78**	0.13	0.05	2.84**
行为控制→外显问题	-0.13	0.04	-3.38***	-0.04	0.04	-0.85
行为控制→内隐问题	-0.07	0.04	-2.02*	-0.07	0.04	-1.72
行为控制→学习问题	-0.21	0.04	-4.77*	-0.13	0.05	-2.72**
适应能力→行为控制	0.05	0.05	1.06	0.12	0.05	2.40*
外显问题→行为控制	0.02	0.06	0.41	0.02	0.06	0.28
内隐问题→行为控制	0.01	0.05	0.24	-0.07	0.06	-1.28
学习问题→行为控制	-0.02	0.06	-0.25	-0.07	0.05	-1.35
心理控制→适应能力	-0.01	0.04	-0.23	-0.03	0.04	-0.68
心理控制→外显问题	0.01	0.04	0.28	0.05	0.04	1.48
心理控制→内隐问题	-0.004	0.04	-0.12	0.03	0.03	0.98
心理控制→学习问题	-0.006	0.04	-0.15	0.10	0.04	2.58*
适应能力→心理控制	0.16	0.06	2.82*	-0.05	0.06	-0.71
外显问题→心理控制	0.08	0.07	1.14	0.16	0.07	2.23*
内隐问题→心理控制	-0.09	0.06	-1.55	0.002	0.07	0.03
学习问题→心理控制	0.11	0.07	1.63	-0.08	0.07	-1.13

4　讨论

本研究考察了流动儿童和城市非流动儿童的社会适应和父母养育行为，以及二者之间的关系。研究结果表明，与城市非流动儿童相比，流动儿童的父母对孩子的日常活动的行踪了解得较少，对孩子的监管不足，而流动儿童也确实比城市非流动儿童表现出更多的外显问题行为。

结构方差模型的结果表明，父母的行为控制对儿童的发展总体来说是有益的，可以增强儿童的适应能力，减少儿童的适应问题，这一结果与在西方国家中发现的结果一致。而父母的心理控制，除了会影响儿童的学习问题外，总体来说对儿童的行为适应的影响并不显著。这与西方国家的结果不一致，西方国家的研究发现，父母的心理控制会导致儿童的心理问题。造成这种不一致的原因可能是，中国文化历来强调人与人之间的联系甚于个体的独立性，父母对儿童的心理控制并不被儿童认为是侵犯他们独立性的表现。

本研究的结果表明，流动儿童与非流动儿童社会适应方面的差异很大程度上是由于二者在父母养育行为上的差异造成的。流动儿童的家庭经济压力较大，父母从事的工作大多报酬低、劳动时间长、劳动强度大，因而父母缺乏足够的时间和精力来对儿童的行为进行监管，而青春期的学生一旦缺少了父母的监管，很有可能发展出各种问题行为。若要改善流动儿童的适应状况，最好是从流动儿童的家庭入手，提高父母的养育质量。

致谢

本文为江苏省哲学社会科学基金青年项目（11JYC011）的阶段性成果。

References

[1] J Fang. A study on the structure and group intervention of self-esteem on emigrant-workers'children. Shanghai: East China Normal University, 2008.

[2] X Li, H Zou, C Jin, et al. The relations among problem behaviors, personalities and family functioning of migrant children. Psychological Development and Education, 2008, 2: 54 - 59.

[3] X Lin, X Fang, Y Liu, et al. The effect mechanism of stigma perception on mental health among migrant children in Beijing. Acta Psychologica Sinica, 2009, 41: 967 - 979.

[4] M Kerr, H Stattin. What parents know, how they know it, and several forms of adolescent adjustment: Further support for a reinterpretation of monitoring. Developmental Psychology, 2000, 36: 366 - 380.

[5] B K Barber, H E Stolz, J A Olsen. Parental support, psychological control, and behavioral control: Assessing relevance across time, culture, and method. Monographs of the Society for Research in Child Development, 2005, 70: 1 - 137.

[6] Q Wang, E M Pomerantz, H C Chen. The role of parents' control in early adolescents' psychological functioning: A longitudinal investigation in the united states and china. Child Development, 2007, 78: 1592 - 1610.

[7] A D Hightower, W C Work, E L Cowen, et al. The teacher-child rating scale: A brief objective measure of elementary children's school problem behaviors and competencies. School Psychology Review, 1986, 15: 393 - 409.

Problems and Solutions in K-2 STEM Education: A Chinese Case

Zhaoning Ye[1,a,*], Yan Ye[2,b], Yu Chen[2,c]

[1]Research Center for Learning Science, Southeast University, Nanjing, China

[2]Education Center for "Learning by Doing" Science Education Reform Pilot Program, China Association for Science and Technology

[a]yezhaoning@seu.edu.cn, [b]kenshin19841129@163.com,

[c]chenyusummer@gmail.com

[*] Corresponding author

Keywords: STEM; engineering education; K-2; young children learning progression

Abstract: STEM education has been spreading all over the world. Research and policy indicates that students should be engaged in STEM courses from kindergarten. The pilot project for science education reform of China, Learning by Doing, has published a range of STEM modules. During the developing and implementing of these modules, problems typically met by K-2 students were recognized and dealt with. Young children are often short of experience of the engineering products, materials and process, and they are likely to present too much or too little imagination. In the instruction, opportunities for children to develop their understanding of what they'll use and design, as well as what engineers' work looks like, is key to solve these problems. Besides, these opportunities also offer a natural way to appreciate the connection between STEM fields. Other teaching strategies, e.g., introducing contexts and brainstorming, support children to fully participate in STEM activities too. A Learning by Doing module, My little boat, is involved to illustrate these problems and solutions. This effort is expected to contribute to the future development and practice of STEM education.

Introduction

STEM, the acronym for science, technology, engineering and mathematics, has been increasingly highlighted in the past decade[1]. It is argued that STEM subjects raise informed citizens, and particularly, sustain the capacity of STEM related workforce. While science and mathematics presented to be two traditional courses, engineering and technology have been contained in science curriculum. In the latest science education framework of the United States and the derived standards[2,3], engineering and technology is specialized across the K-12 learning expectation. In 2006, the pilot project for science education reform of China, Learning by Doing (LBD), launched its content standards[4], which also integrated engineering and technology as a part from kindergarten to elementary level. This effort is prospective to be introduced into the forthcoming new edition of national science education standards of China.

LBD has developed a series of teaching and learning modules, including several engineering and technological ones. During the planning and practice phases of these modules, it was recognized that young children encountered typical problems when challenged by designing and constructing tasks, though science standards acknowledge that they have the ability to engage in such activities. In this paper, these problems are described and addressed, using the LBD module My Little Boat as an example[5], in the hope to support future development of early childhood STEM materials and enrich the limited database of early engineering curricula[6].

Content and practice of My Little Boat module

My Little Boat is an LBD engineering and technology module developed for K-2 students, which is basically an engineering module, while offering an appropriate way toward integrated STEM education. It contains 3 main activities (Table 1).

Table 1 My Little Boat module

Activity	Description
Various Boats	To discuss different boats and ships in the surrounding world.
Make a Boat	To design a boat or ship and build it with daily materials.
Make a Robust Boat	To design and build a boat holding weight.

When teaching this module, the teacher firstly ask children to share what they know about boats or ships, i. e., the types, shapes, structures, materials, and uses. This activity provides students with the opportunity of scientific discourse, and the students make a glance at the connection between the properties of materials (scientific finding) and their usage (engineering for particular purposes).

In the second activity, students creatively design boats, with the constraints of available resources. The requirements of a boat are fixed by students, which simulates the first step of solving an engineering problem—defining the problem. As an engineering process, children plan, build, check, share and improve their design. Science and technology is also involved, when children experiencing the materials, and testing and carrying out their design.

Students are expected to build a boat that bears as much weight as possible in Activity 3. This could be seen as an aspect of improvement to their first product in Activity 2. The new task refers to load bearing and volume of the boat. In addition, it helps children consider the relation between barycentre and stability, which points to the crosscutting concepts of structure and function in LBD Standards[4] and NGSS[3].

Before the publication of the module, it was tried out in 23 kindergartens and elementary schools in Beijing, Shanghai and Nanjing, with about 1 000 students aged 5—7 engaged. After that, as the spread of LBD, more schools have been practicing it.

During the process, several problems typically presented by the students were recognized, and relevant solutions to these problems were carried out, so that the module could get refined and teachers could be informed when planning and implementing such curriculum.

Typical problems of students and corresponding solutions

Problem 1 Lack of experience of the engineering products and materials

Young children do not know much about boats or ships, except that they can float. The types, structures and purposes of different boats are not quite clear to them, or they might have not thought of it. But in engineering education, it is emphasized that students realize people create varieties of artefacts to satisfy particular needs. So before the children build a boat, they should have defined what a boat is used for and what the derived requirements are.

In addition, if children are asked to make a boat without much knowledge about it, their creativity would be limited. Some children would just copy what the others do without thinking.

Compared to what children know about the boat, no more is understood regarding the materials they can use to make a boat, for example, what materials float, what shapes help an object float, what materials are waterproof.

So, before making a boat, the module offers the children enough time to get familiar with different boats and ships in the surrounding world in Activity 1. Although some of the children may not have seen a real boat, some of them have taken a ferryboat, or have been on a boat or raft in the parks, and others may have watched large ships on TV or in pictures. It's possible for them to share what they know. A sheet that organizes types, shapes, sizes, structures and functions could support them to analyze and conclude. There are also opportunities to go out of school to view real boats in their real environments.

Moreover, in the second activity, children have to predict and test the relevant properties of materials, in order to make reasonable choices of what to use to build the boats. This looks much like what's in an inquiry-based science classroom. It's science threaded in the module, which demonstrates the natural connection between science and engineering, and helps to illustrate how a fully integrated STEM curriculum could be[1].

Problem 2　Lack of experience of engineering process

Engineering is fundamentally an iterative process of design to meet human needs. Although engineers sometimes fabricate, operate, inspect, and maintain new technologies, an emerging consensus is that design is a central practice of engineering, which begins with defining and delimiting an engineering problem, and involves then developing possible solutions and optimizing the design solution[2].

On the contrary, young children appear ignorant about this process. They are used to directly making something before designing it explicitly.

In this module, when introducing the task of making a boat, children are asked to think over in advance what the criteria a boat should meet. Based on their discussion of different boats, children can summarize that a boat floats, it holds people or freight which is kept away from water and it is strong and good-looking. Then, children are allowed to choose surrounding objects and tools that could be made into a boat meeting their criteria.

This step simulates defining and delimiting an engineering problem, after which children draw pictures to communicate their design in groups (Figure 1). Discourse and negotiation, an important skill of scientists and engineers, is inevitable here. When necessary, children even need to be guided to make some trials of their designs, especially in the third activity, to make sure their boats would not turn over with that many loads (Figure 2). These steps support the children to appreciate the K-2 grade band endpoints outlined in NRC's framework: because there is always more than one possible solution to a problem, it is useful to compare designs, test them, and discuss their strengths and weaknesses[2].

Figure 1 Children's design and product

Figure 2 Children are testing their designs

An engaging context is useful when young children defining the problem. For example, a little chicken is planning to see his friend resident at an islet in the middle of a pond, and he comes to you for help.

Teachers can tell children that the materials for using are limited. As a result, it is not clever to build a boat before the design is approved by an "engineers board".

It is also recommended to show the students video clips or pictures to demonstrate how engineer groups design in authentic circumstances, such as architects designing a house, automotive engineers designing a car, or environmental engineers design a sewage treatment plant.

Problem 3 Too much or too little imagination

As designing, children often love to think much about details on or inside the boats, while the basic criteria or constraints are neglected. For example, a kindergarten kid just watched a TV program about aircraft carriers before the lesson, so he insisted to make a model aircraft carrier. He spent much time to design different types of aircrafts on the surface of the carrier, but paid no attention that the body of his carrier—an iron box—was not sealed and at the risk of sinking. Besides, he did not have enough time or resources to make that many planes.

Imagination is welcomed in learning and helpful to STEM. But children should also realize that engineers always face constraints when designing. They may have limited time, certain kinds of materials, inadequate funding, or requirement of the size or weight of the products. During the instruction, teachers must remember to remind students of these limits and criteria, and compare it with real engineers' work. Sometimes, a storyline to focus the students on such issues is supportive.

On the other hand, it's probable that young children tend to be far from creative. On cause is the insufficiency of experience with the surrounding world, as discussed above. Giving children chances to gain the relevant knowledge is important. In this module, before deciding what to use to build their boats, children are encouraged to look for any possible resources not only within what teachers prepare, but also at home, where plenty of suitable resources (e. g., radish, watermelon rinds and recycled bottles) could be found. Sharing ideas, i. e., brainstorming, is another effective way for inspiration. Once by brainstorming, children figured out to design a raft by Calabash, which was classical in Chinese myth.

Discussion and Conclusions

In this paper, three typical problems met by children as participating in STEM modules were identified and the solutions were presented. There are other problems as well, one of which is when they set out to implement their designs, and there would be no more design. In other words, they throw their designs away, and never refer to them again. Such problems, including those described above, coordinate with young children's experiences of the world and their cognition characteristics. On the other hand, traditional pedagogy that emphasizes the process of making something rather than the process of designing seems another factor. This reveals the significance of essential engineering education study together with teachers' and administrators' professional development in the future. The solutions to these problems are related to children's age too, such as interesting contexts. Dorie et al. (2013) reported using puppets, a kids' toy, to elicit talking during interviews on engineering with young children[7].

Schunn (2009) proposed four principles for early engineering[8]. The first principle suggested to engage children in solving significant design problems from the beginning, rather than learning basic engineering, science or mathematics in advance. My Little Boat module is coherent with this viewpoint, which helps promoting the motivation for learning and recognizing connection between STEM fields. The task of making a boat is introduced before coping with material science. However, given the fact that young children are interested in showing off what they know, the module allows them to share their ideas about boats and ships before the task.

References

[1] National Research Council. Engineering in K-12 Education: Understanding the Status and Improving the Prospects. Washington D. C. : The National Academies Press, 2009.

[2] National Research Council. A Framework for K-12 Science Education: Practices, Crosscutting Concepts, and Core Ideas. Washington D. C. : The National Academies Press, 2012.

[3] National Research Council. Next Generation Science Standards: for States, by States. Washington D. C. : The National Academies Press, 2013.

[4] Research Center for Learning Science of Southeast University, Key Laboratory of Child Development and Learning Science of Ministry of Education, Think tank: Handsbrain Education. Content Standards (trial edition) for Inquiry-based Science Education Pilot Project in Kindergarten and Elementary School "Learning by Doing". Beijing: People's Education Press, 2006.

[5] Thinktank: Handsbrain Education, Key laboratory of Child Development and Learning Science of Ministry of Education, Research Center for Learning Science of Southeast University. Curricula of Inquiry-based Science Education Pilot Project in Kindergarten and Elementary School "Learning by Doing": Fruit Basket and My Little Boat. Beijing: People's Education Press, 2008.

[6] Bagiati A, Yoon S, Evangelou D, et al. Engineering curricula in early education: Describing the landscape of open resources. Early Childhood Research & Practice, 2010, 12(2): 12-17.

[7] Dorie B, Tranby Z, Van Cleave S, et al. Using Puppets to Elicit Talk During Interviews on Engineering with Young Children. 2013 ASEE Annual Conference papers, 2014.

[8] Schunn C. How kids learn engineering: The cognitive science perspective. K-12 Engineering Education, 2009, 39(3): 32-37.

The Importance and Social Policies of Early Environment and Experience for Children: A Review of Brain Based Researches

Yanwei Li[1,2,a], Dongchuan Yu[1,2,b,*]

[1]Research Center for Learning Science, Southeast University, Nanjing, Jiangsu, China

[2]Key Laboratory of Child Development and Learning Science of Ministry of Education, Southeast University, Nanjing, Jiangsu, China

[a]lyw8739@gmail.com, [b]dcyu@seu.edu.cn

[*]Corresponding author

Keywords: early environment; early experience; genes; brain development

Abstract: With the popularization of invasive neuroimaging tools used in children, researchers have carried on a lot of experiments on child's brain development. As is known to all, the brain starts to develop in uterus and continues to mature until the early adulthood. During the period, early experience plays a crucial role in child's development.

Early experience refers to the environment in the first 6 or 8 years after birth and the experience children have had in their early life. It includes a large variety of factors. For instance, the nutrient for babies and pregnant mothers, the environment in the womb, maternal habits of living and social interaction, the children's living environment after birth, and the interaction between children and their parents, neighbors, teachers and peers, etc. By reviewing the EEG, fNIRS, fMRI studies and gene studies in biology which are experimented on young animals and children, this article has summarized the researches focusing on exploring the effects of children's early experience well before their birth and their early childhood. Particularly, the article has highlighted the terrible effects of some risk factors such as toxic substances, neurotoxin, toxic stress, neglect, poor parenting and so on.

Although people thought the gene blueprint inherited from the parents is unchangeable, scientific findings show that genes can be turned on and off by child's early experience. So the supposition that we thought the brain development process was determined only by the genes inherited from the parents would be wrong. In fact, early experience is a critical factor for whether and how the genes are expressed. The article shows that the risk of early experience can not only affect the gene blueprint inherited from the parents, but also disturb the development of the brain architecture by altering of genes indirectly. Worse still, the irreversible process will leave a life-long effect on children and will probably pass down to the next generation. Besides, the article shows that the risk factors of experience in early life will also damage the development of brain directly and maybe lead to a disease with a long incubation period.

The growing scientific proofs show us that a good foundation of early life will contribute to the bright future for children. Early damages can bring about a large range of physical and mental problems which will impair the children's capacities for cognitive and academic skills, and even the social and emotional competence. The intervention with these defects needs much more financial costs and will be a lager expenditure of time and effort. So the urgency to improve the circumstances and experience in children's early life is worthy of attention for politicians, educators, parents and other relevant people.

People must identify the difficulties in pursuing the protection of maternal environment and children's early life. Scientific researches should be given much more investment in time, money, human resources and so on. Politicians should pay special attention to child welfare programs since some children are severely neglected and badly parented. Educators should make know to the public the importance of early experience and parenting skills. The sincere cooperation of all fields by relevant people is in great urgency.

脑科学视角下儿童早期环境和经验的重要性及建议

李艳玮[1,2,a]，禹东川[1,2,b,*]
[1]东南大学学习科学研究中心，南京，江苏，中国
[2]东南大学学习儿童发展与学习科学教育部重点实验室，南京，江苏，中国
[a]lyw8739@gmail.com，[b]dcyu@seu.edu.cn
[*]通讯作者

关键词：早期环境；早期经验；基因；脑发育

中文摘要：儿童早期环境和经验包括营养，孕妇的生活环境和习惯，个体出生后与母亲、邻居、同伴之间的交流等。通过总结国内外近二三十年来在生物学和脑科学领域的相关研究成果发现，儿童早期的环境和经验不仅会影响脑的发育，还会通过影响基因的表达与否来改变脑的建构，甚至还会将这些影响遗传给孩子的下一代。由此可见，早期环境和经验的重要性必须引起社会各界人士的重视，文章最后针对当前早期教育的问题给出了建议。

1 引言

儿童早期（胎儿期和0—6岁）的发展和生理紊乱是成年期各种疾病的罪魁祸首，早期环境和经验对个体造成的伤害在显现之前可能会有几年甚至几十年的潜伏期，并且这些伤害还可能遗传给下一代，所以早期发展不容忽视。[1]

由于研究手段和技术的限制，以往关于早期发展的研究仅着手于健康、行为及影响因素，根本无法探究深层次的环境、基因及脑发育之间的关系。但自20世纪90年代以来，国外就开始大力推进脑科学研究，例如，美国的“脑的十年”计划（The Decade of Brain）、欧洲的“EC脑十年计划”（European Community，Decade of Brain Research）、日本的“脑科学时代”计划（The Age of Brain Science）以及前不久奥巴马提出的“脑成像计划”（Brain Mapping Project）等。这些使得研究者对儿童早期的探究更加深入，有关儿童早期脑发育的规律及影响因素、与行为和健康之间关系的研究等也日益受到关注。

近二三十年脑科学的研究成果告诉我们，脑的结构和功能受到基因、环境和经验的影响：基因为脑发育提供了最基本的参考框架，负责引导神经细胞在特定时间内显现自己的特性，并按照一定的规则在脑中搭建回路；环境涉及营养、物理生活环境等，会对脑的建构产生重大影响；经验指孩子成长过程中与环境之间的交流，最早的经验是胎儿对子宫环境的感知和回应，随着个体的降生，经验还包括与父母、邻居、同伴之间的交流。[2]

值得强调的是,环境和经验不仅会影响脑的发育,还会通过影响基因的表达来改变脑的建构,母亲子宫内的环境、婴儿期和儿童早期的环境和经验都能够减弱或加强通过遗传获得的“基因蓝图”(Gene Blueprint)。[3] 所以,脑发育的过程是一个随时间而不断演变的进程,这期间内,环境和经验中任意一个微小的成分都会与我们最初遗传得到的基因蓝图产生千丝万缕的联系。

文章在综述国内外有关环境和经验对儿童早期基因与脑发育影响研究的基础上,指出了未来科学实践和政策制定中应当注意的几个问题,并有针对性地对我国儿童早期教育提出了建议。

2 早期环境和经验通过影响基因的表达改变脑的发育

基因为脑提供了最初的发展图谱,决定了神经元的基本属性,制定了脑发育过程中神经回路之间建立联系应遵循的基本原则,所以说基因能够控制脑的基本建构,基因的改变也会带来脑发育的改变。

基因有结构基因和表观基因之分,结构基因指通过遗传得到的基因,类似计算机硬件系统,决定个体发展的轮廓,表观基因则是相应的操作系统,用来决定结构基因如何或在何时表达。[4]

结构基因和表观基因在个体发展过程中相互作用,早期的环境和经验会在基因上留下印记,并很有可能将这些印记遗传给孩子的下一代。尤其是胎儿或儿童早期的“毒性压力”、化学物质、药物、营养物质过剩或匮乏等,都可能会造成表观基因的改变,并进一步影响脑的发育。

2.1 早期“毒性压力”会改变表观基因

由经验引发的生理活动能够改变脑的化学特性,并改变神经元的基因编码:由积极经验引发的生理激活会促使神经元出现有利有效学习的基因表达,[5] 但早期“毒性压力”会导致个体出现持续一生的表观基因改变,使躯体不得不响应生命中的困境。

胎儿期母亲压力过大或出生后遭受的过多压力被称为“毒性压力”,这些压力有害神经回路和机体的荷尔蒙系统,从而使个体的压力应激系统更差。以儿童为研究对象的实验结果表明,拥有安全依恋关系的儿童在失落或受到惊吓时均显示出了更好的应激能力,表明他们能够更好地探索世界、更理智地面对挑战,在偶尔受到惊吓时也不会因遭受困境而产生过多的皮质醇;相反,没有安全依恋关系的儿童在遭受同等水平的惊吓时却要承受更高的压力激素水平,导致他们的神经回路发生改变,无法有效地处理成长中所面对的压力。[6] 另外,一些动物和人类研究的实验结果表明,母亲孕期遭受过大压力会导致其孕育的后代在遭受压力时更容易害怕或出现过度反应,并且这一现象已被证明成为一种稳定的遗传模式,[7] 即在“毒性压力”下暴露的个体的表观基因会发生改变,并且会遗传给他的下一代。

2.2 化学物质、药物、营养过剩或匮乏会改变个体的表观基因

长期或在关键期内暴露于有毒物质会导致表观基因改变，导致基因表达或不表达，这与个体身心疾病发生率的增高有关。近来，有关动物和人类研究的实验结果表明，空气污染、非诱变毒素、饮食选择、行为模式等都会造成基因表型变化、DNA 甲基化。[8]一些食物补充物质，例如过量的酸、碱或维生素 B_{12}等可能会导致某些基因不表达，而母亲孕期的营养状况和服用的药物等环境因素也会造成胎儿表观基因的改变，并且这些改变会遗传给胎儿的下一代。[9]

另外，研究者还发现，原本被认为是永久性的基因改变在某些条件下可被修改。[10]动物实验研究结果也表明，幼仔出生后早期某些压力导致的表观基因型改变会引发其成年后出现过度的压力反应，但是当服用药物之后，这些负面的 DNA 变化消失，也就是说，通过药物的作用，原有的基因表达发生了改变。[11]

3 早期环境和经验会改变其大脑发育

儿童早期蕴含了感知、语言、认知、情感等发展的多数敏感期，该时期内神经回路对各种化学和电信号非常敏感，被称为神经回路形成的敏感期。由于敏感期结束后再改变神经回路非常困难，所以，在敏感期内为孩子提供适宜的环境和经验以维持大脑的正常建构显得尤为关键。

3.1 神经毒素(Neurotoxin)有害正常的脑发育

神经毒素指那些能够造成神经元或神经回路受损，从而导致脑的结构和功能受损的生物或化学物质，分为自然化学物质、兴奋剂和处方药物这三类。[11]无论在出生前还是出生后暴露于这些物质，发育尚不成熟的大脑都会受到伤害。

自然化学物质，也叫环境化学物质，包括重金属、铅、水银、有机磷酸酯类等。其中，重金属会扰乱神经元从一个脑区迁移到另一个脑区，或者阻碍神经元之间突触的形成，从而影响到脑的发育、建构及塑造，此外，它还会干扰神经元之间的信息传递，进而影响脑的多种复杂回路，例如学习、情绪及基本的视觉、听觉、运动回路等，脑中最复杂、最高级的功能回路(如思维和情感)最容易受到这些重金属的干扰。[12]

常见的兴奋剂，例如酒精、尼古丁和卡洛因也会损害脑的正常建构。例如，母亲在怀孕期间吸烟或摄入尼古丁会造成胎儿在青春期时患肥胖症，并且这类孩子的奖赏回路发育受损，他们奖赏回路中的杏仁核脑区相对正常青少年体积偏小。[13]

某些营养补充物和处方药物，例如维生素 A、2-丙戊酸钠、控制痉挛障碍的抗痉挛药等也有损脑的发育。例如，2-丙戊酸钠是一种抗癫痫药物，但如果胎儿暴露于 2-丙戊酸钠会导致动物幼仔的神经元损伤和神经回路的改变，并进一步破坏它们的认知功能。[14]

3.2　忽视和贫乏的教养会导致大脑发育异常

2000年秋,鉴于罗马尼利福利院出现极度困境的现实,研究者开展了布加勒斯特早期干预项目(Bucharest Early Intervention Project, BEIP),用以研究那些经历着忽视、贫乏交流和互动以及糟糕至极的教养的孩子的发展情况。

研究者发现,长期在福利院生活的儿童脑体积小于正常儿童[15],并且一直在福利院长大和2岁左右被领养的儿童灰质体积小于正常儿童,被领养儿童的白质体积高于一直在福利院的儿童。[16]另外,一直在福利院生活的儿童显示出了较低的 α 波和 β 波,[17]通常,较高的 α 波和 β 波则被证明是与较好的认知、注意状态和唤醒相关,他们出现的这种脑电波又与家庭经济条件贫困的儿童[18]以及被确诊患有ADHD的儿童[19]出现的脑电波类似,所以这种脑电波被解释为与脑发育迟缓有关。可见,福利院中忽视和贫乏的教养已经直接影响到了孩子的脑发育。

不仅如此,研究者还发现,这种环境带造成的大脑损伤很难得到补偿或需很长时间才能得到补偿。因为当BEIP项目中的一些孩子被生活条件较好的家庭收养18个月后,他们的脑电波并没有得到改善,[20]直到这些儿童在较好生活环境中度过了约6.5年后,他们的 α 脑电波才与正常儿童没有差别。[21]

类似BEIP项目研究环境的人类研究毕竟罕见,所以利用动物模型探讨环境与经验的对行为和脑发育影响的研究也应当受到研究者的重视。例如,在啮齿类和灵长类动物身上所做的实验结果也正巧验证了上述结论,研究发现,幼鼠刚出生时与母鼠的分离会导致其一系列的行为变化和压力控制系统中关键DNA的改变。[22]

3.3　早期毒性压力会破坏孩子的大脑结构

个体应对压力的能力是由脑中一套关联性较高的回路和应激系统共同控制的,当个体受到威胁时,应激系统会将躯体或情感上的压力转换为化学信号,并通过躯体细胞传递到脑,在一些大脑回路的参与下完成对压力的调控。个体在受到压力时会调动由"下丘脑—垂体—肾上腺"构成的压力应激系统,简称HPA轴,它会在肾上腺外部分泌皮质醇,用以缓解压力。

如果在早期长期遭受毒性压力,个体就无法有效地控制HPA轴的开关,当再次面对压力和威胁时,只能较差地操纵自己的压力应激系统,做出过激或长时间无法回到平息状态的反应。[9]研究者采用人类被试证明了皮质醇水平长时间过高会导致海马体积减小,同时,需要依赖于海马来完成的记忆任务成绩也低于控制组,不仅如此,他们还发现,海马体积缩小的比例与皮质醇水平的高低以及皮质醇水平异常的持续时间有关。[23]所以,长期处于较高皮质醇水平状态有损大脑结构的发育,同时还会影响个体的认知功能。此外,研究者还发现当个体在发展的关键期中被施予极大的压力时,压力给它的大脑结构和神经回路带来的伤害会趋向稳定,并一直会持续到成年期。[24]

4 儿童早期发展的政策指导和建议

我国在推动儿童早期教育方面已经取得了一定的成果,例如《3—6岁儿童学习与发展指南》的推动和落实。但相比国外的早期教育,我国儿童早期教育仍存在较多弊端,因此,政策制定者在开展儿童早期教育,确保儿童早期环境和经验的安全性和支持性的过程中,应做到以下几点:

第一,明确保护孕期和儿童早期生活环境是一项长期而艰巨的任务。由于某些表观基因的改变可以遗传给孩子下一代,所以只有为孕妇和早期儿童提供支持性的生活环境,才有可能保证儿童从亲代遗传的危险基因不得以表达,减免儿童未来出现躯体疾病、学习能力差、对下一代的教养不适等问题。认同并保障儿童早期生活环境的安全性、支持性,以此来促进儿童的健康发展、造福子子代代是一项长期而艰巨的任务。

第二,加大科学研究投入,寻找儿童早期正常发展的保护伞。政策制定者可颁布某些化学物质使用的公共政策、规范或法律条例,以强制要求处理某些毒素或规范某些药物的使用;同时,应加大对科学研究的投入,帮助科学工作者确定儿童发展的关键期中有害物质的暴露阈限,并研发新的、安全的药物来修正不良基因改变造成的后果,这一研究成果如果能够成功运用在人类身上,我们的获益将不可估量。

第三,关注儿童保育和福利,重视改善福利院的教养结构。困境生物学的实验研究结果告诉我们,与在安全环境中生活的孩子相比,易感性儿童在营养、安全和稳定教养关系等方面需要更多的关注。[15]而生长在福利院、孤儿院的孩子大多是无依无靠的孤儿、弃婴或残疾儿童,自身缺陷导致他们比其他孩子更加敏感。因此,实现对这些孩子生活环境的监管,完善对他们的福利制度、改善福利院结构应该尤其受到重视。

第四,加强对父母进行早期科学教育知识的普及。父母作为孩子的第一任教师,在儿童早期发展的过程中发挥着不可估量的作用。母亲在孕期应避免各种伤害,为孩子的基因表达和器官塑造奠定基础;在孩子出生以后,应与孩子建立有响应的、温暖关爱的亲子交流关系,避免孩子受到忽视和过大的压力;应为孩子提供丰富积极的生活环境,因为孩子是天生的科学家,有效的刺激有利于孩子的学习、探索和模仿,甚至还可以弥补忽视和压力造成的伤害。[25]

2003年,伴随着国际“脑、心智和教育学会”的成立,一门基于实证的应用学科——神经教育学(Neuroeducation)应运而生,该学科主张综合应用基础学科中发现的规律与知识以解决教育中的实践问题。[25]研究者认为,在早期教育的过程中,若能通过立法手段巩固实证性教育研究的地位,把握神经教育学带来的新机遇,我国早期教育定会取得重大飞跃。[25]

致谢

本文为国家自然科学基金《基于脑网络拓扑估计的中国儿童社会情绪能力评测

研究》(项目编号:61273224)、《复杂动态网络系统结构辨识研究》(项目编号:61074126)、"973"计划项目《基于影像的脑网络研究及其临床应用》(项目编号:2011CB707800)的阶段性成果之一。

References

[1] F A Champagne. Epigenetic influences of social experiences across the lifespan. Developmental Psychobiology, 2010, 52: 299 - 311.

[2] National Scientific Council on the Developing Child. The timing and quality of early experiences combine to shape brain architecture. Working Paper No. 5, 2007. http://www.developingchild.net.

[3] National Scientific Council on the Developing Child. Early experiences can alter gene expression and affect long-term development. Working Paper No. 10, 2010. http://www.developingchild.net.

[4] D C Dolinoy, J R Weidman, R L Jirtle. Epigenetic gene regulation: Linking early developmental environment to adult disease. Reproductive Toxicology, 2007, 23: 297 - 307.

[5] J D Sweatt. Experience-dependent epigenetic modifications in the central nervous system. Biological Psychiatry, 2009, 65: 191 - 197.

[6] M M Loman, M R Gunnar. Early experience and the development of stress reactivity and regulation in children. Neuroscience & Biobehavioral Reviews, 2010, 34: 867 - 876.

[7] T Zhang, T Parent, I Weaver, et al. Maternal programming of individual differences in defensive responses in the rat. Annals of the New York Academy of Science, 2004, 1032: 85 - 103.

[8] J R Seckl, M C Holmes. Mechanisms of disease: Glucocorticoids, their placental metabolism and fetal "programming" of adult pathophysiology. Nature Clinical Practice Endocrinology & Metabolism, 2007, 3: 479 - 488.

[9] P N Bocock, K M Aagaard-Tillery. Animal models of epigenetic inheritance. Seminars in Reproductive Medicine, 2009, 27: 369 - 379.

[10] F A Champagne, J P Curley. Epigenetic mechanisms mediating the long-term effects of maternal care on development. Neuroscience and Biobehavioral Reviews, 2009, 33: 593 - 600.

[11] P O McGowan, A Sasaki, A C D' Alessio, et al. Epigenetic regulation of the glucocorticoid receptor in human brain associates with childhood abuse. Nature Neuroscience, 2009, 12: 342 - 348.

[12] C D Klaassen. Heavy metals and heavy-metal antagonists//L S Goodman, A Gilman. The Pharmacological Basis of Therapeutics. New York: McGraw-Hill, 1996.

[13] A Haghighi, D H Schwartz, M Abrahamowicz, et al. Prenatal exposure to maternal cigarette smoking, amygdala volume, and fat intake in adolescence. JAMA Psychiatry, 2013, 70(1): 98 - 105.

[14] L G Costa, M Aschner, A Vitalone, et al. Developmental neuropathology of environmental agents. Annual Review of Pharmacology and Toxicology, 2004, 44: 87 - 110.

[15] C A Nelson. The effects of early life adversity on brain and behavioral development. DANA 2013-03-16. http://dana.org/news/features/detail_rop.aspx? id = 39774.

[16] M A Sheridan, N A Fox, C H Zeanah, et al. Variation in neural development as a result of exposure to institutionalization early in childhood. Proceedings of the National Academy of Sciences, 2012, 109(32): 12927 - 12932.

[17] P J Marshall, N A Fox, the BEIP Core Group. A comparison of the electroencephalogram between institutionalized and community children in Romania. Journal of Cognitive Neuroscience, 2004, 16: 1327 - 1338.

[18] G Otero, F B Pliego-Rivero, J Ricardo. EEG development in children with sociocultural disadvantages: A follow-up study. Clinical Neurophysiology, 2003, 114: 1918 - 1925.

[19] R J Barry, A R Clarke, S J Johnstone. A review of electrophysiology in attention-deficit/hyperactivity disorder: I. Qualitative and quantitative electroencephalography. Clinical Neurophysiology, 2003, 114: 171 - 183.

[20] P J Marshall, B C Reeb, N A Fox, et al. Effects of early intervention on EEG power and coherence in previously institutionalized children in Romania. Developmental Psychopathology, 2008, 20: 861 - 880.

[21] R E Vanderwert, P J Marshall, C A Nelson, et al. Timing of intervention affects brain electrical activity in children exposed to severe psychosocial neglect. PLoS ONE, 2010, 5: e11415.

[22] C Murgatroyd, A V Patchev, Y Wu, et al. Dynamic DNA methylation programs persistent adverse effects of early-life stress. Nature Neuroscience, 2009, 12(12): 1559 - 1566.

[23] S J Lupien, M J de Leon, S D Santi, et al. Cortisol levels during human aging predict hippocampal atrophy and memory deficits. Nature Neuroscience, 1998, 1: 69 - 73.

[24] B A Linkenhoker, C G von der Ohe, E I Knudsen. Anatomical traces of juvenile learning in the auditory system of adult barn owls. Nature Neuroscience, 2005, 8: 93 - 98.

[25] Y Wei. The impacts of neuroeducation (Translational Education) on inquiry based science education. Peking University Education Review, 2011, 9: 97 - 117.

The Intervention and Assessment of High-Risk Infants: A Review

Chen Li[1,a], Xuejun Kang[1,b,*], Yuan Song[2,c]
[1]Key Laboratory of Child Development and Learning Science of Ministry of Education, Research Center for Learning Science, Southeast University, Nanjing 210096, China
[2]Suzhou Mother and Child Health Care Center, Suzhou 215002, China
[a]chenlee1203@163.com, [b]xjkang64@163.com,
[c]yuanyuan-sy@163.com
[*]Corresponding author

Keywords: high-risk infants; intervention; assessment

Abstract: This paper focused on the early-stage development of infants and reviewed the researches on interventions of high-risk infants and assessments of their development. The situations of this area were briefly introduced. Then, some intervention methods aiming at early-stage development of infants were listed. Along with the emergence of intervention methods, three kinds of assessments were developed earlier or later, i. e. psychological measurement and observation method, biochemical determination method, and physiological detection method.

1 Introduction

1.1 The current situation of high-risk infants in China

High-risk infants are infants who are faced with risk factors in growth and development (especially brain development) in the prenatal period, delivery period and neonatal period. There were several standards to define high risk infants: (1) gestational age less than 37 weeks or more than 42 weeks; (2) birth weight less than 2500 g; (3) small for gestational age or large for gestational age; (4) Apgar score less than 7; (5) intrapartum infection; (6) c-section births; (7) severe neonatal diseases medical history or neonatal death in brothers and sisters[1].

High-risk infants have potential brain damage which will cause brain paralysis, low intelligence, epilepsy, abnormal sensory, perception and behaviors. These are the main reasons leading to disability. However, brain damage is likely to be misdiagnosed and treated late due to the unobvious clinical symptoms. According to the statistical data in 2000, there were about 20,000,000 newborns in China. Among them, 5% to 10%

experienced asphyxia, above 30% improved after 20 min salvation, 5% to 6% premature delivery, 0.5% to 1.2% very low birth weight, respectively. In another word, there were hundreds of thousands of infants may grow up disabled in the future every year. The data indicated that high-risk infants become a large special group in China[2].

1.2 The key period of children development

Human brain develops fastest in the following several years after birth. A number of researches showed that 0 to 3 years old is the key period of physical and intelligence development. Meanwhile, 0 to 3 years old is the best time to intervene[3]. China has the most population in the world, so it is urgent to improve the quality of population (especially children). Early-stage intervention helped prevent from the abnormal development of nervous system of high-risk infants.

2 Interventions to high-risk infants

A lot of researches focused on early-stage intervention which is deemed as a feasible way to improve high risk infants. Intervention methods include action training, language training, cognitive function training and individual-social association training[4]. Stimulating vestibular function, auditory sense, tactile sense and visual sense is also good for infants' development. Intervention on social communication, language development, cognitive competence and motor development is also very necessary[5].

Craig et al. summarized four aspects of infants' early-stage development, i. e., cognitive/fine motor, social/ego, movement and language. And early-stage intervention methods should include many kinds of knowledge, transfer between generations, fuse situations, be personalized and be cooperative. In this pattern, interventions can promote infants' cognitive development effectively[6]. Another researcher proposed that children's development is associated with the self-discipline regulation of neurons. The purposes of early-stage interventions were to build and form this regulation[7].

Spessato et al. proposed that hygiene and nutrition were also important to infants' new manipulative skills, postural control and social interaction. Their research convinced that enrichment of environment was crucial for early child education[8].

3 Assessment of the development of high-risk infants

After giving high-risk infants some interventions, it was necessary to assess the developmental situations to decide whether the intervention functioned or not. The assessments could feedback messages to modify the interventions in reverse. There were mainly three methods to assess the development of infants. It mainly refers to psychological measurement and observation, biochemical determination and physiological detection.

3.1 Psychological measurement and observation method

Several widely accepted scales had been used to assess early-stage development of infants. Bayley Scales of Infant Development (BSID) assess the motor (fine and gross), language (receptive and expressive), and cognitive development of infants and toddlers, ages 0—3[9].

Based on this assessment, Chinese psychologists developed the CDCC Infant Intelligence Development Scale. This scale was localized and more suitable for Chinese infants[10].

Another assessment, Gesell Developmental Schedules (GDS) measured the development of infants and young children. But this assessment was not used now[11].

3.2 Biochemical determination method

Many biochemical matters are crucial to human body and associated with infants' development. Researchers studied the relationship between high-risk infants' development and neuro-transmitters, hormones et al.

γ-aminobutyric acid (GABA) was a marker of infant development. Shortage of GABA in cerebrospinal fluid could cause severe mental diseases, tension weaken, and reflection hyper functioning. And dissociative GABA level showed an obvious increase when growth and development accelerated[12].

Blood iron was also associated with brain development. Deficiency of blood iron influenced nerve metabolism, neuto-transmitters and form of myelin sheath. Supplement could not solve the influence[13]. Deficiency of iron also lead to change of dopamine receptors and transformation proteins, which would change the behavior related to this neuro-transmitter[14].

Heavy metals were environmental toxicants existed widely in the earth, water and gas. Researchers found that heavy metals causing kinds of abnormal symptoms in infants, such as pore health situations and impairment of cognitive function[15].

3.3 Physiological detection method

With the rapid development of neuroimaging technology, various physiological detection methods were used in the assessment of infant development[16].

Another research confirmed the ultrasound abnormality in high-risk preterm infants, which was a prediction of cerebral palsy[17]. Magnetic resonance imaging was used to predict and assess the neurodevelopment[18].

Continuous electroencephalogram could predict electrographic seizures for neonatal infants[19]. Event-Related Potentials was also used in high-risk infants' assessment, premature and low-birth-weight infants showed some larger possibility to get some disease. Cortical potentials offered a special way to assess the development of brain function[20].

4 Conclusions

It must be emphasized that much more attention should be paid to high-risk infants because children are the future. It's fortunately that more and more researchers are studying deep in this area. A lot of valuable conclusions were drew in both intervention and assessment of high-risk infants.

With the development of various analysis methods, it is better to do some conjunct research or use multi methods. For example, biochemical determination and physiological detection can be combined because human neural signals were transmitted through two pathways: electric signal and chemical signal. In addition, some biochemical determination methods still need blood samples or even cerebrospinal fluid samples. These methods are invasive, painful and hard to sample. It can be seen from this that noninvasive analysis methods are superior. Samples like saliva and urine shall be used more and more widely.

Acknowledgements

This work was supported by Colleges and universities in Jiangsu Province plans to postgraduate research and innovation projects and Infants' health promoting projects in Suzhou city.

References

[1] M J Gu. Women's Health Study. Beijing: Science Press, 1997.

[2] Y K Han, Z Z Xu, R J Yu. Neonatal Hypoxic-is Chemic Encephalopathy. Beijing: People's Health Publishing House, 2000: 51 - 52, 57 - 65, 184 - 198.

[3] H T Chugani. A critical period of brain development: Studies of cerebral glucose utilization with PET. Preventive Medicine, 1998, 27: 184 - 188.

[4] P Zhao, X B Zou, C M Zhou, et al. Effect of early intervention on behavioral development of high-risk neonate. Chinese Journal of Child Health Care, 2004, 12: 204 - 205.

[5] T D Tjossem. Intervention strategies for high risk infants and young children. Baltimore: University Park Press, 1976.

[6] C T Ramey, S L Ramey. Prevention of intellectual disabilities: Early interventions to improve cognitive development. Preventive Medicine, 1998, 27: 224 - 232.

[7] S W Porges. Physiological regulation in high-risk infants: A model for assessment and potential

intervention. Development and Psychopathology, 1996, 8: 43 - 58.

[8] B C Spessato, N C Valentini, R J Krebs, et al. Early childhood education and motor intervention: A view based on the bioecological theory of Bronfenbrenner. Journal Movimento, 2009, 15: 147 - 173.

[9] N Bayley. Bayley Scales of Infant Development: Manual. New York: Psychological Corporation, 1993.

[10] C R Fan. Establishment of CDCC infant intelligence development scale. Acta Psychologica Sinica, 1989, 2: 130 - 140.

[11] R S Ball. The Gesell developmental schedules: Arnold Gesell (1880—1961). Journal of Abnormal Child Psychology, 1977, 5: 233 - 239.

[12] J Jaeken, P Casaer, P De Cock, et al. Gamma-aminobutyric acid-transaminase deficiency: A newly recognized inborn error of neurotransmitter metabolism. Neuropediatrics, 1984, 15: 165 - 169.

[13] B Lozoff, M K Georgieff. Iron deficiency and brain development, seminars in pediatric neurology. WB Saunders, 2006, 13: 158 - 165.

[14] J Beard. Iron deficiency alters brain development and functioning. The Journal of Nutrition, 2003, 133: 1468S - 1472S.

[15] M Lewis, J Worobey, D S Ramsay, et al. Prenatal exposure to heavy metals: Effect on childhood cognitive skills and health status. Pediatrics, 1992, 89: 1010 - 1015.

[16] A H Hoon Jr. Neuroimaging in the high-risk infant: Relationship to outcome. Journal of Perinatology: Official Journal of the California Perinatal Association, 1994, 15: 389 - 394.

[17] L S de Vries, I L C van Haastert, K J Rademaker, et al. Ultrasound abnormalities preceding cerebral palsy in high-risk preterm infants. The Journal of Pediatrics, 2004, 144: 815 - 820.

[18] L J Woodward, P J Anderson, N C Austin, et al. Neonatal MRI to predict neurodevelopmental outcomes in preterm infants. New England Journal of Medicine, 2006, 355: 685 - 694.

[19] N Laroia, R Guillet, J Burchfiel, et al. EEG background as predictor of electrographic seizures in high-risk Neonates. Epilepsia, 1998, 39: 545 - 551.

[20] D Kurtzberg. Event-related potentials in the evaluation of high-risk infants. Annals of the New York Academy of Sciences, 1980, 338: 557 - 571.

Association of Hair Cortisol with Somatic Complaints and Schizoid Behavior among Autistic Children

Xinliang Qi, Qiaozhen Xie, Wei Gao, Hengzu Pan, Xiaoyan Ke, Huihua Deng[a,*], Zuhong Lu

Key laboratory of Child Development and Learning Science of Ministry of Education (Southeast University), Research Center for Learning Science, Southeast University, Nanjing, 210096, China

[a]dengrcls@seu.edu.cn

[*] Corresponding author

Keywords: autism; hair cortisol; somatic complaints; schizoid behaviors

Abstract: Autism individuals were thought to suffer from cortisol-secreting disturbances. However, relationship between cortisol levels and behavior problems has not yet been explored among autistic children. Using hair cortisol as a biomarker of one-month HPA axis activity, this study aimed to explore the relationship between HPA axis activity and behavior problem in the Child Behavior Checklist among autistic children. Hair samples were collected from 8 autistic children and 6 normal children. The results revealed that hair cortisol concentrations significantly positive correlated to the scores of somatic complaints ($p<0.05$) and schizoid behaviors ($p<0.01$) among autistic children, but such association was not found among normal children.

1 Introduction

Autism is a neuron-developmental disorder, which is characterized by deficits in social interaction, impairments in language usage, narrow interests and stereotyped behaviors[1]. Autistic individuals usually show indifferent and unresponsive to the external stimulus[2].

Usually, when normal individuals face stresses, cortisol as the stress hormone would be increased then mobilizes energy to cope with the stress[3]. Long-term cortisol is also gaining attention in becoming a biomarker of behavioral problems now[4]. So far lots of studies have shown that cortisol reactivity was associated with behavior problems in normal children[5-7]. Because autistic individuals showed the unique behavioral characteristics in the response to external stresses, it is essential to explore whether cortisol played a role in building these abnormal behaviors. Circulating cortisol level may be able to predict behavioral and emotional dysregulation. Cortisol modulates individuals to react to the stress from a novel or challenging environment. Thus, disorders of cortisol secretion might cause "the resistance to change" in individuals [8]. "Resistance to change" is common problems which individuals with autism displayed, which may linked with stereotyped behaviors or social withdrawal. This study will investigate the link between the cortisol activity and behavioral problems among autistic children.

The Child Behavior Checklist (CBCL) is a device which can be used to measure behavioral problems of normal children[9] and autistic children[10]. The subscales in which, such as schizoid behaviors, dissociableness and compulsive behavior, can reflect the common behavioral problems of autistic children. In this study, we link between behavioral problems and cortisol activities by means of correlations between traits of CBCL and hair cortisol. Hair cortisol will be used to evaluate the cortisol exposure in one month, which matches the CBCL in time[11].

2 Methods

2.1 Participants

Fourteen male children aged 12 to 15 years joined this study. Of them, eight participants were autistic children and six were normal children. Autistic children (average age = 13.38 years, *SD* = 1.06 years) had received a formal clinical diagnosis. Control group included healthy boys, without psychiatric and endocrinology disorders, matching autistic children regarding their age (average age = 12.17 years, *SD* = 0.41 years).

2.2 Psychological measures

Emotional or behavioral problems of normal children and autistic children were measured with the 130-item Child Behavior Checklist (CBCL) achenbachs developed for 11—16 year-old adolescents[5,6]. Chinese version CBCL[7] measures behavioral or emotional problems including somatic complaints, schizoid behaviour, dissociableness, immature behavior, compulsive behavior, aggressive behavior, disciplinary offence, hostile behavior and hyperactivity. All items were rated by 5-point Likert system from 0 to 4. In China where the Cronbach's α coefficients of all the traits were greater than 0.6 and the agreement between CBCL assessment and pediatrician's diagnosis was ranged from 0.61 to 0.76[12]. In this study, parents of autistic children and normal children rated children's problem behaviors and reported baseline information sub-scale record information of name, age, gender and occupation of parents.

2.3 Hair cortisol measurement

Hair samples with longer than 1cm were cut with fine scissors as close as possible to the scalp from a posterior vertex position. Hair cortisol concentrations were analyzed by LC/MS/MS.

2.4 Statistic analysis

A Mann-Whitney U test for two independent samples was run to investigate differences in concentration of hair cortisol and scores of CBCL between children with autism and normal children. Spearman rank correlation was conducted to investigate association between hair cortisol content and CBCL scores and its nine traits.

3 Results

Autistic children showed significantly higher score than normal children in bad communication ($Z = -2.07$, $p < 0.05$), immature behavior ($Z = -2.23$, $p < 0.05$), aggressive behavior ($Z = -2.48$, $p < 0.05$) and disciplinary offence ($Z = -2.30$, $p < 0.05$). However, there was no significant difference between autistic children and control in total score of behavioral problem subscale ($Z = -1.42$, $p = 0.18$) and its other five traits. Autistic children showed lower hair cortisol concentration [(22.61 ± 18.39) pg/mg] than normal children [(26.32 ± 24.00) pg/mg], but it was not significant ($Z = -0.39$, $p = 0.76$).

More importantly, hair cortisol concentration was significantly positively correlated with CBCL somatic complaint ($r = 0.72$, $p < 0.05$) and CBCL schizoid behavior ($r = 0.90$, $p < 0.01$) among autistic children, but it was not true for normal children. It indicated that, the more cortisol accumulation autistic children were exposed to, the more likely they would experience somatic complaints and schizoid behaviors. Additionally, there were no significant correlations between hair cortisol and other seven traits of CBCL for both autistic and normal children.

4 Discussions

The present study showed that hair cortisol concentrations of autistic children were positively related to the score of somatic complaints and schizoid behaviors. It meant that, the more cortisol autistic children were exposed to the more likely they would experience somatic complaints and schizoid behaviors. However, such significant correlation did not appear among normal children in the present study. It indicated that biological mechanism influencing the two behavioral problems, somatic complaints and schizoid behaviors, was different for autistic children and control.

The previous studies demonstrated that normal individuals tend to get physical discomfort, such as pain and weakness, when they were long-term exposed to higher levels of cortisol[13]. Although somatic complaints in CBCL Chinese version used in the present study mainly referred to the somatic symptoms, which represent psychological distress that manifests itself as bodily ailments. It was inferred that autistic children exposed to higher levels of cortisol were more likely to feel sick than those who exposed to lower level of cortisol. Previous research has shown that autistic individuals had a significant lower dehydroepiandrosterone sulfate (DHEA-S) levels compared to healthy ones[14]. DHEA-S is a sulfate form of DHEA and DHEA-S level is an index of DHEA. In fact, dehydroepiandrosterone (DHEA) is a neuroactive steroid with anti-glucocorticoid properties and can protect the body organ from the damaging effects of cortisol[15]. If the DHEA-S level is lower in autistic children, the cortisol would have a much bigger effect on them, resulting in stronger association between cortisol levels and somatic symptoms.

Schizoid behaviors in CBCL Chinese version used in the present study mainly contain the behavioral characteristics of cold and bizarre. According to cognitive theory, the schizoid behavior is a result of the dull response to the emotional clues provided by other people[16]. In the present study, the positive correlation between hair cortisol and schizoid behaviors meant that the autistic children with higher cortisol levels would react more difficultly to other people's emotions. The HPA axis is actually the system responses to the environmental stimuli, the cortisol is actually one of the reaction product. Therefore, the blunting response of HPA axis would cause the schizoid behaviour. This is also consistent with the hypothesis of some investors that defect of cortisol response may cause defect of emotional response[8]. This result support the E-S theory of autism which acknowledges autistic individuals is defective in emotional response to others[2].

References

[1] American Psychiatric Association. DSM IV -TR//APA. Diagnostic and Statistical Manual of Mental Disorders. Washington D. C. : American Psychiatric Press, 2000.

[2] S Baron-Cohen. Autism: The empathizing-systemizing (E-S) theory. Ann Ny Acad Sci, 2009, 1156: 68 - 80.

[3] B S McEwen. Seminars in medicine of the beth Israel deaconess medical center: Protective and damaging effects of stress mediators. New Engl J Med, 1998, 338: 171 - 179.

[4] A M Dettmer, M A Novak, S J Suomi, et al. Physiological and behavioral adaptation to

relocation stress in differentially reared rhesus monkeys: Hair cortisol as a biomarker for anxiety-related responses. Psychoneuroendocrino, 2012, 37: 191-199.

[5] B A Corbett, C W Schupp, S Levine, et al. Comparing cortisol, stress, and sensory sensitivity in children with autism. Autism Res, 2009, 2: 39-49.

[6] K McBurnett, B B Lahey, P J Rathouz, et al. Low salivary cortisol and persistent aggression in boys referred for disruptive behavior. Arch Gen Psychiat, 2000, 57: 38-39.

[7] S J Yang, D W Shin, K S Noh, et al. Cortisol is inversely correlated with aggression for those boys with attention deficit hyperactivity disorder who retain their reactivity to stress. Psychiat Res, 2007, 153: 55-60.

[8] S Lightman. The neuroendocrinology of stress: A never ending story. J Neuroendocrinol, 2008, 20: 880-884.

[9] T M Achenbach. The child behavior profile: I. Boys aged 6—11. J Consult Clin Psych, 1978, 46: 478.

[10] L Rescorla. Cluster analytic identification of autistic preschoolers. J Autism Dev Disord, 1988, 18: 475-492.

[11] E Russell, G Koren, M Rieder, et al. Hair cortisol as a biological marker of chronic stress: Current status, future directions and unanswered questions. Psychoneuroendocrino, 2012, 37: 589-601.

[12] Y F Wang, Y C Shen. Comprehensive study on behaviour problems in school children: (Ⅰ) The epidemiological report. Chinese Mental Health Journal, 1989, 3: 104-110.

[13] M Ebrecht, J Hextall, L G Kirtley, et al. Perceived stress and cortisol levels predict speed of wound healing in healthy male adults. Psychoneuroendocrino, 2004, 29: 798-809.

[14] R D Strous, P Golubchik, R Maayan, et al. Lowered DHEA-S plasma levels in adult individuals with autistic disorder. Eur Neuropsychopharm, 2005, 15: 305-309.

[15] M Kalimi, Y Shafagoj, R Loria, et al. Anti-glucocorticoid effects of dehydroepiandrosterone (DHEA). Mol Cell Biochem, 1994, 131: 99-104.

[16] A T Beck, A Freeman, D D Davis. Cognitive Therapy of Personality Disorders. New York: Guilford Press, 2006.

The Antecedents and Consequence of Perceived discrimination among Chinese Migrant Children

Ning Jiang[1,a], Guangzhen Zhang[1,b,*]

[1]Key Laboratory of Child Development and Learning Science of Ministry of Education, Southeast University, Nanjing, Jiangsu, China

[a]jiangning199243@163.com, [b]zhangguangzhen2004@126.com

[*]Corresponding author

Keywords: migrant children; perceived discrimination; mental health

Abstract: As a result of the rapid development of economy, the number of migrant children has been expanding substantially and migrant children's adjustment obtained extensive attention. Previous research indicated that migrant children adjust poorer than nonimmigrant children and perceived discrimination is the most essential risk factors. Based on previous research, the present study aims to review the antecedents and consequences of perceived discrimination. This paper also points out the limitation of existing studies and future direction of study in this field.

流动儿童歧视知觉的成因与其对心理健康的影响

姜宁[1,a],张光珍[1,b,*]
[1]东南大学儿童发展与学习科学教育部重点实验室,南京,江苏,中国
[a]jiangning199243@163.com, [b]zhangguangzhen2004@126.com
[*]通讯作者

关键字:流动儿童;歧视知觉;心理健康

中文摘要:经济社会的快速发展使我国人口流动性加大并导致流动儿童规模不断扩大,其心理健康问题也引起各界广泛关注。研究显示我国流动儿童总体心理健康水平较差,而歧视知觉与体验则是最普遍也是隐性伤害最大的心理健康影响因素之一。本文在整合相关领域研究结果的基础上分别从歧视知觉的成因、产生机制、对流动儿童心理健康的影响以及其作用效果的影响因素几方面进行论述,并从研究方法、研究内容与研究工具三方面对现有研究的不足与今后相关领域的研究方向进行探讨。

1 引言

近年来,随着经济社会的快速发展,我国流动人口的规模不断扩大。第六次全国人口普查数据显示,2010年我国目前流动人口已有2.61亿,同2000年相比增加了81.03%[1]。同时流动人口家庭化趋势亦日益明显,因此催生了一个新的群体——流动儿童的出现[2]。流动儿童是指6—18周岁随父母或其他监护人在流入城市暂时居住半年以上,且在当地学校就读的儿童或青少年[3]。学习、生活环境的巨大变化以及生活方式与文化价值观念的差异,对流动儿童的心理发展有着深刻影响。流动儿童的社会适应面临巨大的挑战,其心理健康水平越来越引起各界的关注与重视。

目前,针对流动儿童的研究主要都集中在进城务工的农民工子女上。以往研究发现,由于流动人口身份以及由此带来的不公平待遇而产生的歧视知觉是对儿童心理健康隐形危害性最大且最普遍的因素。歧视知觉是相对于客观歧视而言的一种主观体验,是指个体知觉到由于所属的群体成员资格(如性别、户口身份等)而受到有区别的或不公平的对待,这种不公正的对待可以表现为实际的行为动作,也可以表现为拒绝性的态度或者某些不合理的社会制度等[4]。由于农民工文化程度较低且大多从事低层的体力劳动,因此与其一起生活在城市边缘的流动儿童极易受到各种不公正待遇。目前虽无法确定歧视知觉是否真正反映了客观歧视的情况,但作为弱势群体成员的一种“重要心理现实”[5],流动儿童的歧视知觉体验相当普遍,调查表明,75.5%的

农民工子女报告曾受到过歧视[6],近80%的农民工子女因为感觉被瞧不起而“不愿意”将来过父母现在的生活[7]。因此,有关歧视知觉的研究与探讨对于提高流动儿童心理健康水平以及经济社会的全面发展有着重要的理论与实践意义。

2 歧视知觉的产生机制及对流动儿童的影响

2.1 歧视知觉产生的原因

歧视知觉的产生与发展是个体心理世界与外界客观现实相互作用的结果,其成因主要可分为以下三个方面:(1) 社会层面。作为流动儿童生活的宏背景,社会中的不合理因素为流动儿童歧视体验的产生提供了温床,如城乡二元户籍制度,升学就业福利等的差别待遇,城乡间物质文化发展的巨大差异,教育资源的城乡分布不均,公共媒体不合理观念的宣传,城市居民对待农民工以及其子女的不恰当态度以及相关社会支持机构与部门对流动儿童心理健康问题的忽视等都客观上增强了流动儿童的歧视知觉体验。(2) 家庭与学校层面。农民工家庭相对较低的经济收入、社会地位与父母受教育水平是流动儿童歧视体验产生的客观基础;老师与同学的不当言行往往是其歧视体验最主要的客观来源;作为流动儿童主要集聚地的打工子弟学校的软硬件设施的相对落后亦是歧视体验产生的重要客观因素。(3) 个人层面。个体的自身条件,如外貌、年龄、能力、认知等因素均会对歧视知觉的产生造成影响,其中个体认知因素作用巨大。作为个体对于客观歧视的主观反应,歧视知觉的产生与体验强度在很大程度上是由个人的敏感性以及对外界言行的判断与归因方式有关的。此外,人格的作用也不可忽视,积极健全的人格有利于个体采用积极方式解释、应对歧视问题。

2.2 歧视知觉的产生机制

关于歧视知觉的产生机制,以往理论大致可分为两类:(1) 认为认知变量起主要作用[8],即从内部归因的角度去解释歧视知觉,认为其产生是由于个体对当前情景或者事物的认知观念或评价导致,如心理理论、社会比较等;(2) 认为环境变量起主要作用[8],这一类主要是采用外部归因的方式,认为外界客观环境对歧视知觉的产生起决定性作用,如家庭的社会经济地位、生活学习环境等。目前,最具有影响力的则是社会比较理论。

社会比较就是个体把自己的身心特质、处境和地位等与他人进行比较而得到相应认知或者评价的过程[9,10]。社会比较在儿童自我概念的形成中起重要作用,是儿童自我认知与自我评价发生、发展的重要来源。社会比较为个体所提供的关于比较结果的信息,如是否受到公平的对待等,对歧视知觉的产生是非常重要的。人们关于是否受到歧视的判断与体验往往是通过与外部参照物相对比而引发的。流动儿童家庭的社会地位和物质精神生活条件与城市儿童相比往往差距较大,而城乡二元的户籍制度以及升学、就业、社会福利保障等方面人为的差异与壁垒更加深了社会不公平感。处在学龄期的儿童,信息接触面较广,极易体验到落差感,尤其是与城市儿童处于同一学校的流动儿童,社会比较更是无法避免,高比较的情境更易导致歧视知觉的产生。

2.3 歧视知觉对心理健康的影响

目前国内关于流动儿童心理健康状况研究的所得结果基本一致,即流动儿童心理健康水平相对较差,存在着诸多的心理适应性问题,如抑郁水平高、孤独感强、缺乏安全感等,并且伴随着一系列的外化行为问题,如问题行为、成瘾行为、青少年犯罪等。大量研究发现,歧视知觉体验是影响流动儿童心理适应性水平的最重要因素,会对其心理发展产生消极作用,并主要体现在以下几方面。

2.3.1 身份认同危机

流动儿童的年龄多在6—18岁之间,该阶段正是发展自我评价与自我认同感的关键时期,而较强的歧视知觉体验易导致身份认同危机与角色混乱。由于城乡二元户口制度以及地区发展的差异,儿童被贴上“城市人”与“农村人”的标签。流动儿童处境尴尬,他们随父母迁入城市,受城市文化熏陶,对农村的认同逐渐减弱,但是由于“农村人”的身份与差异,他们也不能成为城市人眼中的真正同类,因而长期在农村人与城市人的边缘徘徊,成为了夹缝中的人。调查研究表明,78%的农民工子女喜欢和城市小朋友一起玩,但不愿意让别人知道自己的流动人口身份[11],75.7%的流动儿童报告在日常生活中被嘲笑和讽刺,可见“外来人口”的身份与歧视已对其身心造成一定程度上的困扰[12]。

2.3.2 自我评价较低与低自尊

社会比较是自我评价的重要来源,而同辈群体则是继父母、教师之后的又一种重要影响力,同龄人的言行与评价会对儿童的心理与行为产生巨大的影响。与城市儿童相比,流动儿童除了物质条件的差异外,其学业成绩与综合能力也往往较差,客观差异再加上歧视体验进一步削弱了他们的自我评价,导致自卑现象较为普遍,并且随着歧视知觉体验的增强,个体对自身及其所在群体的价值感会越来越低。调查显示,大部分农民工子女存在自我评价偏低的问题,自认为“低人一等”、“先天不足”、“无能”[13],并且流动儿童的自我效能感也显著低于非流动儿童[14]。此外,歧视知觉对自尊显著的负向预测作用亦得到大量研究的证明[15,16]。

2.3.3 孤独感

在流动儿童的诸多心理问题当中,孤独感是最突出、最普遍的问题。孤独感是个体的社会关系在数量上不足、质量上低下时感受到的一种广泛弥漫的、严重的痛苦状态[17]。跨文化研究表明,个体在迁移到新的文化环境中时会面临诸多的社会适应性问题,原有的社会支持系统的断裂与新的社会文化生活的挑战使孤独感出现可能性大大增强[18],歧视知觉体验更加剧了这一适应过程的艰难性。研究表明,歧视知觉与孤独感的发生发展之间呈现出一种动态的交互作用的过程[19]。歧视知觉体验易引起儿童不恰当的自我评价,同时表现出停留在原有群体内部、不主动与外界交往等回避性的行为,并体验到强烈的排斥与孤独感,而这种消极情感与举动又会进一步加剧儿童的歧视或排斥感,从而陷入了一种恶性循环,并由此导致一系列人际交往与适应不良的问题行为。

2.3.4 焦虑感

流动儿童的高焦虑感也是很普遍的问题,研究发现,流动儿童的焦虑感显著高于城市儿童与留守儿童,其中最明显的是社交焦虑。社交焦虑是一种与人交往的时候,觉得不舒服、不自然,紧张甚至恐惧的情绪体验。调查显示,流动儿童中患有"对人焦虑"者高达33%[20],31.7%流动儿童会因非常紧张而无法当众说话[21]。歧视知觉体验加重了流动儿童的焦虑程度,一方面它影响儿童的自我认同感,削弱了儿童进行人际交往时的信心与兴趣,另一方面歧视体验也可能引起较高的动机水平,导致儿童在社交时有较大心理压力与负担,增强了紧张、恐惧与不可控制感,削弱儿童的表现。除社交焦虑以外,学业焦虑也比较突出。城乡教育资源、教学进度与方法等的差异,使流动儿童的学习成绩相对较低,压力较大。

2.3.5 幸福感

幸福感是体现个体心理健康水平的重要方面,是个体根据自定的标准对生活质量进行整体性评估而产生的体验,由认知和情感两种成分组成,可分为个体幸福感及群体幸福感。其中,个体幸福感反映了个体对自己生活境况的总体评价;群体幸福感则反映了个体对所属群体的积极评价程度,主要指个体的群体价值感[22]。大量研究显示,歧视知觉对个体和群体主观幸福感都表现出直接的显著的负向预测作用,随着歧视知觉的增加,流动儿童的积极情感体验、生活满意度与群体价值感降低,消极情感体验增多[23],但二者影响机制不同,歧视知觉直接负向作用于流动儿童的个体幸福感,而对群体幸福感则通过情感认同、群体地位等中介变量的间接作用而影响。歧视知觉对群体幸福感直接影响效应的缺失可能是与流动儿童身份的暂时性、可变性,以及其对群体的低认同度有关[24]。

2.3.6 社会适应不良与问题行为

社会适应指社会环境发生变化时,个体的观念、行为方式随之而改变,使之适应所处的社会环境的过程[25]。学习生活环境的巨变作为强烈的应激源,易引发个体不同程度的适应不良行为,最突出的便是人际关系的紧张。研究表明,公立学校与民工子弟学校流动儿童都表现出较多的人际关系敏感与紧张的心理问题[26]。歧视体验加剧了该问题的严重性,它像一道围墙,使双方各自固着在群体内部,使彼此误解加深并造成流动儿童社会支持资源的减少。此外,学习适应性较差也是一个比较普遍的问题。研究表明导致城市农民工子女学习适应性不良的主要是非智力因素以及学习方法方面存在问题[27],其中歧视知觉与由此引发的自卑、自我效能感低下以及意志力缺乏等因素的作用不能忽视[21,28]。

问题行为指个体表现出的妨碍其社会适应的异常行为[25],它不仅阻碍儿童社会性的发展,也会给家庭与社会带来消极影响。和老家联系的阻断以及城市的排斥与歧视阻碍了流动儿童的城市适应进程,也易化了问题行为的发生。研究发现,歧视知觉会显著负向预测流动儿童高自尊组的亲社会行为[29]。

2.4　影响歧视知觉作用效应的因素

回顾过往研究发现,歧视知觉对于流动儿童心理健康的作用受多种因素影响,它往往不是单独的直接的作用,而是受到其他变量的调节或者通过中介作用来影响其心理健康水平的,并且作用效果亦不仅仅只局限于单一的消极的方面。部分研究结果显示,歧视知觉对于流动儿童的某些心理特质发展存在促进作用。这也揭示出歧视知觉对流动儿童心理发展的影响是一个非常复杂的作用机制。通过大量研究的比较,影响歧视知觉作用效应的因素,可归纳为以下几方面:

(1) 时间因素。歧视知觉对于流动时间不同的儿童的心理健康的影响力是不同的,其作用大致可以看作是一种倒U形曲线。以儿童的自尊发展情况为例,研究揭示了歧视知觉对于自尊的负向预测力在流动时间为3.5—10.5年的儿童身上最强,对流动时间低于3年或者高于10年的儿童的影响则相对较弱[16]。这表明歧视知觉对心理发展的作用是一个长期的动态的过程,在特定时间段内存在累积效应,同时也揭示了个体的心理调节与适应的能动作用。

(2) 不同领域的差别。大量研究都表明在不同的领域,歧视知觉的作用效应是不同的。在学业领域,歧视知觉对于流动儿童的学业成绩呈非常显著的消极影响,而在社会生活领域,其影响力则相对较弱。这可能与学龄期儿童的主导任务是学习,以及学校是该阶段儿童最为重要的微环境也是同辈群体最为密集的地区之一有关。

(3) 不同学校与不同性别的差异。流动儿童所处的学校大致可分为两类,一类是普通公立学校,一类是民工子弟学校。研究显示不同学校类别的儿童的歧视知觉水平有显著差异,其对心理健康水平的影响力亦不同。但究竟哪类学校对儿童心理发展更好,现有研究结果截然相反,大量研究显示公立学校中的流动儿童歧视体验较少,心理健康水平较高[20,26,30],而蔺秀云等人的研究则表明打工子弟学校学生同质性高歧视体验少,较少地暴露在高比较的情境中更有利于儿童心理的健康发展[15,31]。这也提示了研究者需要进一步探明学校中哪些因素会促进儿童高歧视体验的产生进而影响其心理健康水平。与学校类型影响的研究结果相类似的是关于该领域性别差异的研究,其结果亦存在较大分歧,蔺秀云等人研究发现歧视知觉在男女性别上的差异并不显著[15],而刘霞等人的研究则指出男性流动儿童歧视知觉体验显著高于女性[32,33],这可能是由于歧视知觉与其他心理品质一样也有不同的组成部分,而男性女性在社会化过程中被灌输的责任与敏感点不同,因此可能带来影响效应的差异。

(4)发展阶段的影响。研究表明,不同的发展阶段歧视知觉的作用效果不同,大量研究都得出相似结论:不同年龄段歧视知觉存在显著差异,并且是一个动态的变化的过程。其中,在小学阶段,六年级学生的歧视体验要显著高于五年级的学生[32];初中阶段学生的歧视体验与作用效应都显著强于小学阶段[34]。这可能与青春期学生认知能力的提升,敏感性的增加,注重自我体验与责任感的增强有关。

(5)认知、应对方式等个体差异的影响。认知行为理论认为,个体的情绪、情感、态度、体验和行为在很大程度上是由自身认识世界、处世的方式和方法决定的,也就是说一个人的认知因素在某种程度上决定了他内心的体验和反应。因此对于歧视与否的判断与体验强度也因个体的认知差异而不同,同时,不同的应对方式与态度也会对歧视知觉的影响作用产生截然不同的效果,这也解释了有些研究表明的歧视知觉对心理品质发展的某些侧面存在促进作用的结果,也启发研究者进一步探明不同中介变量的作用以及歧视知觉影响效应的内部机制。

3 现有研究的不足与展望

3.1 研究对象方面

在研究对象方面,现有研究的局限主要体现在以下三方面:(1)流动儿童与城市农民工子女概念的混淆。根据流动儿童定义,我们发现它包含以下群体:a. 根据监护人可分为:与父母居住和由其亲友抚养;b. 根据来源地可分为:由农村迁入城市与不同城市间的迁移;c. 根据父母收入来源可分为工资收入与自主创业等。而城市农民工子女是指户籍身份还是农民,有承包土地,但主要从事非农产业、以工资为主要收入来源的进城务工人员的子女[35]。两个概念相比,流动儿童概念的外延更广,城市农民工子女只是其中的一个组成部分,而现有研究不是将两个群体完全等同,就是将针对农民工子女的研究结果盲目推广到整个流动儿童群体中去,忽视了对流动儿童其他组成部分的调查研究。这都是研究者没有明确二者概念与内涵的结果。这也提示我们今后需进一步细化研究对象,并将研究扩展到流动儿童的其他群体中去。(2) 研究对象年龄阶段的局限。目前关于流动儿童歧视知觉领域的研究主要集中在小学与初中阶段,而针对学龄前与高中这两个重要的发展阶段的研究则相对稀少,因此研究对象年龄段的扩展也是未来研究的课题。(3) 研究对象所属城市的局限。目前相关研究多集中在北京、上海等这样的一线大城市,而针对其他的二三线城市流动儿童的研究则相对稀少。因此,今后需进一步扩大流动儿童研究的地域范围,全面了解不同地区流动儿童的心理特征与发展情况。

3.2 研究内容方面

在研究内容方面,现有研究主要存在以下局限:(1) 比较研究不足。根据已有研究可以发现,城市、领域、学校类型、年龄阶段、流动时间等因素的差异都会对流动儿童的歧视知觉体验及作用结果造成影响,而针对不同的特定领域的比较研究以及其差异的成因探析则相对缺失。(2) 研究变量的局限。歧视知觉对心理健康的影响是一个复杂的过程,除去歧视知觉的直接作用外,一些中介变量的作用也不容忽视,但现有研究关于研究变量的选取往往局限在年龄、流动时间、自尊等变量上,而忽略了对个体认知变量、应对方式、人格等变量以及不同变量间交互作用的影响的研究,以至于歧视知觉的作用机制目前仍不明了。此外研究发现流动儿童的学业领域歧视知觉体验最强,而针对学业成绩这一变量的研究则较为稀缺。(3) 积极心理关注的缺失。现有研究大多集中于揭示歧视知觉体验对儿童心理健康的危害,将流动儿童划为弱势群体,并且其研究都遵循着"不利环境—过高压力—适应不良的"路线进行,即认为处境不利一定导致发展不利,然而根据心理弹性的相关理论,个体的心理发展也可能遵循着"处境不利—心理弹性—适应良好"的轨迹[36]。任何变量对于心理发展的作用都不是单级单向的,对于心理弹性儿童而言,歧视知觉有可能是促进其自我整合并实现提升的推动力,而大量逆境中成才的儿童的案例也揭示了该理论的现实可能性。因此想要全面地揭示歧视知觉对于心理健康的影响,只关注其消极方面是必然不够的。

3.3 研究方法方面

在研究方法方面,现有研究的不足表现在:(1) 研究方法的单一。现有研究多采取的是问卷法,并主要使用流动儿童自我报告的方法,而缺乏访谈、情境观察与实验等其他方法的研究。单一的研究方法与单一的数据来源可能无法全面反映研究对象的客观情况,增大误差。(2) 缺乏统一的研究工具。不同的研究者往往采用完全不同的歧视知觉与心理健康水平的测量工具,其研究结果也往往差别较大。缺乏相对统一且完善的研究工具不仅使研究的信效度大大降低,也为不同研究间的比较与交流增大了难度。同时流动儿童是一个涉及年龄阶段非常广泛且具有相对特殊性的群体,而现有测评工具往往针对的是普通的青少年或者成人,专门针对流动儿童的和适用于其不同的年龄阶段的有效量表较为缺乏。高信效度的研究工具的缺失不利于真实客观地考察流动儿童的歧视知觉与心理健康状况。(3)纵向研究的缺乏。歧视知觉对流动儿童身心的影响往往是一个长期的动态的累积过程,而现有研究多为横断研究,无法客观地揭示歧视知觉随着时间的变化而对流动儿童身心发展产生影响的动态规律与因果关系。因此,今后需推进相关领域的纵向研究,进一步揭示歧视知觉对于流动儿童身心发展影响作用的动态规律。

致谢

本文为江苏省哲学社会科学基金青年项目(11JYC011)的阶段性成果。

References

[1] National Bureau of Statistics of China. 2010 Sixth National population census data Gazette (No. 1), 2010.

[2] Migrant Children Research Group. Investigation report regarding education status of migrant children in Beijing. Beijing: School of Psychology, Beijing Normal University, 2006.

[3] J L Shen. Disadvantaged Children's Psychological Development and Education. Beijing: Economic Science Publishing House, 2009.

[4] B Major, W Quinton, S McCoy. Antecedents and consequences of attributions to discrimination: Theoretical and empirical advances. Advances in Experimental Social Psychology, 2002, 34: 251-329.

[5] K L Dion, K Kawakami. Ethnicity and perceived discrimination in Toronto: Another look at the personal/group discrimination discrepancy. Canadian Journal of Behavioral Science, 1996, 28: 203-213.

[6] X L Fang, X H Fan, Y Liu. Perceived discrimination and loneliness: Moderating effects of coping style among migrant children. Psychological Development and Education, 2008, 4: 94-99.

[7] Y G Lei. The big world on villagers' eyes—The investigation of the urban floating population children's social cognition. Educational Science Research, 2004, 6: 27-31.

[8] X W Li, H Zhou, J Zhang, et al. Qualitative study on the generating mechanism of migrant children's perception of discrimination: Form a social comparison's perspective. Psychological Research, 2008, 1: 66-70.

[9] C S Brown, P S Bigler. Children's perception of discrimination: A developmental model. Child Development, 2005, 76: 533-553.

[10] D N Ruble, N S Feldman, A K Boggiano. Social comparison between young children in an

achievement setting. Developmental Psychology, 1976, 12: 192 - 197.

[11] W F Bai, L Xu. A research on identity of floating children integrating into society—A case study of Beijing. Journal of Graduate School of Chinese Academy of Social Science, 2009, 2: 18 - 25.

[12] Migrant Children's Academic and Mental Condition Research Group. The study of migrant children's and their teacher's mental condition. New Vision, 2006, 3: 62 - 64.

[13] W P Sun, D Hu, Y L GUO, et al. Migrant children's mental health in a primary school of Chongqing. Chinese Journal of School Health, 2007, 28: 68.

[14] D F Liu, Z L Wang, W B Li, et al. The relationship between self-efficacy, social support on loneliness among migrant children. Chinese Journal of School Health, 2010, 31: 180 - 181.

[15] X Y Lin, XY Fang, Y Liu, et al. The effect mechanism of stigma perception on mental health among migrant children in Beijing. Acta Psychologica Sinica, 2009, 41: 967 - 979.

[16] X Q Deng, B G Shi. Migrant children's perceived discrimination and self-esteem: The effect of social support and migration duration. Chinese Journal of Special Education, 2013, 158: 48 - 54.

[17] R S Weiss. Reflections on the present state of loneliness research. Journal of Social Behavior & Personality, 1987, 2(1): 1 - 16.

[18] C Fisher, S Phillips. Who is alone? Social characteristics of people with small networks//L Peplau, D Perlman. Loneliness: A Sourcebook of Current Theory, Eesearch, and Therapy. New York: Wiley-Inter, Science, 1982: 21 - 39.

[19] S M Hou, X J Yuan, Y Liu, et al. The effect of social support and perceived discrimination on loneliness among migrant children: A longitudinal study. Psychological Development and Education, 2011, 4: 401 - 411.

[20] Z Lin, Y Y Weng. The study of juniors' mental health among floating population. Chinese Mental Health Journal, 2004, 18: 116.

[21] K Xiao, B Feng. Mental health problem of migrant children. Hebei Education, 2008, 3: 18 - 19.

[22] X Liu. Migrant children's perceived discrimination-trait, mechanisms causing and influencing factors. Beijing: Beijing Normal University, 2008.

[23] X Liu, J X Zhao, J L Shen. Perceived discrimination and subjective well-being among urban migrant children: The effect of mediator and moderator. Acta Psychologica Sinica, 2013, 45: 568 - 584.

[24] S F Xing, X Liu, J X Zhao, et al. The effect of perceived discrimination on collective well-being among migrant children in China. Psychological Development and Education, 2011, 6: 655 - 661.

[25] C D Lin, Z LYang, X T Huang. The Comprehensive Dictionary of Psychology. Shanghai: Shanghai Educational Publishing House, 2005.

[26] L X Yuang, J J Zhang, X L Su. Comparison between public school and migrant school students' mental health. Chinese Journal of School Health, 2009, 30: 851 - 853.

[27] G F He. Learning problems and education intervention of floating population's children. Educational Science Research, 2002, 11: 53.

[28] Y L Ou. On urban mobile preschooler's mental health education. Studies in Preschool Education, 2008, 1: 69-71.

[29] X Liu. The relationship among perceived discrimination, self-esteem and behavior tendency of Chinese migrant children. Abstract book of the fourteenth national academic conference of psychology, 2011.

[30] Z R Zheng. Research on mental health problems among migrant children. Yangzhou: Yangzhou University, 2006.

[31] D M Qiu, D Y Cao, H W Yang. A study on status of migrant children's mental health in Nanchang. Chinese Journal of Health Education, 2008, 1: 33-37.

[32] X Liu, J L Shen. Chinese migrant children's perceived discrimination and its relation to self-esteem. Psychological Science, 2010, 33: 695-697.

[33] W Hu, F Wang, L X Ma, et al. Discrimination perception, adversity appraisal and psychological adjustment in rural-to-urban migrants. Chinese Journal of Clinical Psychology, 2012, 5: 679-683.

[34] X Liu, J L Shen. Chinese migrant children's attributions to discrimination and its effect on affect. Chinese Mental Health Journal, 2009, 23: 599-608.

[35] M Xiong, Y D Ye. Mental health for the children of farmers who worked in city in China. Advances in Psychological Science, 2011, 19: 1798-1813.

[36] S J Zhao, X J Zhen, J B Liu. Research on the floating children's resilience: Status quo and enlightenment. China Journal of Health Psychology, 2009, 17: 1020-1022.

Progress in Research of Non-invasive Biomarkersin Autism Children

Kangwei Shen[a], Dongchuan Yu[b,*], Chen Li[c]
Key Laboratory of Child Development and Learning Science of Ministry of Education, Research Center for Learning Science, Southeast University, Nanjing 210096, China
[a]13505163516@139.com, [b]dcyu@seu.edu.cn,
[c]chenlee1203@163.com
[*]Corresponding author

Keywords: autism; non- invasive; biomarker

Abstract: Children's physiological and psychological health may benefit from the determination of biomarkers in non-invasive samples because they are easily obtainable and more practicable compared to other commonly used matrices in diagnoses and stress research. This review summarizes current knowledge about research of biomarkers in non-invasive samples of autism, such as saliva, urine, hair and nail.

孤独症儿童无创伤生物样本中标志物研究进展

沈康维[a], 禹东川[b,*], 李晨[c]
东南大学学习中心,儿童发展与学习科学教育部重点实验室,南京,江苏,中国
[a]13505163516@139.com, [b]dcyu@seu.edu.cn,
[c]chenlee1203@163.com
*通讯作者

关键词:孤独症;无创伤;生物标志物

中文摘要:儿童的生理和心理健康得益于无创伤生物样本中标志物检测,因为在诊断和行为研究中,相对于常用的有创伤生物样本,这些样品容易获取并且更容易被接受。本文对孤独症相关的无创伤生物标志物研究进展作一个综述。

1 引言

孤独症(Autism spectrum disorders, ASD)是广泛性发育障碍的代表性疾病,通常起病于3岁内,主要核心症状为:社会交往障碍、交流障碍、兴趣狭窄和刻板重复的行为方式。目前学界认识到ASD是一种在一定遗传因素作用下受多种环境因子刺激导致的弥漫性中枢神经系统发育障碍性疾病,已开展了从分子遗传到神经免疫、功能影像、神经解剖和神经化学等多方面的研究,但直至目前,仍没有任何一种假说能从根本上完美地解释ASD的病因。尽管孤独症的原因尚无确切定论,但所有研究都认为既有原发性的生物学因素,又受到心理因素的影响。因此,对孤独症的治疗与干预研究应从生物、医学、心理和教育等方面进行。孤独症的早期诊断关系到干预策略和效果,而生物样本标志物检测是ASD诊断、干预和治疗研究的必要手段。临床生化对生物标志物检测大都采用有创样品,如血液、组织等。但有创采样难以被儿童及家长接受,采样过程也对人体造成应激,使得拟检测的指标变化而干扰检测结果,因此无创样品,如唾液、尿液、毛发等更符合检测需要。本文就近年来一些无创伤生物样品中ASD相关标志物研究成果进行梳理,以期为ASD诊断、治疗与干预研究提供素材和思路。

2 无创伤生物样本中标志物研究

2.1 唾液样本

意大利科学家研究发现孤独症患儿至少有一种唾液缩氨酸与健康儿童不同,特别是磷酸多肽、组胺以及酸性蛋白类等唾液蛋白的磷酸化水平显著低于对照组,因此,研究人员表示,唾液缩氨酸分析将有助于早期识别出有孤独症倾向的人群[1]。Corbett

发现与正常对照相比，ASD 患儿唾液皮质醇(SCor)的生理节律没有显著的变化，然而 ASD 组内儿童 SCor 差异要大于对照组[2]。对于 HPA 轴功能的标志——皮质醇觉醒反应(The cortisol awakening response，CAR，醒后 30 分钟唾液皮质醇浓度与觉醒时的浓度差)，ASD 儿童与正常对照组间也没有显著差异[3,4]。Kidd 对学龄前儿童 SCor 和唾液 α-淀粉酶(SAA)水平进行研究，他将 ASD 患儿根据 IQ 不同分为极低功能组(IQ < 55)、低功能组(55 < IQ < 69)和高功能组(IQ > 70)。采集早上醒来后 30 min 内、下午 2:00 以及晚上上床前 30 min 内唾液样本，结果发现 ASD 组儿童 SCor 和 SAA 水平都高于对照组。并且两种标志物水平随功能组级别降低而逐步升高[5]。

应激刺激中 SCor 变化也有不同报道，Corbett 在环境应激实验(柔和环境噪声刺激)中发现 ASD 组 SCor 反应性显著高于对照组[6]。但 Jansen 在演讲应激实验中发现 ASD 与对照组没有显著差异[7]。而 Levine 用标准特里尔社会应激测试(TSST)证实 ASD 儿童的 SCor 没有显著升高，且响应曲线更钝化，表明面对社会应激，ASD 患儿 HPA 轴功能减弱[8]。Gabriels 对比研究重复性行为高(H 组)低(L 组)不同的两组 ASD 患儿白天 SCor 水平，统计分析表明全部的皮质醇水平 H 组低于 L 组 36%，说明重复性行为与 HPA 功能下调有关[9]。

此外也有氧化应激标志物研究方面的报道，通常精神障碍(包括 ASD)患者氧化应激水平升高可归因于生理和心理应激升高体内氧化物质，如活性氧(reactive oxygen species，ROS)或游离基浓度，进而降低唾液抗氧剂水平[10]。ASD 儿童唾液总抗氧化剂浓度显著低于对照组[11]，作者认为这是由于 ASD 儿童难以与社会交流、交往等情绪和生理应激导致的。

2.2 尿液样本

Geetha 针对 ASD 开展了包括尿皮质醇(UCor)在内的多种皮质激素以及单胺代谢物水平与 ASD 严重程度相关性的研究。被试 45 个 ADS 患儿(4—12 岁)，其中低功能组(LF)、中功能组(MF)和高功能组(HF)各 15 人，在 3 个时段收集尿液(Ⅰ：21:00—7:00；Ⅱ:7:00—14:00；Ⅲ：14:00—21:00)。与控制组相比，尿液中前列腺素 E2、中性 17-氧代类固醇、全 17-羟皮质类固醇、17-生酮类固醇、全 17-氧代类固醇和 11-羟基皮质甾醇类激素分泌都升高；5-羟吲哚乙酸和香草扁桃酸这两种单胺代谢物也都升高，且这些指标升高程度与 ASD 严重程度显著相关(r = 0.787—0.902)。作者认为高水平的尿液皮质激素分泌是由于 HPA 轴功能变化的结果，这可能是病症的通路，也影响 ADS 症状程度。而已报道的单胺代谢物的研究结果比较混乱，Geetha 的结果是仅 LF、MF 组显著高于对照组[12]。

尿液中重金属元素与 ASD 相关性研究有较多报道，Adams 的实验发现 ASD 儿童有更高的尿铅、铊、锡、钨浓度，并且浓度升高与 ASD 症状程度有对应关系[13]。而 Albizzati 研究却发现两组儿童尿铅、汞、镉和铝的含量没有显著差异[14]。此外尿液中有机酸α-酮戊二酸、异柠檬酸、4-羟基苯甲酸、对羟基苯乙酸、马尿酸、脂肪酸、辛二酸浓度两组间有显著差异,提示尿液有机酸无创检测可以指示ASD儿童营养或代谢问题[15]。

Damodaran考察ASD儿童尿液中氧化应激指标,包括硫代巴比妥酸反应物、脂质过氧化物、4-羟基壬烯醛、羰基蛋白、巯基化合物、总抗氧化能力、总过氧化物含量、氧化损伤指数、尿酸/肌苷比(UA/Cr)。结果全部的氧化指标都显著高于对照组,其数值与ASD严重程度呈正相关(LFA > MFA > HFA);抗氧化指标都显著低于对照组,其数值与ASD严重程度呈负相关。结果表明尿液氧化应激标志物可以指示ASD儿童氧化应激水平,也可作为ASD的生物标志物[16]。还有报道尿液中低水平的必需氨基酸[17]、较高水平的同型半胱氨酸[18]和尿单胺及其代谢物(多巴胺DA、高香草酸HVA、3,4-二羟基苯乙酸DOPAC、3-甲氧基多巴胺、去甲肾上腺素和肾上腺素)异常与ASD有关[19]。

2.3 头发和指甲样本

Yasuda检测了一个ASD儿童大样本头发样品(1 967人)中26种痕量元素含量,发现29.7%的儿童缺乏锌、17.6%的儿童缺乏镁;而17.2%、8.5%、4.8%和2.8%的儿童分别表现出头发中铝、镉、铅和砷、汞高。说明锌、镁缺乏和毒性重金属水平升高可能诱发幼儿(0—3岁)神经发育的基因和遗传调控机制变化,并且推测对于神经发育以及可能的治疗存在一个时间限制因素(婴儿窗口期)[20]。Damodaran测试了儿童头发和指甲中蛋白和硝基化蛋白含量,与正常对照组相比,ASD儿童头发和指甲中高硫和低硫蛋白的含量显著降低,而硝基化低硫蛋白含量升高。还观察到酶和非酶抗氧剂浓度降低,而血中硫代巴比妥酸反应物和一氧化氮浓度增加,并且低功能组ASD儿童这种现象更明显[21]。

3 总结

综上所述,从无创伤生物样本开展ASD的发生和发展以及诊断、干预和治疗研究已经成为理论和实践的一个重要方向。探究孤独症的生化特征对于了解环境和基因的协同作用机制可能带来新的思路,为阐明和实施医教结合理念提供生物学依据。但是孤独症特异性生化指标筛选、检测的方法和技术仍然有待进一步提高。

致谢

本文由江苏省普通高校专业学位研究生科研实践计划项目和江苏省普通高校学术学位研究生科研创新计划项目经费资助。

References

[1] M Castagnola, I Messana, R Inzitari, et al. Hypo-phosphorylation of salivary peptidome as a clue to the molecular pathogenesis of autism spectrum disorders. Journal of Proteome Research, 2008, 7: 5327-5332.

[2] B A Corbett, S Mendoza, J A Wegelin, et al. Variable cortisol circadian rhythms in children with autism and anticipatory stress. J Psychiatry Neurosci, 2008, 33: 227-234.

[3] B A Corbett, C W Schupp. The cortisol awakening response (CAR) in male children with autism spectrum disorder. Hormones and Behavior, 2014, 65: 345-350.

[4] K Zinke, E Fries, M Kliegel, et al. Children with high-functioning autism show a normal cortisol awakening response (CAR). Psychoneuroendocrinology, 2010, 35: 1578-1582.

[5] S A Kidd, B A Corbett, D A Granger, et al. Daytime secretion of salivary cortisol and alpha-amylase in preschool-aged children with autism and typically developing children. J Autism Dev Disord, 2012, 42: 2648-2458.

[6] B A Corbett, S Mendoza, M Abdullah, et al. Cortisol circadian rhythms and response to stress in children with autism. Psychoneuroendocrinology, 2006, 31: 59-68.

[7] L M Jansen, C C Gispen-de Wied, R J van der Gaag, et al. Differentiation between autism and multiple complex developmental disorder in response to psychosocial stress. Neuropsychopharmacology, 2003, 28: 582-590.

[8] T P Levine, S J Sheinkopf, M Pescosolido, et al. Physiologic arousal to social stress in children with autism spectrum disorders: A pilot study. Res Autism Spectr Disord, 2012, 6: 177-183.

[9] R L Gabriels, J A Agnew, Z Pan, et al. Elevated repetitive behaviors are associated with lower diurnal salivary cortisol levels in autism spectrum disorder. Biol Psychol, 2013, 93: 262-268.

[10] S Tsaluchidu, M Cocchi, L Tonello, et al. Fatty acids and oxidative stress in psychiatric disorders. BMC Psychiatry, 2008, 17(1): S5.

[11] K Rai, A M Hegde, N Jose. Salivary antioxidants and oral health in children with autism. Arch Oral Biol, 2012, 57: 1116-1120.

[12] M D Lakshmi Priya, A Geetha, V Suganya, et al. Abnormal circadian rhythm and cortisol excretion in autistic children: A clinical study. Croat Med J, 2013, 54: 33-41.

[13] J B Adams, T Audhya, S McDonough-Means, et al. Toxicological status of children with autism vs. neurotypical children and the association with autism severity. Biol Trace Elem Res, 2013, 151: 171-180.

[14] A Albizzati, L Morè, D Di Candia, et al. Normal concentrations of heavy metals in autistic spectrum disorders. Minerva Pediatr, 2012, 64: 27-31.

[15] J Kaluzna-Czaplinska. Noninvasive urinary organic acids test to assess biochemical and nutritional individuality in autistic children. Clin Biochem, 2011, 44: 686-691.

[16] L P Damodaran, G Arumugam. Urinary oxidative stress markers in children with autism. Redox Rep, 2011, 16: 216-222.

[17] C Evans, R H Dunstan, T Rothkirch, et al. Altered amino acid excretion in children with autism. Nutr Neurosci, 2008, 11: 9 - 17.

[18] J Kaluzna-Czaplinska, M Michalska, J Rynkowski. Homocysteine level in urine of autistic and healthy children. Acta Biochim Pol, 2011, 58: 31 - 34.

[19] J Martineau, J Herault, E Petit, et al. Catecholaminergic metabolism and autism. Dev Med Child Neurol, 1994, 36: 688 - 697.

[20] H Yasuda, T Tsutsui. Assessment of infantile mineral imbalances in autism spectrum disorders (ASDs). Int J Environ Res Public Health, 2013, 11: 6027 - 6043.

[21] M D Lakshmi Priya, A Geetha. A biochemical study on the level of proteins and their percentage of nitration in the hair and nail of autistic children. Clinica Chimica Acta, 2011, 412: 1036 - 1042.

Guardian Role Weakening Restriction and Auxiliary Measures of Left-behind Children's Social Development

Xiaorong Wang *

Xi'an University, Xi'an, Shanxi, China

xrongwang@126.com

* Corresponding author

Keywords: left-behind children; social; restriction; interpersonal communication; parent-child relationship

Abstract: Young children's sociality is on the basis of its biological characteristics, interaction with the social life environment, gradually grasp the social norms, the formation of social skills, learning social role, has developed from a natural person for the society produced in the process of socialization of people's psychological and behavioral characteristics. Left-behind children's one or both parents working for a long time, can't live together with the children, the guardian weakening effect, it will have negative impact on children's social development, based on the investigation and analysis on the basis of the rural left-behind children socially in development of the age of three to four characteristics, to explore the parents role weakening influence on children's social development, put forward the government work, family, preschool education institutions for rural left-behind children's humanistic care, promote children's social health.

监护人作用弱化对留守幼儿社会性发展的制约与辅助措施

王晓戎*

西安文理学院,西安,陕西,中国

xrongwang@126.com

*通讯作者

关键词:留守幼儿;社会性;制约;人际交往;亲子关系

中文摘要:幼儿的社会性是在其生物特性的基础上,与社会生活环境相互作用,逐渐掌握社会规范,形成社会技能,学习社会角色,由自然人发展为社会人的社会化过程中所形成的心理及行为特征。留守儿童的父母双方或一方长期在外务工,不能与儿童共同生活,监护人作用弱化,这将对儿童的社会性发展产生诸多不利影响,文章在调查的基础上分析了农村三到四岁留守儿童社会性发展的特点,探究父母作用弱化对幼儿社会性发展的影响,提出政府、家庭、幼儿教育机构发挥作用给予农村留守幼儿人文关怀,促进幼儿社会性健康发展。

1 制约农村留守幼儿社会性提高的因素

家庭是幼儿社会性发展的重要场所,父母是幼儿社会化的首要影响人。幼儿期是人的社会化的关键期。由于父母常年在外务工,导致父母职责弱化,是留守幼儿产生各种问题的直接原因。在长期与祖辈或其他亲戚生活中,他们的需要和情感无法得到关注,因而容易对幼儿的亲社会行为发展产生不利影响。

1.1 3—6岁幼儿留守经历对幼儿社会性发展的影响

1.1.1 幼儿留守经历

幼儿留守形式有父母外出的留守、单亲外出的留守。幼儿留守的形式对留守幼儿生活习惯、人际交往、人格发展产生深远的影响。父母都出去打工对留守幼儿社会性发展不利影响最大,母亲缺位影响次之,父亲缺位、母亲在家的留守幼儿社会性发展负面影响较少。

1.1.2 幼儿留守时间与距离

幼儿留守时间越长对留守幼儿社会性发展的不利影响越大。父母外出务工地距离家乡越近,回家的频率相对较高,与幼儿联系较为密切,对幼儿社会性发展不利影响较弱。

1.2 留守幼儿看护形式与质量

1.2.1 留守幼儿看护形式

看护形式对留守幼儿社会性发展有重要作用。母亲或父亲看护的留守幼儿社会性发展不利方面较少，祖辈看护次之，而寄养、亲朋代养的留守幼儿因寄养家庭问题对幼儿造成的不利影响更为突出。

1.2.2 监护人知识水平与教育理念

监护人知识水平高低直接影响留守幼儿社会性发展。监护人知识水平、社会化程度越高，留守幼儿社会性发展越好，监护人教育理念越先进，越有利于留守幼儿的成长与发展。

2 留守幼儿社会性发展的基本特征

幼儿社会性发展具体表现为生活自理能力和良好生活习惯的养成；适当的社会行为规范的习得；学习其社会角色的职责，正确发展自我意识；发展恰当的社会态度，与他人建立良好的关系，发展社会交往能力。社会性发展是幼儿心理发展的重要方面，它对儿童的人格、心理健康、智力发展等具有重要的影响[1]。

2.1 留守幼儿社会认知发展的特点

社会认知是指人对社会性客体及其之间关系，如对人（他人和自我）、人际关系、社会群体、社会角色、社会规范和社会生活事件的认知，以及对这种认知与人的社会行为之间的关系的理解和判断。幼儿社会认知的发展除受一般认知水平的影响外，还和幼儿的社会互动经验密切相关。

2.1.1 留守幼儿自我意识的发展趋势

自我意识包括自我认知、自我情感体验、自我调控等。随着幼儿年龄的增长，其自我意识的发展是逐步递增的，且在水平上存在显著差异[2]。留守幼儿的自我意识发展也遵循如此规律，但是留守幼儿的自我意识发展水平整体略低于被调查幼儿的总体平均水平，也明显低于非留守幼儿的自我意识发展水平。研究表明留守幼儿与非留守幼儿在自我评价、自我体验和自我控制方面均有差异，自我评价和自我体验方面，同班级组的非留守幼儿比留守幼儿发展水平略高，但留守幼儿随着年龄的增加，其自我控制方面发展水平比非留守幼儿更好。

2.1.2 留守幼儿自我调控能力的发展

自我调控是个体对自身的心理与行为的主动掌握，是个体不受外界因素的影响，自觉地选择目标，控制自己的情感和行为，从而保证目标的实现[3]。学龄前幼儿期是自我控制品质发展的敏感期。3—4 岁发展较快，4—5 岁发展迅速。这是因为 3 岁幼儿的大脑皮质抑制机能尚未完善，兴奋过程占优势，表现为活泼好动，自我控制水平较低。随着年龄的增长，幼儿大脑皮质的抑制机能逐渐完善，兴奋与抑制过程逐渐平衡；

同时,随着认知能力的发展和外在的各种教育因素的介入,幼儿对行为规则的理解与掌握逐步深入与内化,形成自觉的规则意识,并且不断约束与控制自己的行为。亲子之间的相互行为会影响幼儿的自我调控能力发展。因父母常年与幼儿分离,父母与孩子之间的相互影响降低,隔代监护容易对幼儿迁就、放任和过分宠爱,导致孩子较少有意识地调控自己的情绪和行为,故其抑制性控制明显差于同龄的非留守幼儿。

2.2 留守幼儿生活习惯与行为能力的发展

幼儿生活习惯与行为能力的发展是幼儿自我发展的一项重要内容。也是幼儿社会化的重要方面。由于父母与孩子长期分离,三到四岁留守幼儿缺少了生活中可模仿的父母的榜样和指导,三到四岁留守幼儿与其他幼儿的生活自理能力没有明显区别,四岁之后留守幼儿自我服务能力的发展弱于有父母指导的幼儿,但父母外出务工也让部分留守幼儿生活独立性增强。

2.3 留守幼儿人际交往的发展

人际交往是幼儿社会化能否顺利实现的必要条件,人际交往还将影响幼儿的人格发展[4]。3—6岁留守幼儿生活圈子主要有家庭、邻里和幼儿教育机构,其中家庭成员与幼儿的关系、幼儿之间的关系是幼儿重要的人际关系,对幼儿社会性发展影响深远。

1. 3—6岁留守幼儿亲子关系的现状

调查发现在父母与留守幼儿关系方面,男孩比女孩与父母的密切程度更高。父母对男孩更为牵挂,对女孩有较多担心。父母与男童的联系多于与女童的联系。留守幼儿年龄越小,家庭的亲子关系越淡化,留守幼儿年龄越大,幼儿逐渐能用语言与父母交流,五到六岁幼儿较三到四岁幼儿与父母的语言交流次数与质量都更高,因此其父母与孩子的关系也更为亲密。

2. 3—6岁留守幼儿与同龄群体交往的特点

幼儿同龄群体交往是幼儿社会化的重要途径[5]。留守幼儿在处境孤独、被拒绝、被欺负等方面比非留守幼儿更为突出,留守幼儿人际关系较为紧张,应该注重留守幼儿同伴关爱的培养。

(1) 留守幼儿与人交往缺乏信心,主动性不强

留守幼儿由于缺少父母的支撑与指导,怯于与他人打交道。幼儿期的交往障碍会使幼儿对人际交往产生逃避,不但会妨碍他们幼儿期的人际交往,也会影响幼儿成年后的人格发展。

(2) 交往对象受限,喜欢结交处境相似的幼儿

调查结果显示:留守幼儿普遍喜欢与其处境相似的幼儿交往,他们有共同语言,能够产生认同感。留守幼儿被欺负时寻求小学生的援助,也容易被问题幼儿同化。

(3) 调节情绪的能力不强,致使攻击行为增多

调查发现留守幼儿的攻击行为多于非留守幼儿,留守幼儿由于缺乏交往技巧,行

为容易变得放任、冲动或具攻击性。

2.4 留守幼儿亲社会行为发展的特点

社会性行为是人们在交往活动中对他人或某一事件表现出的态度、言语和行为反应。根据其动机和目的，可以将社会性行为分为亲社会行为和反社会行为两类。亲社会行为是指人们在社会交往中所表现出来的谦让、帮助、合作、共享等有利于他人和社会的行为。反社会行为是指违反社会法律、法规或为社会所不能接受的行为，在学前幼儿身上主要体现为一种不受欢迎但却经常发生的不良行为，通常表现为对他人打、抓、撞、骂、威胁等问题行为。幼儿很早的时候就表现出亲社会行为，但这种行为是随着幼儿的社会认知水平而发展变化的[6]。观察发现，一岁以前，幼儿已经能够通过微笑或发声表达对别人的友好。在人生的第二年，幼儿的亲社会行为越来越明显地表现出来，他们常常把自己的玩具同其他小朋友分享，也能帮妈妈做些简单的事情。两岁以后，随着生活范围和交往经验的增多，幼儿的亲社会行为进一步发展，他们逐渐能够根据一些不太明显的细微变化来识别他人的情绪体验，推断他人的处境并做出相应的抚慰或帮助行为。留守幼儿由于父母的缺位，亲社会行为的发展缓慢于非留守幼儿[7]。

3 促进农村留守幼儿社会性良性发展的策略

3.1 教育主管部门要创新教育方式，引领社会资源参与留守幼儿的教育

教育主管部门要积极创新教育方式，多渠道、全方位地帮扶农村留守幼儿，引领社会资源参与留守幼儿的教育，引导教育机构与社会公益组织联合开发留守幼儿教育资源，促进农村留守幼儿健康、快乐地成长发展。

3.2 父母应强化情感沟通功能

父母要转变观念，重视孩子的亲情教育和成长。在外出致富与养育子女之间慎重考量得失。父母生活所迫必须外出打工时，最好能选择父亲或母亲一方外出，给予孩子母爱或父爱，让孩子健康成长。父母双方如果万不得已都必须外出，外出父母要给孩子多打电话，多安慰鼓励，尽量减少分离对孩子的负面影响。利用节假日多回家陪伴孩子，给予孩子贴心的温暖。引导孩子明白父母离开孩子是迫不得已，争取孩子的理解。

3.3 幼儿教育机构要重视留守幼儿教育，开展多种形式的人文关怀

幼儿教育机构是留守幼儿社会性发展的重要场所，教育机构在日常工作中要增设留守幼儿教育内容，开展形式多样的留守幼儿关爱活动。教师应给予留守幼儿生活和学习上的帮助和指导，多和留守幼儿谈心，引导班级成员相互关心，积极交往，让留守幼儿体验到集体的温暖和产生心理归属感。还可与当地中小学校联合组成留守幼儿

互助小组,让留守幼儿在与同伴和大龄幼儿良性互动中健康成长。

3.4 社会公益组织积极参与留守幼儿帮扶行动

社会公益组织包括民间自助组织、大学生志愿者、代理家长等,发挥社会责任感与同情心投身到关爱留守幼儿的活动中。志愿者通常可以采取这些关爱行动;走进留守幼儿的生活世界,和他们一起吃住,和留守幼儿谈心、交朋友;假期组织留守幼儿进行集体活动、玩游戏,教孩子唱歌画画等;为留守幼儿募捐生活和学习用品以及玩具[8]。

致谢

本文系西安市社科规划基金项目“西安地区农村留守儿童教育问题与对策研究”(项目编号:12WL07)、陕西省社科联重大理论与现实问题研究项目(项目编号2013C008)、陕西省教育科学“十二五”规划项目(项目编号:SGH13197)阶段性成果。

References

[1] Li ying. “Left-behind children” in rural areas to the social development research. Beijing: Central China Normal University, 2009.

[2] Li na. Rural left-behind children's social adaptation research. Tianjin: Tianjin University of Technology, 2010.

[3] Jiang Xiaona. Rural preschool left-behind children's emotional state research. Kaifeng: Henan University, 2011.

[4] Chen Xinhua. An empirical study of the border region of Guangxi rural left-behind children socialization. Guilin: Guangxi Normal University, 2008.

[5] Lin Shaoling. Left-behind children's family education way on its peer interaction. Contemporary Preschool Education, 2009(4): 18 - 19.

[6] Wang Gonglei, Yao Lixia. Left-behind children's peer interaction problem investigation. Journal of Early Childhood Education (Education Science Edition), 2007(4): 20 - 22.

[7] Bang, Yang jie. The problem of rural left-behind children's interpersonal conflict analysis. Journal of Tenet, 2012, 6: 23 - 25.

[8] Li Yubo. Northwest minority areas rural left-behind children socialization research. Changchun: Jilin Agricultural University, 2011, 6: 2 - 8.

A Study on Teaching of Using Conflict Strategy to Promote Preschool Children's Conceptual Change: Taking the "Sinking and Floating" Concept as an Example

Fang Wang[1, a, *]

[1]Department of Preschool Education, Teachers College of Qingdao University, Qingdao, Shandong, China

[a]wf2210@126.com

[*]Corresponding author

Keywords: conceptual change; conflict strategy; preschool children; sinking and floating

Abstract: Conceptual change teaching is an effective way to improve preschool children's concept learning, their thinking level and problem-solving abilities. The study chose the "sinking and floating" concept as the specific teaching content. Through the teaching experiment, the study testified the actual effect of conflict strategy which is a common conceptual change teaching strategy in primary and middle school in promoting preschool children's conceptual change. The study also discussed the internal mechanism and the reasons, and summarized the essential elements of teaching. The results showed that using conflict strategy under the guidance of science education idea can effectively promote preschool children's conceptual change. Therefore, the conflict strategy is suitable for kindergarten's conceptual change teaching.

运用冲突策略促进幼儿概念转变的教学研究
——以“沉浮”概念为例

王芳[1,a,*]
[1]青岛大学师范学院学前教育系,青岛,山东,中国
[a]wf2210@126.com
[*]通讯作者

关键词:概念转变;冲突策略;幼儿;沉浮

中文摘要:概念转变教学是促进幼儿概念学习、提高其思维水平和问题解决能力的一种有效方式。本研究以沉浮概念为具体内容,通过教学实验验证了当前中小学常用的概念转变教学策略——冲突策略促进幼儿概念转变的实际效果,并探讨了内在机制和原因,总结了教学指导要点。实验结果表明,在科学教育理念指导下的冲突策略能有效促进幼儿概念的转变,适用于幼儿园的概念转变教学。

1 引言

概念是抽象逻辑思维的细胞,是人类进行一切认知活动的基础[1],也是任何一个学科知识体系最基本的构成元素。以前概念为起点并促进其向科学概念转变的“概念转变教学”能有效提高学生概念学习的效率,已成为当前科学教学的主流[2]。但是,已有研究绝大多数集中在中小学阶段,幼儿概念转变教学尚未得到应有的关注。鉴于概念学习是一个连续性的过程且研究者已开始注意到幼儿概念学习的重要性,因此十分有必要对幼儿概念转变教学进行深入的研究,以寻求促进幼儿概念学习、提高其思维水平和问题解决能力的有效方式和途径。

笔者在借用学习心理学、教育学研究成果全面分析幼儿概念转变教学的必要性和可能性的基础上,对几种中小学常见的概念转变教学策略在幼儿园的适用性进行了深入的探究。现将其中的运用冲突策略转变幼儿沉浮概念的研究展示如下。

2 教学研究的设计与实施

2.1 研究目的

验证“冲突策略”促进幼儿概念转变的实际效果。

2.2 研究内容——“沉浮”概念的选择

本研究之所以选择“沉浮”作为运用“冲突策略”促进幼儿概念转变的“内容”,主要基于以下几方面的考虑:

首先,沉浮是幼儿比较感兴趣的现象,他们在日常生活中可以经常观察到物体的沉浮

并有许多机会动手操作,已经具备了和沉浮有关的一些经验,对沉浮形成了一定的认识。

其次,“沉浮”是物理学的基本概念之一,是国内外幼儿科学教育的常见内容。虽然不少研究表明,幼儿阶段不可能真正理解决定物体沉浮的根本原因——密度,但是,沉浮现象与影响沉浮的各种因素(相关的、不相关的)之间的关系又具有一定的“可见性”,可以通过引导幼儿猜测、实际验证(证实和证伪)和归纳,在逐步接近科学概念的过程中发展科学探究的态度、方法和能力。

最后,沉浮是最容易产生错误认识的科学现象之一,且这些认识往往比较顽固。如果运用冲突策略能有效打破幼儿的认知平衡,使其沉浮概念产生转变,那将使本文的立论更加有说服力。

2.3 研究方法

2.3.1 教育实验法

研究采用准实验设计,自变量为教学策略,包括两个水平:实验班采用冲突教学策略,对比班采用普通的教学策略。因变量为幼儿的沉浮概念水平。

在青岛市S幼儿园(该幼儿园为省级示范幼儿园)A分园随机抽取两个中班共58名幼儿作为研究对象。在实验的过程中,少量幼儿未能参加全部实验活动。完整参与全部实验过程的有效被试实验班为23人,对比班为25人,共48人。

表1 运用冲突策略促进幼儿概念转变教学实验的有效被试

	男	女	合计
实验班	11	12	23
对比班	12	13	25
合计	23	25	48

为了尽可能地反映实验的效果,本研究还比较严格地控制了两班幼儿的沉浮前概念水平(前测无显著性差异)以及两班教师的年龄、工作经验和教学水平。实验班和对比班的教师都是参加工作刚满3年的教师,学历皆为本科。

实验前对实验班的老师进行培训,内容为幼儿沉浮概念发展的一般规律,以及冲突策略的内涵和应用等。

2.3.2 访谈法

访谈的对象为教师和幼儿。对幼儿主要采用“事件访谈法”,即“有操作辅助的访谈法”。研究者在访谈过程中,以具体操作方式,实际呈现相关情境或现象,让儿童对所发生的现象进行观察;然后询问问题,并在其回答或说明之后,依儿童的反应情形,弹性回应;以及经确认再确认的过程,以了解其真正想法[3]。这种访谈分别在前测、后测和延迟测验时运用。另外,也会在教学的过程中针对有关问题对幼儿进行访谈。

对教师的访谈贯穿于教学实验的整个过程。访谈的主要内容为教师对冲突策略的认识、将冲突策略应用于幼儿园教学带来的变化和遇到的挑战,以此探讨冲突策略促进幼儿概念转变的作用机制,总结教学指导要点。

2.4 幼儿沉浮概念转变评价工具的研制

本实验只研究“漂浮”和“沉”两种状态,暂不涉及“悬浮”现象;而且仅仅涉及物体在常态水中的沉浮,不涉及液体密度的改变。

儿童发展研究发现,个体沉浮概念的发展是一个长期的、渐进的过程。Piaget 将儿童对物体沉浮的预测和因果解释划分为四个阶段:阶段一(5 岁),将船浮在水上解释为道德和动力的原因,并认为是船的制作者和船自身的意愿;阶段二(5—6 岁),认为船浮在水上是因为它重;阶段三(6—8 岁),认为船浮在水上是因为它轻,同时仍将动力原因包含在内;阶段四(9 岁),开始理解船的重量与其所在液体重量之间的真正关系[4]。Havu-Nuntinen 将儿童沉浮概念的发展概括为如下趋势:(1) 无关的和非科学的解释(Non-relevant and Non-scientific explanations),儿童没有提出任何关于沉浮现象的物理特征或回答;(2) 非本质相关判断(Non-relational but relevant justifications);(3) 和水相关的判断(Water-related justifications),即通过比较物体和水的重量提供物体沉浮的证据[5]。袁美英探讨了 259 名 5—7 岁儿童的沉浮概念的发展趋势。她认为沉浮概念具有以下发展路径:(1) 用心理因素判断和解释物体的沉浮发展;(2) 开始将物体的多种物理属性与物体的沉浮建立联系;(3) 找到影响物体沉浮的某一种本质因素(轻重或大小),以此去预测和解释各种沉浮现象;(4) 进一步思考物体的其他特征对物体沉浮的影响,并将这些特征与轻重(大小)相结合;(5) 开始思考物体重量和大小这两重特征对物体沉浮的影响,产生原始的密度直觉[6]。

综合以上研究结果,通过与有经验的幼儿园教师的讨论,本研究将儿童浮沉概念的发展分为以下五个阶段:(1) 用心理因素来判断和解释沉浮现象;(2) 用物体的颜色、软硬、表面光滑程度等无关因素判断和解释沉浮现象;(3) 用单一的轻重或大小的标准判断或解释沉浮现象;(4) 用物体的材质(木头、铁等)来判断和解释沉浮现象;(5) 初步将轻重和大小结合起来解释物体的沉浮。将这五个阶段作为评价幼儿沉浮概念发展水平的标准,分别赋值 1—5 分。

2.5 研究程序

2.5.1 前测

本研究采用袁美英在幼儿沉浮概念研究中所使用的操作材料[6],通过“有辅助操作的访谈法”来测查两班幼儿的沉浮前概念(操作材料和访谈程序见附录 1)。测查者两人一组,其中一人提问和呈现相关物体,另一人做重点记录。访谈全程录音,随后转化为文字,再根据沉浮概念发展水平评价标准给每个幼儿打分(两个测查者的评分一致性信度为 91%),最后将数据输入 SPSS 进行显著性差异检验。结果显示,两班幼儿沉浮概念水平无显著性差异(详见研究结果)。

2.5.2 教学干预

实验班和对比班各自开展为期 5 周的沉浮探究活动,每周 1 次,共 5 次。两班教学内容基本相同,但实验班运用的是冲突教学策略,对比班运用的是普通教学策略。

在教学期间就冲突策略的相关问题对实验班教师进行访谈。

2.5.3 后测

教学实验结束 1 周后进行后测，材料、程序与前测基本相同。

2.5.4 延迟测验

为了进一步考察冲突策略促进幼儿沉浮概念转变的教学效果的持久性和稳定性，探究实验班幼儿教学后的沉浮概念水平变化是因为认知结构得以重组还是简单地记住了活动中的某些现象和结论，特在实验结束后 2 个月后变换测试材料进行延迟测验。

将所有结果输入 SPSS 进行统计处理，考察组间差异。

2.6 教学活动的实施

2.6.1 教学的基本步骤

首先，暴露或引出幼儿的沉浮前概念。

将全班幼儿随机分为 5 组，每组提供一个大水盆，提供大小、轻重、空心实心、材质、颜色、光滑程度等物理属性各不相同的物体，请幼儿进行操作，观察、记录各种物体的沉浮状况，并解释其原因。

或由教师集中出示一个物体，让幼儿预测其沉浮状况并解释原因，从中了解幼儿沉浮概念的水平和具体特点。

其次，提供“反例”，有效激发幼儿的认知冲突。

所谓“反例”，指的是当前理论不能加以解释、说明的例子、事实。当幼儿的沉浮前概念明确呈现出来后，教师要么直接呈现“反例”，要么提供相应的材料，让幼儿在个人操作中发现“反例”的存在。当“反例”出现后，请幼儿思考“反例”与原有认识之间的矛盾和不一致之处。

第三，解决认知冲突，建构新概念。

鼓励幼儿进行认知调整，建构新的沉浮概念。教师和幼儿围绕着新旧概念进行讨论，探明两者之间的差异。对于幼儿感到迷惑的地方，可再次提供“反例”进行验证，以进一步强化新概念。

第四，提供多种机会，通过探究活动进一步促进幼儿对新概念的理解和应用。

个体的概念转变具有长期性、反复性，幼儿在小组活动中由于受到冲突挑战而产生的对前概念的怀疑和对新概念的肯定，必须经过更多的练习才能得到强化。我们在每次小组活动之后，都会有针对性地根据他们的新概念提供相应的材料，鼓励他们进一步进行沉浮现象的自主探究，加深对新概念的理解和应用。

2.6.2 冲突策略的使用方式

及时地提供“反例”，挑战幼儿的已有知识经验，是使用冲突策略的关键所在。在本教学实验中，教师始终扮演着反例提供者的角色，她们灵活运用了各种方式来展示反例。下面分别就物体的“大小”、“轻重”、“表面光滑程度”以及“材质”的反例提供进行具体说明。

(1) 提供“大小”的反例

大小是实验班幼儿用来判断物体沉浮的一个主要依据。他们有的认为大的物体会浮,小的物体会沉;有的则恰恰相反,认为大的物体会沉,小的物体会浮。无论是哪种情况,教师都会通过操作精心选择的物体,使其观看到完全不同的现象。即,如果幼儿认为大的沉,小的浮,则教师提供大而浮、小而沉的物品;如果幼儿认为大的浮、小的沉,则教师提供大而沉,小而浮的物品。如下例:

个人探究完毕后,教师请小朋友报告发现什么东西浮上来了,什么东西沉下去了,为什么。

依云:我发现,比较大的东西都沉下去了,比较小的东西都浮上来了。

教师拿出一个皮球和一颗围棋子。

教师:皮球和围棋子谁大谁小?

依云:皮球大,围棋子小。

教师:你刚才说大的东西在水里会沉下去,小的东西会浮上来,对不对?

依云:是的。

教师:那大皮球和小围棋子放到水里,哪一个应该是浮的,哪一个应该是沉的?

依云:大皮球沉,围棋子浮。

教师:我们现在实验一下,看是不是和你想的一样。

教师把皮球和围棋子轻轻放进水盆里,请依云观察。

依云:皮球是浮在水面上的,围棋子沉到水底了。

教师:和你刚才想的一样吗?

依云:不一样。

……

(2) 提供“轻重”的反例

“轻重”是实验班幼儿用来判断和解释沉浮现象的另一主要依据。同“大小”的判断类似,同处于这个水平的幼儿观点也大不相同:有的认为重的沉,轻的浮;有的认为重的浮,轻的沉。为了激发幼儿的认知冲突,教师同样需要针对不同的情况提供不同的材料:对前者提供重而浮、轻而沉的物体;对后者提供重而沉、轻而浮的物体。另外,由于涉及轻重,在活动中准备一个天平是非常重要的。如下例:

教师出示一个玻璃球,让小朋友预测它的沉浮状况并说明理由。

泽晨:我觉得玻璃球会沉下去,因为它很重。

教师把玻璃球放进水里,果然沉到了水底。

泽晨:重的东西就是要沉到水底的,轻的东西才会浮在水面。

教师拿出一个篮球和一个小铁块,放在天平上,请泽晨称一称两个物品哪个更重一些。

泽晨:篮球重,铁块轻。

教师轻轻地把篮球和铁块放进水里,请泽晨观察并告知沉浮结果。

泽晨:篮球是浮着的,铁块沉下去了。

教师:你刚才是不是说重的东西会沉,轻的东西会浮?

泽晨:是的。

教师:那现在比较重的篮球为什么浮起来了,比较轻的铁块反而沉下去了?

……

(3) 提供“表面光滑程度”等无关因素的反例

同理,如果幼儿以物体表面的光滑或粗糙程度、颜色以及软硬等与沉浮无关的因素作为预测和解释沉浮现象的标准,教师也会及时通过实验、演示等方式让幼儿感觉到与原有理解相反的事实。如下例:

德青:铁块能沉到水里,是因为它太光滑了,“嗖”地一下就掉到水底去了。

教师拿出表面十分光滑的木块、皮球、空心玻璃瓶。

教师:木块、皮球、空玻璃瓶的表面是不是也很光滑?是不是和铁块的表面一样?

德青:对啊,它们也是很光滑的。

教师让德青把“也是很光滑”的木块、皮球和空心玻璃瓶放进水里,看看它们是否和铁块一样沉下去了。

德青:老师,它们哪个也没沉下去,都浮上来了。

……

(4) 提供“材质”的反例

教师把玻璃球放入水中,玻璃球沉到了水底。

浩天:玻璃球能沉下去,是因为它是玻璃做的。玻璃做的东西都能沉下去,我爷爷的烟灰缸是玻璃做的,放进水里也是沉下去的。

教师拿出几个空心玻璃瓶。

教师:它们是不是都是玻璃做的?

浩天:都是玻璃做的。

教师:你把它们放进水里,看看是沉还是浮。

浩天把玻璃瓶一个一个地放进水中,发现它们都是浮着的。

教师:请你想想,为什么都是玻璃做的,玻璃球沉下去了,玻璃瓶却浮上来了呢?

……

2.7 研究结果

2.7.1 实验班和对比班幼儿沉浮概念发展水平的差异检验

由表2可知,在后测和延迟测验中,实验班和对比班幼儿的沉浮概念水平皆在0.05的水平上达到了显著差异。这说明运用冲突教学策略比普通策略更有利于幼儿沉浮概念的转变,且这种转变具有一定的持久性和稳定性。值得注意的是,尽管在延迟测验中,两班幼儿沉浮概念水平的平均得分均低于后测,实验班幼儿的沉浮概念也出现了“回归”现象,但这种概念的反复并没有消减冲突教学策略的效果,两个班级的沉浮概念发展水平仍然显现出显著性差异。

表2　实验班和对比班幼儿沉浮概念的前测、后测和延迟测验差异检验

		M	*SD*	Sig.
前测	实验班	2.57	1.50	0.472
	对比班	2.52	1.61	
后测	实验班	3.39	0.68	0.043*
	对比班	2.88	0.85	
延迟测验	实验班	3.26	0.93	0.038*
	对比班	2.72	0.72	

*表示在0.05水平上显著($p<0.05$)。

2.7.2　实验班和对比班幼儿沉浮概念水平变化具体情况

两班幼儿在三次测验中的沉浮概念发展水平具体情况如表3和图1所示。

表3　三次测验中两班幼儿各种沉浮概念水平的人数分布

	实验班						对比班					
概念水平	前测	百分比（%）	后测	百分比（%）	延迟测验	百分比（%）	前测	百分比（%）	后测	百分比（%）	延迟测验	百分比（%）
1	3	13.04	1	4.35	1	4.35	4	16.00	2	8.00	2	8.00
2	6	26.09	3	13.04	3	13.04	6	24.00	4	16.00	5	20.00
3	12	52.17	9	39.13	11	47.83	13	52.00	15	60.00	16	64.00
4	2	8.70	6	26.09	5	21.74	2	8.00	3	12.00	2	8.00
5	0	0	4	17.39	3	13.04	0	0	1	4.00	0	0
合计	23	100.00	23	100.00	23	100.00	25	100.00	25	100.00	25	100.00

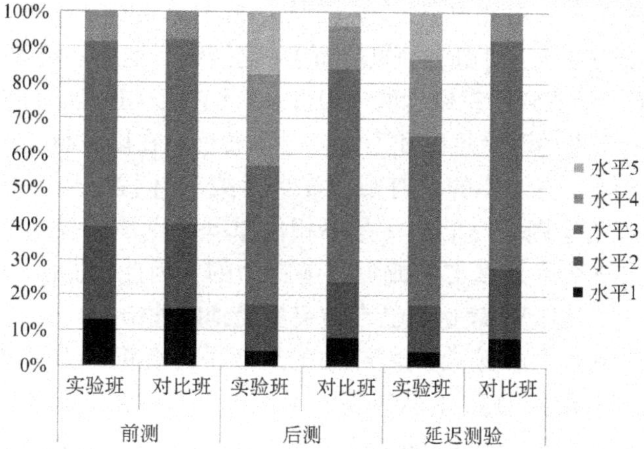

图1　三次测验中两班幼儿各种沉浮概念水平的人数百分比

如果将1、2水平视为沉浮概念发展的较低水平，3水平视为中等水平，4、5水平视为较高水平的话，那么由表3、图1可以看出，教学后，两班幼儿处于较低水平的人数比例都在下降，处于较高水平的人数比例都在上升。与前测相比，实验班幼儿后测中沉浮概念处于1、2水平的人数比例大幅降低（分别由13.04%、26.09%降为4.35%、

13.04%),同时4、5水平的人数比例大幅上升(分别由8.70%、0上升为26.09%和17.39%)。对比班幼儿1、2水平的人数比例也有所下降(分别从16.00%、24.00%降为8.00%和16.00%),4、5水平的人数比例有所上升(分别由8.00%、0上升为12.00%和4.00%),但两种幅度都不如实验班大。

在延迟测验中,实验班和对比班幼儿沉浮概念的总体水平都有所下降。实验班幼儿处于3水平的人数由后测时的9人上升为11人,处于4、5水平的人数由6人、4人降为5人、3人;对比班幼儿处于4、5水平的人数由3人、1人降为2人、0人,处于2、3水平的人数由4人、15人上升为5人、16人。这表明在后测中两班有一些幼儿可能凭借对相关情境和现象的记忆而提高了概念水平,在经过两个月的时间后,其沉浮概念又回归到教学前的水平。

3 讨论

3.1 运用冲突策略促进幼儿概念转变的内在机制和原因

运用冲突策略之所以能促进幼儿的概念转变,最主要的原因在于它打破了幼儿的内在认知平衡,使他们产生了不协调和不满足感。

皮亚杰认为,儿童的认知是通过适应而实现的,适应的本质在于主体能取得自身与环境间的平衡。而任何一次平衡的发生,都包含着三个阶段:(1) 儿童满足自己现有的认知模式,处于暂时的平衡状态;(2) 儿童意识到自己现存的认知模式具有不足的地方,因此产生了不满足感,平衡状态被打破;(3) 克服了原有的认知模式,又达到了一种新的平衡状态[7]。由此可见,个体的认知结构总是处在平衡与不平衡的转换变化之中,不满足感的产生是促成这种转化的关键因素。运用冲突策略能激发幼儿对原有概念的"不满",意识到原有概念的局限性,因此它能促进幼儿的概念转变。

幼儿在冲突中产生的不满足感和不协调感主要反映在以下行为中:

(1) 惊讶与追问。当幼儿的原有观点受到挑战,他们首先就会有一种惊讶的反应。这种反应大致透露了两个信息:一是不相信原有观点是错误或有限的,二是不相信面对的新情境或新结论是真实的或更有解释力的。因此,幼儿会通过各种面部表情、声音变化和不停的追问来表达自己在冲突中受到的冲击。

小凯认为在水中大的东西一定会浮,小的东西一定会沉。为了挑战他这种认识,教师提供了一个大可乐饮料瓶(里面装满沙子)和一个小木片,先让他预测一下两者的沉浮状况。结果是装满沙子的可乐瓶浮,小木片沉。然后教师让幼儿把两样东西都放进水里,观察实际沉浮结果。小凯的眼睛一下子就睁大了,他一会看看浮着的小木片和沉下去的可乐瓶,一会看看老师,又把两者拿出来重新放了一遍,最后才在记录单上记录下实验结果。他看着我问了3遍:"老师,为什么大瓶子没有浮起来?为什么大海船就能浮起来?"我和老师把可乐瓶里面的沙子倒出来,然后再次放进水里,大可乐瓶也浮了起来。小凯更惊讶了,因为他看到了大的瓶子和小的木片都是浮着的!活动结束后,教师让每个孩子用符号表征出自己的问题,小凯提的问题是:“它俩为什么都能浮着呢? 为什么大瓶子也能浮也能沉呢? 小木片是不是也能沉下去?”看样子,这个问题确实让小凯困惑不已。

(2) 沉思和自言自语。然而,并不是所有的幼儿都能像小凯一样能大胆、及时地表达自己的困惑,寻求教师和同伴的帮助。在实验中,我们发现有一些幼儿在观察到与个人预测结果相反的沉浮现象之后,虽然并没有什么太多的惊讶反应,但他们将结果记录下来以后,会不断地在预测结果和实验结果之间进行比对,同时小声地说些什么,但外人很难听清楚。

当教师问正在思考的翰文在想些什么时,翰文似乎有些迟疑:“我还没想好。”教师又问:“是不是你在想为什么预测结果和实验结果不一样?” 翰文才点点头:“是啊,我觉得挺奇怪的。”

(3) 反复的实验。另有一些幼儿直接借助多次的实验来应对自己的困惑和认知不平衡状态。他们会利用各种机会,来验证原有概念是否一定是错误的,新概念是否一定是正确的。

艾凝认为物体的颜色可以决定物体的沉浮,因为发黑的东西大都能沉下去,比如铁、石头等等,而其他颜色的物体大部分是浮的,如花皮球、西红柿等等。当同伴对她这个观点提出反对意见后,为了证明到底谁说得对,她采取了实验证明的方式。在区域活动时,她经常挑各种颜色的物体放进水里,然后拉反对她观点的小朋友来看。

3.2 运用冲突策略的注意事项

3.2.1 冲突的产生要建立在幼儿对相关现象的观察之上,因此在教学中要有针对性地提供多种材料,给予幼儿充分的验证的机会

Kammi 等人认为,沉浮活动属于“中间型活动”,即这种活动既需要幼儿操作物体,又需要对物体的变化进行观察[8],两者对幼儿建构沉浮概念都是非常关键的。因此,无论是个人新旧概念之间的冲突,还是同伴之间、师幼之间冲突的激发和解决,都应建立在具体可见的物体操作和物体变化观察的基础上,而绝不是强调个人的冥思或群体间的口舌之争。仅仅依靠热烈的讨论和争辩,提示幼儿“你这样想不对”或“听听别人的意见”,是无助于幼儿概念转变的。

沉浮概念说到底是对物体的物理属性与沉浮状态之间关系的一种认识,因此教师在提供“反例”以激发幼儿认知冲突时,必须要认真研究所提供材料的物理属性。只有出示与幼儿提及的物理属性相同但沉浮状态相反的物体,才能有效地帮助幼儿在操作中发现“反例”,意识到已有观点的不足。比如,当幼儿坚持“大的沉,小的浮”的看法时,教师就应该提供大而浮、小而沉的物体;当幼儿认为“大的浮,小的沉”时,教师应该提供大而沉、小而浮的材料。让幼儿来操作这些物体,观察它们在水中的实际沉浮状态,才会对其前概念形成强大的挑战,使他们明白大小并不是决定物体沉浮的唯一因素,进而思考其他物体属性对沉浮的影响。如果是随意地提供材料,那不仅无助

于幼儿概念的发展，还有可能进一步强化其现有认识。

3.2.2　在冲突教学中要注意幼儿认知和情感的融合，通过多种途径激发幼儿的学习动机和探索热情

冲突与发展之间并不存在一种必然的促进关系，冲突能否发挥促进概念转变的作用，还取决于个体的学习动机和态度等因素。积极的态度、较高的热情和责任感有利于认知冲突的产生，对问题漠不关心的学生很难产生认知冲突感。另外，不成功的学生会由于消极的自我印象、过度的焦虑或消极的态度等躲避认知冲突的产生[9]。因此，在运用冲突策略的教学过程中，教师要把激发幼儿的学习动机和热情放在重要位置。

首先，教师确定的活动目标要难度适中，给幼儿带来的挑战要处于其“最近发展区”里，避免因任务过难或过易给幼儿带来消极情绪。要做到这一点，需要教师去准确把握幼儿的沉浮前概念以及这个前概念进一步发展能达到的水平。

其次，教师在教学中要灵活采用多种教学方式，比如角色扮演、智力竞赛或故事创编等等，要给予幼儿充分的观察、操作、记录、交流机会，以激发他们活动的热情、积极性和主动性。

致谢

本文为作者博士论文《幼儿概念转变教学研究——以科学领域为例》的部分内容，指导教师为北京师范大学教育学部冯晓霞教授。

附录1　幼儿沉浮概念测查工具

一、操作材料

前测与后测所用材料：

篮球、网球、健身球、高尔夫球、木球、玻璃弹子球。

延迟测验所用材料：

玩具车轮胎、网球、大石块、化妆品瓶子、U形木板、围棋子。

二、访谈和操作程序

	访谈情境与程序	主要目的
1	将玩具雪花片和矿泉水瓶同时放进水中。 提问：玩具雪花片、矿泉水瓶在水中怎么了？	了解幼儿是否具备基本的沉浮概念，能否正确地分辨“沉”与“浮”。
2	出示篮球、网球、健身球、高尔夫球、木球和玻璃弹子球。 提问：如果把这些球放入水中，你觉得哪些会浮上来，哪些会沉下去？为什么？	了解幼儿对物体沉浮的判断依据，确定他们沉浮概念发展的水平等级。
3	把所有球放入水中，请幼儿观察。 对于与幼儿预先猜测结果相反的结果，请幼儿进行解释。如“你刚才说篮球会沉下去，但我们看到它现在是浮着的。你觉得可能是什么原因呢？”	了解幼儿面对与个人猜测相矛盾的情况时对物体沉浮的判断依据，进一步确认其沉浮概念发展水平。

后测与延迟测验时去除第一步,即直接出示相关材料,请幼儿预测其沉浮状态,解释原因。

References

[1] Yinghe Chen. Cognitive Developmental Psychology. Hangzhou: Zhejiang People's Publishing House, 1996: 179.

[2] Tiequan Cai, Jiang Xuying, Hu Mei. Education of Conceptual Change in Science Teaching. Beijing: Science Press, 2009.

[3] Shuhui Zhou. Children's Natural Science Concept and Thinking. London: Psychology Press, 2005.

[4] Piaget. The Children's Conception of Physical Causality. New York: Routledge Kagan Paul, 1930.

[5] Havu-Nuntinen S. Examining young children's conceptual change process in floating and sinking from a social constructive perspective. International Journal of Science Education, 2005, 27: 259 - 279.

[6] Meiying Yuan. The development of 5 - 7 years old children's concept of floating and sinking. Nanjing: Nanjing Normal University, 2008.

[7] Yinghe Chen. Cognitive Developmental Psychology. Hangzhou: Zhejiang People's Publishing House, 1996: 61.

[8] Kammi. Physical Knowledge in Preschool Education. Taibei: Kidsandyou Co., Ltd, 1999.

[9] Dreyfus A, Jungwirth E, Eliovitch R. Applying the "cognitive conflict" strategy for conceptual change-some implications, difficulties, and problems. Science Education, 1990, 74: 555 - 569.

The Role of Stigma Experience and Perception in Chinese Migrant Children's School Adjustment

Guangzhen Zhang[1,a,*], Ning Jiang[1,b], Zongbao Liang[1,c], Huihua Deng[1,d]

[1]Key Laboratory of Child Development and Learning Science of Ministry of China, Southeast University, Nanijng, 210096, China

[a]zhangguangzhen@seu.edu.cn, [b] jiangning199243@163.com,

[c]liangzongbao225@163.com, [d]dengrcls@seu.edu.cn

[*] Corresponding author

Keywords: migrant children; stigma; externalizing problem; internalizing problem; learning problem

Abstract: As a result of the growing number of migrant children in China, more and more attention was paid to migrant children's adjustment. Unlike migrants in western countries, migrant children in China do not have equal access to educational and other welfare resources as urban residents. In addition, migrants are stigmatized by some urban residents. The present study used longitudinal design and multiple informants to investigate the influence of stigma experience of migrant on children's adjustment. Two hundred and eighty-one children (157 boys and 124 girls) and their parents and teachers participated in the study. When these children were in grade 7 ($M_{age}=13.09$ years, $SD=1.13$), they were asked to report their experience of stigma, and their parents and teachers were asked to report their problem behaviors in school. One year later, data was collected again. The results of independent sample t-test demonstrated that boys experienced more stigma and had more behavioral problems than girls, and the results of structural equation modeling showed that children's stigma perception in the first year positively predicted children externalizing problems, internalizing problems and learning problems in the second year, after controlling the stability of problem behaviors. These results indicated that the stigma experience and perception of migrant children had detrimental effect on children's adjustment.

流动儿童的歧视知觉与其社会适应之间的关系

张光珍[1,a,*],姜宁[1,b],梁宗保[1,c],邓慧华[1,d]
[1]东南大学儿童发展与学习科学教育部重点实验室,南京,210096
[a]zhangguangzhen@seu.edu.cn, [b]jiangning199243@163.com,
[c]liangzongbao225@163.com, [d]dengrcls@seu.edu.cn
[*]通讯作者

关键词:流动儿童;歧视;外显问题;内隐问题;学习问题

中文摘要:本研究采用追踪研究设计来考察流动儿童的歧视知觉对其学校适应的影响。在儿童初一上学期期中考试之后,邀请儿童填写歧视知觉问卷,同时邀请流动儿童的父母及老师评价儿童在学校的适应情况。一年之后,再次收集数据。结果表明,男孩知觉到的歧视要显著高于女孩,男孩的学校适应问题也显著高于女孩。结构方程模型的结果表明,在控制了问题行为本身的连续性之后,流动儿童第一年知觉到的歧视显著正向预测其第二年的外显问题、内隐问题和学习问题。本研究表明,流动儿童的歧视体验和知觉对流动儿童的学校适应具有非常消极的影响。

1 引言

近年来,随着我国市场经济的发展,流动人口的规模快速增长,家庭式流动日益盛行,流动儿童的规模也日益壮大。随之而来的流动儿童的适应问题也越来越受到人们的关注。以往研究发现,与城市儿童相比,流动儿童表现出更多的行为和情绪问题[1-3]。在众多影响流动儿童心理适应的因素中,由于流动人口的身份及由此而带来的不公正待遇所产生的歧视体验是很重要的一个因素[3]。歧视直觉是相对于客观歧视而言的一种主观体验,是指个体知觉到由于自己所属的群体成员资格而受到有区别或不公平的对待[4]。在我国,流动儿童的教育安置和其他社会福利资源不同于城市非流动儿童,流动儿童面临着福利制度排斥、社会关系排斥、文化排斥、消费排斥,因此,他们的歧视体验和知觉是非常明显的。国内的一些研究者曾经研究了歧视知觉对儿童的心理适应如自尊、抑郁等的影响,结果发现歧视知觉与低自尊、高焦虑、高孤独感和高抑郁相关[3,4]。然而,目前的为数不多的有关流动儿童歧视知觉的研究存在以下问题:(1)以往大多数研究都是横断研究,难以确定变量间的因果关系;(2)大多数研究只让儿童报告,可能存在共同方法偏差;(3)大多数研究只关注内在心理问题,对外显问题关注得较少。因此在结果的生态效度上可能会存在一些问题。

针对以往研究中存在的这些不足之处,本研究采用追踪研究设计,从儿童、父母和教师多个来源收集数据,同时关注儿童的外显行为问题、内隐行为问题和学习问题,以此来考察歧视知觉与儿童的问题行为之间的关系。我们预测,儿童知觉到的歧视能够正向预测其外显问题、内隐问题和学习问题。

2 方法

2.1 被试与研究程序

被试来自于苏州的初中,共281名流动儿童(157名男孩,124名女孩)及其父母和教师参与了研究,儿童初次参与本研究时的平均年龄为13.09岁($SD=1.13$)。父亲和母亲的教育水平为小学以下、初中、高中、大学以上的分别为14.5%和35.5%,63.8%和51.8%,17%和8%,5%和5%。

在儿童初一上学期期中考试结束两个星期之后开始第一次数据收集。儿童的数据收集由受过培训的主试以班级为单位展开,让儿童报告他们在日常生活中体验到的歧视情况。然后让儿童的班主任和父母分别填写问卷,报告儿童在学校的适应情况。一年之后(初二上学期),再次进行数据收集工作。两次数据收集中,有效的儿童问卷分别是255份、246份,有效的教师问卷分别是253份、256份,有效的父母问卷分别是249份、233份。数据收集之前,我们征得了儿童、家长及教师的同意。

2.2 研究工具

2.2.1 歧视知觉问卷

采用刘霞[5]等编制的“个体歧视知觉”。问卷列举了流动儿童在城市生活中可能遇到的遭受歧视的情况,内容涵盖言语歧视、政策歧视等方面,询问被试句子所描述的情况是否与其现实符合。答案为4点量表:1为“一点都不符合”,4为“完全符合”,以考察儿童主观觉察到的自己因为外地人身份而受到歧视或者不公平对待的程度,得分越高,代表感受到的歧视越多。本研究两次测查中问卷的内部一致性系数分别为0.84和0.89。

2.2.2 社会适应问卷

采用Hightower等人[6]的教师—儿童评价量表,该问卷分为儿童学校适应能力和儿童学校适应问题两大部分,其中学校适应能力又包括挫折耐受、任务定向、果敢社交、自我控制等纬度,学校适应问题又包括内隐问题、外显问题、学习问题三方面。在本研究中,我们只选用学校适应问题下的内隐问题、外显问题、学习问题三个维度。教师和家长分别填写了该问卷,其中家长版问卷在表述上有细微改动。教师报告和父母报告的内隐问题、外显问题、学习问题在第一年和第二年的信度在0.79—0.85之间,信度良好。

3 结果

流动儿童在歧视知觉和问题行为各维度上的平均值和标准差见表1。独立样本 t

检验的结果表明，男孩第二年知觉到的歧视显著地高于女孩。男孩在第一年和第二年的学习问题和外显问题均显著地高于女孩，在内隐问题行为上的性别差异不显著。

表 1　儿童歧视知觉和学校适应各变量的平均值和标准差

变量	女孩		男孩		t
	平均值	标准差	平均值	标准差	
歧视知觉—儿童报告—第一年	1.28	0.38	1.37	0.36	−1.88
歧视知觉—儿童报告—第二年	1.24	0.26	1.48	0.51	−4.73***
学习问题—父母报告—第一年	2.37	0.80	2.80	0.84	−4.16***
外显问题—父母报告—第一年	1.91	0.65	2.25	0.76	−3.72***
内隐问题—父母报告—第一年	2.16	0.72	2.25	0.71	−1.03
学习问题—父母报告—第二年	2.42	0.86	2.81	0.86	−3.38***
内隐问题—父母报告—第二年	2.14	0.71	2.30	0.73	−1.63
外显问题—父母报告—第二年	1.93	0.64	2.31	0.78	−4.03***
外显问题—教师报告—第一年	1.60	0.55	2.03	0.85	−4.71***
学习问题—教师报告—第一年	2.16	0.83	2.45	0.89	−2.58**
内隐问题—教师报告—第一年	2.01	0.64	1.92	0.62	1.12
外显问题—教师报告—第二年	1.68	0.56	2.14	0.88	−5.07***
内隐问题—教师报告—第二年	1.83	0.63	1.86	0.61	−0.43
学习问题—教师报告—第二年	2.17	0.72	2.73	0.96	−5.31***

用 Mplus7.0 软件分别对歧视知觉与父母报告的问题行为和教师报告的问题行为进行交叉滞后回归分析，用极大似然法来对缺失值进行估计。由于正态检验表明儿童的歧视知觉是明显的正偏态分布，因此在进行回归分析之前先对儿童的歧视知觉进行对数转换，将儿童原始的歧视知觉分数取自然对数后的分数作为新的歧视知觉的分数。结构方程模型的结果见表 2。由表 2 可以看出，在控制了问题行为各自的连续性之后，第一年的歧视知觉能够显著正向预测第二年教师报告的和父母报告的外显问题、内隐问题和学习问题。第一年的问题行为对第二年的歧视知觉的预测作用不显著。

表 2　儿童歧视与问题行为的交叉滞后回归分析的标准化路径系数

路径	父母报告		教师报告	
	β	t	β	t
第一年歧视知觉→第二年外显问题	0.18	3.46***	0.15	2.18*
第一年歧视知觉→第二年内隐问题	0.12	1.87+	0.14	1.98*
第一年歧视知觉→第二年学习问题	0.20	3.83***	0.15	2.24*
第一年外显问题→第二年歧视知觉	0.09	1.15	0.06	0.64
第一年内隐问题→第二年歧视知觉	−0.08	−1.23	0.04	0.49
第一年学习问题→第二年歧视知觉	−0.04	−0.48	0.07	0.83

4　讨论

随着我国流动儿童的规模的不断扩大,流动儿童的社会适应正受到越来越多的关注。与西方大多数国家不同的是,在我国,流动儿童无法像城市儿童那样享受到同等的教育资源和其他福利资源,此外,部分城市市民对流动人群带有一定的偏见和歧视。这些不利因素都可能会影响流动儿童的适应。然而,目前此领域的实证研究还比较少,仅有的一些研究也是以横断设计和儿童报告为主,难以揭示歧视体验和知觉对儿童社会适应的影响。本研究采用追踪研究设计和多数据来源的方法,考察了流动儿童的歧视知觉对其学校适应的影响。结果显示,整体而言,我国流动儿童所感受到的歧视水平是较低的,其中男孩感受到的歧视要显著多于女孩。儿童在第一年感受到的歧视能够显著正向预测他们在第二年的各种问题行为,但他们在第一年表现出的问题行为不会影响他们第二年的歧视知觉。本研究的结果证实了歧视对儿童发展存在诸多消极影响。

本研究的结果表明,歧视体验和知觉不仅会使儿童产生内在的心理问题,如抑郁、焦虑,也可能使儿童以一种指向外部的消极的方式表现出来,如攻击、违纪等。歧视既不利于流动儿童内在的心理和谐,也不利于儿童外在社会关系的建立和维持。

尽管本研究为我们带来了一些启示,但本研究也存在不足之处。例如,本研究未能说明歧视体验和知觉影响流动儿童学校适应的内在过程。未来的研究可进一步分析歧视体验和知觉影响儿童适应的中介变量和调节变量,弄清歧视影响儿童适应的内在机制。

致谢

本文为江苏省哲学社会科学基金青年项目(11JYC011)的阶段性成果。

References

[1] J Fang. A Study on the Structure and Group Intervention of Self-esteem on Emigrant-Workers' Children. Shanghai: East China Normal University, 2008.

[2] X Li, H Zou, C Jin, et al. The relations among problem behaviors, personalities and family functioning of migrant children. Psychological Development and Education, 2008, 2: 54 - 59.

[3] X Lin, X Fang, Y Liu, et al. The effect mechanism of stigma perception on mental health among migrant children in Beijing. Acta Psychologica Sinica, 2009, 41: 967 - 979.

[4] X Liu, J Shen. Chinese migrant children's perceived discrimination and its relation to self-esteem. Psychological Science, 2010, 33: 695 - 697.

[5] X Liu. The characters, predictors and effect mechanism of stigma perception among migrant children. Beijing: Beijing Normal University, 2008.

[6] A D Hightower, W C Work, E L Cowen, et al. The teacher—child rating scale: A brief objective measure of elementary children's school problem behaviors and competencies. School Psychology Review, 1986, 15: 393 - 409.

Analysis on Preschoolers' Fine Motor Skills for Self-caring

Yibin Zhang[a], Jiabin Li[b], Chao Xue[c], Jinliang Qin[d,*]
Hangzhou College of Early Childhood Teacher's Education of Zhejiang Normal University, Hangzhou, Zhejiang, China
[a]zybzjnu@126.com, [b]641239957@qq.com,
[c]249982032@qq.com, [d]qjlzjnu@126.com
* Corresponding author

Keywords: fine motor skills; spoon using; chopsticks manipulation; EMG

Abstract: Spoon using and chopsticks manipulation, as important fine motor skills for living, are of benefit to children's self-caring and other fine motor skills' development. Plenty of researches on spoon using and chopsticks manipulation focused more on patterns of reaching and grasping the utensils, and made adults as subjects frequently. This study picks up 8 preschoolers ($M_{Age} = 4.01$, $SD = 0.17$) to explorer characteristic change of AEMG signals in flexor carpi radialis (FCR), flexor carpi ulnaris (FCU), extensor digitorum (ED) and flexor digitorum superficialis (FDS) when using spoon and manipulating chopsticks to transfer dices. Results indicate that, a) chopsticks manipulation differs from spoon using in only FCU'S AEMG signals for children at preschool; and b) chopsticks manipulation and spoon using have significant correlation in other three muscles' AEMG signals.

幼儿生活技能精细动作分析

张义宾[a],李佳斌[b],薛超[c],秦金亮[d,*]
浙江师范大学杭州幼儿师范学院,杭州,浙江,中国
[a]zybzjnu@126.com, [b]641239957@qq.com,
[c]249982032@qq.com, [d]qjlzjnu@126.com
*通讯作者

关键词:精细动作;用勺;用筷;表面肌电

中文摘要:作为儿童生活中主要的精细动作技能,用勺和用筷动作的发展不仅对提高儿童自理能力具有重要作用,也是其他精细动作能力发展的重要前提和基础。以往研究的对象主要为成人,研究内容多集中于对用勺用筷抓握模式的分析上。为了获取年幼儿童在用勺和用筷时上臂肌肉的肌电特征,本研究通过筛选能够熟练用筷的幼儿 8 名($M_{年龄}=4.01$,$SD=0.17$)作为被试,要求幼儿分别完成用勺转移骰子和用筷转移筛子的任务,记录其右手桡侧腕屈肌、尺侧腕屈肌、指伸肌、指浅屈肌四块肌肉的平均肌电值。结果表明,(1) 用勺、用筷动作之间在尺侧腕屈肌的平均肌电值上存在显著差异,用筷高于用勺;(2) 用勺与用筷在桡侧腕屈肌、指伸肌以及指浅屈肌平均肌电值上存在显著相关。

1 问题的提出

精细动作发展是儿童入学准备的重要内容,也是儿童在家庭和幼儿园发展的重要基础。精细动作的发展在提升儿童生活自理能力、促使儿童学会独立、增加儿童的社会认可以及提高身体掌控度方面都发挥着重要作用,是儿童终生学业成功的前提之一。

研究发现,幼儿花费将近一半的时间参与到精细动作活动中[1],这其中生活技能占据了 45%,比如穿衣、饮食等,可以说儿童生活技能能够反映精细动作的发展水平。用勺和用筷作为儿童重要的生活技能吸引了大批研究者的关注,但这些研究多集中在用勺用筷的动作模式上[2,3],较少关注用勺用筷动作的内部肌肉运作机制,更少涉及年幼儿童被试。本研究拟采用表面肌电技术探索年幼儿童在用勺和用筷转移任务时上臂肌肉的肌电属性,从而丰富该领域的研究。

2 研究方法

2.1 被试

从浙江省某省一级幼儿园挑选 8 名幼儿,其中 4 名男孩、4 名女孩。幼儿平均年

龄为(4.01±0.17)岁(3.75—4.25岁),平均身高为(114.13±6.51)cm(105—121 cm),平均体重为(22.18±3.47)kg(17.3—26.3 kg)。所有幼儿身体健康,均为右利手,为防止肌肉疲劳,8名幼儿在实验前24小时内均未进行任何剧烈运动。

2.2 实验设计与过程

本实验采用单因素被试内设计,自变量为任务类型:用勺、用筷。因变量为表面肌电指标:右手的桡侧腕屈肌、尺侧腕屈肌、指伸肌、指浅屈肌四块肌肉的平均肌电值(AEMG)。

(1)被试筛选

被试主要通过儿童主观报告是否会用筷,经由两名主试对儿童在用筷转移骰子的情况进行筛查,选取能够较为熟练地成功完成该任务的幼儿若干,作为实验被试。

(2)贴肌电贴

在实验开始前,根据BTS公司提供的标准,在右手桡侧腕屈肌、尺侧腕屈肌、指伸肌、指浅屈肌放置无线电极,在电极放置之前使用酒精棉对皮肤进行消毒处理。

(3)熟悉实验任务

在进行正式实验前,向被试说明实验要求与任务,直至被试理解,并给被试一定练习机会,熟练整个实验流程,包括用勺、用筷时握勺、握筷的位置。

(4)正式实验

被试用主试提供的两种工具,用右手完成用勺转移、用筷转移任务,左手平放桌面,且不能帮忙。

主试需关注被试的肌电波线,当记录仪出现正常波线后,主试喊开始,被试再完成相应任务。实验使用的桌椅均是根据幼儿发展的特点设计的。

用勺:实验之前将两个碗碟放在一儿童桌上,确保碗碟与桌面距离为10 cm,且两个碗碟间的平行间距为25 cm;被试坐在小桌前,正对两个碗碟中线,双肘与桌面齐高;向被试介绍实验任务,要求被试根据主试口令以每次一个的速度将骰子从一个碗碟舀起并放入到另一个碗碟中;为保证数据有效收集,该任务完成2次。

用筷:实验之前将两个碗碟放在一儿童桌上,确保碗碟与桌面距离为10 cm,且两个碗碟间的平行间距为25 cm;被试坐在小桌前,正对两个碗碟中线,双肘与桌面齐高;向被试介绍实验任务,要求被试根据主试口令以每次一个的速度将骰子从一个碗碟夹起并放入到另一个碗碟中;为保证数据有效收集,该任务完成2次。

2.3 实验材料

儿童筷两双(长18 cm),木制;儿童用勺两只(长15 cm),勺柄长10 cm,铁制;瓷质碗碟一对,直径9 cm,高2 cm;骰子若干,1 cm见方。

2.4 数据收集与分析

选取"幼儿握勺、握筷准备好,主试提示任务'开始'的时间"作为启动时间,儿童完成任务的时间记为结束时间,对儿童完成两种任务时肌肉活动的时域进行分析。本实验采用无线表面肌电系统(FreeEMG,BTS公司,Milan,Italy)记录被试4块肌肉的肌电数据，撷取频率为 4 000 Hz，电极大小 23.8 mm × 37 mm × 10 mm，模拟数字转换 14 bit，灵敏度 1 μV，脱机测试记忆卡容量 4 MB，信噪比 110 d，输入阻抗 10 GΩ。原始肌电数据收集至工作站之后，采用 BTS EMG-Analyzer 分析软件获取用勺、用筷和书写过程中的平均肌电值（即积分肌电值与时间的比值，积分肌电值计算公式如下）。

$$iEMG = \int^{t+T} |EMG(t)| \times dt$$

随后，将原始数据导入 Excel 2010 进行分类整理，使用 SPSS 22.0 数据处理软件进行分析。

3 实验结果

3.1 用勺用筷动作肌电值的差异性分析

幼儿在用勺、用筷两种精细动作任务完成过程中的平均肌电值如图 1 所示。从图上可以看出，两种精细动作的肌肉激活程度各不相同。用筷过程中桡侧腕屈肌和指浅屈肌平均肌电值要高于用勺，尺侧腕屈肌和指伸肌平均肌电值高于用勺。此外，在两种精细动作任务过程中，右手的桡侧腕屈肌和指伸肌的平均肌电值最大，用勺时是 19.37 μV、17.98 μV，用筷时是 26.43 μV、26.04 μV。

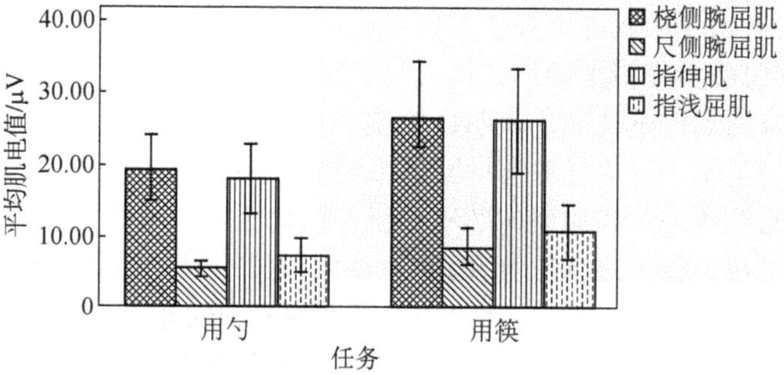

图 1 幼儿用勺、用筷动作的平均肌电值

对幼儿用勺、用筷过程中右手四块肌肉（桡侧腕屈肌、尺侧腕屈肌、指伸肌、指浅屈肌）的平均肌电值分别进行独立样本 t 检验。结果显示，幼儿用勺、用筷只有在尺侧腕屈肌的平均肌电值存在显著性差异（$p < 0.05$），用筷显著高于用勺。

3.2 用勺用筷动作肌电值的相关性分析

第一，桡侧腕屈肌平均肌电值相关分析

对幼儿用勺、用筷时桡侧腕屈肌的平均肌电值进行相关分析。结果显示，幼儿用勺与用筷时桡侧腕屈肌的平均肌电值呈现显著相关（$r = 0.841$，$p < 0.01$）。

第二，尺侧腕屈肌平均肌电值相关分析

对幼儿用勺、用筷时尺侧腕屈肌的平均肌电值进行相关分析。结果显示，在幼儿用勺、用筷过程中，尺侧腕屈肌的平均肌电值无显著相关。

第三，指伸肌平均肌电值相关分析

对幼儿用勺、用筷时指伸肌的平均肌电值进行相关分析。结果显示，幼儿用勺和用筷时指伸肌的平均肌电值呈现显著相关($r=0.768$, $p<0.05$)。

第四，指浅屈肌平均肌电值相关分析

对幼儿用勺、用筷时指浅屈肌的平均肌电值进行相关分析。结果显示，幼儿用勺和用筷时指浅屈肌的平均肌电值呈现极显著相关($r=0.909$, $p<0.01$)。

4 讨论

4.1 两种精细动作特征差异性比较

从用勺、用筷动作肌电特征的考察来看，平均肌电值较好地反映出了幼儿不同动作的发力特点。通过肌电放电情况，我们发现实验所选取桡侧腕屈肌、尺侧腕屈肌、指伸肌和指浅屈肌都得到了激活，而且在两种精细动作任务过程中肌电值都随任务过程发生变化。实验发现两种精细动作过程中肌肉放电的情况并不相同，就肌肉激活来看，我们发现桡侧腕屈肌和指伸肌的激活程度最强。高桥房慧(Takahashi)在1984年对用勺和用筷的肌电研究发现了拇指屈肌和手腕伸肌在动作任务过程中会变化这一属性[4]，本研究丰富了其结论，发现在精细动作过程中其他肌肉如桡侧腕屈肌、尺侧腕屈肌、指伸肌和指浅屈肌等也都会不断变化。此外，结合Pang在2012年的研究[5]，研究者推断，伸肌确实在精细动作的执行中发挥着重要的作用。

肌电值反映的动作电位变化表明桡侧腕屈肌、尺侧腕屈肌、指伸肌和指浅屈肌四块肌肉共同参与了精细动作任务，其协同为动作任务的熟练化提供了共同保障。

实验发现幼儿用勺时四块肌肉的平均肌电值均比用筷都要低一些。研究者认为，勺子是幼儿最早接触到的进食工具，因此幼儿用勺技能必然非常熟练，在使用勺子转移骰子过程中不需要施较大的力；实验中研究者观察到幼儿用勺时基本使用成熟的握勺模式来舀取骰子完成转移任务，研究者推断，平均肌电值所反映的肌肉激活情况可以代表握勺成熟模式的某些特征。

从肌肉反映的动作机制来看(尺侧腕屈肌主要负责屈腕和腕关节内收动作[6])，用筷在尺侧腕屈肌的平均肌电值上较用勺有显著差异，可以说用筷时幼儿内收腕关节肌肉激活模式与用勺存在差异，研究者认为，幼儿用筷时腕关节相应肌肉激活要比用勺时高，换句话说，幼儿用筷时腕关节内收动作更为明显。

4.2 两种精细动作特征相关性比较

实验通过两种精细动作不同肌肉肌电值的相关性分析发现，用勺与用筷之间存在一定的关联度。用勺与用筷在桡侧腕屈肌、指伸肌以及指浅屈肌平均肌电值上的相关性反映了幼儿用勺和用筷肌肉激活模式的相似性，即这二者都涉及腕关节的外展以及手指的动作。对比前人对用勺和用筷对比研究结果，我们发现用勺和用筷动作的确包含同样的动作模式，即腕关节动作上。

实验前我们假设用筷动作比用勺动作会产生更多手指相关肌肉上的激活,但事实上并没有,我们推测这可能由于本实验选取的任务以物体转移为主,这更多的涉及了动作的稳定性成分,转移过程中手指活动度较低,手腕活动高。综上分析,用勺与用筷之间存在着动作机制上的共同性,这为动作技能迁移提供了基础。

5 小结

右手桡侧腕屈肌、尺侧腕屈肌、指伸肌和指浅屈肌四块肌肉的平均肌电值能合理地反映两种精细动作的属性。实验发现,用勺、用筷动作存在着显著差异,这反映在用勺动作效率更高、平均肌电值也最低,表明幼儿已经获得了较好的用勺技能;用筷肌电值最大,反映出幼儿没有发展出较好的用筷能力,动作执行时力量控制不善,往往用力过分;就肌电反映的肌肉机能来看,用筷与用勺之间在尺侧腕屈肌激活强度上存在显著差异,反映出用筷与用勺的内收腕关节模式之间的差异性,换句话说,幼儿腕关节内收更多地参与到幼儿的用筷动作之中,但用筷时的手指动作参与少,当然这可能与实验任务有关。此外,研究发现两种精细动作不同肌肉肌电值之间存在着相关性,笔者认为,这能够反映出用勺与用筷两种精细动作之间存在一定的关联度,因此,从训练用筷稳定度的角度来看,用勺应该是一项不错的选择。

References

[1] D Marr, M M Windsor, S Cermak. Handwriting readiness: Locatives and visuomotor skills in the kindergarten year. Early Childhood Research and Practice, 2001, 3: 1-3.

[2] A Henderson. Self-care and hand skill//A Henderson, C Pehoski. Hand Function in the Child: Foundations for Remediation. Amsterdam: Elsevier Health Sciences, 2006.

[3] L Lin, Q Dong, Y Q Sun, et al. Comparison of chopstick using skills between 3—7 year-old children and adults. Acta Psychologyica Sinica, 2001, 33: 231-237.

[4] Fusae Takahashi, Mari Enomoto, Yukiko Miyakoshi, et al. Electro-geographical studies of usage of eating utensils. Journal of Japanese Society of Nursing Research, 1984, 7: 3-10.

[5] J A Pang. Comparative biomechanical analysis of independent finger movement—Between skilled and unskilled chopsticks users. Massachusetts: University of Massachusetts Lowell, 2013.

[6] X S Gu. Human Anatomy. Beijing: Science Press, 2009.

Interventions of Children's Executive Function: A Review

Lei Zhao[1], Yuankui Yang[1,a,*]

[1]Key Laboratory of Child Development and Learning Science of Ministry of Education, Research Center for learning Science, Southeast University, Nanjing, 210096, China

[a]yuankui@seu.edu.cn

[*]Corresponding author

Keywords: intervention; executive function; computerized training; aerobics; ping-pang training; mindfulness; music training; school curricula

Abstract: Executive function is a central component of children's cognitive development. Executive function is critical for success in school and life and for positive mental and physical health. In general, executive functions begin to develop around the age of 1, have important changes in 2—5 years old, and are similar to the adult level at the age of 7. When around 12 years old, the development of executive functions can reach the adult level in some standard executive functions tests, but some abilities will still develop until adulthood. Diverse activities have shown to improve children's executive functions: computerized training, aerobics, martial arts, yoga, Ping-Pang training, mindfulness, music training and school curricula. All effective programs involve repeated practice and progressively increase the change to executive functions. To improve executive functions, focusing narrowly on them may not be as effective as also addressing physical development and emotional and social development.

儿童执行功能干预研究进展

赵蕾[1],杨元魁[1,a,*]

[1]东南大学学习科学研究中心,儿童发展与学习科学教育部重点实验室,南京

[a]yuankui@ seu. edu. cn

[*]通信作者

关键词:干预;执行功能;计算机训练;有氧运动;武术;瑜伽;乒乓球;冥想;音乐训练;学校课程

中文摘要:执行功能是儿童认知发展的重要方面之一,对儿童的学业、身心健康以及今后事业的成功都至关重要。总体看来,执行功能最早是在1岁左右开始发展的,重要的发展变化出现在2—5岁,到7岁时已与成人基本相似,到12岁左右会在许多标准执行功能测验中达到成人水平,但仍有一些指标要持续发展到成人期。研究表明计算机训练,有氧运动、武术、瑜伽、乒乓球训练等体育活动,冥想,音乐训练以及学校课程等都能改善儿童的执行功能。有效的干预活动应该在不断增加难度的基础上反复进行训练,同时还应强调儿童身体、情感和社会性的发展。

执行功能(Executive Function, EF)是儿童认知发展的重要方面之一,包括一系列与前额叶联系紧密的高级认知功能,是指在完成复杂的认知任务时,对其他认知过程进行控制和调节的高级认知过程,其根本作用是产生协调有序、具有目标性的行为(Funahashi, 2001)。目前普遍认为执行功能有三个核心成分:工作记忆、抑制控制和认知灵活性(Miyake 等, 2000)。它们是更加复杂的执行功能的基础,比如推理、问题解决和计划(Christoff, Ream, Geddes, & Gabrieli, 2003; Collins, & Koechlin, 2012; Lunt 等, 2012)。

学前期是儿童执行功能发展的关键期,儿童的执行功能会发生质的飞跃。总体看来,执行功能最早是在1岁左右开始发展的,重要的发展变化出现在2—5岁,到7岁时已与成人基本相似,到12岁左右会在许多标准执行功能测验中达到成人水平,但仍有一些指标要持续发展到成人期。不过儿童的执行功能存在较大的个体差异,需要在实践中得到发展。在具备了抑制冲动、牢记规则、注意导向等基本的执行功能后,随着进一步的练习,儿童会不断发展更有效的执行功能,以适应更加复杂的情境,完成更具挑战性的任务,执行功能的发展会一直持续到青春期甚至成年早期(栾文双,王静梅和卢英俊, 2013)。

执行功能对儿童在学校中的成就起着十分重要的作用。执行功能对儿童入学准备性的重要性要大于智商对入学准备性的重要性(Blair & Razza, 2007)。执行功能能长久预测儿童的数学和阅读能力(Gathercole, Pickering, Knight, & Stegmanm,

2004)。执行功能对儿童其他方面的发展也起着十分重要的作用,比如今后的事业(Bailey, 2007; Prince et al., 2007)、婚姻(Eakin et al., 2004)、友谊(Rotenberg, Michalik, Eisenberg, & Betts, 2008)以及身体健康和心理健康(Baler & Volkow, 2006; Miller, Barnes, & Beaver, 2011)。

1 干预活动

研究发现很多活动能够提高儿童的执行功能,比如计算机训练、体育活动(比如有氧运动、武术、瑜伽、乒乓球训练等)、冥想、音乐训练、学校课程以及补充课程。

1.1 计算机训练

计算机训练是通过计算机呈现一些特别设计的项目来训练儿童某些能力的方法。CogMed 是目前最广泛使用的计算机训练方法,其也是被反复证明有效的办法。CogMed 通过计算机呈现逐渐增加工作记忆容量的电脑游戏来训练工作记忆(Diamond & Lee, 2011)。

计算机训练能有效改善儿童的工作记忆和推理能力,能帮助那些患有注意力缺陷多动障碍和工作记忆广度较小的儿童(Klingberg et al., 2005; Holmes et al.; 2010)。两次研究(Holmes et al., 2009; Holmes et al., 2010)发现在训练之后,儿童在工作记忆上的提高能持续 6 个月,并且在数学成绩上,虽然当时没有明显的提高,但 6 个月后,数学成绩明显提高。CogMed 训练能够提高儿童的工作记忆,并且这种提高能够泛化到那些没有训练过的工作记忆的任务上(Klingberg et al., 2005; Thorell et al., 2009)。Thorell 等发现儿童在视觉空间工作记忆上的提高能泛化到没有训练过的空间工作记忆和言语工作记忆任务上,并且儿童在注意任务上的成绩也得到了提高(Thorell et al., 2009)。CogMed 训练也能提高儿童的推理能力或者解决问题的速度。Mackey 等使用计算机游戏和非计算机游戏结合的方法来提高儿童的推理或者速度能力。在他们的这个项目中,游戏的难度逐渐增加,并且儿童可能自己单独玩耍或者在一个小团队中一起玩耍。结果发现,推理组的儿童在推理测验上得到了提高,并且在智力测验上的成绩也得到了提高,但在速度测验上没有提高,而速度组的儿童在速度测验上得到了提高,但在推理测验上并没有提高(Mackey et al., 2011)。

虽然计算机训练能提高儿童的工作记忆和推理能力,但是对儿童抑制控制的影响很小。Thorell 等发现在 5 周的抑制控制能力训练之后,4 岁和 6 岁的儿童只在 3 项测试中的 2 项上得到了显著性的提高,并且训练的效果不能泛化到没有训练的工作记忆任务或者注意任务上(Thorell et al., 2009)。Rueda 等用电脑游戏训练儿童的抑制控制能力和视觉运动动力。结果发现,除了在卡夫曼简短智力测验(K-Bit)上的成绩得到提高外,4 岁和 6 岁的儿童在其他认知作业上并没有表现出明显的提高,他们的父母也没有发现孩子的执行功能有明显的变化。但是,研究者发现在训练之后,当儿童在进行选择性注意的任务时,他们的大脑中出现了更加成熟的脑电反应,这或许意味着以后认知能力的提高(Rueda, Rothbart, McCandliss, Saccomanno, & Posner, 2005)。Karbach 和 Kray 发现,年长的孩子(9 岁)在接受基于计算机的任务转换训练之后,他们在转换任务和抑制控制任务上的成绩都得到了提高。因此,可能是因为计算机训练对提高年幼孩子抑制控制能力的效果很小,或者也可能因为研究者还没有设计出一个最佳的电脑游戏(Karbach & Kray, 2009)。

1.2 体育活动

1.2.1 有氧运动

有氧运动能够提高前额皮层功能和执行功能。三篇研究持续有氧运动对儿童执行功能影响的文章支持了以上观点。

Tuckman 等将被试随机分配到实验组和控制组。实验组是跑步,每周 3 次,每次 30 分钟,持续 12 周。控制组则进行平常的活动。结果表明,训练后实验组的认知灵活性和创造性都得到了提高,并且显著高于控制组(Tuckman & Hinkle, 1986)。

Davis 等将坐惯的、超重的 7 到 11 岁的儿童随机分配到没有训练的控制组和每天 20 分钟或者每天 40 分钟的有氧运动组(有氧运动的形式有跑步、跳绳、足球和篮球)。在实验的过程中,研究者要求被试注重过程而不是比赛结果或者技能的提高。结果表明,与控制组相比,只有高强度的有氧运动组在执行功能(仅在执行功能需求量最大的测验上)和数学成绩上得到了提高。但是,在执行功能中的选择性注意或者非执行功能技能上,有氧运动组和控制组之间并没有显著性差异(Davis et al. , 2011)。

Kamijo 等将 7 到 9 岁的儿童随机分配到每天 2 小时的适当训练组(70 分钟的有氧运动,接着是发展运动技能的训练)和没有训练的控制组中。结果发现,比起控制组,训练组的儿童在心肺适能和工作记忆任务上得到了显著的提高,并且当对工作记忆的需求量越多时,成绩的提高越明显。同时研究者还发现,在后测中,训练组儿童的前额叶电极部位能引发更强的伴随负电位(CNV),但在前测中,两组被试间没有显著性差异(Kamijo et al. , 2011)。

研究表明,短暂的有氧运动也能改善儿童的执行功能。我国学者陈爱国借助磁共振成像技术(fMRI)、心理测量技术和体育测量技术研究短时中等强度有氧运动对儿童执行功能的影响。结果表明,一次 30 分钟的有氧运动能改善儿童的执行功能,其脑机制是短时中等强度有氧运动诱发儿童执行功能脑激活模式的变化(陈爱国等, 2011)。

1.2.2 武术

单独训练对执行功能的效果可能会比那些既包括训练又包括性格发展的活动(比如传统武术)或者既包括训练又包括冥想的活动(比如瑜伽)的效果要小。传统的武术强调自我控制、纪律性(抑制控制)和性格的发展。

Lakes 和 Hoyt 将幼儿园到 5 年级(5 到 11 岁)的儿童随机分配到跆拳道训练组(伴随着难度的增加)和一般体育课组。除了体育锻炼,跆拳道课程以 3 个强调自我监控和规划的问题为开端:我在哪儿(即强调此时此刻)? 我在做什么? 我应该做什么? 后两个问题引导学生选择一些特定的行为,将他们的行为与目标相比较,并为改变制订具体的计划。结果发现,比起一般体育课组的儿童,跆拳道组的儿童在工作记忆和抑制控制上都得到了较好的改善。这种改善泛化到了各种不同的环境中,并且儿童在不同测量方法上成绩也得到了提高。他们在心算(需要工作记忆)上的成绩也得到了改善。年长儿童(4 年级和 5 年级)的提高最多,而年幼儿童(幼儿园和一年级)的提高最少,并且男孩的成绩比女孩好(Lakes & Hoyt, 2004)。

武术也能用于改善儿童的犯罪现象。Trulson 将少年罪犯随机分配到传统跆拳道训练组、现代武术训练组以及控制组。传统的跆拳道强调尊重、谦虚、责任心、坚持、荣誉、身体状况以及自我控制和自卫,而现代武术则是一种竞争性的运动,控制组则进行一般性的体育运动。结果表明,比起控制组,传统跆拳道组的儿童表现出降低的攻击性和焦虑水平,以及提高的自尊水平和社会能力;而现代武术组的儿童则表现出更强的犯罪趋势和更高的攻击性,以及降低的自尊水平和社会能力(Trulson, 1986)。

1.2.3 瑜伽

瑜伽也能改善儿童的执行功能。Manjunath 和 Telles 的研究证明了这个观点。他们将 10 岁和 13 岁的儿童随机分配到瑜伽组(包括体育训练、放松和意识感觉)和一般训练组。瑜伽组每天训练 1 个小时 15 分钟,一周 7 次,一般训练组在每天同样的时间进行一般的体育训练。结果表明,瑜伽组儿童在伦敦塔任务(伦敦塔任务涉及执行功能的 3 个核心成分)的计划和执行操作上得到了改善,尤其是在那些难度和复杂性较高的任务上,而一般训练组在执行功能上并没有改善(Manjunath & Telles, 2001)。

1.2.4 乒乓球训练

乒乓球训练能改善儿童的抑制控制,提高儿童的执行功能。张劲松、季星等随机选取参加乒乓球训练的(乒乓球组)和参加游泳训练的(游泳组)儿童进行实验。结果表明,比起游泳组,乒乓球组在 NOGO 任务上的正确率要显著高于游泳组,乒乓球组 N2 的波幅要显著高于游泳组。因此,乒乓球训练有助于提高儿童的抑制控制能力(张劲松,季星等, 2009)。

1.3 冥想

冥想能改善儿童的执行功能。在 Flook 等的研究中,冥想训练课程包括了三个部分:静坐冥想,促进意识感觉、注意控制或者意识他人或环境的活动以及全身扫描。随着时间的延长,冥想的需求量增加,同时第一部分和第三部分延长,而目的性较强、反思性较少的中间部分缩短。第一部分和第三部分训练的技能包括注意自上而下的控制能力。注意自上而下的控制能力能将注意带到目前的状态、发现注意的游离(监控）和将其带回到有意的目标上。结果发现，比起控制组，在接受冥想训练的儿童中，那些起初执行功能就较差的儿童在执行功能上得到了较大的改善。并且，这些起初执行功能较差的儿童在行为管理、元认知和认知控制的所有方面都得到了较明显的提高，使他们的得分都达到了平均分。老师和家长也发现了儿童的这些变化，这意味着儿童行为管理的改善泛化到了其他环境中（Flook 等，2010）。

1.4 音乐训练

音乐训练能改善儿童的执行功能。Bergman Nutley 等和韩明鲲等的研究支持了这个观点。

Bergman Nutley 采用纵向研究设计探讨音乐训练和认知发展的关系。结果表明，受过音乐训练的儿童在视觉空间工作记忆和非言语推理能力上都得到了较大的改善。改善的程度与他们训练的乐器以及每周训练的时间有关（Bergman Nutley et al.，2011）。

在韩明鲲和吕静的研究中，他们随机选取 16 名受过 3 年以上音乐训练的儿童（音乐组）和 16 名没有受过音乐训练的儿童（控制组）进行实验，记录他们在进行 GO/NOGO 实验范式时的脑电信号，并对收集到的 N2、P3 波幅进行统计分析。结果发现，音乐训练不能提高对冲突的监控能力，但是能够显著改进反应抑制能力，继而改善儿童前额叶执行功能（韩明鲲和吕静，2013）。

1.5 学校课程

心智工具（Tools of Mind）和蒙台梭利（Montessori）这两个学校课程能改善儿童的执行功能。

心智工具（Tools of Mind）是 Bodrova 和 Leong 基于 Vygotsky 的研究发展起来的针对学前儿童和幼儿园儿童的课程。Vygotsky 强调社会角色扮演游戏对早期执行功能发展的重要性。在角色扮演中，儿童必须克制表现出自己的个性，记住他们自己和他人的角色，并根据他人的行为灵活地做出应对。这样的游戏锻炼到了执行功能的 3 个核心成分：抑制控制、工作记忆和认知灵活性。Bodrova 和 Leong 最先尝试将心智工具作为现有课程的一种补充。儿童在那些受过训练模块上的成绩得到了改善，但这种改善并没有泛化。为了促进改善的泛化，对儿童的支持和训练以及对执行功能不断的挑战应该贯穿于儿童全天的学习活动中。

Diamond 等将学前儿童随机分成两组，一组接受心智工具训练，另一组接受另一个质量较高的训练项目（District's version of Balanced Literacy curriculum：dBL）。通过分析两组儿童最后的测验结果来比较两者的效果。结果表明，受过心智工具训练的儿童在所有测量执行功能测验上的得分都要高于控制组，当测验所需的工作记忆容量较大时，这种优势更加明显。因此，在改善儿童执行功能方面，角色扮演的方式要比直接指导的效果好（Diamond et al.，2007）。

蒙台梭利(Montessori)课程虽然表面上看没有涉及执行功能,但蒙台梭利教育者所强调的"正态化"原则是包含着好的执行功能的。正态化是儿童从冲动、缺乏注意状态到自我纪律、独立、有秩序、平静状态的转换。在蒙台梭利的课程中,每种材料都只有一份,所以只能等一个儿童用完某个材料,另一个儿童才能接着使用。一些蒙台梭利的活动实质上是行走冥想。与心智工具一样,老师要仔细观察每个儿童,当儿童准备好迎接新的挑战,老师就要给他呈现新的任务。在心智工具课程中,儿童之间彼此轮流讲授或者检查任务。在蒙台梭利课程中,学习形式采用的是跨年龄的导师制,就是将3岁到6岁不同年龄的儿童放在同一个班内游戏、生活和学习。许多研究证明,比起传统的教师主导的教学方式,这种儿童对儿童的学习方式能取得更好的成绩。

Lillard等随机选取59名在蒙台梭利公立学校上学的儿童和53名接受其他教育方法(比如能力学习、发现学习等)的儿童进行比较。结果表明,在儿童5岁的时候,接受蒙台梭利课程的儿童比接受其他教育课程的儿童拥有更好的执行功能。他们在阅读成绩和数学成绩上表现得更好,并且更加关注公平正义。但是在延迟满足任务上,两组之间没有显著性差异。在儿童12岁的时候,比起接受其他课程的儿童,接受蒙台梭利课程的儿童在论文写作上,表现出更高的创造性。同时他们在学校中也感受到更强的社会责任意识(Lillard & Else-Quest, 2006)。

1.6 学校课程的补充

作为对现有学校课程的补充,拥有不同哲学宗旨的PATHS(Promoting Alternative Thinking Strategies)和CSRP(Chicago School Readiness Project)同样能改善儿童的执行功能。PATHS训练教师培养儿童在自我控制、自我认识和管理情绪以及处理人际关系问题上的能力。在年幼儿童能够用语言描述情绪之前,他们就能体验到情绪,并对其做出反应,但他们经常直接做出反应,不涉及自上而下的控制。因此,PATHS十分强调培养儿童用语言描述自己情绪的能力以及有意识地使用自我控制的策略。当孩子们心烦的时候,他们应该静下来,深呼吸,思考一下这个问题是什么、他们现在的感觉如何,然后制订一个行动计划。老师需要学习专门的技术,帮助儿童将在PATHS课程上学习到的知识技能迁移到其他课程上去。Riggs等的研究发现,经过一年的PATHS学习,比起控制组,7岁到9岁的实验组儿童表现出更好的抑制控制和认知灵活性。在后测中抑制控制能力较好的儿童在一年之后表现出更少的内化或者外化问题(Riggs et al., 2006)。

CSRP(Chicago School Readiness Project)的教学方法不同于PATHS,CSRP为老师提供大量行为管理训练和减压的方法。CSRP不会有意去训练教师在传授知识上的技能或者开设关于学校知识的课程,它强调发展有利于儿童管理情绪的言语策略。心理健康顾问全年为老师组织减压的研讨会。外化行为较差的儿童会受到一对一的辅导。Raver等的研究发现,那些接受CSRP教育的4岁儿童的执行功能要显著高于控制组，并且一直在提高。同时，在词汇、字母命名以及数学成绩上，CSRP组的儿童都要显著高于控制组(Raver et al. , 2008; Raver et al. , 2011)。Li-Grining等的研究也发现，比起控制组，那些起初学习成绩较差的儿童在接受CSRP教育后，他们的执行功能得到了很大的改善。同时，在接下去的3年中，他们的数学成绩和阅读成绩也要高于控制组(Li-Grining, Raver, & Pess, 2011)。

2 干预原则

2.1 起初执行功能较差的儿童将得到最大程度的改善。

执行功能较差的儿童能从任何干预项目中获益(Flook et al. , 2011; Karbach & Kray, 2009; Lakes & Hoyt, 2004)。因此，对执行功能早期的训练能为儿童的发展营造公平的竞争条件，从而缩小儿童日后的成就差距和社会差距。

2.2 改善效果的泛化是有限的。

Thorell等的研究表明，对儿童视觉空间工作记忆的训练也能使没有被训练到的言语工作记忆的成绩得到改善，但是抑制控制成绩没有受到影响(Thorell et al. , 2009)。Bergman Nutley等的研究也发现，对推理能力的训练能提高其他推理任务的成绩，但不能改善工作记忆；对非言语推理的训练改善了同种类型非言语推理任务的成绩，但没有影响不同类型非言语推理任务的成绩；对非言语工作记忆的训练能提高其他测量非言语工作记忆任务的成绩，但不能影响言语工作记忆任务上的成绩(Bergman Nutley et al. , 2011)。武术、瑜伽或者学校课程可能有助于执行功能的泛化，因为这些项目本身包含了更多执行功能的成分。

2.3 执行功能必须在训练全程中一直受到挑战。

当儿童的执行功能得到提高后，干预项目的难度也要相应增加，否则执行功能将不再有所改善。一方面，如果儿童自身不要求自己不断提高的话，儿童就会习惯当前的状态，拒绝继续提高。另一方面，如果任务的难度总是没有提高的话，儿童就会对它失去兴趣。

2.4 全面训练。

压力、孤独以及身体不健康等都会影响前额皮层功能，从而影响执行功能。最有效改善执行功能和学习成绩的方法并不是仅仅单一地训练某一方面，而是同时强调儿童身体方面的发展以及情感和社会性的发展。

2.5 反复练习是关键。

执行功能能否提高的关键在于儿童是否自愿参加某个活动，并且花大量的时间反复练习。这与Ericsson等的研究结果一致。Ericsson等的研究表明，对人们目前现有能力之上的知识进行反复训练是人们成功的关键(Ericsson, Nandagopal, & Roring,

2009)。因此,对执行功能的强调应贯穿课程始终,并且应该通过多样的形式来改善执行功能,而不是某个单独的活动。即使是那些最有用的活动,如果不反复练习的话,也是几乎没有成效的。所以武术、瑜伽、有氧运动和冥想这些干预项目可以纳入到学校的课程中,学校也应该尽可能地让孩子接触到这些活动,让儿童的执行功能一开始就沿着良好的轨迹发展。

总之,为了改善执行功能,提高儿童的学业成绩,一方面,学校应吸收多样的干预项目,调动儿童浓烈的兴趣,在不断增加难度的基础上反复练习。另一方面,学校也要关注儿童身体的发展、情感的发展和社会性的发展,给予儿童归属感和社会认同感。

References

[1] Bailey CE. Cognitive accuracy and intelligent executive function in the brain and in business. Annals of the New York Academy of Sciences, 2007, 1118(1): 122 - 141.

[2] Baler RD, Volkow ND. Drug addiction: The neurobiology of disrupted self-control. Trends in Molecular Medicine, 2006, 12(12): 559 - 566.

[3] Bergman Nutley S. Development and training of higher order cognitive functions and their interrelations. (Unpublished doctoral dissertation) Karolinska Institute, Stockholm, Sweden, 2011.

[4] Bergman Nutley S, derqvist S, Bryde S, et al. Gains in fluid intelligence after training non - verbal reasoning in 4 - year - old children: a controlled, randomized study. Developmental science, 2011, 14(3): 591 - 601.

[5] Blair C, Razza R P. Relating effortful control, executive function, and false belief understanding to emerging math and literacy ability in kindergarten. Child Development, 2007, 78(2): 647 - 663.

[6] Christoff K, Ream J M, Geddes L, et al. Evaluating self-generated information: Anterior prefrontal contributions to human cognition. Behavioral Neuroscience, 2003, 117(6): 1161.

[7] Collins A, Koechlin E. Reasoning, learning, and creativity: Frontal lobe function and human decision-making. PLoS Biology, 2012, 10(3): e1001293.

[8] Davis CL, Tomporowski PD, McDowell JE, et al. Exercise improves executive function and achievement and alters brain activation in overweight children: A randomized, controlled trial. Health Psychology, 2011, 30(1): 91.

[9] Diamond A, Barnett WS, Thomas J, et al. Preschool program improves cognitive control. Science, 2007, 318 (5855): 1387.

[10] Diamond A, Lee K. Interventions shown to aid executive function development in children 4 to 12 years old. Science, 2011, 333 (6045): 959 - 964.

[11] Eakin L, Minde K, Hechtman L, et al. The marital and family functioning of adults with ADHD and their spouses. Journal of Attention Disorders, 2004, 8(1): 1 - 10.

[12] Ericsson KA, Nandagopal K, Roring RW. Toward a science of exceptional achievement. Annals of the New York Academy of Sciences, 2009, 1172(1): 199 - 217.

[13] Flook L, Smalley S L, Kitil M J, et al. Effects of mindful awareness practices on executive functions in elementary school children. Journal of Applied School Psychology, 2010, 26(1): 70-95.

[14] Funahashi S. Neuronal mechanisms of executive control by the prefrontal cortex. Neuroscience Research, 2001, 39(2): 147-165.

[15] Gathercole S E, Pickering S J, Knight C, et al. Working memory skills and educational attainment: Evidence from national curriculum assessments at 7 and 14 years of age. Applied Cognitive Psychology, 2004, 18(1): 1-16.

[16] Hillman C H, Erickson K I, Kramer A F. Be smart, exercise your heart: Exercise effects on brain and cognition. Nature Reviews Neuroscience, 2008, 9(1): 58-65.

[17] Holmes J, Gathercole S E, Dunning D L. Adaptive training leads to sustained enhancement of poor working memory in children. Developmental Science, 2009, 12(4): F9-F15.

[18] Holmes J, Gathercole S E, Place M, et al. Working memory deficits can be overcome: Impacts of training and medication on working memory in children with ADHD. Applied Cognitive Psychology, 2010, 24(6): 827-836.

[19] Kamijo K, Pontifex MB, O'Leary KC, et al. The effects of an afterschool physical activity program on working memory in preadolescent children. Developmental science, 2011, 14(5): 1046-1058.

[20] Karbach J, Kray J. How useful is executive control training? Age differences in near and far transfer of task - switching training. Developmental Science, 2009, 12(6): 978-990.

[21] Klingberg T, Fernell E, Olesen PJ, et al. Computerized training of working memory in children with ADHD-A randomized, controlled trial. Journal of the American Academy of Child & Adolescent Psychiatry, 2005, 44(2): 177-186.

[22] Lakes KD, Hoyt WT. Promoting self-regulation through school-based martial arts training. Journal of Applied Developmental Psychology, 2004, 25(3): 283-302.

[23] Lillard A, Else-Quest N. The early years: Evaluating montessori. Science, 2006, 313(5795): 1893-1894.

[24] Lunt L, Bramham J, Morris RG, et al. Prefrontal cortex dysfunction and "jumping to conclusions": Bias or deficit? Journal of Neuropsychology, 2012, 6(1): 65-78.

[25] Mackey A P, Hill S S, Stone S I, et al. Differential effects of reasoning and speed training in children. Developmental Science, 2011, 14(3): 582-590.

[26] Manjunath N, Telles S. Improved performance in the Tower of London test following yoga. Indian Journal of Physiology and Pharmacology, 2001, 45(3): 351-354.

[27] Miller H V, Barnes J, Beaver K M. Self-control and health outcomes in a nationally representative sample. American Journal of Health Behavior, 2011, 35(1): 15-27.

[28] Miyake A, Friedman N P, Emerson M J, et al. The unity and diversity of executive functions and their contributions to complex "frontal lobe" tasks: A latent variable analysis. Cognitive Psychology, 2000, 41(1): 49-100.

[29] Raver C C, Jones S M, Li - Grining C, et al. CSRP's impact on low-income preschoolers'

preacademic skills: Self-regulation as a mediating mechanism. Child Development, 2011, 82(1): 362-378.

[30] Riggs N R, Greenberg M T, Kusché C A, et al. The mediational role of neurocognition in the behavioral outcomes of a social-emotional prevention program in elementary school students: Effects of the PATHS curriculum. Prevention Science, 2006, 7(1): 91-102.

[31] Rotenberg K J, Michalik N, Eisenberg N, et al. The relations among young children's peer-reported trustworthiness, inhibitory control, and preschool adjustment. Early Childhood Research Quarterly, 2008, 23(2): 288-298.

[32] Rueda M R, Rothbart M K, McCandliss B D, et al. Training, maturation, and genetic influences on the development of executive attention. Proceedings of the National Academy of Sciences of the United States of America, 2005, 102(41): 14931-14936.

[33] Thorell L B, Lindqvist S, Bergman Nutley S, et al. Training and transfer effects of executive functions in preschool children. Developmental Science, 2009, 12(1): 106-113.

[34] Trulson M E. Martial arts training: A novel "cure" for juvenile delinquency. Human Relations, 1986, 39(12): 1131-1140.

[35] Tuckman B W, Hinkle J S. An experimental study of the physical and psychological effects of aerobic exercise on schoolchildren. Health Psychology, 1986, 5(3): 197.

[36] Vygotskii LLS. Mind in society: The development of higher psychological processes. Cambridge NA: Harvard University Press, 1978.

[37] Chen Aiguo, Yin Hengchan, Wang Jun, et al. The FMRI study of acute moderate exercise on children's executive function. Sports Science, 2011, 31(10): 35-40.

[38] Han Mingkun, Lv Jing. Effects of music traing on improving prefrontal executive function of children. China Journal of Health Psychology, 2013(4): 542-545.

[39] Luan WenShuang, Wang JingHai, Lu YingJun. A review of preschool children executive function. Preschool Education, 2013(7): 81-85.

[40] Zhang Jinsong, Ji Xing, Yan Chonghuai, et al. Primary study on executive function in children with ping-pang training and swimming training. Journal of Shanghai Jiao tong University (Medical Science), 2009, 29(7): 782-784.

Literature Review on the Relationship between Internet Addiction and Family Factors among Adolescents

Shuang Ji[1,a,*]

[1]Key Laboratory of Child Development and Learning Science of Ministry of Education, Southeast University, Nanjing 210096, China

[a]shuangd313@163.com

[*]Corresponding author

Keywords: adolescent; internet addiction; family factors; review

Abstract: Internet Addiction Disorder (IAD) is an addiction phenomenon that will result many problems of mind and body because of the overusing of the internet. As the Internet is spreading, adolescents are using the Internet more and more and can come across dangerous content, this could bring negative impact on the development of physical and mental health for those adolescents. Therefore, effective intervention to adolescents' internet addiction problems is of great significance, and the research of adolescents' internet addiction has been a focused point to many psychologists. Family plays a significant role in adolescents' daily life, it is also an important factor that can influence adolescents' internet addiction. This paper is a review of the related researches in this respect in recent years, highlighting those which address the contents, influencing factors, measurement tools and some new progress of the general situation of internet addiction and explore its family related factors among adolescents. This paper also points out the problems in current studies and predicts the future direction of study in this filed.

青少年网络成瘾中的家庭因素的研究综述

季爽[1,a,*]
[1]东南大学学习科学研究中心，儿童发展与学习科学教育部重点实验室，南京，210096
[a]shuangd313@163.com
[*]通讯作者

关键词：青少年；网络成瘾；家庭因素；回顾

中文摘要：网络成瘾(Internet Addiction Disorder，IAD)是指由于过度使用网络而导致明显的社会、心理功能损害的现象。随着互联网的普及，青少年群体逐渐成为互联网使用者的中坚力量。由于青少年心理发育尚未成熟，极易导致网络成瘾，网络成瘾产生后会对青少年身心健康的发展带来极大的负面影响。在这一背景下，越来越多的研究者开始从不同角度对青少年网络成瘾现象进行研究，试图找到更有效的干预措施。家庭作为青少年日常活动的主要场所，是人生最初始、最基础的教育场所。它也是青少年网络成瘾问题的重要影响因素之一。本文旨在从青少年网络成瘾问题中家庭相关因素的影响的角度出发，回顾总结现有研究中已有的研究成果，并指出当前研究中尚存在的一些问题，提出未来进一步研究的新方向。

1 引言

《第32次中国互联网络发展状况统计报告》显示，截至2013年6月底，我国网民规模达5.91亿，互联网普及率为44.1%，较2012年底提升2个百分点。手机网民用户达4.64亿。网络在中国的普及一方面给人们提供了获取知识与信息的新渠道，促进了科技的进步与经济的发展，另一方面网络也给人类社会生活带来了一些负面效应。由于网络所形成的虚拟空间有着同真实的社会完全不同的特质，所以它会给人造成十分明显的心理冲击[1]。这种心理冲突表现为以网络成瘾为主的一系列心理问题。网络成瘾(Internet Addiction Disorder，IAD)，也称为网络过度使用或病理性网络使用。Goldberg(1994)借用DSM-Ⅳ中关于药物依赖的判断标准首先对网络成瘾进行了定义[2]。在Goldberg的基础上，随后的研究者对这一概念进行了发展，现在网络成瘾是指由于过度使用网络而导致明显的社会、心理损害的一种现象[3]。其主要特征是：无节制地花费大量时间上网，必须增加上网时间才能获得满足感，不能上网时出现异常情绪体验，学业失败、工作绩效变差或现实人际关系恶化，向他人说谎以隐瞒自己对网络的迷恋程度，症状反复发作等[4]。

青少年处在个体发展的重要期，极易受新奇刺激的影响，再加上青少年自身认识能力发展有限，对新奇信息缺乏抵抗力，这些特点使他们成为网络成瘾的高发人群。

有研究表明,英国大学生中网络成瘾的比例为18.3%[5]。Kim K 等[6]对1 573 名韩国高中生进行了调查,结果表明,1.6%的学生被诊断为网络成瘾,38.0%被诊断为可疑的网络成瘾。在我国,中国民主同盟北京市委员会进行了一项关于网络游戏与未成年人教育的调查(2000 年)显示,北京市有近22 万中学生在玩网络游戏,而中学生上网成瘾者比例达14.8%,初中生为11.8%,高中生为15.97%。中国互联网络信息中心(CNNIC)调查表明,我国大学生中网络成瘾发生率为4%—13%,中学生为6%—15%,我国青少年网民(10—19 岁)占网民总数的24%以上。这些数据表明,青少年已成为网络成瘾人群的主体人群。青少年是个体发展的重要阶段,是人生观、价值观等重要心理特征形成和发展的重要时期。在青少年期的经历很有可能会影响个体今后的健康发展。在这一背景下越来越多的研究者开始关注青少年的网络成瘾问题,并试图发现这一现象的影响因素,以找出针对青少年的网络成瘾问题的有效干预措施。不少研究发现,青年自身的人格特征、气质类型、应对方式等会影响其网络成瘾的产生[7,8]。对于青少年来说,家庭仍是其进行日常活动的主要场所。作为人生最初始、最基础的教育场所,家庭环境的良好与否在青少年的成长过程中起着重要的作用,它也对青少年的心理健康产生着重要的影响[9]。由于与家庭有关的相关因素对青少年的成长起着重要的作用[10],越来越多的研究者开始关注家庭对青少年网络使用和成瘾的影响。本文对近年来青少年网络成瘾中家庭因素的相关研究中的研究方法、已有研究成果等相关内容进行回顾。

2 青少年网络成瘾的研究现状

2.1 研究方法

对网络成瘾中家庭相关因素的研究多采用问卷法,因为不同研究中所涉及的家庭因素不同,研究者会采用不同的相关问卷,所以主要对现在国内外研究中主要使用的网络成瘾的测量问卷进行回顾总结。

2.1.1 网络成瘾问卷(Internet Addiction Test, IAT)

网络成瘾问卷(IAT)是现阶段研究者尤其是国外研究者比较多使用的用于测量网络成瘾的问卷[11-13]。该问卷由 Jimberly. S. Young 对其早期参照 DSM-Ⅳ中赌博成瘾鉴别标准编制成的8 个项目的网络成瘾筛查量表进行修订而得[3]。量表由20 个条目组成,采用 Likert 式5 点计分。该量表上的总分表示测试者对网络的依赖程度,分数越高,网络成瘾的程度越严重。其中20—49 分表明测试者是个一般上网者,只是有时会上得多一些,但总体上是能够自我控制的,尚未沉溺于此。50—79 分表明测试者由于上网似乎开始引起了一些问题,应该谨慎对待上网给测试者带来的影响,以及对家庭和其他成员带来的影响。80—100 分表明上网已经给测试者和其家庭带来了很多问题,必须马上正视并解决这些问题。不同研究者对该问卷的信效度进行验证,该问卷具有良好的信效度[14,15]。

2.1.2 中文网络成瘾量表(Chinese Internet Addiction Scale,CIAS)

国内研究者多采用由台湾学者陈淑惠(2003)编制的中文网络成瘾量表(CIAS)对网络成瘾进行测评[16,17]。该量表包含耐受性、戒断症状、强迫上网、时间管理和人际健康五个维度,共26个条目。问卷采用4点计分,1=极不符合,4=非常符合。各维度分由各维度的题目得分相加而得,总分由各维度分相加而得,分数越高,表明网络成瘾越严重,量表信效度良好。

2.2 已有研究成果

2.2.1 父母教养方式与青少年网络成瘾

父母教养方式是父母的教养观念、教养行为及其对儿童的情感表现的一种组合方式。这种组合方式是相对稳定的,不随情境的改变而变化,它反映了亲子交往的实质。父母教养方式在子女发展过程中的作用是深刻而长远的,已有研究表明,父母教养方式在子女的认知发展、性格形成、社会化、心理健康等多方面具有不可忽视的影响[18]。不少研究者从父母教养方式的角度出发来探讨青少年网络成瘾问题。前人研究发现,在父母投入越多,对孩子有明确要求,越讲究策略的教养方式下,青少年沉迷于网络的风险越低且投入与社交网络活动及下载网络视频的行为越少[19]。职晓燕等[14]采用父母教养方式评价量表对88名网络成瘾青少年和90名健康青少年进行调查研究,结果表明父母教养粗放是导致网络成瘾的重要影响因素。此外,不少研究表明网络成瘾青少年的父母双方都存在对子女管教过严、惩罚过多、拒绝否认[20]、对孩子缺少理解和支持[21]、父母双方情感投入低[20,22,23]等教养方式上的问题。

2.2.2 家庭功能与青少年网络成瘾

个体的社会适应能力与其所在家庭的功能状况有着密切联系,个体社会适应能力的发展水平很难超越其家庭功能的发挥水平多少。家庭治疗临床实践表明,家庭功能不良会导致子女出现更多的外显和内隐问题。大部分实证研究也得到了与此一致的结论:家庭功能和青少年的问题行为存在负相关[24]。因此不少研究者开始关注家庭功能对青少年网络成瘾的影响。大多数研究者采用家庭功能评定量表(Family Assessment Device,FAD),研究发现家庭解决问题的能力低下、成员之间沟通低效[25]、情感反应淡漠[26]、介入行为控制方式粗暴单一[27]等因素都与青少年的网络成瘾呈显著相关[28]。同时,父母关系恶劣、离异[27]、单亲家庭[29]、离守儿童家庭[30]及重组家庭[31]中青少年的网络成瘾率较高。在这些研究成果基础上,不少研究者也开始从家庭功能理论的视角出发对青少年网络成瘾进行干预,并取得了不错的成果[25,32]。

2.2.3 家庭环境与青少年网络成瘾

研究发现家庭结构的稳定性、家庭生活条件、亲子关系和父母监护者的文化素质等家庭环境因素会对青少年的发展产生显著影响[33]。不少研究者利用家庭环境量表

(Family Environment Scale,FES)等相关工具来探究家庭环境对青少年网络成瘾的影响。研究发现家庭环境中的成功性、组织性、控制性三因素与青少年的网络成瘾有关[34],且家庭亲密度能显著预测青少年的网络成瘾,父子依恋中的父子信任和母子依恋中的母子疏离可以分别负向和正向预测青少年的网络成瘾[35]。此外研究还发现家庭经济水平及父母受教育水平的高低都对青少年的网络成瘾问题产生影响[28,34,36]。

3 总结

近年来对青少年网络成瘾的研究已经取得了不少成果,研究发现家庭是影响青少年网络成瘾行为的重要因素。但在现有研究中仍存在许多不足。首先,从研究方法上来说,针对这一问题的研究多采用问卷法进行研究,研究方法单一,很容易造成共同方法偏差。而且研究者采用的工具并未统一,也使一些研究结果间很难进行比较。其次,现有研究中多采用横断研究设计,很少有研究者采用纵向追踪研究,使研究结果缺少信服度。最后,在研究内容方面,学者们还是比较侧重于青少年网络成瘾中家庭因素相关表现上的研究,而对家庭因素在这一问题中如何应用的研究较少。如何从根源上减少青少年网络成瘾,如何有效干预和控制这一问题,这些还有待今后的进一步研究。

References

[1] X G Liu, J Y Liu. Youth network of mental health education model. Educational Research and Experiment, 2013, 2: 89 - 92.

[2] C Chien, C Ming. Internet addiction, usage, gratification, and pleasure experience: The Taiwan college students' case. Computers & Education, 2000, 35: 65 - 80.

[3] K S Young, R C Rodgers. Internet addiction personality traits associated with its development. Bostin: The 69th annual Meeting of the Eastern Psychological Association, 1998.

[4] H Petrie, D Gunn. Internet "addiction": The effects of sex, age, depression and in reversion. London: The British Psychological Society, 1998.

[5] K Niemz, M Griffiths, P Banyard. Prevalence of pathological internet use among university students and correlations with self-esteem, the general health questionnaire (GHQ), and disinhibition. Cyber Psychology & Behavior, 2005, 8: 562 - 570.

[6] K Kima, E Ryub, et al. Internet addiction in Korean adolescents and its relation to depression and suicidal ideation: A questionnaire survey. International Journal of Nursing Studies, 2006, 43: 185 - 192.

[7] P Ugo, Z Carla. Internet Addiction, Temperament, and the Moderator Role of Family Emotional Involvement. Int J Ment Health Addiction, 2014, 12: 52 - 63.

[8] J Tang, Y Z Yu, et al. Prevalence of internet addiction and its association with stressful life

events and psychological symptoms among adolescent internet users. Addictive Behaviors, 2014, 39: 744 – 747.

[9] B Deng, H Luo, X J Wang. Behavior Problem and Family Background of Children in Guiyang. Chinese Mental Health Journal, 2000, 14: 267 – 268.

[10] R Beavers, R B Hampson. The beavers systems model of family functioning. Journal of Family Therapy, 2000, 22:128 – 143.

[11] E K Argyroula, B John. The impact of early parenting bonding on young adults' Internet addiction, through the mediation effects of negative relating to others and sadness. Addictive Behaviors, 2014, 39: 733 – 773.

[12] I Adiele, W Olatokun. Prevalence and determinants of Internet addiction among adolescents. Computers in Human Behavior, 2014, 31: 100 – 110.

[13] K S Young. Caught in the Net: How to Recognize the Signs of Internet Addiction and a Winning Strategy for Recovery. New York: Wiley, 1998.

[14] X Y Zhi, C S Wang, et al. Coping style, social support and parenting style in adolescent with Internet addiction. Chinese Journal of School Health, 2013, 34: 426 – 429.

[15] W Li E L Garland, O M Howard. Family factors in Internet addiction among Chinese youth: A review of English- and Chinese-language studies. Computers in Human Behavior, 2014, 31: 393 – 411.

[16] L Y Deng, X Y Fang, M M Wu, et al. Family environment, parent-child attachment and adolescent internet addiction. Psychological Development and Education, 2013, 3: 305 – 311.

[17] S H Chen, L Z Weng, et al. The preparation of Chinese Internet addiction scale, and psychometric characteristics research. Chinese Journal of Psychology, 2003, 45: 279 – 294.

[18] L Leung, P S Lee. The influences of information literacy, internet addiction and parenting styles on internet risks. New Media and Society, 2012, 14: 117 – 136.

[19] C M Ohannessian, J V Lerner, et al. Adolescent-parent discrepancies in perceptions of family functioning and early adolescent self-competence International. Journal of Behavioral Development, 2000, 24: 362 – 372.

[20] X Huang, H Zhang, M Li, et al. Mental health, personality, and parental rearing style of adolescents with Internet addiction disorder. Cyberpsychology, Behavior, and Social Networking, 2009, 13: 401 – 406.

[21] P Amato, F Fowler. Parenting practices, child adjustment, and family diversity. Journal of Marriage and the Family, 2002, 64: 703 – 716.

[22] H Yang, Y E Lay, et al. Impact of language anxiety and self-efficacy on accessing internet sites. Cyberpsychology and Behavior, 2007, 10: 226 – 233.

[23] Y Peng, S J Zhou. Relationship of internet addiction and family environment and parental rearing patterns in adolescents. Chinese Journal of Clinical Psychology, 2007, 15: 418 – 439.

[24] H Wang, X Zhou, C Lu, et al. Problematic internet use in high school students in Guangdong province, China. PloS One, 2011, 6: 106 – 112.

[25] C Y Liu, F Y Kuoa. Study of Internet addiction through the Lens of the interpersonal theory.

Cyberpsychology and Behavior, 2006, 10: 799 - 804.

[26] F Fan, L Y Su, et al. Relationship between middle school students' Internet over use tendency and their academic achievement, mental problems and family function. Chinese Mental Health Journal, 2006, 10: 635 - 638.

[27] J Song, F C Yang. Internet addiction of college and high school students in Beijing and its influential factors. Chinese General Practice, 2007, 10: 559 - 561.

[28] H Luo, Y Peng. Relationship of Internet addiction and family environment and attachment of the youth. Chinese Journal of Clinical Psychology, 2008, 16: 319 - 321.

[29] L Y Liang, D H Tang, R Tao. Family function of the adolescents with excessive Internet usage. Chinese Mental Health Journal, 2007, 21: 507 - 510.

[30] G Yang, P Li, et al. The Impact of Parental Migration on Health Status and Health Behaviour Among Left Behind Adolescent School Children in China. BMC Public Health, 2010.

[31] X Zhong, R Tao, et al. Effect of group psychological intervention in adolescents on Internet addiction. Journal of Capital Medical University, 2009, 30: 494 - 499.

[32] X H Chen. Teenagers network addiction family intervention with social work involvement in family functioning theory angle of view. Journal of Shandong Youth Administrative Cadres College, 2010, 1: 29 - 33.

[33] H P Luo, Y Peng. Relationship of Internet addiction and family environment and attachment of the youth. Chinese Journal of Clinical Psychology, 2008, 16: 332 - 345.

[34] Z Yu, P Sun, J M Huang. Internet game addiction and inflectional factors of middle school students in Guangzhou. Chinese Journal of Clinical Psychology, 2009, 17: 473 - 475.

[35] Y B Xie, P Zhou, L P Xu, et al. Prevalence of internet addiction and the related factors in middle school students in Guangzhou. Journal of Southern Medical University, 2010, 30: 1801 - 1804.

[36] Y Lang, F J Jia, H F Li, et al. Investigation and analysis of related factors of junior middle school students with Internet addiction disorder. Chinese Journal of Clinical Psychology, 2008, 16: 417 - 419.

Developmental Cognitive Neuroscience of Arithmetic Ability: Implication for Math Training

Yolanda Binglei Zhao[1,a,*]
[1]University of York, York, UK
[a]yolandabzhao@gmail.com
[*]Corresponding author

Keywords: developmental cognitive neuroscience; arithmetic ability; training

Abstract: The aim of this work is to offer an overview and a systemic analysis of cognitive and neuroimaging studies on the development of arithmetic ability in children and describe how these results could be applied for neural training to enhance children's arithmetic performance. However firstly we summarize the mature neural mechanism behind arithmetic ability as a baseline including inferior parietal cortex (IPC) and prefrontal cortex (PFC). Based on the adults' model in numerical and arithmetical cognition, in the second part, the children's ability in number processing is considered as a potential but vital predictor for their concurrent and future mathematical performance. The brain studies afterwards show a shift in brain activation pattern from PFC to IPC with the age increasing. In the last part, arithmetic related trainings are described for both typical and atypical children, which draws a blue print for applying advanced neural technique in training, especially for those who suffer from severe developmental dyscalculia (DD) in the future.

1 Introduction

The acquisition of arithmetic ability is of great value for the current society, not only individuals, but also for educational and economic systems. For individual level, low math ability means much narrow career choice, which seems more harmful than dyslexia or other learning difficulties. In UK, for example, nearly 7% of the population exhibit difficulties in dealing with numbers and have low mathematical performance back in school. It has been argued that low arithmetic ability might lead to a large amount of cost. The 7% low math skill population in UK might generate around £ 2.4 billion in general. Therefore, it is important to know how people do mental calculation or number processing. While more and more research pointed out the low arithmetic ability might trace back to adulthood or children called developmental dyscalculia (DD). Hence to know the developmental procedure of how children learn this math ability is vital to more effectively enhance people's math performance. In this paper, we firstly summarize the neural mechanism of how adults processing numerical tasks. Following that we focus on the development of arithmetical ability by reviewing recent cognitive and brain research. In that last part, some advanced neural techniques are introduced which might be useful and practical for evaluation of math teaching intervention or even direct neural training in the future.

2 Arithmetic Ability in Adults

Inferior parietal cortex (IPC) and prefrontal cortex (PFC) are consistently considered to be highly involved in numerical and arithmetic processing by a large amount of lesion and cognitive neuropsychological studies with adult participants involved. With rapid development of the brain imaging techniques in the last two decades, neuroimaging studies recently have focused on detecting the functional role of these key neural areas in number processing (see for reviews) and mental calculation. Based on these data, several models are built up from different aspects explaining the mature neural mechanism behind numerical cognition.

According to the highly influential triple-code model, three circuits in the IPS are involved in number processing and mental calculation. The left angular gyrus (lAG) shows more activation in multiplication task than subtraction in many functional magnetic resonance imaging (fMRI) studies, suggesting that it is involved in arithmetic fact retrieval. This functional role is also confirmed by neuropsychological research by detecting the calculation deficiency in the patient with lesion to the lAG as well as showing unabiding disrupted in math tasks after repetitive transcranial magnetic stimulation (rTMS) over lAG. However it seems not responsible for quantity-based estimation and number comparison. The activation of horizontal segment of the intraparietal sulcus (hIPS) is thought to be domain-specific for number processing. Regarding to calculation, it is revealed holding the opposite pattern with lAG and associate with procedural strategies that it fires more in subtraction compared to multiplication task. However its functional role is still unclear that an fMRI guided TMS research found its role in arithmetic fact retrieval as well. More research could be done in the future to distinguish to what extent hIPS takes part in the retrieving arithmetic fact by using advanced analytical method [multi-voxel pattern analysis (MVPA) etc.]. The third circuit posterior superior parietal lobule (PSPL) was proved not only activated in specific arithmetic strategy, but saccade tasks as well, suggesting partially participants in attention system.

On the other hand, PFC is also involved in mental arithmetic, engaging in supportive function, for example working memory and control retrieval. Based on Baddeley's multicomponent model of the working memory, behavior research has revealed that all the three elements are considered associated with mental calculation: The central executive which is shown activation in dorsolateral PFC plays its role in both fact retrieval and procedural strategy, but showed more involvement in procedural one. The phonological loop which is relevant to the neural firing mainly in left Broca's area (BA) 44 suggested to responsible for retrieving arithmetic fact, for example, the times table which is taught and practiced verbally. But it has been argued by Imbo et al. that it is only involved in procedural procedure to maintain intermediate arithmetic result. The visual-spatial sketchpad associating with the activation in BA 9/ 46 is considered involved in the procedure of multi-digit problem by reflecting the representation of quantities on a mental number line. Therefore, the PFC as a whole area has been largely detected, leaving an unsolved issue about the subdivision neural correlate to mental calculation, since there is always overlap brain activation pattern across different operations.

3 The Development of Arithmetic Ability

It has been pointed out the perils of neglecting the role of development by roughly applying the existing neurocognitive model of arithmetic cognition to interpret the children's arithmetic ability development and disorder. While progress in research on the development of children's math learning or developmental dyscalculia, a math learning disorder, continues lag behind advance understanding of mature neural mechanism behind arithmetic ability, there now exists a growing body of studies concern about how children develop this ability or the neural mechanism of their math suffering (please see the reference list 29, 31, 32 and 33).

The predictor role of numerical magnitude, either non-symbolic or symbolic format for later calculation development, as one of the outstanding questions in this emerging body of research has been underlined recently. Non-symbolic numerical comparison (dots, etc.) is thought to index the acuity of representation in the approximate number line (ANS). This is a system allows individuals to represent and manipulate the representations of the approximate number of items. Individual with more precise ANS representations perform more accurately and faster on magnitude comparison tasks. The newborn infants have been revealed mastering the ability to compare numerical magnitude in ANS that they could discriminate between small sets of objects that differ in their numerosity. With their development, typical children show an increase in the precision of ANS representations. The results of developmental fMRI studies are consistent with this result that showing a differential neural pattern between adults and children in inferior and superior parietal lobe that adult's brain network activate more strongly than children in this brain areas. However it is still not clear whether the non-symbolic numerical comparison could predict the concurrent and future mathematic achievements. Behavioral research failed to find a significant relationship with two possibilities. One is the no standardized criterion for number comparison task; the other the existing multiple calculation ways [Weber Fraction (ω) estimate, distance or ratio effect, etc.] based on the accuracy and the response time (RT).

Symbolic number comparison task involves Arabic digits. Performance on this task might reflect the nature of the development of ANS. However, behavioral research show consistent result that the performance on symbolic number comparison is a good predictor for the concurrent and future math academic performance. Unfortunately till now no cognitive neuroscience research has been done to investigate the neural correlation of this symbolic number comparison and mathematic level.

As a whole, the non-symbolic and symbolic number processing functioned as vital step-stones for future calculation acquisition. The universal cerebral circuits have been suggested by recent reviews devoted in number processing in early childhood, rather than a domain-specific neural mechanism involved in mature numerical cognition system, Kaufmann and his colleagues by reviewing eight developmental fMRI studies so far and to some extend confirmed this suggestion by showing that in the typical development, the acquisition of arithmetic ability is a shift from activation from PFC to IPS. However more research are needed concern about the sub brain areas involved in the development of children's arithmetic ability and how they shift with the increase of age from infants to adults.

4 The Arithmetic Related Training

Various math teaching interventions or behavioral trainings have been designed to foster the development of typical children's learning as well as the children with DD. In recent two decades, researchers have specifically assessed the effect of targeted training on cerebral structures and brain activity patterns. Pauli and his colleagues ran the first evoked-related potentials (ERPs) study related to math training providing neural evidence showing that intensive practice of arithmetic leads to significant modification of brain activity. Following that, more research use fMRI to trace training related modification of the brain activation. Hence, it is promising to apply advanced neural technique, like ERPs as assessment tools for evaluating the teaching interventions or trainings in either academic or educational context.

With the understanding that IPS is mainly responsible for mental calculation and numerical cognition, neural training in these recent years have been considered to apply for those who suffer severe DD to help them enhance their math performance to some extent. Iuculano and Cohen Kadosh ran such a training session for two DD participants. They combined a numerical learning paradigm with transcranial direct current stimulation (tDCS), a non-invasive technique to assess the potential benefits of this methodology to remediate their math difficulties. One participant received anodal stimulation to the right posterior parietal cortex (PPC) and cathodal stimulation to the left PPC. The second participant received anodal stimulation to the left PPC and cathodal stimulation to the right PPC. Both of these two DD participants' performances after tDCS were compared to the controls. The results showed that anodal stimulation to the left PPC improved both indices of numerical proficiency. This result foretells the useful and applicable of applying neural techniques into training at least for those who suffer from DD.

References

[1] B Butterworh. The Mathematical Brain. London: Macmillan, 1999.

[2] S Dehaene, L Cohen. Towards an anatomical and functional model of number processing. Mathematical Cognition, 1995, 1: 83-120.

[3] S E Hennschen. Clinical and anatomical contributions in brain pathology. Archives of Neurological Psychiatry, 1925, 13: 226-249.

[4] M McCloskey, A Caramazza, A Basili. Cognitive mechanisms in number processing and calculation: Evidence from dyscalculia. Brain and Cognition, 1985, 4(2): 171-196.

[5] E M Brannon. The representation of numerical magnitude. Current Opinion in Neurobiology, 2006, 16: 222-229.

[6] R Cohen Kadosh, J Lammertyn, V Izard. Are numbers special? An overview of chronometric, neuroimaging, developmental and comparative studies of magnitude representation. Progress in Neurobiology, 2008, 84(5): 132-147.

[7] M Delazer, F Domahs, L Bartha, et al. Learning complex arithmetic- an fMRI study. Cognitive Brain Research, 2003, 18(1): 76-88.

[8] A Ischebeck, L Zamarian, K Egger, et al. Imaging early practice effects in arithmetic. Neuroimage, 2007, 36(3): 993-1003.

[9] D Ansari. Effects of development and enculturation on number representation in the brain. Nature Reviews Neuroscience, 2008, 9(4): 278 - 291.

[10] S Dehaene, M Piazza, P Pinel, et al. Three parietal circuits for number processing//Campbell J I D. The Handbook of Mathematical Cognition. Hove: Psychology Press, 2005.

[11] K M Lee. Cortical areas differentially involved in multiplication and subtraction: A functional magnetic resonance imaging study and correlation with a case of selective acalculia. Annals of Neurology, 2000, 48(4): 657 - 661.

[12] V Menon, S M Rivera, C D White, et al. Functional optimization of arithmetic processing in perfect performers. Cognitive Brain Research, 2000, 9(3): 343 - 345.

[13] M Delazer, A Ischebeck, F Domahs, et al. Learning by strategies and learning by drill-evidence from an fMRI study. Neuroimage, 2005, 25: 838 - 849.

[14] R H Grabner, D Ansari, K Koschutnig, et al. To retrieve to or to calculate? Left angular gyrus mediates the retrieval of arithmetic facts during problem solving. Neuropsychologia, 2009, 47: 604 - 608.

[15] E Rusconi, V Walsh, B Butterworth. Dexterity with numbers: rTMS over left angular gyrus disrupts finger gnosis and number processing. Neuropsychologia, 2005, 43: 1609 - 1624.

[16] M Hirnstein, U Bayer, A Ellison, et al. TMS over the left angular gyrus impairs the ability to discriminate left from right. Neuropsychologia, 2011, 49: 29 - 33.

[17] M Andres, B Pelgrims, N Michaux, et al. Role of distinct parietal areas in arithmetic: An fMRI-guided TMS study. Neuroimage, 2011, 54: 3048 - 3056.

[18] O Simon, J F Mangin, L Cohen, et al. Topographical layout of hand, eye, calculation, and language-related areas in the human parietal lobe. Neuron, 2002, 33: 475 - 487.

[19] M Rosenberg-Lee, M C Lovett, J R Anderson. Neural correlates of arithmetic calculation strategies. Cognitive, Affective & Behavioral Neuroscience, 2009, 9(3): 270 - 285.

[20] M Arsalidou, M J Taylor. 2 + 2 = 4? Meta-analyses of brain areas needed for number and calculations. Neuroimage, 2011, 54: 2382 - 2393.

[21] A Baddeley. The episodic buffer: A new component of working memory? Trends in Cognitive Neuroscience, 2000, 4(11): 417 - 423.

[22] E E Smith, J Jonides. Storage and executive processes in the frontal lobes. Science, 1999, 283: 1657 - 1661.

[23] I Imbo, A Vandierendonck, E Verguwe. The role of working memory in carrying and borrowing. Psychological Research, 2007, 71: 467 - 483.

[24] P Trbovich, J LeFevre. Phonological and visual working memory in mental addition. Memory & Cognition, 2003, 31: 738 - 745.

[25] S Rotzer, T Loenneker, K Kucian, et al. Dysfunctional neural network of spatial working memory contributes to developmental dyscalculia. Neuropsychologia, 2009, 47: 2859 - 2865.

[26] A Knops, K Willmes. Numerical ordering and symbolic arithmetic share frontal and parietal. Neuroimage, 2014, 84: 786 - 795.

[27] D Ansari. Neurocognitive approaches to developmental disorders of numerical and mathematical

cognition: The perils of neglecting the role of development. Learning and Individual Differences, 2010, 20: 123 – 129.

[28] G Karagiannakis, A Baccaglini-Frank, Y Papadatos. Mathematical learning difficulties subtype classification. Frontiers in Human Neuroscience, 2014, 8: 1 – 5.

[29] B Butterworth. Foundational numerical capacities and the origins of dyscalculia. Trends in Cognitive Neuroscience, 2010, 14: 534 – 541.

[30] M G von Aster, R S Shalev. Number development and developmental dyscalculia. Developmental Medicine & Child Neurology, 2007, 49: 868 – 873.

[31] V Menon. Developmental cognitive neuroscience of arithmetic: Implications for learning and education. ZDM Mathematics Education, 2010, 42: 515 – 525.

[32] L Zamarian, A Ischebeck, M Delazer. Neuroscience of learning arithmetic- evidence from brain imaging studies. Neuroscience and Biobehavioral Reviews, 2009, 33: 909 – 925.

[33] L Kaufmann, G Wood, O Rubinsten, et al. Meta-analyses of developmental fMRI studies investigating typical and a typical trajectories of number processing and calculation. Developmental Neuropsychology, 2011, 36: 763 – 787.

[34] B D Smedt, M Noel, C Gilmore, et al. How do symbolic and non-symbolic numerical magnitude processing skills relate to individual differences in children's mathematical skills? A review of evidence from brain and behavior. Trends in Neuroscience and Education, 2013, 2: 48 – 55.

[35] C Gilmore, N Attridge, B De Smedt, et al. Measuring the approximate number system in children: Exploring the relationships among different tasks. Learning and Individual Differences, 2014, 29: 50 – 58.

[36] K Wynn, P Bloom, W C Chiang. Enumeration of collective entities by 5-month-old infants. Cognition, 2002, 83: B55 – B62.

[37] K S Mix, J Huttenlocher, S Levine. Quantitative Development in Infancy and Early Childhood. New York: Oxford University Press, 2002.

[38] K S Mix, J Huttenlocher, S C Levine. Multiple cues for quantification if infancy: Is number one of them? Psychological Bulletin, 2002, 128: 278 – 294.

[39] D Ansari, B Dhital. Age-related changes in the activation of the intraparietal sulcus during non-symbolic magnitude processing: An event-related functional magnetic resonance imaging stud. Journal of Cognitive Neuroscience, 2006, 18: 1820 – 1828.

[40] J F Cantlon, E M Brannon, E J Carter, et al. Functional imaging of numerical processing in adults and 4-year-old children. PLoS Biology, 2006, 4: 844 – 854.

[41] J F Cantlon, M E Libertus, P Pinel, et al. The neural developmental of an abstract concept of number. Journal of Cognitive Neuroscience, 2009, 21: 2217 – 2229.

[42] I D Holloway, D Ansari. Developmental specialization in the right intraparietal sulcus for the abstract representation of numerical magnitude. Journal of Cognitive Neuroscience, 2010, 22: 2627 – 2637.

[43] L Kaufmann, S E Vogel, G Wood, et al. A developmental fMRI study of nonsymbolic

numerical and spatial processing. Cortex, 2008, 44: 376 - 385.

[44] K Kucian, M von Aster, T Loenneker, et al. Development of neural networks for exact and approximate calculation: A fMRI study. Developmental Psychology, 2008, 33: 447 - 473.

[45] S Toll, J E H Luit. Accelerating the early numeracy development of kindergartners with limited working memory skills through remedial education. Research in Developmental Disabilities, 2013, 34: 745 - 755.

[46] P Pauli, W Lutzenberger, H Rau, et al. Brain potential during mental arithmetic: Effects of extensive practice and problem difficulty. Cognitive Brian Research, 1994, 2: 21 - 29.

[47] A Ischebeck, L Zamarian, M Schocke, et al. Flexible transfer of knowledge in mental arithmetic- an fMRI study. Neuroimage, 2009, 44: 1103 - 1112.

[48] T Iuculano, R Cohen Kadosh. Preliminary evidence for performance enhancement following parietal lobe stimulation in developmental dyscalculia. Frontiers in Neuroscience, 2014, 8: 1 - 10.

[49] S Parsons, J Bynner. Does Numeracy Matter More? London: National Research and Development Centre for Adult Literacy and Numeracy, 2005.

[50] T Link, K Moeller, S Huber, et al. Walk the number line—An embodied training for numerical concepts. Trends in Neuroscience and Education, 2013, 2: 78 - 84.

[51] J Beddington, C I Cooper, J Field, et al. The mental wealth of nations. Nature, 2008, 455: 1057 - 1060.

Association of chronic stress and the ratio of cortisol to cortisone for mothers with children in developmental disorders

Xingliang Qi, Jing Zhang, Yapeng Liu, Zheng Chen, Huihua Deng[a,*]

Key laboratory of Child Development and Learning Science of Ministry of Education, Southeast University, Research Center for Learning Science, Southeast University, Nanjing 210096, China

[a] dengrcls@seu.edu.cn

[*] Corresponding author

Keywords: chronic stress; disable children; 11β-hydroxysteroid dehydrogenase; cortisol/cortisone ratio

Abstract: The current study aimed to examine whether hair cortisol, hair cortisone or cortisol/cortisone ratio in hair can be biomarkers of the chronic stress. Participants were 41 mothers who rear a child with developmental disability and 31 mothers with one normally developing children as controls. Hair samples closest to the scalp were collected. Cortisol and cortisone were extracted from the hair samples with methanol, and cortisol and cortisone concentrations were measured with high performance liquid chromatography-tandem mass spectrometry. Chronic perceived stress and parenting stress were measured with the Perceived Stress Scale and the Parenting Stress Index. The results revealed that mothers with disable children showed significantly higher perceived stress and parenting stress, and significantly lower cortisol/cortisone ratio in hair than mothers with normally developing children. There were no significantly differences on hair cortisol and hair cortisone between the two groups of mothers. These results suggested that high chronic stress levels might reduce the ability of metabolizing cortisol to cortisone. Cortisol/cortisone ratio in hair would possibly be a new biomarker of chronic stress, at least for mothers with disable children.

慢性应激与头发皮质醇与可的松比值的关联:以发育障碍儿童的母亲为例

齐星亮,张静,刘亚鹏,陈峥,邓慧华[a,*]

东南大学儿童发展与学习科学教育部重点实验室,南京,210096

[a]dengrcls@ seu. edu. cn

[*]通讯作者

关键词:慢性应激;发育障碍儿童;头发皮质醇与可的松的比值;11β-脱羟基酶

中文摘要:本研究的目的是探索头发皮质醇、头发可的松以及头发中的皮质醇/可的松比值能否成为发育障碍孩子母亲慢性应激的生物指标。分别采集41位发育障碍儿童母亲和31位正常发育儿童母亲贴近头皮1 cm的头发,并用高效液相色谱串联质谱法检测头发样本中的皮质醇和可的松含量。压力知觉量表和养育压力量表测量其知觉压力和养育压力。结果显示,发育障碍儿童母亲的知觉压力和养育压力高于正常发育儿童母亲,头发中的皮质醇/可的松比值低于正常发育儿童母亲。两组母亲的头发皮质醇和可的松含量没有显著差异。这些结果提示,慢性应激会降低发育障碍儿童母亲将皮质醇代谢成可的松的能力。头发中的皮质醇/可的松比值可以作为发育障碍儿童母亲慢性应激的生物指标。

1 引言

教养发育障碍孩子给其家长带来沉重的心理、身体、经济和时间负担[1]。例如,相对于正常发育孩子的家长,发育障碍孩子的家长承受更高的慢性心理应激,身心健康水平更低[2,3]。长期处于高水平应激状态会增加个体应激系统的负荷,久而久之会损害应激系统的功能,进而引起疾病[4]。由此,大量研究关注应激系统所分泌的激素与慢性应激的关联,试图理解慢性应激导致疾病的生物机制,寻找监测慢性应激人群健康的有效生物标记。

皮质醇是下丘脑—垂体—肾上腺(HPA)轴的终端产物,也已被公认为应激的生物标记[5]。发育障碍孩子的家长是典型的高水平慢性应激群体,但关注该群体应激系统的生物标记的相关研究还相当缺乏。近来,一些研究以唾液皮质醇含量为生物标记,考察发育障碍孩子的家长皮质醇分泌情况。这些研究的结果显示,相对于正常发育孩子的家长,发育障碍孩子的家长日间唾液皮质醇分泌量更低[6,7],且皮质醇觉醒反应曲线更为平坦[6-10]。这些结果提示,发育障碍孩子的家长经长期高水平慢性应激状态后,其皮质醇的分泌功能和分泌节律调节功能减弱。但是,该高应激群体皮质醇异常的机制有待探索。过去许多研究从HPA轴的激活和负反馈调节等视角考察其机制。本研究拟从代谢的视角探索皮质醇异常的机制。可的松是皮质醇的代谢物,没有生物活性。皮质醇在

11β-脱羟基酶(11β-HSD)的不可逆催化作用下转化为可的松[11],皮质醇与可的松的比值(β 值)是 11β-HSD 的酶活性水平的生物标记[12]。以往研究表明,在应激状态下,皮质醇/可的松的比值会上升[13,14],说明应激状态下皮质醇的代谢功能降低。目前,尚无研究报道高应激水平的家长可的松含量和 11β-HSD 活性水平。

近来,来自头发基质中的生物标记水平可反映一段时间内的累积量。例如,头发皮质醇可提供较长时段内激素暴露总量的信息,相对唾液皮质醇具有采样方便和与时间上心理量表匹配更好的优点[15,16]。头发皮质醇已被证明是一种可靠的反映慢性应激的手段[15]。本研究通过检验发育障碍儿童的家长头发皮质醇含量是否低于正常发育儿童家长来验证头发皮质醇是否可以作为发育障碍孩子的家长慢性应激的生物指标。此外,本研究通过考察发育障碍儿童家长与发育正常儿童家长头发 β 值之间的差异,来探究高应激群体皮质醇水平异常的机制。基于文献报道,本研究假设发育障碍儿童的家长头发皮质醇和 β 值均较低。

2 方法

2.1 被试

发育障碍儿童母亲 41 名（其中自闭症儿童母亲 33 人,智障儿童母亲 8 人),正常发育儿童母亲 31 名。发育障碍儿童平均年龄(4.55 ±1.55)岁,发育障碍儿童母亲平均年龄(33.12 ±3.84)岁。正常发育儿童平均年龄(4.42 ±0.90)岁,正常发育儿童母亲平均年龄(33.45 ±3.44)岁。两组儿童或其母亲的年龄均无统计上的显著差异。

2.2 心理测量

母亲所感知的压力由压力感知量表(Perceived Stress Scale, PSS)[17]测得。该量表共 14 个项目,采用 Likert 式 5 点评分,从“从不”到“总是”五个等级分别给予 0、1、2、3、4 分。得分越高,表示父母的养育压力越高。本研究中,该量表的信度为 0.85。

母亲的养育压力由养育压力量表简缩版(Parenting Stress Index-short Form, PSI-SF)[18]测得。该量表共 36 个项目,采用 Likert 式 5 点评分,从“非常不同意”到“非常同意”五个等级分别给予 1、2、3、4、5 分。得分越高,表示父母的养育压力越高。本研究中,该量表的信度为 0.92。

2.3 头发的采集与分析

被试交回问卷时采集头发。头发取自被试后脑枕部,取贴头皮 1 cm 发段,可反映一个月之内的总体皮质醇水平。采用高效液相色谱串联质谱法对头发样品进行检测[19]。

2.4 数据统计

使用独立样本 t 检验,分别计算两组母亲年龄、孩子年龄、养育压力、头发皮质醇、头发可的松以及 β 值的差异。

3 结果

如表 1 所列，发育障碍儿童母亲的知觉压力和养育压力均显著高于发育正常儿童母亲($p<0.001$)，两组母亲头发中的皮质醇和可的松含量差异不显著($p>0.14$)，发育障碍儿童母亲的 β 值显著高于发育正常儿童母亲($p=0.03$)。

表 1 两组母亲的压力和生物标记水平之间的差异

$M \pm SD$	发育障碍儿童家长 ($n=41$)	正常发育儿童家长 ($n=31$)	统计值(t)
知觉压力	30.54 ±8.15	20.86 ±5.46	7.17***
养育压力	114.07 ±18.43	82.69 ±16.98	5.91***
皮质醇	11.62 ±8.87	16.62 ±22.06	-1.19
可的松	27.93 ±22.82	42.69 ±42.71	-1.51
β	0.51 ±0.34	0.37 ±0.13	2.29*

注：*$p<0.05$，**$p<0.01$，***$p<0.001$。

4 讨论

本研究结果显示，发育障碍与发育正常儿童母亲头发内皮质醇的含量没有显著差异。这个结果与研究假设不一致，也与以唾液皮质醇为生物标记的相关研究不符。以前研究发现，发育障碍孩子的母亲日间唾液皮质醇水平低于正常发育孩子母亲[6,7]。长期高水平的应激会导致低皮质醇症，而在低皮质醇症产生之前，皮质醇水平会经历一个短暂上升[20]。Bella[6]和 Seltzer[7]的研究中，发育障碍孩子的平均年龄分别为 8.3 岁和 24.7 岁，而本研究中发育障碍孩子平均年龄仅为 4.6 岁。我们推测，唾液研究[6,7]反映了长期看护发育障碍孩子所导致家长的低皮质醇症，而本研究中发育障碍儿童的母亲经受慢性应激的时间相对较短，可能还处于低皮质醇症出现前的阶段，所以没表现出较低的头发皮质醇水平。

本研究的另一个结果是，发育障碍儿童母亲头发内 β 值小于发育正常儿童母亲，提示发育障碍儿童母亲皮质醇在体液中的代谢弱于正常发育儿童母亲。这个结果与之前研究发现的高水平应激状态中 β 值上升的结果一致[13,14]，可见头发中的 β 值有可能成为发育障碍儿童母亲慢性应激中皮质醇代谢能力的生物指标之一。11β-HSD 的降解是皮质醇水平降低的途径之一[21]。唾液研究所得出的发育障碍孩子母亲皮质醇日间曲线相对平坦[6-9]或者觉醒 30 分钟至睡觉前皮质醇降低量较少[10]的结果表明发育障碍孩子母亲的皮质醇代谢功能较差，而 11β-HSD 的降解皮质醇的功能减弱可能是产生这一现象的原因之一。

References

[1] G I Orsmond, L Y Lin, M M Seltzer. Mothers of adolescents and adults with autism: The contribution of disability in siblings to maternal well-being and family adjustment. Intellectual and Developmental Disabilities, 2007, 45: 257 – 270.

[2] J Blacher, L L McIntyre. Syndrome specificity and behavior disorders in young adults with intellectual disability: Cultural differences in family impact. Journal of Intellectual Disability Research, 2006, 50: 184 – 198.

[3] A S Eisenhower, B L Baker, J Blacher. Preschool children with intellectual disability: Syndrome specificity, behavior problems, and maternal well-being. Journal of Intellectual Disability Research, 2005, 49: 657 – 671.

[4] B S McEwen. Stress, adaptation, and disease: Allostasis and allostatic load. Annals of The New York Academy of Sciences, 1998, 840: 33 – 44.

[5] J Hellhammer, E Fries, O W Schweisthal, et al. Several daily measurements are necessary to reliably assess the cortisol rise after awakening: Tate- and trait components. Psychoneuroendocrinology, 2007, 32: 80 – 86.

[6] G P Bella, M C Garcia, R C Spadari-Bratfisch. Salivary cortisol, stress, and health in primary caregivers (mothers) of children with cerebral palsy. Psychoneuroendocrinology, 2011, 36: 834 – 842.

[7] M M Seltzer, J S Greenberg, J Hong, et al. Maternal cortisol levels and child behavior problems in families of adolescents and adults with ASD. Journal of Autism and Developmental Disorders, 2010, 40: 457 – 469.

[8] E Gonzalez-Bono, S DeAndres-Garcia, L Moya-Albiol. The cortisol awakening response in caregivers of schizophrenic offspring shows sensitivity to patient status. Anxiety Stress Coping, 2011, 24: 107 – 120.

[9] M M Seltzer, D M Almeida, J S Greenberg, et al. Psychosocial and biological markers of daily lives of midlife parents of children with disabilities. Journal of Health and Human Behavior, 2009, 50: 1 – 15.

[10] E T Barker, J S Greenberg, M M Seltzer, et al. Daily stress and cortisol patterns in parents of adult children with a serious mental illness. Health Psychology, 2012, 31: 130 – 134.

[11] M Quinkler, P M Stewart. Hypertension and the cortisol-cortisone shuttle. Journal of Clinical Endocrinology and Metabolism, 2003, 88: 2384 – 2392.

[12] A Plenis, L Konieczna, I Oledzka, et al. Simultaneous determination of urinary cortisol, cortisone and corticosterone in parachutists, depressed patients and healthy controls in view of biomedical and pharmacokinetic studies. Molecular Biosystems, 2011, 7: 1487 – 1500.

[13] R Gatti, E Cappellin, B Zecchin, et al. Urinary high performance reverse phase chromatography cortisol and cortisone analyses before and at the end of a race in elite cyclists. Journal of Chromatography B-analytical Technologies in The Biomedical and Life Sciences, 2005, 824: 51 – 56.

[14] A Plenis, L Konieczna, I Olędzka, et al. Simultaneous determination of urinary cortisol,

cortisone and corticosterone inparachutists, depressed patients and healthy controls in view of biomedical and pharmacokinetic studies. Molecular Biosystems, 2011, 7: 1487 - 1500.

[15] T Stalder, C Kirschbaum. Analysis of cortisol in hair—State of the art and future directions. Brain, behavior, and immunity, 2012, 26: 1019 - 1029.

[16] E Russell, G Koren, M Rieder, et al. Hair cortisol as a biological marker of chronic stress: Current status, future directions and unanswered questions. Psychoneuroendocrinology, 2012, 37: 589 - 601.

[17] H Luo, J Ma. Relation among college student' s depression symptom, problem solving appraisal and perceived stress. Chinese Journal of Clinical Psychology, 2004, 12: 367 - 368.

[18] Y Liu, G Zhang, Z Liang, et al. Stability and association with toddler's behavioral problems of father's parenting stress. Psychological Development and Education, 2011, 27: 599 - 606.

[19] X L Qi, J Zhang, Y P Liu, et al. Relationship between effort-reward imbalance and hair cortisol concentration in female kindergarten teachers. J Psycho Res, 2014, 76: 329 - 332.

[20] G E Miller, E Chen, E S Zhou. If it goes up, must it come down? Chronic stress and the hypothalamic-pituitary-adrenocortical axis in humans. Psychological Bulletin, 2007, 133: 25 - 45.

[21] J W Tomlinson, E A Walker, I J Bujalska, et al. 11 beta-hydroxy steroid dehydrogenase type 1: A tissue specific regulator of glucocorticoid response. Endocrine Reviews, 2004, 25: 831 - 866.

A Case Study on Primary Problem Student in Yemen

Alhashedi Sena Abdulkarem Noman*
Key Laboratory of Child Development and Learning Science of Ministry of Education, Research Center for Learning Science, Southeast University, Nanjing, 210096, China
senaseu@ hotmail. com
* Corresponding author

Nowadays, problem student is a common phenomenon exiting in primary and secondary school, Yemen. However, current unknown is why problem students appear and how to make an effective intervention way for reducing the problem behaviors. Although there have been many researches about problem student's problem behaviors researches on causes, developmental mechanism and educational strategies of problem students mainly stay on the theoretical research stage. This study aimed to investigate main reason for the formation of problem students and then make an effective intervention way and examine the invention effect.

Materials and Method

Participants

This study selected study cases according to the real status of problem students in primary schools. The specific selection process is listed as follows:

Firstly, I interviewed Grade-three and Grade-four teachers to get the name list of problem students in their eyes. Then, I targeted the name list of problem students in their classes and screened totally six headachy students (Category A), eight students who are not so good (Category B) and 15 students who have some problems (Category C).

Generally, these students were born between the years of 2004 and 2005 and now are studying at schools of Yemen. Of them, the academic performance of Category A problem students is always hovering in the penultimate one, two, three or so, and their behaviors are mainly seen as follows: firstly, they do not listen in class, regularly fall asleep or doze off in class. The general situation is that if the teacher just politely goes up to them and prompted them to listen carefully, at the beginning, they just take standoffish attitude. Only when the teacher is burned up and becoming serious, they will sit up and listen for a while. Once the teacher walks away, they will continue to lie on the table. Secondly, when they do not fall sleepy, they will talk with students around, make noise, trouble others or disrupt the class. Of course, partly because the students sitting in the back of the middle classroom are basically in the similar circumstances, only the degree of severity is different. Some of them will also learn a little, but some simply do not listen in class. Basically substitute teacher cannot control them. In some teachers' classes, they will convergence themselves. However, they usually have poor academic performance. They still keep disturbing students around them. Thirdly, they tend to have group fighting and steal from others. Sometimes they bully relatively honest classmates, and group fight with others. In addition, commonly they have poor interpersonal relationships, which have few friends, belonging to solitary type.

The performance of Category B is relatively better than Category A, mainly in their academic scores. But their problem behaviors mainly focus on the following aspects: Firstly, they do not listen carefully in class, whisper, discuss with classmates or just slinking read novel, or secretly admire themselves in the mirror and so on. Secondly, when Category A tease the teacher, or deliberately provoke, they will follow to stir up troubles; when Category A bully other students, they will follow a mild bullying. Thirdly, they are addicted in the internet, which are often caught in internet cafes by parents. They lie to parents that they look for extra tutoring learning from their classmates. Sometimes they also would like to bully some honest classmates, and fight with others. In addition, generally their interpersonal relationship is average; they have several relatively good friends.

Behavior problems of Category C students are relatively much fewer, occasionally they play games in class, read novels, and academic scores are fluctuating. Their performance will improve after positive communication and education, but the condition is repeated. They have poor willpower. Many behavioral problems are mainly due to Category A and Category B students' negative influences.

Secondly, after several lessons' observation on the screened students and a relatively simple inquiry with their classmates and an interview with them as well as their follow-up investigations, I decided to choose ten problem students (6 boys and 4 girls) as study cases, in which 3 students (2 boys and 1 girl) were from Category A, 3 students (2 boys and 1 girl) from Category B, as well as 4 students (2 boys and 2 girls) from Category C.

Methods

Interviews were used to investigate the reasons of the formation of problem students. Based on problem behaviors of study cases, Intervention methods were educational ideas of Humanism Education and Behavior Modification Method. The former emphasizes to take student as the main body and pay attention to their needs, interests, feelings, and attitudes etc. The latter is mainly based on Skinner's operant conditioning and Bandura's social learning theory to deal with the problem behavior.

Regarding absent-minded behaviors in class, the first step is to care about the study cases' physiological needs, and to build up good relationship with study cases, which is prepared for the later depth interviews and entering their inner world. First of all, starting from caring about their physiological needs. The second is to meet the study cases' sense of achievement. The third is to respect the study cases' personality and self-esteem. After establishing good relationship with students, they realize that I am a teacher who care and understand them, therefore I think it is the ripe time for me to chat with them one by one. The next step is to make the study cases realize the seriousness of their problems by facts and figures (Horner, Day & Day, 1997). After building up a good relationship with study cases, I chose a right time to gather them together, and showed them the observation form which had recorded their behaviors in class. Finally, I communicated and cooperated with other teachers to help the study cases, and gave them special courses.

Regarding interpersonal problems, the main reason was that the problem students often make trouble in class and disturb students who want to study and the way they speak is rude, their cranky temper and frequent bully weak and honest students, resulting in poor interpersonal relationship with their classmates. The intervention measures were listed as follow. Firstly, teach them some basic communication skills by chatting with them, and help the study cases to deal with interpersonal issues, so that the study cases can learn how to get along well with other people and realize the importance of good interpersonal relationship. Secondly, I organize class activities, such as class discussions and games, making them involved in class activities to strength their collection sense of honor and increase their understanding of classmates. Thirdly, let the study cases to be aware of their own character defects by the way of bringing out the facts and reasons, citing examples, taking personality test etc.

Regarding willpower problems, I strength the contact with parents, and persuade them to give their children more economic support and teachers, classmates and parents work together to enhance their self-controlability.

After three months, I made tracked records for the intervention effect, using their classmate's observations and interviews with parents and teachers on the study cases.

Results and discussion

The main reason was that their parents tend to use an indifferent and laissez-faire parenting style as listed in Table 1. This result was consistent with that in previous study which had found that severe punishments of parents and neglected indifferent attitudes will cause more children's problem behaviors.

Table 1 The parenting styles for the 10 students

Category A	Students	AM1	AM2	AF1	
	Parenting style	Indifferent	Indifferent	Indifferent	
Category B	Students	BM1	BM2	BF1	
	Parenting style	Authoritarian	Indifferent	Negligent	
Category C	Students	CM1	CM2	CF1	CF2
	Parenting style	Authoritarian	Negligent	Indifferent	Negligent

Based on the interview with the study cases' teacher, substitute teacher, schoolmates and my one-week observation of the classroom behaviors on the study cases, the main causes preventing him from learning are the five kinds of problem behaviors below: the absence of mind in class, distracting, sleeping, talking and joking randomly with other students around them, to spend too much time playing games and to not finish their homework.

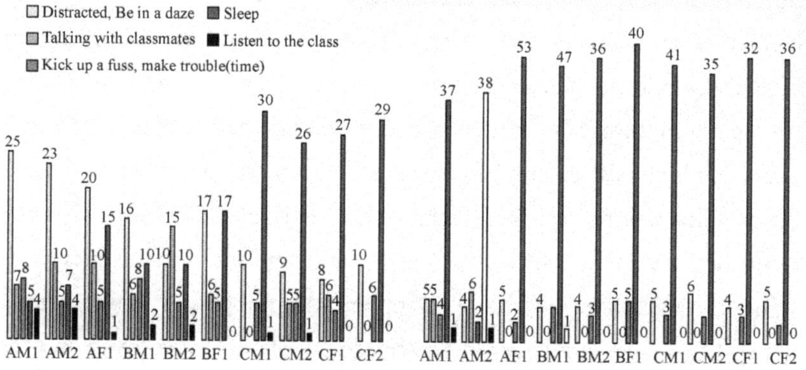

Figure 1 Time distribution of absent-minded behaviors among three kinds of problem students in a 45-min lesson before (left) and after (right) the invention

As listed in Figure 1, the problem students greatly improve their absent-minded problem behaviors in a 45-min lesson. This is because most of their parents have realized their negligence of children and they can better understand children and their teaching methods have changed greatly. Teachers feel that the methods are good enough to be worthy of trying. Classmates notice that they have changed a lot because they are more easily to get along than before. The study cases themselves also feel they have made great progress and led more fulfilling and meaningful life.

Conclusions and Reflections

From the entire process of the fellow-up study, I find that the problem behaviors of study cases are not as serious as my first thought. All teachers hate them mainly because they often make trouble in class, and do not abide by the rules. They discipline the trouble maker with punishment and criticism, which cause case students becoming indulgence and rebellious. With time goes on, they also feel themselves disturbing and annoying. They become so numb, and grow accustomed to the punishment and criticism from teacher. So, it is no wonder that they take the attitude of "abandoning themselves as hopeless and acting recklessly" for their future.

When at home, because of study cases' poor self-control, parents' busyness at work, long absence from home and many children in family, parents are harder to take good care of them and keep the contact with study cases. So, they become disengaged and indulgent. As for their problem of poor grades in school or lack of study discipline, their teachers can't pay too much attention to them or give guidance to their problems because of teacher's limited energy, or inappropriate education methods. At the same time, parents cannot effectively deal with and timely supervise. And students also lack of effective ways to communicate with their classmates. For these kinds of problems, I think, the knocking brick is sincere communication. From the entire research process, I find that giving them basically concerns and respects, and communicating with them equally as they are individuals play the greatest role in the intervention. This discovery not only makes study cases open their mind to me and get along well with me, but also provides foundation for me to put forward and implement the idea of intervention.

As a pupil, their inner world is complicated, no matter how many "problem behaviors" they have, they are eager to be concerned about, to be loved and respected by their classmates and teachers. I am so sorry that sometime it is difficult for me to avoid the mistakes of carrying some inappropriate topics or discussing the topics at the wrong time during the conversation. I hope the study case can forgive me for that kind of mistakes. At the end of the semester, I am really happy and sincerely proud what the study cases have changed. After that, when I calm down, I reflects the days I get along with study cases, I suddenly find that theoretical approaches is important to solve the problem of problem students, but even more importantly, teachers shall have a responsible and respectful attitude of treating all students alike.

After the research, I think a case study is necessary on the matter of problem students by using the method of qualitative research, by which I can enter the inner world of study cases easily and understand their real situations. Based on the qualitative research, it is more easily to find a solution to help study cases out from their problems. What's more, it also makes the theory have more closely connections with the actual relation, which leads an innovative significance.

References

[1] Gershoff E T. Corporal punishment by parents and associated child behaviors and experiences: A meta-analytic and theoretical review. Psychological Bulletin, 2002, 128(4): 539 - 579.

[2] Guajadoa N R, Snyderb G, et al. Relationships among parenting practices, parental stress, child behavior, and children's social-cognitive development. Infant & Child Development, 2009, 18: 37 - 60.

[3] DeCarvalho R J. The Founders of Humanistic Psychology. New York: Greenwood publishing Group, Inc., 1991.

[4] Horner R H, Day H M. Using neutralizing routines to reduce problem behaviors. Journal of Applied Behavior Analysis, 1997, 30(4): 601 - 614.

[5] Campbell S B, Pierce E M. Boys' externalizing problems at elementary school: Pathways from early behavior problems, maternal control, and family stress. Development and Psychopathology, 1996, 12 (3): 19 - 26.

[6] Khine Myint Swe, Fisher Darrell L. Teacher-Student Interactions in Science Classrooms in Brunei. Journal of Classroom Interaction. 2003.

Design and Algorithm Implementation of Children's Arm Motion Detection System

Liang Sheng[1,a], Yangtao Li[1,b], Dongchuan Yu[1,c,*]
[1]Southeast University, Nanjing, 210096, China
[a]shengliangcumt@163.com, [b]klfzlyt@outlook.com,
[c]dcyu@seu.edu.cn
[*]Corresponding author

Keywords: motion capture; sensor; data processing

Abstract: For needs of children's upper extremity movement signal perception, designing a system of multi-dimensional motion capture via Bluetooth wireless transmitting data, to monitor Subjects of upper limbs motion state to study the motion coordination index. The system is based on three-axis acceleration and other sensors to collect multidimensional data, to process it in the use of Cortex-M3, to transmit data via Bluetooth wireless, and achieve portable systems, After weighting algorithm of data real time display in PC, provide the basis for subsequent data analysis. The experiment shows that the system can capture the upper limb motion accurately and easy to carry and operate.

儿童上肢运动检测系统设计与算法实现

盛亮[1,a], 李杨韬[1,b], 禹东川[1,c,*]

[1]东南大学儿童发展与学习科学教育部重点实验室,江苏,南京,210096

[a]shengliangcumt@163.com, [b]klfzlyt@outlook.com,

[c]dcyu@seu.edu.cn

[*]通讯作者

关键词:运动捕捉;传感器;数据处理

中文摘要:针对儿童上肢运动信号检测的需要,设计一种通过蓝牙传输数据的多维运动捕捉系统,监测被试的上肢运动状态,研究其协调运动指标。本系统基于三轴加速度等传感器进行多维数据采集,以 Cortex-M3 为核心进行处理,通过蓝牙传输数据,实现便携式操作,通过权值算法后的数据在 PC 机上实时显示,为后续数据分析提供依据。实验证明该系统可以较好地捕捉手臂运动状态,且方便携带与操作。

1 引言

人体协调运动研究既是技能学习、行为科学、运动控制等众多学科的基础理论问题,又在机器人运动科学、儿童技能发展和运动训练等领域具有很大应用空间。人体上肢运动最为复杂、灵活,对上肢协调运动的分析与探究和许多前沿研究领域相关,研究儿童上肢的协调运动对儿童早期发展与健康成长具有重要的意义。近年来关于上肢协调运动的成因、特征表现、量化和研究手段等方面形成研究热点,研究成果显著。早在很久以前澳大利亚的 Daen 等就提出了“上肢意愿运动协调模式”。后来美国 Jaric 等进行多种任务需求的触点运动实验研究。近些年的 Mitnitski 和 Marin 等对上肢协调运动模式做了很多实验研究,这些实验主要分析上肢与躯干之间的整体性协调关系[1],但没有具体研究上肢协调运动的相关指标。这些实验也局限于探索上肢运动中共有的协调特征,实验方法主要是做一些固定的几个动作,在往复运动中分析运动规律或肌电变化。为了更加全面地、准确地、深入地对上肢协调运动进行研究,对上肢空间运动信息的实时采集很有必要,利用这些量化的数字信息,通过数学方法来研究协调运动指标,就具有了重要的意义。因此本文设计了基于 STM32 的便携式上肢多维运动捕捉系统,这为儿童早期发展和教育的评测方法提供了一个方案。

本文重点在于设计出便携式运动捕捉设备和能实时处理数据的上位机系统,通过群传感器进行准确的上肢运动数据采集,在 STM32 上进行数据算法处理,由蓝牙以无线的方式把捕捉的动作数据传输到上位机实时显示并存储运动数据以便长期跟踪研究。本系统是为后续理论研究实验方案提供的一个采集、数据处理设备。

2 系统架构设计

基于对模拟电路和 PCB 设计以及对电磁兼容特性的研究，设计出了运动捕捉的便携式硬件设备，底层用 STM32 基于 ST 库编写各器件的驱动代码以及数据传输代码，利用 C#在 Winform 上编写了上位机来处理由下位机传输来的九轴运动数据，通过数据变换以及利用权值算法，在上位机得到了较为满意的运动信息，通过拟合出的三轴数据可以实时显示上肢运动的细微变化。该运动捕捉系统结构如图 1 所示，在电路设计时，因为三轴地磁传感器（HMC5883）、三轴陀螺仪（ITG-3200）和三轴加速度传感器（LIS3DH）的 I2C 传输速率满足最低 I2C 总线速率要求，因此它们可以并行挂载在 IIC 总线上。通过 I2C 的总线仲裁机制实现数据的有效传输，数据采样频率为 5 000 Hz，经过 STM32 处理过的数据由串口 1 通过蓝牙并向安装了蓝牙设配器的上位机传输数据，在上位机可以显示平滑的运动曲线。串口 1 以有线的方式与上位机对接，避开蓝牙，用于测试系统。系统结构如图 1。

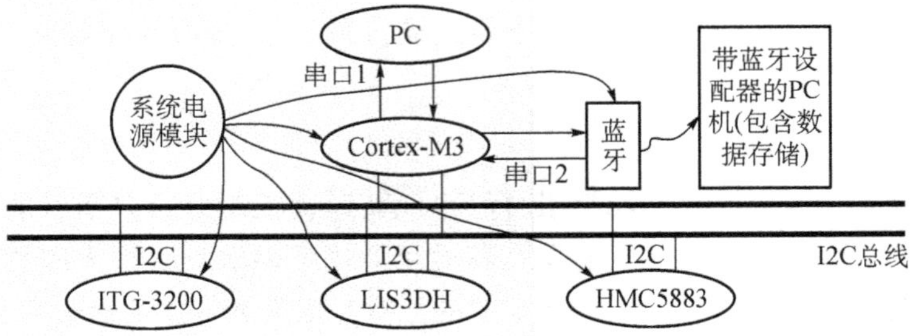

图 1 系统总体结构图

3 系统分析

3.1 系统的核心电路设计

基于 Cortex-M3 内核的 STM32 系列具有低成本、高性能和低功耗特点，这就为实时采集处理数据提供了保障。本系统通过蓝牙与 PC 机进行通信，蓝牙采用 GFSK 技术，通信协议采用 TDMA 时分多址协议，是一种支持设备短距离通信（一般 10 m 内）的无线电技术。在进行 PCB 设计时，三个传感器的信号易受到干扰，因此它们共用一个数字地（GNDA），系统的其他模块电路共用模拟地（GND），最后用 0 阻值电阻进行全 PCB 板地线连接。布线时，STM32 可以不用外部晶振，在蓝牙模块使用中其高频部分不附铜并且尽量不走线[2]。系统的核心电路设计如图 2 所示，三个传感器共同连接在 I2C 总线上。

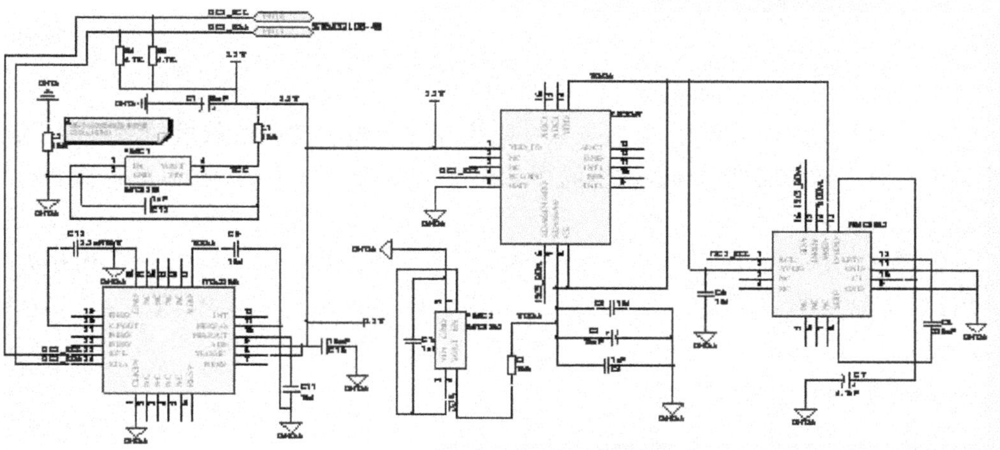

图2　系统核心电路设计图

3.2　系统的多维运动数据捕捉策略

为了更准确地测出手臂的动作,系统运用了三个集成度很高的传感器。加速度传感器重量轻、体积小,在未知物体运动方向的情况下检测空间的加速度,可以准确全面地反映上肢的运动性质。陀螺仪可以检测物体旋转,它对机械运动不敏感但会发生漂移。地磁传感器利用霍尼韦尔各向异性磁阻(AMR)技术,在没有磁场的状况下,材料的电流场为线性状,有磁场时矢量将偏移,材料电阻值增加,从而可以检测出物体的航向角。加速度器测量的惯性力由重力引起,也可由物体的加速度运动产生,它对一般的机械噪声和震动很敏感,为了使加速度器输出更平滑,需要陀螺仪来修正[3]。陀螺仪可以测量沿几个轴的运动角速度,与加速度传感器协同配合,再配合能矫正设备磁场干扰的地磁传感器,这样我们就能得到一个相对准确的测量信息,这就能准确地检测儿童上肢的运动情况了。

4　数据处理算法及软件实现

4.1　STM32对采集数据数字滤波的算法设计

FIR数字滤波器经常用来过滤时间离散信号,对抽样数据的时域信号经傅立叶变换到频域滤波。FIR采用非递归的滤波方式,具有输出稳定的特点并且它在获得严格线性相位特性的同时满足幅频要求。

FIR滤波器主要是设计出系数矩阵 $h[k]$,通过对采集信号的分析设计出低通滤波器和窗函数,利用Matlab的FDATool工具就可以得到这个系数矩阵了。N 阶FIR滤波器的系统函数 $H(z)$ 为:

$$H(z) = \sum_{k=0}^{M} h[k]z^{-k} \tag{1}$$

FIR 滤波器的频率响应为：

$$H(e^{j\Omega}) = \sum_{k=0}^{M} h[k]e^{-jk\Omega} \tag{2}$$

随着滤波器阶数的增加，幅度函数在阻带和通带振荡的波纹数量随之增加，为了使 FIR 的频率响应逼近理想滤波器的频率响应，我们加了 Kaiser 窗，以下是我们设计的 $h[k]$：

$h[k]$ = [0.010 1, −0.000 4, −0.026 9, −0.044 6, −0.015 3, 0.077 4, 0.202 1, 0.291 9, 0.291 9, 0.202 1, 0.077 4, −0.015 3, −0.044 6, −0.026 9, −0.000 4, 0.010 1]

其相频特性和幅频特性如下：

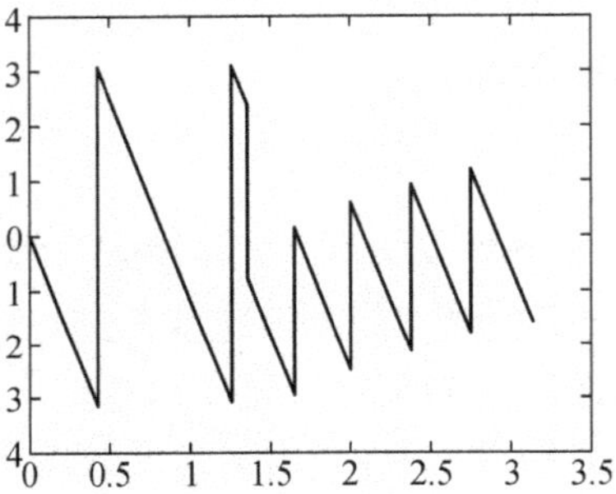

图 3　离散系统相频特性曲线

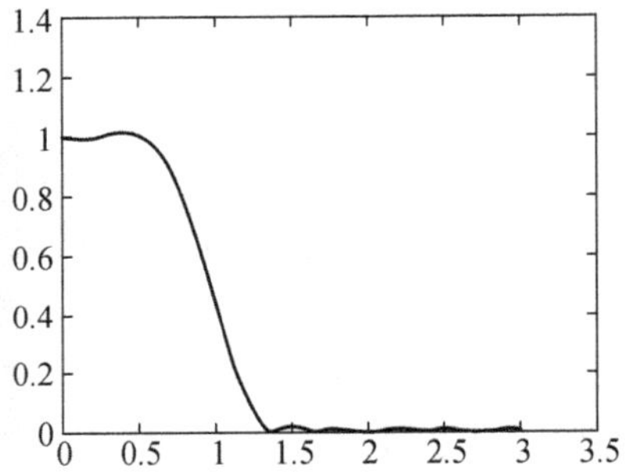

图 4　离散系统幅频特性曲线

4.2　PC 机上的数据融合算法

我们得到 Racc-加速度计读取的当前值、Rgyro-当前陀螺仪读取值和 Rhmc-地磁传感器的当前值。更新融合值 $Rst(n)$，我们利用它们的加权平均值得到：

$$Rst(n) = (R_{Acc} * w_1 + R_{Gwr_0} * w_2 + r_{Hmc} * w_3)/(w_1 + w_2 + w_3) \tag{3}$$

分子、分母同除以 w_1，公式简化为：

$$Rst(n) = (R_{Acc} + R_{Gwr_0} * w_2/w_1 + r_{Hmc} * w_3/w_1)/(1 + w_2/w_1 + w_3/w_1) \tag{4}$$

令 $w_2/w_1 = w_{Gyro}$，$w_3/w_1 = w_{Hmc}$，分别为我们对加速度器和陀螺仪的相信程度及对加速度器和地磁传感器的相信程度。这两个值根据经验确定在 5—20 之间。由最新得到的估算值还需再量化一次：

$$Rxt(n) = (Rx_{Acc} + Rx_{Gyr_0} * w_{Gyr_0} + Rx_{Hmc} * w_{Hmc})/(1 + w_{Gyr_0} + w_{Hmc}) \tag{5}$$

$$Ryt(n) = (Ry_{Acc} + Ry_{Gyr_0} * w_{Gyr_0} + Ry_{Hmc} * w_{Hmc})/(1 + w_{Gyr_0} + w_{Hmc}) \tag{6}$$

$$Rzt(n) = (Rz_{Acc} + Rz_{Gyr_0} * w_{Gyr_0} + Rz_{Hmc} * w_{Hmc})/(1 + w_{Gyr_0} + w_{Hmc}) \tag{7}$$

标准化矢量：

$$R = \sqrt{Rxt(n)^2 + Ryt(n)^2 + Rzt(n)^2} \tag{8}$$

$$Rx(n) = Rxt(n)/R \tag{9}$$

$$Ry(n) = Ryt(n)/R \tag{10}$$

$$Rz(n) = Rzt(n)/R \tag{11}$$

根据这样的数据我们就可以在 PC 机上实时显示运动动态了。

4.3 软件设计

底层 STM32 上和 PC 机 winform 平台上软件设计流程图如下:

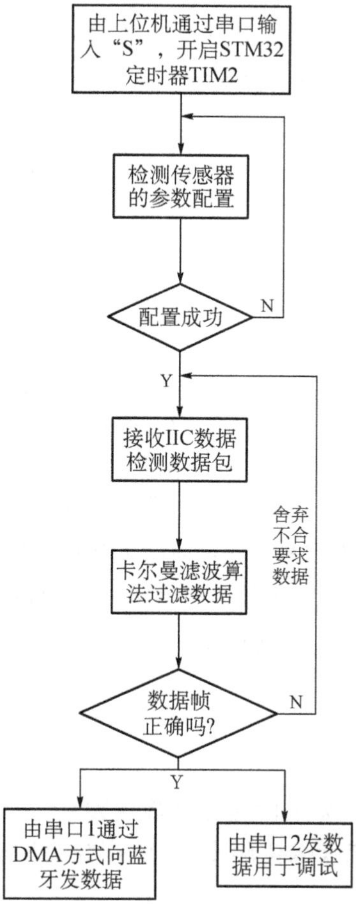

图 5 下位机程序流程图

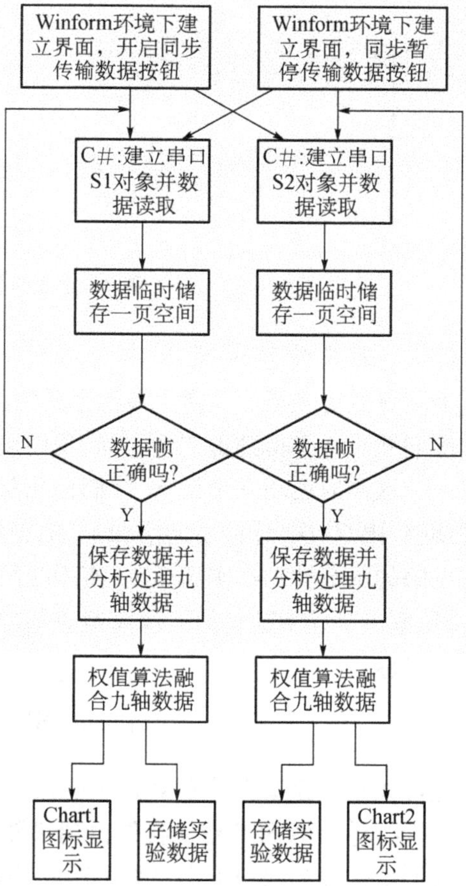

图 6 PC 机上程序设计流程图

5 数据采集及分析算法

5.1 实验数据采集

如图 7 所示,在被试的左右手臂各佩戴一个检测设备。图中为开启设备状态,蓝牙匹配成功后指示灯处于常量状态,设备传输数据时系统首先进行平衡校准,双臂持平并检查设备在保持平衡状态时的实时曲线,若 X、Y、Z 轴不在平衡零点,那么就在程序中修改参数,使这两个设备在不运动且平衡放置的情况下拟合后的 X、Y、Z 三轴都保持在平衡零点。双臂在空间的一个维度运动,在上位机的对应轴上会出现明显的运动规律曲线,由实验可以看出经过滤波算法处理后的数据,输出较为稳定和平滑,达到了设计目的。图中,运动曲线下方的两个曲线图为运动向量图,用来显示上肢运动的平稳性,这可以实时监测手臂在运动时的节奏性。

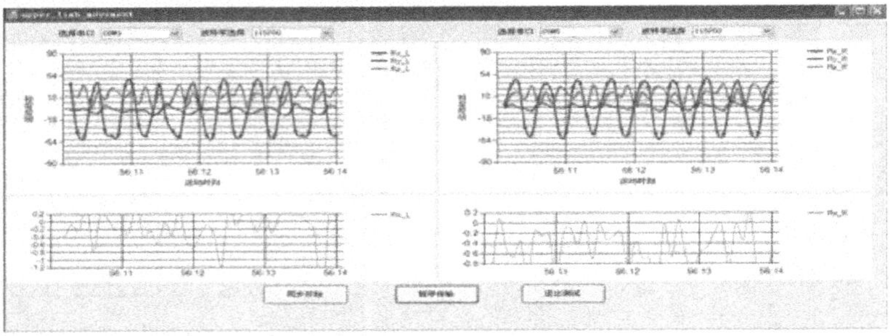

图 7　上位机显示运动数据

5.2　数据分析算法设计

为了有效地表征出儿童上肢运动的协调性,我们设计了三个指标:精确度,稳定性以及协同性。为了得到这三个指标,我们设计了一个实验方案:让儿童左右手腕各自携带一个这样的运动采集设备,我们让儿童在一分钟内做完 120 次反手正手动作(次数可调整,由 60 次/分钟逐渐增加)。电脑给出示范性动作,每分钟做 120 次,让儿童跟着电脑的示范性动作来做运动,实验时间为 3 分钟[5]。由图 7 所示时间轴为触发时间 t_1,儿童正手反手运动的运动曲线正值向负值运动过零点时间设为 t_2,由此可得出准确度指标:

$$\delta = \frac{1}{n}\sum_{i=1}^{n}(|t_1 - t_2|) \tag{12}$$

通过离散快速傅立叶变换 FFT 变换,我们得到 X 轴上的角速度峰值频率,以此作为稳定性指标。由 FFT 变换我们得到 Z 轴上的加速度峰值频率,以此作为协调性指标。我们由这些算法可以得出如下图的分析样图:

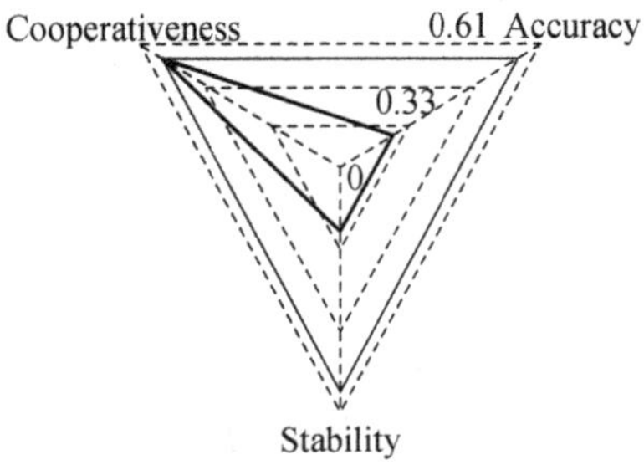

图 8　运动数据三指标分析图

图 8 所示最外围三角形框表示一个标准的协调运动基线,我们做了一组实验数据得出图 8 内部的三角形图例,由图中我们可以直观地分析出,这个运动的协同性比较好,而准确性和稳定度得分较差。

6 结论

对儿童上肢协调运动的研究有助于发现儿童在运动协调方面的缺陷,以便进行医学干预。对上肢运动的研究越深入,其用途也会更加广泛。本文利用成熟的传感器技术,设计出了上肢数据采集处理设备,文中也给出了数据算法处理方案。通过反复矫正和改进设备,目前该设备能正确地捕捉上肢运动信息并实时在 PC 机上处理显示。当然,本文对儿童上肢协调运动的研究方案也有许多不足之处,在以后的实验中会慢慢改进。本文介绍了系统的总体设计和数据的处理算法,最后也给出了部分实验情况,实验结果表明该便携式系统的稳定性满足实验需求,这有助于检测儿童的先天性发育不良以及小脑的共济失调,对儿童早期进行医学治疗提供了一定的科学依据。

References

[1] Yang yiyong, Wang rencheng, et al. Progress in the study on synergetic control principle of human upper extremity and related issues. Journal of Biomedical Engineering, 2003, 20(4): 738-741.

[2] Pillage L T, Rohrer R A, Visweswariah C. Electronic circuit and system simulation methods. New York: McGraw-Hill, 1955.

[3] Li, et al. Based on six accelerometer gyroscope drift compensation algorithm study. Journal of Sensors and Micro Systems, 2009, 28 (12): 42-44.

[4] Xu jingshuo, et al. Adaptive kalman filter fading factor selection method research. Journal of systems engineering and electronics, 2005, 26(11): 1153-1154.

[5] M Kaneko, H Okui, et al. Aging Curve of Neuromotor Function bu Pronation and Supination of Forearms using Three-dimensional Wireless Acceleration and Angular Velocity Sensors. Annual International Conference of the IEEE, 2012: 4676-4679.

The Mediation Effect of Adolescents' Study and Interpersonal Stress on the Relationship between Positive School Climate and Depression

Youyun Xu[1,a], Huihua Deng[1,b,*]

[1] Key Laboratory of Child Development and Learning Science of Ministry of Education, Southeast University, Nanjing, China, 210096

[a]youyunxu@126.com, [b]dengrcls@seu.edu.cn

[*] Corresponding author

Keywords: stress; positive school climate; depression; senior high school students

Abstract: In order to investigate the effect of school climate on adolescents' depression, this study focused on a mediation effect of adolescents' study stress and interpersonal stress. The variables were self-reported by 431 adolescents from a senior high school with Perceived School Climate Questionnaire, Adolescent Self-Rating Life Events Checklist and Self-rating Depression Scale. SPSS16.0 and AMOS17.0 were used to analyze the data. Results showed that classmate support and depression scores of Female students were significantly higher than male students; interpersonal stress of male students was significantly higher than Female students. School climate not only had a direct influence on depression, but also suppressed adolescents' depression indirectly through the mediation effect of adolescents' stress.

高中生学习和人际压力在积极学校氛围和抑郁关系中的作用

许有云[1,a],邓慧华[1,b,*]
[1]东南大学儿童发展与学习科学教育部重点实验室,南京,江苏,中国
[a]youyunxu@126.com,[b]dengrcls@seu.edu.cn
[*]通讯作者

关键词:压力;积极学校氛围;抑郁;高中生

中文摘要:为了考察高中阶段青少年所感知到的学校氛围与其抑郁的关系,本研究关注了高中生的学习压力和人际压力在其中的中介作用。采用问卷法,调查431名高中生所感知的学校氛围、压力和抑郁;采用SPSS16.0和AMOS17.0进行数据统计分析。结果显示,女生的同学支持和抑郁得分均显著高于男生;男生的人际压力显著高于女生。学校氛围既可直接负向预测抑郁,也可通过缓解压力感从而负向预测抑郁。

1 引言

学校氛围(School Climate)是指学校中被成员所体验并对其行为产生影响的相对持久而稳定的环境特征[1]。目前已有大量的研究关注学校氛围对于学校适应性的影响,但是大多数研究关注的是学校氛围与学业成绩的关系,这些证据也为研究学校氛围和抑郁之间的关系提供了间接证据。诸如近期的研究发现,当学生在校园中受到他人的支持,体验到安全感,往往会出现更高的学业成就[2]。在对包括中国在内的大样本中发现学校氛围对学生的数学成绩具有显著地预测作用[3]。除了以上研究学校氛围对学业成就直接效应的,也有研究探讨学校氛围对适应性的作用机制。有研究发现学校依恋在学校氛围与学业成就之间起到中介作用[4,5]。积极的学校氛围对适应性的影响还表现在学校氛围可以显著地降低青少年自杀的意念意图[6],而自杀意念和意图本身就是抑郁的重要表现之一,所以该研究也为积极学校氛围与抑郁之间的关系提供了间接证据。基于以上分析得出假设1:学校氛围可以负向预测青少年抑郁,也就是说感受到更多的教师同学支持和获得更多的自主权利,可以降低青少年抑郁的风险。

在青少年学生群体感受到的人际关系和学习压力表现最为明显和突出[7],同时大量研究发现男女生在对生活事件的感知方面存在显著性差异。青少年生活事件量表具有较高的测量学指标和中学生的适应性,在这些研究中压力事件对于青少年抑郁的影响已得到证实。但是生活事件和生活事件的影响不同,压力事件是客观存在的,而这些压力事件对于个体的影响是具有个体差异性的主观感受,所以有必要在研究中将此进行区分。据此可以推断得出假设2:对于压力事件的感受可以预测抑郁,同时

学校氛围在学生对压力事件的感受上也具有直接的预测作用。

综上可知,积极的学校气氛作为一种学生发展的保护性因素,它对抑郁影响的作用机制目前还不清晰,是否会受到学生对压力事件感受的中介作用的影响则需进一步验证。学校氛围和负性生活事件均影响抑郁,但是目前尚没有研究基于一个完整的框架内对学校氛围、生活事件和抑郁三者之间的关系进行考察。从间接证据可以得出假设3:积极的学校氛围可以通过抑制负性压力事件的影响而作用于青少年抑郁。

2 研究方法

2.1 研究对象

整群抽取南京某一般中学高一学生,共460人,剔除有作答明显规律或者缺失超过三分之一的被试,获得有效被试431人,其中男生178人,女生253人,男女人数差异未达到显著性水平。研究开始前在征得研究对象同意后获得研究对象监护人(父亲或母亲)的书面知情同意。以班为单位,由经过统一培训的心理学专业硕士生进行集体施测,施测时间不超过30分钟。

2.2 研究工具

2.2.1 学校氛围问卷

该问卷由Jia等人(2009)修订,该问卷分为三个维度:教师支持,包含7个项目,如"我能对老师讲我的困难和问题";同学支持,包含12个项目,如"同学们相互帮助";自主机会,包含5个项目,如"学生对学校的事情有发言权"。该问卷在中美青少年样本的研究中发现具有跨文化的适应性[8],在国内近期有研究也证实了该问卷适用于中国中学生人群[6]。

在本研究中问卷修订后的结构效度良好,验证性因素分析的拟合指数:$\chi^2/df=3.06$,$TLI=0.84$,$CFI=0.85$,$RMSEA=0.067$。各维度的a系数为0.784(教师支持)、0.849(同学支持)、0.710(自主机会)。

2.2.2 生活事件量表

该量表由刘贤臣(1987)等编制[9]。该量表由27项可能给青少年带来心理反应的负性生活事件构成,分为人际压力、学习压力、受惩罚、丧失、健康适应、其他6个维度。鉴于已有研究发现学习压力和人际压力是青少年学生最主要的两种压力,所以本次研究重点只关注学习压力和人际关系2个维度。学习压力和人际压力a系数分别是0.732、0.719。

2.2.3 抑郁自评量表

该量表由Zung于1965年编制[9],用于衡量抑郁状态的轻重程度。量表由20个条目组成,每个条目相当于有关症状,按1—4级评分。该量表在中国具有较好的信效度。本次研究中Alpha系数为0.760。

2.3 共同方法偏差

本研究中，问卷均由被试自我报告，这可能会导致预测变量与结果变量因同一报告源而出现共同方法偏差的问题。本研究在施测的过程中采用反向计分题、平衡项目顺序、匿名问卷和增加多个问卷施测的间隔等方式来进行程序控制。在数据回收后，又采用 Harman 单因子检验的方法，将研究变量纳入一个探索性因素分析中，检验未旋转的因素分析结果，结果表明未旋转和旋转都得到 17 个因子特征根大于 1，未旋转得到的第一个因子解释的变异量为 14.83%，旋转得到的第一个因子解释的变异量为 8.71%，皆远小于 40% 的临界值。因此，共同方法偏差的影响并不严重。

2.4 测试过程

以班级为单位，由研究者本人和经过统一培训的研究生担当主试。采用 SPSS16.0和 amos 进行数据的录入和分析。

3 结果分析

3.1 变量的初步分析和相关

除了性别外的其他变量均是 likert 计分方法，所以将性别作为哑变量，与其他变量一起进行了相关分析。结果详见下表。

表 1 各变量的描述统计和相关分析结果

	M	*SD*		1	2	3	4	5	6
1. 性别	0.590	0.493							
2. 学习压力	3.554	0.929	*r*	−0.014	1				
			p	0.777					
3. 人际压力	2.665	0.905	*r*	−0.169***	0.432***	1			
			p	0.000	0.000				
4. 教师支持	2.761	0.496	*r*	0.004	−0.196**	−0.184***	1		
			p	0.928	0.000	0.000			
5. 同学支持	3.315	0.387	*r*	0.113*	−0.321***	−0.299**	0.385***	1	
			p	0.019	0.000	0.000	0.000		
6. 自主权利	2.071	0.615	*r*	0.014	−0.131**	−0.095	0.434***	0.285***	1
			p	0.781	0.007	0.053	0.000	0.000	
7. 抑郁	39.215	7.410	*r*	0.145**	0.405**	0.327**	−0.384***	−0.368***	−0.194***
			p	0.004	0.000	0.000	0.000	0.000	0.000

注:性别为虚拟变量，女生 =1，男生 =0，均值表示女生所占比例; $^{*}p<0.05$, $^{**}p<0.01$, $^{***}p<0.001$，下同。

从上表可以看出，学校氛围各分维度与抑郁均呈显著的负相关，学习压力和人际压力与抑郁是正相关。性别与人际压力、同学支持和抑郁均有显著的相关，进一步的独立样本 t 检验发现，女生的同学支持和抑郁显著高于男生，而人际压力显著低于男生。抑郁与压力事件呈显著的正相关，而抑郁与学校氛围的各个维度之间均呈显著的负相关，尤其是同学支持和教师支持维度达到了中等程度的相关。

3.2　人际压力和学习压力在学校氛围与抑郁之间的中介作用

为了检验人际压力和学习压力在学校氛围对抑郁影响过程中的中介效应，采用结构方程模型进行分析。根据中介效应检验程序[10]，先分析学校氛围对抑郁的直接效应，然后检验加入中介变量后模型的拟合情况及各路径系数的变化显著程度。直接效应的模型拟合指数：$\chi^2/df = 4.10$，$CFI = 0.99$，$TLI = 0.93$，$RMSEA = 0.085$。直接效应的路径分析发现，学校氛围对抑郁的路径系数显著（$r = -0.50$，$p < 0.001$），说明学校氛围可以直接负向预测抑郁。

在学校氛围与抑郁之间同时加入人际压力和学习压力这两个变量后，模型的各项拟合指数良好（$\chi^2/df = 1.64$，$CFI = 0.99$，$TLI = 0.98$，$RMSEA = 0.039$），说明该模型可以接受。对模型中的各个路径进行分析（见图 1），结果发现学校氛围对抑郁的路径（$r = -0.37$，$p < 0.001$）、学校氛围分别对人际压力和学习压力的路径（学校氛围 - 人际压力 = -0.22，$p < 0.001$；学校氛围 - 学习压力 = -0.24，$p < 0.001$）、人际压力和学习压力分别对抑郁的路径（人际压力 - 抑郁 = 0.13，$p < 0.01$；学习压力 - 抑郁 = 0.13，$p < 0.001$）都非常显著。这一结果说明，学校氛围既可以直接负向预测抑郁，也可以通过抑制人际压力和学习压力对抑郁发挥作用，即人际压力和学习压力分别在学校氛围与抑郁之间起着部分中介作用。

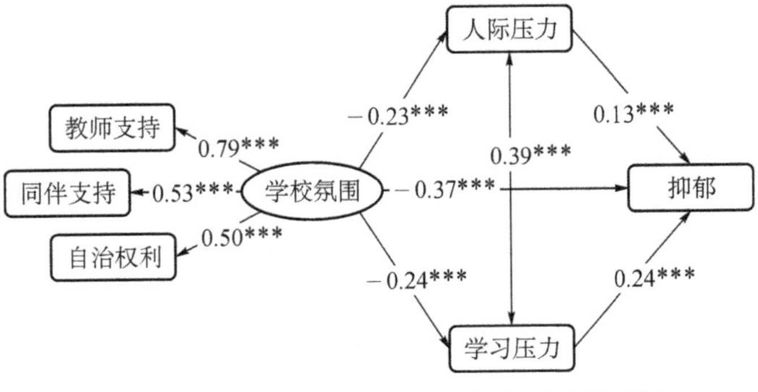

图 1　压力事件中介学校氛围对抑郁影响模型图

为了检验中介效应的显著性，采用 Bias-Corrected Bootstrap 程序进行检验（Preacher & Hayes, 2008）。首先利用重复随机抽样的方法在原始数据（$N = 431$）中抽取 5 000 个 Bootstrap 样本，然后根据这些样本拟合图 1 的模型，生成并保存 5 000 个中介效应的估计值，形成一个近似抽样分布，将这些效应值按数值大小排序，用第 2.5 百分位数和第97.5百分位数估计95%的中介效应置信区间。如果中介效应95%的置信区间没有包括0，表明中介效应显著。使用Bias-Corrected Bootstrap方法得到学校氛围通过人际压力对抑郁的间接效应95%置信区间为-0.084至-0.025之间、学校氛围通过学习压力对抑郁的间接效应95%置信区间为-20.116至-20.037之间，这些结果上述中介效应显著。中介效应值为-20.088[(-20.200.13)+(-0.240.24)]，占总效应的19.1%。

4 讨论分析

本研究发现抑郁的性别差异与以往研究是一致的，青少年期的女生较男生有更多的抑郁风险，这可能与女性的生理激素水平和应对压力的风格都有较大的关系。

在研究中发现人际压力的影响存在显著的性别差异，男生感受到更高的人际压力，但是在学习压力上男女生并无显著差异，这与对初中生群体研究结果[11]不尽相同。高一学生处于青春后期，高中同学之间交往深度要高于初中同学，而这种深入的交往可能需要更多情感沟通，但是男生对此可能并不擅长。同时无论是男生还是女生，高中生活的最大任务就是参加高考，这使所有同学都需要保持对学习的高度重视和对自己成绩的关注，男女生都有类似的表现，从而使得初中发现的学习压力的性别差异在高中阶段不再显现。

本次研究发现了学校氛围与抑郁的关系，高的学习压力和人际压力会增加抑郁的风险，同时发现积极的学校氛围可以缓解学生的压力感，从而减少抑郁。高中生的高考一直被家庭、学校和社会所强调，同时高一学生还处于青春后期，还出现对人际关系的关注和对异性的好奇，这些人际和学习压力客观存在，但是如果处于充满支持的民主的学校氛围中，这些客观事件所带来的影响就会被缓解，甚至可以变压力为动力。这个研究结果说明，在目前高中生普遍压力较大的情况下，可以通过营造积极民主的学校氛围，师生之间、同学之间提供更多的人际支持，学校给予学生更多的民主选择的机会，以此减少高中生出现抑郁的风险。

5 结论

（1）女生的同学支持和抑郁得分均显著高于男生；男生的人际压力显著高于女生。

（2）学校氛围既可直接负向预测抑郁，也可通过减轻压力感而负向预测抑郁。积极的学校氛围除了直接减少青少年抑郁外，也可通过缓解学生的人际和学习压力感水平而减轻青少年抑郁。

References

[1] W K Hoy, J W Hannum. Middle school climate: An empirical assessment of organizational health and student achievement. Educational Administration Quarterly, 1997, 33: 290-311.

[2] J Cohen, L McCabe, N M Michelli, et al. School climate: Research, policy, practice, and teacher education. The Teachers College Record, 2009, 111: 180-213.

[3] P P Zhang, L Y Li, T Xin. Cross-cultural comparison of linkage between school climate and students' mathematical achievement: A multilevel analysis. Psychological Development and Education, 2011, 6: 625-632.

[4] Z Z Bao, W Zhang, D P Li. School climate and academic achievement among adolescents: A moderated mediation model. Psychological Development and Education, 2013(1): 61-70.

[5] Z J Teng, Y L Liu, Y G Pan, et al. Media violence and aggression: A social cognitive neuroscience perspective. Psychological Development and Education, 2013(6): 664-672.

[6] X Yang, Y H Wang, D P Li, et al. School climate and adolescents suicidal ideation and suicide attempts: The mediating role of self-esteem. Psychological Development and Education, 2013(5): 541-555.

[7] X H Ding, J S Wang. A study on the relationship between life events and anxiety among secondary school students. Chinese Mental Health Journal, 2002, 16: 788-790.

[8] Y Jia, N Way, G Ling, et al. The influence of student perceptions of school climate on socioemotional and academic adjustment: A comparison of Chinese and American adolescents. Child development, 2009, 80: 1514-1530.

[9] X D Wang, X L Wang, H Ma. Rating Scales for Mental Health: Expanded Edition. Beijing: Chinese Mental Health Journal Publisher, 1993.

[10] Z L Wen, L Chang, K T Haui, et al. Testing and application of the mediating effects. Acta Psychologica Sinica, 2004, 36: 614-620.

[11] H Chen, Z B Liang, P Zhong, et al. Longitudinal study of life events in early adolescents in Nanjing. Chin J School Health, 2012, 33: 427-430.

议 题

神经科学视野下儿童社会情绪能力发展的研究

What Can We Learn from the Longitudinal and Genetically Informed Study of Birth Cohorts? Findings from Two Quebec Cohorts

Michel Boivin

Canada Research Chair on Child Social Development at the School of Psychology of Laval University

Longitudinal studies are key to examining developmental processes. However, many of the long-standing studies lack information on the early years and on family process. A new generation of prospective longitudinal studies have raised the ante regarding the heuristics of developmental research by describing developmental trajectories from birth on, and by taking advantage of natural experiment to more precisely document the role of gene-environment interplay and family processes. This presentation will review findings from the Quebec Longitudinal Study of Child Development (QLSCD) and the Quebec Newborn Twin Study (QNTS), two ongoing longitudinal birth cohorts of infants from Quebec that have been prospectively assessed since age 5 months. These findings will illustrate the extent to which (1) developmental trajectories are established very early in life; (2) early child and family risk factors reflecting adversity predict these trajectories, (3) a complex and dynamic gene-environment interplay underlies these trajectories, and (4) early childhood programs and services can change these trajectories. The implications of these finding for our understanding of early developmental processes, as well as for prevention and child and family policies, will be discussed.

The Behavioral Features and Brain Mechanisms of Emotional Cognition in Infants

Yuejia Luo
Institute of Affective and Social Neuroscience, Shenzhen University

The current measurement of the behavioral, electrophysiological and blood oxygen level dependent (BOLD) signals provides a rich source of information about the neural mechanisms underlying ongoing cognitive events in the infants' brain. The goal of this lecture is to give an introduction and to provide an overview of how neuroscience methods can be used to elucidate brain and cognitive development in infants in the aspect of emotion, social cognition, language, learning, mathematics, music, and movement cognition.

More importantly, we introduction a novel emotional voice experiment carried out in our lab. Appropriate processing of human voices with different threat-related emotions is of evolutionarily adaptive value for the survival of individuals. Nevertheless, it is still not clear whether the sensitivity to threat-related information is present at born. Using an oddball paradigm, the current study investigated the neural correlates underlying automatic processing of emotional voices of fear and anger in sleeping neonates. Event-related potential data showed that the frontocentral scalp distribution of neonatal brain could discriminate fear voices from anger voices; the mismatch response (MMR) was larger in response to the deviant stimuli of anger, compared with the standard stimuli of fear. Furthermore, this fear-anger MMR discrimination was observed only when neonates were in active sleep state. Although the neonates' sensitivity to threat-related voices is not likely associated with a conceptual understanding of fearful and angry emotions, this special discrimination in early life may provide a foundation for later emotion and social cognition development.

Early Experience, Brain Development, and Early Childhood Education

Nathan A. Fox
Distinguished University Professor
University of Maryland

A great deal of discussion and debate surrounds the issue of the importance of the first years of life on fostering adaptive brain and behavioral development. Preparing young children for school and providing them with an optimum environment for learning should be critical issues for a society in which children are the future scientists, workers, and educators. In this talk I will briefly review the data on the effects of early experience on brain and behavioral development and the evidence for sensitive periods during which experience plays a critical role. A framework for thinking about society's role in early childhood education will be presented.

Development and Social-Cultural Learning of Cooperation: Sharing Behaviors in China's Only Children and Children with Siblings

Liqi Zhu

Institute of Psychology of the Chinese Academy of Sciences

China's one-child policy makes it a special field to study the prosocial behavior of the only child. There is a great concern in the society that the only child would be more self-centered for being spoiled. In a longitudinal study conducted in rural China where there are almost equal numbers of only children and children with sibling, we examined the development of 960 young children's sharing behavior towards friends or strangers in a dictator game. The study examines the developmental origin of reciprocal altruisms. We hypothesize that social relationships besides kinship start with strangers and then differentiate into reciprocal friendship. Only children although may be more self-centered but would have a higher need for friendship than children with siblings. Results showed that most of the 3-4-year-old children in rural areas have behaved more altruistically, measured by willingness to share stickers with both friends and strangers. However, two years later, the same children became more willing to share with friends but less willing to share with strangers. These findings suggest a human developmental trend towards favoritism of reciprocal relations or cronyism, starting as early as age 3. We found no significant difference in the sharing behavior between only children and children with siblings, indicating a higher need for friendship and social networking for the only children than children who have siblings.

Maternal Depression Moderates Effects of Early Child Emotionality on Parenting Styles

Ying Zhu, Yapeng Liu, Yinping Zhang, Guangzhen Zhang, Zongbao Liang, Huihua Deng[a,*]

Key Laboratory of Child Development and Learning Science of Ministry of Education, Southeast University, Research Center for Learning Science, Southeast University, Nanjing 210096, China

[a] dengrcls@seu.edu.cn

[*] Corresponding author

Keywords: child emotionality; maternal depression; parenting style

Abstract: This study examined maternal depression as a moderator of the effect of early child emotionality on parenting styles of 301 mothers. Mothers rated child emotionality and self-reported their depression at children age of 6 months, as well as their parenting styles at children age of 24 months. Results revealed that both child negative emotionality and maternal depression negatively predicted maternal positive parenting style, while child positive emotionality positively predicted maternal positive parenting style. When mothers displayed low depression, both child positive and negative emotionality significantly related to maternal negative parenting style.

Introduction

Parenting styles are defined as "parents' attitude, values and behavior about rearing"[1]. Previous studies emphasized that parenting styles have significant effects on child future development. However, ecological system theory and the theories of determinants of parenting emphasized that children themselves are not passive receptacles for environmental influence, and their characteristics as an independent subsystem play an important role in dictating parental parenting styles[2]. Among child characteristics, early child temperament might be an important factor influencing parenting styles. As Rothbart defined, child temperament is constitutionally based individual difference in reactivity and self-regulation, influenced over time by heredity, maturation, and experience[3]. Child emotionality, including both positive and negative emotionality, is the key component of reactivity, which develops particularly rapidly during early childhood[4].

Recently, some studies start to consider the effect of child temperament on parenting styles. However, the conclusions are not always consistent. Some studies have shown that child positive emotionality promotes positive parenting styles and reduces negative parenting styles, and negative emotion has opposite effects[5-7]. In contrast, Scaramella et al. (2008) found that children's level of distress did not predict change in harsh parenting responses[8]. Kopala-Sibley et al. (2012) also found that child temperament did not predict maternal rejection and control[9]. The key reason for the inconsistency might be that the effect of maternal psychological attributes was ignored in the above studies.

Belsky (1984) proposed that among all determinants, maternal psychological characteristics should be the most influential and should buffer the effect of child psychological characteristics on parenting styles[2]. As differential susceptibility model predicted[10], the interaction between environment and characteristics influences individual future development. In other words, whether, how, and how much child temperament (as environment for mother) influences maternal parenting may depend on the maternal psychological characteristics. Among psychological attributes, maternal depression received the most attention[2]. Individuals with high depression showed a tendency to immerse themselves in negative state. However, only a few cross-sectional studies have tested the moderating effect of maternal depression on association of child emotionality and parenting style. For instance, Kopala-Sibley et al. (2013) found that child temperament correlated with maternal control only in mothers with low self-esteem (i. e. high depression)[9]. Therefore, a longitudinal research needs to examine moderates effects of maternal characteristics (e. g. depression) between child emotionality and parenting styles (including both positive and negative parenting styles).

This study utilized a longitudinal design for examining the role of child emotionality and maternal depression in infancy and their interaction in predicting maternal parenting styles at toddler age. In the previous, most of studies had been focused on older children. This study pays more attention on infants and toddlers because experience during early childhood has a significant effect on outcomes in the future[11]. We expected that maternal depression could moderate the effect of child temperament on parenting styles and hypothesized that the effect was particularly pronounced for low level of maternal depression.

Materials and Method

Participants

Participants were obtained from a large longitudinal international study, Nanjing Metro Baby Project. A total of 301 mothers and child (154 boys and 147 girls) participated in this research.

Procedure

Data were collected at two assessment time points. When children were 6 months old, mothers rated child positive and negative emotionality, and self-reported their own depression. When children were 24 months old, mothers self-reported their parenting styles.

Measures

Child emotionality was assessed with the infant behavior questionnaire (IBQ)[12]. Each item in IBQ describes a specific infant reaction. Mothers were asked to indicate on a 5-point Likert-type scale how often in the past week each response occurred. It showed good reliability and validity in Chinese population[13]. This study focused on 26-item child emotionality including three subscales, distress to limits, fear, smiling and laughter. Negative emotionality combined by distress to limits and fear subscales showed Cronbach's alpha coefficient at 0.60 and positive emotionality (i. e., smiling and laughter subscale) showed Cronbach's alpha at 0.62.

Maternal Depression was assessed with depression subscale of 5-point Likert SCL-90 that showed good reliability and validity in China[14]. Cronbach alpha of depression subscale was 0.87 in this study.

Maternal parenting styles were assessed with the adopted Child-Rearing Practices Report Q-Sort (CRPR) that consists of 91 socialization statements. The measure has been proved to have good reliability as well as construct validity in Chinese population[15, 16]. This study merged punishment and rejection into negative parenting style and set acceptance as positive parenting style. Cronbach's alpha coefficients of negative and positive parenting styles were 0.77 and 0.73.

Statistical methods

Hierarchical multiple linear regression was conducted to examine the main effects of child emotionality and maternal depression, as well as interactions (emotionality × depression) on parenting style. Child gender was controlled in Step 1, followed by child negative and positive emotionality in Step 2, maternal depression in Step 3, and the interactions in Step 4.

Results

As listed in Table 1, child negative emotionality and maternal depression positively predicted negative parenting style, and negatively predicted positive parenting style. Child positive emotionality positively predicted positive parenting style. The effect for negative parenting style was qualified by a significant interaction of child emotionality and maternal depression.

Table 1 Child emotionality, maternal depression and their interaction as predictors of parenting styles

	Negative parenting style		Positive parenting style	
	ΔR^2	β	ΔR^2	β
Step 1	0.005		0.001	
Child gender		−0.067		−0.027
Step 2	0.031**		0.037**	
Negative emotionality (NE)		0.159**		−0.137*
Positive emotionality (PE)		−0.062		0.125*
Step 3	0.083***		0.014*	
Maternal depression (MD)		0.293***		−0.120*
Step 4	0.035**		0.004	
NE × MD		−0.138*		0.036
PE × MD		0.110*		−0.048

Notes: *$p < 0.05$, **$p < 0.01$, ***$p < 0.001$. ΔR^2 is the change of the square of the correlation coefficient and β is standardized regression coefficient.

To probe the nature in the interaction between child emotionality and maternal depression, we estimated the simple slopes for mothers with low depression (−1.5*SD* below the mean) and high depression (+1.5*SD* above the mean), respectively. As depicted in Figure 1 (the left one), the simple slope was significant for mothers with low depression ($b = 0.32$, $t = 3.21$, $p < 0.01$), but it was not significant for mothers with high depression ($b = -0.10$, $t = -0.93$, ns). As depicted in Figure 1 (the right one), the simple slope was significant for mothers with low depression ($b = -0.15$, $t = -2.04$, $p < 0.05$), but it was not significant for mothers with high depression ($b = 0.10$, $t = 1.31$, ns).

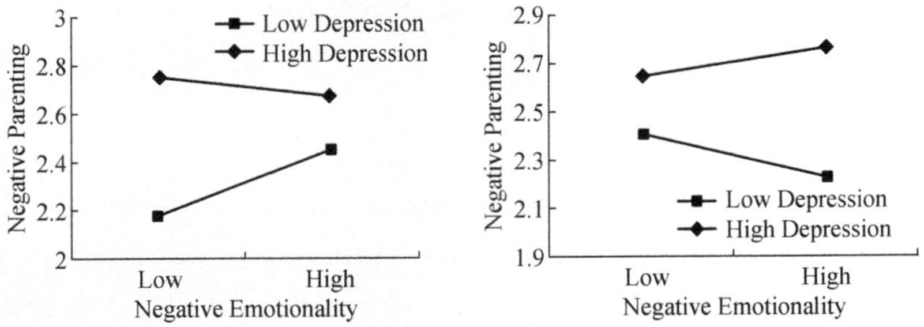

Fig. 1 Maternal depression as a moderator of association between child emotionality and negative parenting style. Left: negative emotionality and right: positive emotionality.

Discussion

This study found that maternal positive parenting style was directly increased by child positive emotionality and directly decreased by child negative emotionality. It was consistent with earlier result[7]. Lengua et al. (2005) found that child positive emotionality positively predicted maternal acceptance[7]. These results indicated that child positive emotionality always directly elicited maternal positive parenting style. If mothers have loving heart to child, whether mothers prefer to show positive parenting depends on child regardless of their own psychological attribute. In addition, this study found that maternal negative parenting style was directly increased by child negative emotionality.

This study found that maternal depression directly increased maternal negative parenting style and decreased maternal positive parenting style. This is consistent with previous cross-sectional study showing that maternal neuroticism promotes maternal negative parenting style[17]. These results indicated that maternal depression predicted parenting beyond the variance accounted for by child emotionality even though child temperament was important to understand maternal parenting.

More importantly, this study found that maternal depression moderates the effect of child positive and negative emotionality on maternal negative parenting styles. Both positive and negative child emotionality predicted negative parenting only for mothers with low depression. This finding was consistent with previous finding that child dominance (temperament) predicted maternal control only when mothers has low self- esteem[9], which is negative related to depression. Mothers with high depression immersed in their own negative emotions so that they might not be influenced by external environment keenly and instantly. In contrast, mothers with low depression perceive child emotionality accurately and timely, so that their child emotionality can predict maternal parenting significantly. Therefore, relevant research in the future needs to consider moderating effect of maternal personal psychological attributes, or take it as a control variable at least.

There were some limitations in this study. All variables were reported by mothers, which may cause common method bias. This research focused on mothers with the exclusion of fathers. Much research work needs to be done in the future. However, the current results add to the extant body of research and have certain theoretical and practical significance.

Acknowledgement

This study is supported by the Cultivation Fund of the Key Scientific and Technical Innovation Project, Ministry of Education of China (704025), the Research Innovation Project in Universities Graduate Students of Jiangsu Province (CXLX13_115) and the Special Funds of Basic Scientific Research Operating Expenses in the Central University.

References

[1] D Baumrind. Current patterns of parental authority. Developmental Psychology Monograph, 1971, 4: 1-103.

[2] J Belsky. The determinants of parenting: A process model. Child Development, 1984, 55: 83-96.

[3] M K Rothbart. Measurement of temperament in infancy. Child Development, 1981, 52: 569-578.

[4] M K Rothbart. Temperament, development, and personality. Current Directions in Psychological Science, 2007, 16: 207-212.

[5] D J Bridgett, M A Gartstein, S P Putnam, et al. Maternal and contextual influences and the effect of temperament development during infancy on parenting in toddlerhood. Infant Behavior & Development, 2009, 32: 103-116.

[6] J Laukkanen, U Ojansuu, A Tolvanen, et al. Child's difficult temperament and mothers' parenting styles. Journal of Child and Family Studies, 2014, 23: 312-323.

[7] L J Lengua, E A Kovacs. Bidirectional associations between temperament and parenting and the prediction of adjustment problems in middle childhood. Applied Developmental Psychology, 2005, 26: 21-38.

[8] L V Scaramella, S L Sohr-Preston, S P Mirabile, et al. Parenting and children's distress reactivity during toddlerhood: An examination of direction of effects. Social Development, 2008, 17: 579-595.

[9] S Kopala, C Daniel, D C Zuroff, et al. The determinants of negative maternal parenting

behaviors: Maternal, child, and paternal characteristics and their interaction. Early Child Development and Care, 2012, 182: 683-700.

[10] J Belsky, J B Marian, H Marinus. For better and for worse: Differential susceptibility to environmental influences. Current Directions in Psychological Science, 2007, 16: 300-304.

[11] B B Lahey, C A Van Hulle, K Keenan, et al. Temperament and parenting during the first year of life predict future child conduct problems. Journal of Abnormal Child Psychology, 2008, 36: 1139-1158.

[12] M K Rothbart. Measurement of temperament in infancy. Developmental Psychology, 1981, 52: 569-578.

[13] H Yu, M H Zhang, X Y Chen, et al. Study of the consistency and its influence factors between laboratory observation and maternal- report on infant temperament. Psychological Development and Education, 2011, 27: 247-254.

[14] Z Y Wang. Self-report symptom inventory-symptom checklist 90. Shanghai Archives of Psychiatry, 1984, 2: 68-70.

[15] X Y Chen, P D Hastings, K H Rubin, et al. Child rearing attitudes and behavioral inhibition in Chinese and Canadian toddlers: A cross-cultural study. Developmental Psychology, 1998, 34: 677-686.

[16] X L Ding, G Z Zhang, L Z Bao, et al. The relation among behavioral inhibition, maternal parenting and toddlers' behavioral problem. Psychological Development and Education, 2013, 29: 174-182.

[17] C L Smith. Multiple determinants of parenting: Predicting individual differences in maternal parenting behavior with toddlers. Parenting: Science and Practice, 2010, 10: 1-17.

Study on Clinical Efficacy of Early Development in High-risk Infants by Health and Education Partnership

Xinglian Liu, Qiong Dai, Haiqing Xu[a,*]

Department of Children Health Care, Hubei Hospital of Maternal and Children, Wuhan, 430070

[a]xuhq0526@ yahoo. com. cn

[*] Corresponding author

Keywords: high-risk infant; early intervention; Health and education partnership; emotion

Abstract: Objectives: To explore a better way of early intervention on High-risk infants. Methods: One month old infants with high risk who were followed-up in out-patient clinic from June 2010 to January 2011 were enrolled in the research. Group of education with medical treatment (140 cases), group of medical treatment (142 cases), group of health control (125 cases). Children in three groups were evaluated their Mental development and Psychomotor development in 6、12 and 24 months old. Children in three groups were evaluated their emotional sociality in 24 months old. Results: Mental that of in the medical treatment group in different ages ($p<0.05$); motor development index in the education with medical treatment group were dramatically improved than that of in the medical treatment group in 6 and 12 months old ($p<0.05$); No different of MDI and PDI between in the education with medical treatment group and in the health control group. The positive ratio of four dimensions of toddler emotion in the education with medical treatment group were dramatically reduced than that of in the medical treatment group in 24 months ($p<0.01$). No different of the positive ratio of extroversion region, introversion region and imbalance region between the education with medical treatment group and the health control group ($p>0.05$). But the positive ratio of ability region was dramatically reduced than that of in the health control group ($p<0.05$). Conclusions: Comparison with simple medical treatment, Patten of early intervention of education with medical treatment can promote mental development, social-association ability and good emotion development of high-risk infants to a great extent.

医教结合促进高危儿早期发展的临床效果研究

刘兴莲，戴琼，徐海青[a,*]
湖北省妇幼保健院，湖北，武汉，430070
[a]xuhq0526@yahoo.com.cn
*通讯作者

关键词：高危儿；医教结合；早期干预；情绪

中文摘要：

【目的】探索一种更有效的早期干预方法，促进高危儿早期康复和身心全面发展。

【方法】选取2010年6月—2011年1月在湖北省妇幼保健院儿童保健科高危儿门诊进行随访的1个月的高危儿为研究对象。高危儿医教结合140例，医学干预组142例，健康对照组125例。6、12、24月龄时三组进行智力和运动发育测评，24月龄时进行幼儿情绪社会性评估。

【结果】医教结合组各月龄MDI均高于医学干预组（$p<0.05$），6、12月龄PDI均高于医学干预组（$p<0.05$），与健康对照组比较MDI与PDI均无统计学差异（$p>0.05$）。24月龄医教结合组幼儿情绪4个维度的阳性率均明显低于医学干预组（$p<0.01$）；与健康对照组比较，外化、内化、失调三个维度的阳性率无统计学差异（$p>0.05$），能力域阳性率医教结合组低于健康对照组（$p<0.05$）。

【结论】医教结合的早期干预模式，可更大程度地促进高危儿智力发展、早期社会交往能力及良好情绪形成。

【中图分类号】R722

【文献标识码】A

1 前言

围产期高危儿发育偏离的表现是多方面的，除体格发育外，还有心理、语言及随年龄增加表现愈加明显的情绪行为问题、学习障碍、运动协调障碍等方面[1]。但对后者偏离，仅靠医学干预并不能完全解决，教育干预有自身优势，可以有效弥补医学干预不足。医教结合是发育行为儿科学的必然趋势。医疗和教育的结合在发育行为障碍的诊治中是一条捷径和坦途[2,3]。如何在高危儿早期干预这一领域，将医疗和教育进行完美结合，将这些干预措施融合为一个完整体系，使高危儿无论近期还是远期发育偏离得到全面的最佳干预效果，国内未见一家机构有这方面的研究和探索。为此，本研究旨在从高危儿长远的生存质量出发探索一种更有效的干预模式。

2 研究对象及方法

2.1 研究对象

选取2010年6月—2011年1月在湖北省妇幼保健院儿童保健科高危儿门诊进行随访的月龄为1个月的高危儿为研究对象。高危儿定义参照《儿科学》第7版的诊断标准。本研究涉及的主要高危因素包括:羊水污染、宫内生长迟缓、宫内缺氧、高龄产妇、妊高征、新生儿窒息、早产、低出生体重、颅内出血、缺血缺氧性脑病等。对纳入的高危儿,根据家长自愿的原则设立医教结合干预组(140例,男75,女65)、医学干预组(142例,男78,女64);同时在儿保门诊按性别因素配比,抽取同期出生的无任何高危因素的婴儿作为健康对照组(125例,男67,女58)。

2.2 研究内容与评价方法

2.2.1 智力发育和运动发育评估

三组儿童6、12、24月龄时,采用由中国儿童发展中心修订的《婴幼儿智能发育检查》(CDCC)进行智力发育和运动发育评估。测评结果记录智力发展指数(MDI)和运动发展指数(PDI)。将CDCC测评结果分为六个等级,得分130以上为非常优秀、120—129为优秀、110—119为中上、90—109为中等、80—89为中下、70—79为临界状态、69以下为智力缺陷。

2.2.2 情绪社会性评价

采用已经标化的《中国12—36个月幼儿情绪社会性发展》量表[4]对24个月幼儿进行外化(反映活动性/冲动性、攻击性/反抗性)、内化(忧郁/退缩、焦虑等)、失调(睡眠、负性情绪等)和能力(依从性、移情、注意力等)4个维度的情绪社会性评价。评分方法:首先计算出每个维度的原始分,然后转化为T分;外化、内化及失调维度>63分为阳性,能力维度<37分为阳性。

2.3 早期干预方法

2.3.1 高危儿医教结合组干预模式

建立高危儿专案,实行系统管理,平均1—2个月高危儿门诊随访一次:① 神经—运动检查:采用由鲍秀兰主持修订的"0—1岁52项神经运动检查表"对高危儿进行脑瘫筛查。② 神经—心理发育评估:采用CDCC进行智力发育和运动发育评估,并根据综合评估结果给高危儿提供个性化早期干预方案;③ 康复训练:由医生采用鲍秀兰教授编导的《0—2岁婴幼儿运动落后和姿势异常的家庭康复训练法》进行康复训练,并指导家长坚持家庭训练;④ 早期发展训练:采用在儿保医生的指导下,由接受过医学培训的高级婴幼教师根据3岁前婴幼儿身心发育特点和各种能力发展的关键期,再结合每个高危儿当前发育水平和医学评估结果专门设计的亲子活动游戏课程[5]。该课程采取团课(每周1—2次)和个训课(每日1次)相结合的形式,由教师引导,家长和孩子共同参与,在轻松愉快的氛围中发展高危儿的大运动、精细动作、适应能力、语言、社会交往能力,同时传授家长育儿知识和技能。

2.3.2 高危儿医学干预组和健康对照组的干预模式

对医学干预组儿童,除了不参与早期发展训练外,其余干预措施同医教结合组。健康对照组记录基本资料,按照体检规定程序进行常规检查。

2.4 统计分析

资料输入后,采用 SPSS11.0 版统计软件进行分析,采用χ^2 检验和方差分析等统计方法。

3 结果

3.1 各组儿童一般情况及可比性

3.1.1 医教结合组和医学干预组高危因素分布情况

经统计学分析,医教结合组和医学干预组的高危因素分布情况经卡方检验,差异无统计学意义($\chi^2=9.047$,$p=0.538$),两组资料具有可比性(见表1)。

表1 医教结合组和医学干预组高危因素分布情况 [n(%)]

高危因素	医教结合组	医学干预组
早产	25(17.85)	22(15.49)
低出生体重	13(9.28)	12(8.45)
窒息	10(7.14)	8(5.64)
早产+低出生体重	11(7.85)	9(6.34)
缺血缺氧性脑病	5(3.57)	6(4.23)
颅内出血	4(2.86)	2(1.40)
窒息+颅内出血	5(3.57)	4(2.81)
先兆流产	15(10.71)	18(12.67)
羊水污染	13(9.28)	15(10.56)
高胆红素血症	21(15.00)	23(16.19)
前置胎盘	9(6.43)	12(8.45)
宫内窘迫	9(6.43)	11(7.75)
合计	140	142
χ^2	9.047	
P	0.538	

3.1.2　各组儿童失访情况

随访过程中,因各种原因医教结合干预组失访7人,医学干预组失访7人,健康对照组失访8人,各组失访率均<5%。随访至2周岁时,医教结合组133人,医学干预组135人,健康对照组117人。

3.1.3　各组儿童一般情况的比较

医教结合组男童75人、女童65人,医学干预组男童78人、女童64人,健康对照组男童67人、女童58人,经比较,性别分布无显著性差异($\chi^2=0.865, p>0.05$)。

将三组儿童父母的文化程度划分为三个等级:大学及以上、大专、高中及以下,分别比较三组间父母文化程度等级分布情况,经统计学分析,三组儿童的父亲文化程度差异无显著性($\chi^2=1.597, p>0.05$),母亲文化程度差异无显著性($\chi^2=3.212, p>0.05$)。见表2。

表2　各组儿童父母文化程度分布　[n(%)]

项目	医教结合组	医学干预组	健康对照组
父亲			
大学及以上	38(27.14)	36(25.35)	30(24.00)
大专	55(39.28)	59(41.54)	53(42.40)
高中及以下	47(33.57)	45(31.69)	42(33.60)
母亲			
大学及以上	32(22.85)	28(19.71)	28(22.40)
大专	55(39.28)	54(38.02)	44(35.20)
高中及以下	53(37.85)	58(40.84)	53(42.40)

3.1.4　各组儿童智力发展指数(MDI)和运动发展指数(PDI)的比较

表3显示,经方差分析,三组儿童MDI差异均有统计学意义($p<0.05$),三组儿童1岁以内PDI差异均有统计学意义($p<0.05$)。经SNK-q检验,医教结合组各月龄MDI均高于医学干预组($q_{6月}=5.23, q_{12月}=4.67, q_{24月}=6.53, p_{均}<0.05$),和健康对照组比较差异无统计学意义($q_{6月}=2.77, q_{12月}=5.62, q_{24月}=4.58, p_{均}>0.05$)。医教结合组6、12月龄PDI均高于医学干预组($q_{6月}=5.98, q_{12月}=7.65, p_{均}<0.05$),24月龄PDI两组比较差异无统计学意义($q=2.35, p>0.05$),各月龄PDI与健康对照组比较差异无统计学意义($p>0.05$)。医学干预组儿童6月龄MDI、PDI均低于健康对照组($qMDI=7.53, qPDI=6.65, p_{均}<0.05$),12月龄PDI与健康对照组差异无统计学意义($q=3.23, p>0.05$),而MDI低于健康对照组($q=8.57, p<0.05$),24月龄MDI、PDI与健康对照组比较差异无统计学意义($p>0.05$)。

表 3　三组间智力和运动发展指数的比较

组别	月龄	例数	*MDI*	*F* 值	*p*	*PDI*	*F* 值	*p*
1	6	140	89.67 ±8.03			88.58 ±8.46		
2	6	142	85.89 ±10.97 *ΔΔ			85.33 ±10.24 *Δ		
3	6	125	90.21 ±9.61			90.50 ±9.01		
1	12	138	95.52 ±9.12			94.34 ±9.55		
2	12	139	90.76 ±11.89 *Δ	36.574	<0.05	90.68 ±11.23 *	46.514	<0.05
3	12	123	95.58 ±10.02			92.85 ±9.24		
1	24	133	102.79 ±13.86			99.73 ±13.45		
2	24	135	96.64 ±16.91 **	30.427	<0.05	98.64 ±14.52	20.458	>0.05
3	24	117	99.25 ±15.95			100.86 ±11.46		

注:组别 1 为医教结合组,2 为医学干预组,3 为健康对照组。
* 表示医教结合组与医学干预组的比较,* 表示 $p<0.05$,** 表示 $p<0.01$;Δ 表示医学干预组与健康对照组的比较,Δ 表示 $p<0.05$,ΔΔ 表示 $p<0.01$。

3.1.5　24 月龄各组儿童智力发育指数等级分布

表 4 显示,医教结合组均未发生智力缺陷,医学干预组和健康对照组均有不同比例智力缺陷的发生。同时,处于智力发育临界状态的儿童,医教结合组的比例均低于健康对照组和医学干预组。

表 4　24 月龄三组智力发育指数等级分布　[n(%)]

智力发展指数等级	医教结合组		医学干预组		健康对照组	
	例数	百分比(%)	例数	百分比(%)	例数	百分比(%)
非常优秀	0	0.0	0	0.0	0	0.0
优秀	3	2.2	0	0.0	4	3.4
中上	13	9.8	5	3.7	12	10.3
中等	87	65.4	70	51.8	71	60.6
中下	25	18.8	49	36.4	24	20.5
临界	5	3.8	8	5.9	5	4.3
智力缺陷	0	0.0	3	2.2	1	0.9

3.1.6　24 月龄时各组幼儿情绪社会性评价的比较

表 5 显示,医教结合组幼儿情绪四个维度阳性率均明显低于医学干预组($\chi^2_{外化}=87.11$,$\chi^2_{内化}=29.15$,$\chi^2_{失调}=23.28$,$\chi^2_{能力}=64.35$,$p_{均}<0.01$)。与健康对照组比较,外化

域、内化域、失调域阳性率差异无统计学意义($\chi^2_{外化}=13.28$,$\chi^2_{内化}=15.49$,$\chi^2_{失调}=14.86$,$p_{均}>0.05$),医教结合组能力域阳性率低于健康对照组($\chi^2=34.75$,$p<0.05$)。医学干预组外化域、失调域、能力域阳性率均高于健康对照组($\chi^2_{外化}=47.14$,$\chi^2_{失调}=35.48$,$\chi^2_{能力}=59.35$,$p_{均}<0.05$),内化域与健康对照组差异无统计学意义($\chi^2=19.05$,$p>0.05$)。

表5　三组间幼儿情绪社会性评价的比较　[n(%)]

维度	组别	例数	阳性例数	阳性率(%)	χ^2值	p值
外化域	1	133	19☆	14.28	84.95	<0.01
	2	135	38	28.15**△		
	3	117	23	19.65		
内化域	1	133	10	7.51	22.38	<0.05
	2	135	20	14.81**		
	3	117	15	12.82		
失调域	1	133	13	9.77	30.14	<0.05
	2	135	27	20.00**△		
	3	117	17	14.53		
能力域	1	133	15	11.27	60.257	<0.01
	2	135	33	24.44**△		
	3	117	22	18.8☆		

注:*表示医教结合组与医学干预组的比较,*表示$p<0.05$,**表示$p<0.01$;△表示医学干预组与健康对照组的比较,△表示$p<0.05$。☆表示医教结合组与健康对照组的比较,☆表示$p<0.05$。

4　讨论

高危儿是指在胎儿期、分娩期和新生儿期存在对生长发育(尤其是脑发育)有危险因素的婴儿。据统计,高危儿占新生儿总数的10%—20%,高危儿有脑损伤的潜在危险,脑损伤将导致脑瘫、智力低下、癫痫及情绪行为异常等疾病,是婴幼儿时期致残的主要病因[6]。0—3岁,中枢神经系统发育最迅速,可塑性最强,代偿能力最好,是脑发育的关键时期,如能提供良好的早期干预,对脑功能和结构的发育都有重要的影响,能发挥其最大的潜能。因此,早期教育工作者如能在医学干预的基础上第一时间介入到高危儿的早期干预工作中,发挥医学及教育对高危儿早期干预不同层面的促进作用,将有助于高危儿身心全面发展。

4.1　医教结合干预模式与儿童智力发展

近年来,脑科学的发展为早期干预奠定了理论依据,国内外许多报道也证明了早期干预对因环境或生物学因素所致的智力落后或高危儿有显著效果[7,8]。国内很多研究结果显示,高危干预组儿童的智力发育指数明显高于高危对照组,进一步证明了对高危儿进行早期干预的效果[9]。本研究在传统医学干预的基础上结合早期教育——亲子游戏课程，经过科学系统的早期干预，结果显示医教结合组儿童各月龄MDI、PDI均高于医学干预组。传统的医学干预方法由于干预过程比较单调和枯燥，儿童易哭闹，家长缺乏长期的依从性，医教结合的干预方法克服了医学干预的缺点，结合早期教育的优势，在轻松愉快的亲子游戏活动中，老师引导家长对孩子进行大运动、精细运动、适应能力、语言、社会交往等五大能区的训练，从而促进高危儿智力发展水平。医教结合组儿童均未发生智力缺陷，医学干预组和健康对照组均有不同比例智力缺陷的发生，更加说明对高危儿采用医教结合干预模式的必要性。

4.2 医教结合干预模式与儿童运动发展

对高危儿在发育的关键期和代偿期进行早期干预，尤其是对一岁之内的婴儿预防和减少脑瘫的发生率，提高人口素质，减轻社会及家庭负担起到了积极作用[10]。本研究结果表明，通过科学系统的早期干预，医教结合组高危儿的MDI和PDI能更早的在一岁以内追赶上健康对照组儿童。而单纯医学干预组高危儿MDI到一岁以后才逐渐追上健康对照组儿童，PDI基本能在一岁达到健康对照组水平。

4.3 医教结合干预模式与儿童情绪

早期是儿童人格和身心发育的关键期，其社会性和情绪发展对今后的成长有着重要的影响。现代神经科学和心理学研究已经证实情绪与儿童认知发展、动机形成、创新能力以及突发性暴力等有关。美国学者研究发现，1—3岁儿童社会情绪行为问题的发生率大约为7%—24%，且问题将持续存在，影响儿童能力的发展。儿童早期情绪和社会性问题有可能预测到小学低年级儿童的情绪行为问题[11-13]。高危儿发育偏离是多方面的，其中包括随年龄增加表现愈加明显的情绪行为问题。本次调查结果显示，医教结合组幼儿情绪4个维度阳性率均明显低于医学干预组。主要表现在儿童攻击性、社会退缩行为及负性情绪明显降低，而注意力和移情明显增强。结果说明在医学干预的基础上结合早期教育，通过亲子游戏活动形式可促进家长和孩子建立和谐的亲子依恋关系，建立儿童早期社会交往意识，同时在干预过程中让家长接受科学、专业的育儿知识和技能，提高家长自身素质和情绪行为能力，从而促进孩子良好情绪行为能力的发展。与健康对照组比较，外化、内化、失调三个维度阳性率无显著性差异，而能力阳性率医教结合组低于健康对照组。进一步证实了亲子游戏无论对高危儿还是健康儿童能力的培养都有重要作用。

本研究证明在高危儿生命体征稳定、各项生理指标基本正常后就应及时进行系统干预，采用医教结合的早期干预模式，通过定期的医学评估、合理的功能训练、轻松愉快的亲子游戏活动，不仅可降低高危儿智力低下和伤残的发生率，还能从更大程度上促进高危儿智力和运动的发展，培养良好的情绪行为能力。从干预和治疗的角度来看，医教结合的模式能增加疗效。总之，高危儿干预是一个系统工程，医教结合干预模式有助于发挥各自优势，合力作用于高危儿，是早发现、早干预的有效途径，有助于高危儿获得身心全面发展,提高高危儿生存质量。今后我们会逐步完善这种医教结合的综合干预模式,增加随访例数及长期追踪随访,探索出适合中国国情的高危儿早期干预模式。

References

[1] Bhutta A T, Cleves M A, Casey P H, et al. Cognitive and behavioral outcomes of school aged children who were born preterm-A meta-analysis. JAMA, 2002, 288(6): 728 - 737.

[2] JING Xingming. The trend of combining medical treatment with education in developmental-behavioral pediatrics. Chinese Journal of Child Health Care, 2008, 16(5): 497 - 506.

[3] SHEN Xiaoming. Health and education partnership for a healthy young generation: China's perspective. Journal of Bio-education,2013, 1(4): 241 - 244.

[4] WANG Huishan, ZHANG Jianduan, HUANG Xiaona. Reliability and validity of standardized chinese version of urban infant-toddler Social and Emotional Assessment(CITSEA) scale. Chinese Journal of Child Health Care,2009, 17(3): 271 - 274.

[5] Joseph Sparling, Isabelle Lewis. The Creative Curriculum? Learning Games (Birth-12 months) Teaching Strategies Incorporated, 2008.

[6] Paramleen Kaur, B S Chavan, Sneh Lata, et al. Early intervention in developmental delay. Indian Journal of Pediatrics, 2006, 73(5): 405 - 407.

[7] N de Souza V, Sardessai K, Joshi, et al. The determinants of compliance with an early intervention programme for high-risk babies in India. Child Care, Health & Development, 2006, 2(1): 63 - 72.

[8] Richard C Adams, Carl Tapia M D. Early Intervention, IDEA Part C Services, and the Medical Home: Collaboration for Best Practice and Best Outcomes. Pediatrics, 2013, 13(4): 1073 - 1088.

[9] McCormick M C, Brooks G J, Buka S L, et al. Early intervention in low birth weight premature infants: Results at 18 years of age for the infant health and development program. Pediatrics, 2006, 117(3): 771 - 780.

[10] Tucker S, Klotzbach L, Olsen G, et al. Lessons learned in translating research evidence on early intervention programs into clinical care. MCN, 2006, 31(5): 325 - 331.

[11] Briggs-Gowan M J, Carter A S. Socia-l emotional screening status in early childhood predicts elementary school outcomes. Pediatrics, 2008, 121(5): 957 - 962.

[12] American Academy of Pediatrics. Identifying infants and young children with developmental disorders in the medical home: An algorithm for developmental surveillance and screening. Pediatrics, 2006, 118(1): 405 - 420.

[13] Campbell S B, Spieker S, Burchinal M, et al. Trajectories of aggression from toddlerhood to age 9 predict academic and social functioning through age 12. J Child Psychol Psychiatry, 2006, 47(8): 791 - 800.

Predictive Models of Autism Spectrum Disorder (ASD) of Children Based on Neuroimaging Technology

Kun Bi[1,a], Chu Liu[1,b], Qing Lu[1,c,*], Zhijian Yao[2,d]

[1]Key Laboratory of Child Development and Learning Science of Ministry of Education, Research Centre of Learning Science, Southeast University, Nanjing 210096, China

[2]Academic Department of Psychiatry, Nanjing Brain Hospital, Nanjing Medical University, Nanjing 210029, China

[a]bk.90@163.com, [b]chuliu1990@gmail.com,

[c]luq@seu.edu.cn (Q Lu), [d]zjyao@njmu.edu.cn (Z. Yao)

* Corresponding author

Keywords: predictive model; autism spectrum disorder; children; feature selection; machine-learning classifier

Abstract: Autism spectrum disorder (ASD) of children is a neurodevelopmental disorder with a wide phenotypic range, often affecting personality and communication. Currently, ASD is diagnosed based on behavioral criteria. Given the VBM and SBM findings, an MR-based diagnostic model holds the promise of enhancing, perhaps complementing, behavioral assessment. The most important parts of the model are feature selection and machine-learning classifier. Many methods of feature selection are applied in the predictive models of ASD of children. First, some useful feature selection methods and classifiers which can be used in this field are introduced. Then many applications are introduced and prove that the predictive model is an effective tool for diagnosis of the autism of children.

1 Introduction

Neuronavigational systems[1] are widely used in conjunction with transcranial magnetic stimulation techniques[2] for thorough investigation of children brain function, and to treat several neurological disorders, such as ASD[1,3,4].

Autism spectrum disorder (ASD) is a neurodevelopmental disorder with a wide phenotypic range, often affecting personality and communication. It is approximately in 1 in 150 children with a prevalence[5]. Children with ASD have impaired communication, language skills, abnormal social behavior and repetitive behavior[6,7]. Affected individuals exhibit stereotypical repetitive movements, restricted interests, lack of impulse control, speech deficits, impaired intelligence and social skills compared to typically developing (TD) children .

Imaging studies have been instrumental in mapping aberrant connections in the brains of ASD children. Several studies revealed both structural and functional connectivity deficits in ASD[8]. In studies of cognition, ASD has been defined as fundamental deficits in central coherence, executive function, and empathizing[3]. MR examination has revealed that children with ASD have subtle structural changes in many brain structures[9]. Some have also reported that anatomical differences in some of these regions are correlated with clinical severity[10].

Many morphological studies of ASD have used voxel-based morphometry (VBM), which measures voxel-wise gray- and white-matter volume changes across the entire brain. These VBM-based studies identified both gray- and white-matter volumetric changes[10]. Differences in gray matter (GM) volume have been reported by several previous studies using "regions of interest" (ROI) approaches involving manually tracing brain regions as well as automated voxel-based morphometry (VBM) of the entire brain[11]. However, VBM cannot directly measure the intrinsic topology due to a 2-D sheet with a highly folded and curved geometry[12]. Surface-based morphometry (SBM), which centers on the computation of cortical topographic measurements, has the potential to provide information complementary to that provided by VBM. SBM can derive features such as regional gray-matter thickness and accuracy rate was based on reclassification of the training set, rather than on cross validation or classification of an independent test set. Other[13] investigated the predictive value of whole brain structural volumetric changes in ASD, using SVM classifiers, and obtained 81% classification accuracy based on cross-validation. A study[14] developed a diagnostic model generated by the LPboost based algorithm to distinguish autistic children from control subjects, based on voxel-wise cortical thickness, based on approximately 40, 000 points for each subject; they reported 89% classification accuracy[15].

Currently, ASD is diagnosed based on behavioral criteria. Given the VBM and SBM findings described above, an MR-based diagnostic model holds the promise of enhancing, perhaps complementing, behavioral assessment. A research[16] entered six preselected brain volume-based features into discriminate analysis and correctly classified 95% of very children with ASD.

For the predictive model, feature selection and machine-learning classifier are most important parts. Feature selection reduces possible classifier overfitting and improve generalization. It is one effective means to identify relevant features for dimensionality reduction. At the same time, machine-learning classifiers are also introduced as follow, the accuracy of the model can be improved by an appropriate classifier.

2 Method

2.1 Feature selection

Many methods of feature selection are applied in the predictive models of ASD of children. Here, some feature selection methods are introduced that have been used in ASD of children and others that can be used in this field.

Feature selection is an important and frequently used dimensionality reduction technique that select a subset of original features according to certain criteria[17,18], reducing possible classifier overfitting and improve generalization. It removes irrelevant, redundant, or noisy data, reduces the number of features, and brings the immediate effects for applications: speeding up a data mining algorithm, and improving mining performance such as predictive accuracy and result comprehensibility. Feature selection is one effective means to identify relevant features for dimensionality reduction . Various studies show that features can be removed without performance deterioration[19].

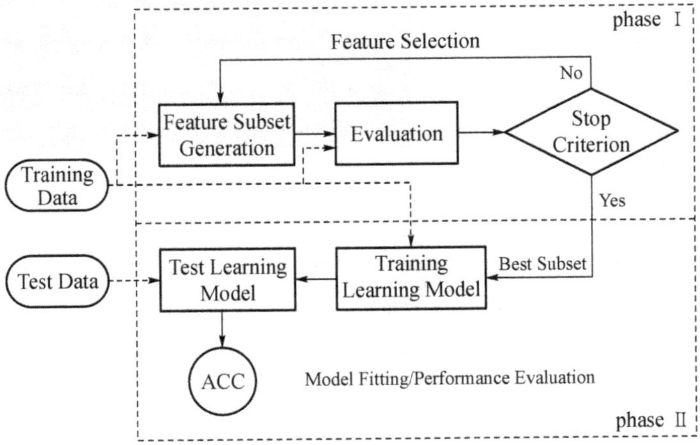

Figure 1 A unified view of feature selection process

Zheng Zhao, et al. Advancing Feature Selection Research—ASU Feature Selection Repository 2010.

PCA

Principal component analysis (PCA) is a statistical procedure . An orthogonal was used to transform to convert possibly correlated variables into the values of linearly uncorrelated variables which called principal components. The first principal component has the largest possible variance . Under the constraint that it is orthogonal to the preceding components, each succeeding component in turn has the highest variance possible. The number of principal components is less than or equal to the number of original variables. When the data set is jointly normally distributed, principal components are guaranteed to be independent. PCA is sensitive to the relative scaling of the original variables. It was used in the feature selection of children ASD[4].

Fisher Score

Fisher Score[20] is used to select features. The different values to samples from different classes and similar values to the samples from the same class for the class labels $y = \{y_1, \cdots, y_n\}$. The evaluation criterion used in Fisher Score can be formulated as:

$$SC_F(f_i) = \frac{\sum_{j=1}^{c} n_j(\mu_{i,j} - \mu_j)^2}{\sum_{j=1}^{c} n_j \sigma_{i,j}^2} \tag{1}$$

Above μ_i is the mean of the feature f_i, n_j is the number of samples in the jth class, and $\mu_{i,j}$ and $\sigma_{i,j}$ are the mean and the variance of f_i on class j, respectively. Fisher Score is a special case of Laplacian Score, when n_l is the number of instances in l-th class and when K is defined as:

$$K_{ij}^{FIS} = \begin{cases} 1/n_l, & y_i = y_j = l \\ 0, & \text{otherwise} \end{cases} \tag{2}$$

Fisher Score is widely applied in many real applications. It is an effective feature selection algorithm[21].

Chi-square Score

Chi-square[22] is used to test of goodness of fit and test of independence. In feature selection, it is used as a test of independence to assess whether the class label is independent of a particular feature. Chi-square score for a feature with r different values and C classes is defined as

$$\chi^2 = \sum_{i=1}^{r} \sum_{j=1}^{C} \frac{(n_{ij} - \mu_{ij})^2}{\mu_{ij}} \tag{3}$$

where n_{ij} is the number for samples with the ith feature value. And

$$\mu_{ij} = \frac{n_{*j} n_{i*}}{n} \tag{4}$$

where n_{i*} is the number for samples with the ith feature value for the particular feature, n_{*j} is the number of samples in class j and n is the number for samples[21].

Kruskal Wallis

Kruskal Wallis test is a non-parametric method. It is based on ranks for comparing the population medians among groups. The first step here is to rank all data points across all groups together. And the measurement can be formulated as:

$$K = \frac{12}{N(N+1)}\sum_{i=1}^{g} n_i\left(r_i - \frac{N+1}{2}\right)^2 = \frac{12}{N(N+1)}\sum_{i=1}^{g} n_i(r_i)^2 - 3(N+1) \qquad (5)$$

From the equation, we can see that the test metric contains only the squares of the average ranks[21].

Gini Index

Gini index[23] is a test for quantifying a feature to distinguish between classes. Given C classes, Gini Index of a feature f can be calculated as

$$GiniIndex(f) = 1 - \sum_{i=1}^{C}[p(i \mid f)]^2 \qquad (6)$$

Gini Index can take the maximum value of 0.5 for a binary classification. Smaller the Gini Index, more relevant the feature. Gini Index of each feature is calculated independently and the top k features with the smallest Gini index are selected[21].

Information Gain

Information Gain[24] is one of the most popular feature selection techniques which calculates dependence between the feature and the class label. It is easy to compute and simple to interpret. Information Gain (IG) of a feature X and the class labels Y is calculated as:

$$IG(X,Y) = H(X) - H(X \mid Y) \qquad (7)$$

Entropy(H) is a measure of the uncertainty associated with a random variable. $H(X)$ and $H(X \mid Y)$ is the entropy of X and the entropy of X after observing Y, respectively.

$$H(X) = -\sum_{i} P(x_i)\log_2(P(x_i)) \qquad (8)$$

$$H(X \mid Y) = -\sum_{j} P(y_i)\sum_{i} P(x_i \mid y_i)\log_2(P(x_i \mid y_i)) \qquad (9)$$

A feature with a high information gain is relevant. Information gain is evaluated independently for each feature and the features with the top-k values are selected as the relevant features[21].

Minimum-Redundancy-Maximum-Relevance (mRMR)

Minimum-Redundancy-Maximum-Relevance (mRMR) selects features that are mutually far away from each other, while they still have "high" correlation to the classification variable. mRMR is an approximation to maximizing the dependency between the joint distribution of the selected features and the classification variable.

For discrete variables, the relationship between two variables x and y are defined as

$$I(x,y) = \sum_{i,j} p(x_i,y_i)\log\frac{p(x_i,y_i)}{p(x_i)p(y_i)} \quad (10)$$

Where $p(x, y)$ is their joint probabilistic distribution and $p(x)$ and $p(x)$ are the respective marginal probabilities. The goal of the minimum redundancy condition is to select those features that are most dissimilar. If we denote S as the subset of features and $|S|$ as the number of features in S, then the minimum redundancy condition is

$$\min W_1, W_1 = \frac{1}{|S|^2}\sum_{g_i,g_j\in S} I(g_i,g_j) \quad (11)$$

The aim of the maximum relevance condition is to maximize the total relevance of all features in S:

$$\max V_1, V_1 = \frac{1}{|S|}\sum_{i\in S} I(h,g_i) \quad (12)$$

Where $I(h,g_i)$ represents the mutual information between the targeted classes $h = \{h_1, \cdots, h_k\}$ and the features g_i. We optimized the conditions in Eq. (11) and (12) simultaneously using the following criterion function:

$$\max(V_1 - W_1) \quad (13)$$

In this algorithm, the first feature is selected according to Eq. (12), and the remaining features are selected in an incremental way (that is, the features that were selected earlier remain in the feature set). If m features are selected for set S, the additional features are selected from the remaining set using the criterion function shown in Eq. (13)[25].

2.2 Machine-Learning classifier

Machine-Learning classifier is important for the predictive model. Now introduce some classifier that have been applied for ASD of children.

support vector classifier(SVM)

The most popular machine-learning method for the prediction of children disorder is the support vector classifier[3,4,26]. The basic SVM is linear classifiers, assuming separable data. The SVM separates the classes by constructing a hyperplane with maximal margin, which is defined by the distance from the hyperplane to the nearest data points of the classes[27]. It can be proven that this particular solution has the highest generalization ability[3].

SVM can be expressed as follows. Assume each training samples Z_n, $N = 1, \cdots, N_s$, which belongs to a label $c_n \in \{1, -1\}$. Then a linear classifier $g(z) = w^T z + b$ is sought, such that:

$$w_T z_n + b \geqslant 1 \text{ if } c_n = +1$$
$$w_T z_n + b \leqslant -1 \text{ if } c_n = -1 \quad (14)$$

These two constraints can be rewritten into one inequality:

$$c_n(\mathrm{w}^{\mathrm{T}}\mathrm{z}_n + \mathrm{b}) \geqslant 1 \quad (15)$$

The gradient vector of $g(z)$ is w. Therefore, the square of the margin is inversely proportional to $\|w\|^2 = w^T w$. To maximize the margin, we have to minimize $\|w\|^2$. Using Lagrange multipliers, we can incorporate the constraints Eq. (15) into the minimization:

$$L = \frac{1}{2}\|w\|^2 + \sum_{n=1}^{N_S} \alpha_n(c_n[w^T z_n + b] - 1),\ \alpha_n \geqslant 0 \quad (16)$$

L should be minimized with respect to w and b, and maximized with respect to the Lagrange multipliers α_n. Setting the partial derivates of L, w and b to zero results in the constraints:

$$w = \sum_{n=1}^{N_S} \alpha_n c_n z_n$$
$$\sum_{n=1}^{N_S} c_n \alpha_n = 0 \quad (17)$$

Resubstituting this into Eq. (16) gives the so-called dual form:

$$L = \sum_{n=1}^{N_S} \alpha_n - \frac{1}{2}\sum_{n=1}^{N_S}\sum_{m=1}^{N_S} c_n c_m \alpha_n \alpha_m z_n^T z_m,\ \alpha_n \geqslant 0 \quad (18)$$

After optimization, the α_n are used to find w. In typical problems, the solution is sparse, meaning that many of the α_n become 0. Samples z_n for which $\alpha_n = 0$ are not required in the computation of w. The remaining samples z_n (for which $\alpha_n > 0$) are called support vectors[28].

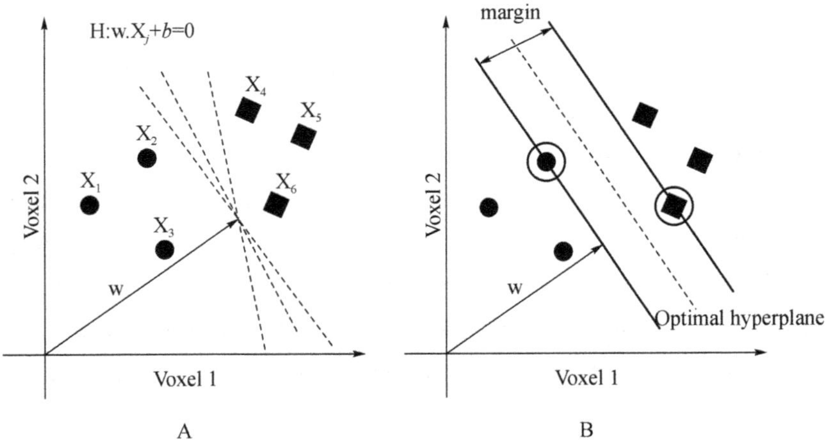

Figure 2 Classification and support vector machine (SVM)

Ecker C, et al. Investigating the predictive value of whole-brain structural MR scans in autism: A pattern classification approach. Neuroimage, 2009.

Naive Bayes

Naive Bayes classifiers are a family of simple probabilistic classifiers based on applying Bayes' theorem with strong independence assumptions between the features. Naive Bayes is a popular method for text categorization, the problem of judging documents as belonging to one category as the features. With appropriate preprocessing, it is competitive in this domain with more advanced methods including SVM. Training naive Bayes can be done by evaluating an approximation algorithm in closed form in linear time, rather than by expensive iterative approximation[29].

Enhanced Probabilistic Neural Network (EPNN)

Enhanced Probabilistic Neural Network (EPNN) is proposed by Ahmadlou and Adeli[30] using local decision circles. EPPN is a robust classifier in terms of noise in the data with higher accuracy than conventional probabilistic neural network (PNN). EPNN incorporated local information and non-homogeneity existing in the training population by local decision circles. The circle has a radius which limits the contribution of the local decision. The spread parameter and the radius of local decision circles are optimized to maximize the performance of the model. Using the one-way ANOVA to discover the features that as inputs of EPNN. EPNN consists of an input layer with number of nodes equal to the number of the selected features. Using two local and global Bayesian rules, a pattern layer which computes the likelihood of the input data to each training data, a summation layer which computes the likelihood of the input data to each class, and an output layer with one node which assigns the input data to the class with maximum likelihood are obtained[26].

3 Application

ASD is diagnosed based on behavioral criteria. The MR-based diagnostic model holds the promise of enhancing, perhaps complementing, behavioral assessment.

The SVM classifier is the most popular one for the classification of ASD in children. Ecker et al.[13] examined neuroanatomical networks implicated in ASD using a whole-brain classification approach employing a support vector machine (SVM) and investigated the predictive value of structural MRI scans with ASD. The results were compared between SVM and VBM. The study reported that the result of SVM is better than the single morphological methods. VBM revealed few significant between-group differences at conventional levels of statistical stringency. In contrast, SVM identified spatially distributed networks discriminating between ASD and controls. SVM applied to gray matter scans correctly classified ASD individuals at a specificity of 86.0% and a sensitivity of 88.0%. Cases (68.0%) were correctly classified using white matter anatomy. SVM can detect subtle and spatially distributed differences in brain networks between ASD and controls. Also, these differences provide significant predictive power for group membership, which is related to symptom severity. Erdem et al.[31] use support vector machine classifiers (SVM) for classification of structural magnetic resonance images (MRI) of the brain. Then voxel subsets are selected based on the rank value using a forward feature selection scheme. Finally, an SVM classifier is trained on each subset of image voxels. The class label of a test subject is calculated by combining individual decisions of the SVM classifiers using a voting mechanism. The method is applied for classifying patients with neurological diseases such as autism spectrum disorder (ASD). The results on datasets demonstrate superior performance as compared to two state of the art methods for medical image classification. Bloy et al.[4] use Principal component analysis (PCA) and support vector machine (SVM) classifier for creating abnormality classifiers from high angular resolution diffusion imaging (HARDI) data and utilized the fiber orientation distribution (FOD) diffusion model to represent the local WM architecture of each subject. The classifier assigns each test subject a probabilistic score indicating the likelihood of belonging to the patient group. The method was validated using a 5 fold validation scheme on a population containing autism spectrum disorder (ASD) patients and typically developing (TD) controls. A clear distinction between ASD patients and controls was obtained with a 77% accuracy.

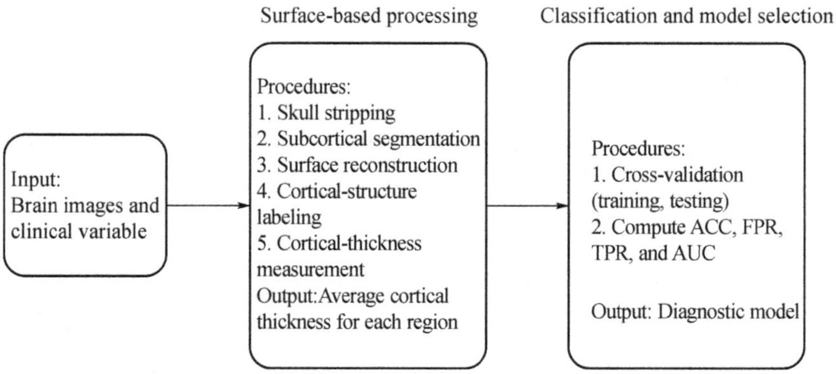

Figure 3 Data-analysis pipeline for diagnostic models based on volumetric morphometry

Jiao Y, et al. Predictive models of autism spectrum disorder based on brain regional cortical thickness. Neuroimage, 2011.

Except SVM classifier, other classifiers are also applied in discriminating between

ASD and controls. Jiao Y et al. [18] constructed diagnostic models for ASD, based on regional thickness measurements extracted from SBM; and to compare these models to diagnostic models based on volumetric morphometry (Figure 3). To generate diagnostic models, they employed four machine-learning techniques: support vector machines (SVM), multilayer perceptrons (MLP), functional trees (FT), and logistic model trees (LMT). For thickness-based classification, LMT achieved the best classification performance, with accuracy = 87%, area under the receiver operating characteristic (ROC) curve (AUC) = 0.93, sensitivity = 95%, and specificity = 75%. Justin Eldridge et al. [32] use support vector machine (SVM), logistic regression, and a naive Bayes classifier for the classification of ASD. The best classification accuracy of 79% was achieved by naive Bayes, making the method competitive with other automatic diagnosis methods based on EEG. Uddin LQ et al. [33] explored between-group differences in intrinsic functional connectivity of large-scale brain networks, performance of a classifier built to discriminate children with ASD from TD children based on specific brain networks, and correlations between brain networks and core symptoms of ASD (Figure 4). The study showed stronger functional connectivity within several large-scale brain networks in children with ASD compared with TD children. Using maps of each individual's salience network, children with ASD could be discriminated from TD children with a classification accuracy of 78%, with 75% sensitivity and 80% specificity. The salience network showed the highest classification accuracy among all networks examined, and the blood oxygen-level dependent signal in this network predicted restricted and repetitive behavior scores. The classifier discriminated ASD from TD in the independent sample with 83% accuracy, 67% sensitivity, and 100% specificity. It showed Salience network hyperconnectivity may be a distinguishing feature in children with ASD. Mehran Ahmadlou et al. [27] use an Enhanced Probabilistic Neural Network classifier to make an accurate diagnosis of ASD based on the detected differences in the regional functional connectivity of autistic and healthy EEGs. A high classification accuracy of 95.5% was achieved for distinguishing autistic EEGs from healthy EEGs.

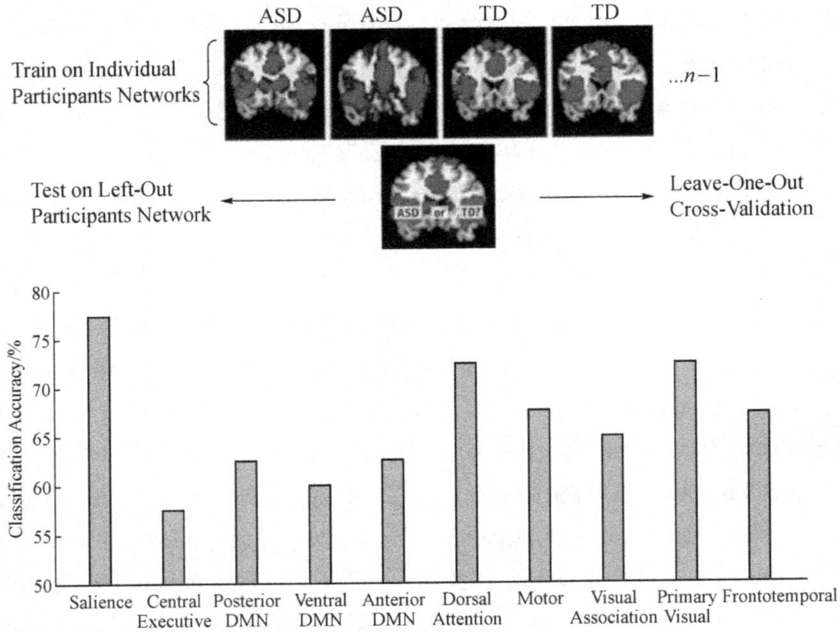

Figure 4 Classification Analysis and Accuracy

Lucina Q Uddin, et al. Salience Network - Based Classification and Prediction of Symptom Severity in Children With Autism. JAMA Psychiatry, 2014.

4 Conclusion

It is concluded that feature selection is an important and frequently used dimensionality reduction technique. It is one effective means to identify relevant features for dimensionality reduction and can be removed without performance deterioration.

The classifier methods mentioned above can be used as an effective tool for diagnosis of the autism of children. The machine-learning approaches perform high classification accuracy for distinguishing ASD and controls. SVM can detect subtle and spatially distributed differences between ASD and controls, which can also be used to provide significant predictive power for group membership. Other classifiers also investigated the predictive value of gray and white matter MRI scans in children with ASD and proved good group separation overall.

Acknowledgement

This work was supported by the following grants: the National Natural Science Foundation of China (81071135,61372032), the Jiangsu Clinical Medicine Technology Foundation (BL2012052), and the Jiangsu Natural Science Foundation (BK2012740, BK20131074).

References

[1] Julkunen, Petro, Laura Säisänen, et al. Comparison of navigated and non-navigated transcranial magnetic stimulation for motor cortex mapping, motor threshold and motor evoked potentials. Neuroimage, 2009, 44(3): 790-795.

[2] Barker, Anthony T, Reza Jalinous, et al. Non-invasive magnetic stimulation of human motor cortex. The Lancet, 1985, 325(8437): 1106-1107.

[3] Jiao, Yun, Rong Chen, et al. Predictive models of autism spectrum disorder based on brain regional cortical thickness. Neuroimage, 2010, 50(2): 589-599.

[4] Bloy, Luke, Madhura Ingalhalikar, et al. HARDI based pattern classifiers for the identification of white matter pathologies. Medical Image Computing and Computer-Assisted Intervention - MICCAI 2011, 2011: 234-241.

[5] Amaral, David G, Cynthia Mills Schumann, et al. Neuroanatomy of autism. Trends in neurosciences, 2008, 31(3): 137-145.

[6] Belmonte, Matthew K, EH Cook, et al. Autism as a disorder of neural information processing: directions for research and targets for therapy. Molecular psychiatry, 2004, 9(7): 646-663.

[7] Nordahl, Christine Wu, Donna Dierker, et al. Cortical folding abnormalities in autism revealed by surface-based morphometry. The Journal of Neuroscience, 2007, 27(43): 11725-11735.

[8] Uddin, Lucina Q, Kaustubh Supekar, et al. Reconceptualizing functional brain connectivity in autism from a developmental perspective. Frontiers in human neuroscience, 2013(7): 458.

[9] Courchesne, Eric, CM Karns, et al. Unusual brain growth patterns in early life in patients with autistic disorder an MRI study. Neurology, 2001,57(2): 245-254.

[10] Rojas, Donald C, Eric Peterson, et al. Regional gray matter volumetric changes in autism associated with social and repetitive behavior symptoms. BMC psychiatry, 2006, 6(1): 56.

[11] Ashburner, John, Karl J Friston. Voxel-based morphometry—the methods. Neuroimage, 2000, 11(6): 805-821.

[12] Fischl, Bruce, Martin I Sereno, et al. Cortical surface-based analysis: Ⅱ. Inflation, flattening, and a surface-based coordinate system. Neuroimage, 1999, 9(2): 195-207.

[13] Ecker, Christine, Vanessa Rocha-Rego, et al. Investigating the predictive value of whole-brain structural MR scans in autism: a pattern classification approach. Neuroimage, 2010, 49(1): 44-56.

[14] Singh, Vikas, Lopamudra Mukherjee, et al. Cortical surface thickness as a classifier: boosting for autism classification//Medical Image Computing and Computer-Assisted Intervention - MICCAI 2008. 2008: 999-1007.

[15] Voets, Natalie L, Morgan G Hough, et al. Evidence for abnormalities of cortical development in adolescent-onset schizophrenia. Neuroimage, 2008, 43(4): 665-675.

[16] Akshoomoff, Natacha, Catherine Lord, et al. Outcome classification of preschool children with autism spectrum disorders using MRI brain measures. Journal of the American Academy of Child & Adolescent Psychiatry, 2004, 43(3): 349-357.

[17] Guyon, Isabelle, André Elisseeff. An introduction to variable and feature selection. The Journal of Machine Learning Research, 2003(3): 1157 – 1182.

[18] Liu, Huan, Hiroshi Motoda. Computational methods of feature selection//CRC Press. 2007: 115 – 128.

[19] Donoho, David L. For most large underdetermined systems of linear equations the minimal. Communications on pure and applied mathematics, 2006, 59(6): 797 – 829.

[20] Duda, Richard O, Peter E Hart, et al. Pattern Classification. New Jersey: John Wiley & Sons, 2012.

[21] Zhao, Zheng, Fred Morstatter, et al. Advancing feature selection research-ASU feature selection repository. School of Computing, Informatics, and Decision Systems Engineering, Arizona State University, 2010.

[22] Liu, Huan, Rudy Setiono. Chi2: Feature selection and discretization of numeric attributes// 2012 IEEE 24th International Conference on Tools with Artificial Intelligence. IEEE Computer Society, 2012.

[23] Gini C. Variabilite e mutabilita. Memorie di metodologia statistica, 1912.

[24] Cover, Thomas M, Joy A Thomas. Elements of Information Theory. New Jersey: John Wiley & Sons, 2012.

[25] Lu, Qing, Kun Bi, et al. Predicting depression based on dynamic regional connectivity: A windowed Granger causality analysis of MEG recordings. Brain Research, 2013, 1535(1): 52 – 60.

[26] Ahmadlou, Mehran, Hojjat Adeli, et al. Fuzzy synchronization likelihood-wavelet methodology for diagnosis of autism spectrum disorder. Journal of neuroscience methods, 2012, 211(2): 203 – 209.

[27] Sajda, Paul. Machine learning for detection and diagnosis of disease. Annu. Rev. Biomed. Eng., 2006, 8: 537 – 565.

[28] Van Der Heijden, Ferdinand, Robert Duin, et al. Classification, Parameter Estimation and State Estimation: An Engineering Approach Using MATLAB. New Jersey: John Wiley & Sons, 2005.

[29] Rennie, Jason D, Lawrence Shih, et al. Tackling the poor assumptions of naive bayes text classifiers. ICML. Washington DC, 2003.

[30] Ahmadlou, Mehran, Hojjat Adeli. Enhanced probabilistic neural network with local decision circles: A robust classifier. Integrated Computer-Aided Engineering, 2010, 17(3): 197 – 210.

[31] Varol, Erdem, Bilwaj Gaonkar, et al. Feature ranking based nested support vector machine ensemble for medical image classification. Biomedical Imaging (ISBI), 2012 9th IEEE International Symposium, 2012.

[32] Eldridge, Justin, Alison E Lane, et al. Robust features for the automatic identification of autism spectrum disorder in children. Journal of Neurodevelopmental Disorders, 2014, 6(1): 12.

[33] Uddin, Lucina Q, Kaustubh Supekar, et al. Salience network – based classification and prediction of symptom severity in children with autism. JAMA psychiatry, 2013, 70(8): 869 – 879.

Association of Paternal Mental Health and Preschoolers' Behavioral Problems: The Moderating Role of Child Negative Emotionality

Yapeng Liu, Guangzhen Zhang, Zongbao Liang, Zuhong Lu, Huihua Deng[a,*]
Key Laboratory of Child Development and Learning Science of Ministry of Education (Southeast University), Research Center for Learning Science, Southeast University, Nanjing 210096, China
[a]dengrcls@ seu. edu. com
[*]Corresponding author

Keywords: depression; somatization; negative emotionality; behavioral problems

Abstract: This study examined the interaction between child negative emotionality and fathers' mental health in predicting preschoolers' behavioral problems. Fathers reported their mental health and mothers rated on child negative emotionality at the child age of 14 months. Preschoolers' behavioral problems were rated by child's mother and father at 48 months. The results showed that preschoolers with higher negative emotionality exhibited more externalizing and internalizing problems than those with less negative one if their fathers were in high level of somatization, but they showed no difference in behavioral problems if paternal somatization was low. The result supported the diathesis-stress model. Additionally, paternal depression positively predicted preschoolers' internalizing problems.

Introduction

Behavioral problems have high prevalence rate among young children and can predict a large range of adulthood negative outcomes from antisocial behaviors to suicide. Parental mental health is an important factor influencing preschooler's behavioral problems. Previous studies showed that children whose mothers were in poor mental health have high level of externalizing and internalizing problems[1-4]. For example, O'Donnell and colleagues have found that prenatal maternal depression and anxiety has a direct and persisting effect on their children's behavioral and emotional symptoms across childhood into adolescence[2].

Negative emotionality as a core of difficult temperament refers to children's tendency to react to stressors including fear and distress to limitations[5]. According to the differential susceptibility or diathesis-stress model, unfavorable environmental conditions may be particularly negative for children with certain difficult temperamental traits[6]. Prior studies have showed that children with more difficult temperaments had more behavioral problems than all other children if they experienced poor parenting[7,8]. However, the former model stresses that individuals vary in their susceptibility to both favorable and unfavorable environmental conditions, and the latter highlights that only poor developmental experiences are most likely to impact the development of individuals with vulnerability factors[9]. Most previous studies failed to further distinguish the differential susceptibility from diathesis-stress model.

Furthermore, relatively few studies pay close attention to the role of paternal mental health in the child social emotional development. As an important member of the family, the fathers' mental health may play an irreplaceable role on preschoolers' behavioral problems. The main aim of the present study was to examine the interactions between paternal mental health and child negative emotionality in predicting preschoolers' behavioral problems, and further examine whether the interactions fit with differential susceptibility or diathesis-stress model. Specifically, we hypotheses that: (a) among preschoolers' with high negative emotionality, fathers' poor mental health positively predicted preschoolers' externalizing and internalizing problems; (b) the interactions were consistent with diathesis-stress model.

Methods

Participants

The participants came from an ongoing longitudinal study in Nanjing, China. At 14 months, 365 children including 190 boys (52.1%) and 175 girls (47.9%) and their parents participated in the present study. They were Han Chinese and primarily from middle- and high-income families (monthly family income range of ¥6 000—¥10 000). At 48 months, 248 children came for another visit to the laboratory (127 boys and 121 girls).

Attrition occurred after 24 months because of busy work and moving out. To examine the variables related to attrition between 24 and 48 months, χ^2 analyses was conducted. There were no significant differences between participants at 48 months and those who drop out after 24 months on fathers' mental health.

Procedures

When the child was 24 months old, the toddlers and their fathers were invited to the laboratory. All families signed informed consent forms after the experimenter fully explained the procedure to them. Fathers reported on their mental health scales and mothers rated on toddlers' negative emotionality. At 48 months, mothers and fathers were invited back to fill out the questionnaires on behavioral problems, respectively.

Measures

Paternal mental health was measured with two subscales of Symptom Checklist 90 (SCL-90), somatization (13 items) and depression (6 items). Each item was rated on a 5-point Likert format (from 1 = never or seldom to 5 = nearly always). It has been consistently demonstrated that the reliability and validity of SCL-90 is satisfactory in Chinese sample[10]. In the present study, the Cronbach's alphas of somatization and depression were 0.90 and 0.84, respectively.

Child negative emotionality was rated by mothers with 19 items from the Infant Behavior Questionnaire (IBQ)[11]. Items were constructed in a 5-point Likert format (from 1 = never or seldom to 5 = nearly always). Its Cronbach's alpha was 0.69.

Children's behavioral problems were assessed with Child Behavior Checklist (CBCL)[12]. Items measuring social withdrawal and depression/anxiety were used to assess internalizing problems, and items measuring aggression and defiance were used to assess externalizing problems. Each item was rated as 0 = if not true, 1 = if somewhat or sometimes true, or 2 = if often true. The internal consistencies of internalizing problems for maternal and paternal ratings were 0.76 and 0.76, and of externalizing problems were 0.85 and 0.86, respectively. Data from maternal and paternal reports were averaged to avoiding the same-reporter deviation.

Statistical analyses

A series of hierarchical multiple regression analyses were conducted to examine the effect of fathers' mental health, negative emotionality, and their interactions in predicting child outcomes. At the first step, child gender was controlled. Then, fathers' mental health and negative emotionality were entered to the second step. At the final step, the interaction mental health and negative emotionality was entered. At last, we conducted simple slope analysis to further analyze the nature of the interaction and the "region of significance" analysis to examine the differential susceptibility model.

Results

As listed in Table 1, fathers' depression positively and significantly predicted preschoolers' internalizing problems. The interaction between somatization and negative emotionality significantly predicted preschoolers' externalizing and internalizing problems.

Table 1 Father's mental health, negative emotionality, and their interactions as predictors of children's behavioral problems

Predictors	Externalizing problems			Internalizing problems		
	ΔR^2	F	Beta	ΔR^2	F	Beta
Step 1	0.01	1.258		0.19	55.166**	
Child gender			-0.07			0.46
Step 2	0.05	3.821**		0.06	6.158**	
Somatization			0.07			0.05
Depression			0.10			0.17*
Negative emotionality (NE)			0.11			0.10
Step 3	0.02	4.776**		0.02	6.442*	
Somatization × NE			0.14*			0.14*

Note: In the step 3, predictors were entered by stepwise. $^{**}p < 0.01$, $^{*}p < 0.05$。

To further investigate the nature of the interactions, simple slope analyses were conducted at one standard deviation above and below the mean of fathers' somatization. As showed in Figure 1 and Figure 2, for toddler's with high negative emotionality, fathers' somatization positively and significantly predicted preschoolers' externalizing ($slope = 0.06$, $t = 2.064$, $p < 0.05$) and internalizing problems ($slope = 0.05$, $t = 2.504$, $p < 0.05$), but it was not for those with low negative emotionality ($slope = -0.02$, $t = -0.675$, $p > 0.05$ for externalizing problems and $slope = -0.01$, $t = -0.567$, $p > 0.05$ for internalizing problems).

In order to distinguish differential susceptibility model from diathesis-stress model, the "regions of significance" analysis was conducted[13]. As showed in the shaded area of Figure 1, the slope between negative emotionality and externalizing problems of preschoolers was significant when the score of fathers' somatization was higher than 0.03 s.d. than the mean score, but there was no significant difference below this value. Similarly, preschoolers' internalizing problems only differed significantly between children with high and low negative emotionality when fathers' somatization was higher than -0.01 s.d. than the mean score (see the shaded areas in Figure 2). Consequently, the interactions were more fit with diathesis stress than differential susceptibility model.

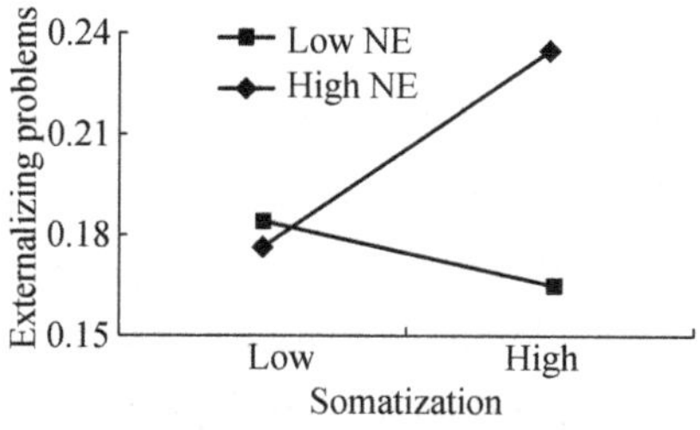

Figure 1 Child negative emotionality moderated the effect of fathers' somatization on externalizing problems

The solid line represents a significant simple slope

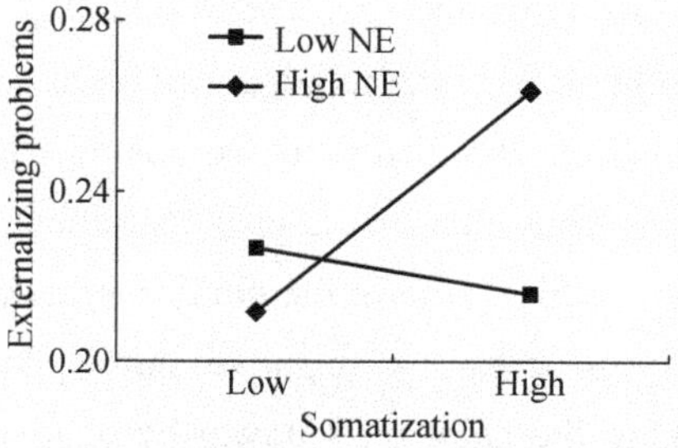

Figure 2 Child negative emotionality moderated the effect of fathers' somatization on internalizing problems

The solid line represents a significant simple slope

Discussion

This longitudinal study examined the moderating effect of child negative emotionality in the associations between fathers' mental health and preschoolers' behavioral problems. The results showed that fathers' somatization interacted with child negative emotionality in predicting preschoolers' externalizing and internalizing problems. This cross-over interaction seems to consistent with differential susceptibility model, but the results from "regions of significance" analysis indicated that preschoolers with high negative emotionality have more behavioral problems than those with less negative emotionality if their fathers were in high level of somatization, but there was no difference if fathers somatization was low, which fitting with diathesis-stress model rather than differential susceptibility model.

This findings were consistent with the study of Belsky and Pluess[14] showing those 15-year-old adolescents who were highly negative at infancy exhibited more externalizing problems when they were in low-quality child care, but not fewer problems when in high-quality child care when comparing with those who were less negative. But it was not consistent with the finding of Kim and Kochanska[15], where infants with high negative emotionality were less self-regulated when the parent—child mutually responsive orientation (MRO) was unresponsive, but more self-regulated when it was responsive, but there was no link between MRO and self-regulation for less negative infants. One interpretation for these inconsistent findings involves a possibility that behavioral problems and self-regulation call for different biological foundations. Compared to behavioral problems, self-regulation was strongly associated with nervous systems which causing the child is highly sensitive to both positive and negative experience[16].

Additionally, we also found that fathers' depression was positively associated with preschoolers' internalizing problems. Previous evidence has showed that maternal depression was positively associated with child's behavioral and emotional symptoms[1-4]. The present study expanded to fathers' mental health and found that fathers' depression play a critical role in the child internalizing problems. On one hand, fathers' depression is likely to create a negative atmosphere endangering children's emotional security by making the child feels unworthy of love, which result in child internalizing problems[17]. On the other hand, the father and child may share the common genes that cause fathers' depression and child internalizing problems such as social withdrawal and depression/anxiety.

This study has several limitations. First, the participants in the current sample were recruited from middle- to high- income, highly educated families. The results in this study are limited to generalize to low-class populations. Second, data on negative emotionality, fathers' mental health, and behavioral problems were collected using questionnaire data. Other sources such as observational ratings are needed to avoid possible problems of method variance.

In conclusion, this longitudinal study showed that fathers' depression positively predicted preschoolers' internalizing problems. More importantly, fathers' somatization interacted with child negative emotionality in predicting preschoolers' externalizing and internalizing problems. Further "regions of significance" analysis indicated that highly negative preschoolers exhibited more externalizing and internalizing problems than less negative ones if their fathers were in high level of somatization, but there were not fewer problems if fathers' somatization was low, supporting the diathesis-stress model.

Acknowledgments

This study is supported by the Cultivation Fund of the Key Scientific and Technical Innovation Project, Ministry of Education of China (704025), the Research Innovation Project in Universities Graduate Students of Jiangsu Province (CXLX13_115) and the Special Funds of Basic Scientific Research Operating Expenses in the Central University.

References

[1] J A Leis, J Heron, E A Stuart, et al. Associations between maternal mental health and child emotional and behavioral problems: Does prenatal mental health matter? Journal of Abnormal Child Psychology, 2014, 42: 161 - 171.

[2] K J O'Donnell, V Glover, E D Barker, et al. The persisting effect of maternal mood in pregnancy on childhood psychopathology. Development and Psychopathology, 2014, 26: 393 - 403.

[3] M P Santelices, F Perez, C Rivera, et al. Maternal mental health and preschool adaptation to play groups in chile. Revista Argentina De Clinica Psicologica, 2012, 21: 75 - 84.

[4] K Turney. Pathways of disadvantage: Explaining the relationship between maternal depression and children's problem behaviors. Social Science Research, 2012, 41: 1546 - 1564.

[5] M K Rothbart, S A Ahadi, K L Hershey. Temperament and social-behavior in childhood. Merrill-Palmer Quarterly-Journal of Developmental Psychology, 1994, 40: 21 - 39.

[6] M Pluess, J Belsky. Children's differential susceptibility to effects of parenting. Family Science, 2010, 1: 14 - 25.

[7] R H Bradley, R F Corwyn. Infant temperament, parenting, and externalizing behavior in first grade: A test of the differential susceptibility hypothesis. Journal of Child Psychology and Psychiatry, 2008, 49: 124 - 131.

[8] J Mesman, et al. Predicting growth curves of early childhood externalizing problems: Differential susceptibility of children with difficult temperament. Journal of Abnormal Child Psychology, 2009, 37: 625 - 636.

[9] J Belsky, M J Bakermans-Kranenburg, M H van Ijzendoorn. For better and for worse: Differential susceptibility to environmental influences. Current Directions in Psychological Science, 2007, 16: 300 - 304.

[10] C Shulin, L Linjiang. Re-testing reliability, validity and norm applicability of SCL-90. Chinese Journal of Nervous and Mental Diseases, 2003, 29: 323 - 327.

[11] M K Rothbart. Measurement of temperament in infancy. Child Development, 1981, 52: 569 - 578.

[12] T Achenbach. Child behavior checklist/4-18. Burlington: University of Vermont, 1991.

[13] A F Hayes, J Matthes. Computational procedures for probing interactions in OLS and logistic regression: SPSS and SAS implementations. Behavior Research Methods, 2009, 41: 924 - 936.

[14] J Belsky, M Pluess. Differential susceptibility to long-term effects of quality of child care on externalizing behavior in adolescence? International Journal of Behavioral Development, 2012, 36: 2 - 10.

[15] S Kim, G Kochanska. Child temperament moderates effects of parent-child mutuality on self-regulation: A relationship-based path for emotionally negative infants. Child Development, 2012, 83: 1275 - 1289.

[16] E N Aron, A Aron. Sensory-processing sensitivity and its relation to introversion and emotionality. Journal of Personality and Social Psychology, 1997, 73: 345 - 368.

[17] R M Rapee. Potential role of child rearing practices in the development of anxiety and depression. Clinical Psychology Review, 1997, 17: 47 - 67.

A Quantitative Analysis on the International Literatures about Emotional Development in Early Childhood Base on WOS Database

Yufei Yang[1,a,*], Lin Ye[2,b], Yangyang Liu[3,c]

[1]Nanjing University, School of Information Management, Nanjing 210093, Peoples R China

[2]Nanjing University, School of Information Management, Nanjing 210093, Peoples R China

[3]Nanjing University, School of Social and behavioral sciences, Nanjing 210093, Peoples R China

[a]yang841841@gmail.com, [b]411081445@qq.com, [c]liuyangyang@nju.edu.cn

[*]Corresponding author

Keywords: emotional development; early childhood; bibliometric; co-occurrence analysis

Abstract: Early childhood is an important period of an individual's emotional development, during which emotional development plays a critical role in the development of an individual's other competences. By using the method of bibliometric and social network analysis, the present study did quantitative analysis on literature samples collected from Web of Science published from 2004 to 2014, trying to explore the research characteristics, development trend, and hotspot distribution of emotional development in early childhood. The results indicated that the research of this area was in a steadily developing period; the regional difference of research was significant; authors and journals were scatterly distributed; and the topics such as social-emotional development, parenting, and emotion intervention were hotspots in this area.

国际儿童早期情绪发展的文献定量分析

杨宇菲[1,a,*]，叶琳[2,b]，刘阳阳[3,c]
[1]南京大学信息管理学院,南京,江苏,中国
[2]南京大学信息管理学院,南京,江苏,中国
[3]南京大学社会学院,南京,江苏,中国
[a]yang841841@gmail.com，[b]sarah8671@163.com，[c]liuyangyang@nju.edu.cn
[*]通讯作者

关键词:情绪发展;儿童早期发展;文献计量学;共现分析

中文摘要:儿童早期是个体情绪发展的重要阶段,该时期的情绪发展对个体各方面能力的发展起着关键性的作用。本文以 web of science 数据库为文献来源,采集 2004—2014 年儿童早期情绪发展领域文献作为样本,运用文献计量学和社会网络分析方法展开定量分析,从而探索该领域目前的研究特点、发展趋势和热点分布。研究结果表明该领域目前处于稳定发展期,研究的地域差异较显著,作者和期刊分散,研究热点集中在社会性情绪发展、亲子教育及情绪问题干预。

1 引言

情绪是人对客观事物的态度体验,是人的需要获得满足与否的反映,是人的整体发展至关重要的部分。儿童早期是情绪发展的重要阶段,这一阶段情绪的发展将影响个体各方面能力的发展,对个体未来的成长有很大影响。社会的发展导致社会环境、社会价值产生了大的变化,在这样的情况下,儿童情绪的发展也出现了新的特点。针对新的形势,心理学界关注与探索的儿童早期情绪发展的相关问题也有所改变,例如,从关注个体的情绪的生理过程、调控机制转向关注情绪互动、社会化发展、人际交流的影响等。关注儿童早期情绪发展的主要研究成果,对促进新时期儿童的健康发展有着重要的意义。

近年来有关儿童早期情绪发展的研究表现为不同情绪发展观点并行的特点,影响较大的观点包括生物观点、机能主义观点、认知观点等,同时,这些观点的共同主题也表明了儿童早期情绪发展研究的主要趋势。借助文献计量的方法,定量分析儿童早期情绪发展领域的研究文献,归纳该领域研究特点与规律,总结研究热点,对推动儿童早期情绪发展的进一步研究具有重要的实践价值。一方面,定量分析结果可以反映儿童早期情绪发展研究的发展轨迹,揭示其在一定时间内的研究水平与发展状况,为下一阶段的研究提供指导;另一方面,通过引文分析、关键词分析,以及一定程度上的可视化,突出现阶段的研究热点,可为广大研究人员提供参考。

2 数据来源

本文以 WOS 数据库作为文献来源数据库，该数据库收录了包括 SCI、SSCI 引文数据库在内的 8 000 多种世界范围内最有影响力的学术期刊，以一周为更新频率，所收录的期刊多采用同行评审机制，具有时效性强、收录全面、权威性高的特点。采用该数据库的文献进行定量分析，能够客观、准确、全面地反映国际儿童早期情绪发展领域的最新进展和发展趋势。

为了全面、准确地检索有关儿童早期情绪发展的国际文献，笔者经过文献调研，构建了以下检索式在 WOS 数据库中的主题字段进行检索：

(("child*") or ("year* old") or ("toddler") or ("bab*")) and ("emotion* develop*")

该检索式将"child"（儿童）、"year * old"（各年龄段）、"toddler"（幼儿）和"bab *"（婴儿）这四个表征儿童早期涵义的字段分别与"emotion * develop *"（情绪发展）进行匹配检索，是经过术语筛选和检索式优化后试检索中效果最优的检索式表达。为了对目前的儿童早期情绪发展研究成果进行时序分析的同时保证结论的时效性，本研究将文献样本的发表时间控制在近十年以内，即将选取的文献发表时间控制在 2004 年至 2014 年间。因此，根据选定的检索式和时间段在 WOS 数据库的核心合集数据库的主题字段进行检索，检得文献 728 篇（截至 2014 年 5 月 22 日）。经过人工抽检，这批文献均与儿童早期的情绪发展研究高度相关，能够作为本文文献计量分析的最终样本。

本节运用文献计量学的基本定律对儿童早期情绪发展的 728 篇文献从年份分布、作者分布、期刊分布和引文分布四个方面进行定量分析。

3 文献量分析

3.1 年份分布

对检出的 728 篇文献按照出版日期的年份分布进行统计，得到这批文献的年分布量和累积分布量如表 1 所示。根据文献计量学的文献增长定律普赖斯定律，对年份分布趋势进行相关公式拟合，得到拟合结果如图 1(1) 和图 1(2) 所示。

根据表 1 和图 1，我们可以分析得到以下结论：

(1) 儿童早期的情绪发展领域文献量在近十年呈现规律的稳定增长趋势。使用一次线性函数对文献年分布量进行拟合，得到的拟合方程为 $Y = 7.5636X - 15122$，相关系数 r 高达 0.95。这说明近十年内儿童早期的情绪发展研究呈现稳定发展的态势，文献量逐步增长，领域研究稳步成熟，研究成果呈现上升趋势。有趣的是，该领域的文献量呈现较明显的周期性突增，在 2008 年、2011 年两个年份出现与之前相比较为明显的分水岭；而在其他年份之间文献量基本保持稳定。这一现象通常意味着在断层年份领域内的如下情况：① 研究出现了突破性进展；② 领域的实际应用出现新的需求和研究热点；③ 与其他领域的交叉结合出现了进展，甚至出现了新兴的交叉学科。

（2）根据文献计量学的普莱斯定律，当该领域处于稳定发展期时，文献的年累积分布量和与时间呈现指数相关，即满足公式 $F(t)=ae^{bt}$（其中 F 为文献累积量，t 为年份，a，b 为常数）。使用这一公式对儿童早期的情绪发展文献的年份累积量进行拟合，相关系数 r 高达 0.97，说明儿童早期情绪发展的研究处于稳定发展时期，符合文献计量学的相关描述。

表1　文献量年份分布

年份	文献量	累计文献量	累计百分比	年份	文献量	累计文献量	累计百分比
2004	41	41	5.632%	2009	77	328	45.055%
2005	45	86	11.813%	2010	73	401	55.082%
2006	46	132	18.132%	2011	103	504	69.230%
2007	48	180	24.725%	2012	99	603	82.829%
2008	71	251	34.478%	2013	97	700	96.153%

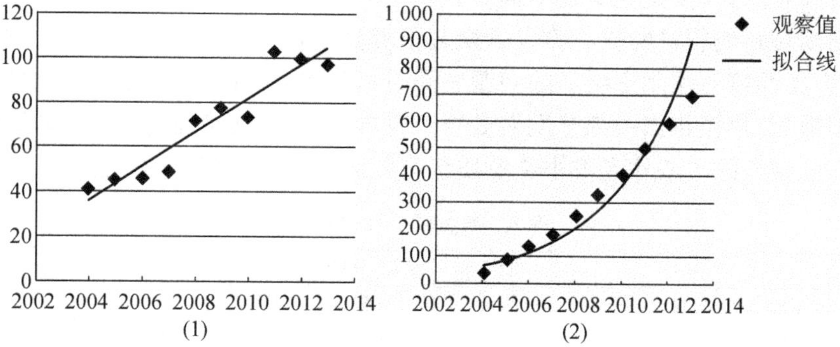

图1

3.2　作者分布

某领域内文献的作者分布情况是文献计量学中衡量一个领域的学者质量、研究人员组成的重要指标，同时也能间接反映出该领域的研究现状。对本次的728篇文献样本的作者及其发文情况进行统计，结果如表2所示：

表2　作者的发文情况及分布

作者群体	作者数	发文数
高频核心作者	1	8
	3	6
	3	5
	9	4

续表 2

作者群体	作者数	发文数
重要作者	29	3
	168	2
非核心作者	1 758	1

本次的 728 篇文献中，共涉及 1 971 位作者，人均文献量为 0.369 4 篇。较小的人均文献量说明云计算研究领域可能存在文献著者较为分散的现象。同时，根据洛特卡定律，在某一研究领域中，仅发表一篇文献的偶然作者应约占总作者数的 60%；而在本批文献中这一比例高达 89.19%，远远超过了洛特卡定律的估计。这说明儿童早期情绪发展的国际研究界普遍存在作者分散的现象，核心作者群尚未形成，偶然作者(包括交叉学科或相关领域的研究学者)较多。这可能导致领域研究的向心力和领军力量不足，影响领域的纵向发展。

经过整理，儿童早期的情绪发展领域的高频核心作者群如表 3 所示。该表按发文量多少选取了领域发文量前 16 位的作者，并对这些作者的文章总被引量进行了统计。从表中可以看出，即使是发文量最高的作者 FELDMEN R 也只发表了 8 篇相关文章，这一数据相对其他领域的核心作者来说并不算多。这一现象也反映了该领域作者分散，中坚力量的核心作用不明显的问题。同时可以看到，发文量与总被引量的正相关关系并不强烈，存在相当一部分发文量较少但被引量，尤其是篇均被引量较高的作者。这说明在该领域的核心作者群中文章质量与数量之间存在较大的偶然性。

表 3　高频核心作者列表

作者	发文量	总被引量	作者	发文量	总被引量
FELDMEN R	8	192	DOYLE LW	4	30
HOLODYNSKI M	6	16	GUNNAR MR	4	90
MACCALLUM F	6	158	HEMMETER ML	4	100
PETERMANN F	6	41	INDER TE	4	30
ANDERSON PJ	5	32	LUBY J	4	32
GOLOMBOK S	5	154	RESCH F	4	87
VAN IJZENDOORN MH	5	51	STEIN A	4	282
BAKERMANS-KRANENBURG MJ	4	51	TREYVAUD K	4	30

表 4 反映了儿童早期情绪发展领域的作者合作情况。该领域的文均作者数十年间保持在 3 人左右，相对其他社会科学研究领域处于正常水平。

另外从表中可以看出，大体上说该领域的作者合作在近十年间呈现增长的态势，从头 3 年的篇均不足 3 人增长至最后两年的 3.5 人以上。这表明近十年间该领域的合作研究成果在增加，这可能反映了以下趋势：(1) 研究中的合作性实证研究在增加；(2) 领域内的学术交流与学术合作增多；(3) 领域研究的重心从理论假设向实际应用偏移。事实上，由于近十年来儿童早期的情绪发展研究更多地侧重于社会性情绪的发展和儿童在不同社会环境,如亲子关系、同伴关系中的情绪发展的实证性研究,因此这一现象的出现可以得到解释。

表4　作者合著的年份分布情况

年份	文章总数	作者总数	文均作者数	年份	文章总数	作者总数	文均作者数
2004	41	120	2.93	2009	77	254	3.30
2005	45	128	2.84	2010	73	249	3.41
2006	46	136	2.96	2011	103	349	3.39
2007	48	144	3	2012	99	376	3.80
2008	71	208	2.93	2013	97	360	3.71

3.3　期刊分布

某个领域的文献的期刊分布可以在一定程度上反映出该领域研究成果的呈现情况,同时也反映出该领域核心期刊的组成和数量。根据布拉德福定律,如果将涉及某领域的期刊按照发文量降序排列并计算所有期刊的累计发文数量,最终按照累积发文量大致相等的原则,将文献期刊分为三个区域,其中发文量较多的期刊所属区域为核心期刊群。

根据这一划分法则,本文对儿童早期情绪发展的文献进行了期刊发文量统计及累积发文量计算,并进行了期刊区域的划分,如表5所示。

从表5中可以看到,被划分为核心期刊区域(即第一区域)的共约占总数8%的期刊(32种)发表了总量的30%左右的文献,而发文量较少的第三区域的共约占总数69%(281种)期刊也发表了总量30%左右的文献。

表5　文献期刊的载文量分布(布拉德福定律区域分析法)

区域	期刊种数	期刊载文量	累计期刊数	累计文献量
一	2	13	2	26
	2	12	4	50
	1	11	5	61
	1	10	6	71
	2	9	8	89
	2	8	10	105
	5	7	15	140
	7	6	22	182
	10	5	32	232
二	12	4	44	280
	28	3	72	364
	56	2	128	476
三	281	1	409	757

布拉德福定律同时指出,按照以上原则对期刊进行划分后,三个区域的期刊数量

应大致呈现指数增长分布，即三个区域的期刊数量比应符合 1∶ n∶ n^2 的比值且 n 等于 5 左右。对本批文献进行该比值的拟合，得到 n 为 3.58，拟合系数 r 高达 0.998。这说明这批文献高度符合布拉德福定律给出的描述，但核心期刊的比例相对较低，n 比值比布拉德福定律给出的成熟领域参考值低，说明核心期刊群相比其他成熟领域来说相对较小，文献散布在众多相关学科期刊中的情况较为突出。

3.4 引文分布

文献的被引情况是文献质量和对领域研究的贡献程度的重要衡量指标。根据对本批文献的引文分布情况统计，本次 728 篇文献中，总共被引 7 355 次，除去自引（即本批次文献内部互相引用的次数）外共被引 7 168 次，篇均被引 10.10 次，H 指数高达 41。从这个数据上看，儿童早期情绪发展的文献总的来说质量较高，被引频次较高；同时自引只占较小的比例，说明领域的开放度较高，该领域的文献频繁地被其他领域的研究文献所引用；但同时也说明领域内部可能存在互引不足，研究过于发散而系统性、承接性较差的问题。

对这批文献的被引情况分别按照年份分布和国别分布进行统计，结果如表 6 和表 7 所示。

表 6　文献被引次数年度分布

年份	被引次数	被引累计	累计篇均被引	年份	被引次数	被引累计	累计篇均被引
2004	8	8	0.20	2010	875	2 468	6.15
2005	38	46	0.53	2011	1 161	3 629	7.20
2006	180	226	1.71	2012	1 443	5 072	8.41
2007	299	525	2.92	2013	1 713	6 785	9.69
2008	415	940	3.75	2014	570	7 355	10.10
2009	653	1 593	4.86				

表 7　引文相关指标的国别分布

国别	总发文量	总被引量（除自引）	被引与发文比例	H 指数
美国	363	4 609	12.70	34
英国	63	1 652	26.22	17
德国	60	457	7.62	11
加拿大	43	667	15.51	13
荷兰	34	273	8.03	10
澳大利亚	27	160	5.93	8
以色列	25	227	9.08	9
西班牙	20	73	3.65	4
意大利	16	124	7.75	5

从表6可以看出,文献的被引次数和累计篇均被引均呈现逐年上升的趋势。其中累计篇均被引指的是当年及以前所发表的总文献量在当年及之前的时间内被引的总次数。如果某领域的文献质量保持不变,出于文献被引时延的缘故,该值会呈现先稳定增长再逐渐趋于平稳的变化趋势;而在本批文献中该值呈现稳定增长的趋势,这说明领域内的文献从被引上看质量在十年内不断上升,得到了较大的改善。截至2014年,累计篇均被引达到10篇左右,对于社会科学领域的文献平均水平来说相对较高,显示了该领域的文献质量以及该领域对其他学科的贡献度、权威性都相对较高。

从引文指标的国别分布来看,表7选择了按照总发文量降序排列之后的前9个国家,对其文献的总被引量、篇均被引量和 H 指数进行了统计。从表7可以看出,美国的发文量远远领先于其他国家,而从篇均被引量来说也位于9个国家中的第三位,仅次于英国和加拿大。这说明美国儿童早期情绪发展领域的研究在发文数量和质量上都处于比较领先的地位。发文量居于次位的英国则在篇均被引指标上远远领先于其他国家,达到26.22,这说明英国在该领域上虽然发文量不多,但发文质量相当高,在该领域中处于相对领先且权威的地位。其他国家的发文量和被引指标相差不大,其中加拿大的篇均被引位列第二,表征着比较高的发文质量。

4 研究热点分析

4.1 关键词频次统计

关键词是文献重要内容和涉及领域的最为精简的提炼与表述,在通过格式化的词组或术语提供读者准确、快捷地检索到文献的线索和途径。在文献计量中,常常通过对关键词的出现频率、共现情况等方面进行统计,以此反映某个研究领域的研究热点分布和它们之间的关系。表8中对728篇文献的关键词词频进行了统计,并列出其中词频最高的20个高频核心关键词。

表8 关键词词频分布

关键词	词频	关键词	词频
emotional development	67	adolescence	16
parenting	30	anxiety	15
social-emotional development	28	cognitive development	14
children	26	preschool	14
emotion	25	socio-emotional development	13
attachment	25	temperament	13
development	22	early intervention	13
child development	21	social and emotional development	12
depression	17	infant	11
emotion regulation	16	social competence	11

从表8中可以看出，高频关键词中除了与儿童早期情绪发展直接相关的检索词，如“emotional development”、“children”等外，相当一部分高频词反映了儿童早期情绪发展领域内近十年的研究热点和侧重方面，例如亲子教育与亲子关系、社会性情绪发展、情绪发展问题及干预等主题均在高频关键词中有所反映，可能是近十年内儿童情绪发展研究的热点。而最终研究热点的确定以及各个热点之间的相互关系和相对地位则应结合下文的共现网络进行分析。

4.2 研究热点的可视化

使用社会网络分析方法中的共现分析，可以研究文献关键词之间的共现规律，从而分析关键词及其所代表的领域研究热点之间的相互关系和组成结构。[8] 在使用共现矩阵表示出关键词之间的共现规律后，可以使用知识图谱可视化软件生成以关键词为节点，关键词之间的贡献关系为连接线的共现网络，从而形象地表现关键词之间的共现关系和各自在共现网络中的地位。图2中是根据本次728篇文献中的前20个高频词之间的共现矩阵，使用知识图谱可视化软件Ucinet生成的共现网络，表9是在该共现网络中各个节点（即各个关键词）在网络中的中心度指标。

图2中各个节点的大小代表了节点的媒介中心度数值的大小。媒介中心度也称为中介中心度，表征了各个节点对其他两个节点的传递效应的大小，媒介中心度值高的节点通常在某个领域中处于各个研究热点的交叉节点，对领域研究热点有着重要的桥梁作用，往往是领域未来研究新热点的潜在切入点，对领域的未来发展有着重要的潜在作用。节点之间的连接线疏密则代表了该节点与其他节点共同出现的频率大小。

表9中统计了各个节点的绝对中心度。所谓绝对中心度，就是将某一点的点度中心度等同于该点的度数，即与该点有直接联系的点的个数。

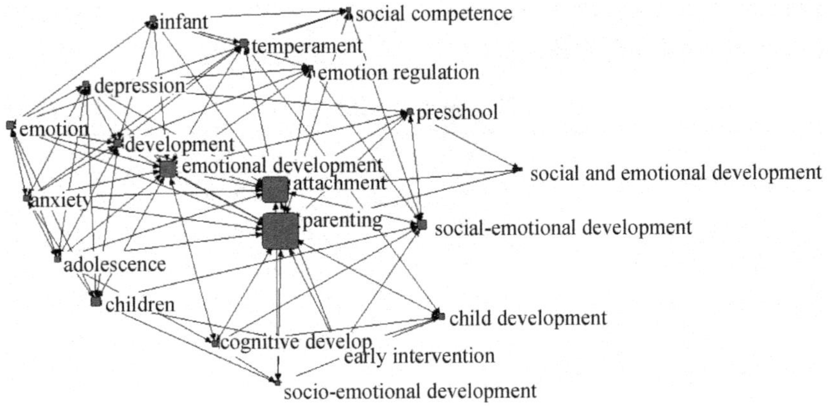

图2　高频关键词共现网络图

表9　共现网络的各节点中心度指标

关键词	绝对中心度	关键词	绝对中心度
emotional development	35	preschool	12
attachment	24	cognitive development	11
depression	21	infant	11
anxiety	21	emotion regulation	11
development	20	adolescence	9
emotion	18	social competence	7
parenting	16	early intervention	6
children	15	child development	6
social-emotional development	15	socio-emotional development	6
temperament	12	social and emotional development	4

结合图2和表9,可以得出以下分析和结论:

(1)社会性情绪发展是儿童情绪发展研究的热点之一。从高频词分布上可以看出,社会情绪发展、社会能力、社会和情绪发展等关键词均出现在核心高频词中,同时亲子关系、依恋、早期干预等从社会性角度切入的情绪发展研究内容也出现在高频关键词中,说明近十年来从社会过程角度切入的儿童早期情绪发展成为一个比较侧重的研究热点。事实上,以情绪发展理论的社会文化观点为理论基础的实证研究是目前儿童早期情绪发展研究的重点之一,本批文献中存在相当大一部分基于特定社会情境如亲子关系、同伴关系等环境下儿童情绪发展的实证性研究。

(2)亲子教育与亲子关系虽然是一个更为细分的研究主题,但其中心效应却相当显著,是一个值得关注的研究热点。一方面高频关键词中的"parenting"和"attachment"与该主题直接相关,另一方面从关键词共现网络中可以看出,这两个关键词的媒介中心度是所有关键词中最大的,这可能是因为亲子教育相关的研究主题既是社会性情绪发展研究的重要切入点,同时从儿童早期发展的角度看,也是儿童早期发展的重要干预途径和研究情景。这说明亲子教育相关的主题,如亲子教育对儿童早期情绪发展的调节手段,亲子依恋对儿童情绪发展的影响机制等,不仅是目前儿童早期情绪发展的研究热点,更可能会成为该领域内未来一段时间稳步发展的侧重点之一。

(3)针对儿童情绪发展的问题及干预的研究可能是该领域的另一个研究热点。亲子依恋、沮丧、情绪调节、焦虑、早期干预等关键词均出现在高频核心关键词中,说明针对这类儿童早期情绪发展的主要问题,尤其是负面情绪及其应对方法,是近十年来儿童早期情绪发展的又一个主流研究主题。事实上在本批文献中,相当一部分文献(尤其是后期文献)在儿童早期情绪问题及其调节与干预上进行了大量实证研究并取得了一定的成果,相信这一研究趋势将在未来一段时间内持续。

(4)然而,总的来说,从高频核心关键词的词频和绝对中心度来看,除了检索关键词“情绪发展”之外,其他关键词的词频最多只有30次,并不算非常显著的高频频率;绝对中心度也维持在一个较低的数值。这说明儿童早期的情绪发展领域可能存在研究热点较分散,没有形成显著的核心研究主题的情况。当然也不能排除由于领域的新兴热点尚未成熟,某些研究术语尚未统一,导致无法准确将这些关键词通过词频统计挖掘出来的情况。

5 结论

通过上文的统计分析,我们可以总结出国际儿童早期情绪发展领域的以下特点:

(1) 儿童早期情绪发展的研究近十年来处于稳定发展阶段。文献的年份分布量以稳定的比率逐步上升,同时文献的质量(主要由文献被引频次表征)也保持逐步上升的趋势。同时,该领域的作者分布较为分散,文献散布在较大范围的期刊中,这说明儿童早期情绪发展领域仍存在较大的上升空间,将在今后迎来较好的发展前景和更多的挑战。

(2) 该领域研究的地域差异较显著。从发文量上看,美国的发文量远远领先于其他国家;而如果将发文量和文献质量综合起来看,美国、英国和加拿大也领先其他国家相当一段距离。导致这一情况的原因有很多,如各国对该领域研究的资金、硬件和人才投入比例不一,各国的儿童情绪研究应用情景差异(如亲子关系、社会文化、社交氛围等)导致各国对儿童早期情绪发展的研究需求不一致等。值得注意的是,我国在这一领域的研究从发文量上看并不突出,发文量排名在前十名之外,这说明我国对这一领域的研究投入和重视程度还有待加强。

(3) 该研究存在作者和期刊分散、系统性缺乏的特点。这一特点可能与该领域的学科交叉性较强、应用情景广泛有关。从作者上看,该领域的研究成果过多地来自于偶然作者,而成熟的、具备一定规模的核心高频作者群尚未完全形成。同时领域内互引较少,说明作者之间相互研究的纵向承接性、横向对比和参照较少,不利于形成系统的学科研究体系。而从期刊分布上看,过多的文献散布在大量非该领域专门期刊上,说明该领域缺乏权威的、针对性的核心期刊群。

(4) 该领域较为显著的研究热点有:① 儿童早期的社会化情绪发展;② 亲子教育与亲子关系;③ 儿童早期的情绪问题及其干预。根据关键词词频分析,相当一部分文献侧重于从社会化情绪发展的角度切入对儿童早期情绪发展进行研究,同样的,也有相当一部分文献标注为情绪问题相关的高频关键词。事实上,近十年来从社会性情绪发展角度切入儿童早期情绪发展的研究逐渐进入实证阶段,并涌现了大量实际社会情境中的儿童早期情绪发展实证研究,这对本文的研究热点分析提供了例证。另外,根据关键词共现网络的中介中心度度量,亲子教育相关的关键词“parenting”的高中介中心度可能意味着亲子教育对儿童早期情绪发展有着重要的潜在作用。

致谢

We are grateful to the National Natural Science Fund of China (31301027), the Fundamental Research Funds for the Central Universities The 12th Five Year Plan of Jiangsu Education (C-c/2013/01/003) for supporting this study.

References

[1] Yang Xiaoling. A research on children's emotion development and their socialization. The Journal of Yan'an Vocational & Technical Institute, 2009(1).

[2] Liu Guoxiong, Fang Fuxi, Yang Xiaodong. Advances of studies on children's emotional development. Journal of Nanjing Normal University (Social Science Edition), 2003(6).

[3] Wang Chongde. Bibliometric. Tianjin: Nankai University Press, 1990.

[4] Price D S. A general theory of bibliometric and other cumulative advantage processes. Journal of the American Society for Information Science, 1976, 27(5): 292 – 306.

[5] Subramanyam K. Bibliometric studies of research collaboration: A review. Journal of Information Science, 1983, 6(1): 33 – 38.

[6] Gao Jianqun, Zhang Rongan, Chen Jiping, et al. Periodical citation analysis and its information value. Library and Information Service, 2004, 48(1): 58 – 61.

[7] Wang Jing, He Shousen, Wang Hui, et al. Study on the influence factors of the toddler's emotional and social competence development. Chinese Journal of Child Health Care, 2013(12).

[8] Garfield E. Bradford's law and related statistical patterns. Current Contents, 1980, 19(8): 5 – 12.

[9] Moed H F, De Bruin R E, Van Leeuwen T N. New bibliometric tools for the assessment of national research performance: Database description, overview of indicators and first applications. Scientometrics, 1995, 33(3): 381 – 422.

[10] De Bakker F G A, Groenewegen P, Den Hond F. A bibliometric analysis of 30 years of research and theory on corporate social responsibility and corporate social performance. Business & Society, 2005, 44(3): 283 – 317.

Behavioral and Event-related Potential Studies of Preschoolers' Expression Cognition of Cartoon Face and Real Face

Jingmei Wang[a], Xian Zheng, Xiaoqun Zhang, Xiaoya Zheng, Yingjun Lu[b,*], Jinliang Qin[c]

Laboratory of Developmental Cognitive Neuroscience, Zhejiang Normal University, Hangzhou, Zhejiang, China

[a]cathywang1201@hotmail.com, [b]luyingjun@zjnu.edu.cn, [c]qjlzjnu@126.com

* Corresponding author

Keywords: children; cartoon faces; facial expression recognition; expression recognition and labels; event-related potential

Abstract: The ability of facial expressions recognition, which often plays a remarkable role in daily communication, is the highlight of emotional psychology and cognitive neuroscience studies in recent years. Cartoon faces, as an important part of children's daily life, are exercising an invisible, formative influence on children's cognitive and social development. Facial expression recognition and labeling tasks and implicit facial expression processing tasks during ERP recording were used to explore the differences in time courses of brain responses and in accuracy rates of behavioural reactions. It demonstrated that: (1) Children's cognitive ability of cartoon facial expression is better than real faces, sadness, fear and neutral expressions in special, which is due to the exaggerated expressions and simplified features on cartoon faces that in line with the children's development on facial cognition; (2) The neural mechanisms between cartoon and real faces is significantly different, corresponding to the Bruce & Young's face processing model; the intensity of real faces is larger than cartoon faces at early encoding stage on 6-year-old children suggesting the higher degree of automotive processing on real faces; the intensity of cartoon faces is larger than real faces at late features processing stage suggesting that cartoon faces are more attractive for young children and children put more attention resources; (3) Behavioral and ERP experiments showed that it is imbalance on the development of 6-year-old children's ability to identify different expressions; according to the results of this study, using cartoon faces as learning materials of facial expressions, will promote face cognitive ability of children.

幼儿对卡通与真人面孔表情认知的行为与 ERP 研究

王静梅[a],郑娴,张筱群,郑潇雅,卢英俊[b,*],秦金亮[c]
发展认知神经科学实验室,浙江师范大学,杭州,浙江,中国
[a]cathywang1201@hotmail.com, [b]luyingjun@zjnu.edu.cn, [c]qjlzjnu@126.com
*通讯作者

关键词:幼儿;卡通面孔;面孔表情认知;表情识别与标签;事件相关电位

中文摘要:面孔表情认知的能力在日常交往中至关重要,卡通在儿童日常生活中不可或缺,影响了幼儿认知和社会性发展。本研究采用行为方法和 ERP 技术,探究儿童对卡通和真人表情面孔进行加工的差异及其背后的脑机制。研究结果表明:(1) 幼儿对卡通面孔表情认知能力优于真人面孔,特别是悲伤、恐惧和平静表情,原因可能为卡通面孔的夸张的表情与简化的五官等表征更符合幼儿的认知发展水平;(2) 幼儿对卡通与真人面孔加工的神经机制存在差异,对应于 Bruce & Young 的面孔加工模型,在早期结构编码阶段,真人面孔的加工强度显著高于卡通面孔,提示幼儿对真人面孔的自动化加工程度更高,可能反映了其社会学意义;在晚期精细加工阶段,卡通面孔的加工强度显著高于真人面孔,提示卡通面孔对幼儿更具吸引力,使其投入了更多的注意资源;(3) 行为与 ERP 实验均表明,6 岁幼儿对不同表情的识别能力发展不平衡,根据本研究的结果,使用卡通面孔作为表情学习的材料,将有助于促进幼儿表情认知能力的发展。

1 引言

面孔提供表情、年龄、性别、姓名和个体识别等信息,承载大量社会信息。面部表情(facial expression)作为一种非言语信号,是情绪交流实现和情绪体验产生的重要基础和前提。对面孔表情的认知能力可以反映出个体通过情绪表情推测他人心理状态的能力[1]。

Denham (1986)对 2—4 岁幼儿高兴、悲伤、愤怒和害怕表情的研究发现,识别高兴的能力优于消极情绪,在消极情绪中最难识别的是害怕[2]。王军利等以 3—5 岁儿童为被试,要求儿童对静态和动态表情进行识别和标签,发现了幼儿表情标签与识别能力发展最好的是高兴,其次是愤怒和伤心,再次是害怕、惊讶和厌恶[3]。王振宏等(2010)用 Matsumoto 和 Ekman 编制的面部表情图片,让 3—6 岁幼儿进行标签和识别,结果发现,幼儿最先较好识别的是高兴表情,其次是愤怒和悲伤表情,最后是恐惧、惊奇和厌恶表情[4]。

近年来,卡通动画在幼儿日常生活中扮演了重要角色,成为幼儿感知、认识世界的

重要媒介,有着独特的价值。研究发现卡通面孔和真人面孔存在共同的面孔加工脑机制,Miyahara 在亚斯伯格症儿童与正常儿童对面孔表情加工差异的研究中,没有发现卡通面孔与真人面孔加工存在差异[5]。但是也有部分研究表明这两者之可能存在脑区与加工机制的差异。如王玲(2012)等人[6]在卡通面孔与真实面孔识别的 ERP 比较研究中,发现在早期加工阶段,大学生对卡通面孔与真实面孔加工强度不存在差异;在晚期加工阶段,真人面孔在枕区与颞区存在加工强度优势;卡通面孔加工表现出明显的右半球偏侧化,揭示成人在面孔结构加工阶段对卡通与真人面孔进行相似脑加工,而在面孔特征加工阶段,成人对卡通与真人面孔加工存在差异。韩世辉等人以 10 岁儿童为被试,利用 fMRI 研究发现,正常儿童观看虚拟现实中的卡通角色时,与观看真实人物一样会激活内侧前额叶皮(MPFC),而成人没有类似的脑激活[7],揭示儿童对卡通人物进行了与真实人物相似的脑加工,此外,尽管以往研究表明 4—6 岁幼儿已具有心理理论能力,但 10 岁儿童其 MPFC 尚未自动区分真实与虚拟角色。

比较不同类型面孔表情之间加工的差异研究有助于理解面孔表情认知的脑机制。本研究利用行为方法和 ERP 技术,来探究儿童对真人和卡通表情面孔进行加工的差异及其背后的脑机制。随机选取大班幼儿,以情绪类型(恐惧、生气、悲伤、高兴和平静)、面孔类型(卡通和真人)和被试性别作为自变量因素,使用不同的实验任务,考察这些因素对儿童表情标签和识别以及儿童卡通和真人面孔表情在注意和非注意条件下加工的 ERP 成分(如 N170、N2、P2、LPC 等)的潜伏期和波幅的影响。

2 幼儿对卡通与真人面孔表情认知的行为研究

2.1 研究方法

2.1.1 被试

随机选取大班幼儿 50 名,男女各半[平均月龄为(75.2 ±3.1)个月]。所有被试均为右利手,视力或矫正视力正常,无色盲,无精神病史,语言发展正常。

2.1.2 实验材料

真人儿童面孔照片来源于美国国家心理卫生研究中心的儿童表情面孔图片库(National Institute of Mental Health-Child Emotional Faces Picture Set, NIMH-ChEFS)[8],面孔的平均年龄为 13.6 岁,图片在平均年龄上无性别差异,该图库用于早期儿童焦虑障碍的 fMRI 研究,以保证所有刺激图片均为被试首次呈现。该图库包含正视(Direct Gaze)的平静(Neutral)、高兴(Happy)、悲伤(Sad)、恐惧(Afraid)和生气(Angry)面孔图片 266 张,剔除个别面孔表情缺失的,使用其中的 250 张(5 ×50 张)。每张平静儿童面孔均通过 Microsoft Cartoon Maker 软件转换为卡通面孔,并使用 Adobe Photoshop CS4 将卡通的脸覆盖到原图上进行微调,即保留相同的衣服、发型等,共合成情绪图片 250 张,控制所有图片高与宽均为 400 像素 ×260 像素,居中显示,所有图片背景统一为灰色,调整分辨率、明暗、对比度等一致。

500张儿童面孔表情图片由50名成人(平均年龄20.0岁,女性26名)进行情绪类型(1—平静,2—高兴,3—悲伤,4—恐惧,5—生气)和情绪强度(1—9分)的判断与评分,结果见表1。选取表情图片共180张[18×2(真人,卡通)×5(平静、高兴、悲伤、恐惧和生气),情绪强度均值为(5.68±0.53),准确率均值为89.5%]。

表1　大学生对5种表情标签的正确率与正确情绪强度的评价

刺激类型	情绪类型	正确率($M \pm SE$)	Max	Min	情绪强度($M \pm SE$)
真人	平静	0.87±0.02	0.98	0.40	4.81±0.07
真人	高兴	0.98±0.00	1.00	0.86	5.55±0.09
真人	悲伤	0.81±0.02	0.98	0.32	4.04±0.11
真人	恐惧	0.89±0.01	1.00	0.60	5.17±0.15
真人	生气	0.84±0.03	1.00	0.26	4.27±0.16
卡通	平静	0.88±0.02	1.00	0.46	4.83±0.09
卡通	高兴	0.96±0.01	1.00	0.68	5.78±0.09
卡通	悲伤	0.90±0.01	1.00	0.60	5.02±0.09
卡通	恐惧	0.85±0.01	0.96	0.70	5.57±0.12
卡通	生气	0.82±0.04	1.00	0.04	4.34±0.17

2.1.3　实验过程

(1)幼儿卡通与真人面孔情绪标签能力实验

面孔图片由E-prime程序随机呈现(见图1),每次呈现一张。请幼儿说出这张面部表情图片的情绪,即要求幼儿对表情面孔进行命名。幼儿报告的同时,主试立即按键并记录成绩,正确计1分,错误计0分。实验分为真人表情标签和卡通表情标签两个block,每个block包含15张图片,呈现顺序被试间交替。实验前另取表情面孔图片进行练习,以确定幼儿充分理解实验要求。

(2)幼儿卡通与真人面孔情绪识别能力实验

面孔图片由E-prime程序随机呈现(见图2),每次一组,每组5张图片(5种表情各1张)。主试随机指定一种情绪,请幼儿从五种表情中指认。幼儿指认同时,主试立即按键并记录成绩。正确计1分,错误计0分。实验分为真人表情识别和卡通表情识别两个block,各15组,呈现顺序被试间交替。实验前另取表情面孔图片进行练习,以确定幼儿充分理解实验要求。

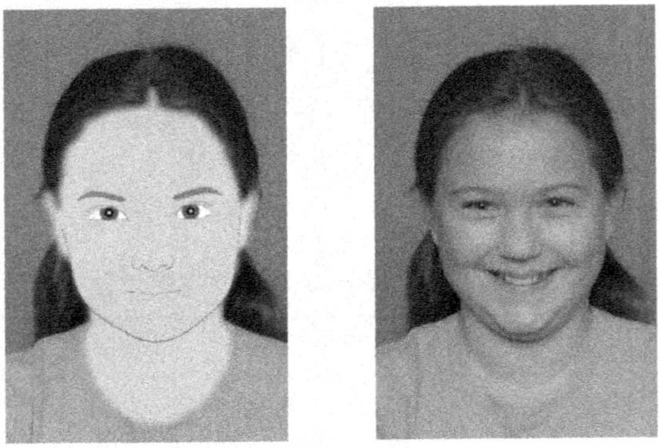

图1　表情标签任务刺激材料(左图为卡通,右图为真人)

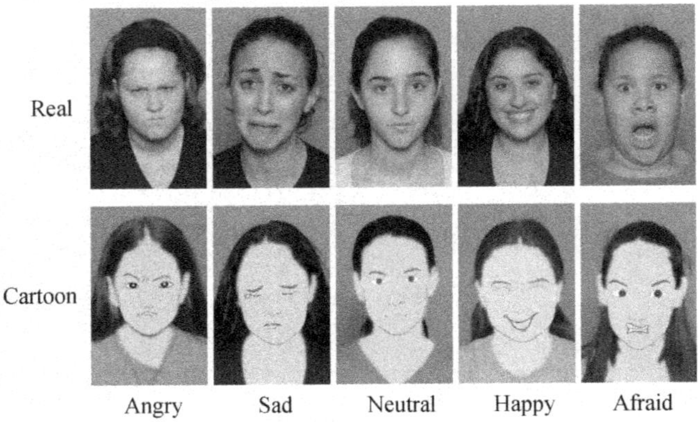

图2　表情识别任务刺激材料

2.1.4　数据分析

运用SPSS13.0统计分析软件对数据进行处理分析。表情标签和识别任务比较:以真人、卡通表情标签和识别的正确率作为因变量,进行2(任务类型:标签和识别)×5(表情类型)×2(性别)的重复测量方差分析,其中性别为被试间变量。表情标签任务:以真人与卡通表情标签正确率和反应时作为因变量,进行2(图片类型:真人和卡通)×5(表情类型)×2(性别)的重复测量方差分析,其中性别为被试间变量。表情识别任务:以真人和卡通表情的正确率与反应时作为因变量,进行2(图片类型:真人和卡通)×5(表情类型)×2(性别)的重复测量方差分析,其中性别为被试间变量。若不符合球形检验,则采用Greenhouse Geisser法校正。

2.2　结果与分析

2.2.1　幼儿表情标签与识别能力的差异

真人表情结果显示:情绪类型主效应显著,$F(4,388)=29.396$,$p<0.01$。事后检验表明,悲伤(0.729±0.03)的正确率显著低于其他各种表情,高兴(0.995±0.005)

的正确率显著高于平静(0.903 ±0.021)和恐惧(0.918 ±0.018)。任务类型和表情类型交互作用显著,$F(4,388)=6.359$,$p<0.01$。简单效应分析显示,恐惧与生气表情在两种任务下存在显著差异,恐惧识别的正确率(0.990 ±0.01)显著高于标签(0.846 ±0.036),$F(1,98)=13.84$,$p<0.001$;生气识别的正确率(0.990 ±0.010)也显著高于标签(0.950 ±0.022),$F(1,98)=4.13$,$p<0.05$;其他主效应和交互作用均不显著。任务类型的主效应虽不显著,但真人表情识别正确率(0.907 ±0.012)略高于真人表情标签正确率(0.899 ±0.014)。整体来说,6 岁幼儿表情认知能力发展稳定,识别能力发展优于标签能力,主要体现在恐惧与生气情绪上。

卡通表情结果显示:情绪类型的主效应显著 $F(4,388)=5.178$,$p<0.01$,事后检验表明,恐惧表情的正确率(0.945 ±0.016)显著低于高兴(0.995 ±0.005)和平静(0.995 ±0.005)。其他主效应和交互作用均不显著,但卡通表情识别得分(0.986 ±0.005)略高于卡通表情标签得分(0.972 ±0.009)。

2.2.2 幼儿对真人和卡通表情认知能力的差异

(1) 真人和卡通表情标签能力的差异

正确率结果显示,图片类型主效应显著,$F(1,98)=34.553$,$p<0.01$,事后检验表明,卡通表情正确率(0.98 ±0.01)显著高于真人表情(0.90 ±0.01)。表情类型主效应显著,$F(4,392)=15.445$,$p<0.01$,幼儿对表情标签的正确率由高到低依次为高兴(0.995 ±0.01)、生气(0.975 ±0.01)、平静(0.955 ±0.02)、恐惧(0.939 ±0.018)和悲伤(0.833 ±0.024),事后检验表明,悲伤表情标签得分显著低于其他四种表情,恐惧表情标签得分显著低于高兴表情。图片类型和表情类型交互作用显著(见图 3),$F(4,392)=23.122$,$p<0.01$,简单效应分析显示,悲伤的图片类型差异显著,幼儿对卡通悲伤表情的标签能力显著高于真人。这说明,卡通和真人表情标签能力差异主要体现在悲伤表情上。其他主效应和交互作用均不显著。

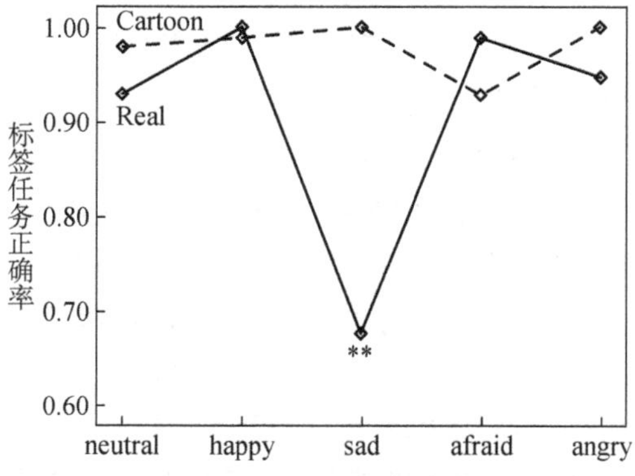

图 3 卡通和真人表情标签任务正确率比较(:$p<0.01$)**

反应时结果显示:图片类型主效应显著,$F(1,98)=34.879$,$p<0.01$,事后检验表

明,卡通标签反应时[(2 946.6 ±86.7)ms]显著短于真人[(4 272.0 ±220.3)ms];情绪类型主效应显著,$F(4,392)=7.941$,$p<0.01$,事后检验表明,悲伤表情反应时[(4 610.5 ±331.5)ms]显著长于高兴表情[(2 820.0 ±239.9)ms],生气表情[(3 077.3 ±178.9)ms]、恐惧表情反应时[(3 722.2 ±182.2)ms]显著长于高兴表情;图片类型和表情类型交互作用显著(见图4),$F(4,392)=4.110$,$p<0.05$,简单效应分析显示,悲伤表情下,卡通反应时显著短于真人反应时,$F(1,98)=18.86$,$p<0.01$。其他主效应和交互作用均不显著。上述结果说明,卡通和真人表情标签能力的差异主要体现在悲伤表情上。

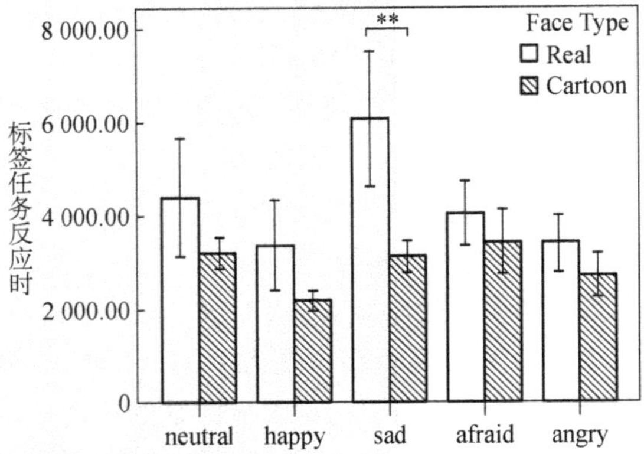

图4　卡通和真人表情标签任务平均反应时差异(:$p<0.01$)**

(2) 真人和卡通表情识别能力的差异

正确率结果发现:图片类型主效应显著,$F(1,98)=41.295$,$p<0.01$,事后检验表明,真人情绪识别(0.899 ±0.014)显著低于卡通情绪识别(0.986 ±0.005)。表情类型主效应显著,$F(4,388)=8.6$,$p<0.01$,事后检验表明,幼儿对表情识别的正确率由高到低依次为高兴(0.995 ±0.005)、生气(0.984 ±0.009)、平静(0.939 ±0.016)、恐惧(0.904 ±0.022)和悲伤(0.889 ±0.022);高兴表情识别的正确率显著高于其他四种表情,生气、平静和恐惧表情识别正确率显著高于悲伤,生气表情的识别的正确率显著高于恐惧。表情类型与图片类型交互作用显著(见图5),$F(4,392)=8.311$,$p<0.01$。简单效应分析结果:卡通面孔表情下,正确率差异不显著;真人面孔下,幼儿表情识别能力在情绪类型上存在显著性差异,$F(4,392)=9.52$,$p<0.01$;此外,当表情类型为平静、悲伤、恐惧时,卡通面孔表情识别正确率显著高于真人[平静:$F(1,98)=13.52$,$p<0.01$;悲伤:$F(1,98)=24.81$,$p<0.01$,恐惧:$F(1,98)=8.69$,$p<0.05$],详参图5;性别与表情类型交互作用显著 $F(4,388)=3.33$,$p<0.05$,简单效应分析表明:女孩和男孩对各种表情识别的正确率差异显著,其中高兴和生气情绪正确率显著高于其他情绪。此外,女孩的悲伤情绪识别正确率(0.938 ±0.031)显著高于男孩(0.843 ±0.030),$F(1,95)=5.84$,$p<0.05$。其他主效应及交互作用不显著。

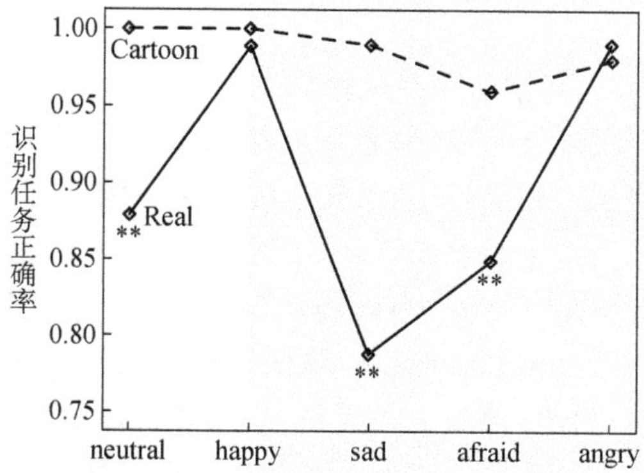

图5　卡通和真人表情识别任务正确率比较（ * ： $p<0.05$ ， ** ： $p<0.01$ ）

上述结果表明，幼儿表情识别能力受到图片类型显著影响。整体来说，幼儿卡通表情识别能力优于真人表情识别能力，且女孩表情识别能力发展要优于男孩。

识别反应时结果发现：表情类型主效应显著， $F(4,392)=4.45$ ， $p<0.05$ ，事后检验表明，反应时由短到长依次是高兴[（4 760.2 ±548.3）ms]、生气[（4 959.4 ±200.7）ms]、平静[（4 984.4 ±286.4）ms]、恐惧[（5 003.1 ±168.1）ms]和悲伤[（6 379.30 ±381.67）ms]（见图6），其中悲伤表情反应时显著高于其他类型表情反应时，其余表情类型两两之间差异均不显著。图片类型主效应显著， $F(1,98)=23.065$ ， $p<0.01$ ，事后检验表明，真人图片类型识别反应时[（5 966.2 ±217.1）ms]显著长于卡通图片[（4 468.4 ±291.5）ms]，表明幼儿对卡通表情识别显著快于真人。情绪类型与图片类型交互作用显著（见图6）， $F(4,392)=7.771$ ， $p<0.01$ 。简单效应分析表明，悲伤表情下，卡通面孔反应时显著短于真人， $F(1,98)=44.38$ ， $p<0.01$ 。

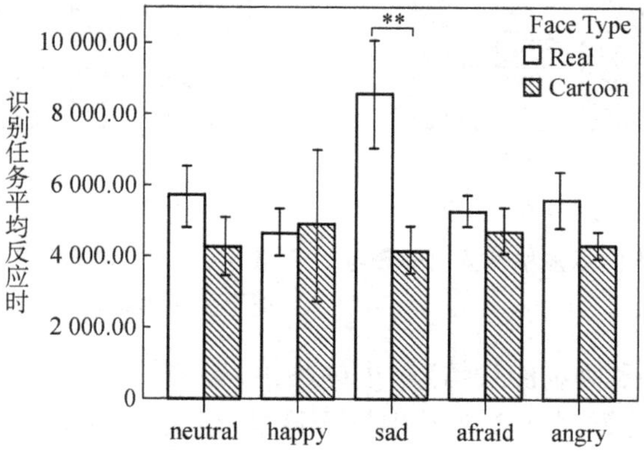

图6　卡通和真人表情识别任务平均反应时差异（ ** ： $p<0.01$ ）

上述结果表明，整体来说卡通表情识别速度快于真人表情识别能力，且主要体现在悲伤表情上。

2.3 讨论

2.3.1 卡通面孔相较于真人面孔表情认知更具优势

从图7和图8可以发现,幼儿对卡通面孔表情的认知在反应时和正确率上均优于真人面孔表情。具体来说,幼儿对卡通面孔五种表情识别能力均较高,尤其在识别卡通面孔平静、恐惧、悲伤表情上显著优于真人;此外,幼儿对卡通面孔悲伤表情标签能力显著优于真人。这与 Hoptman & Levy(1988)利用嵌合图片发现卡通和真人面孔认知加工没有差异及王玲等在早期结构编码阶段发现卡通和真人面孔认知不存在差异的研究结果不尽一致。差异可能源于刺激材料,本研究运用的卡通面孔包含了表情,而王玲等人(2012)的刺激材料都是中性无表情的卡通面孔。

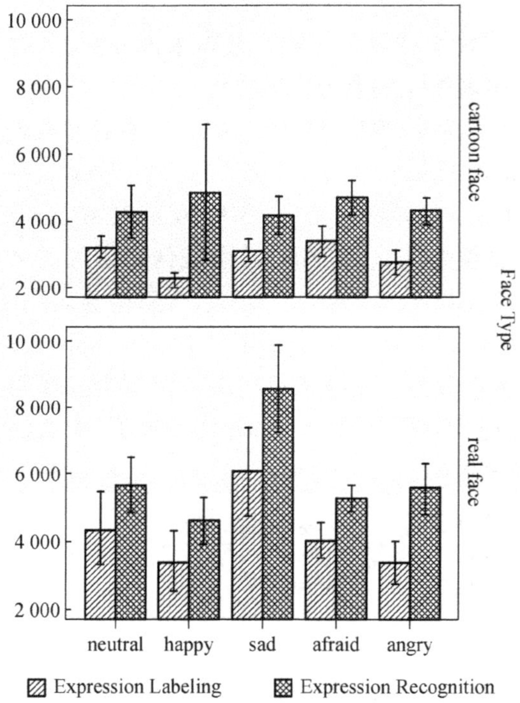

图7 卡通和真人在表情标签和表情识别任务下的反应时比较

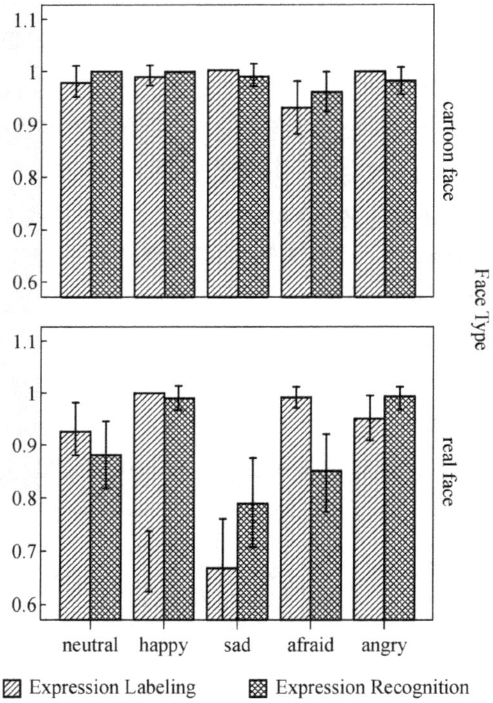

图8 卡通和真人在表情标签和表情识别任务下的正确率比较

达尔文在《人类和动物的表情》一书中指出,人类的一些最基本的原始情绪带有遗传性,如高兴、生气等,在儿童生活中体验最早,因而其认知发展也最早。本研究显示,幼儿对卡通和真人面孔的高兴和生气两种表情认知能力均甚好,不存在显著差异,是由于6岁幼儿高兴或生气表情的认知已发展成熟,如果对2—3岁的幼童进行测试,可能会得出不同的结论。

幼儿对卡通平静、恐惧与悲伤表情的认知显著优于真人。推测这种差异源自面孔识别晚期阶段,是由于实验刺激材料的类型(卡通、真人)差异导致脑区激活不同所致[9]。面孔五官体现了个体的具体相貌,直接传递情绪,且真人面孔的额眼、眉、鼻、嘴、耳的大小特点颇具差异。通常卡通面孔表情设计,是生活积累与艺术再创造的结果,对面部五官都采用了简化和夸张,能增强表情的力度和气势。这种夸张的刻画,能够鲜明传达出各种表情的特征,推测幼儿对真人与卡通面孔表情的认知差异,是基于五官的固定表征差异。幼儿对卡通面孔表情认知优于真人是源于卡通面孔的夸张的表征,更易于或更大程度上刺激了大脑的颞枕区。如改用动态表情刺激,则差异可能主要反映在顶叶背侧通路上。该假设可以进一步通过 ERP 或脑成像研究加以验证。

2.3.2 幼儿面孔表情识别能力优于表情标签

从图 8 可以看出,6 岁幼儿的面孔表情认知能力发展比较成熟,识别的平均正确率高达 90.7%,标签的平均正确率高达 89.9%。面孔表情的识别能力略优于标签能力,尤其体现在恐惧和生气情绪上。这与王军利等以 3—5 岁儿童为被试,进行静态和动态表情识别和标签任务,发现幼儿表情识别能力好于标签能力结果一致[10]。姚端维(2004)等人研究 3—5 岁儿童情绪能力的年龄特征、发展趋势和性别差异,发现 4 岁幼儿已基本上获得了情绪理解能力[11]。本研究发现 6 岁幼儿的情绪认知能力已经处于稳定且发展较好的状态。6 岁儿童对面孔情绪的标签能力弱于识别能力,可能是因为面部表情识别需要幼儿掌握一定的情绪词汇,而且面部情绪标签也可能要求更高的认知能力[12]。

比较真人与卡通面孔的两项任务,我们发现,幼儿对恐惧、伤心和生气的识别和标签能力均弱于平静和高兴表情,这与 Denham(1986)的结果一致。使用高兴、悲伤、生气和恐惧四种表情,2—4 岁幼儿标签和识别高兴的能力优于消极情绪,其中,对恐惧表情的识别能力最弱[13],究其原因可能是因为 6 岁儿童认识体验情绪需要与过去经验相联系,而幼儿处于人生早期阶段,生活经验不足。在日常生活中,在极少的机会之下,父母会使得儿童在感到恐惧的情境中,并且父母也较少在儿童面前表现出恐惧情绪。此外,幼儿生气表情识别能力也显著高于标签能力,依据 Woodworth(1938)建立的六种面部表情的系统量表中的基本情绪为(1) 喜爱,幸福,快乐;(2) 惊讶;(3) 恐惧,痛苦;(4) 生气,决心;(5) 厌恶;(6) 蔑视。生气与恐惧情绪在系统量表里的位置相邻近,痛苦(伤心)和恐惧则被归为一类,因而推测幼儿对于伤心、恐惧和生气表情的反应速度和准确率也相似。

2.3.3 6 岁幼儿对面孔不同表情的认知特点

幼儿对不同的面部表情认知存在差异,表情标签任务中表现为高兴 > 生气 > 平静 > 悲伤 > 恐惧,在表情识别任务中表现为高兴 > 生气 > 平静 > 恐惧 > 悲伤;综合识别与标签实验结果发现,幼儿对面孔五种表情的认知能力由高到低依次为高兴、生气、平静、恐惧、悲伤,对生气和恐惧表情的认知显著高于悲伤表情。幼儿对高兴表情认知能力出现天花板效应，与王异芳和赵怡菲(2009)的研究一致，他们认为产生这一结果的原因是高兴表情在社会交往中的表现稳定，与其他消极情绪相比，在社会化修饰、掩盖或夸大的过程中高兴表情没有显著的变化。

本研究发现幼儿对生气的认知优于悲伤，幼儿最难对悲伤表情进行识别和标签。然而 Camras 等(1990)发现：美国白人幼儿对悲伤的认知能力高于生气与恐惧[14]。这种差异可能基于文化差异，中国的父母极少会在孩子面前表露悲伤，而美国的父母会把自己的悲伤表现出来，并让孩子体会到父母的悲伤情绪。这种东西方文化的差异使得中美幼儿表情认知发展规律存在差异。

2.3.4　女孩较男孩对悲伤情绪更具易感性

情绪易感性(emotional susceptibility)是指个体感知情绪能力的大小，及其认知过程容易受情绪影响的程度[15,16]。大量研究表明，性别差异影响了情绪加工，即女性在识别情绪时具有优势，相比于男性，情绪记忆能力更好，负性情绪易感性更强。不管是面孔表情还是情绪场景，女性都能既准确又快速地对表情进行识别，并且对情绪的敏感性也更高。本研究发现 6 岁女童对悲伤表情的识别正确率显著高于男童，这说明女童比男童更易识别悲伤情绪，该结论验证了负性情绪易感性具有性别差异的假设，根本原因是表情加工的神经基础存在性别差异，而该差异也与两性之间皮层体积的大小、半球间的信息沟通以及荷尔蒙水平变异等因素有关[17]。

Lee 等人(2002)采用 fMRI 技术研究发现，在悲伤情绪的识别中，女性相比男性较少卷入前额叶皮层的活动，提示女性可能更为自动化地识别悲伤情绪。进一步研究发现男性人群倾向于通过回忆过去情绪经验，激活岛叶皮层；女性则是通过即时情绪感受来识别眼前不同刺激材料(如场景、表情与词汇)的情绪内容[18]。研究发现，与男性相比，女性的眶额皮层较大[19]，因而推测女性拥有更大的脑容积来调节杏仁核的表情信息的输入，导致女性在表情加工方面具有优势。面部表情识别的功能磁共振成像研究发现，负性情绪刺激下，女性的额叶和小脑激活更明显[20]。女童较男童对悲伤情绪更具易感性，不仅受到遗传、激素与大脑活动等生理因素的影响，也与儿童先天不同的气质特征及性别角色认知有关，还受到教育文化传统等社会背景的影响。

一项关于幼儿认知、个性发展的性别差异研究发现，6 岁男童在好奇心及情绪稳定性两方面优于女童。女童对悲伤情绪的易感性体现了其情绪的不稳定性，这与家长、幼儿保教人员对待男女幼儿的不同教育方式有关。父母有意无意地按着社会所给予的性别规范，去期望和要求儿女。在父母的态度和行为影响下，男童从小就被唤起“男儿有泪不轻弹”的意识，并努力表现出勇敢、顽强的性格。性别角色的社会认知理论在解释儿童性别角色发展中强调了模仿的作用，指出模仿从婴儿一出生就开始起作用。婴儿能通过模仿进行学习，尤其在互动情境中。当儿童依据环境行为获得性别角色适应性的时候，便开始扮演与社会性别相符的行为，体验社会的反映，并管理其相应的行为。因而,男童潜意识中深藏着的悲伤情绪经常处于压抑状态,不能得到有效的宣泄和疏导,对其缺乏体验。

3 研究二:表情判断任务下幼儿卡通与真人面孔表情加工的ERP比较研究

3.1 研究方法

3.1.1 被试

随机选取大班幼儿18名[平均月龄(75.1±4.6)个月],男女各半。所有被试均为右利手,视力或矫正视力正常,无色盲,无精神病史,测试前家长签下知情同意书。

3.1.2 实验材料

选取NIMH-ChEFS中平静、高兴、悲伤、恐惧和生气的真人以及合成的卡通面孔图片共200张[20×2(真人,卡通)×5(平静、高兴、悲伤、恐惧和生气),情绪强度均值为5.20±0.81,准确率均值为95.5%](见图9)。因实验任务为面孔表情判断,即判断两张表情面孔是否一致,将刺激材料随机组合,其中真人和卡通面孔不同时出现在一个组。最终生成刺激材料100组,控制所有图片的像素为600×452,居中显示,视角为16.9°×11.1°,其他控制因素同研究一。

图9 表情判断任务刺激材料

3.1.3 实验过程

实验要求幼儿判断两张图片的情绪是否一致,须认真注视每一张呈现的面孔,正式实验前先进行练习。反应键在被试间进行左右手交叉平衡设计。100组图片由Stim²(Neuroscan)程序随机呈现,每次呈现一组,呈现时间为1 000 ms,若被试在1 000 ms内做出判断,图片自动消失,呈现白屏直至下一张图片出现,若被试未能在1 000 ms内做出判断,图片自动消失呈现白屏直至下一张图片出现。刺激间隔ISI在1 800—2 000 ms之间随机,实验同时记录脑电。实验分为真人表情判断和卡通表情判断两个 block，每个 block 包含 50 组面孔，每个 block 之后休息 5 分钟。

3.1.4　脑电记录参数

Neuroscan 32 导系统记录脑电，脑电采样率为 1 000 Hz，DC 采样，带宽：0—70 Hz。以双侧乳突平均为参考，前额接地，同时在两眼外侧记录水平眼电（HEOG）和左眼上下记录垂直眼电（VEOG），电极与皮肤接触阻抗小于 5 kΩ。使用 Scan4.3 软件对 EEG 数据进行离线分析。EOG 信号相关法去除眼电伪迹，分析时程选取 -200—1 000 ms，将波幅大于 ±120 μV 的视为伪迹而剔除。对 EEG 进行波形叠加平均，30 Hz 低通滤波。

3.1.5　数据采集与分析

为考查 N170 成分，采用 2（面孔类型：卡通、真人）×2（表情组合：一致、不一致）×2（左右半球：T5、T6）×2（被试性别：男、女）重复测量方差分析的实验设计；考查 LPC 成分，采用 2（面孔类型：卡通、真人）×2（表情组合：一致、不一致）×3（偏侧化：左侧、中央、右侧）×3（脑区：中央区、顶中央区和顶区）×2（被试性别：男、女）重复测量方差分析的实验设计。自变量是不同面孔类型、表情组合以及左右半球和被试性别，因变量是被试反应时和正确率，N170 的潜伏期、波幅以及 LPC 平均波幅。参考以往研究，32 导脑电记录选取颞枕区的 T5、T6 电极分析 N170 成分，选取中央区的 C3、Cz 和 C4，顶中央区的 CP3、CPz 和 CP4 以及顶区的 P3、Pz 和 P4 电极分析 LPC 成分。若不符合球形检验，则采用 Greenhouse Geisser 法校正。

3.2　结果分析

3.2.1　行为结果分析

在反应时上，主效应和交互作用均不显著，其中被试对真人面孔的反应时[（882.7 ± 15.1）ms]大于卡通面孔[（856.0 ± 16.1）ms]，$p = 0.057$。在正确率上，真人面孔[（36.6 ±2.6）%]显著低于卡通面孔[（47.4 ± 3.4）%]，$F(1,16) = 26.439$，$p < 0.001$；其他主效应和交互作用均不显著（见表 2）。

表 2　表情判断任务的幼儿平均反应时与正确率　　*M*（*SD*）

	卡通面孔		真人面孔	
	表情相同	表情不同	表情相同	表情不同
反应时（ms）	855.3（65.8）	856.7（84.7）	884.1（66.1）	881.3（66.8）
正确率（%）	50.2（18.4）	44.7（21.4）	39.6（16.3）	33.6（17.8）

3.2.2　ERPs 结果分析

（1）N170

N170 潜伏期：主效应和交互作用均不显著。

N170 波幅：面孔类型主效应显著，$F(1,16) = 9.988$，$p < 0.01$，真人面孔诱发的

N170 波幅[(−8.87±0.94)μV]显著大于卡通面孔[(−6.11±0.83)μV]；偏侧化主效应接近显著，$p=0.052$，左半球的 N170 波幅[(−9.10±1.11)μV]小于右半球[(−5.88±1.06)μV]（见表3，图10）。其他主效应和交互作用均不显著。

表3　表情判断任务的 N170 波幅(μV)　　*M*(*SE*)

刺激类型	T5	T6
卡通面孔		
表情相同	−3.32(1.26)	−7.96(1.21)
表情不同	−5.08(1.08)	−8.07(1.14)
真人面孔		
表情相同	−8.67(1.24)	−9.81(1.78)
表情不同	−6.43(1.27)	−10.58(1.54)

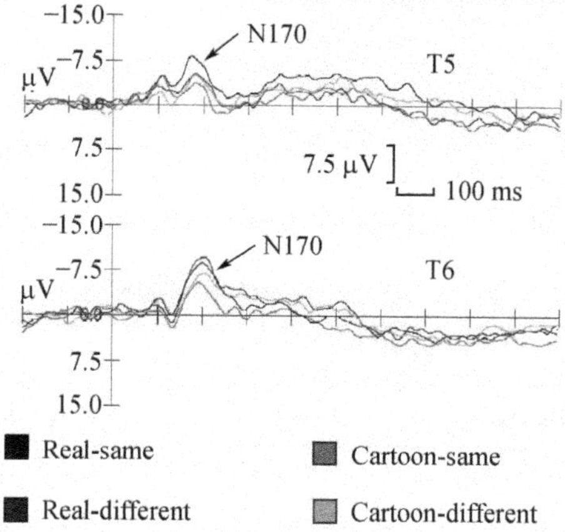

图10　表情判断任务的 N170 波形图

（2）LPC

根据每个被试各电极上的 ERP 波形图，同时参考所有被试平均反应时，其值 869.4 ms，选取 550—850 ms 为 LPC 分析时段，该时间段所记录到的 LPC 波形仍处于面孔识别的加工阶段。LPC 平均波幅的方差分析结果如图11。

真人面孔诱发的 LPC 平均波幅[(11.23±1.45)μV]显著小于卡通面孔[(17.15±1.34)μV]，$F(1,16)=12.117$，$p<0.01$。半球主效应显著，$F(2,32)=9.450$，$p<0.01$，其中中央的 LPC 平均波幅[(17.82±1.47)μV]显著高于左半球[(11.99±1.57)μV，$p<0.001$]和右半球[(12.76±1.51)μV，$p<0.001$]。脑区差异也极其显著，$F(1.238,19.807)=35.369$，$p<0.001$，中央区[(8.22±1.38)μV]、中央顶区[(13.96±1.40)μV]与顶区[(20.39±1.73)μV]的三者之间的差异也极其显著，$p<$

0.001。此外，脑区与偏侧化的交互作用极其显著，$F(4,64)=7.340$，$p<0.001$。简单效应分析表明：不同脑区的 LPC 平均波幅在左半球、中央和右半球的差异均极其显著，$p<0.001$；在中央顶区和中央区，LPC 平均波幅的偏侧化差异极其显著，$p<0.001$，而在顶区无差异（见表4）。

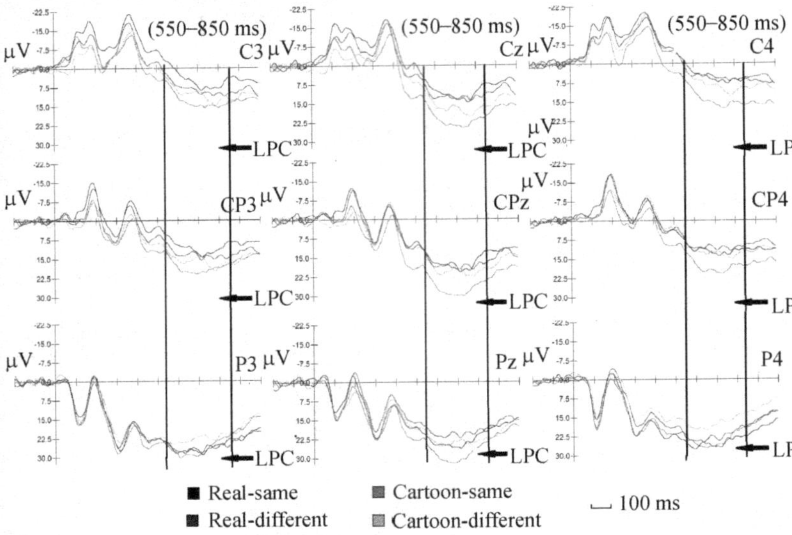

图 11　表情判断任务的 LPC 波形图

表 4　表情判断任务的 LPC 平均波幅（μV）　　$M(SE)$

电极点	卡通面孔		真人面孔	
	表情不同	表情相同	表情不同	表情相同
C3	9.45(1.69)	7.96(1.96)	2.49(2.10)	1.43(2.72)
Cz	17.93(2.41)	15.71(2.05)	10.33(1.96)	8.55(2.60)
C4	11.16(1.69)	8.89(1.81)	3.89(2.05)	0.87(2.74)
CP3	14.92(2.05)	13.90(2.03)	8.20(2.02)	7.21(2.28)
CPz	22.97(2.49)	20.55(2.17)	17.10(2.23)	14.76(1.97)
CP4	16.23(1.66)	14.51(2.16)	10.99(1.83)	6.19(2.69)
P3	21.05(2.40)	20.62(2.31)	18.33(2.81)	18.34(2.77)
Pz	25.04(2.43)	23.32(2.13)	20.23(2.30)	17.39(1.84)
P4	23.14(2.05)	21.43(2.82)	19.67(2.51)	16.17(3.13)

表情判断任务下诱发的时程为 550—850 ms 的 LPC 广泛分布于顶区。当面孔表情不一致时，卡通面孔加工出现明显偏侧化，主要在左侧，而对真人面孔的加工主要在双侧顶区，但相比于右侧，左侧加工更深；当面孔表情一致时，卡通面孔的加工更广泛，

而真人面孔加工则主要在双侧顶区(见图12)。

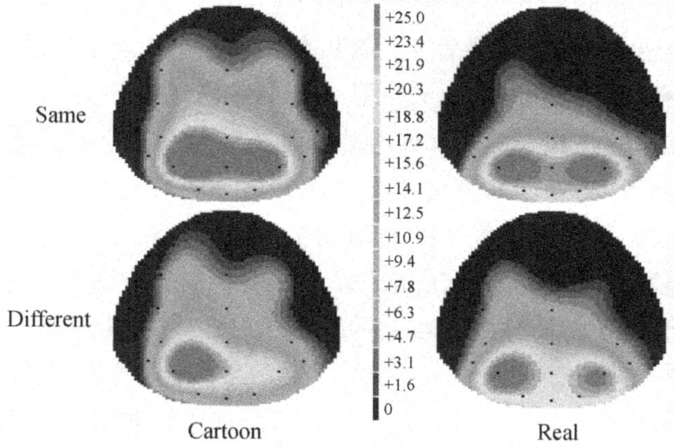

图12　表情判断任务的LPC地形图(550—850 ms)

3.3　讨论

3.3.1　幼儿对卡通面孔表情认知优于真人

行为数据表明,在判断任务中,对卡通面孔表情反应的正确率显著高于真人,且与研究结果一致,表明实验使用的面孔材料具有一定代表性。判断任务中,对真人面孔的反应时稍长于卡通,面孔信息附带有经验信息,幼儿在日常生活中能够接触大量卡通形象,幼儿对卡通面孔较真人面孔更加熟悉,因此反应时较短。

3.3.2　幼儿卡通与真人面孔表情在早期加工阶段存在显著差异

在面孔识别早期阶段,卡通面孔与真人面孔表情均诱发了N170,两者在潜伏期上没有显著性差异,但真人面孔表情诱发的N170波幅要显著高于卡通,显示了在早期的面孔结构加工阶段,幼儿真人面孔加工强度要高于卡通。这与王玲等在早期结构编码阶段发现成人对卡通和真人面孔认知不存在差异的研究结果不尽一致。可能原因有三:一是与王玲等人研究被试的年龄、社会经验不同。Bruce和Young[20]认为面孔识别第一阶段是对面孔整体结构的识别,卡通与真人面孔整体面孔结构相似,因此在王玲等人的研究中发现面孔识别早期阶段不存在差异。本研究发现真人面孔所诱发的N170比卡通面孔所诱发的N170波幅大,可能是由于卡通面孔附带的经验信息与幼儿的社会经验有直接联系,幼儿在提取时的卡通面孔表情识别动用较少的心理资源,在提取真人面孔表情时动用较多的心理资源,加工过程也更加复杂。二是任务不同。本研究要求幼儿被试对两张面孔表情进行判断,而王玲等要求成人被试从面孔及非面孔图片中识别面孔图片。再次,差异也可能源于刺激材料,本研究采用的卡通面孔包含了表情,整体结构更加夸张,而王玲等的刺激材料都是中性无表情卡通面孔,整体结构单一。依据Bruce和Young的面孔识别加工模型可知,表情分析在早期面孔结构加工之后,早期面孔识别加工不受表情影响[20]。李围(2012)通过比较愉快、愤怒及中性面孔表情诱发的 N170,也发现其差异不明显,证实了 N170 不受面孔表情内容的调制。因此,参照本实验的方法和结果,是由于静态图形面孔的质地类型即卡通与真人对产生 N170 波幅的差异,结果表明,幼儿在对早期面孔加工阶段,幼儿更易识别整体夸张的卡通面孔,也证实了 N170 是面孔识别的特异性成分[21]。

3.3.3 幼儿卡通与真人面孔表情在晚期加工阶段存在显著差异

在晚期加工阶段,卡通面孔表情比真人面孔表情诱发了更正的 LPC,表明卡通面孔表情比真人面孔表情涉及更复杂的心理加工。可能反映了儿童的脑更加关注卡通面孔,幼儿对卡通面孔具有显著的认知偏好。韩世辉等研究发现,儿童观看卡通人物与真实人物时都激活了与心理理论相关的脑区 MPFC,表明儿童在观看卡通时能够置身其中"感同身受"[24]。分析其原因可能在于:虽然卡通与真人面孔在年龄、角色等因素上保持一致,但通过真人转化的卡通面孔表情添加了各种夸张元素,在面孔基本结构、表情等方面明显区别于真人面孔,根据 Bruce-Young 模型[20],面孔认知加工的第二阶段是对表情分析、面孔语言分析、面孔视觉特征分析与面孔身份识别等加工,所以早期成分差异体现了对卡通与真人面孔的粗略信息加工;而晚期成分的差异则体现了对卡通面孔与真人面孔的精细信息加工的差异。在对面孔特征进行编码后,进入后继视觉处理单元,对面孔的精细特征进行分析。卡通面孔与真实面孔在 ERP 晚期成分 LPC 平均波幅上的差异可能反映了对面孔的表情、五官等精细信息进行加工的差异,而且儿童对卡通面孔的细节特征加工投入了更多的注意资源,相对增加了被试的认知负荷,Van Schie 等人的研究表明注意资源和认知负荷能够影响 LPC[22]。实验结果与 Bruce-Young 模型吻合较好。总体而言,面孔加工是整体加工先于特征加工,粗略信息加工先于精细加工。

此外,晚期正成分(LPC)的波幅与背景更新的分类加工的程度有关。陈安涛等人的研究表明,类别判断在晚期正成分(LPC)上有明显的反应[23]。因此,550—850 ms 时间窗口内 LPC 的差异证明了幼儿对卡通与真人面孔表情是否一致的判断存在差异,卡通面孔对幼儿产生更大的影响。从信息加工的角度来讲,幼儿对卡通面孔认知偏好伴随大脑信息加工的出现。这种偏好可能由于卡通在幼儿日常生活中扮演重要角色,反映的是幼儿对熟悉刺激的偏好。

4 结论与展望

4.1 结论

卡通对儿童表情认知的社会性发展具有显著的影响,结论如下:(1) 幼儿对卡通面孔表情认知能力优于真人面孔,特别是悲伤、恐惧和平静表情,原因可能为卡通面孔的夸张的表情与简化的五官等表征更符合幼儿的认知发展水平;(2) 幼儿对卡通与真人面孔加工的神经机制存在差异,对应于 Bruce & Young 的面孔加工模型,在早期结构编码阶段，真人面孔的加工强度显著高于卡通面孔，提示幼儿对真人面孔的自动化加工程度更高，可能反映了其社会学意义；在晚期精细加工阶段，卡通面孔的加工强度显著高于真人面孔，提示卡通面孔对幼儿更具吸引力，使其投入了更多的注意资源；(3) 行为与ERP实验均表明，6岁幼儿对不同表情的识别能力发展不平衡，根据本研究的结果，使用卡通面孔作为表情学习的材料，将有助于促进幼儿表情认知能力的发展。

4.2 展望

现今大多数关于表情面孔的研究中，所使用的刺激材料为静止面孔，但表情具有社会性，是动态变化的，从图片到视频，让表情动起来，使得研究更生态化；另外，关于基本表情的研究已经几近饱和，研究幼儿对复杂表情（如尴尬等）的识别将会更有效的补充和完善表情面孔加工的脑机制。

此外，ERPs因具有很高的时间分辨率而备受青睐，但在空间分辨率上却略显不足，未来的研究可以考虑将其与功能性成像技术如fMRI、fNIRs等结合起来以获得更准确脑源定位。

References

[1] C A Nelson. Recognition of Facial expressions by 7-month-old infants. Child Development, 1979, 50: 58 - 61.

[2] S A Denham. Social cognition, prosocial behavior and emotion in preschoolers: Contextual validation. Child Development, 1986, 57: 194 - 201.

[3] J L Wang. The developmental research on 3—5 year old children's abilities of facial expression recognition, facial expression labeling and cognition of emotional display rules. Hangzhou: Zhejiang Normal University, 2012.

[4] Z H Wang. The developmental characteristics of recognition and free labeling of facial expression of emotion in 3-6-year-old children. Journal of Psychological Science, 2010, 33: 325 - 328.

[5] M Miyahara, A Bray, M Tsujii, et al. Reaction time of facial affect recognition in Aspersers disorder for cartoon and real, static and moving Faces. Child psychiatry and Human Development, 2007, 38: 121 - 134.

[6] L Wang, J M Wang, J L Wang, et al. A comparative event-related potential study on recognition of cartoon face and real face. Psychological Research, 2012, 5: 19 - 28.

[7] S H Han, Y Jiang, W H Glyn. Watching cartoons activates the medial prefrontal cortex in children. Chinese Sci Bull, 2007, 52: 3371 - 3375.

[8] H L Egger, D S Pine, E Nelson, et al. The NIMH Child Emotional Faces Picture Set (NIMH-ChEFS): A new set of children's facial emotion stimuli. International Journal of Methods in Psychiatric Research, 2011, 20: 145 - 156.

[9] S M Ji, W Li, P Liu, et al. Studies of visual mismatch negativity elicited by cartoon facial expression. Journal of Biomedical Engineering, 2013, 3: 476 - 480.

[10] J L Wang, J M Wang, J T Ren, et al. A comparative event-related potential study on cartoon face classification and perception processing. Journal of Psychological Science, 2013, 36: 320 - 327.

[11] D W Yao, H Y Chen, Y Q Zhao. The study on the age characters, development trend and sex differences of preschoolers' emotion competence. Psychological Development and Education, 2004, 2: 12 - 16.

[12] Y F Wang, Y F Zhao. On developmental features of ability to denominate facial expressions in 3-5-year-old children. Early Childhood Education: Educational Sciences, 2009, 6: 39 - 43.

[13] L A Camras, S Ribordy, J Hill, et al. Maternal facial behavior and the recognition and production of emotional expression by maltreated and non-maltreated children. Developmental Psychology, 1990, 26: 304 - 312.

[14] C L Rusting, R J Larsen. Extraversion, neuroticism and susceptibility to positive and negative affect: A test of two theoretical models. Personality and Individual Differences, 1997, 22: 607 - 612.

[15] J M Zelenski, R J Larsen. Susceptibility to affect: A comparison of three personality taxonomies. Journal of Personality, 1999, 67: 761 - 791.

[16] J J Yuan, H Li. The human susceptibility to the valence strength of emotional stimuli: Neural mechanisms. Advances in Psychological Science, 2012, 20: 10 - 18.

[17] T M C Lee, H L Liu, R Hoosain, et al. Gender differences in neural correlates of recognition of happy and sad faces in humans assessed by functional magnetic resonance imaging. Neuroscience Letters, 2002, 333: 13 - 16.

[18] R C Gur, F G Dixon, W B Billker, et al. Sex differences in temporo-limbic and frontal brain volumes of healthy adults. Cerebral Cortex, 2002, 12: 998 - 1003.

[19] X C Me. Functional MRI study on recognition of facial expression in the healthy subjects. Tianjin: Tianjin Medical University, 2010.

[20] V Bruce, A Young. Understanding face recognition. British Journal of Psychology, 1986, 77: 305 - 327.

[21] W Li. The ERP studies of facial expressions recognition under attentional and non- attentional conditions. Haerbin: Yanshan University, 2012.

[22] H T Van Schie, A A Wijers, R B Mars, et al. Processing of visual semantic information to concrete words: Temporal dynamics and neural mechanisms indicated by event-related brain potentials. Cognitive Neuropsychology, 2005, 22: 364 - 386.

[23] A T Chen, H Li, J Qiu, et al. Time course of visual classification: An ERP study. Chinese Sci Bull, 2006, 11: 1281 - 1286.

The Impact of Internet on Youth Socialization

Liu Yang[1,a,*], Xuesong Li[1,2,b]

[1]Research center for learning science, Southeast University

[2]Key Laboratory of Child Development and Learning Science of Ministry of Education

[a]974392783@qq.com, [b]xuesongli66@gmail.com

[*]Corresponding author

Keywords: youth socialization; positive effect; negative effect; measures

Abstract: Socialization is the process of teenagers from the "natural person" turn into the "social person". In modern society, the impact of Internet on youth socialization can not be overlooked. While the Internet of adolescent socialization brings positive effect, it also produces many negative effects. In view of this, we should take corresponding measures to prevent the harmful effects of Internet on youth socialization.

互联网对青少年社会化的影响

杨柳[1,a,*]，李雪松[1,2,b]
[1]东南大学学习科学研究中心，南京，江苏，中国
[2]东南大学儿童发展与学习科学教育部重点实验室，南京，江苏，中国
[a]974392783@qq.com，[b]xuesongli66@gmail.com
[*]通讯作者

关键词：青少年社会化；积极影响；消极影响；对策

中文摘要：社会化是青少年从“自然人”转变为“社会人”的过程。在当今社会，互联网对青少年社会化的影响不容小视。互联网对青少年社会化带来积极效果的同时也产生了许多负面影响。对此，我们应该采取相应的对策，防止互联网对青少年社会化的不良影响。

1 引言

中国互联网络信息中心报告的统计数据显示，我国25岁以下的网民用户占到了总体的52.5%。青少年作为最积极的潮流跟随群体，已经成为网民最大的组成部分之一。因此，在网络发达的时代背景下，青少年的个性社会化进程也不可避免地受到互联网的影响。

1.1 社会化的定义

社会化就是一个人内化社会价值标准、学习角色技能、适应社会生活的过程。是由自然人到社会人的转变过程，每个人必须经过社会化才能使外在于自己的社会行为规范、准则内化为自己的行为标准。用弗洛伊德的话说，社会化就是个人学习控制天性的冲动，就是“把野兽关到笼子里”的过程。所谓青少年社会化，是从社会化衍生出来的一个概念，就是指12—19岁的青少年群体在特定的社会与文化环境中，形成适应于该社会与文化的人格，掌握该社会所公认的行为方式的过程。青少年时期是人的社会化的一个重要时期，因此，探讨此问题具有非常重要的现实意义。

1.2 互联网的特点

互联网，又被简称为“网络”。它有五大特征：(1) 开放性。网络的开放性体现在对用户开放和对服务者开放；(2) 全球性。网络突破了国家、种族等有形或无形的“疆界”，真正体现了全球范围内的信息共享和人际互动；(3) 虚拟性。网络是一个虚拟空间。在网上，网民的一切行为都是伪实的，不具备实体性特征；(4) 匿名性。网络中，每个网民都是一个信息代码。正如彼得·斯坦纳创作的漫画——“在网络中，没

人知道你是一条狗";(5) 平等性。网络的平等性更多地体现在网民间的平等。

2 互联网对青少年社会化的积极影响

第一,互联网有利于青少年观念的创新、个性的发展和形成健康的心理。

上网是人机对话的过程,它是不受任何外来因素支配的平等交流。在虚拟的网络世界中,网民可以隐蔽自己的真实身份,能充分表达自己的真实理想,没有什么顾虑,十分有利于青少年的独立个性。尤其是那些缺乏自信、不善于交际的青少年,可以在网上的交流中体会人际交往的乐趣,找到信心。

第二,互联网促进青少年教育方式的改变。

互联网是信息、人以及文化三位一体的组合,是人类社会科技发展和社会发展的产物,且以互联网作为依托极大地加快了文化传播的速度,各种知识更新的周期也被大大缩短。网络已经取代传统的书本,正在成为青少年获取信息与知识的主要方式。网络的出现和发展,使得青少年的知识视野得到了前所未有的拓展,且伴随着网络技术的发展,形成了许多新的教育方式,这些都促进了青少年个性社会化。

第三,互联网为青少年角色扮演提供新途径。

网络创造的虚拟环境使青少年能够在其中不断进行角色学习、角色理解,从中进一步了解角色扮演的各种行为规范,检验角色扮演过程中互动的准则,把握不同社会角色扮演的尺度。

第四,互联网带来青少年生活方式的改变。

在网络环境中,青少年的课余文化生活得到极大的丰富,青少年以声音、文字、图像等丰富多样的形式,接受来自世界各地的娱乐节目和文化信息。一些生活方式、思潮、学习方式、观念、娱乐方式、消费方式等都会通过各种渠道对青少年产生间接或直接的影响。

3 互联网对青少年社会化的消极影响

第一,对青少年心理有负面影响。

首先,身处网络,以情感为纽带的人际依存被人、机关系所取代,易导致青少年情感淡漠; 其次,信息全球化进程的加快以及网站的社会背景不同,会使青少年产生认知偏差,易导致青少年价值取向模糊;最后,网络的虚拟环境,使得人们在网上的行为表现出一种解除抑制的特点,从而易导致青少年的去抑制性。

第二,网络交往易导致青少年对现实交往的冷漠化。

网络交往角色的匿名性和虚拟性、交往关系的平等性、交往途径的便捷性在一定程度上满足了青少年对交往的需求,使他们在交往中产生愉悦感和成就感。而这种理想化的感觉非常容易上瘾,久而久之,青少年就会只热衷于网络交往,而忽视物理空间中的现实交往，甚至产生对现实交往的冷漠。因此，网络所引起的人际交往方式的改变对青少年社会化的影响是不可低估的。

第三，网络文化导致青少年角色规范与行为方式相脱节。

一般来说，青少年社会角色的培养包括角色规范社会化和行为方式社会化两个方面。两者是相辅相成的关系，青少年必须要一方面知道社会对他的期望是什么，进而做出相应的角色行为和规范行为；另一方面，青少年还要接受社会的规范。如果只有角色期望而没有行为规范，必然会导致青少年的行为失衡。然而，网络文化并没有为青少年的角色学习提供与之相适应的行为规范，使得青少年常常出现角色认知上的认知失调，进而导致青少年的行为失范。

第四，网络沉溺易引发青少年人格障碍。

青少年沉溺网络可能引发的人格障碍，比较突出的有攻击型人格障碍和双重或多重人格障碍。由于网络角色具有虚拟性、匿名性特征，青少年在网上可以不负责任地攻击、诽谤他人，这会强化他们人格特质中的攻击性因子，导致攻击型人格；同时，青少年在网上还可扮演不同的角色，网络中的“我”未必是真实的“我”，有些青少年网上网下判若两人。这种双重或多重角色，如果处理不当，就容易诱发双重或多重人格障碍。

4　防止互联网对青少年社会化消极影响的对策

第一，青少年自身应树立正确的人生观和价值观。

接受并认同社会价值观是青少年社会化的一项重要内容。互联网中良莠并存，多元的价值观念会导致青少年价值观的迷离，因此，青少年只有树立正确的人生观和价值观，才能在网络的世界中有效地控制自己的社会化偏离行为。

第二，强化青少年的道德责任感。

通过强化青少年的道德责任感，增强他们抵制和识别各种诱惑以及不良思潮的能力。因为青少年是网络文化的先导，只有青少年自身加强主观上的道德意识和道德观念，才可提高自身对于不良思潮的免疫力。具体来说，可以从以下两个方面入手：首先培养青少年有强烈的道德责任感，网络文化极大地拓展了青少年的思维空间，使得他们的道德行为的灵活性和自由度明显增强，这同时也为青少年提供了放弃道德责任和行为规范的可能。因此，在网络时代下，学校和教师应教育青少年牢记自身肩负的社会的期望和社会责任，形成良好的道德习惯和行为规范。其次，青少年也要不断提高自己的道德修养和行为规范，使自身在缺乏监督的网络文化环境中坚守符合社会要求的道德规范。

第三，优化网络环境。

措施包括：(1) 加强网络监管。在管理上，信息管理部门需要加强与国际组织的合作，共同研究解决网络不良信息泛滥问题；在技术上，要研制更高水平的网络过滤系统,对不利于青少年健康成长的网络垃圾进行严格监控。(2) 多提供优质的信息资源。面对网络信息的纷繁庞杂,青少年工作者要树立强烈的社会责任感,努力为青少年提供更多优质的网络资源,促进青少年健康成长。

第四,强化网络环境管理,控制越轨:法规是必要的保障。

开放的网络文化跨越了主流文化的民族地域、制度界限,缺少凌驾其上的统一的文化控制机构,因而制定必要的法规或规范,才能有效控制网络中违规现象甚至是犯罪的行为的发生。

致谢

本文得到北京市教育委员会共建项目(sys1002706601)的支持。

References

[1] Xue Liu, Minjie Hu. The negative impact of network on youth and countermeasures. Journal of Hohai University, 2002, 1: 88-91.

[2] Hongqin Hua. Under the influence of network dual mechanism of youth socialization and way of life. Society, 2007, 27(2): 147-158.

[3] Ruiping Xu. The negative effect on the adolescent socialization and its countermeasures. Journal of Foshan institute of science and technology (Social Science), 2002, 21(4): 31-33.

[4] Fukun Li, Xinhai Zhong, Xiongfeng Chen. Symptoms, causes, prevention and therapy of teenagers Internet addiction. Journal of Hebei youth management cadre institute, 2003, 3: 12-13.

[5] Chuhong Chen. The syndrome of the Internet addiction in campus—Implement channel of the Internet addiction and achievement identity. Research on Adolescence, 2001, 10: 70-72.

[6] Lijuan Pang, Juan Hu. Socialization and its significance in modern education. Journal of Beijing Normal University (Social Science), 2003, 1: 46-53.

[7] Weicai Huang. The challenge of youth socialization and countermeasures. Hubei Social Sciences, 2003, 1: 70-72.

[8] Huibo Wang. The analysis of adolescent socialization deviation in Network era. Politics and Sociology, 2010(3): 63-66.

Advances in Brain Mechanism of Social Exclusion

Jili Zhang[1,a], Yue Leng[2,b,*]

[1]Research Center for Learning Science, Southeast University, Nanjing, China

[2]Key Laboratory of Child Development and Learning Science of Ministry of Education, Southeast University, Nanjing, China

[a]zhangjili1989@126.com, [b]lengyue@seu.edu.cn

[*]Corresponding author

Keywords: social exclusion; paradigm; brain mechanism; influence factors

Abstract: Social exclusion refers to the phenomenon and process that people's need of belongingness and social relationships is thwarted as the one is excluded by a group or other people. As a common social phenomenon, social exclusion has an important influence on individual health and social security. This article introduces the paradigms, brain imaging and neuro-electrophysiological studies of social exclusion based on carding domestic and foreign related research papers in recent years, and the possible future directions are also discussed.

社会排斥的脑机制研究进展

章吉利[1,2,a]，冷玥[1,2,b,*]
[1]东南大学学习科学研究中心，南京，江苏，中国
[2]儿童发展与学习科学教育部重点实验室(东南大学)，南京，江苏，中国
[a]zhangjili1989@126.com，[b]lengyue@seu.edu.cn
*通讯作者

关键词：社会排斥；研究范式；脑机制；影响因素

中文摘要：社会排斥是由于为某一社会团体或他人所排斥或拒绝，一个人的归属需求和关系需求受到阻碍的现象和过程。它普遍存在于人们的社会生活之中，对个体健康和社会安全都具有重要影响。本文通过介绍社会排斥的研究范式、脑成像和神经电生理研究及其影响因素的研究，对近年来社会排斥相关的国内外研究进行梳理，并探讨了未来可能的研究方向。

1 引言

从进化的角度来看，人类作为一种哺乳动物，经历长时间的成熟过程，在这个过程中，几乎要完全依靠他人(照料者)来获取必要的食物和保护。在成熟之后，仍然需要通过获取食物、防御野兽、照顾后代等责任的分担与社会团体进行联结，从而增加生存的机会。社会依恋系统(social-attachment system)可能在长期的进化过程中纳入了疼痛系统，借用疼痛信号来强调社会分离并促进社会联结的恢复。因此，当个体察觉到自己所渴望的社会联结面临威胁或社会关系遭受贬损时，就会产生一种特定的情绪反应——社会性疼痛[1]。近年来越来越多的认知神经科学研究成果都支持了这样一种假设，即社会性疼痛与生理性疼痛具有共享的神经生理机制，涉及阿片肽系统、前扣带回皮层和右腹侧前额叶皮层[2]。

社会性疼痛的产生往往与关系贬损(relational devaluation)有关，同时，窘迫、羞耻、内疚或嫉妒等情感状态也会引发社会性疼痛[1]。社会排斥(social exclusion)是社会性疼痛的主要诱因之一，目前对社会性疼痛的研究也主要集中在由社会排斥引起的社会性疼痛。本文通过介绍和总结社会排斥的概念、研究范式、脑成像和神经电生理研究及其影响因素的研究，对近年来社会排斥的脑机制研究成果进行梳理，并探讨未来可能的研究方向。

2 社会排斥概述

社会排斥是一种古老且普遍存在的社会现象，但直到最近 30 年，才成为社会学

者、社会政策研究者所感兴趣的课题，随后又引起了学者对社会排斥心理的关注。随着脑成像技术的成熟和发展以及在社会性疼痛与生理性疼痛共享神经生理机制上的发现，对社会排斥的神经机制的研究成为近年来的热点。

心理学界对社会排斥这种现象尚没有统一的界定，最常用的词是 social exclusion（社会排斥）、social rejection（社会拒绝）和 social ostracism（社会放逐），但心理学研究者普遍倾向于将社会排斥视为一个与社会接纳相对立的概念。国内学者杜建政和夏冰丽对社会排斥的概念进行了较为系统的总结，认为社会排斥（social exclusion）是由于为某一社会团体或他人所排斥或拒绝，一个人的归属需求和关系需求受到阻碍的现象和过程，有多种表现形式，如排斥、拒绝、孤立、无视等[3]。

3 社会排斥的研究范式

生活经验告诉我们，引发个体产生排斥感的刺激种类很多，比如语言上的拒绝、行为上的排斥，甚至一个眼神都能给人造成排斥感。相应地，在社会排斥研究中给被试以拒绝、排斥反馈的方式也非常多，常见的研究范式有拒绝范式、放逐范式和孤独终老范式等，其中又以拒绝范式和放逐范式最为常用。

3.1 社会排斥研究的常用范式

拒绝范式以明确、直接的方式向被试传达拒绝信息，例如让被试通过讨论相互认识后选择同伴，然后给予被试虚假的反馈，即告知被试没有人愿意选他作为合作伙伴，又或者用视频的方式让被试相互了解，继而告知被试对方不愿意进行下一轮面对面交流。总的来说，这种范式的拒绝反馈及时、明确、直接，比较接近真实生活情境，其缺点在于讨论中的熟悉程度、人数的多少和其他额外变量都容易对研究结果造成混淆。

放逐范式的特点是有意忽视被试或者无应答反应，包括面对面的放逐，即当面传达放逐信息，如抛球游戏（ball tossing）和火车谈话（train ride conversation）等；也包括网络放逐，即通过网络或者其他通讯手段传达放逐信息，如聊天室范式（chatroom paradigm）、网络投球范式（cyberball）和手机短信范式（cell phone text messaging method）等。这种范式所产生的社会排斥不像拒绝范式那么明确、直接，且容易受到拒绝敏感性（rejection sensitivity）等个体差异的影响，但研究证明这种范式可以引发适度的受排斥感，并较为容易改编为适用于脑成像研究的版本，为研究社会排斥的神经机制提供便利。

3.2 网络投球范式（cyberball）：社会排斥脑机制研究的常用范式

在社会排斥的 fMRI 和 ERP 研究中，应用最为广泛的是网络投球范式（cyberball），它改编自 Williams 于 1997 年发明的传球游戏。该范式在不同的研究中实现方式会略有不同，大致程序为：邀请被试参与在线式三人虚拟投球游戏，指导语说明该游戏是用来训练心理想象能力(mental visualization skills)，需要将游戏场景想象得越真实越好，后面的实验需要该能力。投球游戏分为公平游戏阶段(fair play)和排斥阶段(exclusion)。公平游戏阶段被试接到球的次数为投球总次数的三分之一；排斥阶段被试只在开始阶段接到其他玩家投来的球，以及在过程中很少的次数接到球以保持注意力，其他情况均为另外两个玩家相互投球而将他忽视。实际上并不存在其他玩家，玩家的投球操作是事先设定好的。在被试进行网络投球游戏的同时记录其脑部的活动，最后将公平游戏阶段和排斥阶段被试的脑部活动进行对比以发现被试对社会排斥信号的加工方式和时程特点[4,5]。网络投球范式由于其简单易行，目前被广泛地应用于社会排斥的脑成像研究。但这种范式对于成年人的吸引力程度不高，更适合在儿童和青少年中人群中进行研究。

3.3 眼神注视范式(eye-gaze)：社会排斥研究的新范式

作为人类固有的一种特质，人们总是在社会交往中倾向于关注他人的眼神。眼神回避是用以表达排斥的常见的非语言线索。因此，有研究者通过眼神注视范式(eye-gaze)对眼神注视方式(直视/回避)在关系评价中的作用进行了研究[6]，该研究包含三个实验：实验一中，向被试呈现一段2.5分钟的简短视频，视频中的人物的眼神为直视或回避。结果表明，相对于眼神直视，参与者接受眼神回避后感到被排斥和忽视，并且报告了更低的归属感和自尊心，以及更强的消极情绪。在实验二中，也发现同样的结果，相对于眼神直视而言，眼神回避标志着更低的关系评价。此外，实验二还表明，相对于直视者而言，眼神回避使得参与者对回避者表现出更多的攻击性，并且对回避者给予更低的人格评价。实验三发现，与眼神直视相比，眼神回避导致了内隐自尊的降低，这表明短暂的眼神回避至少能够暂时改变自我评价。总的来说，与接受眼神直视相比，参与者在面对回避眼神时感到被排斥，表现为基本的需求满足受挫，外显和内隐自尊降低，关系价值降低，以及在行为上对互动的另一方表现出更多的攻击倾向。

该研究有效地证明了眼神回避是传达排斥信号的有效方式，目前这种范式还只应用于行为研究，未见相关的脑机制研究。但由于眼神表达的简易性，研究者很容易通过控制其他面部表情等额外变量来标准化视频或图片刺激，从而发展出相应的fMRI和ERP版本的眼神注视范式。另外，这种范式在成年人群的行为研究中已经得到了验证，为成年人社会排斥的神经生理机制研究奠定了可靠的基础。

4 社会排斥的脑机制

目前对社会排斥的研究不断深入，但理论解释尚未成熟，而脑成像技术为研究者采用相对客观稳定的生理指标来探究社会排斥现象提供了便利。

4.1 社会排斥加工的重要脑区

关于社会排斥脑机制的研究,始于 MacDonald 等对生理性疼痛与社会性疼痛关系的研究,随后引起了学界的广泛关注。Eisenberger 等[5]用功能磁共振成像手段对“社会性疼痛与生理性疼痛有着相似的脑机制”这一假设进行了检验。实验采用了上文所述的网络投球范式,首先让被试观看他人在投球游戏中遭受排斥,再让被试自己参与到游戏中,经过一段时间的公平游戏后,被试遭到排斥(游戏同伴极少将球投给被试)。相比社会接纳(social inclusion)的条件,观看他人遭遇社会排斥以及自己经历社会排斥都会引起背侧前扣带回(dorsal anterior cingulate cortex, dACC)的激活;相比接纳条件,自己遭受社会排斥,还引起了右腹侧前额叶(right ventral prefrontal cortex, rVPFC)的激活,并且这个脑区的激活与 dACC 的激活以及被试主观报告的悲伤感呈负相关。这一模式与生理性疼痛的神经反应[7]十分相似,因此 Eisenberger 等认为 dACC 的活动与社会排斥引起的社会性疼痛体验有关,而 rVPFC 可能在个体被社会排斥的时候起到了自我调节以及抑制负性情绪的作用。

一些研究者认为被社会排斥时 dACC 的激活可能反映了被试自身产生了负性情绪,也可能表明被试对自己能融入投球游戏的预期的违反。在 Sommervillie 等[8]的研究中,被试需要先报告对照片中的人是否接受自己的预期,然后得到对方对自己的反馈。结果发现,dACC 对预期违反更为敏感,而腹侧前扣带回(ventral anterior cingulate cortex, vACC)对对方的反馈更为敏感,即在对方接受自己的时候比在对方拒绝自己的时候激活更强。该结果支持了社会排斥研究中所发现的 dACC 的激活更多地反映了人们在认知上的预期违反的观点。

Eisenberger 及其同事[5]使用网络投球范式开启了社会排斥的 fMRI 研究,之后,其他范式也逐渐被研究者们相继用于社会排斥的脑机制研究,这对发现人脑如何识别社会排斥信息、产生悲伤体验并进行情绪调节的相关脑区具有重要意义。除了 ACC 和 VPFC 以外,研究还发现内侧前额叶皮层(medial prefrontal cortex, mPFC)、后扣带回皮层(posterior cingulate cortex, PCC)[9,10]和脑岛(insula)[5,9,10]都可能与社会排斥引起的悲伤情绪有关。这种被激活脑区的差异可能是由研究范式的不同而造成。比如有研究者认为,一些研究报告了社会排斥只激活与生理疼痛共享疼痛情绪评估的脑区,而没有激活疼痛感知相关的脑区,是因为这些范式不足以诱发被试足够强烈的痛苦感受,这一观点也得到了近期一项研究结果的支持,该研究让被试将自己被前任伴侣抛弃的感受和被一个朋友拒绝的感受相比较,结果发现被前任伴侣抛弃时除了负责疼痛情绪加工的区域得到了激活以外,负责疼痛感知的次级躯体感觉区(secondary somatosensory)和背侧脑岛(dorsal posterior insula)也得到了激活[11]。

4.2 社会排斥加工的时程特点

在社会交往中,人们常常需要迅速地对社会排斥信息进行知觉和反应,因而“人脑是如何快速体验并对社会排斥进行反应的?”成为社会认知神经科学需要解决的问题。fMRI研究为社会排斥加工的脑区定位提供了大量而重要的线索,但由于其时间分辨率较低,且大多数网络投球范式的研究都采用对整个排斥区组的脑活动进行平均,因而未能对人脑加工社会排斥的时程特点提供有力证据。鉴于此,近年来研究者开始采用事件相关电位技术(event-related potentials, ERPs)对社会排斥的脑机制进行研究,从而将社会排斥脑机制的研究从整体加工的探讨转向对排斥事件神经反应的时间进程的研究。与认知—情感和评价加工相关的ERP成分,如反馈相关负波(feedback related-negativity, FRN)、P3以及晚期慢波(late slow wave)等,引起了社会排斥研究者的特别关注。

4.2.1 反馈相关负波

FRN大约出现在反馈刺激呈现后250—350 ms的额中头皮区域,一般出现于反馈结果与预期不相符的情况[12],且溯源分析结果[13]显示,FRN产生于与目标冲突、预期违背相关的ACC,因此,被认为与反馈警示系统有关。

一项儿童中期的Cyberball研究[14]将公平游戏中的“这轮不是我投球”事件和排斥阶段的排斥事件进行了对比,发现了刺激呈现后264—656 ms内的位于前额叶的负波,这与经典的FRN成分在空间位置上十分相似,且相比接受事件,该成分对社会排斥事件似乎更为敏感(统计学差异接近显著)。然而,该负波比经典的FRN出现得更晚一些,这可能与反馈的复杂性有关,因为网络投球游戏的排斥反馈依赖于一定的情景才能让被试知觉到,不像经典FRN研究中呈现的反馈刺激那么简单直接。接受条件和排斥条件下的FRN波幅差异在统计学上只达到边缘显著,可能是由于被试在排斥阶段极少接到传球因而降低了期望。总的来说,被试在网络投球游戏中遭到游戏同伴的排斥,很可能引发了游戏前对“自己能够融入游戏并且被同伴接受”的预期的违反。

4.2.2 P3

通常所说的P300/P3是指P300的一种亚成分P3b,它的幅度比较大且跨度范围较宽,由稀少的、任务相关的刺激(靶刺激)诱发,潜伏期一般在310—380 ms左右,分布于中央—顶区,且以中线附近幅度最大,与事件分类、背景更新等过程相关[15]。另外,稀少的、任务不相关的刺激(新异刺激)也可以在300 ms左右诱发出一个正成分,即P3a。P3a的头皮分布比P3b更靠前,最大波幅位于Fz点附近(额叶后部),且潜伏期提前(220—280 ms)。P3a对新异刺激的朝向反应[16]能使机体觉知与应对不测事件,使之优先进入认知加工,对机体有重要保护意义。

Crowley等的研究[14]发现了刺激呈现后264—656 ms内,分布于头皮后部,类似于 P3b 的正波,相比“这轮不是我投球”事件,拒绝事件引发的波幅显著更正。P3b 成分被普遍认为与注意资源分配有关,对出现概率稀少的刺激更为敏感,按照背景更新理论,P3 应当对次数较少的“这轮不是我投球”条件更为敏感。然而,P3 也会对刺激的凸显性反应更加强烈,例如对有毒瘾的人来说,包含毒品线索的视觉刺激会比出现概率小的刺激诱发更强烈的 P3 成分[17]。由于社会联结对生存具有重要的适应价值,人类可能在长期的进化过程中发展出了对社会排斥事件进行突出标记的倾向,从而促进社会联结的维持和恢复,因此拒绝或排斥事件会引起更加强烈的 P3 反应。

4.2.3　晚期慢波

额区慢波往往出现于对各种唤醒刺激的预测,因此被认为与评估加工有关。Crowley 等用网络投球范式在儿童中期的样本中进行研究[14],发现刺激呈现后 500—900 ms 内,在额区内侧出现晚期慢波,该成分与之前 Crowley 等在成年早期样本得到的结果[18]相似,即排斥事件诱发了左半球前额叶区域在 580—900 ms 的慢波,且该神经活动与被试自我报告的悲伤感呈显著的正相关。这种额区的晚期慢波可能反映了被试对“小球会再次被投向其他人”的评估和预期。

该研究还发现了刺激呈现后 500—900 ms 内,位于枕顶区域的正性慢波,在排斥条件下波幅更正,表明被试对排斥事件进行了更多的评估和注意加工。这与晚期正波(late positive potential, LPP)的模式非常相似。但作者并没有将这一成分直接定义为 LPP,首先是由于该研究不像以往诱发 LPP 的研究那样采用图片刺激,而是通过投球游戏来传达社会排斥的信号;第二,该成分的出现还伴随着额区的慢波活动;第三,该成分可能与以往研究中发现的 LPP 有着不同的神经发生源。尽管 Crowley 等发现的正性慢波与经典的 LPP 可能并非同一种成分,但该成分仍然值得引起社会排斥研究者们的关注,因为大量研究表明 LPP 反映了对情绪刺激的注意偏向[19],无论在儿童研究[20]还是成人研究[19]中,都发现具有情绪唤醒的刺激比中性刺激诱发更强烈的 LPP,而这种效应在对消极情绪进行自发的抑制—重评后减小[21]。因而,在今后对社会排斥的 ERPs 研究(特别是用图片刺激的方式诱发社会排斥感的研究)中,排斥条件很可能会诱发更大的 LPP 效应。

4.2.4　N400

N400 是一个大约开始于目标词呈现后 250 ms,并在 400 ms 左右达到峰值的负成分,属于对语义和概念进行协调性分析的特异性成分,一般认为 N400 反映了由一个目标词诱发的对句子进行整体语义的加工,波幅更负、持续时间更长表明这种语义加工更多[22]。例如与预期不符的结果相对于符合预期的结果,错误的陈述相对于正确的陈述,都会诱发更负的 N400 成分。

一项使用文字材料的 ERP 研究[23]发现,在依恋(attachment)相关的语境中,与拒绝相关的词汇比与接受相关的词汇引发了中央顶区更负的N400，而在非依恋相关的语境中则没有出现这种效应。这种差异大约在250—300 ms就开始出现，表明大脑在300 ms以内即对同伴的拒绝/接受线索做出了区分，更负的N400可能反映了被试对拒绝情境投入了更多的语义加工和一定程度的预期违反。

4.3 社会排斥脑机制的影响因素

4.3.1 年龄

研究者采用网络投球范式分别以成人[18]和儿童[14]为样本进行了ERP研究，发现两者在前额区域头皮的电活动存在差异。具体来说，成人的脑地形图有明显的左侧化倾向，受排斥后悲伤感更少的被试在左半球前额区域的慢波活动更正。Kross等的研究[9]也发现了这种偏侧化效应，低拒绝敏感性的个体在拒绝条件下，左侧额下回会有更多的激活。由于情绪调节可能会涉及单侧和内侧前额叶的活动，Crowley等把这种神经加工解释为对社会排斥体验的调节。因此，成人的左侧化倾向可能源于前额发育的成熟，能够更好地使用更大范围的前额网络来应对社会排斥和拒绝。

Sebastian等[24]的研究则发现了成年人相对于青少年的右侧化偏向。他们认为，青少年本身就比成年人具有更高的拒绝敏感性，而根据以往研究，情绪管理依赖于前额叶皮层，特别是腹外侧区域，以及它与边缘系统（如杏仁核）的联系[25]，青少年对于社会排斥引起的痛苦情绪管理可能尚未达到成熟，因此，导致了青少年组右半球腹外侧前额叶皮层的活动比成年组更弱。

此外，在青少年人群中年龄差异也会带来对社会排斥神经生理反应程度的差别。例如2010年，Silk等[26]采用虚拟的同伴互动范式——聊天室互动范式（Chatroom Interact Task）对9—17岁的青少年开展了社会排斥的眼动研究，主要考察的神经生理指标是瞳孔扩张程度，以往研究表明，瞳孔扩张指示了大脑的认知和情感加工区域的活跃。参与者被告知他们正在网络聊天室与其他年轻人进行互动，获得来自虚拟同伴的接受或拒绝反馈。结果显示，与接受条件相比，拒绝条件会引起瞳孔扩张，而且这种现象在年纪大一些的青少年中表现得更为明显。

以上这些研究表明，人脑对社会排斥信息的加工是一个随年龄增长而不断发展的过程，这使得成年人能够更好地应对和处理社会排斥事件。

4.3.2 拒绝敏感性

Downey和Feldman等人对拒绝敏感性进行了大量而细致的研究，于1996年将拒绝敏感性定义为“个体对拒绝所表现出焦虑的预期，准备性觉知及过度反应的倾向”。认知神经科学家将拒绝敏感性视为影响大脑对社会排斥信息进行加工的主要因素之一。2004年的一项行为研究通过两个实验来观察被试对不同拒绝/接受程度和不同的拒绝/接受模式的反应[27]，包括情绪、自我评价和他人评价，以及行为方面的反应，发现拒绝敏感性高的个体(相比拒绝敏感性低的个体)在遭受拒绝后会产生更多的消极反应(如愤怒、悲伤、受伤感、焦虑、对他人的负性评价,以及反社会倾向)。

2007年,Kross等[9]使用fMRI技术来探索拒绝敏感性不同的个体在进行情感评价和认知控制加工时,所涉及的脑区是否存在不同的模式。结果发现,相对于接受图片,拒绝敏感性高和低的两组在观看拒绝图片时,都激活了涉及情感刺激加工的PCC、insula和认知控制加工的dACC、mPFC。而观察拒绝和接受两种条件下的大脑活动差异,却发现两组被试并不一致:低拒绝敏感性的个体相对于高拒绝敏感性的个体在左脑下额皮质和右脑背侧额叶(left inferior and right dorsal frontal)区域表现出显著的激活,并且这些区域的活动与被试自我报告的悲伤程度成负相关。总的来说,这些研究结果表明不论拒绝敏感性的强弱,涉及情感加工和认知控制脑区的反应都对拒绝事件敏感,但拒绝敏感性低的个体可能会通过激活前额结构来调节看到拒绝图片时产生的悲伤感,而拒绝敏感性高的个体通过自下而上的认知控制来调节对社会排斥的反应的能力则较弱。

4.3.3　分裂型人格特质

分裂(schizotypy)是一种人格特质,它处在精神分裂谱系的正常范围之内,但是分裂型人格特质与精神分裂症在临床、基因、神经心理和神经生理水平都存在关联。因此,对健康人群的分裂型人格特质进行研究,既可以排除病症和药物的影响,又可以为精神分裂症患者的社会排斥加工机制提供有意义的参考。Premkumar等根据分裂型特质将被试分为高低两组,进行社会排斥研究[28]。研究发现,在观看拒绝场景(相对于中性场景)图片时,低分裂型人格特质组激活而高分裂型人格特质组抑制两侧的背侧前扣带回皮层(dACC)、右半球额上回(superior frontal gyrus, SFG)和左半球腹侧的前额叶皮层(prefrontal cortex, PFC)的活动,表明高分裂型人格特质的人群对拒绝刺激给予更少的注意,让自己远离这种刺激,从而应对自己高于常人的拒绝敏感性。

4.3.4　依恋

依恋(attachment)是指人与其他人之间在互动中逐步建立起来的,给予彼此支持、安全感和亲密感受的关系。依恋理论由心理学家Bowlby最先提出,他认为个体关于自我和与重要他人之间关系质量的内部认知模型在婴儿期和童年期不断发展,并在毕生发展过程中对影响和指导个体的社会行为起着重要的作用 。近年来,关于依恋如何影响人们对社会排斥事件的加工取得了一些新的进展。

White等[29]对Cyberball范式进行调整,在公平游戏(fair paly)和排斥(exclusion)区组之后又增加了一个类似于公平游戏的重聚(reunion)区组,在11—15岁的儿童样本中进行研究。发现对于不安全—排拒型(insecure-dismissing)依恋的儿童,重聚阶段的接受事件比公平游戏阶段的基线诱发了更大的N2成分,而安全型(secure)依恋的儿童则没有出现这种效应。这可能是由于不安全—排拒型依恋的儿童在经历了社会排斥阶段之后,预期自己会很少接到同伴的传球,而随后的重聚阶段则违背了这种预期,因而产生更大的 N2 成分。该结果表明,相对于安全型依恋的儿童,社会补偿(social reparation)对不安全—排拒型依恋的儿童来说是一个更大的挑战。在成人的社会排斥研究中,也发现了依恋对社会排斥的调节作用。例如 Zayas 等[23]的研究不仅发现了拒绝词的 N400 效应,还发现高依恋焦虑、低依恋回避的女性对拒绝线索表现出更负的 N400。

除上述因素之外,社会排斥的脑机制还可能受到其他因素的调节,如一项视觉监测任务的 ERP 研究[30]发现拒绝线索引发了低自尊个体更显著的 N2pc 成分,而在高自尊个体中却没有出现这种效应,从脑机制的角度证明了低自尊个体对社会排斥信号的注意偏向。

综上所述,人脑可以快速察觉到社会排斥信号,体验到社会排斥带来的悲伤感,并对由此引发的社会性疼痛进行调节。然而脑机制研究也证明人们对社会排斥的认知策略存在着个体差异,如拒绝敏感性低的个体通过激活前额结构来主动调节社会排斥带来的负性情绪,而高分裂型人格特质的个体则通过回避这种社会排斥信号来进行自我保护。

5 未来研究展望

社会排斥是人们社会生活中常见的现象,对个体的健康和社会安全具有重要影响。例如,Leary 等[31]研究了 1995 年至 2001 年间的 15 起校园枪击案,发现社会排斥与攻击行为之间可能存在密切联系。近年来,我国大学生投毒、自杀、行凶等现象再次引起社会各界的广泛关注,这些事件的出现是否与社会排斥有关还有待研究。总之,由于社会排斥的普遍性及其对人们心理和行为的巨大影响,这一领域值得研究者进行持续关注和深入研究。采用生理反应指标对社会排斥进行研究,已经越来越成为相关研究的趋势,下面将从社会排斥脑机制的角度出发,对未来研究进行展望。

第一,根据研究目的选用恰当的研究范式并探索新的研究范式。目前网络投球范式得到了广泛的应用,尤其在认知神经科学研究中多采用该范式。但 Gutz 等[32]发现,在投球游戏中,将“排斥”和“接受”两个区组的顺序进行调换,被试的 ERPs 反应和自我报告的情绪都会发生变化,表明大脑对社会互动信息的加工依赖于先前的体验,因此在今后研究范式的使用应当考虑被试的期望基线。此外,网络投球范式引发的是放逐,其所得结论能否推广到所有排斥现象还有待验证。眼神回避是一种十分常见的社会排斥的表现形式,能够真实地给研究对象造成适度的排斥感和悲伤感,并且方便在实验室条件下达成,同时也克服了网络投球范式等对成年被试吸引较弱的缺点。因此眼神注视范式可以通过适当的改进,从而方便地与脑成像技术相结合,以获取对社会排斥神经过程的证据。

第二，提高研究的生态效度。如上文所述，拒绝范式较为接近真实生活，实验结论推广程度较大。但是拒绝范式往往操作复杂，在行为实验中应用较多，难以直接改编为适用于脑成像研究的版本。研究者不妨在脑成像实验之前先创造一些真实的社会场景，比如让被试相互认识，然后在接下来的脑成像研究中反馈被拒绝的信息，从而提高社会排斥神经机制研究的生态效度。

第三，近年来很多认知神经科学的证据表明社会性疼痛和生理性疼痛有着共享的脑机制。那么对生理性疼痛敏感的人群是否也对社会排斥信息更敏感？缓解生理性疼痛的方法，如一些药物和社会支持，是否同样对社会性疼痛有效？这些问题都有待于研究者进行进一步探讨。

第四，关于社会排斥的影响因素，目前研究主要集中在内部因素，比如年龄、人格特质等，而外部因素的研究甚少。对于内部因素的研究，可以在以下方面进行拓展：哪些特质人群容易遭受社会排斥，加入生化检测手段来区分人群，做好对易感人群的鉴别和区分，从而尽早发现、提前干预，减少由遭遇社会排斥而引起的反社会行为的发生。加强外部因素的研究，可以从成长经历、教育背景等方面入手，改善儿童的成长环境。

References

[1] M Shu, P Liu, Y H Wu. Social pain: Evidence from physical pain. Acta Scientiarum Naturalium Universitatis Pekinensis, 2010, 46: 1025 - 1031.

[2] N I Eisenberger. Broken hearts and broken bones: A neural perspective on the similarities between social and physical pain. Current Directions in Psychological Science, 2012, 21: 42 - 47.

[3] J Z Du, B L Xia. The psychological view on social exclusion. Advances in Psychological Science, 2008, 16: 981 - 986.

[4] M J Crowley, J Wu, E R McCarty, et al. Exclusion and micro-rejection: Event-related potential response predicts mitigated distress. Neuroreport, 2009, 20: 1518 - 1522.

[5] N I Eisenberger, M D Lieberman, K D Williams. Does rejection hurt? An FMRI study of social exclusion. Science, 2003, 302: 290 - 292.

[6] J H Wirth, D F Sacco, K Hugenberg, et al. Eye gaze as relational evaluation: Averted eye gaze leads to feelings of ostracism and relational devaluation. Pers Soc Psychol Bull, 2010, 36: 869 - 882.

[7] G Macdonald, M R Leary. Why does social exclusion hurt? The relationship between social and physical pain. Psychol Bull, 2005, 131: 202 - 223.

[8] L H Somerville, T F Heatherton, W M Kelley. Anterior cingulate cortex responds differentially to expectancy violation and social rejection. Nature Neuroscience, 2006, 9: 1007 - 1008.

[9] E Kross, T Egner, K Ochsner, et al. Neural dynamics of rejection sensitivity. Journal of

Cognitive Neuroscience, 2007, 19: 945 -956.

[10] C L Masten, N I Eisenberger, L A Borofsky, et al. Neural correlates of social exclusion during adolescence: Understanding the distress of peer rejection. Social Cognitive and Affective Neuroscience, 2009, 4: 143 -157.

[11] E Kross, M G Berman, W Mischel, et al. Social rejection shares somatosensory representations with physical pain. Proceedings of the National Academy of Sciences of the United States of America, 2011, 108: 6270 -6275.

[12] G Hajcak, C B Holroyd, J S Moser, et al. Brain potentials associated with expected and unexpected good and bad outcomes. Psychophysiology, 2005, 42: 161 -170.

[13] W J Gehring, A R Willoughby. Medial prefrontal cortex and rapid processing of monetary gains and losses. Science, 2002, 295: 2279 -2282.

[14] M J Crowley, J Wu, P J Molfese, et al. Social exclusion in middle childhood: Rejection events, slowwave neural activity and ostracism distress. Soc Neurosci, 2010, 5: 483 -495.

[15] A Kok. On the utility of P3 amplitude as a measure of processing capacity. Psychophysiology, 2001, 38: 557 -577.

[16] M J Crowley, J Wu, C A Bailey, et al. Bringing in the negative reinforcements: The avoidance feedback-related negativity. Neuroreport, 2009, 20: 1513 -1517.

[17] D I Lubman, N B Allen, L A Peters, et al. Electrophysiological evidence of the motivational salience of drug cues in opiate addiction. Psychological Medicine, 2007, 37: 1203 -1209.

[18] M J Crowley, J Wu, E R McCarty, et al. Exclusion and micro-rejection: Event-related potential response predicts mitigated distress. Neuroreport, 2009, 20: 1518 -1522.

[19] B N Cuthbert, H T Schupp, M M Bradley, et al. Brain potentials in affective picture processing: Covariation with autonomic arousal and affective report. Biological Psychology, 2000, 52: 95 -111.

[20] G Hajcak, T A Dennis. Brain potentials during affective picture processing in children. Biological Psychology, 2009, 80: 333 -338.

[21] J S Moser, G Hajcak, E Bukay, et al. Intentional modulation of emotional responding to unpleasant pictures: An ERP study. Psychophysiology, 2006, 43: 292 -296.

[22] M Kiefer, D Brendel. Attentional modulation of unconscious "automatic" processes: Evidence from event-related potentials in a masked priming paradigm. Journal of Cognitive Neuroscience, 2006, 18: 184 -198.

[23] V Zayas, Y Shoda, W Mischel, et al. Neural responses to partner rejection cues. Psychological Science, 2009, 20: 813 -821.

[24] C L Sebastian, G C Y Tan, J P Roiser, et al. Developmental influences on the neural bases of responses to social rejection: Implications of social neuroscience for education. Neuroimage, 2011, 57: 686 -694.

[25] K N Ochsner, J J Gross. The cognitive control of emotion. Trends in Cognitive Sciences, 2005, 9: 242-249.

[26] J S Silk, L R Stroud, G J Siegle, et al. Peer acceptance and rejection through the eyes of youth: Pupillary, eyetracking and ecological data from the Chatroom Interact task. Social Cognitive and Affective Neuroscience, 2012, 7: 93-105.

[27] K E Buckley, R E Winkel, M R Leary. Reactions to acceptance and rejection: Effects of level and sequence of relational evaluation. Journal of Experimental Social Psychology, 2004, 40: 14-28.

[28] P Premkumar, U Ettinger, S Inchley-Mort, et al. Neural processing of social rejection: The role of schizotypal personality traits. Human Brain Mapping, 2012, 33: 695-706.

[29] L O White, J Wu, J L Borelli, et al. Play it again: Neural responses to reunion with excludes predicted by attachment patterns. Developmental Science, 2013, 16(6): 850-863.

[30] H J Li, V Zeigler-Hill, J Yang, et al. Low self-esteem and the neural basis of attentional bias for social rejection cues: Evidence from the N2pc ERP component. Personality and Individual Differences, 2012, 53: 947-951.

[31] M R Leary, R M Kowalski, L Smith, et al. Teasing, rejection, and violence: Case studies of the school shootings. Aggressive Behavior, 2003, 29: 202-214.

[32] L Gutz, C Kupper, B Renneberg, et al. Processing social participation: An event-related brain potential study. Neuroreport, 2011, 22: 453-458.

议 题

神经科学视野下儿童语言发展的研究

Neuroimaging Studies of Early Language Development, Reading and Reading Disability: An Update on Recent Findings

Kenneth R. Pugh
Haskins Laboratories

Good reading skills are crucial for success in the modern world. Reading disability (RD) is characterized as a brain-based difficulty in acquiring fluent decoding skill, associated with problems in operating on the phonological structures of language. We review recent findings from ongoing longitudinal studies in our lab with low and high risk children that indicate that RD children fail to develop a coherent left hemisphere reading circuitry that in typically developing (TD) readers comes online to support fluent word reading. New longitudinal findings on gene-brain-behavior pathways in early language development are discussed in detail (including new findings on links between abnormal neurochemistry and atypical language and reading development). We also provide an update on the latest research on reading remediation studies. Treatment studies from our group and others have examined the effects of intensive reading remediation in at-risk children and adolescents, revealing substantial gains in both reading scores and corresponding development of key LH reading networks for readers afforded this treatment. We will also discuss new directions in research on language development research including our ongoing studies of learning and consolidation, birth to five neurodevelopment in challenging environments, and second language learning across contrastive languages.

Deficits of Visual Magnocellular Stream in Chinese Children with Developmental Dyslexia

Hongyan Bi

Institute of Psychology of the Chinese Academy of Sciences

Developmental dyslexia (DD) is the most common learning disability and is characterized by a poor reading ability (e. g. impairments in word coding, reading fluency) in children who have normal intelligence, sufficient sociocultural opportunities, and have not known neurological damage or organic injury. The magnocellular (M) deficit theory proposes that dyslexia is due to abnormality in the M stream.

Our research group has conducted a series of experiments to explore the visual M function of Chinese dyslexic children. In order to explore how the M deficit in dyslexic individuals impeded reading, we firstly examined the possible role of visual M stream in Chinese reading. We directly manipulated the spatial frequency of Chinese characters to separate the visual M condition from visual control condition, and adopted the global/local decision task to investigate the global and local processing of Chinese characters in one visual condition (Zhao, et al., 2013). Our results showed that, university students exhibited a global precedence effect in M condition, i. e. shorter reaction time and higher accuracy for global decision relatively to local decision. These results revealed that the low spatial frequency associating with M stream might contribute to the global recognition of Chinese characters (Zhao, et al., 2013). Moreover, Qian et al. submitted using fMRI technique further explore the relationship between visual M stream and Chinese reading skills in Chinese adults. Results exhibited that the activation in left MT area was significantly correlated with performance in reading fluency and rapid naming; and the activation in right PPC was correlated with orthographic skills. All the above findings were the basis for our further researches to explore the underlying mechanism of visual M deficit in developmental dyslexia.

In summary, the present studies showed that Chinese children with DD exactly had dysfunction in visual M stream, and the visual M stream might play a role in Chinese character recognition, which further related with reading speed and orthographic processing. We will explore the possible influence of visual M stream in Chinese reading in the future.

The Child as a "Naive Engineer": How the Brain Extracts Phonology from the Speech Signal and Implications for Dyslexia

Vicky Leong

Research Fellow in Psychology at the University of Cambridge

Dyslexia is a neurodevelopmental disorder that affects the acquisition of skilled reading in 7% of children. The process of learning to read builds on pre-existing neural representations of speech sounds (phonology), which are acquired during the child's early years. In dyslexia, a poor foundation in phonology hampers reading development, however, the neurobiological origins of the phonological deficit have yet to be elucidated. I will discuss phonological development from the perspective of the child as a "naive engineer". Young children develop awareness of large-grain phonological structure spontaneously, without explicit adult instruction. By 2 years of age, children are able to count the number of syllables in a word, and to say whether two words rhyme. Remarkably, even 7.5-month-old infants show the ability to use prosodic stress patterns (motifs of strong and weak syllables) to segment words from continuous speech. These are complex feats of speech engineering, requiring the child to de-construct the overt acoustic spectro-temporal structure of the speech signal in order to reveal the latent phonological building blocks of the English language—a nested hierarchy of prosodic stress patterns, syllables and onset-rime units. This ability to hack the acoustic signal for its structural components is particularly crucial for infants, who have to build a phonological system from the speech signal "ground-up". I will present the theory of Acoustic-Emergent Phonology (AEP) which proposes that the naive engineer uses the emergent dimensional structure of the speech signal (a spectro-temporal hierarchy) as an effective blueprint for finding latent phonological structure. I further suggest that this process of acoustic-phonological extraction is mediated neurally by multi-timescale rhythmic entrainment of neuronal oscillations in the auditory cortex. Further, I will address the possibility that poor rhythmic entrainment by the dyslexic brain results in faulty extraction of phonology from the speech signal, producing the classic phonological deficit. Finally, I will describe intervention strategies that utilise music and poetry to support neural rhythmic entrainment in children with dyslexia. Our results indicate that these rhythm interventions are providing benefits for children's language development. Accordingly, adults' spontaneous use of motherese, nursery rhymes, and other rhythmically-enhanced speech could be important in helping children to reverse-engineer the speech signal for phonology.

Development of Reading in Adults with Atypical Hemispheric Dominance for Speech and in Young Children

Qing Cai

Associate Professor at East China Normal University

We investigated the neural machanism of word reading in two population—adults with atypical right hemispheric (RH) dominance for speech, and children in their first year of learning to read. By the first population, we attempted to clarify the influences of language processings in the frontal cortex on visual word recognition in the ventral occipito-temporal (vOT) regions; By tracking the acquisition of reading in young children, we examined the emergence of word-specific response in vOT region, especially when and how it develops.

As reading is a relatively new skill for human beings, an important question is to what extent hemispheric dominance for speech has influences on reading. We therefore investigate whether the functional lateralization of the vOT was correlated to the laterality of the frontal language processing areas or could be explained by other factors such as left hemisphere dominance for fine-grained form perception or the left-right reading direction. We compared the individuals with typical LH or atypical RH dominance for speech, and found a high correlation between inferior frontal lateralization (measured in a silent word generation task) and ventral occipito-temporal (vOT) lateralization (measured in a lexical decision task), which indicates that the interactions between the frontal and occipito-temporal brain areas are important for language processing. This correlation was accompanied by a higher percentage of bilateral language representation in vOT than in frontal regions (Cai et al., 2010; Van der Haegen et al., 2012).

On the other hand, at what age the specialized vOT area for reading develops was still debated: some studies claimed that stable responses to faces and words do not emerge before 10 years of age, whereas other studies demonstrated lateralized vOT responses to words and faces in young children before reading acquisition. We explored this question in a longitudinal study with 6 year-old non-reading first-graders. The preliminary results showed that 4—5 months of reading acquisition are sufficient to induce specific neural response in the reading-related network including left vOT regions, left inferior frontal gyrus, left posterior STS and left SMA, and specific responses to words increases with the time in these regions. At the same time, the site for the right face fusiform area (FFA) responds significantly to faces in 6 year-old, although this response to faces remains weak, in particular in comparison with bodies (Monzalvo et al., in preparation).

The Emotional Processing in Chinese Sentence Comprehension: A Near-infrared Spectroscopy Study

Shengnan Guo[a], Xuesong Li[b,*], Xiaoxiang Chen[c]

Key Laboratory of Child Development and Learning Science of ministry of education, Southeast University, China

[a]511zoe90@gmail.com, [b]xuesongli66@gmail.com, [c]1186044189@qq.com

[*] Corresponding author

Keywords: the prefrontal cortex; near-infrared spectroscopy; emotional processing

Abstract: The near-infrared spectroscopy (NIRS) technology can be used to measure brain blood flow in the prefrontal cortex. In this study, a 16-channel NIRS is used to measure concentration changes of oxygenated hemoglobin (oxy-HB) in the prefrontal cortex while the subjects are reading the emotional sentences. Compared with neutral condition, we find they are more sensitive in negative condition. Besides, the degree of activity in right hemisphere is the same as left hemisphere during the emotional processing in Chinese sentences. These results confirm that using NIRS to detect the brain activation evoked by Chinese emotional words is sensitive and feasible.

Introduction

Emotional cognition and the prefrontal cortex (PFC)

The brain mechanism of emotion is mainly involved with the prefrontal cortex and the limbic system, the emotional processing has a wide range of contacts about both the old skin and new skin layer. Two hemispheres of the brain mechanism of emotion is not consistent, positive emotions and negative emotions have different brain regions, the researches before shows that the left PFC was related with positive feelings and the right PFC associated with negative feelings[1].

Prefrontal locations are suggested to be closely associated with emotional stress and negative emotional reactions[2]. It has ever been reported that the activity in frontoparietal cortical attention networks is modulated by emotional arousal[2].

A lot of researches have done for emotional expression in human communication (i. e., facial, prosodic, and verbal)[3], only a little information is available in the field of emotional word processing by means of NIRS. Even though the ERP studies on the processing of emotional words present a complicated picture[4].

Near-infrared spectroscopy (NIRS)

NIRS is an emerging optical imaging technology, which is developing into a useful tool for noninvasive clinical monitoring of tissue oxygenation. We have confirmed its reliability in estimating regional cerebral blood flow in simultaneous measurements. It can readily detect cortical activation in frontal-temporal cortical surface areas.

Compared with magnetic resonance imaging (MRI), positron emission tomography (PET) and other relatively new functional neuroimaging technology, NIRS requires neither large expensive equipment nor an exogenous contrast medium, it is easy to handle and portable. It also has a high temporal resolution (typically 0.1 s, even 0.01 s in some study).

Recently, NIRS has been rapidly developed to explore the cognitive activities of human brain, such as language, learning and memory etc. So, in the present study, our aim is to verify whether NIRS is suitable for the measurement of blood oxygenation changes in frontal brain areas that are associated with Chinese emotional words processing.

Method

Participants

28 right-handed undergraduate students from Southeast University with normal or corrected-to-normal vision are recruited in the study (16 males and 12 females, aged 20—23); psychiatric illnesses are excluded by a measurement using Symptom Check List-90 (SCL-90). A written informed consent is obtained from each subject prior to the experiment and all subjects receive monetary compensation for their participation.

Materials

The experiment includes two kinds of sentences as materials which are matched by frequency. 60 words are selected from the *Frequency Dictionary of Modern Chinese*[5] as the end word of the sentence to make sentences. All critical words were matched across conditions with respect to frequency and the number of character strokes, as presented in Table 1.

Table 1 Mean Frequency for the Words

	Neutral	Negative
Frequecy[a]	15.26	14.34
Number of strokes	12.17	12.49

[a]Per million, according to Frequency Dictionary of Modern Chinese.

All the words are arranged in two sets (neutral and negative). Hence, there are two emotion conditions which are rated in terms of valence and arousal[6,7] by other 20 students recruited from the same population before the formal experiment. An example in Table 2 illustrates the three conditions. There is a significant difference in the mean rating of valence and arousal between negative and neutral sentence.

Table 2 Example of Design and Materials

Sentence context	Word	Condition
Mike put the notes in hand and drawing comics. 迈克把笔记本放在手边并在上面画漫画。	漫画(comics)	Neutral
Mother put the cat in a tub and poured boiling water. 妈妈把小猫放到木盆里并往里面倒开水。	开水(boiling water)	Negative

Procedure

The experiment is conducted in a quiet dim room. Stimuli are presented by computer positioned approximately 100 cm in front of the subjects with white words and black background. The experiment has two experimental tasks and a baseline task. For one experimental condition, subjects are presented with neutral sentences. In the other condition, subjects are presented with negative sentences. Subjects are instructed to watch them carefully and do not response. During baseline period the subjects passively view "××" for 30 s. Before the sentence, there is a "+" for 500 ms, each sentence consists of 5—8 phrases, the phrase is presented for 500 ms and soon after a blank screen for 200 ms, and each experimental condition includes 60 sentences (30neural, 30negtive). After a sentence, there is a blank screen for 1 500 ms. All participants are given practice with the tasks in order to be familiar to the procedure before NIRS experimental session. All subjects are in a sitting position throughout the measurements and are asked not to change their posture in order to prevent artifacts due to changes in hydrostatic pressure.

Apparatus

The experiment is conducted with a 16-channel NIRS system (The Key Laboratory of Biomedical Photonics of Ministry of Education, Huazhong University of Science and Technology in China). Figure 1 shows the layout of light sources and detectors on the NIRS imager panel. It contains four three-wavelength (735, 805, and 850 nm) light sources and ten detectors. The measurement covers an area of 18.6 cm × 7.4 cm centered over electrode position FPz, and is localized symmetrically and mainly over the prefrontal cortex. The distance between Light source and detector is set at 2.89 cm, which enables cerebral blood volume measurements to be at a 2—3 cm depth from the skin of the head, that is, the surface of cerebral cortices. Since the structure is formed by the infusion of black silicone material fixed detectors and light source in it. Therefore, the probes as a whole are strong and have a good flexibility to adapt to the different contours of the forehead measurement needs.

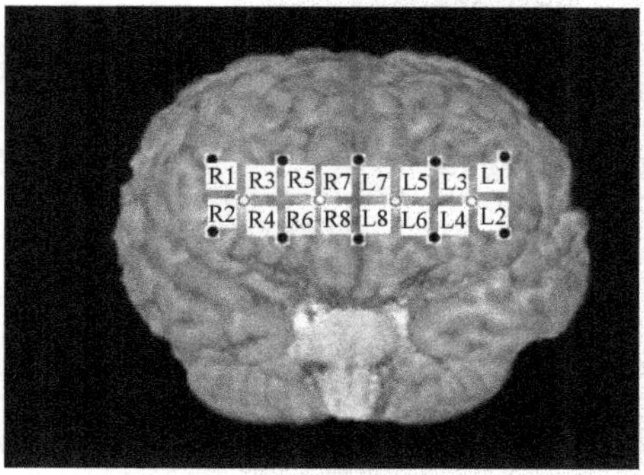

Figure 1 NIRS channel orientation

The detector's output signal, which is proportional to light intensity, is amplified and then is inputted into the computer through an A/D board. The sampling frequency for measurements is 3 Hz[7].

Data Analysis

With the software attached to the 16-channel NIRS system, the relative changes of the concentration of oxy-HB during emotional processing are calculated. The data of 16 channels, which correspond to the prefrontal area, are analyzed. In order to increase signal-to-noise ratio, data of 16 channels are filtered with digital band pass set from 0.000 5 to 0.02 Hz[8].

Hemoglobin is a colored protein in red blood cells, its molecular structure characteristics that make it an excellent transport oxygen carrier. As a result, concentration of oxy-HB plus concentration of deoxy-HB is equal to the concentration of total-HB[9]. Due to oxy-HB in the activated brain regions, deoxy-HB and total-HB concentration in general have a relatively stable relationship. The concentration of oxy-HB is often seen as ideal indicators for evaluation of degree of cortical activation[10].

Therefore, brain activity caused by emotional words, we only need further analyze the changes of oxygenated hemoglobin concentration. As for statistics, a 3 × 2 (task × hemisphere), two-way repeated measures analysis of ANOVA is applied to the changes of the concentration of oxy-HB as a dependent variable using SPSS 11.0, with within-subjects factors of task (baseline, neutral and negative), hemisphere (left and right). We add a baseline condition in order to ensure more accurate results.

Result

Average value of oxy-HB Changes

Table 3 Mean oxy-HB Changes

Condition	*M*	*SD*
Baseline	0.029	0.013
Neural	0.038	0.017
Negative	0.057	0.021

We can see from the table above, the changes of oxy-HB in negative condition is larger than others.

Analysis of variance (ANOVA)

The ANOVA for repeated measurements reveals a signicant main effect for the averaged changes of the concentration of oxy-HB. The experimental main effect of task is significant, $F(2,54) = 13.74$, $p < 0.0005$. It suggests that there must be a notable increase of the concentration of oxy-HB during the processing of negative sentences. The other main effect of hemisphere and the interaction effects are not statistically significant.

The result of LSD post-hoc shows that, no matter under natural condition or negative condition, the changes of concentration of oxy-HB are larger than the baseline condition significantly, the former, $p = 0.042$, the latter, $p = 0.029$. The changes of concentration of oxy-HB between two experimental conditions is of significance, $p = 0.033$, under the negative condition is larger than the natural condition.

Discussion

The present findings suggest that negative words have a larger activity. This result matches strongly with previous studies[2].

No lateralization effects were observed, both hemispheres are involved in emotional word recognition. Inconsistent with the findings from the current study, a study from rhesus monkeys suggests an asymmetric frontal electrical activity[11]. It is also not in line with the view that both hemispheres have access to the meanings of emotional words, although their time course of activation may be different[3]. It may be due to the confusion of the effects of arousal and valence by various kinds of negative emotional components.

In conclusion, we can see that using NIRS to detect the brain activation evoked by Chinese emotional words is a sensitive and feasible method. And we have tested and verified that the PFC is related to emotion processing. What remains unclear, however, is how the cerebral hemispheres contribute to the processing of emotional words. In future studies, MRI should be used to obtain more precise identification of brain regions.

Acknowledgments

This research was supported by grants from the Scientific Research Foundation to the returnees of Ministry of Education, the Social Science Foundation of Jiangsu Province (09YYB008), the topics on Cognitive mechanism of Chinese and English reading and research on the promotion strategy of Jiangsu Province Educational Sciences "Eleven-Five" Project (D/2008/01/013), the Corporation Project of Beijing Municipal Commission of Education (SYS100270661) and a grant from the Natural Science Foundation of China (91132705) to the researches on highly functional autistic children neuropathic central and basis for mood disorders face recognition.

References

[1] Guo Dejun, Ma qingxia. Research on brain mechanisms of emotion. Advances in Psychological Science, 2003, 11(3): 328 - 333.

[2] Andreas Keil, Margarita Stolarova, Stephan moratti. Motivated attention in emotional picture

processing is reflected by activity modulation in cortical attention networks. Neuroimage, 2004(21): 954-964.

[3] Ensie abbassi, Karima Kahlaoui, Maximiliano A Wilson, et al. Processing the emotions in words: The complementary contributions of the left and right hemispheres. Congn Affect Behav Neurosci, 2011(11): 372-385.

[4] Maecel Bastiaansen, Yufang, Yang Lin wang. ERP evidence on the interaction between information structure and emotional salience of words. Congn Affect Behav Neurosci, 2013(13): 297-310.

[5] Language Teaching College of Beijing Language Institute. Modern Chinese Frequency Dictionary. Beijing: Beijing Language Institute, 1986.

[6] Wei Wang, Hongyu yang. Prefrontal hemodynamic response during emotional stress measured with near-infrared spectroscopy. Chin J of Behavioral Med Sci, 2007, 16(5): 396-398.

[7] Zhenyu Zhou, Yun Liu, Zongcai Ruan, et al. Gender difference in hemodynamic responses of prefrontal area to emotional stress by near-infrared spectroscopy. Behavioural Brain Research, 2007(178): 172-176.

[8] Matthias L schroeter, Markus M Bucheler, Karsten Muller, et al. Towards a standard analysis for functional near-infrared imaging. Neuroimage, 2004(21): 283-290.

[9] Li Chengjun. On the prefrontal cortex function in working memory with near-infrared spectroscopy. Academic Degree's Evaluation Committee of Huazhong University of Science and Technology, 2005.

[10] 佚名. Interpretation of near-infrared spectroscopy signals: A study with a newly developed perfused rat brain model. Journal of Applied Physiology, 2001(90): 1657-1662.

[11] Christine Larson Steven, E Shelton, Richard J, et al. Asymmetric frontal brain activity, cortisol, and behavior associated with fearful temperament in rhesus monkeys. Behavioral Neuroscience, 1998, 112(2): 286-292.

Human Identity Verification Based on Heart Sounds

Jinzhou Cai[1,a,*], Lanyi Liu[1,b,*], Jun Xu[1,c], Duyang Li[1,d], Zhuoqian Li[1,e]

[1]College of Information Science Technology and engineering, Southeast University, Nanjing, 211189, China

[a] cjz2zy@126.com, [b]2646907366@qq.com, [c]1352659984@qq.com, [d]875677103@qq.com, [e]827924130@qq.com

[*] Corresponding author

Keywords: heart sound identification system; mel-frequency cepstrum coefficient; the first-to-second ratio; the marginal spectrum; the gaussian mixture mode

Abstract: Recently, many systems and approaches that employ heart sounds as physiological traits for biometric recognition have been investigated. However, there have not been a detailed and complete scheme so far, and the tests just stay in the experimental conditions. This paper designs a heart sound biometric system. This heart sound identification system is consisted of signal acquisition, pre-processing, feature extraction, and identification. The first step is using heart sound sensor HKY06C to extract the heart sounds signal. The second stage is to conduct pre-processing by using Wavelets, etc. Following by the extraction of three high recognition rate features which are (1) Mel—Frequency Cepstrum Coefficient (MFCC), (2) The Marginal Spectrum, (3) The First-to-Second Ratio (FSR). And finally we utilize the classifiers of the Gaussian Mixture Mode (GMM) for matching. We extracted the three features in particular, which have been proven suitable for non-stationary signal processing and capable of achieving correct recognition rate up to 90%. The results prove that the scheme has significant applicability and feasibility.

1 Introduction

Biological recognition technology refers to individual identification based on unique physiological or behavioral characteristics of the human body. There are some common biological recognition technologies such as fingerprint, eyes (retina and iris), palm prints, ear, tooth etc.

Compared with previous traditional biometrics patterns, heart sounds have unique advantages: (1) Easy to process due to the reason that the heart sound is a one-dimensional signal with frequency components that exist mainly in the low-frequency range, thus making the signal processing simple. (2) High universality because every person has a beating heart. (3) High level of safety and reliability because an individual's heart sounds cannot be faked. The recognition rate is less than 70% even if your heart sounds are recorded. It is impossible to reconstruct a new heart in modern technical conditions. The unique physiological characteristics of heart sounds make a promising identification technology.

Heart sound is the reflection of the mechanical movement of the heart and cardiovascular system. This feature contains a large amount of physiological and pathological information about the heart and various parts of the body. Heart sounds are typical non-stationary signals, including two parts. The first heart sound (S1) is mainly produced by the closure of the mitral and tricuspid valves. S1 lasts a period of 65 MS to 150 MS with a frequency of 25 Hz to 45 Hz. The second heart sound (S2) is produced by the closure of the aortic and pulmonary valves. S2 has duration of 60 MS to 120 MS with a frequency of approximately 50 Hz. Heart sound signal information is mainly distributed in the first heart sound and second heart sounds where therefore, contain the main information we need to extract. The third and the fourth heart sound is not obvious due to the low frequency, therefore it is rarely emphasized. A typical waveform of S1 and S2 is shown in Figure 1.

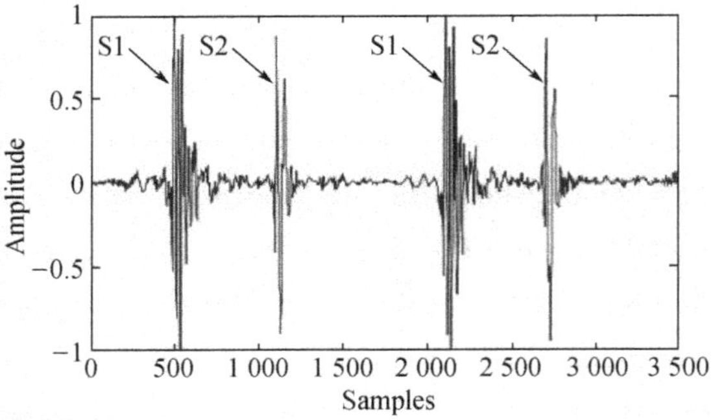

Figure 1 Typical waveform of S1 and S2

This technology has been receiving substantial attention all over the world. In 2010, Cheng Xie Feng research group from the Nanjing University conducted a preliminary study of heart sound biometrics. One method included characteristic analysis, followed by the extraction of characteristic parameters, and then they put forward an "S1—S2—CFS" recognition model and similarity coefficient for matching. The system's best performance in terms of accuracy and identification rate could reach 99%, but the experimental sample was far from adequate because the total sample size was only 10.

In Jasper & Othman (2010), the authors describe an experimental system where the signal is first down sampled from 11 025 Hz to 2 205 Hz; then it is processed using the Discrete Wavelet Transform, using the Daubechies-6 wavelet, and the D4 and D5 sub bands (34 to 138 Hz) are then selected for further processing. After a normalization and framing step, the authors then extract from the signal some energy parameters, and they find that, among the ones considered, the Shannon energy envelope is the feature that gives the best performance on their database of 10 people.

Tao et al. used the signals' cycle-power-frequency drawing and improved the D-S information fusion method to realize identity recognition based on heart sound. Fatemian et al. used a feature set of Mel—Frequency Cepstrum Coefficients (MFCC), Linear Discriminant Analysis (LDA), and Energy Peaks to acquire the heart sound classification information and to realize identity recognition. Cheng et al. presented a synthetic model of heart sounds and then used the heart sounds' linear band frequency cepstrum (HS-LBFC) as a specified configuration with similarity distance to achieve recognition and verification. The three methods are theoretically feasible but involve feature or model integration that can result in a more complicated implementation of the identification system.

The primary studies on this novel biometric method are summarized in Table 1. Given that no standard database exists and because of the use of different performance metrics, the various performances cannot be compared.

Table 1 Comparison of recent works about heart-sound biometrics

Author	Year	Database	Features	Classfication
Beritelli et al.	2007	20 people	STFT	Euclidean distance
Jasper & Othman	2010	10 people	Energy Peaks	Euclidean distance
Tao et al.	2010	5 to 100 people	Cycle Power Frequency	VQ
Fatemian et al.	2010	21 people	MFCC, LDA Energy Peaks	Euclidean distance
El-Bendary et al.	2010	40 people	autocorrelation cross-correlation complex cepstrum	kNN, MSE
Cheng et al.	2012	12 people	HS-LBFC	similarity distance

In this paper, we will study the basic principles of heart sound identification, a practical and feasible scheme by comparing different kinds of solutions, which are presented. Furthermore, we will discuss the extraction of three features in particular which have been proved to have a high recognition rate, and will attempt to solve the low success level of one feature. In the process of recognition, we will use Gaussian Mixture Model for matching and also reducing the effect of features, which has high deviation, by using Euclidean Distance.

2 Heart Sound Identification System

This novel identification system is comprised of five parts: signal acquisition, pre-processing, feature extraction, and identification. A diagram of this identification system is shown in figure 2.

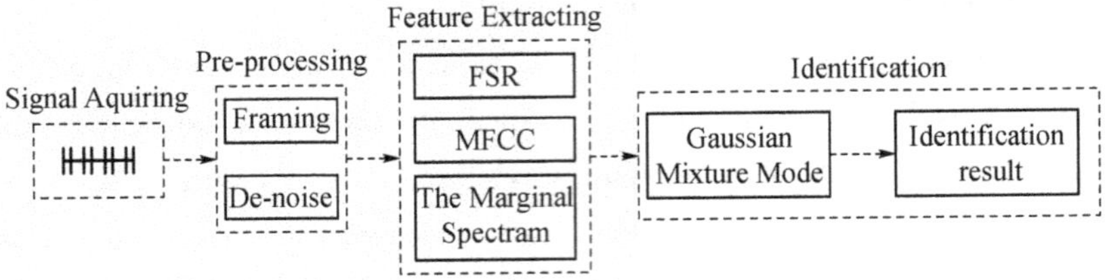

Figure 2 Heart sound identification system

2.1 Signal Acquisition

In this work, the equipment for the acquisition of heart sounds and the waveform through the sensor is shown in Figure 3. The sampling frequency of the sensor is about 1 000 Hz to 8 000 Hz. It is comprised of three parts. The first part is the pole used for collecting heart sounds, which acts like the stethoscope. The second part is the body of heart sound sensor consisted of operational amplifier circuit with high accuracy. It can transport the mechanical vibration on the heart into the electrical signals. The last part is the USB, which can connect the computer to display the waveform through the VB program designed in the computer.

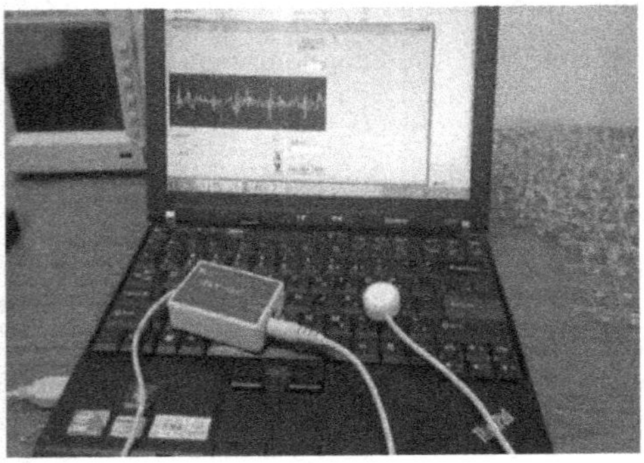

Figure 3 Equipment for signal acquisition

Participants are required to be calm and relaxed during signal acquisition. HKY06C sensor is placed on the participants' chest in the pulmonary auscultation region. The interval between each recorded signal is about one hour. The location on the chest for all recordings should be the same. We collect each person's heart sounds twice, providing convenience for training and we have established a database recording from 200 people's heart sounds signal, which last approximately 20 s.

2.2 Pre-processing

When extracting the heart sound signal with HKY06C, which inevitably includes some noise. In order to eliminate the impact of noise and facilitate follow-up study, we need to pre-process the acquired heart sound signal first. Pre-process is divided into two stages with the first stage of noise reduction and pre-emphasis, while the second stage is decomposing heart sound into frames and adding windows.

2.2.1 Noise Reduction & Pre-emphasis

The specific de-noising steps are listed as follows:

(1) The fifth-order Daubechies wavelet is selected as the mother wavelet to decompose the heart sound signal into six scales;

(2) The WT coefficients at the third, fourth, fifth, and sixth scales are retained based on an energy-based threshold, whereas the coefficients related to other scales are set to zero;

(3) The signal is reconstructed by using inverse DWT (IDWT).

The purpose of pre-emphasis is to compensate for the high-frequency part repressed by sound system of the heart sound signal, the spectrum of heart sound signal becomes flat, so that we can use the same signal-noise ratio for spectrum analysis and channel parameter analysis from low to high frequency in the whole frequency band.

2.2.2 Decomposing heart sound into frames

Heart sound signals are assumed as short-timed stationary signals, which are considered as smooth process only in the short period of time, so we divide heart sound signal into lots of short segments called analysis frame. Each frame contains N sample points, which takes 256 or 512. We use the method of overlapping segments, helping a smooth transition between frames to maintain its continuity. The distance from the beginning of a frame to the beginning of the succeeding one is called frame shift, the rate of the frame length to the frame shift is usually from 0 to 1/2. Sub-frame is carried out with a moveable window of finite length, that is to use a certain window function to multiply heart sound signals $s(n)$, thereby forming windowed heart sound signal $s_w(n) = s(n) * w(n)$. In the field of digital audio signal processing, we usually choose Rectangular window, Hamming window. Due to the fact that hamming window doesn't lose the high frequency part, we use Hamming window in accordance with the following formula to divide acquired signal into frames.

$$w(n) = \begin{cases} 0.54 - 0.46\cos\left(\dfrac{2pn}{N-1}\right) & 0 \leqslant n \leqslant N-1 \\ 0 & n = \text{else} \end{cases} \tag{1}$$

A de-noised heart sound signal along with its corresponding raw signal is depicted in Figure 4.

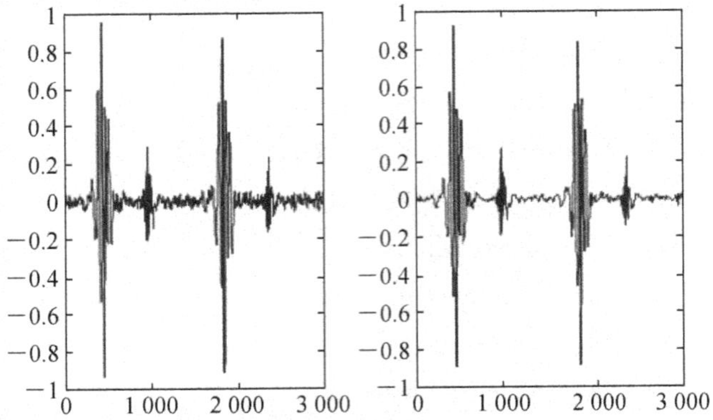

Figure 4 Original heart sound signal and the related de-noised signal

2.3 Feature Extraction

In order to improve the recognition rate of heart sound recognition, we decide to use the idea of evaluation model of mathematical modeling to extract several valid eigenvalues of the heart sound signal to form a feature vector, thus the original heart sound signal is converted to low-dimensional feature matrix, which is easy to match and store. We mainly extracted MFCC (Mel Frequency Cepstrum Coefficient), The First-to-Second Ratio (FSR), and The Marginal Spectrum.

2.3.1 Mel—Frequency Cepstrum Coefficient (MFCC)

Mel Frequency Cepstrum Coefficients are widely used as speech signal processing features, which take full account of the non-linear characteristics of the human ear's auditory system and convert the spectrum of the speech signal into nonlinear spectrum based on Mel frequency, and then convert to the cepstral domain. So MFCC parameters have good recognition performance and noise immunity. Although heart sound signals and voice signals are very different, they are the same in the essence and some characteristics, so MFCC also can be applied to the heart sound signal recognition. The extraction procedure is as follows:

(1) Fast Fourier Transform: Because it's usually hard for us to see the characteristics of the signal in the time domain, so we converted it to the frequency domain to observe it with the energy distribution, the different energy distributions can represent different heart sound feature.

(2) Triangular Band pass Filters: The energy spectrum of the energy is multiplied by a group of 20 Triangle-pass filters to obtain the Log Energy (the logarithm of the energy) output of each filter. Triangle-pass filter has two main purposes: smoothing the spectrum and eliminating the role of harmonics to highlight the formant of original sound. So whether

the tone of some heart sound is high or low, it is not rendered within the MFCC parameters.

(3) Discrete cosine transform: Take above 20 pairs Log Energy into discrete cosine transform, finding L-order Mel-scale Cepstrum parameter, where L is usually taken 12.

(4) Delta cepstrum: We coupled differential cepstrum parameters to display the change of cepstrum parameters on time, which represents dynamical change of cepstral parameters over time.

2.3.2 The Marginal Spectrum

In this part, the marginal spectrum is extracted as the feature. Figure 5 shows the flow chart of the feature extraction procedure.

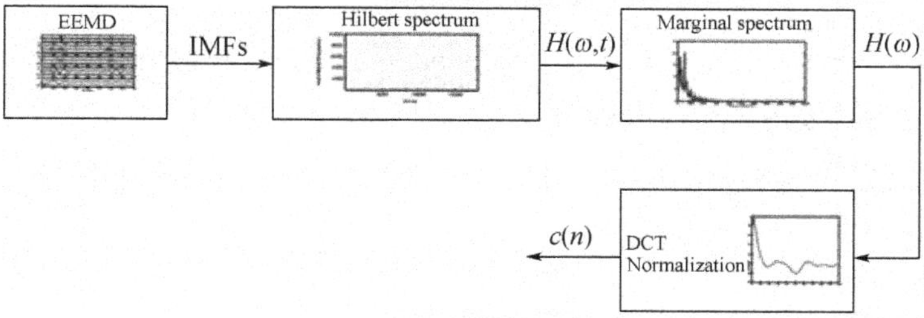

Figure 5 Flow chart of the extraction of The Marginal Spectrum

(1) EEMD is applied to each frame signal of heart to obtain the IMFs of the signal.

(2) Hilbert spectrum $H(\omega,t)$ of each frame will be obtained by applying HT to each IMF, which shows the amplitude and the instantaneous frequency in a three-dimensional plot.

(3) Three-domain Hilbert spectrum $H(\omega,t)$ of each frame signal is integral in the time domain to obtain the Marginal spectrum $H(\omega)$.

(4) Dimension compression and amplitude normalization: the spectrum coefficients $c(n)$ are followed by the Discrete Cosine Transform (DCT). The dimension is reduced to an appropriate dimension for the subsequent training and identification phase.

2.3.3 The First-to-Second Ratio (FSR)

$S1$ and $S2$ signals are the typical features of heart signals. The energy of the two signals keeps changing with the systolic and diastolic process. From the experiment, we can conclude that the ratio of $S1$ and $S2$ energy (first-second ratio) remains stable. So we use the first-second ratio (FSR) as a feature.

The definition of FSR:

$$FSR = \frac{Pf1}{Pf2} \tag{2}$$

Let N be the cycle of $S1/S2$ in a certain digital heart sound, $Pf1$ be the average energy of $S1$, and $Pf2$ be the average energy of $S2$.

Algorithm protocol

We use wavelet to decompose the heart sound signal in order of 4 windows stages and then utilize the normalized average Shannon energy to analyze it. It can be seem from the oscillogram that $S1$ and $S2$ mainly concentrate at A3 (0—138 Hz). Then we calculate the normalized average Shannon energy using A3 as the reconstructed data source.

The data is separated into several segments with each segment of 20 ms and the interval between two segments lasts 10 ms.

$$E_S = \frac{-1}{N}\sum_{i=1}^{N} x_{xom}^2(i)\log x_{xom}^2(i) \tag{3}$$

x_{xom} is the ratio of the sampled value and the maximum absolute value of the signal analyzed. N is the sampling number in 20 ms.

The average Shannon energy of the whole heart sound signal is defined as follow:

$$P_d(t) = \frac{E_{s(t)} - M(E_{s(t)})}{S(E_{s(t)})} \tag{4}$$

$E_{s(t)}$ sequence is composed of E_s in different time segments. $M(E_{s(t)})$ is the average value of $E_{s(t)}$. $S(E_{s(t)})$ is standard deviation of $E_{s(t)}$.

2.4 Identification

The main purpose of this process is to acquire the correspondence of two heart sounds sequences. Following are the main steps:

2.4.1 To form feature vectors from extracted features:

We arrange the features in order and form two vectors in both test heart signals and in signals in the database:

$$S1 = (A, B, C, D\cdots) \quad S2 = (a, b, c, d\cdots) \tag{5}$$

Let $S1$ be the vectors from database, $S2$ be the vectors from test signals and $A(a)$, $B(b)$ be the features.

2.4.2 To compare the similarity of the two sequences:

So far, there are several algorithms have been used in the heart sounds research internationally:

(1) Euclidean distance:

This algorithm has been widely used in the research, which to some degree amplifies the effect of feature, but it has great deviation. Features with little deviation means more similarity, otherwise it has little similarity. In the process of heart sound recognition, it is expected that the effect of features having little deviation could be amplified. Therefore, in conclusion, this algorithm is excluded.

$$d = \sqrt{\sum (x_{i1} - x_{i2})^2} \tag{6}$$

x_{i1} is the ith-dimensional coordinates of the first point, x_{i2} is the ith-dimensional coordinates of the second point. N-dimensional Euclidean space is a set of points, each of its points can be expressed as $(x(1), x(2), \cdots, x(n))$, where $x(I)$ $(I = 1, 2\cdots, n)$ is a real number. The Euclidean distance between the two points is defined as the above formula.

(2) Supporting Vector Machine (SVM)

The vector is mapped to the higher dimensional space and then divides the hyper plane. This algorithm performs well in a small sample group, nonlinear and high dimensional pattern recognition. However, it has two drawbacks. First of all, it is difficult to implement on a large scale training sample. Secondly, classic SVM classification gives only two types of classical algorithm.

(3) Gaussian mixture model:

① Gaussian mixture model uses K (typically 3 to 5) Gaussian models to represent different heart sound signal characteristic variables.

② Training feature vectors from the database into different Gaussian mixture models.

③ Input the test vector, then calculate the probability of the feature vector which belongs to different Gaussian mixture models.

$$N(x;u,\sum) = \frac{1}{\sqrt{2\pi|\sum|}}\exp\left[-\frac{1}{2}(x-u)^T\sum{}^{-1}(x-u)\right] \tag{7}$$

x is column vector of the the dth-dimension, u is the expectation of the model, $\sum$ is variance of the model.

$$Pr(x) = \sum_{k=1}^{K} \pi_k N(x;u_k,\sum{}_k) \tag{8}$$

K needs to be defined in advance like the k in the k-means, u_k is the weight value.

Set a threshold. If the probability is higher than the threshold, the match is successful. Otherwise, the match fails.

3 Conclusion

Although heart sound identification technology research remains at its early stage, this technology has great significance in various research fields and been applied in many different areas.

In this paper, we presented a practical and feasible scheme. Four processing steps signal acquisition, pre-processing, feature extraction, training, and identification are introduced in detail. We extracted the three features in particular, which have been proven suitable for non-stationary signal processing and capable of achieving correct recognition rate up to 80%.

So, there is no doubt that heart sounds could be regarded as a promising future for biometric technology.

Although the proposed system was found to achieve good performance under the experimental conditions, numerous factors have to be considered in practical applications, such as signal stability and a large signal.

References

[1] Phua K, Chen J, Tran H D, et al. Heart sound as a biometric. Pattern Recognit, 2008, 41: 906 - 919.

[2] Beritelli F, Serrano S. Biometric identification based on frequency analysis of cardiac sounds. IEEE Trans. Inf. Forensics Secur, 2007, 2: 596 - 604.

[3] Beritelli F. A multiband approach to human identity verification based on phonocar diagram signal analysis. Proceedings of BSYM '08 Biometrics Symposium. Tampa, FL, USA, 2008.

[4] F Beritelli, S Serrano. Biometric identification based on frequency analysis of cardiac sounds. IEEE Transactions on Information Forensics and Security, 2007, 2(3): 596 - 604.

[5] L Lu. A one-vendor multi-buyer integrated inventory model. European Journal of Operational Research, 1995, 81: 312 - 323.

[6] Cheng X, Ma Y, Liu C, et al. Research on heart sound identification technology. Sci, China Inf. Sci. 2012, 55: 281 - 292.

[7] Besson P, Kunt M. Hypothesis testing for evaluating a multimodal pattern recognition framework applied to speaker detection. Journal of Neuro Engineering and Rehabilitation, 2008, 5: 11.

[8] N El-Bendary, H Al-Qaheri, H M Zawbaa, et al. Haas: Heart sound authentication system//Nature and Biologically Inspired Computing (NaBIC). 2010 Second World Congress, 2010: 351 - 356.

[9] S Fatemian, F Agrafioti, D Hatzinakos. Hearted: Cardiac biometric recognition//Biometrics: Theory Applications and Systems (BTAS). 2010 Fourth IEEE International Conference on Biometrics Compendium, 2010.

[10] Lindo Y, Buzo A, Gray R M. An algorithm for vector quantizer design. IEEE Trans. Commun, 1980, 28: 84 - 95.

[11] Beritelli F, Spadaccini A. Human identity verification based on mel frequency analysis of digital heart sounds//Digital Signal Processing. 2009 16th International Conference on. IEEE, 2009.

[12] K Phua, J Chen, T H Dat, et al. Heart sound as a biometric. Pattern Recognition, 2008, 41 (3): 906 - 919.

[13] D A Reynolds, R C Rose. Robust text-independent speaker identification using Gaussian mixture speaker models. IEEE Transactions on Speech and Audio Processing, 1995, 3: 72 – 83.

[14] D H Tran, Y R Leng, H Li. Feature integration for heart sound biometrics//Acoustics Speech and Signal Processing (ICASSP). 2010 IEEE International Conference on Acoustics Speech and Signal Processing (ISASSP), 2010: 1714 – 1717.

[15] Jain AK, Ross A, Prabhakar S. An introduction to biometric recognition. IEEE Trans. Circ. Syst. Video Technol, 2004, 14(2): 4 – 20.

[16] Jain A K, Ross A, Prabhakar S. A Tool for Information Security. IEEE Trans. Inf. Forensics Secur, 2006, 1: 125 – 143.

[17] Shengli W, Mclean S. Performance prediction of data fusion for information retrieval. Information Processing and Management, 2006, 42: 899 – 915.

[18] Piella G. A general framework for multi-resolution image fusion, from pixels to regions. Information Fusion, 2003, 4: 259 – 280.

[19] Jasper J, Othman K. Feature extraction for human identification based on envelogram signal analysis of cardiac sounds in time-frequency domain//Proceeding of 2010 International Conference on Electronics and Information Engineering (ICEIE). Kyoto, Japan, 2010: 228 – 233.

[20] Tao Y W, Sun X, Zhang H X, et al. A biometric identification system based on heart sound signal//Proceedings of The 3rd Conference on Human System Interactions (HSI). Rzeszow, Poland, 2010: 67 – 75.

[21] Guo X M, Duan Y, Zhong L. Study of human identity recognition based on HMM and WNN. Appl. Res. Comput, 2010, 27: 4561 – 4564.

[22] Chen T-h, Han L-q. Detection and realization of heart sounds signal based an HKY06C sensor. Microcomputer Information, 2009, 6: 167 – 168.

Classification of Emotion in Chinese Words Based on EEG

Minmin Cheng[a], Haixian Wang[b,*], Zuhong Lu[c]
Key Laboratory of Child Development and Learning Science of Ministry of Education
Research Center for Learning Science, Southeast University, Nanjing, Jiangsu 210096, China
[a]mmcheng@seu.edu.cn, [b]hxwang@seu.edu.cn, [c]zhlu@seu.edu.cn
[*] Corresponding author

Keywords: emotion classification; two-character chinese word; EEG; short-time fourier transform (STFT)

Abstract: To classify the emotion induced by human language, this study used EEG signals from the brain to identify the emotional and non-emotional two-character Chinese words. The power spectrums in theta, alpha and beta frequency bands are extracted by short time Fourier transform (STFT). Principal component analysis (PCA) is employed for dimensionality reduction. The mean accuracy rate of LDA classifier is about 63% for 4 subjects. The result demonstrates the identifiability of emotion in Chinese words.

1 Introduction

In human's daily activities, understanding of each other's emotion directly affects the communication. It is particularly important to accurately identify the emotional information in language since language is always the first choice for human's communication. Therefore, classification of emotion induced by language brings a great progress to human-computer interaction which is popular and badly needed.

In earlier studies, emotion recognition of language focused on voice, such as emotive speech[1]. Then, signals from peripheral neurons system increasingly presented in this research area, e.g. EMG, ECG and skin conductivity, etc. Nowadays, more and more attentions are paid to EEG-based emotion recognition since it is the most direct and practical way of measuring brain activities. Many EEG-based researches concentrate on the emotional picture[2], facial expression, videos and even music[3]. Due to the far lower emotional arousal of language compared to pictures', classification of emotion in language is an unsolved problem. It is almost blank in this research area.

Time-Frequency analysis of electroencephalogram (EEG) during different mental tasks received significant attention. As EEG is non-stationary, time-frequency analysis is essential to analyze brain states during different mental tasks. Further, the time-frequency information of EEG signal can be used as a feature for classification. Fourier transform (FT) is a basic and simple method to do time-frequency transform. As the traditional fast Fourier transform (FFT) does not provide time-domain information, short-time Fourier transform (STFT) isolates the EEG signal in time domain by multiplying with a window function and computes the Fourier coefficients in that time interval, and then shifts the time window through the time line to capture the entire time-frequency feature of the EEG signals[4].

In this paper, we focus on how to classify the emotion induced by Chinese words. Two-character word is used in the experiment as it is the most commonly used language elements in Chinese[5]. The framework of this paper is arranged as follows. Section 2 gives details about the data recording experiment. Section 3 describes the feature extraction and classification. Then the results and discussion are presented in Section 4. And finally Section 5 concludes the paper.

2 Experiment

2.1 Subjects

EEG signals were recorded from 4 healthy university undergraduate students (2 males; mean age 23). All participants were native Chinese speaker, right-handed, and had normal or corrected-to normal vision. The study protocol conformed to local ethics guidelines.

2.2 Stimuli and Design

160 two-character Chinese words, half emotional neutral and half emotional negative, were showed to subjects as materials which were all chosen from Modern Chinese Frequency Dictionary and were evaluated by other 25 undergraduate students with the same age as the 4 subjects. The evaluation was made from two dimensions: emotional valence (positive on the one and negative on the other side) and arousal (from calm to excited). Each dimension was divided into nine grades. Then 60 unreal two-character words with no realistic meaning were created as experimental target materials.

Software Stim 2 presented materials at the center of a computer screen. A single trial was shown to subjects as following: a fixation sign (" + ") for 500 ms, followed by a blank screen for 500 ms. After a 500 ms-presentation of a Chinese word, another blank screen was present for 1 500 ms. Then a new trial started. Subjects were asked to press a button when an unreal word was shown to make sure they concentrated on the experiment. All the words were presented in random order.

2.3 EEG Recording and Preprocessing

The EEG data was record from a 64-channel electrode cap (NeuroScan Inc.). All inter-electrode impedance was maintained below 5 kΩ. During the recording, band-pass filtering was between 0.05 Hz and 100 Hz, and sampling rate was 1 000 Hz.

According to the purpose of this research and the related literatures[6], 21 electrodes were selected evenly throughout the whole scalp. Figure 1 illustrates the specific distribution of these 21 electrodes. Epoch of 1 200 ms length was cut from the continuously recorded data. The first 200 ms before onset of the words was used as baseline of EEG. After baseline correction, trials with amplitudes larger than 100 μV were rejected.

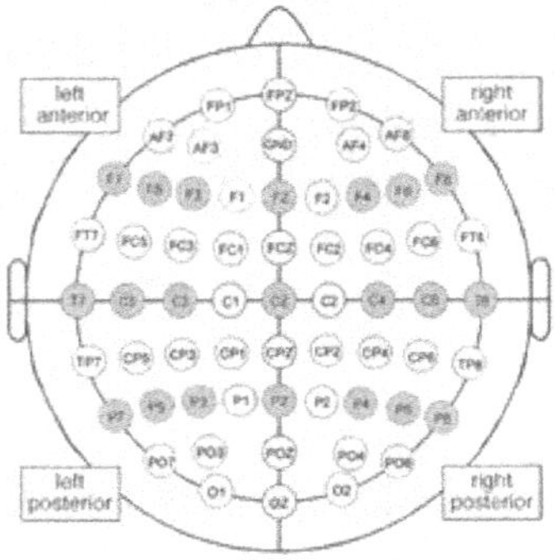

Figure 1 The distribution of the whole 64 electrodes. The gray points are the 21 chosen ones

3 Feature Extraction and Classification

There has been prior evidence that power in theta, alpha and beta frequency bands vary when considering inhibition tasks[7]. Therefore, we consider theta, alpha and beta bands for features extraction in this paper. STFT is an extension of conventional Fourier analysis for non-stationary data. To see how the frequency content of a signal changes over time, STFT performs FFT on consecutive blocks of data that are assumed stationary, and is equivalent to a sliding window that analyzes the local frequency content of the signal. The STFT for signal windowed by a fixed-length function is defined by (1).

$$STFT_x(t,f) = \int_{-\infty}^{\infty} x(\tau)w(t-\tau)e^{-2j\pi f\tau}\mathrm{d}\tau \qquad (1)$$

In our analysis, we use a 0.5s window and 50% overlap for the STFT. The type of window is Hamming window. Output of STFT is the power of signal in different frequency bands and time segments. Features used in this paper are a combination of STFT Output. Each trial is represented with a feature vector containing 189 (21 channels, 3 blocks, and 3 frequency bands) elements. Then PCA is employed for dimensionality reduction. Finally, we use LDA for emotion classification.

4 Results and Discussion

As the purpose of this study is to classify emotional information in Chinese words, the created unreal words are not analyzed. The emotional and non-emotional two-character words are exactly what we needed to compare and identify. The trials are separated into training sets and test sets by 10-fold cross-validation method for classification. The results of emotion classification are shown in Table 1.

Table 1 The accuracy of emotion classification

	Subject				mean
	1	2	3	4	
Accuracy of classification	62.7	64.5	61.3	62.9	62.9

It is said that affective words could induce significantly greater components than neutral ones in event-related potential (ERP) study. That is because more information which activates more cognitive resources is extracted from emotional words. Thus, greater amplitude can be seen in ERP waves[8,9]. We assumed that emotional words can be distinguished from neutral ones using the method of pattern recognition. The recognition result with around 63% accuracy verifies our hypothesis. Maybe it is not a very satisfied result since higher classification accuracy can be achieved by using other materials, such as emotional pictures. But this result does demonstrate the identifiability of emotion in Chinese words. It is consistent with the conclusion of related ERP researches.

5 Conclusion

In this research we use EEG signal to classify emotions elicited by Chinese Words (emotional and non-emotional two-character words). The power spectrums from 3 frequency bands are used as the features. The mean accuracy rate of LDA classifier is about 63%. With the increase of social pressure, more and more negative emotions are involved in normal life, e.g. depression, anxiety. Our study may contribute to identify the negative emotion in computer users' language within BCI system, and then helps to make a fluent communication, even to maintain people's mental health.

The good news is that there is still a lot can be improved in this study. As mentioned above, STFT is a basic method for time-frequency analysis while there are several more comprehensive analysis methods which are widely used, such as wavelet analysis. We intend to try these methods in the next step. In this study, we only compare the emotional neutral words to the negative emotional words. Actually, positive emotion is also an indispensable part in emotion. In a study which focuses on the difference between emotional and non-emotional materials, it will be more precisely to involve both negative and positive elements. This is an important part we should consider in future work. Improvements in these aspects will provide great opportunities to acquire higher classification accuracy.

References

[1] J Chen, C Li. Recent Development in Speech Emotion Recognition. Computer Engineering, 2005, 31(13): 35-37.

[2] P J Lang, M M Bradley, B N Cuthbert. 2008 Technical Report A-8. University of Florida, Gainesville, FL, 2008.

[3] S N Daimi, G Saha. Classification of emotions induced by music videos and correlation with participants' rating. Expert Systems with Applications, 2014, 41: 6057-6065.

[4] D Gabor. Theory of communication. Journal of the Institution of Electrical Engineers—Part Ⅲ: Radio and Communication Engineering, 1946, 93(26): 429-441.

[5] X Sui, X L Zhang. Review about the research of recognition of Chinese 2—Character words. Journal of Liaoning Normal University (Social Science Edition), 2012, 35(6): 768-771.

[6] Y J Luo, Y X Huang, X Y Li. Effects of emotion on cognitive processing: Series of event-related potentials study. Advances in Psychological Science, 2006, 14(4): 505-510.

[7] T Harmony, A Alba, J Marroqun, et al. Time-frequency-topographic analysis of induced power and synchrony of EEG signals during a Go/No-Go task. International Journal of Psychophysiology, 2009, 71(1): 9-16.

[8] S Williamson, T J Harpur, R D Hare. Abnormal processing of affective words by psychopaths. Psychophysiology, 1991, 28(3): 260.

[9] Y N Wang, L M Zhou, Y J Luo. Implicitly processing of affective connotation of Chinese words evidence from event-related brain potential. Journal of Beijing Normal University (Natural Science), 2007-2008, 43(4): 466-470.

Plasticity, Sensitive Period and Language Development

Wei Song[1,2,a,*], Hongli Xue[2,b]

[1] Institute of linguistics, Jiangsu Normal University, Xuzhou, Jiangsu Province, 221009, China

[2] National key lab of cognitive neuroscience and learning, Beijing Normal University, 100875, China

[a] xzhsongwei@163.com, [b] xuehli225@163.com

[*] Corresponding author

Keywords: Brain; Plasticity; Sensitive period; Language Development

Abstract: Language is the specific communication competence of human being and has its biological base. Based on the contemporary research of brain and neuroscience, the paper postulates that the critical period of second language learning has different stages and patterns according to the plasticity, sensitive period and the language development rules. The education and learning strategies and methods should be adapted according to the nature of human languages, the language types, the writing systems in order to achieve the best result of second language learning.

脑可塑性、敏感期与语言发展

宋伟[1,2,a,*]，薛红莉[2,b]
[1]江苏师范大学语言研究所，徐州，江苏，中国
[2]北京师范大学认知神经科学与学习国家重点实验室，北京，中国
[a]xzhsongwei@163.com，[b]xuehli225@163.com
[*]通讯作者

关键词：脑；可塑性；敏感期；语言发展

中文摘要：语言是人类特有的交流能力，具有明显的生物遗传学基础。基于当代神经科学理论和脑科学最新成果，根据人脑可塑性、敏感期的语言发展规律，文章提出学习敏感期具有层次性的观点，要根据人类语言发展的特点、人类语言的不同类型、书面语言的不同系统，建立适合于人脑认知机制和神经机制的语言教育与发展及促进策略。

1 引言

语言能力是人脑最重要的高级功能之一，语言能力的获得是人类进化史上具有重大意义的事件，自从有了语言，人脑其他高级功能如思维、记忆、情绪、注意等才获得了飞跃式的发展。

语言具有神经生物学基础。提出语言与基因遗传关系的是 Hurst 在 1990 年发表的有关英国一个 KE 家族的报告。Enard 在 2009 年通过将人类语言基因 FOXP2 植入老鼠体内的方法，发现植入语言基因的老鼠比正常老鼠在大脑皮层和基底节的联系上要丰富，其在基底节的神经元轴突增长快，树突密度变厚，可塑性增强，能发出较低波段的超声波唧叫声，从而进一步说明了该基因在人类语言能力进化和人类语言器官进化中的重要作用。

人脑不仅能够熟练掌握母语即第一语言，而且还可以学习和掌握第二种语言，甚至第三种语言。因此，母语习得能力和多语言学习能力一直是心理学家、认知神经科学家、脑科学家和教育工作者研究和关注的热点。探究语言的脑机制对于教育具有重要的意义，这些研究成果可以使我们科学地认识母语习得和二语学习的脑机制，认识基于人类亿万年进化所逐渐形成的与语言能力有关的脑结构网络和功能网络是如何在短短几年(0—5 岁)间形成语言能力的，二语学习是如何在母语基础上进行并能达到与母语一样的熟练程度的。可以使我们对语言发展的行为规律、认知规律、脑结构网络、功能网络透彻了解，可以帮助提高学生的母语和二语学习能力，促进语言能力的发展。

人与其他动物的最大区别之一就是人类拥有语言且能在 5 岁左右就能熟练掌握

母语,随着对狼孩、幼年脑损伤儿童、先天聋人儿童的语言能力发展轨迹的研究,以及二十世纪中叶视觉功能关键期概念的提出,学者们逐渐提出语言能力具有关键期的概念,Eric Lenneberg 在 1967 年首次提出母语习得存在关键期,即语言学习必须在某一年龄段(青春期前)进行才能达到最好效果,过了这个阶段,语言学习好像变得困难了。后来,学者们又发现关键期其实与脑的可塑性密切相关,即关键期并不是一个绝对的概念,过了关键期,语言学习虽然困难,但仍可以进行,人脑似乎又有一定的可塑性。

2 人脑的可塑性与语言发展

随着脑科学的发展和研究的逐步深入,学者们发现人脑有着极强的可塑性(plasticity),这不仅体现在脑结构的可塑性上,而且体现在脑功能的可塑性上。在脑结构可塑性上,研究发现,脑的神经元突触数量、突触密度以及突触回路是不断变化的,额叶、颞叶、顶叶和枕叶之间的纤维联结会随着自身结构的成熟和外界经验的变化而发生变化,皮层中枢、皮层下功能核团之间的纤维联结同样也会发生变化;在脑功能可塑性上,研究表明,无论是初级视觉功能还是高级语言功能,都具有随着经验的变化而表现出功能网络发生相应变化的特点。

人脑可塑性对于语言发展有着重要的意义。母语一般在自然状态下习得,觉察不到学习的难度,体现不出训练的过程;而二语学习往往是在有意识的状态下,通过有目的的教与学活动,对语音、单词、语法进行系统的学习和训练,才能逐渐掌握。在行为学层面上,表现出二语学习者对二语知识的掌握和运用能力的提高;在脑机制上,表现为与语言相关的脑区激活模式产生了变化。人脑神经网络的这种变化模式为我们提供了人脑在语言发展过程中具有可塑性的科学依据。

研究发现在语音加工任务中,汉语母语的语音加工任务主要由左侧半球为主的额叶—颞叶—顶叶加工网络执行。以英语为第二语言的人,虽然也主要由左侧半球的网络来加工,但其优势不明显。Q. Dong 和 G. Xue 等(2004)运用功能磁共振成像(fMRI)技术发现非熟练中英双语者在加工英语语音时,后部双侧的顶叶激活要比加工汉语语音时强,而左侧额叶下部布洛卡区的激活却较弱。这说明由于二语语音经验的影响,造成了非熟练中英双语者脑激活模式的差异,反映了脑在语言学习过程中的强大可塑性。这说明,人脑在二语学习中功能网络会产生变化,即脑功能具有可塑性。

Weber-fox 等(1996)发现中英文双语被试由于开始学习二语的年龄不同,学习英语的时间分别为 1—3 岁, 4—6 岁, 7—10 岁, 11—13 岁和 16 岁以后,在阅读句子并判断其语法正确性上的事件相关电位指标(ERPs)上表现出不同的特点。早期双语者集中在左半球颞叶前部, 而晚期双语者的脑电波活动则分散得多。这也表明,人脑具有可塑性,即由于熟练度、习得年龄等因素的影响,同一语言任务可以由不同的脑区和功能网络来完成。

上述两个研究，一个是语音方面的脑机制，一个是句法方面的脑机制，但两者都体现出二语脑功能网络的变化和可塑性。一般来说，人脑从形成过程开始就逐渐形成了一个默认的语言加工网络，即左侧外侧裂核心语言区，包括前部的布洛卡区和后部的威尔尼克区、角回（即颞顶枕区结合部）、颞叶前部等。这个默认的语言加工网络在母语的习得中发挥了巨大的作用。正常情况下该网络应该在二语学习中也发挥作用，不需要其他脑区的参与。而上述研究却发现，除了默认网络，其他脑区也参与了二语加工，这不仅体现在语音加工网络上，也体现在句法加工网络上。人脑为了完成语音或句法任务，调用了所有可能的脑区，这不仅体现出人脑的高度灵活性，也体现出人脑功能的可塑性。

脑功能可塑性的另一个例证来自 Kim 等 1997 年的一个研究。在该研究中，不同母语和二语的被试分别用母语和二语描述前一天发生的事情，结果发现晚期习得二语的双语者两种语言在布洛卡区的激活模式存在差异，而早期习得二语的双语者两种语言在布洛卡区激活模式相同。这表明对于早期学习者而言，母语和二语的加工可能具有相同的脑功能网络；而对于晚期学习者而言，右半球可能参与了第二语言的学习和加工，或者在左半球可能分别有不同的区域负责母语与第二语言的加工。人脑模式的激活同样表现出高度的可塑性，即二语习得年龄越早，熟练程度越高，布洛卡区对二语的加工越表现出同母语一样的激活模式。

从脑可塑性的角度来研究二语学习具有明显的现实意义。通过对人脑二语学习过程中所表现出的语音、句法和语义等方面的脑功能网络变化，总结脑可塑性的具体演变机制，找出母语和二语表征、存储和运算加工方面的异同以及在行为学上的表现差异，由此可以预测二语的熟练程度和二语语音、句法和语义等不同方面的学习水平，这为针对性地进行后续语言训练和学习提供了科学的依据。

对于母语为汉语的中国学生来说，可以在充分认识和了解脑可塑性的基础上，根据汉语和英语语言的各自特点和汉英双语加工过程的异同，来寻找英语作为二语的语言学习的心理机制和脑机制的规律，并在英语学习的过程中，根据英语学习的科学规律来优化教和学的方案，从而使英语学习者在学习运用中逐步习得正确的语言加工策略和加工形式，促进英语语言能力的发展，逐步达到熟练掌握英语的能力。

综上所述，在二语学习中，脑的可塑性其实是神经元的可塑性、突触的可塑性，是脑中神经元根据新的语言学习经验重组神经通路，并在新的语言环境的刺激下做出适应性改变的能力。脑的可塑性非常复杂，不同的语言学习内容在学习的不同阶段具有不同程度的可塑性，正如前面 Kim 的研究所表明的那样，较小年龄阶段学习二语与较晚阶段学习在脑机制上表现出不同的激活模式。这涉及语言学习和二语能力发展中的关键期问题，下面我们就讨论这个问题。

3 人脑的敏感期与语言发展

关键期概念最早源自于1920年Charles Stockard对鱼的胚胎学研究;1937年Konrad Lorenz在小鸭等动物的行为研究中发现了“铭记”(imprinting)现象,开创了行为学领域的关键期研究;1949年Donald Hebb提出突触“学习”假说,也被称为Hebbian突触可塑性,该学说阐述了认知或学习如何通过诱发持续的神经元放电引起长时程的神经元通讯效能的变化机制,为后来关键期的分子生物学方向的研究开创了先河。1965年,David Hubel和Torsten Wiesel通过对小猫视觉研究发现了小猫大脑视觉皮层发育中的关键期现象,开创了关键期的神经科学研究;1967年,Eric Lenneberg首次提出母语习得存在关键期。1998年,Takao K. Hensch等人从分子生物学(molecular biology)角度探讨了脑关键期的分子生物学机理,提出了关键期中脑神经元突触兴奋——抑制平衡神经回路的分子机理观点。从分子生物学视角来看,学者们将关键期与神经元的突触增加(synaptogenesis)和突触修剪(synaptic pruning)联系起来,认为关键期是与突触神经回路的时空分布变化相联系的,在这一时期,神经系统如视知觉系统对于外界有无刺激非常敏感,可塑性最强。

随着对关键期研究的逐渐深入,特别是视知觉关键期研究的深入,Takao K. Hensch和Tommaso Pizzorusso等人提出关键期就是指脑发展在某一时期内神经突触回路从可灵活变化组合到逐渐固化的阶段,过了该阶段,神经回路可变性并未彻底关闭,只是变化的难度加大了。T. K. Hensch将关键期结束比喻为开车减速时的“脚刹”,也就是说,随着关键期的结束,可塑性降低了,“脚刹”踩到底了,但并未完全失去制动,可通过松开“脚刹”来提高可塑性。T. K. Hensch和T. Pizzorusso等人从在分子生物学角度认为关键期发展中存在两种情况,一是神经元形态变化上的结构性关键期,一种是神经元化学结构变化上的功能性关键期。

在结构性关键期研究中,Pizzorusso等人发现随着脑神经元的逐渐成熟发展,特别是随着一种包含小清蛋白(parvalbumin, PV)的中间神经元的发展,产生了大量突触,与原有的周围神经元生成很多突触回路,同时也抑制了原来存在的周围突触回路。在本身成熟发展和外界经验刺激的交互作用中逐渐形成了固定的神经元回路,这时关键期也就逐渐结束了。其原理可如图1中图A所示。

对于功能性关键期发展研究来说,Hensch等人发现存在一种诸如Lynx1的类胆碱蛋白质分子能有效调节皮层中兴奋性神经元和抑制性神经元之间的平衡,即Lynx1能有效阻碍神经递质乙酰胆碱(acetylcholine)的活动,从而有效控制抑制性神经元的活性,获得一种神经元突触回路网络的动态化学平衡,这时,关键期也逐渐结束了。老鼠模拟实验表明,如在已过关键期的成年老鼠脑中有效降低Lynx1的水平,则又发现视知觉的关键期,这说明Lynx1之类的蛋白质分子在功能性关键期发展中的作用。

其原理可如图 1 中图 B 所示。

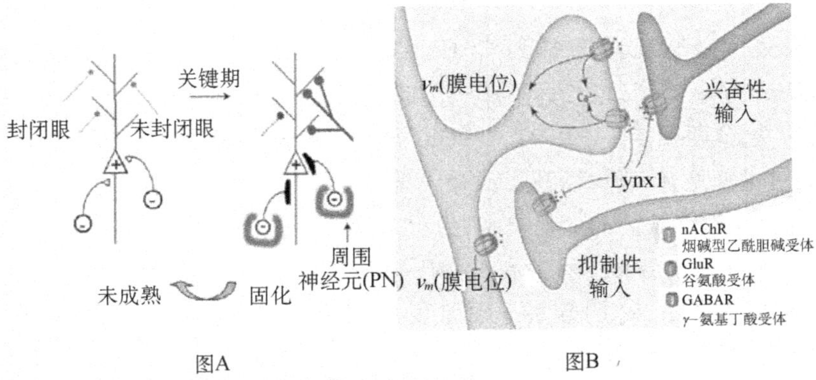

图 1　结构性关键期发展和功能性关键期发展简图

现在学者们倾向于认为随着人脑的不断成熟发展,外界经验刺激的丰富,人脑的不同功能可能有不同的关键期。如感觉关键期是在婴儿出生后几个月之内,肢体协调运动关键期在出生后一年左右。而语言习得和学习的关键期在出生后到青春期这段时间,一般到 12 岁左右结束,6 岁之前学习效果最好。

虽然人脑不同功能具有不同关键期,但并未否定这些功能的关键期是不能改变或对立的,即某一功能关键期结束后,该功能就不可改变了,而只是可塑性降低了;现在学者们普遍认为关键期不是严格限定的,只是在关键期,脑在本身成熟和外界刺激经验的影响下,可塑性最强,然后逐渐降低。现在学者们一般都倾向于采用“敏感期”这个说法,也有部分学者称之为“机会窗”。如图 2 所示:

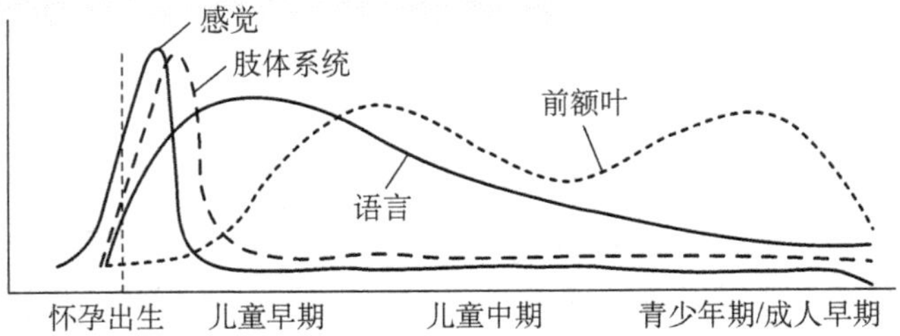

MaCain M N , Mustard J F, McCuaig K. Early Years Study 3:Making Decisions, Taking Action. Toronto: Margaret & Wallace MeCain Family Foundation,2011.

图 2　人脑不同功能的不同关键期

对语言能力来说,利用人脑可塑性和关键期规律,积极探索语言本质,将使我们更好地开展教育实践,更好地促进母语习得和二语学习。人类语言能力包括两个方面,即天生语言学习能力(innate faculty)和后天语言学习能力(postnatal acquired competence)。天生语言学习能力是建立在生命亿万年进化基础上的人脑复杂结构所具有的功能,有其特定的发展发育规律;后天语言学习能力则是指在一定的语言环境和社会环境下习得和应用语言的能力。两者表现为在起始时间、持续时间、表达形式、经验性质、受外界环境诱导与协调作用的影响程度不同。

语言本身是一个非常复杂的系统，最基本的方面包括语音、语义、语法等系统。要掌握运用这些系统需要依靠人脑的相关功能，如语音加工网络、语义网络、语法网络等，除了这些直接的语言加工网络外，语言加工还需相关人脑网络的支持，如声音感知觉系统、视知觉感觉系统等，这些系统本身也受关键期的影响。如图 2 显示的感觉系统的发展就有关键期。因此，探索语言能力和二语学习需要综合考虑各个方面的关系和影响，从而最大化地促进学习和教学实践。

在二语学习关键期的研究中，学者们注意到语音和句法（phonology and syntax）存在起始习得年龄（age of acquisition, AOA）效应，而词义和语义却不明显，即在早期接触和学习二语的人，在语音和句法加工方面要比晚期二语学习者更易于达到母语化的程度。

Snow 等研究发现年龄大的学习者学习发音有初始优势，但是一年后年龄较小儿童开始超过年龄较大的学习者。这表明年龄较大的第二语言学习者的速度优势是短暂的。Thompson 以第二语言获得年龄在 4—42 岁间的成人为被试，发现获得年龄是预测第二语言最终达到的口音等级最强有力的因素。10 岁前到达美国的学习者虽然口音得分显著高于成人组，但没有完全达到母语的水平。这表明习得二语年龄越小，达到母语化发音的可能性就越大，支持第二语言语音学习存在关键期。

Johnson 和 Newport 等通过对第二语言学习年龄为 3—39 岁的朝鲜语母语者为被试，根据他们对 12 类句法规则的错误率进行分析，发现各组被试错误率的句法规则类型效应显著。除母语组和 3—7 岁组在各规则类型的错误率都不超过 10% 外，其他年龄组在限定词、复数规则方面的错误率超过了 30%，表明虽然在青春期前语言获得年龄和句法合理性判断的成绩显著相关，但和母语组相比，第二语言句法获得在 7 岁而不是青春期就开始下降了，比 Lenneberg 提出的语言获得的关键期在 12 岁结束的时间早一些。如图 3 所示。

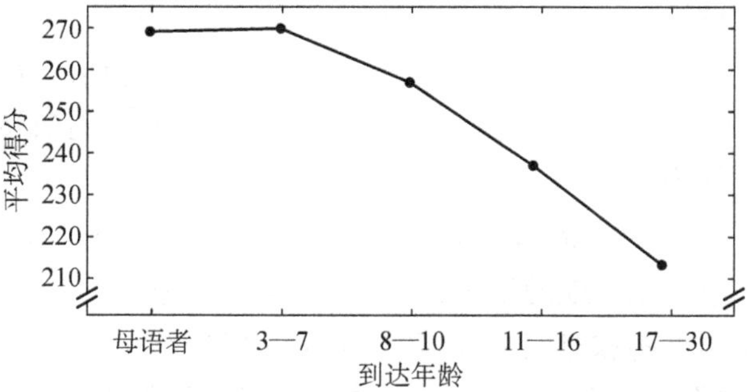

图 3　到达美国年龄与英语语法测验成绩得分之间的关系

John J S, Newport E L. Critical Period Effects in Second Language Learning the Influence of Maturation State on the Acquisition of English as a Second Language Learning. Cognitive Psychology, 1989(22): 60 - 99.

Wartenburger 等通过功能磁共振成像（fMRI）对二语习得年龄与熟练程度在句法

和语义上的脑激活模式研究发现,句法表现出明显的年龄效应,而语义却不明显。G. Xue 和 Q. Dong 等人以低熟练程度母语汉语的中英双语者为被试,让他们进行单词语义和押韵判断任务,发现汉语和英语的行为和脑成像激活模式类似,认为这至少在单词层次上反映出语言习得年龄和熟练程度对语义影响不明显。宋伟对晚期学习英语达到较熟练程度的中英双语者的 fMRI 研究发现,被试在双语句子语义加工上表现出类似的脑激活模式,在简单句法的左额下回脑区激活模式上差别不大,而在复杂句法加工(双层嵌套句)脑激活模式中,发现左侧布洛卡区及其周围脑区、右侧对应脑区存在差异。说明句法(复杂句法)上存在起始习得年龄效应。

通过上面行为和脑成像的二语研究,我们可以看出,由于语言存在语音、韵律、句法和语义、语用等多系统,且每个系统有自己的结构规律和担负的功能,二语学习在关键期问题上表现出分层次多模式现象。即语义与二语学习年龄关联不大,关键期效应不明显;语音、韵律和句法表现出学习起始年龄效应,与关键期有关,学习年龄在 7—9 岁之前最好,在这期间学习,容易获得类似母语化效果,成为熟练双语者。

二语能力促进和学习不仅包括语音、句法和语义的学习,其实还包括一个重要的方面,即对书面文字的阅读和书写能力,即读写能力(literacy capacity),它是一个人社会化过程中最重要的能力之一。读写能力涉及复杂的认知机制和脑机制。相较于人类具有几十万年历史的口语听说能力而言,人类书面文字的出现只有几千年历史,从人脑进化的角度来说,人脑不大可能在这么短的时间内发展出一个特异性的阅读和书写模块。读写功能网络可能是多年学习经验积累的结果,并受到不同语言文字系统和人脑神经机制的影响和制约。

读写能力获得也应存在关键期。有学者认为读写能力关键期一般在 4—5 岁,但这可能存在语言类型学的差异,如表音语言(英语)和表意语言(汉语)之间的差异。在读写能力获得关键期,对儿童进行单词和文字的书写、发音、意义、句法等方面进行教学,将会获得最佳效果。这是对大多数正常儿童读写能力训练而言,但也有少部分儿童患有阅读障碍,则需要额外的阅读干预练习。据估计,患有阅读障碍儿童在普通儿童人群中的比例约为 7%—15%。

对于中国的二语学习来说,要特别注意母语汉语与二语英语在读写认知神经机制上的差异。中文和世界上其他的语言相比有许多特殊的属性。中文的特性,不仅仅表现在形、音、义的基本结构和对应上,而且也体现在书面文字、词汇、句法和语篇结构等方面。相关的 fMRI 研究结果显示,人脑的中文读写脑区与西方语言如英语读写脑区在位置上既有相似性,又有区别。如左脑额中回在中文文字加工时有明显激活,主管英文单词的左脑后部颞顶区在中文加工中作用则很小。因此,基于世界上少量语言样本和文化所得到语言能力和语言学习知识,不能轻易推广到所有语言和读写上面。有关读写能力关键期的研究目前尚未系统深入,仍待将来学者们继续努力,探讨读写能力关键期中更具体更普遍的一些规律和机制,为母语习得和二语学习提供理论支撑。

4 结束语

人脑是极为精细、复杂和完善的信息处理系统。为了更加清晰地认识语言和二语的神经系统结构和功能,揭示语言和二语的神经活动基本规律,一方面需要对神经系统活动的研究深入到分子和细胞水平;另一方面,我们也注意到,脑功能是由神经细胞通过集群活动的整合实现的,要了解语言及二语的认知神经机制,就会不可避免地涉及各种层次。这需要从分子、细胞、突触回路、脑功能柱脑区、全脑和行为等多个水平深入开展多层次多角度的跨学科交叉综合研究。

开发人脑潜能,进行语言发展促进机制和发展策略的研究,旨在进一步发挥人脑潜力,增强智能,从而优化教育质量,满足促进我国人口素质提升这一重大的战略需求,为增强我国综合国力提供坚实的科学支撑。

致谢

本文得到国家社会科学基金重大项目"神经语言学研究及学科建设研究"(2010)(10&ZD126)、江苏省哲社项目"汉语儿童母语习得的认知神经机制研究"(12YYC014)、江苏高校优势学科建设工程资助项目"语言认知科学与文化传承优势学科群"(2010)(PAPD)及江苏师范大学博士科研启动项目的资助。

References

[1] Hurst J, Baraitser M, Auger E, et al. An extended family with a dominantly inherited speech disorder. Dev. Med. Child Neurol, 1990, 32: 347-355.

[2] Enard W, Przeworski M, et al. Molecular evolution of FOXP2, a gene involved in speech and language. Nature, 2002, 418: 869-872.

[3] Lenneberg E. Biological Foundations of Language. New York: John Wiley & Sons, 1967.

[4] Dong Q, Xue G, et al. Brain response is shaped by language experience: Evidence from a fMRI study on beginning second language learners. Acta Psychologica Sinica, 2004, 36(4): 448-454.

[5] Weber-Fox C, Neville H J. Maturational constraints on functional specializations for language processing: ERP and behavioral evidence in bilingual speakers. Journal of Cognitive Neuroscience, 1996, 8(3): 231-256.

[6] Kim K H S, Relkin N R, et al. Distinct cortical areas associated with native and second languages. Nature, 1997, 388(6638): 171-174.

[7] 龚少英,彭聃龄.第二语言获得关键期研究进展.心理科学,2004,27(3):711-714.

[8] 周加仙.基于脑的教育研究:反思与对策.上海:华东师范大学,2004.

[9] Jon Bardin. Neurodevelopment: Unlocking the brain. Nature, 2012, 487: 24-26.

[10] Pizzorusso T, Medini P, et al. Reactivation of ocular dominance plasticity in the adult visual cortex. Science, 2002, 298(5596): 1248 - 1251.

[11] Morishita H, Miwa J M, et al. Lynx1, a cholinergic brake, limits plasticity in adult visual cortex. Science, 2010, 330(6008): 1238 - 1240.

[12] Snow C, Hoefnagel-Hohle M. Age differences in the pronunciation of foreign sounds//S Krashen, R Scarcela, M Long. Child-adult differences in second language acquisition. Rowley, MA: Newbury House, 1982.

[13] Thompson I. Foreign accents revisited: The English pronunciation of Russian immigrants. Language Learning, 1991, 41: 177 - 204.

[14] Johnson J S, New Port E L. Critical period effect in second language learning: The influence of maturational state on the acquisition of English as a second language. Cognitive Psychology, 1989, 21: 60 - 99.

[15] Wartenburger I, Heekeren H R, et al. Early setting of grammatical processing in the bilingual Brain. Neuron, 2003, 37: 159 - 170.

[16] Xue G, Dong Q, et al. Mapping of verbal working memory in nonfluent Chinese-English bilinguals with functional MRI. Neuroimage, 2004, 22: 1 - 10.

[17] 宋伟. 布洛卡区在句法加工和工作记忆中的作用——来自汉英双语者研究的证据. 北京: 北京师范大学,2012.

[18] Shu Hua. Understanding the reading of Chinese children: Critical deficits, development trajectories, and neural correlates? Beijing: The 2012 International Workshop on Brain, Cognition and Learning, Beijing, China, 2012.

议题

儿童早期发展的评测方法与工具

Optical Topography Noninvasive brain imaging method for early child development studies

Hideaki Koizumi

Fellow and Corporate Officer, Hitachi, Ltd.

Vice President, Engineering Academy of Japan (EAJ)

Foreign Member, Chinese Academy of Engineering (CAE)

Observation of Infants' Brain Activities Using Noninvasive Brain Imaging

In recent years, we have seen various methods to measure infants' brain functions. With regard to functional magnetic resonance imaging (fMRI) and magneto-encephalography (MEG), the equipment is so large that the coordinate axes for measurement are fixed to the equipment, which requires that the subject be attached to the equipment, unable to move, during measurement. Therefore, such methods are difficult to adopt for infants who cannot stay still during measurement. Moreover, although traditional electro-encephalography (EEG) allows coordinate axes fixed on the subject, if the electrodes are set on the scalp surface rather than the cerebral cortex it is difficult to obtain the precise location of the signals. Absent decisive methods to observe infants' brain functions, a part of early child development studies has remained an untapped field. At the Central Research Laboratory, Hitachi, Ltd., which has been a pioneer in noninvasive brain imaging methods including superconducting MRI, fMRI and MEG, a recent major focus has been on improvement and applications of Optical Topography (OT).

Observation of Infants' Brain Development Using Optical Topography

We developed Optical Topography, which uses a specific wavelength region (760—830 nm; close to the visible longest wavelength) located between the ultraviolet/visible wavelength regions and the infrared wavelength region, thereby conducting brain function imaging for infants, adults and the elderly. In this narrow region, due to the different light absorption mechanisms (between the wavelength at which electronic transitions occur and the wavelength where the rotational and vibrational transitions occur), almost no substances with a maximum absorption peak exist. Despite the weak light absorption of oxidized and deoxidized hemoglobin in this region (three digits less than the maximum absorption value), an isosbestic point exists on the far wing of the light absorption band. Given these factors, by radiating light onto the subject's scalp surface between hair roots and capturing the returning light caused by intra-brain light scattering at a location distant from the scalp surface, it is possible to constitute a multiple-wavelength absorption spectroscopy imaging system to observe the functional localization of the cerebral cortex. Because near infrared spectroscopy (NIRS) is typically considered to handle a wavelength region of approximately 800—2 500 nm, it is not necessarily correct to abbreviate and call optical brain function imaging methods such as Optical Topography "NIRS." Commercial equipment for Optical Topography is generally of the most basic and simplest mechanism. For research, we developed equipment embedded with improved spatial and time resolutions, a dermis (scalp) blood absorption correction method and inverse solutions to obtain depth resolution. Also, research is continuing in the pursuit of shifting to compact or ultra-compact sizes.

Optical Topography, which has no sound during measurements, unlike fMRI, can be used simultaneously with other noninvasive measurement methods such as fMRI, MEG and EEG. Furthermore, this method is safe in principle because it uses photons with less energy than the lowest molecule bonding energy that constitutes the bio-tissue. In addition, Wearable Optical Topography (WOT) allows measurements while subjects are engaging in activities and the simultaneous measurement of multiple brains (i. e., observation of the interaction among multiple subjects). However, because this method uses cerebral local blood volume changes and light scattering measurements as its basic principles, it has limitations such as a temporal resolution of 0. 5—3 seconds, although measurement can occur every 0. 1 second, and a spatial resolution of 10—20 mm in the evaluation of the point-spread function.

Even Optical Topography in its basic structure has a wide range of applications. In Japan, under the approval of the Ministry of Health, Labor and Welfare, examinations using Optical Topography are covered by insurance, including adults, to identify the dominant hemisphere and epileptic seizure focus in the field of neurosurgery. Furthermore, in March 2014, insurance officially started to cover this method to assist differential diagnoses of mental illness ("Optical Topography examination as an aid for differential diagnoses of symptoms of depression").

Why Optical Topography?

John Locke called the newborn's brain a blank slate, or tabula rasa, believing that local functional areas did not exist during the early development of the brain. However, observation using Optical Topography has shown a partial area already functioning at the stage of newborn. Moreover, observation of the Default Mode Network (DMN) is gradually unraveling the connectivity between functional areas. A broad range of applications of Optical Topography for infants, young children and schoolchildren includes the fields of language development, acquisition of a second language, development of facial expression recognition, working memories, social abilities, and developmental and learning disorders.

With regard to the adult brain, fMRI and DTI (diffusion tensor imaging) are gradually unraveling the detailed structure of each cerebral area and the neural bonding between areas. However, the adult brain, of which development is almost complete, is extremely complex. Probing the adult brain is analogous to observation of a building structure by making one hole after another in a building to investigate its internal structure and intra-wall piping and wire connections. Observation of the development of the infant brain, on the other hand, is akin to observation of the construction process of a building structure along a time axis. To build a house, the foundation is made first, followed by the pillars, the framework and then the roof. If such a process is observed over time, the basic structure of the building structure is clearly understood without seeing the detail.

Optical Topography is well suited for understanding the basic structure of the brain. The infant brain allows light to reach deep inside. However, as the brain develops, the range where light can reach becomes limited to the cerebral cortex. To obtain information extensively up to the cerebral limbic system, we could consider, for example, the amygdala of the limbic system, which shares neural projections with the prefrontal cortex. The development of longitudinal observation along a time axis might lead to cohort studies.

References

[1] The Future Opened by Optical Topography (2009). http://www.film.hitachi.jp/en/movie/movie765.html.

Affective Computing and Social-Emotional Competence Assessment

Wenming Zheng

Key Laboratory of Child Development and Learning Science, MOE

Research Center for Learning Science, Southeast University

Social and emotional competence plays a crucial role in the early Child development. It is recognized that Child's social and emotional competence, rather than their IQ, would be the best predictor of their late success in life. Basically, there are several ways to assess the development of Child's social and emotional competence, which can be summarized as the following four categories: biochemistry approaches; psychological approaches; physiological approaches; behavior analysis approaches. Among the above four categories, both physiological approaches and behavior coding approaches have attracted more and more researchers in the recent years. One of the most commonly used physiological approaches is to use the heart rate for the assessment of emotional competence, which is generally thought to be an effective approach for discriminating the pleasant and unpleasant emotions. However, the traditional heart rate measurement approach needs special device, e. g. , electrocardiogram (ECG), to extract the heart rate signals, which may cause discomfort for Child. Facial expression coding is another commonly used emotional competence assessment approach. It works by observing Child's facial expression of video image sequences and then coding the expressions and emotions. Although this approach has been widely used in the assessment of social emotional competence, it suffers from the drawbacks of time consuming. Another problem of this approach is the possible inconsistence of the assessment, which means that coding the same facial expression video with different person may not obtain the same coding result. The recent development of affective computing makes it possible to use much more efficient and convenient approach to evaluate the social emotional competence. In this talk, I will address the methodology of applying the affective computing to the assessment of social-emotional competence. The presentation will focus more on the facial expression expression recognition and the physiological parameters extraction for emotional competence assessment. In addition, I will also present our work on constructing the multimedia database of Children's individual learning pathway & development.

Assessment and Training of Children's Social Emotion Competency

Renlai Zhou
Principal Investigator and Lab Director

This presentation consists of two parts: assessment and training of children's social emotion competency. The assessment includes behavioral and neural assessments. The Preschool Behavioral and Emotional Rating Scale (PreBERS) was revised in Chinese Preschoolers. The results indicated that PreBERS consisted of four factors, and the total variance explained 61.44%; In confirmatory analysis, $\chi^2/df = 2.487$, $IFI = 0.917$, $CFI = 0.917$, $RMSEA = 0.066$; each subscale had significant correlation with the criterions; Cronbach's α coefficients of the four subscales were between 0.868 and 0.932; the test-retest reliability of the four subscales were between 0.587 and 0.826; the cross-rater reliability of the four subscales were between 0.309 and 0.478. Age had a main effect on all the subscale scaled scores and the strength index, but there was no gender difference on either of them. It concluded that the Chinese version of PreBERS had acceptable psychometric quality and can be applied in Chinese preschoolers.

Neural assessments covers four experiments, experiment one and two focus on performance monitoring. Thirty-three young children participated in these two experiments. There were sixteen children in the younger group (aged from 4 to 7) and seventeen in the older group (aged from 8 to 11). The classic Flanker test and a variant of Flanker test (facial Flanker test) were employed as the experimental tasks. Behavioral and EEG data were recorded during the entire experiment. The results showed that, in the younger group, the largest ERN was found under the negative facial expression condition in the incorrect trials. However, there was no difference among three facial expression conditions in the older group. It concluded that children's error monitoring toward negative facial expressions developed earlier than other variants of emotion. Alternative neural mechanisms of this negative-emotion-advantaged error monitoring and potential ways of application were also discussed.

Experiment three and four are involved in if emotional picture processing is accompanied by the increased amplitude in late positive potential (LPP) in adolescents and adults. Twenty preschoolers of 4—5 years old viewed pleasant, neutral, and unpleasant pictures while their scalp event-related potentials (ERPs) were recorded. Results demonstrate that pleasant and unpleasant pictures elicited significantly larger LPP amplitudes than neutral pictures. This emotional effect on LPP emerged in the posterior region and then gradually extended to the central and anterior regions. Furthermore, the LPP amplitudes in the posterior region elicited by unpleasant pictures were negatively correlated with individual differences in emotion regulation competence. Experiment four examined whether cognitive reappraisal could modulate preschoolers' LPP amplitudes. Results suggested that LPP amplitudes in the posterior region elicited by unpleasant pictures with negative or neutral preceding descriptions were both associated with emotion regulation competence rated by teachers, but the LPP amplitude difference between negative versus neutral description were not related with emotion regulation competence, suggesting that LPP amplitude during negative emotional processing might predict emotion regulation competence in preschoolers, but the ability to use cognitive reappraisal strategy cannot.

The second part of this presentation aims at developing a series of curriculum on children's social emotion competency aged from 3 to 5 years old. Based on the self-emotion, other's emotion and intrapersonal relationship, this curriculum try to train children's emotion from four aspects: recognition, evaluation, expression and regulation. To validate whether the emotional competence training curriculum is feasibly, we selected two Intermediate classes in kindergartens, one is arranged as experimental class and the other as control class. Pre-test and post-test were performed by using PreBERS during one-year emotional competence training courses. While the control class for only teach normal content, not including training related to the emotional content. Before and after the course, teachers and parents conducted two classes were included preschool emotional and behavioral rating scales and questionnaires, including the strengths and difficulties infant emotional competence level testing. The results showed that: (1) the experimental class children in emotional regulation, family integration, emotional problems, conduct problems, hyperactivity problems, peer problems and presocial dimensions of social self-confidence have shown a significant improvement. (2) The dimension of emotion regulation upward trend very quickly. Emotional problems of this dimension decline very fast, but also in the evaluation of parents and teachers in the same assessment.

Development and Education of Academically Supernormal Children in Mainland China in the Last 35 Years

Jiannong Shi

Center for Supernormal Children, Institute of Psychology, CAS

Department of Learning and Philosophy, Aalborg University, Denmark

Abstract: A sophisticated education system for academically gifted students at university, middle school and primary school levels has been developed since 1978. A statistics-based definition of academically supernormal children was suggested by Chinese psychologists. A series of experiments and investigation has been conducted on psychological development of academically supernormal children. Some principles, procedures, and steps of identification, as well as some principles and typical models of education were developed in Mainland China during the last twenty-four years. Dozens of experimental classes for academically gifted children at university, middle school and primary school levels have been set up in China since 1978. Hundreds of high ability students are benefited from the gifted education programs in China. Some essential issues about gifted education in China will be discussed in this presentation.

A Study of K-12 STEM Education in America：A Trend of Integrated STEM Education

Xuan Zeng[1,a], Yi Bai[1,b,*]

[1] Key Laboratory of Child Development and Learning Science of Ministry of Education, Southeast University, Nanjing, Jiangsu, China

[a] aenxuan@163.com, [b] by.rcls@seu.edu.cn

[*] Corresponding author

Keywords: American K-12; STEM; integration

Abstract: Nowadays, the thinking of current economic and social benefits of scientific innovation and STEM (science, technology, engineering, mathematics) education has been widely accepted and recognized. This thesis put emphasis on the new trend of STEM education-integration on the base of the four separate discipline, on the other hand, it provide a recent descriptive framework.

美国K-12阶段STEM教育改革的新趋势——综合

曾旋[1,a]，柏毅[1,b,*]

[1]东南大学儿童发展与学习科学教育部重点实验室，南京，江苏，中国

[a]aenxuan@163.com，[b]by.rcls@seu.edu.cn

[*]通讯作者

关键词：美国K-12；STEM；综合

中文摘要：现今科学创新和STEM(science，technology，environment，mathematics)教育的经济效益和社会效益思考被广泛接受和认同，但一直以来以各单独学科为重点的课程与教育改革占多数，随着美国STEM改革的深入，STEM的综合(integration)成为重点。本文探讨了STEM各科教育的发展、各科素养的定义以及它们之间的联系，并对综合STEM教育的描述性框架进行初步解读，对我国教育改革具有理论与现实意义。

1 引言

STEM教育是一个课程或研究项目序列，以便让学生包括弱势群体为成功就业、进入高等教育做好充分准备，并且为具有数学和科学的技能和概念应用的尖端技术能力做好准备，让他们在我们的技术型社会中成为有竞争力、有能力的公民。STEM教育能成为各学科间的和跨学科的学习方法，在STEM教育中，严谨的学术概念与现实世界基于问题和基于表现的课堂相结合。在这种程度上，STEM教育充分体现了公理"整体大于部分之和"。但是以往的研究往往放在将STEM各科进行单独的研究，或者缺少联结性的总结。

最近的《课堂内外的K-12工程教育概述》和《下一代科学标准》，都明确地将科学概念和工程实践相联系，有将综合作为STEM教育中的潜在组成的趋势。K-12阶段STEM教育综合方法的提倡者们认为，用联系的方式教授STEM科目(尤其是在现实生活背景下)对学生和老师都要更有价值。这反过来可以促进学习动机，提高学生兴趣、成就、持久性。而且这些结果能够应对工作场所和大学的储备需求，同时能增加考虑从事STEM相关领域工作的学生数量。这一切都说明学科间的联合越来越成为重点，综合的STEM教育研究蓄势待发。

2 美国K-12阶段课程中的STEM

STEM各科在K-12各阶段的出现、发展都不一致，数学和科学较早出现，也得到较多关注，技术和工程也晚一些。此外，对STEM各科素养的定义也是一个发展的过程。

2.1 科学教育与数学素养

科学教育通常强调生物、化学、物理以及地球和空间科学——尽管不像数学教育那样在美国学校盛行,但是也是大部分K-12阶段学校课程的常规部分。然而,科学在小学阶段并没有得到很多关注,尤其是在K-12阶段。它通常由同时教授阅读、数学以及社会学的老师教授。与数学一样,专门的科学课程从初中或高中开始出现。

科学是知识产生的一个过程,这个过程取决于对自然现象的仔细观察和发明出使这些观察具有意义的理论,从而使学生有着对自然世界的预先的信仰。44个州毕业生科学科目上的要求是有两年或更长时间的科学课程学习。《不让一个孩子掉队》要求的科学考试从2007年开始执行,在过去的10年,小学中有一个趋势,在科学上花费较少时间而在阅读和数学上花费较多时间,至少有部分原因是该法案的影响。

《国家科学教育标准》和经济合作与发展组织规定,科学素养即个人在做出决定、参与公共事物以及进行经济生产时所需要的科学概念和程序。它包括在有关生命与健康、地球与环境、技术的科学领域中,运用科学知识和程序来理解和参与决策制定的能力。

2.2 技术教育与技术素养

技术相关的教育有多种解释和强调重点。最先在20世纪80年代中期,学校关于技术教育的课程叫做工艺课或手工课。现在技术教育的版本大体相似,它经常与职业教育混淆。另一个对技术的解释是教育或教学上的技术。这一性质的技术包括幻灯片、电影、电视、计算器、电子书等,最具影响力的教育技术要数个人电脑和因特网,包括网上资源和教育软件。还有三分之一与STEM教育相关的技术解释为科学、数学、工程参与者运用的工具,这些工具包括应用于准确测量体积或物质质量的天平、用于研究细小或较远物体的显微镜和望远镜等等。

国家教育发展评估开发了技术和工程素养评估项目,他们将技术素养定义为运用、理解、评价技术的能力,以及在开发解决方案、实现目标时对技术原则和策略的理解。国际技术教育社团又增加了展现创造力和创新,交流与合作,进行研究和运用信息,辩证思考,解决问题,做出决定以及高效运用技术(2000)。第三个组织——国际技术教育协会认为还应该与时俱进,要理解技术如何形成、如何与社会相互作用(2007)。

2.3 工程教育与工程素养

最新和最落后的K-12阶段的STEM组成部分是工程。它在小学和中学的印迹比数学、科学、技术都要少。过去15年以来,很多以教授儿童工程课程为中心的课程已经被设计出来并且在全国的中小学都在实施。有一小部分方案为老师提供专业发展的机会以使他们参与到学生的工程活动中去。

K-12水平的工程知识和技能组成这一问题还没有一致认同,但是对工程设计程序和概念重要性的认同正在增长，这些概念有约束、标准化、最优化和权衡。截至2010年，有9个州已经将工程纳入科学教育标准（NAE2010）。《下一代科学标准》包括与科学相关的工程概念和实践。26个州参与了标准的改进，它们其中有很多都希望采纳这些标准，这就为扩大K-12阶段的工程教育的意义奠定了基础。

经济合作与发展组织将工程素养定义为理解技术通过工程设计程序如何发展。这包含了综合、创造性地应用科学和数学原则来达到目的的能力，如设计、生产、高效经济结构的开发、机器、程序和系统。工程与技术认证委员会认为还应包括通过学习知道的数学和自然科学知识、应用于为造福人类开发使用材料和自然力量的经济高效途径（2010）。

2.4 数学教育与数学素养

数学教育通常都强调算术、几何、代数、三角函数、微积分，自20世纪初开始就一直是美国K-12教育中的常规课程。在初等教育阶段（小学），同一个老师教授所有的核心课程，包括数学。自从2001年《不让一个孩子掉队》法案颁布以后，要求常规的数学考试，使得这一科目在小学得到更大的关注，虽然它并不像阅读和语言艺术占课程的大部分。

从中学或高中以及大学开始，数学被当成独立的课程，由专业教师教授。很多州都要求学生毕业时有良好的代数成绩，而且学生经常学习内容、水平、严谨度不同的数学领域。2008年，43个州的毕业生要求是至少要有两年的数学课程方面的学习。

数学素养在国际数学评估项目（PISA）中被定义为识别、理解、从事数学问题的能力。PISA认为数学素养还包括：在个人生活、职业生活、社会生活以及作为一个具有建设性的、富有思考力的公民的生活中，有能力对数学所发挥的作用做出有理有据的判断。国家数学教师委员会将数学素养定义为阅读、听、创造性思考的能力，还有交流问题情况、数学推导和解决方案来解决和提升数学理解力的能力（2000）。

2.5 STEM学科间的联系

要有更具综合性的方法（不管是学科内还是跨学科原则）来教学和学习的提倡者们注意到专业实践促进了以单独学科为重点的工作站和研究室向跨学科的事业转化，如生物医学工程。此外，进行研究并且开发新的产品和服务的联合企业、学术机构的专家和工程师总是运用综合STEM学科的方式来工作。实际上，在一些研究领域，很需要更多学科间相互作用的方式。科学家用技术工具来进行实验，并进行数学运算和统计以解释实验产生的数据。工程师利用科学知识和数学推理来开发和模拟有潜力的设计发明和解决方案——这些专家相互作用形成多元化跨学科小组。STEM间的联系在工作场所上得到延伸。

1901年成立的学校科学和数学协会已经成为讨论综合的基地。早在20年前，就发起了基于标准的教育改革运动，意识到对综合STEM教育的价值要远远超越数学和科学本身。《科学素养基准》将科学定义为基础和应用自然社会科学,基础和应用数学、工程和技术,以及它们的相互联系。《科学素养基准》和《国家科学教育标准》(1996)呼吁学生在科学课上学习技术和社会、技术设计相关的东西。《技术素养标准》花了大量显著的部分来撰写工程设计目标,以及学生了解技术与科学、工程、数学之间联系的必要性。

《下一代科学标准》更深入地强调了数学、科学、工程之间的联系,并且鼓励在科学的分支间建立联系,如能量在生物和物理中是如何解释的,标准明确规定在科学课上要教授工程学方面的实践和核心观点。关于数学的《州立标准共同核心》也建议提倡建立 STEM 学科间的联系。

3 综合 STEM 教育的描述性框架

Leon Lederman 提出了一个观点,STEM 素养意味着在知识型经济运营时代的一个人有能力适应和接受由于新技术带来的改变,能够与各界人士合作,预见他们行为可能带来的影响,与大众有效地交流复杂的观点,并且找到现今难以想象的问题的测量方法并能提出创造性的解决方案(National Governors Association, 2007)。

但是找到一个精确的综合 STEM 教育定义是一个挑战,因为很多种综合方式都可能发生。它可能包括 STEM 学科间的不同联系,可能更强调某一科,可能出现在正式或非正式的环境中,可能包含一系列教育策略。比如有建议谈到综合的科学教育必须包括技术和工程设计,并将其作为建立科学和数学的概念和实践间联系的基础(Sanders,2009)。

在教育实践和研究中,综合这一名词应用得很宽松,与结合、统一、跨学科、交叉学科或学科间等专业术语不能很好地区分。定义综合 STEM 教育比实际要更难,因为实际上某些联系同时反映在多个水平上(学生思维和行为、教师的指导、课程、老师之间甚至教育系统如整个学校)。如果缺乏严格定义,可能造成参与综合 STEM 教育的学校和项目实际上没有做到,这确实是一个冒险。但是在这一领域发展的早期,比起提出一个在为促进我们理解综合 STEM 教育的研究和实践中所需要的并不限制实验和创造力形式的定义,它的问题更小。

美国综合 STEM 委员会确认和描述出现有的综合 STEM 教育的方法,综合的 STEM 教育在 K-12 教育蓝图中占一个多维的空间,而不仅仅是一个单一的、定义良好的经历,它包括一系列有着某种程度的联系的经历体验。这种经验可能发生在一个或多个课程阶段,或者贯穿整个课程,它们可能反映在某个课程或某个学校中,或者它们将出现在课后或校外的活动中。

每个综合 STEM 教育的变体都暗含了不同的计划方法、资源需求、实施挑战、成果。在这里我们提出一个框架(见图 1),它有四个特点:(1) 综合 STEM 教育目标;

(2) 综合 STEM 教育成果;(3) 综合 STEM 教育的性质和范围;(4) 综合 STEM 教育的实施。每个特点都有具体的组成部分,如图 1 所示,从而为研究人员、参与者和其他人提供一个词汇表来识别、描述和验证美国 K-12 教育系统中专门的 STEM 综合教育方案。

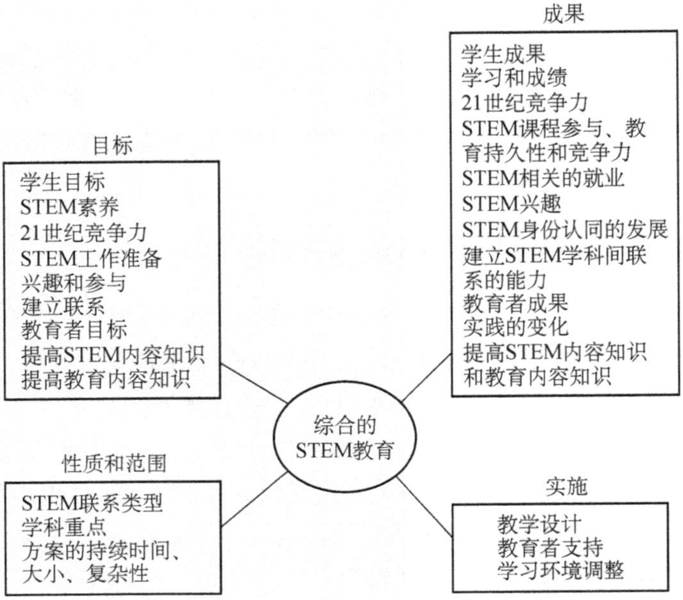

图 1　综合 STEM 教育的大体特征和组成部分的描述性框架

4　总结

虽然 STEM 教育的发展有着漫长的过去,对 STEM 教育的综合理念的思维在以往的研究中或多或少有所体现,但直到最近,综合的 STEM 教育才真正成为焦点。虽然还未曾有明确与扎实的理论基础,但可以确认的是综合必然是未来 STEM 教育改革的趋势。相信在对综合 STEM 教育的理论、框架、实施、评估等一系列的探索中,我们会越来越明确老师、学生、政府在这个进程中所扮演的角色,在有效的通力合作下,综合 STEM 教育也必将促进 21 世纪全民素质的提高,为经济发展提供源源不断的活力。

致谢

本文为教育部人文社会科学研究专项任务项目(工程科技人才培养研究)《基础教育阶段技术和设计教育的国际比较研究》阶段性成果之一,项目批准号为 11JDGC026。

References

[1] Margaret Honey, Greg Pearson, Heidi Schweingruber. STEM Integration in K-12 Education: Status, Prospects, and An Agenda for Research. Washing, D. C.: The National Academies Press, 2014.

[2] The Next Generation Science Standards. http://www.nextgenscience.org/

[3] Paul A. Standards for technological literacy and STEM education delivery through career and technical education programs. Journal of Technology Education, 2012, 23(2): 44 - 48.

[4] Alan Zollman. Learning for STEM Literacy: STEM Literacy for Learning. School Science and Mathematics, 2012, 112(1): 12 - 15.

[5] Duane A Renfrow. The three "faces" of technology education. Journal of STEM Teacher Education, 2011, 48(3): 8 - 10.

[6] Jonathan M Breiner, Carla C Johnson. Shelly Sheats Harkness. What Is STEM? A Discussion About Conceptions of STEM in Education and Partnerships. School Science and Mathematics, 2012, 112 (1): 3 - 7.

[7] Heather B Gonzalez, Jeffrey J Science. Technology, Engineering, and Mathematics (STEM) Education: A Primer. Kuenzi, CRS Report for Congress, 2012: 1 - 3.

Synchronization Likelihood of Whole-brain Functional Connectivity on Resting-state: A MEG Study of Depression

Chu Liu[1,a], Qing Lu[1,c,*], Kun Bi[1,b], Zhijian Yao[2,d]

[1]Key Laboratory of Child Development and Learning Science of Ministry of Education, Research Centre of Learning Science, Southeast University, Nanjing 210096, China

[2]Academic Department of Psychiatry, Nanjing Brain Hospital, Nanjing Medical University, Nanjing 210029, China

[a]chuliu1990@gmail.com, [b]bk.90@163.com,

[c]luq@seu.edu.cn (Q Lu), [d]zjyao@njmu.edu.cn (Z. Yao)

* Corresponding author

Keywords: MEG; resting-state; functional connectivity; depression; synchronization likelihood

Abstract: Depression is closely related with abnormality of functional connectivity between brain regions involved in cognitive process. Recently, influence of depression on cognitive competence and developments have been paid more attention as a result of increasing proportion of adolescent depression. This passage introduces a new method detecting dynamic characteristics of neural activity based on magneto encephalography (MEG) signal in order to explore internal neural mechanisms of depression and provide evidence for early diagnosis of depression. Since MEG is an sensitive and non-invasive equipment, this method provides a general testing method without hurts for many kinds of mental disorder patients, especially for children.

Temporal correlation of different neural activity proved to be important in cognition and emotion process. Functional integration and interaction are modulated by synchronization of relative neural signals. Since MEG has the advantage of a high time and spatial resolution, we use MEG data of resting-state to study the functional connectivity of different bands and different regions by the method of SL. Interested frequency bands was selected as follows: delta(0.5—4 Hz), theta (4—8 Hz), alpha1 (8—10 Hz), alpha2 (10—13 Hz), beta (13—30 Hz) and gamma (30—48 Hz).

Results showed that differences of functional connectivity represented by SL value between depression patients and healthy controls were mainly observed in the posterior region of the brain, such as the parietal and occipital. The difference is relatively prominent in the left hemisphere. In the left parietal-occipital area, the change of functional connectivity was irregular. Furthermore, in most of the interested bands, patients showed a extensively loss of long distance intrahemispheric interactions, which is agree with former studied of depression. These indicated SL algorithm is credible and effective.

1 Introduction

Since depression has become a high-incidence disease for both teenagers and adults, its influence on people's cognitive competence has been paid more and more attention. Quite a number of studies indicated that major depressive disorder (MDD) may be associated with a disability in cognitive domains such as attention, memory and emotional information processing[1,2]. Although the underlying mechanisms are still not quite clear, functional magnetic resonance imaging (fMRI) findings have hypothesized that it may contribute to dysfunctional cortical and subcortical connectivity, such as the interrupted limbic-cortical networks, during resting-state and task performance[3,4].

Recently, many neurophysiologic implements are adopted to detect brain network action, such as functional magnetic resonance imaging (fMRI), magneto encephalography (MEG) and electroencephalogram (EEG). fMRI research suggested that specific patterns of local and large-scale integration of distributed brain areas is essential to most normal cognitive process[5]. Moreover, it is confirmed in electrical studies that the functional networks may still dynamically active even when at rest[6], and appears to have a specific signature involved the combination of diverse electrical oscillations[7,8]. In addition, brain rhythms may also reveal different hierarchical levels of network organization that distinctly existed in health and disease[9]. Therefore, synchronization likelihood (SL), a neurophysiologic index of functional connectivity with higher time resolution, has been adopted to detect the dynamic temporal correlation of different brain regions[10]. SL arithmetic provides us a new alteration to detect the dynamic and simultaneous characteristic of time-frequency signal based on a more general concept of synchronization. This method can be applied to the comparison of numerous kinds of complex systems, no matter on a high or low frequency. It is proved to be sensitive to both liner and non-liner signal correlation.

The evidence of SL alternations in depression is not yet sufficient. In a resting EEG study, MDD subjects showed decreased SL inter-connections at delta and alpha frequencies in the frontal and temporal region[11]. In another study dealing with sleep EEG recordings, the mean SL of acutely depressed patients was lower in the slow wave and sigma frequency bands in the frontal-parietal-temporal circuit[12]. This loss of synchronization might be agreed upon the view that disturbed functionally connected large-scale cortical systems existed in depression, which may partly elicit executive dysfunction. However, all these studies were EEG-based SL calculation; actually, MEG may be more suitable than EEG to evaluate functional connectivity due to its sensitivity to nonlinear correlations and the useless of a reference[10]. Moreover, the application of MEG measures for functional connectivity analysis in resting-state of depression is quite rare up to now.

To this end, the aim of present study is to explore resting state cortico-cortical functional coupling in depressive subjects by using the MEG-based SL application. First, we show the deduction of SL arithmetic and talk about the selection of parameters in SL arithmetic. Then, parameters of SL algorithms were designed. Functional connectivity on different bands was computed between long distance (8 Interhemispheric and 4 Intrahemispheric) and short distance regions respectively. Disorder of functional connectivity of these regions may be correlated with disease severity. At last, differences between depression patients and controls were analyzed via permutation test. In this manner, we attempt to test correctness and availability of SL method. On the other hand, we could also verify the fact that MDD can be primarily considered as an asthenic information transmission of brain.

2 Materials and Methods

2.1 Materials

23 MDD subjects were recruited from inpatient facilities at the Department of Psychiatry, Nanjing Brain Hospital of Nanjing Medical University. All the patients met the diagnostic criteria with the Structured Clinical Interview for DSM-IV (SCID) and currently in a first episode. Diagnosis was confirmed by an expert psychiatrist. Patients had to score 24 at least on the 17-item Hamilton Depression Rating Scale (HDRS) on the day of scanning. Individuals were excluded if they had taken psychotropic medications during the 2 weeks prior to MEG scans.

17 healthy participates were matched with the depression subjects in age and educational level. Healthy subjects had to score less than 7 on the HDRS, have no neurological or psychiatric diseases or family history of mental illness according to SCID diagnosis. There were no significant differences in age ($t = 0.44$, $p = 0.67$) and educational level ($t = -1.26$, $p = 0.21$) between MDD and healthy controls.

2.2 MEG data acquisition and pre-processing

MEG recordings of whole-head were acquired using an Omega 2000 (VSM Med Tech Inc., Port Coquitlam, Canada) 275-channel device placed in a magnetically shielded room, which could provides a considerable amount of shielding from noise and interference. Signal was bandwidth from 0.1 Hz to 100 Hz and was digitized at a sampling rate of 600 Hz. During the experiment, subjects were informed to keep still, with their eyes closed and their mind blank. Subjects with head movements exceeding 0.5 cm were excluded. The incessant scanning lasted exactly for two minutes with eyes close and two minutes with eyes open.

The raw data were processed by SPM8 (London, Welcome Department of Imaging Neuroscience) and segmented into 2 s epoch. Epochs containing artifacts exceeding 3 PT (peak-to-peak) are rejected. The artifact free epochs are averaged and then 0.5—48 Hz bandpass filtered. Butterworth was applied to filter. After that, MEG data were filtered with the following bands: 4—8 Hz (theta), 8—10 Hz (alpha1), 10—13 Hz (alpha2), 13—30 Hz (beta) and 30—48 Hz (gamma). MEG channels are grouped into regions of interest (ROIs) roughly in sensor space corresponding to ten major cortical areas (frontal, central, temporal, parietal and occipital) on both sides[10].

2.3 Synchronization likelihood

The synchronization likelihood (SL) is a general measure based on the concept of generalized synchronization and detected linear and non-linear interdependencies between two signals[11]. Generalized synchronization exists between two dynamical systems X and Y when the state of the response system Y is a function of the state of the driving system X: $Y = F(X)$. When F is continuous, and X_i, X_j are two points on the attractor of X which are very close together, then the corresponding points Y_i, Y_j on Y will also be close together. An important feature of generalized synchronization is that the corresponding time series need not resemble each other. For neuronal systems, recurrent patterns of a neural activity seem common to repeat itself periodically and approximately. Simultaneously, if another neural signal also demonstrates repetitions, the two neural activities are considered to be synchronous according to the Synchronization likelihood algorithm. Compared with other coherence methods, the concept of generalized synchronization provides a new alteration to evaluate the functional connectivity between neuronal systems. The application of Synchronization likelihood measure is more appropriate to detect the non-linear dynamical interactions of two neural activities.

In this study, we used the measure of synchronization likelihood (SL) to detect the functional connectivity of different brain areas. The SL value calculated between each channel represents the degree of general synchronization between two neural signals. It vacillates around P_{ref} (a small positive number) among independent time series, which reaches the value of 1 in case of maximally synchronic signals. P_{ref} is a parameter of the synchronization likelihood algorithms which has to be chosen artificially. In the present study, P_{ref} was set at 0.05 for all frequency bands. We used time-delay embedding vector to represent the MEG time series. Time series were considered as vector i, i denoted discrete time $i = (1, 2, \cdots, N)$ depended on the sampling rate.

$$X_i = (X_i, X_{i+1}, X_{i+2\cdot l}, \cdots, X_{i+(m-1)\cdot l}) \quad (1)$$

The lag l and embedding dimension parameter m were chosen based on Stam's theory of time-frequency priors rationally to pick up the fastest oscillation and also to be long enough to sample the slowest oscillation[12]. Parameters were selected depending on the frequency band of interest and limited by Nyquist sampling theorem. According to the definition of SL, if embedded vectors of time series X_i are closer to each other than a distance ε_X at a certain period of time, embedded vectors of time series Y_i should be closer to each other than a distance ε_Y similarly.

2.4 Process

Average connectivity of MEG channel was grouped into three types. 1) short distance: local synchronization within one region, respectively left and right frontal, parietal, central, occipital, and temporal lobes; 2) long distance intra-hemispheric: correlations between two different regions within one hemisphere, respectively fronto-temporal, fronto-parietal, parieto-occipital, occipito-temporal synchronization; 3) long distance inter-hemispheric: correlations between homologue regions of two hemispheres, respectively central, frontal, occipital and parietal synchronization of both sides.

SL were calculated pair wise between channels of every type of ROI regions and averaged by MATLAB to get the average SL of a certain area. SL values were computed for the following frequency bands: 4—8 Hz (theta), 8—10 Hz (alpha1), 10—13 Hz (alpha2), 13—30 Hz (beta) and 30—48 Hz (gamma).

For the first step, we set time-delay embedding vector to represent MEG time series.

$$X_{k,i} = (X_{k,i}, X_{k,i+L}, X_{k,i+2\cdot L}, \cdots, X_{k,i+(m-1)\cdot L}) \quad (2)$$

Parameter L was calculated based on the frequency of the time series and Nyquist sampling theorem according to Stam.

$$P_{k,i}^{\varepsilon} = \frac{1}{(\omega_2 - \omega_1 + 1)} \sum_{\omega_1/2 < |i-j| < \omega_2/2}^{n} \theta(\varepsilon - | X_{a,i} - X_{a,j} |) \quad (3)$$

Here the $|\cdot|$ is the Euclidean distance and θ is the Heaviside step function, $\theta(X) = 0$ if $X<0$ and $\theta(X) = 1$ for $X>0$. Here ω_1 and ω_2 are two windows in order to avoid autocorrelation effects and should be at least as long as autocorrelation time, ω_2 was chosen to be large enough to allocate a sufficient number of vectors in order to make sense to take P_{ref} of them as recurrences. P_{ref} was set as 0.05.

Synchronization likelihood was calculated between two channels. Repetition of a certain condition at time was detected along the time series in the time window of ω_1 and ω_2, both the left and right sides of i. SL of two channels at a certain time i was computed by the following equations.

$$N = \theta(\varepsilon_{a,i} - |X_{a,i} - X_{a,j}|) \cdot \theta(\varepsilon_{b,i} - |X_{b,i} - X_{b,j}|) \quad (4)$$

$$N_{ab} = \sum_{j=\frac{i-\omega_2}{2}}^{\frac{i-\omega_1}{2}} N_j + \sum_{j=\frac{i+\omega_2}{2}}^{\frac{i+\omega_1}{2}} N_j \tag{5}$$

$$SL_{ab} = \frac{N}{(\omega_2 + \omega_1 + 1) * P_{ref}} \tag{6}$$

Finally, consequential SL value of different brain regions were computed between channels pair wise. Connectivity of short and long distance area are reflected by the average SL of relative brain regions.

2.5 Statistic

Permutation test, a method of nonparametric test, was adopted to detect the significance of SL value of each frequency band and ROIs between MDD and healthy subjects. To correct for multiple comparisons, the maximum t-value across sensors for each permutation was used to construct a distribution of maximum t-values for 20 000 permutations. In this session, $p < 0.05$ or $p > 0.95$ was considered significant.

3 Results

Figure 1 showed that significant difference was found for short distances interactions. There are statistical decrease in temporal area in theta bands and increase in parietal area in alpha2 band of the depression. Besides, SL was greater in patients compared to healthy controls in beta band, while in the occipital of alpha1 band, the SL of patients decreased significantly.

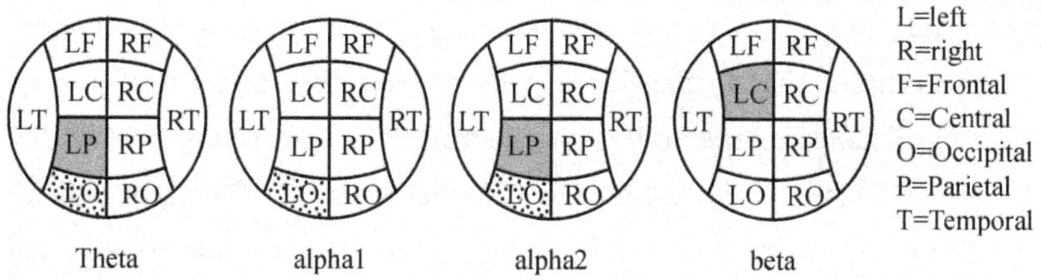

Figure 1 Short distance interaction: regions have statistical differences between control (C) and major depression (MDD) group. The whole-brain is seperated into 10 brain regions (Left frontal lobe, right frontal lobe, left central area, right central area, left occipital lobe, right occipital lobe, left parietal lobe, right parietal lobe, left temporal lobe, right temporal lobe). Shadow area represent average SL value of MDD are greater than the controls significantly in a certain brain region. The region with round dot means that SL of MDD decreases compared to the healthy subjects.

For the long distance connectivity, intrahemispheric interactions of all the regions in all of the frequency bands were significantly increased except the right and left occipital areas at beta band and the frontal areas at theta band. Interhemispheric of the left parietal and occipital areas, the alpha SL and beta SL for patients were decreased significantly.

While in the right temporal-occipital of theta band and in the left parietal-temporal area of alpha2 band, the SL of the parietal and occipital area increased.

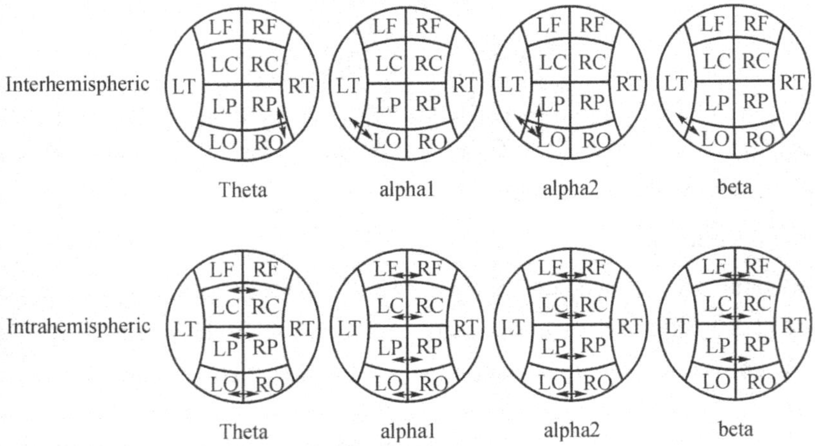

Figure 2　Long distance interaction: regions have statistical differences between control (C) and major depression (MDD) group. The whole-brain is seperated into 10 brain regions (Left frontal lobe, right frontal lobe, left central area, right central area, left occipital lobe, right occipital lobe, left parietal lobe, right parietal lobe, left temporal lobe, right temporal lobe). arrows between two brain regions suggest that average SL value of these area has significant difference.

For short distances interaction at theta and alpha2 bands, statistical decrease was found in temporal area for the depression. While there was obvious increase in parietal area. In beta band, the SL was greater at the central area in patients compared to healthy controls, while in alpha1 band, the SL of patients decreased significantly at occipital.

For the long distance connectivity, intrahemispheric interactions of all the regions in all of the frequency bands were significantly increased except the right and left occipital areas in beta band and the frontal areas in theta band. In the left parietal and occipital areas, the alpha SL and beta SL for patients were decreased significantly in the left temporal-occipital and parietal-temporal areas, while in theta band, the SL of the parietal and occipital area increased.

4　Discussion

4.1　Selection of parameters related to finding recurrent states

SL algorithm is a time-dependent correlation method, which attempts to detect the simultaneously occurring pattern of different time series. The simultaneous pattern of neural activity is complex and wildly different between signals. According to the principle of SL arithmetic, time-frequency characteristics of the underlying physiological process are restrained by six parameters. Here we discuss the definition of these parameters as a function of the time-frequency content of the patterns of interest. A rigorous selection of these parameters leads to a accurate definition of time-frequency characteristic of signals.

According to Stam's study l, m define the lag and dimension of the time series. If l was too large, it can hardly sample the higher frequency, while a too low dimension might lead to "unfolding" of the state space and the existence of false neighbors. These parameters were selected depending on the frequency band of interest and limited by Nyquist sampling theorem.

$$l = \frac{fs}{3 \cdot HF} \tag{7}$$

fs is the sampling rate of HZ, HF is the highest frequency of the signal.

The lowest frequency (LF) has the longest period and thus determines the length of the state vector. m is defined indirectly by parameter l:

$$l \cdot (m-1) = \frac{fs}{LF} \tag{8}$$

SL arithmetic is robust to the choice of ω_1, we imposed only one rule that ω_1 is long enough to allow the system to change state and thereby prevent trivial recurrences caused by the reference state being sampled multiple times. The window ω_1 is not applied around the other embedded vectors.

$$\omega_1 = 2 \cdot L \cdot (m-1) \tag{9}$$

We did not set the value of ω_2 accurately because it depends on the data. ω_2 has to be large enough to allocate a sufficient number of state vectors as potential recurrent states. Choosing ω_2 to be the entire data interval with periodic boundary conditions reduces the free parameters only to P_{ref}, with the only drawback of an increase of the computation time. A higher P_{ref} for the same ω_2 implies a larger number of recurrences. Some of them may be tracked more than once at adjacent samples. However, a larger leads to a large sliding window and a larger ω_2 number of recurrences. On this occasion, the rate of change of the average SL on a certain time i along the time series would be smooth. Additionally, the time window may be too large to tracking some simultaneous changes, which could be detected with a short window. So we should choose a small boundary value on the premise that ω_2 is large enough.

$$(\omega_2 - \omega_1) \cdot P_{ref} > 1 \tag{10}$$

4.2 About results

To our knowledge, although SL arithmetic has obviously advantages adapted to MEG data, there is few study of synchronization likelihood about resting-state MDD.

Apparently, results of our study indicate that differences of functional connectivity between depression patients and healthy controls are mainly observed in the posterior region of the brain, such as the parietal and occipital. The difference is relatively prominent in the left hemisphere. In the left parietal-occipital area, the change of functional connectivity was irregular. Furthermore, in most of the interested bands, patients showed an extensively loss of long distance intrahemispheric interactions. Consisted with our assumption, we can conjecture that MDD patients perhaps display an inefficiency pattern of interaction and integration of information generally.

The present study contributes unique MEG evidence of SL assessment for major depression. Present results indicate that major depressive patients exhibit significant deficits in information transmission among cortical regions in resting condition. Decreased right fronto-parietal connectivity in the 8—10 Hz range seems to be a reliable risk factor for depression, which negative correlated with disease severity according to the HRDS. Several limitations should be commented. First, depression is a heterogeneous disorder with highly variable symptom clusters, but we cannot relate the decreased connectivity to specific depressive subtypes due to the sample size and the psychopathological assessment. Then, as far as SL is a time function with high time resolution, detecting the dynamics underlying the time series is a great advantage. However, it is hard to conclude the dynamical characteristics from the significant distribution of SL value. fMRI studies have indicated that resting-state correlations occur on relatively slow timescale. A feasible hypothesis is to focus on the alpha band with lower frequency.

5 Conclusion

In this study, we introduced and modified an method of SL to explore dynamic functional coupling of resting-state neural activity. Present results suggested that the depression exhibit significant asthenic in information transmission among cortical regions in resting condition. According to SL findings of depression, MDD patients could show the global connectivity reorganization as an a dynamic state, especially in the frontal, parietal, and temporal lobes for devise band frequencies, and these modifications of functional brain connectivity may be correlated with disease severity. Our research provides a new method to explore the pathomechanism of depression. Besides, results of SL are available for imaging diagnosis of depression.

What's more, this algorithm provides a general testing method without hurts for many kinds of mental disorder patients, especially for children. It has already been proved to be effective and creditable for detecting information interaction between regions by experiments on MDD patients. Our next step research is to applied this method on children with cognitive defects, especially children has auditory hallucination.

Acknowledgement

This work was supported by the following grants: the National Natural Science Foundation of China (81071135,61372032), the Jiangsu Clinical Medicine Technology Foundation (BL2012052), and the Jiangsu Natural Science Foundation (BK2012740, BK20131074).

References

[1] S K Goyal. An integrated inventory model for a single supplier-single customer problem. International Journal of Production Research, 1977, 15: 107 - 111.

[2] A Banerjee. A joint economic-lot-size model for purchaser and vendor. Decision Sciences, 1986, 17: 292 - 311.

[3] S K Goyal. A joint economic-lot-size model for purchaser and vendor: A comment. Decision Sciences, 1988, 19: 236 - 241.

[4] R M Hill. The single-vendor single-buyer integrated production - inventory model with a generalized policy. European Journal of Operational Research, 1997, 97: 493 - 499.

[5] S L Kim, D Ha. A JIT lot-splitting model for supply chain management: Enhancing buyer-supplier linkage. Int. J. Production Economics, 2003, 86: 1 - 10.

[6] M Ben-Daya, M Darwis, K Ertogral. The joint economic lot sizing problem: Review and extensions. European Journal of Operational Research, 2008, 185: 726 - 742.

[7] L Lu. A one-vendor multi-buyer integrated inventory model. European Journal of Operational Research, 1995, 81: 312 - 323.

[8] H Siajadi, R N Ibrahim, P B Lochert. A single-vendor multiple-buyer inventory model with a multiple-shipment policy. Int J Adv Manuf Technol, 2006, 27: 1030 - 1037.

[9] M Hoque. Synchronization in the single-manufacturer multi-buyer integrated inventory supply chain. European Journal of Operational Research, 2008, 188: 811 - 825.

[10] T Kim, Y Hong, S Y Chang. Joint economic procurement—production-delivery policy for multiple items in a single-manufacturer, multiple-retailer system. Int. J. Production Economics, 2006, 103: 199 - 208.

[11] M Y Jaber, S K Goyal. Coordinating a three-level supply chain with multiple suppliers, a vendor and multiple buyers. Int. J. Production Economics, 2008, 116: 95 - 103.

[12] Stam C J, van Dijk B W. Synchronization likelihood: An unbiased measure of generalizedsynchronization in multivariate data sets. Physica D: Nonlinear Phenomena, 2002, 163(3 - 4): 236 - 251.

An Overview of Technology and Design Education Development in England

Jing Xu[1,a], Yi Bai[1,b,*]
[1]Key Laboratory of Child Development and Learning Science of Ministry of Education, Southeast University, Nanjing, Jiangsu, China
[a]xujing5392@163.com, [b]by.rcls@seu.edu.cn
[*]Corresponding author

Keywords: England; Technology and Design Education; Development

Abstract: Technology and design education in elementary education stage of implementation is relatively early in England, and its development was long. From the mid-18th century to the present, the period is divided into germination stage and development stage, after more than two centuries of evolution, technology and design education gradually improve and mature in England. With the hope of providing valuable reference for the reform of technology and design education in China.

英国技术与设计教育发展概述

徐静[1,a]，柏毅[1,b,*]
[1]东南大学儿童发展与学习科学教育部重点实验室,南京,江苏,中国
[a]xujing5392@126.com，[b]by.rcls@seu.edu.cn
[*]通讯作者

关键词:英国;技术与设计教育;发展

中文摘要:英国是技术与设计教育在基础教育阶段实施比较早的国家,其发展道路是漫长的。从18世纪中期至今,分为萌芽期和发展期,历经两个多世纪的发展演变,技术与设计教育逐步地完善和成熟,对我国这一教育领域的发展有着重要的启示。

1 引言

技术与设计教育在世界各国的基础教育中普遍存在,在英国,它是从手工训练、手工艺、工艺、技术教育再到“设计与技术”,它的发展不仅是名称上的改变,其意义和内涵也是不断地配合社会的发展而推陈出新。英国完成第一次工业革命,欧洲社会就进入了资本主义的自由竞争期,此后法国最先开始开办了中等、高等的工艺学校和农业学校,其他各个国家开始学习法国创办类似的学校,以发展技术教育。由此,技术与设计教育开始进入学校教育领域并逐渐具有相当规模。英国在1990年一场以实施“国家课程”(national curriculum)为中心的教育改革又明确地把以“设计与技术”、“信息技术”为主要内容的技术与设计教育列为英国5—16岁儿童必修的基本课程之一[1]。回顾英国技术与设计教育的发展历程,对现阶段我国的技术与设计教育的改革有着重要的意义。

2 技术与设计教育的内涵

目前对于技术与设计教育领域并没有一个明确的界定,英国国家课程对“设计与技术”这样说明:是一门启发灵感、严谨的和实用性的课程。学生运用创造力和想象力设计并制作一些产品,这些产品能解决各种情况下真实的、相关的问题,并要考虑到自己的产品和别人的需要、想法和评价。学生们要获得广泛的学科知识还要重点关注如数学、科学、工程、计算机和艺术这些学科。学生学习如何承担风险,成为足智多谋的、创新的、进取的和有能力的公民。通过对以前和现在对设计与技术的评估,学生们对设计与技术在他们的日常生活和世界上的影响形成了重要的理解。高质量的设计与技术教育为创造力、文化、财富和国家的安康都做出了重要的贡献[2]。

技术与设计教育都是培养学生解决现实生活问题的能力和适应社会的能力。要

学生自己动手动脑去完成，设计并制作出解决问题的方案，在设计和制作的过程中运用学生先前的经验和知识。因此认为：(1) 技术与设计教育在基础教育阶段出现，旨在培养学生解决实际生活的能力。在社会日新月异的今天，让学生更好地适应社会。(2) 技术与设计教育并不是一门单独的学科在学校中出现，它和技术教育、科学教育是相互融合的，在它们中得以体现并实施。(3) 技术与设计教育的教学内容是设计和制作方案的过程，是培养学生运用技术、创造力、想象力的过程。在本文，笔者想要说明的技术与设计教育就是英国在不同历史时期的手工艺学、工艺与设计、工艺、技术教育、设计与技术等方面的内容。

3 英国技术与设计教育的发展历程

3.1 萌芽期(18 世纪中叶到 1944 年)

从 18 世纪中叶开始，在英国各地成立了向群众广泛普及知识以促进科学和工艺发展的多种多样的协会。其中有当时为了促进科学和工艺发展而成立的“奖励学习协会”；“工艺促进协会”给工艺关系方面的教育带来很大的影响；“皇家讲习所”的目的就是把科学上的发明创造应用于工业和产业，以提高人们生活水平和为人们带来方便，在各地举办了许多相同类型的讲习所，这种讲习所还设有图书馆、读书室、科学讲座、新式科学机械展览室，可以说是后来成立的职工讲习所的雏形。

英国的技术与设计教育史是在几种不同意义的教育运动中逐渐积累形成的。其中，比较初期的教育运动是以贫苦儿童为对象的“作业学校”的运动。这个运动是由教会组织领导的、以反对统治阶级企图把下层阶级长期置于愚昧无知状态下的传统顽固态度为目的而发起的贫苦儿童的启蒙运动。对于下层阶级的子弟除读、写、算外，还施以手工业方面的教育。然而由于产业革命的结果，贫苦工人集中于城市，儿童也作为一名工人在工厂从事劳动。于是必然地产生劣迹儿童，出现了犯罪者激增的趋势。为了应付这种事态的发展而掀起了“贫民学校运动”。在这种形式下建立起来的贫民学校中，很重视把手工业作为使贫困的、可怜的儿童勤奋起来，并且让他们从事正当职业的手段。作为以勤奋青少年为对象的技术教育机关——伦敦所特有的“工艺学校”也是在贫民学校的基础上发展起来的。其次，另一个具有重要意义的教育运动是“机械工人讲习所”运动，到了 19 世纪 40 年代，随着机械工人讲习所运动的衰退，多数讲习所转为工业学校。

在英国，从 18 世纪开始，就已广泛地在“作业学校”和“贫民学校”中试行开设手工课。统治阶级把让人民大众长期处于无知和贫困状态作为政治的必要条件的这种偏见，大大地推迟了义务教育制的实施。发展手工教育的前提条件是初等教育制度的完善，英国于 1870 年公布了《初等教育条例》(Elementary Education Act)。而手工作为初等教育的课程并为人们所重视，则是在 1880 年以后的事。手工教育引进中等教育的趋势不断高涨,在中学和工业学校中开设实习课的情况已相当普遍。1880 年在舍非尔德(Sheffield)创办了最早的“中央学校”(Central School),以年龄大的儿童为对象,设立了木工、金工实习工厂。紧接着在全国各地都建立了类似学校。《1889 年技术教育法》允许新成立的地方会议建立技术教育委员会,它们得到按照 1 英镑中不超过 1 便士的比例所征收的地方税财政支持。20 世纪中期前,英国的教育对穷苦家庭的孩子存在严重的不平等,他们只能进行初等教育的学习,中等教育主要为中上层阶级子女提供教育。面对这一现象,在第一次世界大战前夕,公会和工党大会提出了“人人受中等教育”的口号,在 1922 年时兴起的“人人受中等教育”的运动,在这些运动的推动下,1926 年教育署委员会主席哈多爵士主持起草并发表了《青少年教育报告》,报告将中等教育分为文法学校、现代中学和技术中学三类,后两者偏重于使用技能和实践方面的知识。这时中等教育中技术与设计教育的发展提上了日程,但二次世界大战再次中断了技术与设计教育的发展。

3.2 发展期(1944 年至今)

二战后,政府以重建教育的目的发布了《1944 年教育法》,开启了英国教育的新篇章,其中技术与设计教育也开始新的阶段。1944 年的教育法提出了中等教育分为三种学校,即文法中学、现代中学和技术中学。手工课程也得以在小学继续发展,中等教育制度也为技术教育的发展提供了广阔的空间。技术教育课程被称为“工艺”,以金工、木工、工业制图和家政为课程内容分别授课,授课内容为如何使用工具进行制作。对于战后发展科学、技术教育方面,英国当时的领导集团是很关心的,在 1994 年教育法发布之前就成立了对战后科学技术教育发展提出建议的专门委员会,在 1945 年委员会就提出了战后科技技术教育的想法。在 1956 年,政府发表了《技术教育白皮书》,提出了二战之前到 1955 年近二十年时间里,英国的技术教育无论在基础教育、中等教育和高等教育中都有很大的发展,但与美国、苏联相比,技术教育的发展并不乐观,认为要继续扩大科学、技术的教育,培养出更多的人才,并且增加对技术人员的培养。白皮书进一步发展了技术教育,带动了学生更加注重学习技术与设计教育。在白皮书发布之后,技术中学并没有得到繁荣,因为很多地方教育当局在现代中学加入工艺、烹调、家政、裁缝、设计、汽车机械、农业、音乐、船舶驾驶、理科、商业、护理等科目,逐渐取代了技术学校的功能。

进入 20 世纪 60 年代后,英国教育部门对技术教育进行了重新组织。对中等教育也提出创办综合中学,并接收所在地的所有儿童入学,并为具备各种能力的儿童提供多种多样课程的学校。关于技术教育的教学在每个综合学校的课程中都能体现出来,在每学年都开设金属加工、木工、家务、裁缝课程给学生学习。这些课程都是技术与设计教育实施的体现。进入 70 年代后,技术教育在英国被称为“手工、设计与技术”,这个课程是以金工、木工等为课程内容的“工艺教育”改为“手工、设计与技术”,并在

1970—1988 年间一直沿用此课程名,“手工、设计与技术”课程在原有强调手工制作的基础上加入“设计”的因素。而作为第一个完成工业革命的国家来说,英国的经济增长持续低迷,1970—1979 年英国经济平均年增长率仅为 2.2%,在主要工业国中最低,而同期内通货膨胀年均率达到 12.5%,在主要工业国中最高。高利率,产品竞争力的下降,严重的失业现象[3],在 1973 年和 1974 年的石油危机中,英国的社会面临内忧外患。政府推行经济改革的同时推动教育改革,1985 年英国发布教育白皮书《更好的学校》,其中认为:“设计与技术”课程应该是中小学校课程中的重要一部分,应该是一门独立的实践课程,而不应该仅作为科学课程的辅助课程或者说应用科学课程而存在。1988 年,英国教育部出台了英国教育史上里程碑式的法案——《1988 年教育改革法》,设置国家课程:数学、英语、科学为核心课程,历史、地理、技术、音乐、艺术、体育和现代外语为基础课程,其中正式把技术课作为必修基础课之一,这在英国中小学课程史上还是第一次,并正式将课程“手工、设计与技术”更名为“设计与技术”,由此开启了技术与设计教育在英国的现代变革。在 1990 年,英国政府下发《国家课程标准:设计与技术》,在中小学全面开设“设计与技术”课程。

20 世纪末期,全球经济、技术、政治格局发生变化,依据国内外的形势,英国在 1995 年和 2000 年分别对《国家课程标准》进行修改。在近十年,英国国家设计与技术课程有两次较大的变化:2003 年 9 月,英国国家课程与资格局(简称 QCA)发布了一篇题为《14—19 岁:机会与卓越》(14—19:*Opportunity and Excellence*)的白皮书,取消了对“设计与技术”课程 14—16 岁阶段的强制性学习[4];2007 年,英国国家课程改革加强了中央对课程的控制,对“设计与技术”的课程标准进行了修订,在 11—14 岁阶段提出了新举措[5]。

4 我国技术与设计教育存在的不足和建议

4.1 注重科学教育,提高技术与设计的地位

技术与设计教育在基础教育阶段主要是在科学教育中体现,要提升技术与设计教育的地位,首先要注重科学教育。科学教育的实施状况直接关系到我国人才的培养和国家科学技术在世界范围内的竞争力。面对全球科学教育改革潮流的形势,我们要改变原有的教育观念,让学校、社会、家庭和学生都认识到科学教育在社会变革中的重要地位。

首先对中小学科学课程标准来说,“设计与技术”是第一次在标准中得到明确的,这说明其已经引起了教育学者和教育部门的重视,但与科学知识相比,这些重视是远远不够的。其次,“设计与技术”在学校的课程中是独一无二的内容,为学生带来了实际的挑战,学生学习时它并不是有单一的“正确答案”,需要学生的创造力和技术能力去解决问题。学生把世界看作一个处处都有可能的地方,而且人们不能控制生活的环

境,这就要培养学生的自尊和自我效能感。对于在激烈竞争行业中的一个人来说,自我效能感是成功的先决条件,"设计与技术"教育能很好地建立学生的自我效能感[6]。对学生的长远发展来说,"设计与技术"教育是关键性的。最后是设计与技术教育对经济复苏的贡献,为全球市场提供创新的产品设计和制造,这被视为经济复苏的一个主要政策。英国的财政大臣曾说过:"我们希望的词语是'英国制造'、'英国创造'、'英国设计'、'英国发明'来推动国家向前发展。"[7]技术与设计教育能为学习者学习现代设计和制造提供引导,也可以给年轻人的技术职业提供一个原汁原味的介绍。

4.2 在科学教育中平衡技术和设计

长期以来,我国的技术与设计教育的课程中都比较注重技术教育的内容,一般以学生的技术能力的发展作为此教育领域的目标。技术与设计教育要通过对学生动手能力的培养,发展和提高学生的思维能力,同时提高其设计能力与解决问题的能力。英国关于技术与设计教育的课程一直都有设计的因素。我国科学教育的主要教学方法是探究式教学,它属于归纳式的教学方法,是一种自上而下的知识建构过程,这与传统的科学教育中教师为中心演绎式的教学方法有很大的不同。在知识建构过程中的教师对学生设计能力的培养和提高比较忽视。产生这种现象的原因是多方面的,一方面在我国的科学课程中,由于教师缺乏对技术和设计本质的认识,很多教师对教学过程两者的共同运用没有把握,教师对技术和设计理解的偏差在教学中会产生一些背离技术教育和设计教育本质的教学方法,另一方面是长期以教师为主体的教学方法影响探究式教学的推进和实施,从而忽视科学课程中的设计教育。

对学生进行设计教育,不仅可以使学生获得知识的建构,也会学习到书本上没有的知识,同时可以应对生活中不同的问题,以进行设计解决。在进行设计时,可以培养学生的创造力、自我效能感、解决问题的能力等。在我国技术与设计教育逐步走上正规化道路的时候,要注意对技术教育和设计教育双管齐下,培养学生的思维和能力。

4.3 提高科学教师的专业水平及职业素养

近年来,我国中小学的科学教师的队伍逐渐壮大起来,但教师职前职后培养的问题也随之而来。因为我国科学教育比欧美等国起步晚,教师的培养也存在很多问题亟待解决和完善。

一是在科学教师职前培养中,小学有很多科学教师自身素质不能够胜任教学活动,很多师范学校不能很好地培养科学教育专业学生的探究精神和探究能力,导致教师上岗后,对科学课程的教学活动不能很好地设计,也难以适应探究式教学的理念和实践能力。我国科学教师的培养应该多借鉴国外对科学教师教育的模式、教材等方面,像英国、美国、芬兰、澳大利亚国家有着多年的教师培养经验,如美国密西根州立大学的5年制本科专业(4年专业学习+1年专业实践)通过综合科学教学主修(Integrated Science Teaching Major for Elementary Teacher Certification)模式培养专家型小学科学教师,连续16年被评为全美排名第一的小学教育专业。二是教师缺乏有效的培训,科学教师的培训质量直接影响着教师的教学活动。在职前教育不完善的情况下,教师走上教学岗位,应多参与培训,加强教学专业知识和实践能力。在职学校和省市教育部门应该重视科学教师的在职培养。地方教育可以开展简单的活动,也可以高等院校和地方教育部门合作,定期对科学教师进行培训,方式可灵活多样。如中国南京市各区每周都会进行科学教育的教研活动,每期都会有不同的教师进行讲课,其他教师听课记录,课程结束后进行讨论和反思。这样的活动简单易行。在一定程度上,对教师进行了反思教学的培养,教师交流教学经验。教师的职前职后培养培训不能分离,在学习内容和学习方法上都要相互衔接,保持连贯性和一致性,真正提高科学教师的专业化水平和职业素养。

致谢

本文为国家社科基金一般项目《基础教育阶段技术与设计教育的国际化比较研究》(11JDGC026)的阶段性成果之一。

References

[1] Mu Jing. A Study on Paradigm Technology Education in Basic Education. Wuhan: Central China Normal University, 2005.

[2] PRIMARY National Curriculum Design and Technology. https://www.gov.uk/government/publications/national-curriculum-in-en.

[3] Zhu Gang. Interpretation of new review of national curriculum in England and inspiration for China. Primary & Secondary Schooling Abroad, 2012, 10: 10-15.

[4] Su Lingli, Lu Wei. Features of a new high school curriculum reform in the UK and inspiration in 2008. Contemporary Educational Science, 2010, 2: 46-47.

[5] D & T Association. https://www.data.org.uk/.

[6] Bandura. A Self-efficacy: The Exercise of Control. New York: W. H. Freeman, 1997.

[7] Ding Bangping. Science teacher education for primary schools in China: Status quo, problems and recommendations. Contemporary Teacher Education, 2011, 4: 1-7.

A Novel Method for Psychological Assessment Based on the Analysis of VOCs in Exhaled Breath

Shibing Yu[1,a], Xuejun Kang[1,b,*], Yan Yan[1,c], Siwei Deng[1,d], Xiaoxiao Wu[1,e]
[1]Key Laboratory of Child Development and Learning Science of Ministry of Education, Research Center for Learning Science, Southeast University, Nanjing, 210096, China
[a]yushibing88@126.com, [b]xjkang64@163.com, [c]yshwqgyy@sina.com, [d]adengsiwei@163.com, [e]wxx2010xiaoxiao@139.com
[*] Corresponding author

Keywords: Stress; Exhaled breath; Biomarkers; VOCs

Abstract: Stressful events may adversely affect a child's physiological and psychological health. To evaluate the impact of stress on children's well-being, it is important to develope valid and reliable stress assessment methods. Exhaled breath is a type of non-invasive biological sample, it can be used to define biomarkers (or breath prints) related to human biological process. In this article, a novel sampling and determination for exhaled breath has been developed and a preliminary exploration has been taken to make clear the relationship between the variation of the content of the VOCs and the psychological behavior of individuals.

1 Introduction

Stressful events may adversely affect a child's physiological and psychological health, with potentially enduring effects into adolescence and adulthood. Over the last two decades, interest in biological research in the social sciences has grown rapidly. Non-invasive biological sample research is appealing as a quick, inexpensive means of determining a range of biological markers, which offer insight into a variety of human responses, for example, stress. To the social researcher these advantages provide exciting possibilities for new transactions between social, behavioral and biological models of development. To evaluate the impact of stress on children's well-being, it is important to develop valid and reliable stress assessment methods. In general, stressor questionnaires and laboratory measurements of markers in non-invasive biological sample, such as saliva and urine have been widely performed in childhood development research.

Exhaled breath is also a type of non-invasive biological samples, similarly to other types of biological samples, exhaled breath can be used to define biomarkers (or breath prints) related to abnormal health status in humans. The metabolites detected in exhaled breath originate from normal and deviant (for instance inflammatory) are Volatile Organic Compounds (VOCs), which are first released into the blood and ultimately in the lungs into exhaled breath. VOCs are chemicals that have sufficiently high vapor pressure of over 133.32 Pa and the boiling point is 50—260 ℃. Exhaled breath contains thousands of VOCs that may be used as biomarkers of many kinds of diseases and cancers. Exhaled breath is a non-invasive, easily performed and rapid sampling, either in the gaseous or condensed state. For example in the gaseous state, there have been studies for asthma, attention deficit hyperactivity disorder in children. However, at the moment there is a general death of literature on the relationship between the variation of the content of the VOCs and psychological behavior of individuals.

In this paper a novel method which gathered collection and enrichment of the human exhaled breath by electrospun nanofibers was set up, and then a capillary gas chromatography was used to monitor the change of exhaled breath when a subject was faced with a psychological stress. The research recruited 9 young students who experience a speech stress. The breathing gas samples of participants were collected before and after stress test and then were determined. The data of anxiety inventory filled out by participants after the speech stress test were collected. It was shown preliminary that breathing gas composition and concentration will vary correspondingly after psychological stress. A new data processing for stress evaluation was developed. In order to understand the baseline levels of human breathing gas, a subject' exhaled breath was collected at different time point on one day. The gaseous samples were determined to obtain preliminary the rhythm of human respiratory gases.

2 Experimental

2.1 Chemicals and samples

THF and DMF are obtained from Kelong (Nanjing, China), both are analytically pure. The polystyrene (PS) is purchased from Shanghai Chemical Agents Institute. The 1 L Tedlar gas sampling bags are purchased from China Dalian delin gas packing co., ltd. Polystyrene (PS) nanofibers were provided by Suzhou Dongqi Biological Technology Company Limited.

2.2 Instruments and apparatus

The equipment used in this study for the analysis of all target VOCs contains a GC system (Agilent 7890A, USA). The target VOCs are separated on a DB-1 column (diameter: 0.2 mm, length: 30 m, and thickness: 0.80 mm). The thermal desorption equipment is a headspace sampler (Zhongdingshichuang, Beijing, China).

2.3 Construction of enrichment equipment for VOCs in exhaled breath

The sample concentrating tube consists of a glass tube that is home-filled with 30 mg of nanofiber into a clean glass tube. The subjects were asked to exhale deeply to the Tedlar gas sampling bag until it is filled with respiratory gases. Each subject collected exhaled breath at the beginning and the end of a speech. After sampling the Tedlar gas sampling bag was connected with the sample concentrating tube, and the latter was connected with a pump which was switched on to draw the exhaled breath out from the bag into the sample concentrating tube (figure 1).

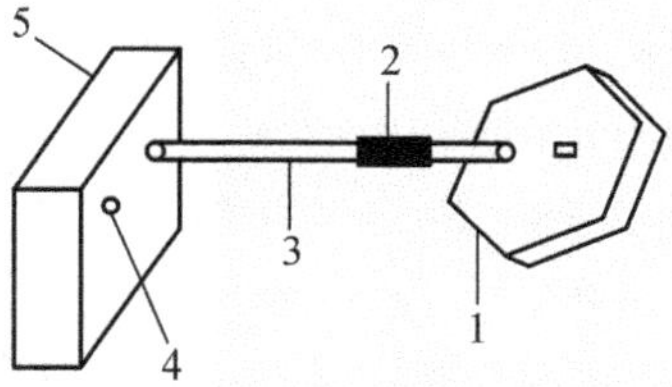

Figure 1 Construction of enrichment equipment for VOCs in exhaled breath: 1. Tedlar gas sampling bag;2. sample concentrating tube;3. connection tube;4. air outlet;5. pump.

2.4 GC condition

The GC experimental condition of analyzing the exhaled breath samples as follows. The gas chromatography was equipped with split injector, the temperature of the injection port was 270 ℃, 1 L of the desorbed solution was injected for analysis. The chromatographic condition were: the column temperature was held at 60 ℃ for 2 min and increased at 3 ℃/min up to 113 for 1 min, subsequently heated to 170 ℃ at 5 ℃/min for 1 min and thereafter to 280 ℃ at the rate of 3 ℃/min for 5min. The flow-rate of the nitrogen carrier gas was constant to 0.3 mL/min.

3 Results and discussion

3.1 Chromatogram and the diurnal changes of VOCs in exhaled breath

The typical chromatogram of VOCs in exhaled breath was shown in Figure 2. It was clear that both the number and the intensity of the peaks of VOCs are varied at the beginning and the end of a speech. To simplify data analysis, the sum of all peak area (F) was defined as the quantitative parameter to evaluate the intensity of VOCs in exhaled breath. Then the diurnal rhythm of human respiratory gases can be presented in Figure 3. It seems that baseline level of breathing gas of human body is fluctuant.

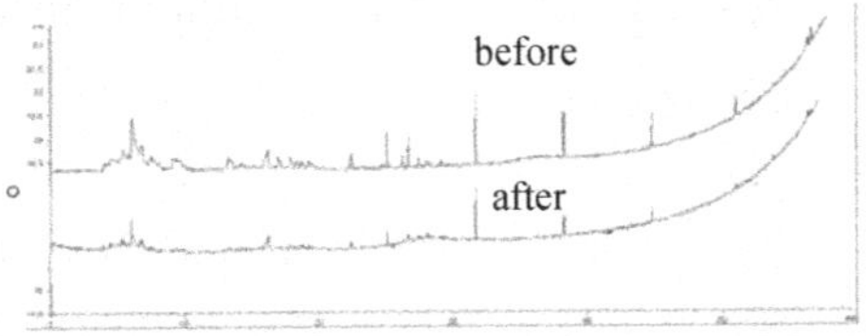

Figure 2 The typical chromatograms of VOCs in exhaled breath before and after the speech

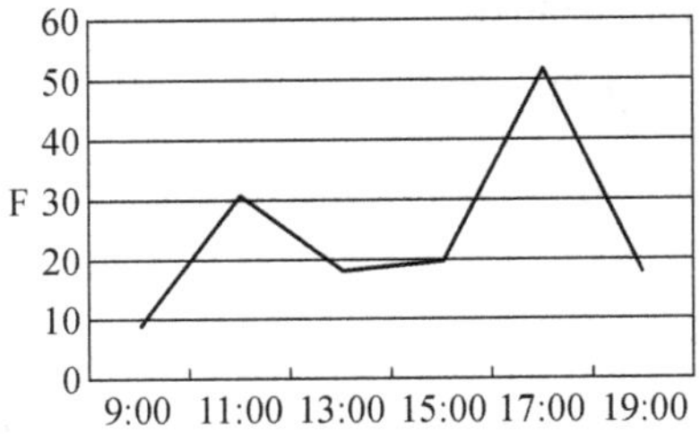

Figure 3 The diurnal rhythm of human respiratory gases

3.2 Data analysis

In order to explore the correlation between psychological behavior and human exhaled breath, a parameter, the ratio of peak intensity (R) was defined as the ratio of sum peak area of the VOCs in exhaled breath before and after the speech. The ratios are compared with the Activities-specific Balance Confidence Scale statistics, the correlation between the score of anxiety score and R was significant ($r = -0.609$, $p = 0.084$) (Figure 4). The results show that the subjects with lower R feel more anxiety than whom with higher R in speech task.

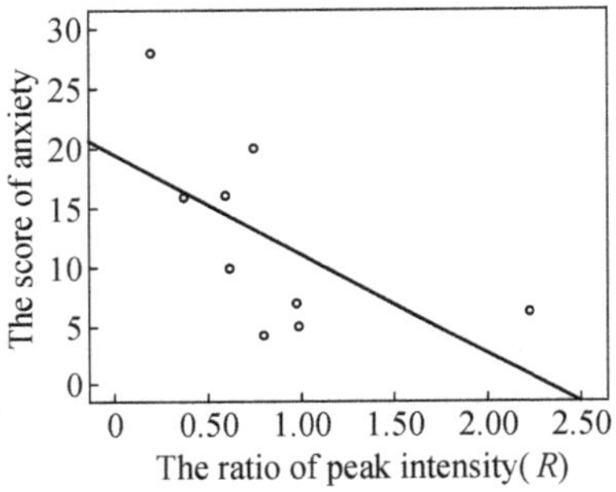

Figure 4 Correlation between the score of anxiety and the ratio of peak intensity

4 Conclusion

A novel method which gathered collection and enrichment of the human exhaled breath by electrospun nanofibers was developed, and the VOCs in exhaled breath were determined successfully. A new data processing basing on the results of chromatographic determination was explored for it use in stress evaluation. It seems that exhaled breath could provide a valuable tool which offer insight into a variety of human responses, for example, stress.

Acknowledgement

This work was supported by the National Natural Science Foundation of China (No. 81172720, and No. 21307086) and Colleges and Universities in Jiangsu Province plans to graduate research and innovation projects (CXLX12_0121).

References

[1] T Stalder, D Bäumler, R Miller, et al. The cortisol awakening response in infants: Ontogeny and associations with development-related variables, hair and urine. Psychoneuroendocrinology, 2013, 38: 552 – 559.

[2] A A Sehgal, L Duma, G Bodenhausen, et al. Fast proton exchange in histidine: Measurement of rate constants through indirect detection by NMR spectroscopy. Chemistry—A European Journal, 2014, 20: 6332 – 6338.

[3] E Archana, P Pai, B K Prabhu, et al. Altered biochemical parameters in saliva of pediatric attention deficit hyperactivity disorder. Neurochem Res, 2012, 37: 330 – 334.

[4] Z Vaghri, M Guhn, J Weinberg, et al. Hair cortisol reflects socio-economic factors and hair zinc in preschoolers. Psychoneuroendocrinology, 2013, 38: 331 – 340.

[5] B Vanaelst, T De Vriendt, I Huybrechts, et al. Epidemiological approaches to measure childhood stress. Paediatr Perinat Epidemiol, 2012, 36: 280 – 297.

[6] A Smolinska, E M Klaassen, J W Dallinga, et al. Profiling of volatile organic compounds in exhaled breath as a strategy to find early predictive signatures of asthma in children. PLoS One, 2014, 9: 95668.

[7]R A García, V Morales, S Martín, et al. Volatile organic compounds analysis in breath air in healthy volunteers and patients suffering epidermoid laryngeal carcinomas. Chromatographia, 2014, 77: 501 – 509.

[8] M Caldeira, A S Barros, M J Bilelo, et al. Profiling allergic asthma volatile metabolic patterns using a headspace-solid phase microextraction/gas chromatography based methodology. Chromatogr A, 2011, 1218: 3771 – 3780.

[9] B M Ross, I McKenzie, I Glen, et al. Increased levels of ethane, a non-invasive marker of n-3 fatty acid oxidation, in breath of children with attention deficit hyperactivity disorder. Nutr Neurosci, 2003, 1218: 277 – 281.

The Research of Technology and Engineering Literacy Assessment and Test Paper Based on Computers for the 2014 National Assessment of Educational Progress in the United States

Yan Xu[1,a], Yi Bai[1,b,*]

[1]Key Laboratory of Child Development and Learning Science of Ministry of Education, Southeast University, Nanjing, Jiangsu, China

[a]seuxuyan@163.com, [b]by.rcls@seu.edu.cn

[*]Corresponding author

Keywords: NAEP2014; Technology and engineering literacy; Assessment based on computers; Test paper

Abstract: In 2009, the Unite States published the document *Technology and Engineering Literacy Assessment and Item Specifications for the* 2014 *National Assessment of Educational Progress*, which have guiding significances to the technology and engineering literacy assessment in the future. Firstly, the article focuses on the change of American technology and engineering literacy definition and the development of the assessment tools. Then the focal point is the presentation of the NAEP2014 framework and the style of the test questions, especially the type of computer-based test questions and assessment methods, aiming at providing references to the design of our technology and engineering assessment.

美国 NAEP2014 技术和工程素养计算机化评测及试题编制研究

徐燕[1,a], 柏毅[1,b,*]
[1]东南大学儿童发展与学习科学教育部重点实验室,南京,江苏,中国
[a]seuxuyan@163.com, [b]by.rcls@seu.edu.cn
[*]通讯作者

关键词:NAEP2014;技术和工程素养;计算机评测;试题编制

中文摘要:美国于2009年发布《2014美国技术和工程素养教育进展评测框架和项目》,对美国今后的技术和工程素养评测具有指导意义。本文关注美国技术和工程素养的定义变革和评测工具的发展,重点研究了NAEP2014的评测框架和试题编制方式,特别是基于计算机的试题类型和评测方式,旨在为我国技术和工程素养的评测提供借鉴意义。

1 NAEP2014 简介

1.1 NAEP 背景

美国教育进展评测(the National Assessment of Educational Progress,以下简称NAEP),作为美国最大规模的成就测验,已经在美国各州实施了超过37年。起初,NAEP的目标是对全美年龄为9岁、13岁和17岁的学生进行数学、阅读、科学和写作等科目的标准化抽样测验。从20世纪90年代开始,NAEP主要考察4年级、8年级、12年级的学业成就,并将结果反馈给国家教育统计中心(National Center for Educational Statistics,NCES),达到全国范围内教育水平监控的目的。从2003年布什政府颁布《不让一个孩子掉队法案》(*The No Child Left Behind Act of* 2001,NCLB)之后,美国所有的州都参与了州一级别的NAEP评测。

1.2 NAEP2014 评测的起源

2006年,布什政府提出了《美国竞争力计划》,认为知识时代具有竞争力的人才是STEM人才(STEM代表科学、技术、工程、数学)。随着科学的发展、技术的进步,人类不断创造产品来满足自身的需要或者用以进一步改进自然。随着工业结构从机械化生产代替简单重复操作,解放人力进行更深层次的创造性改造,这种趋势要求现代社会的人才运用计算机网络等通信设备,依据一定的科学原理、数学计算结果,来进行技术的改进、工程的设计,也就是提出了人才的技术和工程素养要求。

NAEP从2009年开展技术与工程素养评测的计划，并出版了 *Technology and Engineering Literacy Assessment and Item Specifications for the* 2014 *National Assessment of Educational Progress*[1]（以下简称NAEP2014）。NAEP2014作为未来美国技术和工程素养评测的指导性框架，用以指导评测委员会进行评测前的准备，如评测的基本框架、不同年级学生的评测标准、试题编制；评测的实施，例如保证全国范围内计算机化评测的信度和效度；评测结果的报告，如学生成就水平的分类。其中，由于技术和工程素养的表现性、操作性、实践性，以及计算机化测验的优越性，NAEP2014选择了全国范围内基于计算机的评测方式。

1.3 NAEP2014评测报告

NCES会根据NAEP2014对美国学生技术和工程素养的评测结果出具一份全国性的报告，又叫做国家报告卡（The Nation's Report Card）。这份报告将会包括全国学生的素养评测结果，并以各种分类标准（如性别、种族、是否残疾、英语是否为母语等等）来分类报告。同时它会报告每个州学生分别达到基础水平、熟练水平和高级水平的比例，以及每个水平的最低分数。其中，基础水平要求学生能够掌握基础知识、熟练操作基本技能；熟练水平的学生能够应对富有挑战性的问题，富有逻辑地思考分析问题，并将知识运用到问题解决的过程中；而高级水平的学生都有超出一般水平的卓越表现。

2 技术和工程素养及其评测的发展过程

2.1 技术和工程素养概念的发展

美国国际技术教育协会（以下简称ITEA）于2000年发表的 *Standards for Technological Literacy*[2] 详细描述了K-12的学生的技术素养，总共包含20个标准，分别是技术的本质、技术和社会、设计、应付技术世界的能力以及设计世界等五大类。美国学术委员会（the National Academics，NA）在2006年进行的技术素养评测的工具开发研究中，定义了技术和工程素养的概念和评测框架。它认为技术是为了满足人类的需求而进行的对自然状态的改造、创造以及对环境的改造[3]。技术素养则定义为在技术活动中表现出来的能力，包括知识、能力、批判性思维和决策三个维度。

而NAEP2014重新定义了技术和工程素养。它认为技术和工程素养指的是，使用、理解、评价技术的能力，理解技术的原理和策略，开发出问题的解决方案并实现目标。NAEP2014分为技术与社会、设计与系统、信息与通信技术三个领域，这三个评测领域是相互联系的。它们相互之间的关系用表1中的三面金字塔来说明，即为其中的一个领域支持另外两个领域的发展。在技术与社会、设计与系统、信息与通信技术的任意一个领域中表现出来的素养，都需要另外一个领域的素养的支持，才能够外化成为有效的技术和工程的活动。

表1　美国技术和工程素养概念的发展过程

<table>
<tr><th>ITEA-技术素养(2000)</th><th>NA-技术素养(2006)</th><th>NAEP2014 -技术和工程素养(2014)</th></tr>
<tr><td>技术的本质
技术和社会
设计
应付技术世界的能力
设计世界</td><td>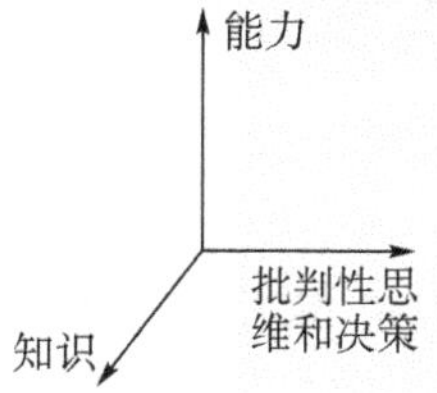
</td><td>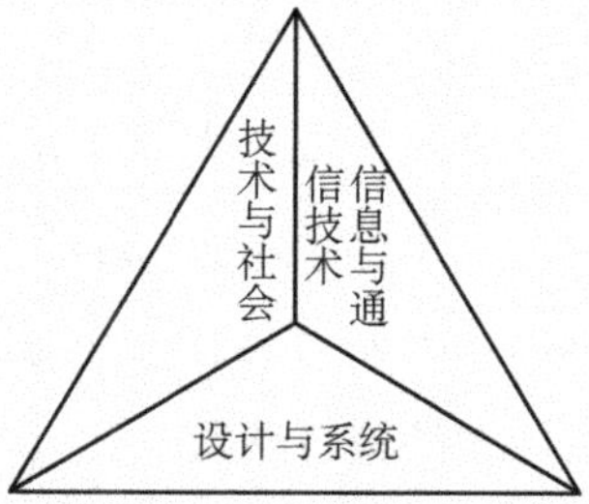
</td></tr>
</table>

表2　NAEP2014技术和工程素养评定的主要区域和分区

技术与社会	设计与系统	信息与通信技术(ICT)
A. 技术与人类的相互作用 B. 技术对自然世界的影响 C. 技术对信息和知识世界的影响 D. 道德、公平和责任	E. 技术的本质 F. 工程设计 G. 系统构想 H. 维修和故障排除	I. 观点与解决方案的构建与交流 J. 信息分析 K. 问题调研 L. 思想与信息的确认 M. 数字化工具的选择和使用

表1罗列了美国技术和工程素养概念的发展过程，表2则对NAEP2014的主要分区做了说明。从表1和表2中可以看出，美国技术和工程素养概念变化的过程中，一以贯之地关注技术对社会产生影响，关注使用技术进行设计的能力，关注思维方式和决策能力。NA的技术素养概念偏重技术素养的表现形式，提出了知识、能力、思维和决策三个维度的综合表现。而NAEP2014的技术和工程素养概念从素养的表现方式、应用领域出发，定义了技术素养在社会影响、在实践操作方面的体现方式[1]。同时引入"工程"这一概念，定义工程为"为满足人类需求，系统地反复地设计对象、进程和系统的方式"，体现技术在工程中的应用，如设计系统、维修系统等等。此外，NAEP2014也强调了信息与通信技术(即ICT)在技术应用、设计系统过程中的搜集信息、问题调研、思想交流等等中的媒介作用。

2.2　技术和工程素养评测的发展过程

总体而言，美国技术课程的发展情况是没有完整体系的K-12的技术课程，专职的技术教师较少，少有针对学生的技术素养评测。Greg等人[3]统计到2012年为止，美国针对学生的已测评的技术素养评测工具有19个，形式有标准参照测验、常模参照测验、基于活动的表现评测等等,大多测量学生某一方面的技术素养,如设计能力、问题解决能力。这些评测工具是由公司、高校研究者或者州立的教育机构开发出来,由于上述评测工具对技术素养概念定义的不一致,测试框架、测试题目也存在差异性,导致评测结果的不可比。因而,NAS 试图在 NAEP 测量数学、阅读、科学和写作等科目的实践经验基础上,评测美国学生的技术和工程素养,旨在评估美国学生技术方面的竞争力。要实现全国范围内 NAEP 的评测,关键在于评测框架、评测试题的开发,同时考虑基于计算机的评测的优越性和呈现方式。

2.3 计算机化评测的发展

张华华[4]对 NAEP 的学业水平测验研究发现,NAEP 采用项目反应理论和公认的参数估计软件进行参数估计,根据学生的作答情况和各种背景变量(如性别、年龄、英语是否为母语)来估计学生的能力得分。此外,NAEP 采用垂直等值的方法把 4、8、12 年级的学生放在同一量尺上进行年级间的比较。这是运用计算机进行海量数据的大样本分析方法,也是 NAEP 一直沿用的评测报告方法。

而 NAEP2014 在计算机大样本分析的基础上,借用 NAEP2009 部分地使用计算机呈现评测的经验,期望全面使用计算机评测技术和工程素养。NAEP2014 只是提出了计算机化评测的设想和部分样题,但是对于计算机化评测的试题开发、呈现方法、评分方式、实现评测的区分度等等都没有具体的说明。在 NAEP 技术和工程素养正式评测之前很难了解到具体的评测试题等细节信息。而且,上述问题也是 NAEP2014 亟须解决的问题。

Randy 等人[5]研究了 2003 年美国在全国 200 多所学校评测 8 年级学生科学和技术方面的问题解决能力的测验,为 NAEP2014 的实施做出示范性研究。这个测试采用了氦气球负载一定重量物体升空的背景,要求学生在虚拟的网络环境中,完成两个场景的测试。第一个场景下,学生需要自己输入关键词在虚拟的搜索引擎上搜索问题答案,计算机在这个过程中监控学生使用的关键词、搜索技术、计算机网页使用技巧、甄别科学信息真伪等等的能力,从学生的科学研究能力、科学综合能力以及计算机应用能力三个维度打分。而第二个场景为模拟场景,要求学生完成三个难度逐步加深的问题,学生或者控制氦气量或者控制气球负重,模拟氦气球的升空,计算机记录气球升空的快慢和最高高度,然后学生对数据进行分析得到结果。计算机全程进行与第一个场景类似的评测监控,在多维度对学生的问题解决能力进行评测。这个问题解决的能力测验具有完整的评估框架和评估细则,运用计算机创造虚拟环境,使学生在虚拟背景下能够通过技术问题的解决过程得到评测。

基于计算机的技术和工程素养评测,提供学生丰富的、现实状态下的背景资料

(以村庄里有需要维修的压水井为例[6]),让学生在没有接触这类机械、环境的基础上也能够运用技术和工程的素养来完成评测。学生在评测过程中根据任务形成假设,并在计算机上进行假设的检验时,计算机对于学生的行为给予及时的反馈,如分别从损坏可能性最大到最小进行压水井的故障排除,计算机对于学生每次操作都会反映是否在维修后打出了清澈的水,从而帮助学生定位需要维修的部位。最后,学生在计算机上形成最后的结论,和计算机虚拟的专家讨论进行结论的修改,形成最终的结论。整个过程中学生在提出问题、假设、假设检验、形成结论的环节中均体现了技术和工程素养。计算机化评测有纸笔测验不可比拟的优越性,特别是在操作性很强的技术领域,能够提供丰富的情境,对学生的反应做出及时的反馈,从而帮助学生调整行为,有助于学生技术和工程素养的表达。

3 计算机化评测框架

NAEP2014 将技术和工程素养的评测领域分为了技术与社会、设计与系统、信息与通信技术三大领域,每一个大领域下分为若干子领域,如设计与系统中包含了技术的本质、工程设计、系统构想、维修和故障排除四个子领域。

3.1 知识和技能的要求

对于上述的 3 大领域和 13 个子领域,如表 2 所示的 A—M 领域,NAEP2014 都提出了细化的评价指标。对于每一个子领域,NAEP2014 框架提出了 4 年级、8 年级、12 年级学生应该知道的知识和应该掌握的能力,作为评测的依据和试题编制的依据。随着年级的增高,4 年级、8 年级、12 年级所要求的目标也从记忆性知识的了解到应用性知识的理解,从简单的技能操作到复合性的工具应用和综合。

3.2 实践应用

一个具有良好技术和工程素养的人,在技术与社会、设计与系统、信息与通信技术三大领域都能够有良好的实践应用。NAEP2014 将技术性的实践应用分为三类:理解技术的原理、开发解决方案并实现目标、交流与合作。这些实践应用会在三个领域都有表达,并且各类实践之间也是相关联的。

理解技术的原理,要求学生能够运用知识,理解技术的组成,并进行思考和推理。这里所指的知识,包括简单的事实性和概念性的知识,到高层次的关于事实、概念和原理的推理及其相互关系。开发解决方案并实现目标,要求学生能够系统性地应用技术知识、工具、技能来解决问题,以实现社会、设计、课程和显示的情境中提出的目标,这种实践包括程序性知识的应用和在战略上知道如何应用。交流与合作,主要要求学生和同伴、专家应用各种现代技术进行交流并达成一致结果。

4 计算机化评测试题

4.1 表现期望

张雨强[7]等人研究了NAEP试题的开发过程，认为开发过程如下：首先确定学生的表现期望，然后根据表现期望的细则和要求编制评价试题，根据评价试题引发的学生相应的反应，作为解释学生在这一领域知道什么和能做什么的证据，也就是评价学生技术和工程素养的依据。同时，在试题编制的过程中，需要预设学生所有可能的行为，以及行为的各种结果，根据学生的行为和结果对应的达到的“表现期望”的程度，给予不同等级的分数，来保证不同能力水平（基础水平、熟练水平、高级水平）的学生具有区分度。

NAEP2014技术和工程素养评测的试题编制同NAEP2009科学课程评价类似，都是基于学生的“表现期望”并以此为中心进行的。三大评测领域（技术与社会、设计与系统、信息与通信技术）和三种实践应用（理解技术的原理、开发解决方案并实现目标、交流与合作）不可能独立地进行评价，也就是说学生不可能脱离评测领域单单进行实践，也不可能只在三大领域中没有实践的活动。这两个维度的交叉表现为学生的“表现期望”。以理解技术的原理为例，它和三大领域的交叉内容即为学生的表现期望。如表3中，在三大领域，要达到理解技术的层面，表现期望为分析现有技术的利弊、描述ICT工具的特征和功能等等。

表3 理解技术的原理这一实践的表现期望

	技术与社会	设计与系统	信息与通信技术
理解技术的原理	分析现有技术的利弊 解释成本与收益 比较两种技术对个人的影响 等等	描述一个系统或过程的特征 识别一个系统或过程的例子 等等	描述信息与通信技术工具的特征和功能 解释一个整体的各部分是如何交互作用的 等等

4.2 计算机化试题类型

NAEP2014使用的试题类型包括两类：第一，独立的条目，即为简单的选择、简答；第二，基于情境的评测题串。其中，基于情境的题串又有长情境和短情境之分，长情境要求学生花费25分钟左右的时间完成10—15个与情境相关的问题，而面对短情境学生要在12—15分钟完成5—10个问题。基于计算机的情境性评测，能够有效提高整个评价的正确性，但是减少了测量的覆盖面，而独立条目的评测能够多题覆盖多个领域。引进情境类评测和独立条目的评测，能够兼顾测量的准确性和独立性。

4.2.1　基于情境的评测

由于独立条目评测和传统的纸笔测验比较接近,本文主要对基于计算机的情境评测进行研究。在情境评测中,首先需要情境的描述,重点反映出技术任务的背景,可能是贴合现实生活环境。这样的情境越具体、详细,越能够保证更多样本的学生即使没有接触过这种环境,也能够调动技术和工程素养来解决问题。计算机通过多媒体、动画的方式呈现动态情境,可以减少文本、减少题目阅读的实践,而且能够传送文本难以传送的背景信息。

其次,在情境中,需要明确提出具有激励性的任务目标,目标能够推进任务的进行、保持任务的连贯性。在多任务情境中,可以在完成了任务一之后,呈现出任务二的目标,以此来保证任务的推进。此外,情境中还可以提供多样的辅助工具,如电脑辅助设计、地理信息系统、录像编制工具等等,一方面用以测量学生 ICT 的维度,另一方面较为真实地提供了技术问题解决的环境。

4.2.2　建构响应

建构响应指的是学习者在进行基于问题解决的知识建构时,外界环境对建构的反馈,"提问—响应"和"阐释—澄清"是主要的响应形式[8]。在长情境评测中,呈现给学生接近于真实世界的情境。学生在完成任务过程中,不同的行为会产生不同的计算机响应,由于这种响应是学生自己建构的,又叫做建构响应。计算机多媒体,使得这种实时建构响应的反馈成为了现实。

在设计长情境的建构响应时,要考虑学生所有可能出现的行为,并且记录下表现出学生技术和工程素养的行为。同时,情境中设计出学生所有可能行为的反馈结果,使得学生对计算机的不同操作得到不同结果,结果反馈给学生,便于学生调整评测的进度。

4.3　计算机化试题举例

下面通过 NAEP2014 试题的实例,对其计算机化试题的编制进行研究。针对 8 年级学生的评测,要求在关于村庄安装风力涡轮机的情境中,学生需要完成下列任务。任务一:利用模型探索风速和轮叶的半径对风能的影响;任务二:选择村庄附近最适合安装风力涡轮机的位置;任务三:在村民大会上做出安装涡轮机的策划报告。

4.3.1　表现期望

在这个系列任务中,体现了技术与社会以及工程设计的领域理解技术的原理、开发解决方案、交流与合作的实践活动。具体的表现期望有:识别风力涡轮机系统的运作方式和影响因素;构建涡轮机模型;选择合适的位置、合适的风速和轮叶大小来解决村庄安装涡轮机的社会问题;调查设计方案对环境的影响并权衡做出决定;利用多媒体展示结果，并和村民交流、讨论。上述的表现期望，都是在这个长情境中能够评测到的。

4.3.2　基于情境的评测

本情境中，会提供村庄附近若干个能够安装风力涡轮机的地点的周边环境，包括风力、离村庄距离、是否影响小鸟生活等等。村庄的平面图便于学生对位置的判断。同时，为了准备村民大会的演示，情境中提供虚拟网络搜索素材和幻灯片制作的软件。

4.3.3　建构响应

学生在任务一中，可以选择不同的风速、轮叶大小，计算机响应出风能大小，从而提供数据给学生建立风力涡轮机模型。学生点击村庄平面图的任意一点，计算机会响应出该点的基本环境信息和生态信息。同时，可以通过虚拟互联网得到各种素材制作幻灯片。

从以上的实例可以看出，计算机在技术和工程素养的评测过程中，增加了评测背景的真实性，提高学生与评测系统的互动过程，更真实地反映出了纸笔测验难以测量出来的潜在的行为和能力，以及学生在应用信息技术方面的能力。

5　对我国技术和工程素养评测的启示

5.1　以实践为核心，确定中国技术和工程素养的教育和评价框架

在部分发达省份如江苏、浙江等，在高中阶段使用通用技术（简称 GT）课程，它指的是信息技术之外的、较为宽泛的、体现基础性和通用性并与专业技术相区别的技术，是日常生活中应用广泛、对广大同学的发展具有广泛迁移价值的技术，中国的基础教育阶段至今为止没有专门的技术和工程课程及相应的评价系统。然而，在基础教育阶段，技术和设计的教育无处不在，从小学阶段科学课程中的科学探究、物理领域、生物领域和地球空间领域，到初中阶段的物理、化学、生物学科，很多部分都能够体现出学生应用技术、设计实验、模拟方案、解决社会问题等等方面的素养。所以，确定中国的技术和工程素养的内涵和外延，从现有的科学课程及其评价中区分出特别能够体现出技术和工程素养的部分，并加以修改，最终确定适合我们中小学学生的评价方式是尤为重要的。

同时，现有的科学课程在评价的时候，由于纸笔测验的束缚和传统评测的思维，侧重于评价学生对知识的记忆和理解，迁移知识解决新问题，很少注重到学生实践的能力，包括动手运作机械的能力、尝试错误并修正的能力、概括分析的能力、交流讨论的能力。基于计算机的评测，能够在模拟方式上提供给学生实践的可能。

5.2 注重评测框架中表现期望的开发

基于计算机的评价,能够全面记录学生在评价过程中的行为,包括搜索关键词的选择、每一次鼠标的点击、图表的修改、搜索网页的保存和分析、操作的反应时等等,这些行为的信息量是远远超过纸笔测验得到的答案。基于计算机的评测, NAEP2014 开发出详细的表现期望,是使评测成为可能的直接方式。

而中国现有的课程标准,作为课程实施的依据和课程评价的标尺,只有内容标准没有表现标准。它们作为理论上的指导效果卓越,但是很难在评测的操作上有细致的指导。至今为止,尚没有专门的评价标准作为评价测试体系的依据颁布出来,以课程标准指导评价,用课程标准和国外的评价标准比较难免会出现偏差。所以,从现有的国家课程标准出发,开发评价标准,并细化评价标准中的学生表现期望,特别是关注学生应用计算机进行评测的表现期望,对学生的素养评测具有重要意义。与此同时,细化表现期望,能够捕捉到每一个与技术和工程素养相关的信号,并对这些信号区分和打分,从而得到具有区分水平的技术和工程素养的评测结果。

5.3 评测试题编制的建设

从 NAEP 将近 40 年的实施时间中,可以得到很多关于全国性评测的经验。对于技术和工程素养而言,它一方面作为课程在中国受重视程度不高,另一方面作为 21 世纪的必备技能对学生的未来发展很重要,我们可以借鉴教育评测发达的国家经验,来对中国学生进行脱离学业水平测试的评测。

第一,应注重评测试题编制团队的建设[9]。美国普遍依赖政府专业命题部门和社会性评价组织进行大规模标准化成就测验,而我国的命题主要由各级学校、教研室和教育局进行命题。同时,题目为了能够兼顾到各个地区、各类不同水平的学生,保证基础题、难题的比例。上述情况容易造成命题的行政干预以及区分度的降低。引用计算机评测,能够提高评测的区分度,而将评测试题的开发交给独立的评测机构或者学术研究机构,能够保证命题的公平公正。

第二,基于计算机的题库建设是发展技术和设计素养评测的重点。采用计算机进行评测成为评测的大趋势,而建设题库能够保证评测资源的充分性和稳定性。到现在为止,中国尚没有哪一科学业水平测试采用计算机的题库抽测,从而导致了每年评测试题难度的波动。基于计算机的题库建设,可以根据难度等级,将历年的技术和工程素养评测试题纳入到题库中,并补充符合技术发展的新试题,在评测的时候随机生成试题,能够保证评测的大样本、大范围、大领域。

致谢

本文为教育部人文社会科学研究专项任务《基础教育阶段技术和设计教育的国际比较研究》(11JDGC026)的阶段性成果之一。

References

[1] National Assessment Governing Board. Technology and Engineering Literacy Assessment and Item Specifications for the 2014 NAtional Assessment of Educational Progress, 2012.

[2] Intenational Technology Education Association. Standards for Technological Literacy_ Content for the Study of Technology. Reston: ITEA, 2003.

[3] Greg Pearson. Assessment of Technological Literacy in the United States. Design and Technology Education:An International Journal, 2012, 2: 87 - 96.

[4] Zhang Huahua. Computerized testing and what we can learn from NAEP. Psychological Exploration, 2013, 5: 387 - 391.

[5] Randy Elliot Bennett, Hilary Persky, Andy Weiss, et al. Measuring problem solving with technology. The Journal of Technology, Learning, and Assessment, 2010, 85: 5 - 9.

[6] National Center for Education Statistics. http://nces. ed. gov/nationsreportcard/tel.

[7] Zhang Yuqiang, Feng Cuidian. The research of NAEP2009 science assessment of the test paper. Global Education, 2007, 10: 59 - 64.

[8] Wang Lu, Yang Hui, Bai Jifang. The knowledge construction based on the problem solving in CSCL. China Educational Technology, 2008, 4: 31 - 34.

[9] Mei Songzhu. Comparative research between U. S. NAEP and Chinese NAEQ. Journal of Tianjin Normal University (Elementary Education Edition), 2013, 1: 59 - 62.

Study on Selection Operator in Feature Selection of Physiological Signals Based on Genetic Algorithms

Yun Liu *

Key Laboratory of Child Development and Learning Science of Ministry of Education, Southeast University, Nanjing, Jiang Su, China

liuy@ seu. edu. cn

* Corresponding author

Keywords: Standard genetic algorithms; Adaptive factor; Feature selection; Physiological signals

Abstract: The feature selection algorithm based on genetic algorithms (GA) is developed for four kinds of physiological signals, including ECG, skin conductance, EMG and respiration. Adaptive factor is increased in order to improve the algorithm in the selection process of standard GA (SGA). Judging criteria of GA is given, and the feature selection results are compared by experimental data among the four operating methods of selection operator including roulette selection, random traversal selection, non-linear ranking selection and tournament selection. A hybrid selection strategy of non-linear ranking and tournament is proposed. From the calculated number of feature amounts, the difference between the maximum and minimum, the trend, and the error of average recognition rate, the operating method has the best performance and the improving effect is optimal.

基于遗传算法的生理信号特征选择中选择算子的研究

刘云*
东南大学儿童发展与学习科学教育部重点实验室,南京,江苏,中国
liuy@ seu. edu. cn
*通讯作者

关键词:标准遗传算法;自适应选择算子;特征选择;生理信号

中文摘要:本文基于遗传算法研究心电、皮肤电、肌电和呼吸等四种生理信号的特征选择算法。在标准遗传算法计算流程的选择环节增加自适应因子,对标准遗传算法进行改进。给出遗传算法的优劣评判准则,应用实验数据对轮盘赌选择、随机遍历选择、非线性排名选择和锦标赛选择等四种选择算子的操作方法进行了特征选择的效果计算和比较分析。给出一种非线性排名和锦标赛混合选择的策略,从计算得到的特征个数、平均识别率最小最大值之差、水平趋势和误差等这几个参数来看,该选择算子的操作方法性能最好,得到了最优的改进效果。

1 Introduction

In recent years, emotion recognition research mainly focuses on the study of human facial and vocal expressions, that the ancients called “the wind blows”. But there is needed to remind that when people stay calm and collected and might even lie, some emotional state is not reflected from these signals. Changes of some physiological signals such as ECG and skin conductance, are only controlled by human autonomic nervous system and endocrine system, not by his subjective control. Therefore for the research of physiological signals emotion classification, data obtained would be more objective, and in some situations it will better reflect the real human emotion.

Feature selection is the key point of emotion recognition research. It is to select the optimal feature subset from the original feature set. And it is essentially a optimization problem of combination. Genetic Algorithm is a random search algorithm which simulates Darwin’s theory of natural selection and nature biological evolution. It was proposed by Professor John Holland of Michigan University, USA. Encoding, generating initial population, individual evaluation, selection, crossover and mutation are included in the calculating process. This method automatically obtains and accumulates the knowledge about space adaptively in the searching process so as to obtain optimal or quasi-optimal solution. It is especially for solving complex and non-linear problems which traditional methods can not solve. But it has some disadvantages such as being easily precocious, so many iterations, very long running time, and not ideal improving effect of recognition rate, and so on. In this paper, the adaptive operator will be added in the selection step of SGA in order to improve the SGA algorithm.

2 Judging criteria of Genetic Algorithms

The key problem must be solved before using SGA in feature selection, that is to determine what kind of genetic algorithms for feature selection is excellent and how to judge the change of a operation is for the better rather than destruction. Seven sets of data are chosen as judging criteria. Among them, *c*_best and *c*_num are the ultimate criteria, that is, the higher recognition rate and the less feature amounts, the more superior the algorithm is. The others are auxiliary for the criteria.

(1) Optimal recognition rate *c*_best. The higher the value after convergence is, the more excellent the algorithm is.

(2) The number *c*_num of feature amounts selected after the ending of selection. When *c*_best is the same, the smaller *c*_num is, the better the algorithm is.

(3) Convergence generations of GA *gen*_stop.

(4) Average value *c*_best_Mean of optimal recognition rate and average value *c*_avg _Mean of average recognition rate after convergence.

(5) Difference *c*_best_Max_Min between the maximum and minimum of optimal recognition rate, and difference *c*_avg_Max_Min between the maximum and minimum of average recognition rate.

(6) Trend *S*_best(1) of optimal recognition rate, and trend *S*_avg(1) of average recognition rate after convergence.

(7) Error *c*_best_Var of optimal recognition rate under limited measurements, and error *c*_avg_Var of average recognition rate under limited measurements.

3 Comparison of GA selection operator

In this paper, experimental data is from the multimedia and signal processing laboratory of University of Augsburg in Germany. Four kinds of physiological signals (ECG, skin conductance, EMG and respiration) are related to four emotional states including happiness, anger, sadness and joy. Physiological data were collected during 25 days, as a total of 100 samples. In the actual feature extraction, some original measurements can be characterized as original features, and the others need to be calculated from time domain and frequency domain. 186 features are extracted as the original feature set. Operating parameters of SGA include the individual coded string length $l = 186$, the initial population size popsize = 50, crossover probability $P_c = 0.7$, the initial mutation probability $P_m = 0.2$, the termination generations $T = 200$, and the generation gap $G = 0.9$ and so on.

According to the selection step of SGA, algorithm performance varies with the different selection strategies. The basic principle is that the strategy should follow the nature's choice, "survival of the fittest". Some common operating methods of selection operator are as followed. They will be implemented and compared so as to get the optimal selection algorithm.

3.1 Roulette selection

Roulette selection method is a playback random sampling method whose basic idea is that the selected probability of each individual is proportional to its fitness. Its implementation result is given as Figure 1. Among them, *c*_num = 74, *c*_avg_Mean = 0.877 55, *c*_avg_Max_Min = 0.037 5, *S*_avg(1) = −1.544e −0.005, *c*_avg_Var = 5.233 2e −0.005.

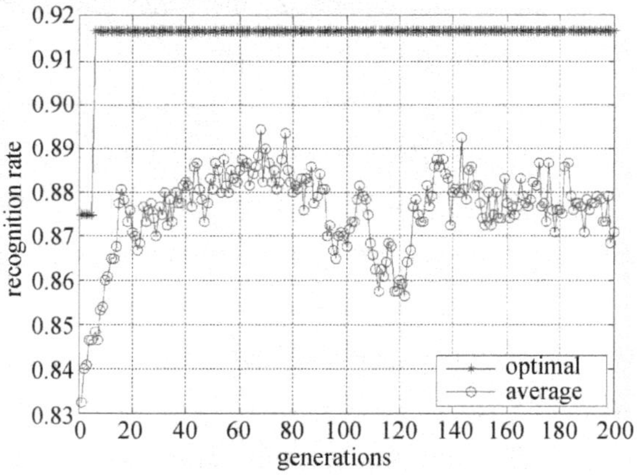

Figure 1 Feature selection result using roulette selection method

As shown in Figure 1, the algorithm converges at the 40th generation around and deteriorate at the 120th generation around.

3.2 Random traversal selection

The basic idea of random traversal selection is to carry out the random selection operation according to the expected survive value which is decided by individual fitness and whether is participated in cross step. Its implementation result is given as Figure 2. Among them, *c*_num = 70, *c*_avg_Mean = 0.876 19, *c*_avg_Max_Min = 0.036 667,

$S\_avg(1) = 6.5359e-0.005$, $c\_avg\_Var = 4.9962e-0.005$.

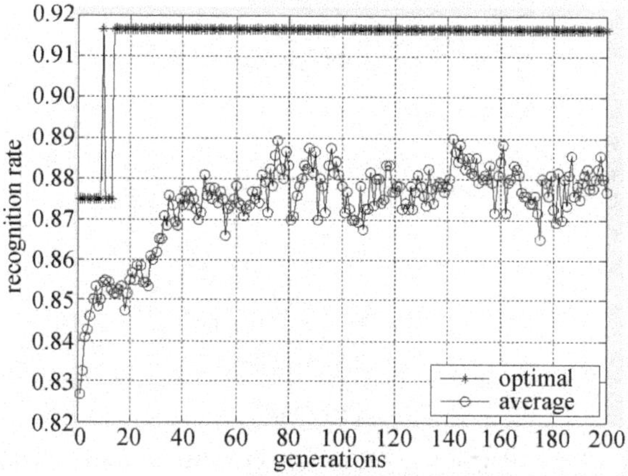

Figure 2 Feature selection result using random traversal selection method

As shown in Figure 2, the algorithm converges at the 60th generation. around and deteriorate at the 120th generation around. The curve of average recognition rate tends to level basically. It is smoother than roulette and has better performance after convergence. But this strategy is also based on the proportion of fitness and often appear premature convergence and stagnation happen. As shown in Figure 2, there is no change when the maximum recognition rate happens at the 10th generation.

3.3 Non-linear ranking selection

The idea of non-linear ranking selection is to sort all individuals according to their descending fitness, to design the probability distribution table and to assign to each individual according to the abovementioned order. Its implementation result is given as Figure 3. Among them, $c\_num = 59$, $c\_avg\_Mean = 0.89445$, $c\_avg\_Max\_Min = 0.036667$, $S\_avg(1) = 2.3098e-0.005$, $c\_avg\_Var = 3.9717e-0.005$.

As shown in Figure 3, the algorithm converges at the 40th generation around. It has much more better performances of feature selection results, the trend to level and the error than abovementioned two algorithms whether it is the average recognition rate or the feature selection number. But the additional computation workload (such as calculating the overall fitness value and sorting) is also considerable when the population size is large.

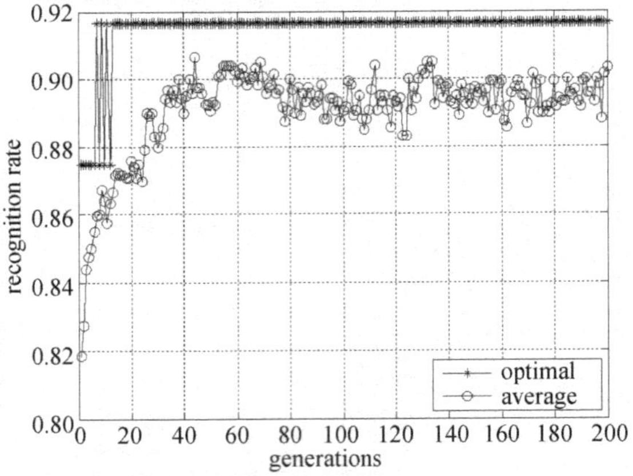

Figure 3 Feature selection result using nonlinear ranking selection method

3.4 Tournament selection

The basic idea of tournament selection is based on individual fitness. It is to pick out a certain number of individuals randomly, and then to choose the best one as father sample from the selected population. This process is repeated until the enough individuals are generated. Its implementation result is given as Figure 4. Among them, $c\_num = 51$, $c\_avg\_Mean = 0.893\ 22$, $c\_avg\_Max\_Min = 0.029\ 167$, $S\_avg(1) = 8.776\ 4e - 0.006$, $c\_avg\_Var = 3.877\ 9e - 0.005$.

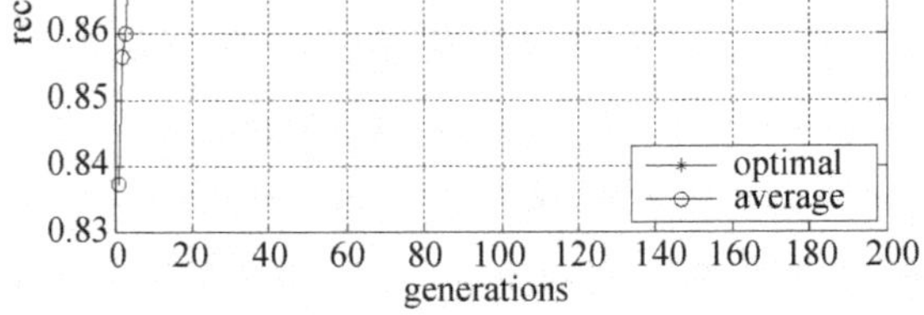

Figure 4 Feature selection result using tournament selection method

As shown in Figure 4, the algorithm converges at the 20th generation around. It has much more better performances of feature selection results than non-linear ranking selection method from the aspects of number of feature amounts, the difference between the maximum and minimum, the trend, and the error of average recognition rate. And the tournament selection method also has nice dynamic performance and can avoid a premature convergence to a certain extent. But this method has poor off line performance.

4 Hybrid selection strategy of non-linear ranking and tournament

Although each of the non-linear ranking and tournament selection method has its advantages, and the effect is more excellent when used separately than selection method based on probability, each of them has its own disadvantages respectively. This paper attempts to adopt a hybrid selection strategy of non-linear ranking and tournament methods. Non-linear ranking algorithm is used in the beginning in order to overcome the premature and stagnation problems, furthermore to improve the tournament search algorithm which has the shortcomings of unfavorable searching other viable regions. In the later genetic algorithm, tournament algorithm is used to enhance the dynamic performance and increase the computing speed so as to overcome its low computational speed disadvantage. Its implementation result is given as Figure 5. Among them, $c\_num = 42$, $c\_avg\_Mean = 0.894\,38$, $c\_avg\_Max\_Min = 0.025$, $S\_avg(1) = -8.203e - 0.006$, $c\_avg\_Var = 2.95e - 0.005$.

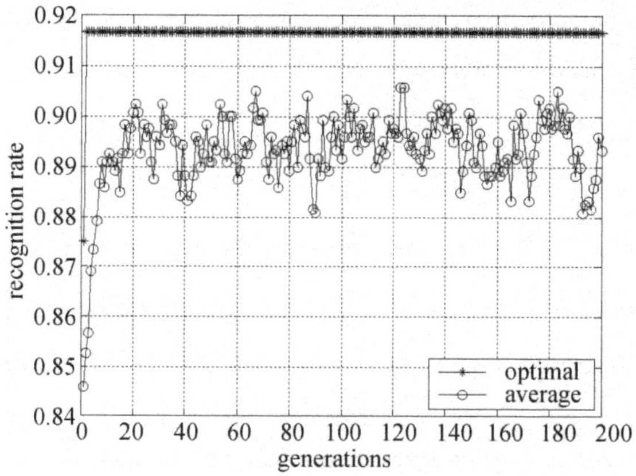

Figure 5 Feature selection result using hybrid selection strategy of non-linear ranking and tournament method

As shown in Figure 5, the genetic algorithm converges at the 20th generation around and the average recognition rate converges to 89.4% around. 42 features are selected. As can be seen from Figure 5, the hybrid algorithm has made great improvements, the features number significantly reduces. The difference between the maximum and minimum of average recognition rate is reduced to 2.5%. The trend tends to level basically and the error is also small. All these indicate that such improvements are very effective.

5 Conclusion

This paper focuses on the adaptive improvement of selection step of SGA. Some common operation methods of selection operator of SGA are implemented and compared. A new hybrid selection strategy of non-linear ranking and tournament is proposed. And experiment result shows that this hybrid selection method. Feature selection results show that there are considerable and more effective improvements of feature amounts, after the hybrid algorithm compares with two separate algorithms from the following parameters, such as the number of feature amounts, the difference between the maximum and minimum, the trend, and the error of average recognition rate.

Acknowledgement

This paper is one of the progressive achievements of Southeast University Natural Science Pre-research Foundation "research of emotion recognition and emotion sensor network based on multiple physiological and behavioral signals for education" (9250180010) and Jiangsu Province Education Science "Eleventh Five-Year Plan" Planning Project "research of wireless sensor network for education application" (D/2009/09/07)

References

[1] Picard R W, Vyzas E, Healey J. Toward machine emotional intelligence, analysis of affective physiological state. IEEE Transactions on Pattern Analysis and Machine Intelligence, 2001, 23(10): 1175-1191.

[2] Multimedia concepts and applications. http://mm-werkatatt.informatik.uni-augsburg.de/project_details.php? id=33, 2008.

[3] Healey J A. Wearable and Automotive Systems for Affect Recognition from Physiology. Cambridge, MA: MIT, 2000.

[4] Zhou Hai-sheng. Research on emotion recognition with physiological signals based on adaptive genetic algorithm. Nanjing: Southeast University, 2011.

[5] Nasoz F, Alvarez K, Lisetti C L, et al. Emotion recognition from physiological signals for

presence technologies. International Journal of Cognition Technology and Work, Special Issue on Presence, 2003, 6(1): 1 -32.

[6] Kim K H, Bang S W, Kim S R. Emotion recognition system using short-term monitoring of physiological signals. Medical and Biological Engineering and Computing, 2004, 42(3): 419 -427.

[7] Haag A, Goronzy S, Schaich P, et al. Emotion recognition using bio-sensors: First step towards an automatic system. Affective Dialogue Systems, Kloster Irsee, Germany, 2004, 3068: 36 -48.

[8] Cai Lianhong. Affective computing. Communications of China Computer Federation, 2010, 6 (5): 5 -8.

[9] Chen Jihua, Li Lan, Qian Kun-xi. Emotion recognition by physiological signals. Journal of Biomedical Engineering Research, 2006, 25(3): 141 -146.

[10] Bian Zhaoqi, Zhang Xuegong. Pattern Recognition. Beijing: Tsinghua University Press, 2000.

[11] Wagner J, Kim J, Andre E. From physiological signals to emotions: Implementing and comparing selected methods for feature extraction and classification. IEEE International Conference on Multimedia & Expo, 2005.

[12] Villon O, Lisetti C. A User Model of Psycho-physiological Measure of Emotion. Berlin: Sprineger, 2007.

[13] Zhou Ming, Sun Shudong. Genetic Algorithms: Theory and Applications. Beijing: National Defence Industry Press, 1999.

[14] Li Minqiang, Kou jisong. Basic Theory and Applications of Genetic Algorithms. Beijing: Science Press, 2004.

[15] Xu Xiaohua, Chen Ling, Chen Hong-jian. Genetic algorithm with variable population size. Journal of System Simulation, 2006, 18(4): 870 -872.

[16] Wang Ning. Urban distribution network structure planning based on adaptive genetic algorithms. Baoding: North China Electric Power University, 2007.

A Pilot Investigations of the Effects of Gender, Diurnal Variation, and Age in Children Salivary Imidazole Compounds Profiles

Zhao Zhang[1,a], Xuejun Kang[1,b,*], Lei Ma[1,c], Yu Wang[1,d], Xiaoxiao Wu[1,e]

[1]Key Laboratory of Child Development and Learning Science of Ministry of Education, Research Center for Learning Science, Southeast University, Nanjing, 210096, China

[a]zhzhzz@qq.com, [b]xjkang64@163.com, [c]mlmyhero@163.com, [d]w.yuer@163.com, [e]wxx2010xiaoxiao@139.com

[*]Corresponding author

Keywords: Histidine; Child; Stress; Age

Abstract: As a non-invasive fluid, saliva has been suggested to reflect the physiological and psychological state of human. Imidazole compounds are present in all mammals in different concentrations which have multiple functions closely related to human health. Imidazole compounds in saliva contain free histidine and histatins, closely related to children development. The present paper is the first report of the concentration level of imidazole compounds in children saliva and it documents the investigations of the effects of gender, diurnal variation, and age in children salivary imidazole compounds profiles. 57 subjects were investigated in this study, and 6 volunteers (3 boys and 3 girls) were chosen to participate in the diurnal changes research. The diurnal changes research indicated that the concentration of imidazole compounds changed with circadian rhythm. The Determination method was based on chromatic reaction with Pauly reagent by flow injection-spectrophotometer, quick, high-precision and reproducible. The mean concentration of all the samples was (28.09 ± 11.87) g/mL. There was a significant difference with age, but no significant difference was observed with gender. In conclusion, salivary imidazole compounds may be a possible biological marker of social psychological stress.

1 Introduction

The advances in analytical technique enable a variety of analytes to be measured in non-invasive fluid which are helpful for behavioral scientists to explore the correlates and concomitants of the interaction between the human response, intrinsic factors, and social forces as they occur naturally in everyday life. Human saliva contains appreciable quantities of substance, and has a good correlation with blood. Saliva sample collection is convenient, fast and inexpensive, thus, in contrast to more traditional biological specimens (e.g., urine or plasma), analytic measurements in saliva seem to afford researchers an opportunity to gather measures of the confluence of biobehavioral processes in response to variation in individuals' everyday interpersonal demands and experiences[1].

Imidazole compounds are present in all mammals in different concentrations which have multiple functions closely related to human health. The imidazole side chain is a common coordinating ligand that controls the transmission of metal ions in biological bases[2]. In human saliva, imidazole compounds mainly contain free histidine and histatins. Histidine is a precursor of histamine which has been established to play a important role as a neurotransmitter in the central nervous system[3,4]. Histatins are a family of histidine-rich proteins found in saliva which have known functions, i. e. antimicrobial action, wound closure, biomarkers of stress, satiety, body mass and incipient Alzheimer's disease, and diagnosis and treatment of addictive disorders[5]. Thus, more investigations are needed for better understanding the mechanisms of action of salivary imidazole compounds before these targets are brought into clinical use or psychic stress assessment for human.

As far as we know, the present paper is the first report of the concentration level of imidazole compounds in children saliva. Furthermore, it documents the investigations of the effects of gender, diurnal variation, and age in children salivary imidazole compounds profiles. This work can be considered a pilot study for the future application of salivary imidazole compounds in the assessment of children psychic stress.

2 Methods

2.1 Subjects

A total of 57 subjects were investigated in this study. 24 children at the age of 6 or 7 and 33 children at the age of 10 or 11 were recruited from a primary school student population, including 29 boys and 28 girls. 6 volunteers (3 boys and 3 girls) were chosen to participate in the diurnal changes research.

2.2 Sample preparation

In the diurnal changes research, the collection of saliva was carried out at 8:00, 9:00, 10:00, 12:00, 13:00, 15:00, 17:00, 18:00, 20:00, 22:00. The three meals were prepared distinctively, and only water was allowed to be drunk. In the age & gender-related research, the saliva collection was at the same time at 15:00. The saliva sample was collected in a very short time (2—3 min), at least 2 h after eating, and after having washed the mouth with water three times. The samples were placed in plastic tubes which were closed immediately to preserve labile markers and frozen at −40 ℃ until use.

Likewise, for the determination of imidazole compounds in saliva, sample was thawed, centrifuged for 5 min at 12 000 r/min. The supernatant was collected for the determination.

2.3 Determination of imidazole compounds concentration

Imidazole compounds determination was based on chromatic reaction with pauly reagent as described in our previous paper[6]. Figure 1 exhibits the determination system constructed in our group, including a flow injection sampler, a spectrophotometer and a PC to collect the data. The linear range of imidazole compounds amount suited for this method is 5—200 μg/mL, and standard curve correlation coefficient is 0.999 1. The determining diagram is shown in Figure 2. This methed is quick (less than 4 minutes per sample), high-precision and reproducible, suitable for a large sample detection.

Figure 1 Photograph of the determination system

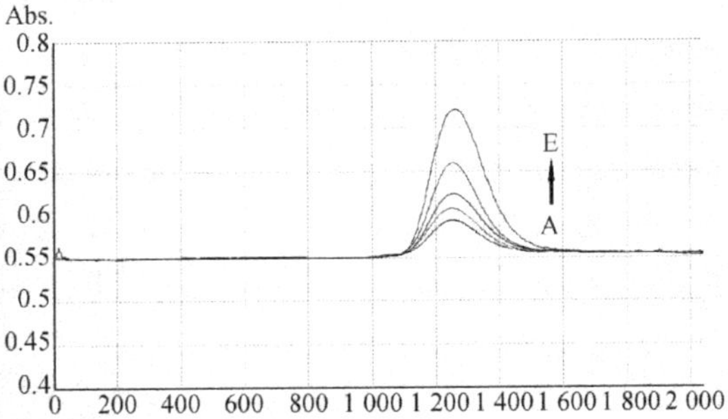

Figure 2 Diagram of flow injection analysis

2.4 Statistical analysis

Basic data processing and analysis were realized in Excel, including histidine levels at different time points. Changes of His levels before and after the experiment were examined by the method of Paired-sample T test. Independent-Sample T test was used to analyze the difference of His levels and its response to exercise stress in saliva of children between two age groups. The results were meaningful and reported if they achieved the level of significance at least $p < 0.05$.

3 Results and discussion

All the samples were determined using the above method. Figure 3 shows the diurnal changes in the mean concentration of imidazole compounds. In general, at 8:00 in the morning, the concentration was at a high level, and then it went down at 10:00. At lunch time (12:00), it increased and kept high till 15:00. Before supper (17:00), the concentration decreased distinctly. It reached another high level at about 20:00.

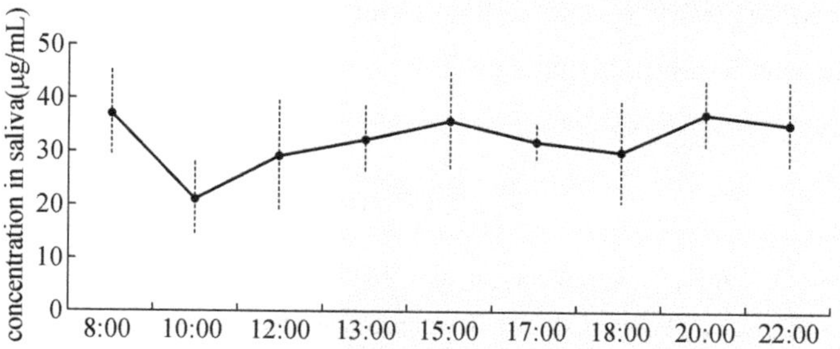

Figure 3 Changes in the mean imidazole compounds concentration and the standard deviations in saliva of the six volunteers

The mean concentration of all the samples was 28. 09 μg/mL, and the standard deviations is 11.87. Salivary imidazole compounds of age brackets and gender are shown in Table 1. There was a significant difference with age ($p < 0.001$). The salivary imidazole compounds concentration of younger children (6—7) was higher than that of elder children (10—11). No significant difference was observed between boys and girls ($p > 0.05$).

Table1 Age & gender-related mean concentrations and standard deviations

		Salivary imidazole compounds(μg/mL)	
		mean concentrations	standard deviations
Age	6—7 ($N=24$)	34.24	10.93
	10—11 ($N=33$)	23.61	10.57
Gender	male ($N=29$)	26.55	11.88
	female ($N=28$)	29.68	11.86

4 Conclusion

It is the first time to report salivary concentrations of imidazole compounds. The present study demonstrated that salivary concentrations of imidazole compounds were significantly related to circadian rhythm and ages. For children the concentrations was decreasing with the growth of age.

It has been reported that stress can affects saliva composition[7,8], therefore salivary imidazole compounds may be a possible biological marker of social psychological stress. In the later research, a large sample stress experiment will be needed to verify this viewpoint.

Acknowledgement

This work was supported by the National Natural Science Foundation of China (No.

81172720, and No. 21307086) and Colleges and universities in Jiangsu Province plans to graduate research and innovation projects.

References

[1] D Granger, L Hibel, C Fortunato, et al. Medication effects on salivary cortisol: Tactics and strategy to minimize impact in behavioral and developmental science. Psychoneuroendocrinology, 2009, 34: 1437 - 1448.

[2] Y Hu, Q Wang, C Zheng, et al. Recyclable decoration of amine-functionalized magnetic nanoparticles with Ni (2 +) for determination of histidine by photochemical vapor generation atomic spectrometry. Analytical Chemistry, 2014, 86: 842 - 848.

[3] Z Chen, C Kamei. Faciletating effects of histamine on spatial memory deficit induced by scopalamin in rats. Acta Pharmacologica Sinica, 2000, 21: 814 - 818.

[4] Z Chen, Y Sugimoto. Effects of intracerebroventracular injection of α-fluoromethylhistidine on radial maze performance in rats. Pharmacology Biochemistry and Behavior, 1999, 64: 513 - 518.

[5] M Caldero' n-Santiago, M D Luque de Castro. The dual trend in histatins research. Trends in Analytical Chemistry, 2009, 28: 1011 - 1018.

[6] Y Wang and Z Zhang. Determination of histidine in saliva by Flow injection—Spectrophotometer. 7th National Instrument Analysis and Sample Preparation Conference Proceedings, 2013.

[7] N M Gomes, M Katsurayama, F Makimoto, et al. Psychological stress and its influence on salivary flow rate, total protein concentration and IgA, IgG and IgM titers. Neroimmunomodulation, 2010, 17: 396 - 404.

[8] H Tsuboi, M Hamer, G Tanaka. Responses of ultra-weak chemiluminescence and secretory IgA in saliva to the induction of angry and depressive moods. Brain, Behavior, and Immunity, 2008, 22: 209 - 214.

The Study on Development Situation of Information and Communication Technology Education in China, Singapore, Korea and Japan—Base on PISA2012 ICT Questionnaire Data

Zhishan Liu[1,a], Yi Bai[1,b,*]

[1]Key Laboratory of Child Development and Learning Science of Ministry of Education, Southeast University, Nanjing, Jiangsu, China

[a]zhishanliu0421@126.com, [b]by.rcls@seu.edu.cn

[*]Corresponding author

Keywords: PISA2012; ICT questionnaire; ICT education; ICT popularization; ICT application

Abstract: It cannot be ignored that the prospect of ICT used in the educational field. ICT is a method providing a better teaching circumstance for the learners and educators through the huge energy of computer and network. Base on PISA2012 database, this paper discussed the popularity of ICT equipment, the use of ICT equipment and student attitudes towards ICT in China, Singapore, Korea and Japan. Through description and analysis of PISA2012 ICT questionnaire data, the study hopes to understand the overall development situation of ICT education and provide references for the sustainable development of ICT education in China.

中新韩日 ICT 教育发展情况研究
——基于 PISA2012ICT 问卷数据

刘枳杉[1,a]，柏毅[1,b,*]
[1]东南大学儿童发展与学习科学教育部重点实验室，南京，江苏，中国
[a]zhishanliu0421@126.com，[b]by.rcls@seu.edu.cn[*]
[*]通讯作者

关键词：PISA2012；ICT 问卷；ICT 教育；ICT 普及；ICT 运用

中文摘要：ICT 在教育领域中的运用具有不可忽视的前景，它是一种通过计算机和网络的巨大能量为学习者和教育者提供更好的教学服务的方式。本文根据 PISA2012ICT 问卷数据分别讨论了中新韩日 ICT 设备的普及情况、ICT 设备的运用情况以及学生对待 ICT 的态度，旨在通过对 PISA2012ICT 问卷数据的描述和分析，得到中新韩日的 ICT 教育发展整体情况，以期对中国 ICT 教育持续发展提供参考与借鉴。

1 前言

ICT，全称 Information and Communication Technology，其中 Information 和 Technology 分别译为“信息”和“技术”，Communication 可理解为“通讯”、“通信”、“传播”、“交流”等，因此 ICT 可相应译作“信息通讯技术”、“信息通信技术”、“信息传播技术”、“信息交流技术”。ICT 最早由英国提出，1999 年英国政府颁布了《信息与交流技术课程标准》（The National Curriculum for England：Information and Communication Technology），并于 2000 年明确把以前的“信息技术（IT）”课程变更为“信息与交流技术（ICT）”课程[1]。

ICT 在教育领域中的运用具有不可忽视的前景，它能通过网络和计算机的巨大能量为学习者和教育者提供更高质量的教学体验，改善教学内容和教学过程，增强师生之间的联系，为学习和教学创建一种全新的、动态的并且能够进行实时交互的讨论空间。在 21 世纪信息化的社会中，英国成为首个将 ICT 教育普及为全民教育的国家，并推动 ICT 教育成为世界各国教育研究的热点，中国国内专家称 ICT 为教育信息化。在教育领域中，ICT 不只是组织学习内容的手段，也不只是传统教育的辅助工具，它更是推动整个教育体系发展的主要因素，它促使教育的目标、内容、方法、形式甚至学校结构等方面都发生深刻的变革，ICT 与教育的整合是当前教育中的一种重要趋势[2]。

PISA（Programme for International Student Assessment）是 OECD（经济合作与发展组织）组织的“国际学生评价项目”，是全球范围进行的一项大型学生学习质量比较研

究[3]。PISA 的测评领域为阅读、数学和科学，每三年一次，九年一个大循环，每次以三个领域中一个为重点测评领域，每次测试都会对被测者学习环境、生活和家庭等方面的背景进行调查，以此来判断被测者背景对其成绩的影响。2000 年 PISA 首测，主要领域为阅读素养，设计了学生问卷、学校问卷、电脑使用能力问卷以及跨学科能力问卷四种调查问卷，分别调查学生的家庭背景、学习环境、技术能力和学科水平。2003 年，PISA 主测数学素养，将电脑使用能力问卷变更为 ICT 问卷，将跨学科能力问卷变更为教育事业问卷，之后 PISA2006（科学）、PISA2009（阅读）、PISA2012（数学）都对 ICT 教育情况进行了调查，其中中国上海从 2009 年开始参与 PISA 测试，并参与 PISA 的问卷调查。

PISA 虽然设计了不同的问卷来对学生进行调查研究，但无论问卷类别如何变化，PISA 每次测试都会设计学生问卷、学校问卷和 ICT 问卷，由此看出，涉及全世界多个国家的国际评测项目 PISA 正持续关注着学生的家庭背景、学习环境以及各国 ICT 教育发展情况对学生能力发展所带来的影响。

2012 年 PISA 测试中约有 51 万学生完成了评估，学生年龄从 15 岁 3 个月到 16 岁 2 个月不等，他们代表着 65 个参与国家和地区学校的 2800 万 15 岁左右的学生[4]。本文将以 2012 年 PISA 测试中 ICT 问卷得出的最新数据为依据，以在 PISA 测试中取得较好成绩的四个亚太地区和国家，即中国上海（第一名）、新加坡（第二名）及韩国（第五名）、日本（第七名）为对象，对亚太地区各地区和国家的 ICT 教育发展情况进行概述，以期对中国 ICT 教育持续发展带来参考借鉴和启示。

2　中新韩日 ICT 教育发展概况

2.1　中国 ICT 教育发展概况

ICT 教育始于西方国家，在西方迅速发展并得以推广。虽然我国的 ICT 教育发展迟于西方国家，但中国并未忽视 ICT 教育的重要性，近年来，ICT 在我国教育领域的应用发展十分迅速。

由于中国的感性思维方式与西方国家的抽象思维方式有所区别，中国的 ICT 教育发展较少关注成效。也就是说，国家对 ICT 教育应用投入了大量资源，并不断进行着各种各样的 ICT 教育实验项目，例如，全国教育科学“十五”规划教育部重点课题广东教育信息技术科研课题网络教育的资源整合研究《基础教育信息化资源开发应用的有效性研究》（广东省电教馆）以及《信息技术在中小学教育中应用的有效性研究》[1]等，但对于 ICT 教育在中国的普及情况以及应用情况却缺乏整体的把握和了解，换句话说，并没有研究表明中国的 ICT 教育普及到底达到了一个怎样的水平。

我国作为一个教育资源不算优厚的发展中国家，相比于国外经费来源广，我国大部分教育经费来源单一——仅来自于政府拨款，可以说，我国发展 ICT 教育的风险是要高于经济发达且教育经费充足的国家。因此在中国 ICT 教育的未来研究中，我们不得不考虑成本以及有效性的问题,清楚把握ICT教育的普及、应用、发展速度、质量等问题,才能为政府、教育部门的ICT教育投入决策提供必要依据。

2.2 新加坡ICT教育发展概况

从20世纪80年代起,新加坡就以信息技术发展作为国家施政目标,有计划地规划信息通信产业发展道路。新加坡教育部1995年提出AICTP计划,明确将信息技术作为初等学校学生的辅助学习工具[5]。1997年新加坡实施了ICT教育总规划,将信息技术结合到教育中,明确信息化教育总体目标,奠定了ICT教育发展的基础。2003、2009年新加坡分别实施了第二个、第三个ICT教育总规划。第二个ICT教育总规划强调信息技术是提升教学水平的有力手段,学校要在信息技术大环境中摸索、试验、探索信息技术与学科教学整合途径,发挥信息技术的作用以满足学生需求,构建思考型学校和学习型社会[6]。而第三个ICT教育总规划则表达了一种愿景,包括要求学校领导者创造条件,教师有能力通过ICT进行教授,学生能够有效应用ICT发展自我和合作学习。

从对教师进行培训,对ICT进行研究,组建实验室到对未来学校的愿景,新加坡一直致力于实现有意义的ICT教育。为了能够推动ICT教育更好地发展,无论是在ICT授权、互联网接入还是在硬件设施、人员与技术支持方面,新加坡政府以及新加坡的各学校都给予了鼎力支持。

2.3 韩国ICT教育发展概况

韩国是亚太地区中较早引入ICT教育的国家。20世纪70年代,韩国教育发展研究所属下的"小学电脑教育问题研究机构"成为研究中小学计算机教育的第一个政府部门。1987年,韩国教育部在教育改革发展计划指导下颁布《韩国计算机教育提高计划》,从政策上扶持ICT教育全面发展[5]。有专家曾提出,韩国经济的迅速发展很大程度上得益于教育信息化的普及深入。韩国对于ICT教育普及给予了高度的重视,不仅推进韩国中小学教育信息化,使学生解决问题的能力和学习能力得到提高,同时也培养了一些能够主导知识经济社会的创造性人才。

韩国是紧随芬兰、英国的脚步,对ICT教育做出了详细规划的国家,它的ICT课程教育特点表现在两个方面:其一是突出ICT课程建设的规范性,建立ICT课程标准;其二是强调ICT和其他课程整合的针对性,针对不同学科开发与之相应的学科整合教材[7]。韩国ICT教育发展一直走在亚太地区前沿,在推动ICT教育发展中,不仅给更多教师配备ICT设备并传授其使用应用技巧,还给更多的学生提供了更便利的接触ICT设备的机会。因此对于其他国家来说,韩国ICT教育的很多做法,例如明确分工各司其职、建立完善的配套设置、对弱势群体采取扶助措施等都是非常值得借鉴和参考的。

2.4 日本ICT教育发展概况

20世纪80年代,日本实行"教员方法开发特别设备"国库补助,出台了促进普通教育和职业教育信息化发展的系列政策。90年代,日本信息素质教育赶超西方,制定了一系列计划和政策,如1990年九年行动计划,为全部学校配备多媒体和软件,1994年建立“百校联网工程”,2006年制定了信息技术改革新战略,明确教育信息化发展方向、具体目标等。

2008年,在日本中央教育审议会报告中,明确提出:“利用ICT进行高效的学习指导是极为重要的。”[8]日本文部科学省认为ICT对于推动教育变革具有积极的作用,因此不断地以各种方式促进ICT教育的发展。在教师使用ICT教学层面上,日本发现即使是参加了各种ICT培训的日本老师依旧很难灵活、合理、高效地运用ICT进行教学,因此日本文部科学省制定了“教师活用指导力比照表”,其对教师ICT活用指导力的各项基本技能都进行了详细的描述,以强调ICT灵活运用的重要性并推进了ICT教育的发展。除此之外,日本还强调并普及了ICT教育应用对外语学习、交流、扩大视野等方面具有正面的影响。在英语教学中应用ICT,学生能够通过网络更加便利地收集外国的各种信息和资料,考察国外文化、语言,不仅增长了知识,而且促进了对其他民族文化的进一步理解[9]。

由此可以看出,日本在扶持ICT教育并促使其快速稳定发展的道路上一直没有停下前进的脚步。

3 中新韩日ICT设备普及情况

根据PISA2012ICT问卷问题IC01“哪些ICT设备是你平常在家能使用的”及IC02“哪些ICT设备是你平常在校能使用的”的调查数据,将ICT设备普及情况分为三类,一是配备了ICT设备并投入使用,二是配备了ICT设备但没有投入使用,三是未配备ICT设备。本文选取问卷中较为典型的四种ICT设备,即台式电脑、笔记本电脑、平板电脑及联网手机,对配备ICT设备并投入使用及配备ICT设备但没有投入使用的数据结果进行研究和分析。

3.1 配备ICT设备,并能够使用ICT设备

根据表1所呈现的数据,可以得到以下信息。首先,从设备所在地来看,中新韩日在家庭和学校配备使用笔记本电脑、平板电脑等未大面积普及的设备上的情况上是一致的,均为在家庭中的配备、使用情况要优于在学校中配备、使用情况。但就台式电脑的配备和使用来看,日本和新加坡为了推动ICT教育的发展,致力于在所有学校里配备台式电脑并鼓励学生使用,因此其普及率不仅高于在家庭中的台式电脑普及率,也远远高于中国上海和韩国在学校的台式电脑普及率。其次,从四个国家或地区来看,通过比较发现仅有新加坡每一项百分比都接近和超过OECD的平均值,不难看出新加坡对ICT教育普及的支持力度比另三个国家更大。而中国上海每一项ICT设备普及率均低于OECD平均值,这说明中国虽然在PISA测试中荣获世界第一,但其ICT教育发展水平却未达到世界第一应该具备的水平。最后,从ICT设备来看,台式电脑

在家庭和学校的普及率要高于笔记本电脑和平板电脑的普及率，这可能是由于台式笔记本电脑的性价比相对于其他 ICT 设备更高。除此之外，表 1 数据还支持了“现代社会手机的普及率非常高”这个结论，四个国家或地区配备和使用联网手机的比例均达到 70% 以上，高于 OECD 平均值。

表 1　中日韩新 15 岁学生家庭及学校配备、使用 ICT 设备的百分比　（单位：%）

选项＼国家		中国上海	新加坡	韩国	日本	OECD 平均值
家庭	台式电脑	64.19	57.03	71.96	43.54	66.45
	笔记本电脑	39.8	74.86	31.29	52.29	56.06
	平板电脑	18.62	34.84	13.52	17.65	22.64
学校	台式电脑	37.3	63.24	38.35	51.76	62.63
	笔记本电脑	2.03	28.37	8.58	11.32	25.2
	平板电脑	1.06	8.55	2.33	5.31	5.27
联网手机		77.64	75.64	86.74	78.59	69.37

数据来源：Database-PISA 2012。

3.2　配备 ICT 设备，但并不使用 ICT 设备

在四个国家或地区中，有部分学校和家庭配备了 ICT 设备但并未投入使用，从表 2 中可以看出，中新韩日在学校配备了台式电脑但并未使用的比例均高于 OECD 平均值，除此之外，其余配备的 ICT 设备未被使用的概率也相对较高，由此可见有一部分 ICT 设备处在被闲置的状况下，并未发挥它的作用。

表 2　中日韩新 15 岁学生家庭及学校配备但不使用 ICT 设备的百分比　（单位：%）

选项＼国家		中国上海	新加坡	韩国	日本	OECD 平均值
家庭	台式电脑	15.65	18.85	5.63	12.52	13.22
	笔记本电脑	19.06	12.68	16.15	15.04	9.47
	平板电脑	10.83	10.03	6.13	6.75	6.86
学校	台式电脑	45.26	31.05	40.82	24.68	22.6
	笔记本电脑	14.3	28.42	37.54	13.53	15.81
	平板电脑	5.29	14.67	10.46	7.36	5.74
联网手机		14.1	7.85	6.29	4.75	9.23

数据来源：Database-PISA 2012。

3.3 小结

在2012PISA测试中获得亚军的新加坡在ICT设备的普及方面做得比中国上海、韩国和日本更好,不仅是在学校中ICT设备普及率相对较高,在设备使用率上也比另外三个地区或国家高。这得益于新加坡政府在国家推动ICT教育发展方面给予了鼎力支持,并且致力于全民普及ICT教育,这是值得其他国家借鉴和学习的。虽然中国上海在PISA测试中获得了冠军,但中国的ICT设备普及相对比较落后,仍然需要大力推动和发展,这样才能够更好地维持世界第一的教育水准。

另外,各国在配备ICT设备的同时,应该加强对ICT设备使用方法和技巧的普及。由PISA2012ICT问卷数据所知,部分配备的ICT设备被闲置,这个现象出现的原因可能是由于使用者自身使用ICT设备的技术所限,或者是教师并未掌握使用ICT设备教授学生的技术,因而放弃使用ICT设备。这不仅是在浪费资源,也是教育事业的止步不前,更使得ICT设备不能够被充分利用,不能更好地帮助学生学习。由此可见,在解决ICT设备闲置的问题上,对教师和学生进行ICT设备使用及应用技术的培训是必不可少的。

4 中日韩新ICT设备运用情况

根据PISA2012ICT问卷问题IC08、IC09"你在家使用ICT设备进行以下活动的频率如何"及IC10"你在学校使用ICT设备进行以下活动的频率如何"的调查数据,将ICT设备运用频率分为5种,分别为每天、几乎每天、1—2次/周、1—2次/月、从不或很少。本文选取问卷中较为典型的使用ICT设备进行的六种活动,即在线聊天、收发E-mail、浏览网页(学习)、浏览网页(娱乐)、完成作业、使用社交网站/小组交流活动,对学生高频使用ICT进行以上活动的数据结果进行研究和分析。

4.1 高频运用ICT设备(几乎每天,每天)

ICT设备能运用于诸多方面,但运用ICT设备进行各项活动的时候存在较为明显的校内校外差异,就OECD平均值来看,学生在校外使用ICT设备进行活动的频繁程度远高于在校内使用ICT设备进行活动,最大相差约为60%。由表3可以看出,除了日本在收发E-mail的频繁程度高于OECD平均值以外,四个国家或地区运用ICT设备进行其余活动的频繁程度均低于OECD平均值,并且频繁使用ICT设备进行活动的人数接近或低于总人数的50%。在线聊天和使用社交网站是学生在校外运用ICT设备的主要活动,频率较高,同时,通过ICT设备进行学习和完成作业此类学习活动的频繁程度则较低。

表 3　中日韩新 15 岁学生校外、校内高频使用 ICT 设备的百分比　　（单位:%）

选项		中国上海	新加坡	韩国	日本	OECD 平均值
校外	在线聊天	50.31	23.33	22.71	26.87	51.84
	收发 E-mail	9.19	26.04	6.26	63.29	35.41
	使用社交网站	46.29	68.54	31.52	34.9	69.86
	浏览网页(学习)	8.71	15.78	4.05	2.78	17.95
	浏览网页(娱乐)	29.36	66.7	28.29	51.16	67.97
	完成作业	4.39	14.44	6.52	0.99	20.19
校内	在线聊天	3.76	3.88	2.36	1.16	7.81
	收发 E-mail	1.34	5.8	0.86	9.05	7.18
	小组活动交流	1.37	4.2	0.79	0.64	7.21
	浏览网页(学习)	1.88	8.34	1.86	1.39	13.87
	完成作业	0.93	4.93	1.01	0.62	7.72

数据来源:Database-PISA 2012

4.2　小结

学生在校外运用 ICT 设备的频率比在校内运用 ICT 设备的概率高,其一部分原因在于校内的 ICT 设备由学校控制,学生并不能随意接触到这些设备,需要通过特殊的方式或者上课来获得使用这些设备的权利,这对学生运用 ICT 设备进行活动产生一些阻碍。从四个国家或地区的数据低于 OECD 平均值来看,四个国家或地区都还没有达到高度的信息化,而要达到频繁运用 ICT 设备进行日常活动还需要一定的促进条件以及充足的时间。当然,由于 ICT 设备具有一定的娱乐性,这必然削弱了 ICT 设备在教育中的优势,当大多数学生选择使用 ICT 设备进行娱乐而不是学习的时候,家长以及学校就应该采取一些措施来控制不良影响的产生,例如,限制使用 ICT 设备的时间等。虽然 ICT 设备的运用会出现负面影响,但我们不能因噎废食,应该采取一定的措施来加强其积极作用、削弱其负面缺点,使得 ICT 设备能够更好地造福学生。

5　中日韩新学生对 ICT 的态度

根据 PISA2012ICT 问卷问题 IC22"你怎么看待 ICT",该题罗列了对 ICT 的六种看法,并给予每一项看法四个选择,分别为非常赞成、赞成、不赞成、非常不赞成。本文根据对这六种看法表示非常赞成及赞成的学生人数百分比数据进行研究和分析。

5.1 对ICT的态度

由图1可知,中新韩日四个国家或地区一半以上的人对ICT持乐观正面的态度,即对学习有帮助、使作业更有意思及作为信息来源这三个选项的赞同度较高。虽然中新韩日均看好ICT,但仅有新加坡一个国家每一个选项持正面看法的人数百分比能够接近和超过OECD平均值。对于中国学生来说,大约91%的中国学生认为ICT主要是作为一种信息来源,赞同人数百分比超过了OECD的平均值,并且赞同负面意见,即制造麻烦、不可信的人数百分比均低于OECD平均值。

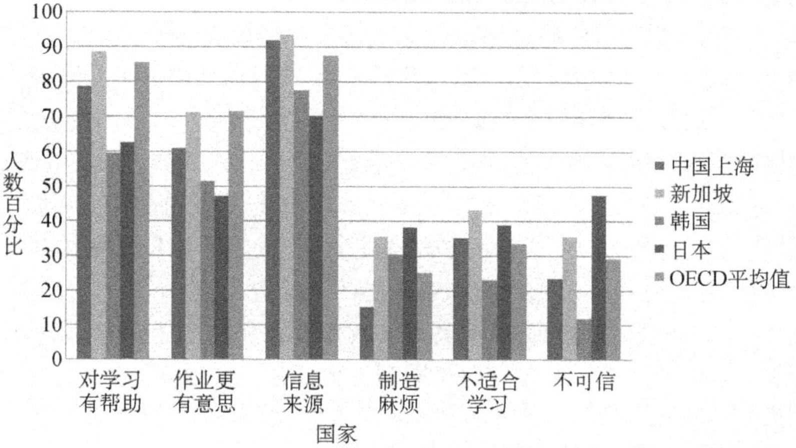

图1　中新韩日15岁学生对ICT的态度(单位:%)

数据来源:Database-PISA 2012

5.2 小结

对于ICT运用于教育领域,大多数学生持积极的态度,支持并认为ICT能够帮助他们更好地学习,这得益于国家的推广力度及各项促进ICT发展的策略。新加坡ICT发展迅速,但持正面看法的人数虽超过OECD平均值,持负面看法的人数也比中国上海、韩国和日本更多,这可以看出,新加坡人对ICT持批判态度,认为ICT能够对学习有帮助但并不是最适合学习的方式,虽然能够让作业更有意思但也会由于ICT设备的其他特性导致出现一些麻烦,是信息的最大来源但也存在信息不可信的情况。而相比于新加坡学生的选择,中国学生赞成正面看法和赞成负面看法的百分比都处在中间位置,这反映了中国人的中庸思想和平均主义。韩国和日本两国在赞成正面看法方面差距不大,但在赞成负面看法方面,近50%的日本人认为ICT不可信,比例远远高于其他三个国家或地区,本文认为出现这个情况的原因之一可能是由于受到日本传统文化的影响。

6 中国ICT教育的启示

从PISA2012ICT问卷数据的分析结果来看，新加坡虽然成绩居于中国上海之下，但其各项教育发展比中国上海更具前沿性，尤其是ICT教育的发展，其普及程度、应用程度都相对较高，学生对待ICT的态度也很明确，有自己看法并不随波逐流。

新加坡之所以能够在ICT教育方面更接近世界水平，这得益于新加坡政府在推进和发展ICT教育上实行的诸多措施。从ICT教育总规划的提出、修改、完善及实施到ICT教育总规划3的愿景及规划指导，新加坡一直按照规划所提出的工作有条不紊的推广着ICT。如今，新加坡已经开始执行ICT教育总规划3，其中包含了新加坡对未来ICT教育发展的愿景，分别为利用ICT实现推动者目标和利用ICT实现成果目标。推动者目标包含学校领导者为ICT在教和学之中的应用指明方向并创造条件；教师要有能力规划并传授通过ICT得以强化的学习经验；ICT基础设施可以随时随地支持学习。这不仅要求推广和普及ICT设备更要求推广ICT设备的使用技巧和方法，防止ICT设备的闲置。成果目标主要指的是学生通过有效应用ICT来发展自我指导与合作学习的能力，并且成为有辨别能力和责任心的ICT应用者。

中国虽获得PISA2012的冠军，但其ICT教育发展并没有达到国际的平均水平，这是中国教育所必须要努力的一个方向。同为亚太国家，新加坡与中国的思维习惯相比西方人来说更为相似，而新加坡ICT教育的发展紧跟国际水平，因此新加坡推广ICT所使用的措施和策略将会成为中国ICT教育的一个非常好的借鉴和参考。

中国在借鉴新加坡ICT教育发展的基础上，推动ICT教育发展还需要以本土教育背景为基础来制定目标，并拟定实现该目标的计划，保证软硬件之间的平衡，结合新时代的要求，实现长期跟踪进展和调查，相信这将会是促进中国ICT教育迅速崛起的一个强有效的方法。

致谢

本文为教育部人文社会科学研究专项任务《基础教育阶段技术和设计教育的国际比较研究》(11JDGC026)的阶段性成果之一。

References

[1] Liu Xiangyu. Research of International Effectiveness Indicators on ICT for Education and Some Inspiration. Jilin: Northeast Normal University, 2007.

[2] Chen Xiaochun, Zhou Caiying. Three attributes of ITC education: Science, morality and artistry. Journal of Hetan Teachers College, 2005(1): 69 - 70.

[3] Chen Qing. Programme for International Student Assessment PISA_The Research of Scientific

Literacy Assessment. Zhejiang: Zhejiang Normal University, 2013.

[4] Wang Xin, Gong Xiaoliang, Zhao Shanjiang, et al. The results analysis of PISA2012. Shanghai Education, 2013(35): 42-56.

[5] Zhang Li. The general situation and the comparative study of ICT education in four Asia countries. Teaching of Forestry Region, 2009(3): 77-80.

[6] Xie Hanwen. Educational informationization promote learning reform in singapore. Journal of World Education, 2013(20): 7-10.

[7] Lian Yang. The enlightenment presented by Korea ICT education for Chinese middle and primary school to develop teaching materials of ICT. China Education Info, 2007(22): 24-26.

[8] Sun Lihui, Li Mang. The research and enlightenment of ICT utilization in primary school teachers in Japan—Base on the statistic analysis of "primary school guidelines". China Educational Technology, 2013(4): 70-74,118.

[9] Hua dan, ShanTian Taizi. The combination of ICT and English teaching in Japanese middle and primary school. Shanghai Research on Education, 2006(8): 47-49.

Rapid and Automated Determination of Salivary α-amylase by Flow Injection Analysis for Children Exercise Stress Response Research

Lei Ma[1,a,*], Yu Wang[1], Yuan Ying[1], Biao Sun[2], Xiaobo Cai[3], Xuejun Kang[1,b]

[1]Key Laboratory of Child Development and Learning Science of Ministry of Education, Research Center for Learning Science, Southeast University, Nanjing, 210096, China

[2]Department of Human Sports Science, Nanjing Institute of Physical Education, Nanjing, 210014, China

[3]Department of physical education, Southeast University, Nanjing, 210096, China

[a]mlmyhero@163.com, [b]xuejunkang64@163.com

[*] Corresponding author

Keywords: exercise stress; Flow Injection Analysis (FIA); salivary α-amylo

Abstract: The aim of the study was to assess/evaluate the applicability of flow injection spectrophotometry in the monitor of the potential biomarker, salivary α-amylase in acute exercise stress. Subjects were 120 healthy graduate students who took a 30 min exercise test. To assess pre and post stress Salivary α-amylase levels, the participants provided three salivary samples (10 minutes before the stress test, 10 minutes after the end of the each test and 40 minutes after the second sample). it was verified that individual's salivary α-amylase secretion was changed under exercise stress, The method could detect saliva α-amylase activities conveniently and accurately. It was concluded that flow injection spectrophotometry might be a reliable method for determination of Salivary α-amylase in the assessment of exercise stress.

流动注射法快速测唾液α-淀粉酶用于儿童应激实验研究

马磊[1,a,*],王羽[1],应媛[1],孙飙[2],蔡晓波[3],康学军[1,b]

[1]东南大学学习科学中心,东南大学儿童发展与学习科学教育部重点实验室,江苏南京,210096

[2]南京体育学院,南京大学南京体育学院联合运动医学实验室,江苏南京,210014

[3]东南大学体育系,江苏南京,210096

[a]mlmyhero@163.com, [b]xuejunkang64@163.com

[*]通讯作者

关键词:运动应激;流动注射;唾液α-淀粉酶

中文摘要:流动注射法测定唾液中α-淀粉酶,探讨儿童在运动应激条件下该指标与运动应激的相关性,考察其作为一种客观地评价运动应激的生物学参数的可能性。被试者为120名小学生(高年级组和低年级组各60名),年龄为6—12岁。在运动应激条件下,采集他们测试前10 min、测试结束后10 min以及测试结束休息30 min后的唾液样品。利用流动注射法测定唾液α-淀粉酶的浓度。本研究的结果显示被试的α-淀粉酶水平在儿童应激实验时明显存在个体差异,也表明流动注射快速测定唾液α-淀粉酶的方法可用于客观评价运动应激。

1 背景

经过对应激反应的不断认识以及科学实验知识积累,人们已经逐渐认识到应激是一种整体的神经内分泌反应。一旦应激反应发生,它可激活下丘脑—垂体—肾上腺皮质(HPA)轴、自主神经系统和胆碱能系统,释放糖皮质激素、儿茶酚胺、神经肽类等物质发挥各类调节作用。由于应激无时无处不在,故机体始终处于这种应激调节中,过弱或过强的应激均会影响执行功能[1]。为了探索人类运动应激现象的本质规律,研究者们采用了多种手段,如心率血压测量,唾液、尿液与血液等生物样品中标志物的测量,等等。唾液α-淀粉酶(salivary α- amylase,SAA)被认为可以反映自主神经活性,刺激交感神经可以增加SAA蛋白的分泌,而刺激副交感神经增加唾液总量[1]。越来越多的研究发现,SAA活性与人体在急性应激时交感神经系统的反应相关[2]。唾液淀粉酶浓度可以预测应激情况下血液儿茶酚胺水平,特别是去甲肾上腺素,并且比心率更直接更简单[3]。此外,相关研究发现唾液淀粉酶与唾液蛋白、血乳酸相关,唾液总蛋白与运动强度相关[4,5]。在竞技运动中,舞蹈运动员唾液皮质醇和唾液淀粉酶显著低于平均值,对于健康的抱怨程度以及白介素—6也较一般人高,说明持续慢性运动应激同唾液淀粉酶活性相关[6]。跆拳道比赛时运动员呈现高应激,交感肾上腺系统反应比下丘脑垂体反应一恢复所需时间更短[5]。在运动相关唾液淀粉酶的研究方面,有越来越多的研究不断开展。有研究发现免疫球蛋白 A 的下降与唾液淀粉酶水平的升高一致[7]。70% 的最大吸氧量强度运动后唾液淀粉酶迅速上升,直到 12 小时、24 小时之后仍在上升。但是唾液总蛋白 12 小时之内快速下降。运动后即刻反应不明显,24 小时之后上升[8]。此外,有关研究发现,运动引起唾液淀粉酶水平升高可能暂时损害老年人的执行功能,但是同时对老人的心理有益[9]。70% 最大吸氧量功率自行车运动显著提高唾液淀粉酶(代表去甲肾上腺能)水平,提高了老年人的执行功能[10]。但是关于儿童运动与唾液淀粉酶的不同年龄对比研究相对较少。除此之外,目前 SAA 的检测主要是采用国外专门的仪器检测,本文基于碘淀粉比色法构建流动注射分析法测试 SAA,并用于人体运动应激实验样本的测试,考察流动注射新技术在应激反应评价体系中的可用性。

2　对象和方法

2.1　被试对象

通过招募形式,筛选出 120 位被试者(在校小学生,男女比例各占一半,一年级和五年级各占一半,年龄为 6—12 岁)签订知情同意书,参加体质测试,之后参加速算应激实验。被试者要求身体健康,在实验准备期间,均没服用药物。

2.2　仪器与试剂

2.2.1　仪器

Polar 多功能心率表(型号:RS800 芬兰),TGL-16C 离心机(上海安亭科学仪器厂);XW-80A 漩涡混合器(上海青浦沪西仪器厂);AL104-IC 分析天平(METTLER TOLEDO);CMFIA—1 流动注射分析仪(山东电讯七厂),恒温水浴(自行组装)。

2.2.2　试剂与溶液

α-淀粉酶标准品(购自北京索莱宝科技有限公司,酶活力 3 700 U/g),可溶性淀粉(分析纯,国药集团化学试剂有限公司)。碘化钾、碘(分析纯,上海申博化工有限公司)。实验用水为二次去离子水。

淀粉溶液:精密称取 0.8 g 可溶性淀粉,加水溶解后定容至 1 000 mL,配成浓度为 0.8 mg/mL 的溶液。

碘液:精密称取 6.5 g 碘与 17.5 g 碘化钾,加水溶解后定容至 1 000 mL,配制成含碘 50 mmol/L 的溶液。

α-淀粉酶工作溶液:精密称取酶标准品加水配制成 10 mg/mL 的溶液,再用水依次稀释成 0 μg/mL、5 μg/mL、12.5 μg/mL、20 μg/mL、50 μg/mL 的酶系列工作溶液。

2.3 方法

2.3.1 体质测试方法

跑(25 m×2 往返跑)、立定跳远、跳绳。

跑(25 m×2 往返跑)、立定跳远、跳绳严格按照《国家体质测试标准》执行。

2.3.2 唾液样品采集

在每位被试者采集第一份样品之前,均被要求用清水漱口,并在此次实验过程中,不能饮用或食用除清水之外的饮料或食品。每份唾液样品采集完后,放于 -20 ℃冰箱避光保存。为了避免测试干扰,被试者从前一天开始禁食兴奋性饮料及食物、不抽烟,测试当日统一饮食。为避免采样应激,先采集唾液样本,后采集其他样本。具体实验流程见表1。

表1 实验流程表

实验流程		
测试前准备	心率(1)	测试前准备
唾液样本(1)	心率(2)	运动前
唾液样本(2)	心率(3)	运动后 10 min
唾液样本(3)	心率(4)	运动后 20 min

2.3.3 样品处理

将唾液离心(3 000 转)后精密量取其上清液 1 mL,加水稀释至 10 mL,混匀,即得到待测溶液。在流动注射流路中,通过载流水将进样阀中的淀粉液和待测溶液带至反应盘管,反应盘管的混合溶液在 37 ℃的水浴锅中反应 20 s,继续被载流带至第二个汇流点与碘液汇合反应,最后反应液流至检测器,于 660 nm 处测量吸光度值。

如图1所示,流动注射分析的程序是:(1) 清洗。用淀粉溶液及载留水消除管路内残留的气泡,增加结果的稳定性,同时,让淀粉溶液充满反应管。(2) 进样。机器经过清洗过程后进行样品的进样,此时主泵工作,副泵不动。进样过程中,由待检测的唾液样品将清洗时注入的淀粉溶液冲入反应管中等待反应,然后借转向阀的转动停止管路中淀粉的进入,同时将采集的淀粉和唾液样品推入反应管。(3) 反应。此时淀粉液和唾液样品都进入了反应管,两个泵都停转,给出充分反应的时间,反应完后的混合溶液遇碘,反应后的液流输到检测器,得到检测信号。

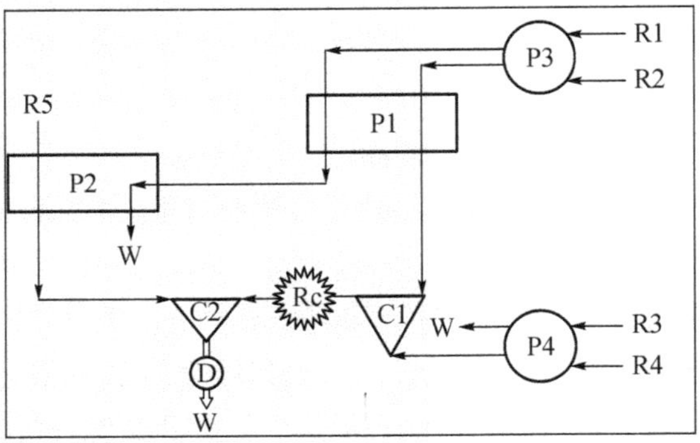

图 1　流动注射反应流路图

P1，P2（蠕动泵，Peristaltic pump）；P3、P4（多通道进样阀，multi-channel injection valve）；D（检测器，detector）；C1，C2（三通阀，three-way valve）；Rc（反应管，reaction coil）；W（废液，waste）；R1（水，water）；R2（淀粉溶液，starch solution）；R3（样品，sample）；R4（水，water）；R5（碘液，iodine solution）

由图 2 所示，随着工作溶液浓度的增加，峰高逐渐降低并与浓度呈线性关系，图 3 所示的工作曲线的线性工作方程为：$y = -0.1094x + 0.8476$；$R^2 = 0.9986$。结果表明：当 SAA 的浓度在 0—50 μg/mL 范围内，具有较好的线性关系。同时做回收率实验，回收率在 92.0%—101% 之间，所有 *RSD* 值均小于 5.0%（见表 2）。

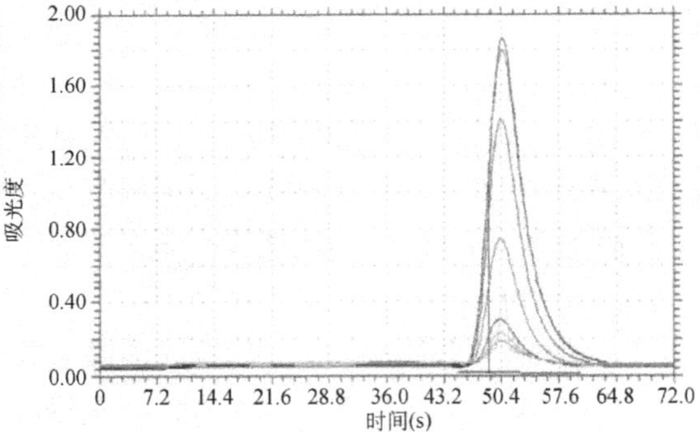

图 2　SAA 工作溶液测定信号图

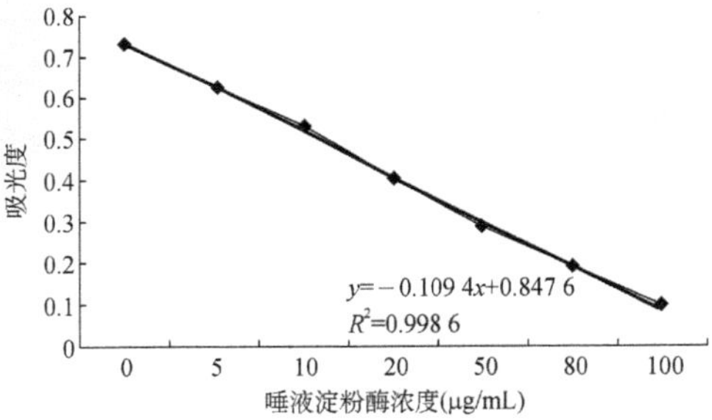

图 3　SAA 工作曲线图

表 2　方法回收率

加入量(μg/mL)	测得量(μg/mL)	回收率%	*RSD*(%)
5	5.05	93.2	3.2
10	10.13	92.5	2.5
40	40.16	100.8	1.1

3 结果

如表3、表4以及图4所示,低年级组的SAA的平均值在测试前后及休息后之间的没有显著性差异,被试者在参加应激测试前后三个阶段高年级组SAA酶活力值均显著低于低年级组($p<0.01$),同时高年级组在测试后休息30 min时SAA酶活力显著下降($p<0.01$)。不同阶段的变化率平均值差异不显著,方差较大,说明被试者个体差异较大。

表3 不同分组测试不同阶段SAA酶活力值(*Mean*±*SD*)

分组	Before-test (A)	10-Minutes Post (B)	30-Minutes Post (C)
低年级组 (Grade 1)	141.60±21.10	139.10±30.94	138.32±21.90
高年级组 (Grade 5)	114.22±36.63	113.09±36.49	102.86±34.59
p value	$p<0.01$	$p<0.01$	$p<0.01$

表4 不同分组测试SAA酶活力变化值(*Mean*±*SD*)

分组	B—A	C—B	C—A
低年级组 (Grade 1)	−2.51±36.20	−0.78±38.79	−3.29±22.58
高年级组 (Grade 5)	−1.13±29.85	−10.22±25.28	−11.36±20.56
p value	—	—	—

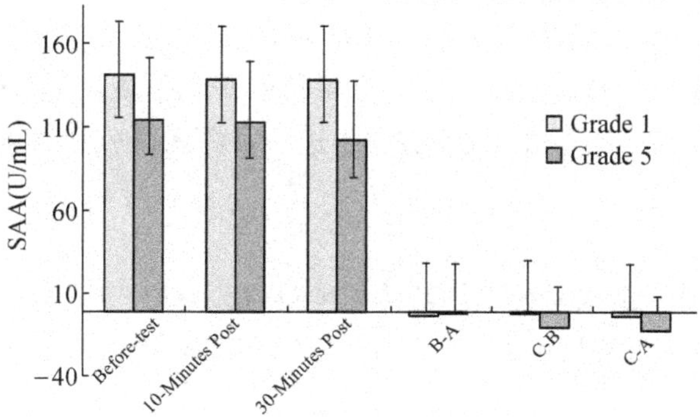

图4 运动应激对SAA的影响

4 讨论

借助于神经科学以及分子技术发展,越来越多的生理学家和心理学家发现,应激反应有其生物学基础。并且也一直在积极寻找与之相关的稳定的生物指标[11]。早期的研究发现,SAA活性水平被认为是反应副交感神经活性的指标[12]。到了20世纪90年代中期,有学者发现SAA水平在应激时同样上升并且与在运动时机体的去甲肾上腺水平相关[13]。近期研究者大多关注人体唾液皮质醇变化与人体应激之间的相关性研究[14,15]。但是,越来越多的研究结果显示,似乎 SAA 更能反映应激系统的调节水平[1]。唾液淀粉酶由唾液腺体中的浆液细胞分泌,受植物神经系统控制,副交感神经兴奋引起唾液腺分泌大量清稀的唾液,促进唾液淀粉酶的合成与分泌,交感神经兴奋,引起小量黏稠唾液的分泌。因此副交感神经对唾液浓度的变化调减似乎起主要作用。有学者认为副交感神经影响 SAA 浓度的通路主要有三条:(1) 通过副交感神经主要控制腺体释放淀粉酶。(2) 通过协同交感神经—副交感神经的交互作用,副交感神经的活动放大了交感神经效果。(3) 通过副交感神经介导唾液流速[2]。由于这种副交感神经的协同以及介导作用存在,因此研究自主神经对 SAA 的调节不是简单的一一对应关系,而可能是像 Berntson 提出的自主神经活动可能存在九种活动搭配模式[16],因此关于 SAA 与自主神经关系还有许多与此相类似的有待解决的问题,这些问题的存在表明研究人员使用 SAA 作为交感神经系统活性标志物的研究有待细化和深入,还需要对其作用机理进一步深入了解。

本研究主要采用小学生体质测试标准运动应激实验,取自然流出的混合唾液作为测试样本,通过自建流动注射法检测 SAA 响应应激反应的情况。实验结果发现,高年级儿童 SAA 浓度在各个阶段浓度均比低年级测试结束后下降快速。结果表明,测试期间的不同神经内分泌反应类型儿童自主神经变化趋势不同,高年级儿童 SAA 酶活性比低年级儿童低且存在显著性差异($p<0.01$)。

总之,唾液淀粉酶可以作为儿童运动应激相关标记物,相对于其他标记物更加便宜、快速和方便[17]。本研究的结果说明用流动注射法快速测定可以用于儿童应激唾液淀粉酶研究,为相关学科研究提供了一个可行的研究手段。实验研究经常采用电生理、心理等多种测试结合本生化方法,有利于进一步深入研究和探索应激反应机制。

致谢

本文为江苏省普通高校研究生创新计划项目(CXLX12_0121)陕西省教育厅科研项目(11JK0443);安康学院高层次人才引进项目(AYQDRW200964)的阶段性成果之一。

References

[1] Ali N, Pruessner J C. The salivary alpha amylase over cortisol ratio as a marker to assess dysregulations of the stress systems. Physiology & Behavior, 2012, 106: 65 - 72.

[2] Proctor G B, Carpenter G H. Regulation of salivary gland function by autonomic nerves. Autonomic neuroscience: Basic & Clinical, 2007, 133: 3 - 18.

[3] Allgrove J E, Oliveira M, Gleeson M. Stimulating whole saliva affects the response of antimicrobial proteins to exercise. Scandinavian Journal of Medicine & Science in Sports, 2013.

[4] de Oliveira V N, Bessa A, Lamounier R P, et al. Changes in the salivary biomarkers induced by an effort test. International Journal of Sports Medicine, 2010, 31: 377-381.

[5] Bocanegra O L, Diaz M M, Teixeira R R, et al. Determination of the lactate threshold by means of salivary biomarkers: Chromogranin a as novel marker of exercise intensity. European Journal of Applied Physiology, 2012, 112: 3195-3203.

[6] Berndt C, Strahler J, Kirschbaum C, et al. Lower stress system activity and higher peripheral inflammation in competitive ballroom dancers. Biological Psychology, 2012, 91: 357-364.

[7] Gill S K, Teixeira A M, Rama L, et al. Salivary antimicrobial protein responses during multistage ultramarathon competition conducted in hot environmental conditions. Applied Physiology, Nutrition, and Metabolism = Physiologie appliquee, nutrition et metabolisme, 2013, 38(9): 977-987.

[8] Rosa L, Teixeira A, Lira F, et al. Moderate acute exercise (70% VO2 peak) induces TGF-beta, alpha-amylase and IgA in saliva during recovery. Oral Diseases, 2013(2): 186-190.

[9] Hatta A, Nishihira Y, Higashiura T. Effects of a single bout of walking on psychophysiologic responses and executive function in elderly adults: A pilot study. Clinical Interventions in Aging, 2013, 8: 945-952.

[10] Muller M P, Hansel M, Fichtner A, et al. Excellence in performance and stress reduction during two different full scale simulator training courses: A pilot study. Resuscitation, 2009, 80: 919-924.

[11] Stalenheim E G, von Knorring L, Oreland L. Platelet monoamine oxidase activity as a biological marker in a Swedish forensic psychiatric population. Psychiatry Research, 1997, 69: 79-87.

[12] Morse D R, Schacterle G R, Furst M L, et al. Stress, relaxation and saliva: Relationship to dental caries and its prevention, with a literature review. Annals of Dentistry, 1983, 42: 47-54.

[13] Bosch J A, Brand H S, Ligtenberg T J, et al. Psychological stress as a determinant of protein levels and salivary-induced aggregation of Streptococcus gordonii in human whole saliva. Psychosomatic Medicine, 1996, 58: 374-382.

[14] Bosch J A, de Geus E J, Carroll D, et al. A general enhancement of autonomic and cortisol responses during social evaluative threat. Psychosomatic Medicine, 2009, 71: 877-885.

[15] Tyrka A R, Wier L M, Price L H, et al. Cortisol and ACTH responses to the Dex/CRH test: Influence of temperament. Hormones and Behavior, 2008, 53: 518-525.

[16] Berntson G G, Bigger J T, et al. Heart rate variability: Origins, methods, and interpretive caveats. Psychophysiology, 1997, 34: 623-648.

[17] Diaz M M, Bocanegra O L, Teixeira R R, et al. Response of salivary markers of autonomic activity to elite competition. International Journal of Sports Medicine, 2012, 33: 763-768.

In Exploring on Science Teacher Training Model in England —A Case Study of York University

Yingsi Qi[1,a], Yi Bai[1,b,*]

[1]Key Laboratory of Child Development and Learning Science of Ministry of Education, Southeast University, Nanjing, Jiangsu, China

[a]qiyingsi@126.com, [b]by.rcls@seu.edu.cn

[*]Corresponding author

Keywords: England; science teacher training; Helsinki University

Abstract: England has a long history of science education and science teacher training. Attaching great importance to the science teacher training, England has an advanced science teacher training model. Taking York University as an example, science teacher training in England emphasizes collaboration between university and practice schools, stressing the importance of teaching practice, paying attention to pedagogical content knowledge learning and subject knowledge learning.

英国科学教师培养模式探析

亓英斯[1,a], 柏毅[1,b,*]
[1]东南大学儿童发展与学习科学教育部重点实验室,南京,江苏,中国
[a]qiyingsi@126.com, [b]by.rcls@seu.edu.cn
[*]通讯作者

关键词:英国; 科学教师培养; 约克大学

中文摘要:英国是科学教育及科学教师培养实施较早的国家,一直以来英国对教师培养十分重视,发展至今,英国已形成先进的科学教师培养模式。以约克大学科学教师PGCE培养为例,英国科学教师培养采取实践学校与大学校本部相结合的培养模式,注重教学实践,注重教学法及学科知识学习。

1 引言

当今社会,科学与技术不断创新,移动互联浪潮及大数据日益刷新着人们的认知能力,不断改变着每个人的生活方式乃至整个社会的运作方式。在科学技术迅速发展的今天,科学教育不仅承担着培养科学人才、推动科技发展的重大历史任务,还应肩负起提高全民科学素养、促进科学思维社会化等具有新时代意义的教育责任。作为科学教育任务的主要践行者和科学社会发展的重要推动者,科学教师培养已成为科学教育发展至关重要的环节。英国作为欧洲四大经济体之一,一直在世界历史的长河中有着举足轻重的影响地位。伴随两次工业革命、科学发展以及功利主义思潮给英国带来的新的影响,经济、科技、思想领域的巨大变革不断对英国的科学教育提出新的要求。英国是科学教育及科学教师培养实施较早的国家,英国长久以来都对教师培养十分重视,发展至今,英国已形成先进的科学教师培养模式。

2 英国科学教师培养概况

在英国,基础教育时期的科学教育被分为KS1(5—7岁)、KS2(7—11岁)、KS3(11—14岁)、KS4(14—16岁)四个阶段。同时,英国科学教育还有综合和分科之分:KS1阶段以综合性科学为主,KS2、KS3、KS4阶段则多以分科的形式进行,3—6年级主要学习生物学知识,7—9年级主要学习化学学科,10—11年级则以物理学的学习为主,还包括零散的地理学及天文学知识。由此,英国的科学教师一般被分为生物学科学教师、化学科学教师和物理学科学教师。英国具有悠久的教师培养历史,英国教师培养发展至今已形成完整的多样化的教师职前培养模式,主要形式有两种:"4+0"的教育学学士(Bachelor of Education, BEd)培养模式、"3+1"的教育学硕士

(Postgraduate Certificate in Education, PGCE)培养模式。教育学学士培养模式学制四年,在四年的学习中,师范生一边学习专业的学科性知识,一边进行教育专业训练;教育学硕士培养模式总学制也为四年,但采取三年专业性学科学习加一年教育专业训练相继进行的模式,这种模式培养下的师范生需先取得主修专业的学士学位,之后完成一年的教育专业训练后取得“研究生教育证书”。PGCE 模式发展较为迅速,已成为近年来英国教师职前培养的重要趋势。

3 英国科学教师培养的基本模式及课程设置

3.1 英国科学教师 PGCE 培养模式

英国的很多大学都提供 PGCE 培养,科学教师 PGCE 培养的形式和类别也比较多样化。下面以英国约克大学的科学教师 PGCE 培养为例来阐述英国科学教师职前培养基本模式。约克大学是英国的新型大学之一,也是一所高质量的研究型学校。约克大学的 PGCE 课程实施是通过大学校本部与多所实践学校共同完成的,约克大学 2013—2014 学年的 PGCE 培养自九月份开始至次年夏季结束,划分为秋季学期、春季学期、夏季学期三个阶段,PGCE 培养模式如下:

约克大学的 PGCE 课程实施是通过大学校本部与多所实践学校共同完成的。这就保证了实践学校可以充分参与到未来教师培养的计划、训练、评估等整个培养过程中来,师范生有三分之二的课程是在实践学校中完成的,并且可以在至少两所实践学校进行实际教学以增加教学经验。大学校本部的学习由大学中的专业导师指导,主要内容是各种理论性知识,实践学校中的学习主要由学科导师指导,同时需完成大学专业导师布置的各项任务,更具实践性:第 1—2 周的培养目标是形成基本的学校教学经验认识;在入学的第 4—8 周和第 13 周中,受训者有近一半的时间在实践学校接受训练,这四周的实践学校培训内容主要包括进行课堂观摩,了解相应的学科设置,与专业导师和学科导师进行交流讨论和初步学习,熟悉学校部门设置和教学资源,尝试与学科教师一起设计、准备及实施教学;第 9—12 周主要是连续四周的迷你模块教学培养,也是对之前教学实践的继续深化,主要包括课堂观摩,在至少两个班级进行每周共 6 小时的跟班接触,加强教学能力,尽量完成 6 次课堂教学,进行教学计划和教学准备并对学生进行每日评估反馈,与班级教师保持沟通学习;第 16—30 周的培训由迷你模块教学转向模块教学,这向受训者提出更高的要求,内容包括了解并对多样化的班级负责,组织教学,接受班级教师监管,与班级教师或其他受训者进行联合教学,继续进行课程观摩学习,针对不同年龄阶段及能力水平的学生开展教学,协助进行学生课堂作业和考试的评估工作,参与家长会及撰写报告以及完成周记录表和标准档案袋自我管理等;第 33—34 周主要是教学的丰富化与专业化加深阶段,受训者可以根据自身的兴趣和需要来完善自己的专业化改进项目,此阶段受训者可以与大学校本部导师及实践学校导师协商自己的训练重点,一般包括微型研究、教材的拓展与采集、经验教师的授课观摩与请教、学科知识的全面深入提升、课外活动的参与运用等。[1]

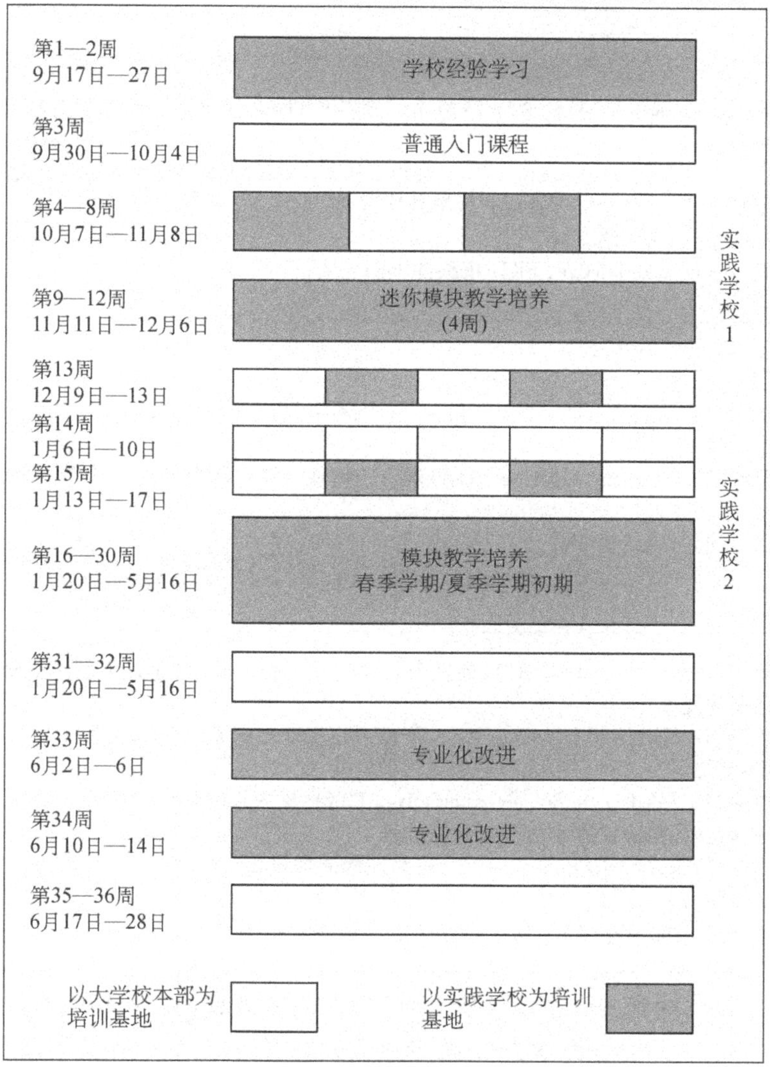

图1 约克大学PGCE培养模式结构(2013—2014)

3.2 英国科学教师PGCE课程设置

英国约克大学科学教师PGCE培养课程设置中包含了学科知识学习和教学法培养内容。以约克大学物理教师培养为例,物理教师PGCE培养项目为受训者提供了丰富的训练内容,包括各种多样化活动、工作坊、导师指导和同伴教学研讨等,旨在提高受训者的学科教学能力,培养出优秀的物理科学教师。约克大学物理教师PGCE课程设置符合约克大学PGCE基本培养模式,也分为秋季学期、春季学期、夏季学期,各学期主要课程内容如下：

表 1　约克大学物理教师 PGCE 课程设置主要内容

秋季学期
• 成为教师(Becoming a teacher, BT)：促进个人发展及 PGCE 课程进展的研讨培养，为获得教学职位做准备 • 教学与学习(Teaching and Learning, TL)：聚焦于物理学等科学学科教与学特定方面的研讨培养 • 实践学校实习：以实践学校为基地的教学技能培养 • 评估考核：定期完成评估考核 • 学科知识(Subject knowledge, SK)：审核并不断更新学科知识
春季学期
• 成为教师(Becoming a teacher, BT)：促进个人发展及 PGCE 课程进展的深化研讨培养，促进教学专业化发展 • 教学与学习(Teaching and Learning, TL)：聚焦于物理学等科学学科教与学各个方面的深化研讨培养 • 评估考核：定期完成评估考核
夏季学期
• 成为教师(Becoming a teacher, BT)：促进个人专业发展及 PGCE 课程进展的深化研讨培养，促进教学专业化发展 • 教学与学习(Teaching and Learning, TL)：聚焦于物理学和其他科学学科教与学各个方面的深化研讨培养，特别是 KS4 阶段之后的物理教学培养 • 学科教学法知识(Pedagogic Subject Knowledge, PSK)：深入理解物理学等科学学科基本理念的学习过程，以及如何通过教学活动促进该过程 • 专业化改进(Professional Enrichment, PE)：为期两周的自我活动计划，以加强和改进自身的科学教学专业能力 • 评估考核：定期完成评估考核，参加外部考试[2]

由表 1 可见，约克大学物理科学教师 PGCE 培养课程内容包括成为教师、教学与学习、实践学校实习、学科教学法知识、专业化改进等内容，其中囊括了基本的学科知识、相应的学科教学法和一般教学法知识。与此同时，约克大学科学教师培养还特别注重跨学科领域科学知识和教学法的普及，如物理科学教师的夏季学期培养计划中不但包含物理学的学科教学法知识，还包括生物学和化学的学科教学法知识，三个学科领域内具体主题如下：

表2 约克大学物理教师PGCE课程学科教学法主要内容

物理学
• 学科教学法知识4:学生科学学习:了解原子 • 学科教学法知识5:力与运动 • 学科教学法知识6:电学 • 学科教学法知识7:能量
生物学
• 学科教学法知识1:繁殖与性教育 • 学科教学法知识2:基因与进化 • 学科教学法知识3:呼吸作用和光合作用
化学
• 学科教学法知识8:放热和吸热反应 • 学科教学法知识9:元素的混合物和化合物[2]

4 英国科学教师培养特点及启示

第一,硕士学位教育修学年限长。英国教育学硕士培养模式已成为近年来英国教师职前培养的重要趋势,该模式学制四年,采取三年专业性学科学习加一年教育专业训练相继进行的模式,这种模式培养下的师范生需先取得主修专业的学士学位,之后完成一年的教育专业训练后取得"研究生教育证书"。由此可见,提高科学教师的学历水平可以有效提高教师的专业水准。

第二,教师教育机构具有较大自主权,培养方式灵活多样。英国的很多大学都提供PGCE培养,科学教师PGCE培养的形式和类别也比较多样化,不同的教育培训机构的科学知识的学习时间、课程设置等培养重点有所差异,因地制宜,具有较强的灵活性。科学教师培养具有很高的灵活性和较高的培养效率。

第三,注重教学实践,注重教学实践学校在教师培养中的作用。英国注重科学教师的教学实践,例如约克大学的PGCE课程实施是通过大学校本部与多所实践学校共同完成的。师范生有三分之二的课程是在实践学校中完成的,保证了实践学校可以充分参与到未来教师培养的计划、训练、评估等整个培养过程。

第四,注重学科知识培养,同时也注重主修学科之外的广泛的科学知识积累。英国科学教师一般分为生物、化学和物理三个学科,培养中注重学科知识积累,同时也要求教师具备其他学科的基本知识,例如约克大学科学教师培养特别强调跨学科领域科学知识和教学法的普及,如物理科学教师的夏季学期培养计划中不但包含物理学的学科教学法知识,还包括生物学和化学的学科教学法知识。

致谢

本文为国家社科基金一般项目《基础教育阶段技术与设计教育的国际化比较研究》(11JDGC026)的阶段性成果之一。

References

[1] University of York. PGCE Trainees' Handbook 2013—2014[EB/OL]. (2014-05-06)[2014-05-28]. http://www.york.ac.uk/media/educationalstudies/pgce/documents/pgcehandbooks/2013-14handbooks/PGCE%20Trainee%20handbook%2013-14.pdf.

[2] University of York. PGCE Physics Handbook 2013—2014[EB/OL]. (2014-05-06)[2014-05-28]. http://www.york.ac.uk/media/educationalstudies/pgce/documents/pgcehandbooks/2013-14handbooks/PGCE%20Physics%20Handbook%202013-14.pdf.

Development of a Parenting Assessment Tool for Chinese Parents of Infants/Toddlers

Lijun Wang[1,a], Zonghan Zhu[2,b], Yaohua Dai[3,c,*], Xiaohua Xie[3,d], Aihua Liu[3,e], Ni Jia[3,f]

[1]Graduate Student School of Peking Union Medical College, Beijing, China

[2]Chinsese Pediatrician Association, Beijing, China

[3]Department of Integrated Early Childhood Development, Capital Institute of Pediatrics, Beijing, China

[a]doctorwlj@163.com, [b]zonghanzhu@263.net, [c]yh.dai@263.net, [d]xiexiaohua@vip.sina.com, [e]liuaihua315@163.com, [f]jiani1981@163.com

[*] Corresponding author

Keywords: infant; toddler; parenting; scale; parenting assessment tool

Abstract: Objective To develop a parenting assessment tool (PAT) for parents of children aged zero to 3 years to assess parenting quality within the Chinese socio-cultural context. Methods The development of PAT fell into three basic stages. Stage 1 was item development. Through a thorough review of the literature, experts consultation and focus group discussion, the item pool was established. Then the deductively generated items were subjected to a sorting process that served as a pretest, permitting the deletion of items that were deemed to be conceptually inconsistent. Stage 2 was scale development, or the manner in which items are combined to form scales. Deductive approach was used to determine PAT subscales, aiming at developing subscales that were conceptually meaningful. Firstly 18 experts developed 10 dimensions of PAT and then evaluated the degree to which each item was representative of the parenting dimension. Data gathered from 5 cities ($n = 284$) was used to purify the items. Stage 3 was scale evaluation. In order to confirm the properties of PAT, a second data collection was conducted ($n = 607$) in ten cities. Confirmatory factor analysis was used to evaluate the latent structure of PAT and to modify the model.

Results: A 78-items pool was developed. Twenty-eight items were deleted that were deemed to be conceptually inconsistent. Experts developed 10 dimensions of PAT. Factor 9 and factor 10 has an alpha below a minimal acceptable level (0.5), so these two factors were not included in this study. Based on this result, we proposed a 8-factor model named PAT. Results of the confirmatory factor analysis suggested that two additional items should be deleted from the scale. After the removal of these two items, the 8-factor model provided good fit ($\chi^2/df < 2.0$, $RMSEA < 0.06$, $CFI = 0.916$, $TLI = 0.906$).

Conclusion: In the current research, we developed PAT for assessment of parenting of infants and toddlers in China.

0—2岁儿童父母育儿评估量表编制

王丽君[1,a]，朱宗涵[2,b]，戴耀华[3,c,*]，谢晓桦[3,d]，刘爱华[3,e]，贾妮[3,f]

[1]北京协和医学院研究生院,北京,中国

[2]中国医师协会儿科医师分会,北京,中国

[3]首都儿科研究所儿童早期发展研究室,北京,中国

[a]doctorwlj@163.com，[b]zonghanzhu@263.net，[c]yh.dai@263.net，

[d]xiexiaohua@vip.sina.com，[e]liuaihua315@163.com，[f]jiani1981@163.com

*通讯作者

关键词:婴幼儿;养育;量表;育儿评估量表

中文摘要:目的:编制适合中国国情的、能全面评价0—2岁儿童父母养育质量的评价量表。方法:通过专题小组讨论、专家咨询及文献查阅等构建PAT条目库,通过一般性筛选和试验性测试筛选建立了PAT初稿。由专家将婴幼儿养育的定义操作化为若干个维度,并把PAT初稿中相关条目归到对应的养育维度,每个维度即形成一个因素。利用初稿进行预试($n=284$),并进一步纯化条目。用生成的PAT测试版进行正式调查($n=607$),用验证性因素分析法进行模型评估及模型修正。结果PAT条目库包含78个条目。通过条目筛选,形成含有50个条目的PAT初稿。专家采用逻辑法提出0—2岁儿童养育测量的10个维度,并把条目归到了最相关的因素下。因素9和因素10的Cronbach α 系数小于0.50,从量表中删掉。PAT测试版模型拟合指数:$\chi^2/df<3.0$,$RMSEA$ 估计值为0.043,$CFI=0.886$,$TLI=0.875$,进一步修正模型。根据修正指数删除条目T42、T6后,$CFI=0.916$,$TLI=0.906$。PAT建立,共含有8个因素36个条目。结论:本研究在提取因素阶段采用逻辑法编制了0—2岁儿童父母育儿评估量表。该研究形成了量表的初始版本,进一步的研究将对量表的信度、效度进行检验。

1 引言

0—2岁是儿童最重要的发展阶段,是生理发育和心理发展最迅速的时期,被称为生长发育的“窗口期”。研究表明,儿童认知和非认知能力的差异在生命的早期即形成,等学龄期时儿童的能力已经存在了很大的差异。许多令人担心的儿童后期行为如好动、肥胖以及学习成绩较差,其实早在婴儿期就已经被其所经受的经历定型。成人后存在的很多问题如心理健康问题、肥胖、心脏病、犯罪、读写能力和计算能力较差等都能在儿童早期找到其根源[1]。

在影响儿童早期发展的诸多因素中,养育是最重要的一个。家庭的养育环境、父母的养育质量与儿童的发展结局存在多种相关性[2-4]。养育可以影响到儿童的健康、

行为、幸福、智力发展及教育所得。因此,养育对儿童、对父母、对社会都有极其重要的作用。在欧美国家,近几十年来政府对育儿表现出了很大的兴趣,并采取了许多育儿干预措施提高父母的养育技能。大量证据表明:父母确实可以根据专业人员的指导和建议改变养育行为,从而改善儿童发展结局[5,6]。近年来国内对儿童早期养育的研究热度也在递增。《中国儿童发展纲要(2011—2020年)》[7]明确提出新时期儿童教育的主要目标:促进0—3岁儿童早期综合发展,积极开展0—3岁儿童科学育儿指导。卫生部于2009年起启动了儿童早期发展促进项目,探讨以父母为中心的儿童早期发展服务模式,提高父母的儿童早期发展相关知识和育儿技能。本研究即是该项目的一部分。

现有的0—2岁儿童养育测评工具并不多,国内更少。国内的研究者常常从国外引进成熟的育儿量表,直接应用于研究。现在国内用以研究的养育量表主要有以下局限性:① 由于养育受传统文化及社会状况的影响,引进国外量表中的条目未必都适合评价中国的父母;② 已有的育儿评估工具往往只是从养育方式、养育环境或育儿知识等孤立的角度出发对养育加以测量,很难揭示出养育的全貌。因此,本研究的目的就在于编制一套适合中国国情的、能全面评价0—2岁儿童养育质量的评价量表,为标准化评估0—2岁儿童父母的养育观念、养育知识的掌握情况、养育行为及养育环境提供客观有效的工具。

2 对象及方法

2.1 编制量表条目库

2.1.1 文献研究

检索Google及Medline、Pubmed、Springer、万方及清华同方等数据库,广泛收集国内外儿童养育相关资料及其评价工具,了解儿童早期发展、婴幼儿养育及养育评估工具的研究现况。

2.1.2 专题小组讨论

举行4次专题小组讨论,每个小组包含5名儿童保健、儿童早期发展专业人员及5名婴幼儿(0—35个月龄)的父母。针对开放式问题“您认为与养育相关的因素主要有哪些”,广泛收集专业人员及家长的意见。

2.1.3 专家咨询

邀请8名来自首都儿科研究所、中国科学院心理研究所、山东省妇幼保健院、山西省妇幼保健院、北京市昌平区妇幼保健院及深圳市妇幼保健院的儿童保健及测量学专家,就0—2岁婴幼儿的养育进行深度咨询,并在专家同意的基础上进行录音,整理咨询结果。

根据专题小组讨论内容及专家咨询结果,结合国内外有关文献描述及已有的婴幼儿养育量表,构建 PAT 条目库。

2.2 条目筛选

2.2.1 一般性筛选

在首都儿科研究所、北京市昌平区妇幼保健院及首都师范大学选择了 2 名儿童早期发展研究人员、2 名儿童保健科医师及 2 名心理学专业在读博士,请以上人员通读 PAT 条目库,指出相关性不强、语义难以理解或者有重复的条目,予以修改或删除。

2.2.2 试验性测试

然后对 23 名 0—2 岁儿童的父母进行试验性测试,测试中注意家长的感受和反应,修改难于理解、语义模糊和容易产生歧义的条目。

条目筛选后,形成 PAT 初稿。

2.3 量表因素的构建及条目归类

邀请 18 名儿童保健、儿童早期发展及心理学专家,就 0—2 岁儿童养育测量的维度进行深入探讨,并审阅已建立的 PAT 初稿。18 名专家最终将 0—2 岁儿童养育的定义操作化为育儿观念、关注、亲子关系、避免限制和干扰、语言刺激、学习环境、外出活动、喂养、安全和护理共 10 个方面,对应于 PAT 的 10 个因素。同时对 PAT 初稿中每个条目最能代表的因素进行评价,至少应有 2/3 的专家均一致同意某一条目归属于某一因素,才会将这一条目放到该因素下。如果多于 2/3 的专家认为某一条目不对应于任何一个因素,则删除该条目。

2.4 预试与条目的纯化

于 2013 年 8 月—2013 年 9 月,在 5 家妇幼保健机构的儿童保健及免疫接种门诊,选择 0—35 月龄儿童及家长 290 名,使用专家归类后的 PAT 版本对家长进行了测试。利用预试数据进行以下分析和研究:计算每个条目与其所属因素的 Spearman 相关系数及每个因素的 Cronbach α 系数。如果条目与所属因素的相关系数小于 0.30,则从该因素中删除该条目。如果因素的 Cronbach α 系数小于 0.50,则删除该因素。通过这一步骤,删除了 10 个条目 2 个因素,形成了含有 38 个条目 8 个因素的 PAT 测试版。

2.5 正式测试与验证性因素分析

于 2013 年 9 月—2013 年 11 月在 11 家妇幼保健机构的儿童保健及免疫接种门诊,每家机构抽取约 60 名 0—35 月龄儿童及家长,使用 PAT 测试版对家长进行了测试。利用正式测试的数据,应用 Mplus 7.0 软件进行验证性因素分析以评估模型即 PAT 测试版,并根据拟合指数决定是否进一步修正模型,形成最终模型即 PAT。

3 结果

3.1 PAT 条目库及初稿形成

PAT 条目库包含78 个条目。通过一般性筛选和试验性测试,初步筛选出50 个条目,形成 PAT 初稿。

3.2 条目的归类、纯化及量表测试版的形成

基于专家评价的条目归类见表1,如表所示,每个因素含有4—6 个条目,比较均匀。另外,多于2/3 的专家认为条目 T49 及条目 T50 不对应于10 个因素的任何一个因素,则删除这两个条目。条目与其所属因素的 Spearman 相关系数及每个因素的 Cronbach α 系数见表1。其中因素6 外出活动、因素9 避免干扰和限制、因素10 护理的 Cronbach α 系数小于0.50,故从量表中删掉因素9 和因素10。因素6 的 α 系数为0.448,略小于0.50,但是我们认为其包含的这些条目对育儿评估量表的组成有重要意义,所以保留了该因素及其条目。其他条目与所属因素之间的相关系数均大于0.30,且所属因素的 Cronbach α 系数均大于0.50,故均予以保留。通过这一步骤,删除了10 个条目2 个因素,形成了含有38 个条目8 个因素的 PAT 测试版。

表1 条目—因素之间的 Spearman 相关系数及各因素的 Cronbach α 系数 ($n=284$)

因素	Cronbach α 系数	条目	相关系数
因素1 育儿观念	0.548	T1	0.540
		T2	0.620
		T3	0.551
		T4	0.419
		T5	0.642
		T6	0.455
因素2 关注	0.582	T7	0.508
		T8	0.660
		T9	0.389
		T10	0.726
		T11	0.734

续表 1

因素	Cronbach α 系数	条目	相关系数
因素 3 亲子关系	0.614	T12	0.668
		T13	0.335
		T14	0.574
		T15	0.713
		T16	0.763
因素 4 学习环境	0.709	T17	0.616
		T18	0.663
		T19	0.667
		T20	0.666
		T21	0.553
因素 5 语言刺激	0.756	T22	0.666
		T23	0.780
		T24	0.828
		T25	0.694
因素 6 外出活动	0.448	T26	0.646
		T27	0.568
		T28	0.661
		T29	0.409
因素 7 喂养	0.526	T35	0.639
		T36	0.748
		T37	0.557
		T38	0.654
因素 8 安全	0.611	T39	0.625
		T40	0.691
		T41	0.626
		T42	0.471
		T43	0.702

续表1

因素	Cronbach α 系数	条目	相关系数
因素9 避免干扰和限制	0.370	T30	0.635
		T31	0.449
		T32	0.389
		T33	0.472
		T34	0.643
因素10 护理	0.397	T44	0.475
		T45	0.643
		T46	0.259
		T47	0.768
		T48	0.350

3.3 验证性因素分析

3.3.1 模型评估

PAT测试版模型拟合指数见表2,模型χ^2值较大(1 367.795),与CFA所用样本量较大($n=607$)有关,但是χ^2/df小于5;*RMSEA*估计值(0.043)在精确拟合范围内(<0.05),*RMSEA*的90%置信区间(0.040,0.047)在拟合良好的范围内,精确拟合优度检验统计不显著($p>0.05$),因此不能拒绝精确拟合的零假设(即*RMSEA*≤0.05),这说明模型拟合还可以。*CFI*和*TLI*的值分别为0.886和0.875,均小于0.90,所以进一步修正模型。

表2 删除条目T6、T42前后的模型拟合指数($n=607$)

模型	PAT测试版模型拟合指数							
	χ^2	df	χ^2/df	*CFI*	*TLI*	*RMSEA*	*RMSEA* 90% CI	Probability (*RMSEA*)≤0.05
修正前模型	1 367.795	637	2.147	0.886	0.875	0.043	0.040—0.047	1.000
修正后模型	1 048.906	566	1.853	0.916	0.906	0.037	0.034—0.041	1.000

3.3.2 模型修正

为了改善数据拟合不良的初始模型,常使用修正指数(modification indices, *MI*)作为诊断指标来帮助修改模型设定[4]。根据修正指数结果,第一个需要修正的参数是因素5和条目T42的误差协方差,其*MI*值为100.066,最大。分析原因,考虑是条目T42放在多个因素下均有理论意义所致,故将条目T42删除,再对模型进行拟合。以此方法又删除了条目T6。删除条目T42、T6后的模型拟合指标见表2。由表可见,修正后模型的拟合指数均有所改善,尤其是 *CFI* 和 *TLI* 的值均大于0.90。这些指标都说明修正后的模型拟合良好。

3.3.3 条目的标准化因素载荷

各条目在所属因素的标准化因素载荷见表3,由表可知,除条目 T35"家长是否在孩子6个月龄时及时添加辅食"外,所有其他条目的因素载荷都大于0.30,满足传统的因素载荷截断值0.30。条目T35的标准化因素载荷较低,为0.198,说明它是因素7喂养的弱标识,但是T35的因素载荷统计显著($p<0.01$),且该条目从理论意义上来说对因素7很重要,因此我们在模型中保留该条目。

至此,PAT建立,PAT共含有8个因素,分别含有5、5、5、5、4、4、4、4共36个条目。

表3 PAT各条目的标准化因素载荷($n=607$)

因素	条目	因素载荷
因素1	T1	0.355
	T2	0.521
	T3	0.675
	T4	0.388
	T5	0.607
因素2	T7	0.496
	T8	0.422
	T9	0.573
	T10	0.694
	T11	0.751
因素3	T12	0.698
	T13	0.461
	T14	0.651
	T15	0.677
	T16	0.529
因素4	T17	0.638
	T18	0.733
	T19	0.740
	T20	0.528
	T21	0.762

续表3

因素	条目	因素载荷
因素5	T22	0.678
	T23	0.807
	T24	0.693
	T25	0.640
因素6	T26	0.464
	T27	0.736
	T28	0.629
	T29	0.670
因素7	T35	0.198
	T36	0.572
	T37	0.715
	T38	0.518
因素8	T39	0.629
	T40	0.591
	T41	0.669
	T43	0.442

4 讨论

4.1 量表编制原则

由于养育不是一个单一的结构,它所包含的内容很广泛,包括父母的养育观念、养育行为及其对儿童的情感表现等,所以在对其进行定量、半定量评价时,必须依据一定的标准,遵循相应的原则。

4.1.1 导向性与独立性原则

编制PAT时,应充分考虑到与儿童发展结局相关的养育观念及养育行为等。要以促进儿童早期发展为方向,体现新的时代背景特色。独立性原则是各个条目之间互不相容,每个条目都独立地提供信息,不能有重叠。重叠、冗余的条目将被重复记分,加大了权重,会影响整个评估的科学性和精确性。

4.1.2 客观性与全面性原则

条目的内容应尽量量化,尽可能剔除不确定因素的影响,明确评价的尺度和标准,如"访谈期间,家长自然地赞扬孩子至少两次"。已有的育儿评估工具往往只是从养育方式或育儿知识等孤立的角度出发对养育加以测量,很难揭示出养育的全貌。为此,本研究在编制育儿评估量表时对构成养育的各个方面加以有效的整合,构建合理的测量维度,并在此基础上构建 PAT 条目库。

4.1.3 普遍性与针对性原则

PAT 所涉及的条目,在父母中应具有普遍性,而不是个别父母的养育行为。同时条目的设计应针对 0—2 岁儿童,因为不同年龄阶段的儿童,其父母采取的养育方式和养育行为也是不同的。该年龄阶段的最佳养育应该包括儿童与养育人之间积极的感情交流,丰富的语言环境,各种各样的与年龄相适应的提供刺激的玩具,没有严厉的或惩罚性的父母行为,积极的喂养及丰富全面的营养提供,规律的日常生活和安全的环境。

4.1.4 可行性与可测性原则

所编制的量表应简单易操作,由于调查对象是婴幼儿及其父母之一,为避免调查时费时太长儿童产生的疲劳感和厌烦感,条目不能太多,结构不能过于复杂,否则会加大被试的负担,使评价过程难以施行。同时量表注意从实用角度出发,注意简化实施和记分方法,方便儿童保健专业人员评价使用。

4.1.5 区分性与准确性原则

PAT 是对婴幼儿的养育状况进行量化评价,评价最终得分要有等级之分,故量表编制时要注意避免没有区分性的条目,如"是否带孩子定期免疫接种"。根据我们在量表编制前进行的准备性问卷调查,98.9% 的父母都能做到这一点,因此该条目不具有区分性。准确性是指条目不能使评价对象难以回答或产生歧义。

4.2 量表编制方法

编制量表的具体方法主要有三种:即合理建构法(逻辑法)、因素分析法和实践标准法(经验法)[8]。合理建构法(逻辑法)就是由专家根据某种专业理论,确定所要测量的特质,用逻辑分析的方法编写和选择一些看起来能测验这些特质的题目[8]。从研究方法上来看,探索性因素分析从可观测变量中探索、发现潜变量和规律量,从为数众多的可观测变量中概括和综合出少数几个因素,用较少的因素变量来最大限度地概括和解释原有的观测信息[9],现已成为心理测验编制发展初步模型和理论建构强有力的心理测量学方法。然而,探索性因素分析也有不足之处,由于该方法是在统计技术的基础上进行的,具有较强的数据依赖性,往往只考虑数据之间的纯数字特征而没有任何理论前提,容易出现一些不合理的分析结果[10]。比如,20 世纪七八十年代 Caldwell 和 Bradley 编制的 IT-HOME 量表,采用探索性因素分析抽取分量表,结果一些条目并不在所属分量表的范畴,像"避免限制和惩罚"分量表,除了 6 条评价"严厉"的条目之外,还包括了这样 2 个条目:家中至少可以看到 10 本书,家里养有宠物[11]。所以探索性因素分析法提取因素的量表编制方法尚需进一步探索和完善,以取得量表既结构合理又有理论意义的效果。

本研究采用第一种方法即合理建构法(逻辑法),就是由专家将婴幼儿养育的定义操作化为若干个维度,并把相关的条目归到对应的养育维度,每个维度即形成一个因素。该方法的目的在于建立一些“概念丰富”的分量表,使其更加合乎养育理论,条目的归组是基于理论联系而不是统计分析。这种方法曾被用于重新建立 HOME“概念丰富”的分量表,我们借鉴了这些文献中建立分量表的方法和步骤。

然而逻辑法编制量表也有缺点[8]:从表面上看能测量某一特质的条目,实际上可能并不测量这一特质,即量表的表面效度并不能保证量表的真正效度。因此,我们通过以下两种方法检测这些表面上同质的条目是否真的测量了养育的某一特质,如果不是则删除之。第一种方法是检测每个条目与其所属因素的相关性,相关性越强,说明条目的鉴别力越高,敏感性越好。如果条目与所属因素的相关系数小于 0.30,则从该因素中删除该条目。第二种方法是检测各个因素的 Cronbach α 系数,反映的是量表内部条目间的一致性,即同质性。如果因素的 Cronbach α 系数小于 0.50,则删除该因素。通过以上 2 个步骤,确保了每一个因素均由相关性高的、具有同质性的一组条目组成。

4.3 模型评估和模型修正

在结构方程模型分析中,人们通常在现有理论、文献或先前研究的基础上提出模型,然后用设定的模型来拟合可用的数据,即模型评估。如果模型对数据拟合良好,则经过该步骤后建模过程可以停止。这种尝试性的初始模型常常并不如所愿的拟合数据。换言之,初始模型常常有设定不当之处,因而需要寻找模型拟合不良的可能原因,确定导致模型设定错误的因素,然后修正模型并用同一数据进行检验。实际研究中的建模过程可能会重复进行多次的模型修正。该过程可称为“模型设定探索”[12]。本研究中经验证性因素分析发现模型拟合数据略有不足之处(*CFI* 和 *TLI* 值低于 0.90 的标准),故经过了一次模型修正,结合理论意义删除了一个条目后,模型精确拟合数据,确立了 PAT 最终版。

综上,本研究通过专家探讨建立 PAT 的结构,并通过专家评价将条目归组,即采用逻辑法编制了 PAT。该量表包括 8 个 “概念丰富”的分量表(因素),包括 36 个条目,基本包括了 0—2 岁儿童养育的内容,具有较好的代表性。进一步的研究将进行 PAT 的信效度检验。

致谢

本文为国家计生委项目《儿童早期发展促进项目》(第二周期)的阶段性成果之一。

References

[1] C Hertzman, T Boyce. How experience gets under the skin to create gradients in developmental health. Annual Review of Public Health, 2010, 31: 329 - 347.

[2] J Rijlaarsdam, H Tiemeier, A Hofman. Home environments of infants: Relations with child development through age 3. Journal of Epidemiology and Community Health, 2013, 67: 14 - 20.

[3] B Bell, J Belsky. Parenting and children's cardiovascular functioning. Child: Care, Health and Development, 2008, 34: 194 - 203.

[4] A Waylen, N Stallard, S Stewart-Brown. Parenting and health in mid-childhood: A longitudinal study. The European Journal of Public Health, 2008, 18: 300 - 305.

[5] M Smith. Early Interventions with Young Children and Their Parents in the UK. London: Jessica Kingsley Publishers, 2006.

[6] C Puckering. The Mellow Parenting Program: Its Methods and Outcome. Parenting Imperatives: A National Parenting Conference, 2004.

[7] Central People's Government of the People's Republic of China. National Programme of Action for Child Development in China in the 2010s. 2013-02-06. http://www.gov.cn/gongbao/content/2011/content_1927200.htm.

[8] Y Jin. Psychological Testing. 2nd ed. Shanghai: East China Normal University Press, 2005.

[9] Z Z Feng, F Wang. Confirmatory factor analysis of armymen's mental quality scale. Chinese Journal of Behavioral Medicine and Brain Science, 2010, 19: 658 - 660.

[10] V Savalei, S Kolenikov. Constrained versus unconstrained estimation in structural equation modeling. Psychological Methods, 2008, 13: 150.

[11] M R Linver, J Brooks-Gunn, N Cabrera. The home observation for measurement of the environment (HOME) inventory: The derivation of conceptually designed subscales. Parenting, 2004, 4: 99 - 114.

[12] J C Wang, X Q Wang, B F Jiang. Structural Equation Models: Methods And Applications. Beijing: Higher Education Press, 2011.

The Revelation of Primary Science Curriculum Evaluation from PISA and TIMSS

Jia Liu[1,a], Yi Bai[1,b,*]

[1]Key Laboratory of Child Development and Learning Science of Ministry of Education, Southeast University, Nanjing, Jiangsu, China

[a]loveinpuff@163.com, [b]by.rcls@seu.edu.cn

[*]Corresponding author

Keywords: PISA; TIMSS; science curriculum evaluation

Abstract: This paper introduced two major international education assessment program: PISA and TIMSS. Based on the evaluation content, the thesis design, testing methods, scientific inquiry of PISA and TIMSS, some revelations were given to primary science curriculum evaluation in China.

PISA 与 TIMSS 对小学科学课程评价的启示

刘佳[1,a]，柏毅[1,b,*]

[1]东南大学儿童发展与学习科学教育部重点实验室，南京，江苏，中国

[a]loveinpuff@163.com，[b]by.rcls@seu.edu.cn

[*]通讯作者

关键词：PISA；TIMSS；科学课程评价；论文；会议

中文摘要：本文介绍了 PISA 和 TIMSS 两大国际教育成绩评估项目，从测评内容、命题设计、测评方式、科学探究几个方面思考了 PISA 和 TIMSS 对我国小学科学课程评价的启示。

《小学科学(1—6 年级)课程标准(修订稿)》评价建议中明确指出：教学和评价是课程实施的两个重要环节。建立评价目的多元、评价内容全面、评价方式多样的评价体系，将促进学生科学素养的全面发展和教师水平的提高，有效地改进教学，以保证科学课程的有效实施[1]。

从课程标准中可以看出，科学课程评价的基本理念包括评价目的个性化，评价内容全面化，评价方法多样化，评价实施过程化。但统一标准后，在真实评价中往往陷入以考定教的怪圈，即考试考什么，老师教什么。如果考试中只评价学生对科学基本原理的掌握，这种评价对于学生的未来无疑是失败的。科学课程中如何评价学生的学习，以使测评实现其基本的功能——预测、比较、评估？本文针对以上问题，分析了国际教育成绩评估项目对我国小学科学课程评价的启示。

1 国际教育成绩评估项目

国际教育成绩评估项目由于参与国的数量多，参与国的经济总量占世界经济总量的比例大，对于各国进行纵向和横向比较有重要指导意义，它们为各国认识本国学生的学业成就、学生适应未来生活的能力和学生在世界上的竞争力提供信息，也为各国借鉴他国优秀的教育模式、学校类型、课程内容和教学方法提供素材。

1.1 国际学生评估项目(PISA)

国际学生评估项目(PISA)是经济发展与合作组织(OECD)发起的国际比较研究，测评 15 岁的学生在多大程度上掌握了全面参与社会所需要的终身学习能力，聚焦在阅读、数学和科学等关键领域上[2]。PISA 除了关于相关素质的标准试题外，还通过问卷调查收集学生个人、家庭和学校背景信息，以全面分析学生素质和其他因素的关系。由于 PISA 关注学生在主要学科领域应用知识和技能的能力，以及在不同情境中提出、解决和解释问题时有效地分析、推理和交流的能力，因此，PISA 的评估框架不同

于学业选拔考试。PISA测评从2000年开始,每三年进行一次,每次从阅读、数学、科学中选择一个作为主要领域,另外两个作为次要领域。迄今已开展4次测评,累计参与测评的成员国和伙伴国已有60多个,这些国家的经济总量占世界经济总量的90%,PISA已成为当前最受瞩目的国际教育成绩评估项目之一。

1.2 国际数学和科学测评趋势(TIMSS)

另一个国际教育成绩评估项目TIMSS是由国际教育成就评价协会(IEA)发起和组织的国际教育评价研究和测评活动。TIMSS主要测试四年级和八年级学生的数学与科学学业成绩,以及达到课程目标的情况。与PISA不同,TIMSS更符合学校学业评价的要求,它是基于课程标准对知识和技能进行的评价。20世纪60—80年代,IEA曾组织十多个国家参加第一次和第二次国际数学和科学测评。1994年IEA在美国国家教育统计中心NCES和国家科学基金会NSF的财政支持下,发起并组织了第三次国际数学和科学评测,这次活动被简称为TIMSS[3]。1999年这项活动继续进行,之后每四年进行一次。为了更好地延续这项有意义的研究活动,2003年,TIMSS成为国际数学和科学测评趋势的缩写。TIMSS测评是当代青少年数学教育和科学教育颇具影响力的比较研究,对我国的科学教育测评有一定的启发和借鉴意义。

2 对科学课程评价的启示

PISA和TIMSS分别代表着对于学生学习能力和学业成就的国际成绩评估项目,在国际上颇具影响力和公认度,它们对我国小学科学课程评价具有诸多启发。

2.1 测评内容应包括广泛的生活情境

以PISA为例,PISA科学素养测评框架由四个相互关联的部分组成:科学背景、科学能力、科学知识和科学态度。其中科学知识涉及“物质系统”、“生命系统”、“地球和空间系统”和“技术系统”四个内容领域。在我国《小学科学课程标准(修订稿)》中对课程内容的界定也包括四个领域,分别为物质科学、生命科学、地球与宇宙科学、技术与工程。通过比较发现,两者覆盖的内容基本相同。但差别主要在于PISA在设计科学试题的背景时,把广泛的生活情境纳入了测评框架中,不仅关注学生个人(包括自我、家庭和同伴群)的生活情境,也包括社会的和全球的情境,在各个情境下都涉及健康、自然资源、环境、危险、科学与技术前沿五个议题。虽然上海学生在PISA测评中的表现不俗,但仔细分析可以发现,上海学生在全球背景的试题上表现不如其他国家,在涉及科学与技术前沿的问题上也有待提高。

在科技发展日新月异的今天,科学教育应更多关注科技前沿问题,让学生了解现代科技发展的最新动态,以开阔学生的视野,激发学生对于科学技术的兴趣。另外,科学技术问题的全球化也是当今科技发展的一个重要议题。包括流行病、大气污染、全球变暖等问题越来越需要在全球化的视角下探讨和解决。在科学课程测评框架中,应全面考虑科学问题的生活背景，特别是加强对全球问题和科技前沿的关注。

2.2 将真实的情境融入命题设计中

PISA 和 TIMSS 科学素养测评中都注重试题设计的情境生活化。这里以 PISA 有关温室效应的一题为例。

温室效应：事实还是幻想？

生物需要能量才能生存，而维持地球生命的能量来自太阳。太阳非常炽热，将能量辐射到太空中，但只有一小部分的能量会到达地球。地球表面的大气层，就像包裹着我们的星球表面的毯子一样，保护着地球，使它不会像真空的世界那样，有极端的温差变化。大部分来自太阳的辐射能量，会穿过大气层进入地球。地球吸收了部分能量，其他则由地球表面反射回去。部分反射回去的能量会被大气层吸收。由于这个效应，地球表面的平均温度比没有大气层吸收能量时的温度高。大气层的作用就像温室一样，因此有了“温室效应”一词。温室效应在 20 世纪越来越显著。事实表明，地球大气层的平均温度不断上升。报纸杂志上常说，二氧化碳排放量增加，是 20 世纪气温上升的主要原因。

小德有兴趣研究地球大气层的平均温度和地球上二氧化碳排放量之间的关系。他在图书馆找到下面两幅曲线图。

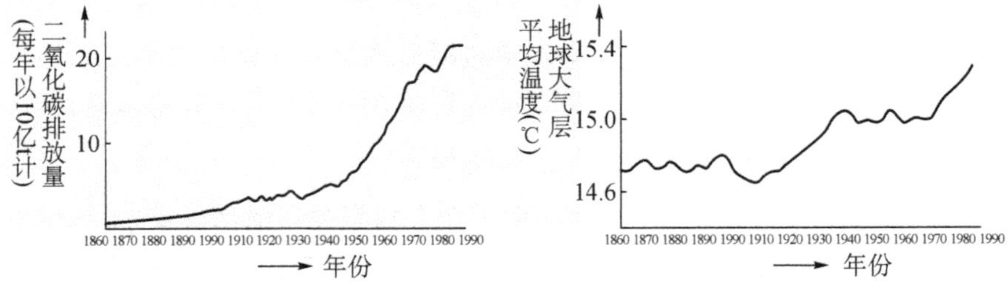

图 1

小德从曲线图中得出结论，认为地球大气层平均温度的上升，显然是由二氧化碳排放增加而引起的。

问题 1：曲线图中有什么数据支持小德的结论？

问题 2：小德的同学小妮却不同意他的结论。她比较两幅曲线图，指出其中有些资料并不符合小德的结论。请从曲线图中举出一项不符合小德结论的资料，并解释答案[2]。

从例题可以看出，测试的每个单元都创设了一个真实的生活情境，一般是一段涉及生活背景的简短文字，加上一张表格、图表、图片或者示意图。测试的任务往往是在表格、曲线图或者图示中找到与答题相关的信息，发现图表中信息的特点，用科学知识来解释这些信息，或者用科学方法对科学证据做出解释从而得出结论。

科学测评的目的不是考查学生是否掌握孤立的科学知识，而是考查学生是否具有运用科学知识解决生活问题的能力。因此,在进行科学课程测评时,应注重命题设计的情境化,这些情境是贴近生活实际、学生可以接受的,而不是命题者为了加强命题设计的情境化而想象或抽象出的情境。

2.3 注重测评方式多样性

《小学科学课程标准(修订稿)》中对于课程评价的方式给出以下建议:纸笔测验、表现性评价、真实性评价和档案袋。表现性评价主要针对学生的行为,如让学生运用实验器材设计并完成一个实验,有的会对实验加上书面的记录,教师可以从中了解学生对于科学知识的掌握、对实验技能的把握及得出结论的合理性等多方面信息。真实性评价检验学生面对真实生活情境时解决问题的能力。相对于纸笔测验是对学生掌握特定教育目标的短期评价,档案袋主要用来做长期的促进式的评价,帮助学生反思或修改自己的学习计划,记录学生的学习进度,以求得更大的进步。档案袋这种评价方式类似于追踪研究,即在比较长的时间内对相同对象进行有系统的定期研究。TIMSS 针对四年级和八年级的学生进行数学和科学学业成绩的测评,如果在四年级和八年级测试的是同一批学生,则 TIMSS 可以看作一项追踪研究。追踪研究可以看到学生在科学课程学习中较完整的发展过程和发展过程中的一些关键转折点,可以有效评价学生学习的稳定性问题,预测学生在科学素养上的发展情况。

但在实际的课堂教学中,纸笔测验仍占据着主导地位。借鉴 PISA 和 TIMSS 的测评方式,在进行纸笔测验的同时可以结合问卷调查。通过问卷调查收集学生的背景信息,从多个方面考虑影响学生学习的因素。单一的纸笔测试,其测试目的过于功利,忽视了价值的多元性。随着社会的不断发展,人们思想的不断更新,人们会逐渐意识到社会在根本上是价值多元的。这种多元不仅深刻地反映在个人生活中,还反映在各国的教育体制中。正是由于价值多元性的存在,在教学测评中应改变测试的功利思想,合理运用多种评价方式,分析影响学生学习的各方面因素,认识学生认知发展的规律,为学生的学习提供合理的建议和反馈。

2.4 注重科学探究能力

我国一直被视为"知识为本"的典范,在以知识为主的国际测评中,我国学生往往能取得卓越的成绩,但实际上我国学生的探究能力或动手能力和批判性思维往往不及其他国家,这也是我国学生缺乏创新精神的一个原因。对于科学探究的测量和评价要比科学知识的测评困难得多,传统纸笔考试中的题目如果有具体答案,那么这个就不是真正的探究,它不能通过多种方法和途径来解决问题。如果答案只是一个数字,与其说是探究不如说是计算[4]。就算计算过程有多么的复杂,它也只是科学探究的工具。之前提到的表现性评价可以作为评价科学探究的方法,但这种方法的不足是花费大,难推广。因此,在科学探究能力的测评上,我国还需要借鉴其他国家的经验,关注学生动手能力和批判性思维的培养,改革评价方式,以提高我国学生的科学学科国际竞争力。

致谢

本文获得教育部人文社会科学研究专项《基础教育阶段技术与设计教育的国际化比较研究》(项目批号:11JDGC026)支持。

References

[1] Y G Jiang, H Z Xiang, P Jin. The construction and practice of the assessment system of scientific inquiry teaching. Curriculum, Teaching, Material and Method, 2005, 25: 60 - 64.

[2] J Lu. The theory and practice of PISA assessment. Shanghai: East China Normal University Publishing, 2013.

[3] J Q Shen, J C Yang. The enlightenment of scientific evaluation in TIMSS and PISA. The Science Education Article Collects, 2011, 6: 95,115.

[4] J Y Wang. The exploration to the science method and significance of academic assessment in America. Global Education, 2008, 37: 3 - 5.

Influence of Sensory Integration Level on Children's Breaststroke Learning Outcomes

Yang Liu[1,a], Lei Ma[2,b,*], Chao Du[3,c]

[1]The Physical Education College of Jiangxi Normal University, Nanchang, China

[2]Key Laboratory of Child Development and Learning Science of Ministry of Education, Research Center for Learning Science, Southeast University, Nanjing 210096, China

[3]The Number 4 Primary School of BinCheng District of Binzhou City, BinZhou, Shandong, China

[a]worldinsight@163.com, [b]mlmyhero@163.com, [c]hainiusdbz@163.com

[*] Corresponding author

Keywords: children; sensory integration dysfunction; breaststroke; skill learning

Abstract: The fact that the negative influence of modern society on children's Sensory Integration Levels has been proved to be true by many experts. SID can influence various aspects in children's daily lives such as school studies or even development of their potential intelligence. However, for experiments that research the effects of SID on children's MSL, majority of them are mainly about its influences on the outcomes of physical education courses with almost no research on its effect on swimming learning. Thus a further study on the influence of SID on children's swimming learning outcomes is necessary. Method: By evaluating the Sensory Integration Level of 108 children by Children's Sensory Integration Evaluating Questionnaire, and calculating the standard scores of their Breaststroke learning outcomes, this article analyzed the influences of Sensory Integration Level on Children's Breaststroke Learning Outcomes. Conclusion: Levels of Sensory Integration can not be a significantly negative factor in Children's Breaststroke Learning, children who suffer Sensory Integration Dysfunction (SID) can also achieve an excellent Breaststroke learning outcomes.

统合水平对儿童蛙泳学习效果影响的探究

刘杨[1,a]，马磊[2,b,*]，杜超[3,c]
[1]江西师范大学体育学院，南昌，江西，中国
[2]东南大学学习科学中心，东南大学儿童发展与学习科学教育部重点实验室，江苏南京
[3]滨州市滨城区第四小学，滨州，山东，中国
[a]worldinsight@163.com，[b]mlmyhero@163.com，[c]hainiusdbz@163.com
*通讯作者

关键词：儿童；感觉统合失调；蛙泳；技能学习

中文摘要：儿童时期正是成才的关键期，有研究显示感觉统合失调除对儿童学业成绩有负面影响外，同样对其体育技能的学习有一定影响；关于调查儿童感觉统合失调对运动技能学习的影响尤其是对于游泳技能学习的影响在国内报道较少。

方法：本文通过“儿童感觉统合能力发展评定量表”评定108名男、女学员各项统合水平得分，并结合学员学期末测得的蛙泳学习效果标准分来探讨统合水平对蛙泳学习效果的影响。

结论：儿童统合水平的高低不影响其蛙泳学习效果，统合失调儿童也可较好地掌握蛙泳技能。

1 引言

现代化社会生活给儿童的感觉统合能力的发展带来负面影响已被许多国内外学者所证实，感觉统合失调会对儿童的正常学习活动产生一定程度的影响，有的甚至严重地阻碍了孩子潜力的开发，长此以往会对儿童的学习活动造成心理创伤。儿童时期正是成才的关键期，有研究证明感觉统合失调除对学业成绩有一定影响外[1]，同样对体育技能的学习也有一定影响[2]。儿童感觉统合失调是儿童神经心理发育上的不同程度缺陷所造成的[3]，统合水平低下的儿童常常会发生诸如在运动中肢体的协调性较差、对体位或空间的感知能力下降、容易失去平衡以及获取相同知识技能较慢等现象，使技术动作练习中的自我监控时视觉和本体感觉的功能得不到相互适应，技术动作间的协调配合不佳[4]。而自我运动监控在游泳技能的学习中却起到关键作用；因此研究儿童统合失调对游泳技能学习的影响具有一定的实践意义。

2 实验对象与方法

2.1 实验对象

选取2011年、2012年文化宫暑期游泳培训班115名6—11岁学员（男68名，女

47名)为教学实验对象,依照招收的学员情况按年龄、性别比例随机分为A、B、C、D共4组进行教学(见表1)。经过对研究对象的教学以及对其成绩和各项指标的测试,最终获得有效被试的基本数据如表2所示。

表1 被试儿童分组年龄情况一览表

组别	组人数(人)学龄儿童			平均年龄(Year)学龄儿童		
	男童	女童	合计	男童($\bar{X} \pm S$)	女童($\bar{X} \pm S$)	合计($\bar{X} \pm S$)
A	17	11	28	9.27 ±1.67	9.49 ±1.64	9.36 ±1.63
B	17	11	28	9.27 ±1.74	9.51 ±1.56	9.36 ±1.64
C	17	12	29	9.37 ±1.69	9.25 ±1.58	9.32 ±1.62
D	17	13	30	9.57 ±1.81	9.29 ±1.44	9.45 ±1.64

表2 有效被试基本信息一览表

性别	组人数(人)	平均年龄(Year)($\bar{X} \pm S$)	平均体重(kg)($\bar{X} \pm S$)	平均身高(cm)($\bar{X} \pm S$)
男	65	9.43 ±1.70	37.37 ±11.66	142.52 ±10.59
女	43	9.55 ±1.40	32.87 ±6.76	141.28 ±9.28

如表2与表3所示,本研究被试儿童人群的年龄均值为男童(9.43 ±1.70)岁、女童(9.55 ±1.40)岁,对应全国常模10岁儿童的体重、身高均无显著性差异。可认为被试儿童在身高、体重指标上可反映全国儿童总体水平。

表3 有效被试与全国常模的单总体平均数假设检验(单尾)

对比方式	平均年龄(Year)($\bar{X} \pm S$)	平均体重(kg)($\bar{X} \pm S$)	平均身高(cm)($\bar{X} \pm S$)	显著水平 sig.
男童学员	9.43 ±1.70	37.37 ±11.66	142.52 ±10.59	
VS 全国常模	10.00 ±0.00	35.50 ±0.00	140.90 ±0.00	$p > 0.05$
女童学员	9.55 ±1.40	32.87 ±6.76	141.28 ±9.28	
VS 全国常模	10.00 ±0.00	33.80 ±0.00	141.30 ±0.00	$p > 0.05$

注:表中全国常模(男、女童10岁组全国平均体重、身高)数据引自国家体育总局官方网站发布的2010年国民体质监测公报。

2.2 实验方法

2.2.1 问卷调查法

本研究以填写《儿童感觉统合能力发展评定量表》[5]为测量儿童蛙泳学员感觉统合水平的主要手段。此量表由Aryes编制,先后由台湾的郑信雄和北京医科大学精神卫生研究所儿经改编,后经国内十个不同区域的实测,已证明其具有良好的效度。信度上,由于本研究所用问卷是儿童长期监护人根据儿童最近半年的生活情况来进行填写,因此考虑到蛙泳教学后距第一次填表日期相隔一个月,可能会导致填写依据产生变化(游泳运动可能会成为干预因素),而本研究仅研究统合水平对游泳学习的单向影响,因此未对儿童进行量表的重测信度检验;然而在实施问卷填写时已对监护人严正叮嘱,在一定程度上也保证了问卷填写人填写时的较严谨态度。

表4　儿童统合失调评判标准[6]

	正常分值	统合不调分值	重度统合不调分值
统合水平标准 T 分	40—69	30—40	<30

将由问卷获得的原始分换算成标准 T 分值,并与儿童统合失调评判标准对照,儿童感觉统合水平的四项分值中只要有一项小于 40 分即判定为轻度感觉统合不调,小于 30 分即为重度感觉统合不调。

经教学试验阶段的初测与补测,本研究共发放 115 份问卷,获得 113 份有效问卷,回收率为 98.26%。由于其他指标测量原因,实际使用问卷 108 份。

2.2.2　实验测试法

(1) 实验指标

A. 蛙泳学习效果 Z 分:学员学会蛙泳所用最少天数的标准分与终期 25 m 运动成绩标准分之和。

B. 感觉统合指标:前庭失衡、触觉过分防御、本体感失调、学习能力发展不足、大年龄的特殊问题。

(2) 实验方案

蛙泳的教学严格按照体育学院通用教材、全国体育院校教材委员会审定的《游泳运动》[7]中所记述的初学者的教学步骤进行蛙泳教学。

学员学会蛙泳所用最少天数的记录必须建立在以较为正确、完整的动作技术独立完成 25 m 蛙泳为准,记录学员能独立以蛙泳游完 25 m 的最少学习天数;技术要求必须是一个蛙泳动作周期内一次蛙泳划臂、一次抬头换气(或两次)、一次蛙泳蹬腿(或两次),且配合顺序正确。运动成绩的测定也必须建立在以较为正确、完整的动作技术独立完成 25 m 蛙泳的基础上,记录其最快完成 25 m 蛙泳的用时,技术要求必须是一个动作周期内一次蛙泳划臂(或两次)、一次蛙泳蹬腿(或两次),且动作配合的顺序正确。

学员学会蛙泳所用最少天数的标准分与终期 25 m 运动成绩标准分之和为蛙泳学习效果标准分。将标准分的前后 27% 定为优秀组和较差组,中间部分为一般组。

2.2.3　数理统计法

本文运用了 SPSS 17.0 对数据进行了两个总体率的假设检验、卡方检验、两独立样本非参数检验和单因素方差检验处理。

3　研究结果

3.1　男、女童学员不同程度统合失调率的特征

对比统合失调评判标准，确定男童患有重度、轻度统合失调人数分别为3人和13人，占其人数比例的4.62%和20.00%，总失调率24.62%；女童患重度、轻度统合失调人数分别为1人和5人，占其人数比例的2.33%和11.63%，总失调率为13.95%（见表5）。

表5　男、女童学员中统合失调发生率情况

性别	总人数（人）	轻度统合失调人数/失调率（人）/%	重度失调人数/失调率（人）/%	总失调者/总失调率（人）/%
男	65	13 / 20.00	3 / 4.62	16 / 24.62
女	43	5 / 11.63	1 / 2.33	6 / 13.95

如表6所示，经男、女统合失调两总体率的假设检验分析表明男、女学员间的轻度统合失调率和重度统合失调率均无显著性差异（$p>0.05$）。

表6　男、女童学员之间统合失调率的总体假设检验

组间对比方式	轻度统合失调率		重度统合失调率	
	Z值（$Z_{0.05}=1.96$）	显著水平（sig. 2-tailed）	Z值（$Z_{0.05}=1.96$）	显著水平（sig. 2-tailed）
男童VS女童	1.14	>0.05	0.62	>0.05

3.2　男、女童学员不同蛙泳学习效果水平组的感觉统合失调率特征

3.2.1　男、女儿童学员各蛙泳学习效果水平组的统合失调率特征

将男、女童学员的不同蛙泳学习效果组内样本的统合水平标准T分与评价标准对比，评定出男、女童学员各组内的统合失调人数，计算各组内不同程度的统合失调比率，汇总如表7和表8所示。女童蛙泳学习效果的优秀组、一般组、较差组中轻度感觉统合失调的比例依次为7.69%、17.65%、7.69%，重度感觉统合失调只在优秀组存在一人，占组内人数的7.69%。男童学员只在优秀组和较差组存在重度感觉统合失调现象，分别占组内人数的5.00%和10.00%，男童学员轻度感觉统合失调率在优秀组为30.00%，在一般组为20.00%，在较差组为10.00%。

表7　男童不同学习效果组感觉统合失调率汇总

组别	组人数（人）	轻度失调人数（人）	重度失调人数（人）	轻度失调比例（%）	重度失调比例（%）
优秀组	20	6	1	30.00	5.00
一般组	25	5	0	20.00	0.00
较差组	20	2	2	10.00	10.00

表8　女童不同学习效果组感觉统合失调率汇总

组别	组人数（人）	轻度失调人数（人）	重度失调人数（人）	轻度失调比例（%）	重度失调比例（%）
优秀组	13	1	1	7.69	7.69
一般组	17	3	0	17.65	0.00
较差组	13	1	0	7.69	0.00

3.2.2　感觉统合失调者在男、女童学员不同蛙泳学习效果组间的分布特征

如表9至表12所示，男、女童学员各蛙泳学习效果组内都发现不同比例的失调人数，男、女童各组失调者与正常者人数分布（比率）在经卡方检验后发现男、女童失调者在各组的人数分布较一致，总体上无显著性差异（$p>0.05$）。

表9　男童不同学习效果组感觉统合失调人数3×2列联表

组别	组人数（人）	轻度+重度失调人数/理论频数（人）	正常人数/理论频数（人）
优秀组	20	7 / 4.92	13 / 15.08
一般组	25	5 / 6.15	20 / 18.85
较差组	20	4 / 4.92	16 / 15.08
合计	65	16	49

表10　各男童蛙泳学习效果组不同统合水平人数分布的卡方（X^2）检验参数表

组间对比方式	卡方值 X^2	自由度 df	显著性水平/临界值 $\alpha/X^2_{0.05(2)}$	显著性 p
优秀组 VS 一般组 VS 较差组	1.68	2	0.05 / 5.99	>0.05

表11　女童不同学习效果组感觉统合失调人数3×2列联表

组别	组人数（人）	轻度+重度失调人数/理论频数（人）	正常人数/理论频数（人）
优秀组	13	2 / 1.81	11 / 11.19
一般组	17	3 / 2.37	14 / 14.63
较差组	13	1 / 1.81	12 / 11.19
合计	43	6	37

表12　各女童蛙泳学习效果组不同统合水平人数分布的卡方（X^2）检验参数表

组间对比方式	卡方值 X^2	自由度 df	显著性水平/临界值 $\alpha/X^2_{0.05(3)}$	显著性 p
优秀组 VS 一般组 VS 较差组	0.638	2	0.05/5.99	>0.05

3.2.3 男、女童学员不同蛙泳学习效果组之间感觉失调率的假设检验

上述卡方检验仅揭示了男、女童各自3组蛙泳学习效果组患统合失调者分布的整体差异情况,并不能说明具体任意两组间的差异或检验是否人数比率具一致性。因此进一步将男、女童学员各蛙泳学习效果组间的统合失调率进行两总体率的差异检验,对比不同蛙泳学习效果组儿童的不同统合水平人群比例是否有差异,检验方式及结果汇总如表13至表16所示。

表13 男童学员轻度统合失调率的组间差异检验

组间对比方式	样本合并率 P_t	抽样误差 δ	对应 Z 值 ($Z_{0.05}=1.96$)	显著水平 (sig. 2-tailed)
优秀组 VS 一般组	0.24	0.13	1.01	>0.05
优秀组 VS 较差组	0.20	0.13	1.82	>0.05
一般组 VS 较差组	0.16	0.11	0.92	>0.05

表14 男童学员重度统合失调率的组间差异检验

组间对比方式	样本合并率 P_t	抽样误差 δ	对应 Z 值 ($Z_{0.05}=1.96$)	显著水平 (sig. 2-tailed)
优秀组 VS 一般组	0.02	0.04	1.13	>0.05
优秀组 VS 较差组	0.08	0.08	0.60	>0.05
一般组 VS 较差组	0.04	0.06	1.61	>0.05

表15 女童学员轻度统合失调率的组间差异检验

组间对比方式	样本合并率 P_t	抽样误差 δ	对应 Z 值 ($Z_{0.05}=1.96$)	显著水平 (sig. 2-tailed)
优秀组 VS 一般组	0.13	0.13	0.79	$p>0.05$
优秀组 VS 较差组	0.08	0.07	0	$p>0.05$
一般组 VS 较差组	0.13	0.13	0.79	$p>0.05$

表16 女童学员重度统合失调率的组间差异检验

组间对比方式	样本合并率 P_t	抽样误差 δ	对应 Z 值 ($Z_{0.05}=1.96$)	显著水平 (sig. 2-tailed)
优秀组 VS 一般组	0.03	0.07	1.17	$p>0.05$
优秀组 VS 较差组	0.04	0.05	1.44	$p>0.05$
一般组 VS 较差组	0	0	—	—

检验结果显示男、女童学员不同蛙泳学习效果组间轻度、重度统合失调率均无显著性差异($p>0.05$),表明男、女童学员各不同蛙泳学习效果组间在不同统合水平的人群比例上无显著性差异,即便是在优秀组与较差组之间在重度感觉统合失调率上也

无显著性差异。

3.3 不同统合水平下儿童蛙泳学习效果的特征

3.3.1 儿童不同统合水平组间蛙泳学习效果的两独立样本非参数检验

将不同程度统合水平组(统合水平正常组、轻度失调组、重度失调组)间的反映蛙泳学习效果的“标准分之和”进行两独立样本非参数检验,探讨是否儿童不同的统合水平会对其蛙泳学习效果产生影响。

表17和表18为男、女儿童学员统合水平正常组与不同程度失调组的蛙泳学习效果标准分之和的两独立样本非参数检验情况,结果显示男、女儿童学员的学习效果在统合水平正常组、不同失调组之间无差异显著性($p>0.05$),认为男、女童轻、重度的感觉失调对其蛙泳学习效果的影响不显著。

表17 男童不同统合水平组间蛙泳学习效果的两独立样本非参数检验

对比方式	组人数(人)	学习效果 Z 分之和 $\bar{X}\pm S$	显著水平(sig. 2-tailed)
统合水平正常组	49	0.08 ± 1.76	
VS 轻度失调组	13	-0.45 ± 1.74	0.28
VS 重度失调组	3	0.63 ± 1.63	0.81

表18 女童不同统合水平组间蛙泳学习效果的两独立样本非参数检验

对比方式	组人数(人)	学习效果 Z 分之和 $\bar{X}\pm S$	显著水平(sig. 2-tailed)
统合水平正常组	37	0.08 ± 1.77	
VS 轻度失调组	5	-0.35 ± 1.10	0.74
VS 重度失调组	1	-1.07 ± 0.00	0.63

3.3.2 不同统合水平下儿童蛙泳学习效果的单因素方差检验

将不同程度统合水平组(统合水平正常组、轻度失调组、重度失调组)作为控制变量,将反映蛙泳学习效果的标准分之和作为观测变量,对男、女童不同统合水平下的儿童蛙泳学习效果进行单因素方差检验,分析是否儿童的统合水平会显著影响其蛙泳学习效果。

如表19至表20的结果显示,不同统合水平对儿童蛙泳学习效果的影响不显著($p>0.05$),对具有不同统合水平儿童学员的划分不会引起划分群体内蛙泳学习效果的显著变化。

表19 男童不同统合水平下的蛙泳学习效果单因素方差检验

控制变量	组人数（人）	学习效果标准分均值 $\bar{X} \pm S$	方差显著水平（sig.）	方差齐性检验（sig.）
统合水平正常组	49	0.08 ±1.76		
轻度失调组	13	-0.45 ±1.74		
重度失调组	3	0.63 ±1.63		
			0.51	0.85

表20 女童不同统合水平下的蛙泳学习效果单因素方差检验

控制变量	组人数（人）	学习效果标准分均值 $\bar{X} \pm S$	方差显著水平（sig.）	方差齐性检验（sig.）
统合水平正常组	37	0.08 ±1.77		
轻度失调组	5	-0.35 ±1.10		
重度失调组	1	-1.07 ±0.00		
			0.72	0.22

4 结果分析与讨论

4.1 被试人群统合失调率特征分析

由3.1结果可知,男、女儿童患感觉失调的人数分别为16人、6人;女童学员感觉统合失调率为13.95%,小于男童学员的24.62%,这与许韶君[8]等的研究结果相一致。男、女学员中重度感觉统合失调人数分别为3人和1人,重度失调率男童学员大于女童学员,其原因除特定区域总体的较为固定的重度失调检出率因素外,女学员样本量较少也可能会导致检出率出现误差造成差异。但经男、女统合失调两总体率的假设检验分析表明男、女学员间的轻度统合失调率和重度统合失调率均无显著性差异($p>0.05$);提示男、女被试统合失调检出率一致,所选取的样本对于研究统合失调对蛙泳学习效果影响及其人群的特征较可靠。

4.2 男、女童学员不同蛙泳学习效果水平组的感觉统合失调率特征分析

由3.2.1和3.2.2可知男、女童学员感觉统合失调者的分布特征,男、女童学员各自的3个蛙泳学习效果组内患感觉统合失调者人数与正常者人数在人数结构上较一致。提示男、女童学员即便蛙泳学习效果整体存有差异的群体中(即优秀组、一般组、较差组),出现感觉统合失调的人数分布(比例)在3组总体上却无差异的显著性。因此从男、女学员整体上讲,最终蛙泳学习优秀者、一般者、较差者当中患统合失调的人数或比例无差异,可以认为一个患有统合失调的孩子在学习蛙泳后可能出现在优秀组、一般组、较差组中的概率是相当的。

由3.2.3的结果提示，蛙泳学习效果优秀组、一般组和较差组内的儿童群体中有相近的感觉统合失调现象，因此可以认为蛙泳学习效果较好的人群不一定都是统合水平正常者，被检测出有统合失调的儿童也可以在蛙泳学习中获得较好的技能绩效体验，这与曹秀菁等[9]得出的体育成绩越差的儿童群体感觉统合失调率越高相违背。由于统合失调所造成的身体运动协调障碍、结构和空间知觉障碍、前庭平衡功能障碍等容易给儿童带来学习技能方面的诸多不便，久而久之会给其学习自信心蒙上阴影[10]。而本研究显示不同蛙泳学习效果水平组之间学员的不同统合水平人群比例无显著性差异，因此建议感觉统合不调儿童可通过多参与游泳运动来提高身体素质，同时也可为改善儿童学习自信心及日后学习其他技能的能力做铺垫。

4.3 不同统合水平下儿童蛙泳学习效果的特征分析

由3.3.1的检验结果进一步提示，统合失调的儿童当中的轻、重度的感觉统合失调患者也可以获得较好的蛙泳学习效果，从中获得基本蛙泳技能的掌握。其原因可能是由于游泳的练习环境对于儿童初学者来说较新鲜，水环境的陌生感和特殊趣味性使学员注意力更趋于集中，大脑皮质运动中枢兴奋性加强，对儿童的触觉防御障碍产生一定抑制作用；同时人体在水环境中的行动受阻力影响加大，动作趋于缓慢，那些反映儿童动作精密性程度较高的运动在水下变得更舒缓，使得小肌肉群发挥运动协调的过程被动延长；统合水平低下造成的前庭统合刺激不良会使人体感知地心引力的敏感性降低，因而人的翻、爬、跑、跳能力受阻[11]，然而游泳时的失重感会改善因前庭问题而产生的不良运动障碍，使孩子有更大的空间施展，发挥并拓展现有的运动能力，从中获得正向的运动情感体验。但此次样本的取样有限，对于能否代表儿童整体统合水平的人群特征还较缺乏样本量的支撑；因此统合失调对于儿童的技能学习的影响尤其是游泳技能学习的影响仍不容忽视。

根据3.3.2检验的结果，提示感觉统合正常、轻度失调、重度失调的男、女儿童在学习蛙泳后有相同的获得较佳技能学习效果的机会，再次证明统合失调儿童可以在游泳运动中获得与统合正常儿童同样的运动情感体验。

5 结论

(1) 男童学员的不同程度统合失调率均大于女童学员，但经两总体率的假设检验显示男、女童学员间不同程度感觉统合失调率均无显著性差异。

(2) 男、女童学员在总体和各组间的感觉统合失调人数的分布一致。

(3) 儿童蛙泳学习效果的好坏与其感觉统合水平无关。轻、重度感觉统合失调的儿童也可以获得较好的蛙泳学习效果，从中获得基本蛙泳技能的掌握。

致谢

本文为江苏省普通高校研究生创新计划项目(CXLX12_0121)陕西省教育厅科研

项目(11JK0443);安康学院高层次人才引进项目(AYQDRW200964)的阶段性成果之一。

References

[1] Luo Liru. The effect of children's sensory integration dysfunction on their learning ability and behavior. Chinese Journal of Clinical Rehabilitation, 2003, 7(28): 3914.

[2] Dai Xi, Ma Tinghui. The effect of sensory integration training on the balanced capacity and exercise ability of children who are suffering autism. Chinese Journal of Rehabilitation Medicine, 2008, 23(5): 436 – 437.

[3] Liu Xiaoli, Jiang Feng, Sun Zhihua. Study on relation between sensory integrative dysfunction of children and neuropsychological function. Chinese Journal of Public Health, 2005, 21(3): 296 – 297.

[4] Dick Hanura. Successful Swimming Teaching. Beijing: Beijing Sports University Press, 2007.

[5] Xue Wei. Statistical Analysis and Application. Beijing: Electronic Industry Press, 2004.

[6] Wei Ping. The relationship between sensory integration and behavior problems of chuang nationality children. Maternal and Children Health Care of China, 2008, 33: 4733 – 4734.

[7] The Compilation Committee of New Century Higher School Sports Teaching Materials. Swimming. Beijing: Higher Education Press, 2006.

[8] Xu Shaojun, Tao fangbiao, Wang Jun, et al. Intelligence, behavior problem and the sensory integration dysfunction of the children with learning difficulties. Chinese Journal of School Health, 2005, 26: 376 – 377.

[9] Cao Xiuqing, Tao Fangbiao, Zeng Guangyu, et al. Study on the relationship between sensory integration dysfunction and subject records in the primary scholar. Chinese Journal of School Doctor, 2002, 16: 492 – 494.

[10] Huang Xiting, Zhang Liwei, Mao Zhixiong. Sports Psychology. Shanghai: East China Normal University Press, 2003.

[11] Mehrdad Jazayeri, J Anthony Movshon. Integration of sensory evidence in motion discrimination. Journal of Vision, 2007, 12: 1 – 7.

A Comparative Study of Elementary School Science Curriculum and TIMSS Test Objective

Yexin Zhang[1,a], Yi Bai[1,b,*]
[1]Key Laboratory of Child Development and Learning Science of Ministry of Education, Southeast University, Nanjing, Jiangsu, China
[a]zyexin1991@126.com, [b]by.rcls@seu.edu.cn
[*]Corresponding author

Keywords: TIMSS; primary school; science curriculum

Abstract: This paper mainly introduces the science courses and evaluation targets of TIMSS. Compare TIMSS's targets with jiang su version teaching material of primary school in our country. This paper aims to give some suggests to the curriculum in our country from the perspective of the international assessment of science education.

我国小学科学课程与TIMSS测评目标的比较研究——以苏教版及TIMSS四年级为例

张叶欣[1,a], 柏毅[1,b,*]
[1]东南大学儿童发展与学习科学教育部重点实验室,南京,江苏,中国
[a]zyexin1991@126.com, [b]by.rcls@seu.edu.cn
*通讯作者

关键词:小学科学;课程;TIMSS

中文摘要:本文主要介绍科学教育国际测评领域影响力较大的TIMSS在四年级科学课程上涉及的领域和评测目标,以及我国小学科学教育教材——苏教版在课程设置上存在的异同,以期从国际测评角度对我国科学教育课程设置提出建议。

1 引言

随着科学技术的进步,很多国家开始重视科学技术教育,国际科学教育的测评不断发展。TIMSS测评是其中影响力较大的,它已明确提出不同阶段课程设置及评价目标,对于我国科学课程的设置有参考意义。

2 TIMSS简介

TIMSS是由国际教育成就评价协会(the International Association for the Evaluation of Educational Achievement,简称IEA)发起和组织的国际教育评价研究和评测活动,其含义为国际数学与科学趋势研究项目。TIMMS评价的领域由数学、科学成就和影响因素两部分组成。数学和科学成就主要考查样本学校四年级和八年级学生对基本概念的掌握情况和推理应用情况。TIMSS每四年测评一次,从1995年至今TIMSS已经组织过五次国际评估。本文主要参照TIMSS最新发布的2015评估框架。

TIMSS系列研究是IEA组织的覆盖面最大、参与人数最多且最严格的国际比较教育研究。2007年全球有48个国家和地区参与TIMSS研究,2011年有70个国家和地区参与。中国大陆没有参加TIMSS测评,但中国香港、台湾地区均参加。作为在科学教育国际测评领域非常有影响力的研究,TIMSS有着完善的评价体系,以科学领域小学四年级为例,它明确提出涉及不同国家的课程中多数主题的三个主要的领域被选来定义科学课程的内容——生命科学、物理科学和地球科学。[1]

虽然我国大陆尚未参与TIMSS评价,但我们仍然可以学习借鉴其课程设置及评价目标。因为TIMSS评价的理念即课程是学生学业成就的重要影响因素,评估的出

发点和落脚点也是课程。课程评价分为三个层次，即准备的课程、实施的课程、掌握的课程。准备的课程即社会认为学生应该学习怎样的数学和科学课程以及学校教育系统怎样满足社会的这种需要。实施的课程指在实际课堂上真正发生了什么，谁来教授这些课程，这些课程是怎样被教授的。掌握的课程指事实上，学生从课程中掌握了多少。

3 我国小学科学教育教材概况——以苏教版为例

2001 年，我国新一轮基础教育课程改革开始实施，开设了半个多世纪的小学自然课程更名为小学科学课程，《自然教学大纲》也由《全日制义务教育科学(3—6 年级)课程标准(实验稿)》取而代之。新课程改革以提高学生科学素养为宗旨，为了达到这一培养目标，小学科学课程的教学方法、教学内容及其呈现方式等都发生了巨大的变化。其中，对科学教材更是提出"一纲多本、教材多样性"的创新思想。目前，我国小学科学教材已经有 10 种。[2]

本文选取江苏教育出版社 2007 年第六版小学《科学》作为与 TIMSS 科学部分对比的教材，苏教版小学《科学》教材经全国中小学教材审定委员会 2001 年审查通过，由郝京华、路培琦主编，苏教版教材使用范围较大，影响力较广，评价较高。

苏教版《科学》教材一共 8 册，从三年级到六级，每学年两册。每册都由五个单元组成，前四个单元均为基础知识，苏教版教材强调科学概念结构化，把相关的科学概念重新组合在单元主题下，每个单元都可以作为一个课题。它强调从问题入手，认为科学的本质就是从提出问题到解决问题，特别是日常生活中人们所关心的问题。[3] 因此，苏教版教材的很多内容都是从生活出发，比如"我们周围的空气"、"白天与黑夜"、"呼吸和血液循环"。

最后一个单元为科学探究方法指导。从三年级到六年级依次为提出问题、观察与测量、排序与分类、调查与预测、解释与建立模型、交流与质疑、假设与实验、拓展与应用。

本文主要比较科学知识的设置，主要关注每册前四单元所涉及的科目领域。

4 科学课程考查科目及比例比较

TIMSS 意识到科学课程的组织在每个国家是不同的，为了进行四年级 TIMSS 2011 评估，TIMSS 选取了涉及不同国家的课程中多数主题的三个主要领域作为科学部分的测评内容，这三个领域为生命科学、物理科学和地球科学，其比例见表 1。

生命科学包括对生物的特点和生命进程以及它们之间的关系、与环境的相互作用的理解。物理科学涉及物质和能量相关的概念，包括化学和物理领域的一些主题。由于四年级的学生仅有关于化学的初步知识，因此这一框架更多地强调物理概念。地球科学主要包括地球的构造、物理性质和资源，地球的进程、周期和历史，太阳系中的地球。

表1 TIMSS四年级科学部分考查科目及比例

科目	比例
生命世界	45%
物质世界	35%
地球与宇宙	20%

苏教版教材内容的编制是依照现行《全日制义务教育科学(3—6年级)课程标准(实验稿)》进行的,课程标准的分目标主要包括五个方面:科学探究、情感态度与价值观、生命世界、物质世界、地球与宇宙,其中涉及具体内容的生命世界、物质世界、地球与宇宙与TIMSS四年级考查科目相同。参照苏教版《小学科学教学参考书》为教师提供的授课课时参考,得到三个科目的授课课时数以及比例,详见表2。

表2 苏教版小学科学课时数及比例

科目	课时数	比例
生命世界	75	37%
物质世界	84	42%
地球与宇宙	42	21%

由表1、表2可见,我国苏教版科学课在内容设置的科目上与TIMSS四年级测评领域相吻合,在具体领域的考查比例上存在一定差异,苏教版在生命世界、地理与宇宙部分所用的课时较少,其重心主要在物质世界,物质世界主要包括物理和化学。

苏教版各年级课时数相差不大,但每个学期的侧重科目有所不同,在低年级物理所占课时明显高于其他科目。化学总的课时数极少,地理科学的课时多分布在高年级。详见表3。

表3 苏教版科学各年级课时分布 (单位:课时)

	生物	化学	物理	地理	合计
三年级上册	7	0	10	2	19
三年级下册	13	0	7	6	26
四年级上册	6	2	17	1	26
四年级下册	9	1	13	1	24
五年级上册	5	0	14	7	26
五年级下册	9	0	13	5	27
六年级上册	5	5	2	13	25
六年级下册	21	0	0	7	28
合计	75	8	76	42	201

由表3可看出生物占总课时的37%,化学占4%,物理占38%,地理占21%。

虽然新的科学教育课程标准提出科学教育应从一年级开始,但现行的教材是从三年级开始的,通过表3可以清楚地看到不同门类知识在各年级的分布及在总知识中所占的比重。

在苏教版教材中生物知识在四个学科领域知识中所占比例最大，而且分布最均匀，每本教材中都包含生物知识。其次，地理和物理学科知识分布也比较均匀，都有过半的教材涉及这两个部分的内容 。

由表1、表2可见，苏教版教材可以适当增加地球与宇宙科学领域的知识。苏教版的教材中涉及地理科学的知识较少，而且多集中在五、六年级，在四年级以前只有10个章节。

5　具体领域比较——以生命科学领域为例

TIMSS评测分为科目、领域、主题、目标四个层次。

生命科学的主题范围一共5个，即生物的特点和生命进程、生命周期，繁殖和遗传，与环境的相互作用，生态系统，人类健康。

选取生命科学主题中的繁殖和遗传，与苏教版教材相关课程做比较。

TIMSS生命科学繁殖和遗传的目标一共有三方面。

(1) 认识到植物和动物在繁殖的时候将自己从父母那里遗传来的特征遗传给自己的后代。

认识并解释，一些特性是与环境相互作用的结果，比如植物的高度与接收到的太阳光量有关，或小动物不增加体重，是因为它没有得到足够的食物。

(2) 认识并解释，从父母那里继承的一些特征可以帮助生物生存，如蜡质涂层植物的叶子帮助植物在干燥的气候条件下生存，或者动物的颜色帮助它躲避捕食者。

(3) 识别并描述不同的增加生物后代存活率的策略，比如植物有许多种子或哺乳动物照顾它们年幼的子女。

苏教版教材相关课程主要分布在四个单元。

三年级下册“植物的一生”包括三小节：果实和种子，根和茎，叶和花。

四年级下册“养蚕”包括四小节：我们来养蚕，给蚕宝宝记日记，我们来抽丝，养蚕经验交流会。

苏教版五年级下册“第三单元　他们是怎样延续后代的”包括三个小节：不同的种子也能繁殖吗，动物怎样繁殖后代，我是怎样出生的。

苏教版六年级下册“第二单元　遗传与变异”包括三个章节：生物的遗传现象，生物的变异现象，寻找遗传与变异的秘密。

我们可以看出TIMSS和苏教版教材在涉及的内容上差异并不大，如果学生认真学习了苏教版课本的全部内容，应具备回答TIMSS题目的知识能力。而且苏教版教材贴近生活，内容涉及人的出生，可以解答学生困惑。

但在内容教授的时间上差异较大，TIMSS2011科学框架中对四年级学生所提出的要求已经涉及生命科学中的繁殖、遗传与变异，但苏教版教材中除了植物讲授的较早以外，其他相关课程大多放置在五六年级，学生掌握此课程的时间相对较晚，如果使用苏教版教材的学生参加 TIMSS2015 测评，很可能因为课程设置的原因而失去相应的分数。

6 总结与启示

（1）苏教版小学科学教材在内容模块设置上与 TIMSS 在四年级的测评领域完全吻合，但苏教版中心主要放在物质世界，在生命世界、地球与宇宙方面课时数较少，应该适当协调三模块比例。

（2）苏教版在课时设置时考虑了学生接受能力，在低年级化学、地球科学的课时数明显较少，可以在低年级课程增加难度较低的化学、地球与科学知识，培养学生对各学科的兴趣，避免出现偏科现象。

（3）小学科学的内容总体较丰富，可以涵盖 TIMSS 测评涉及的领域，但某些内容的时间晚于 TIMSS 的要求，应该增加科学课时数或者提前科学教育开始的时间，如从一年级开始教授科学。

致谢

本文为教育部人文社会科学研究专项任务《基础教育阶段技术和设计教育的国际比较研究》（11JDGC026）的阶段性成果之一。

References

[1] TIMMS. TIMSS 2015 Assessment Frameworks.

[2] Zhang Dan. Comparative Research of Textbooks (3—6 grade) and Their Correlation with Standard for Primary School. Chengdu: Sichuan Normal University, 2012.

[3] Science teaching references books of primary school. Nanjing: Jiang Su Eduction publishing Press, 2007.

Online Science Education Evaluation System Research Based on iOS systems

Ruoyun Xu[1,a], Xiaojun Xia[1,b,*]

[1]Research Center for Learning Science, Southeast University, Nanjing, China

[a]xuruoyun719@163.com, [b]xxj.rcls@seu.edu.cn

[*] Corresponding author

Keywords: Science education; Online evaluation; iOS

Abstract: In this paper we present an iOS application designed for comparative research of technology and design education, adding the evaluation system on the basis of former version. Evaluations stored on the server are accessed via iPhone, and the evaluation questionnaire data is loaded into the APP, then the users' result data will be collected to database for later analysis. This project is designed using C/S architecture, with XCODE IDE and objective-C programming language, and the server-side code is written in PHP and MySQL.

1 Introduction

In recent years, with the rapid development of China's economy and culture, the task of training a new generation of talent becomes increasingly important. Thus, society and government are paying more attention to the science education of young people. And the purpose of science education is increasingly inclined to cultivate students' scientific inquiry ability, scientific attitude and scientific spirit.

According to statistics in recent years, with the popularity of smart phones, the use of third-party applications is also rapidly growing. The classifications of the APPs are also diverse. Although ranked fourth in the proportion of the APP Store accounted for educational applications, most of them are designed for children, and the APPs provided to personnel engaged in education research are rare. So in this project, the innovation is presented by the combination of Science Educational evaluations and mobile devices. The project is designed using C/S architecture, and the client is designed XCODE IDE, with the objective-C programming language to write, and the server-side code is written in using PHP and MySQL. If implanted into the iOS platform, the evaluations will be able to improve the efficiency to process and the coverage of science education evaluation, and it will be easier access to student data for quick analysis with the widespread of iOS devices, their easy accessibility and etc. [1]

2 Interface design and implementation of client systems

2.1 Interface design

2.1.1 Storyboard

Storyboard of the evaluation is presented in Figure 1 above. The Tab Bar is connected to navigation controller, which manages the navigation of hierarchical content. This navigation interface makes it possible to present your data efficiently and also makes it easier for the user to navigate that content. With the Table View Controller being the root of the Navigation View Controller, it presents a list of evaluations to users. Then with the table cell connected to the view controller where the evaluation selected by user from the list is about to be displayed in the following view controller.

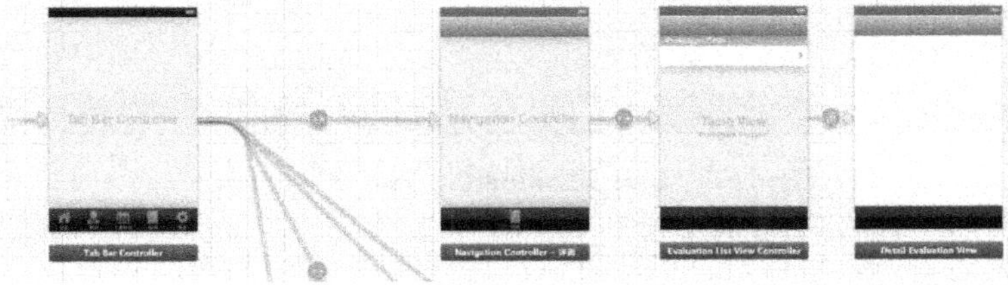

Figure 1 Storyboard of the evaluation

2.1.2 Home Interface

The Home Interface is shown in Figure 2. The top is navigation bar, the tab bar is at the bottom of the screen, which contains five items. This paper focuses on demonstrating the evaluation item in the Tab Bar.

Click evaluation field, and then enter a list of evaluations. This interface's view controller is Evaluation List View Controller and it carries dynamic cell (Dynamic Prototypes) Evaluation List View Controller is also responsible for adding a title to the navigation, and get the evaluation displayed in the table view by order.

Figure 2 Home

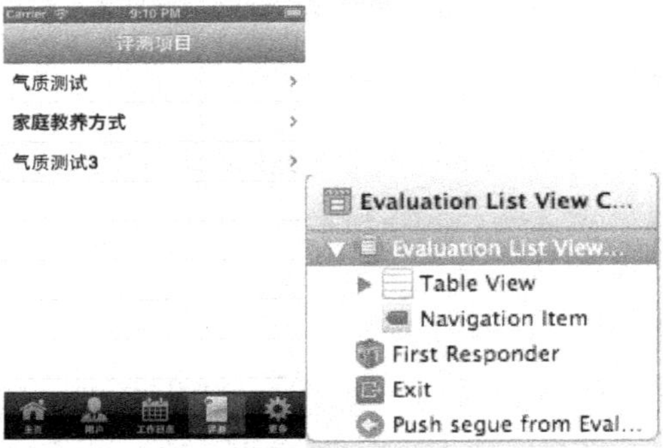

Figure 3　Evaluation List View Controller

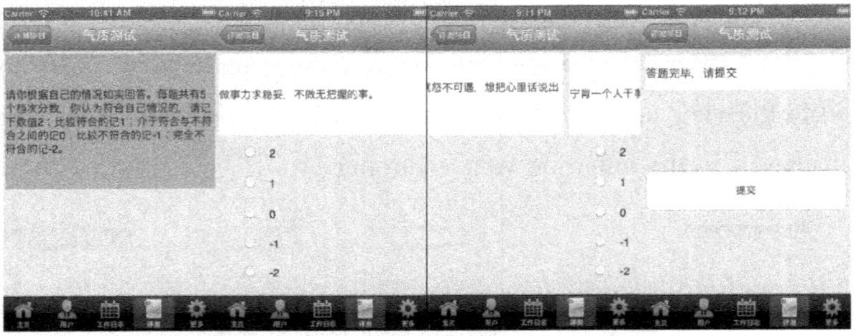

Figure 4　Detail Evaluation View Controller

Click on a table cell to enter the evaluation. The view controller of this interface is Detail Evaluation View Controller. It contains a scroll view defined by the class Detail Scroll View.

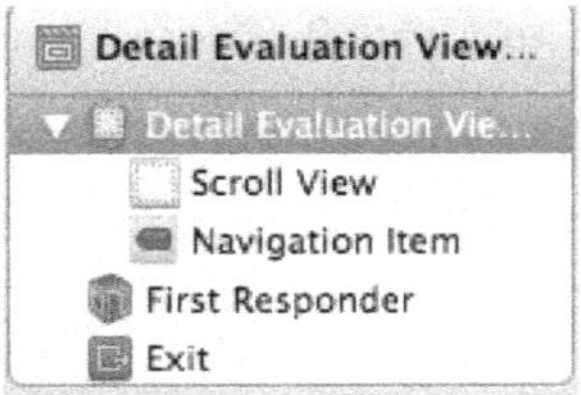

Figure 5　Structure of Detail Evaluation View Controller

2.2　Detailed Evaluation Design

2.2.1　Evaluation List View Controller

According to the http protocol, the data returns to the client's from the server can only be xml or Json format. Therefore, the client returns to the server after receiving the first data used to parse the data. In this view controller, it has the responsibilities to analyze the evaluations in Json format downloaded from the server to transfer the evaluation to something the Xcode can understand then display these evaluations.

Data analysis is accomplished in the method viewDidLoad.

```
NSArray *paths = NSSearchPathForDirectoriesInDomains(NSDocumentDirectory, NSUserDomainMask,
YES);
NSString *path = [paths objectAtIndex:0]; NSString *Json_path = [path stringByAppending
PathComponent:@"evaluation1.json"];
NSData *data = [NSData dataWithContentsOfFile:Json_path];
    //==JsonObject
NSError *error = nil;
id JsonObject = [NSJSONSerialization JSONObjectWithData:data options:NSJSONReadingAllowFragments
error:&error];
  if (JsonObject!=nil&&error==nil) {
    if ([JsonObject isKindOfClass:[NSDictionary class]]) {
      NSLog(@"NSDictionary JsonObject→%@",(NSDictionary*)JsonObject);
    }
    else if ([JsonObject isKindOfClass:[NSArray class]]) {
        NSLog(@"NSArray JsonObject→%@",(NSArray*)JsonObject);
    }
    else{
        NSLog(@"JsonObject not NSDictionary||NSArray Class");
  }
```

And via the method prepareForSegue: sender:, Evaluation List View Controller send these data to Detail Evaluation View Controller.

```
-(void)prepareForSegue:(UIStoryboardSegue*)segue sender:(id)sender
    {
        NSIndexPath *indexPath = [self.tableView indexPathForSelectedRow];
        NSInteger row = [indexPath row];
        Evaluation *evaluation = [self.evaluations objectAtIndex:row];
            DetailEvaluationViewController* detailEvaluationViewController = (DetailEvaluation
ViewController*)[segue destinationViewController];
        detailEvaluationViewController.evaluation = evaluation;
    }
```

2.2.2 Detail Evaluation View Controller

Detail Evaluation View Controller contains a scrollview to perform the function that when user scrolls the views in landscape directions the views display the questions in one evaluation properly.

The code below is manually add labels and buttons to every single subview of the scrollview.

```
for (int i =0; i < totalPage; i + + )
    {
        //UIView * view = [ [ UIView alloc] initWithFrame:CGRectMake(320 * i, 0, 320, 480) ];
        //view. userInteractionEnabled = YES;
        UILabel * label1 = [ [ UILabel alloc] initWithFrame:CGRectMake(320 * i +5, 5, 310, 120) ];
        label1. text = [ [_questions objectAtIndex:i] question];
        label1. backgroundColor = [ UIColor whiteColor];
        if (label1. text. length% (310/12) = =0) {
            a = label1. text. length/(310/16);
        } else {
            a = label1. text. length/(310/16) +1;
        }
        label1. font = [ UIFont systemFontOfSize:16];
        label1. numberOfLines = a;
        //[ view addSubview:label1];
        //NSLog(@ "%@" ,label1. text);
        [ self addSubview:label1];
        int optionNum = [ [ theEvaluation. questionList objectAtIndex:i] optionNum];
        _buttonIndex = [ [ NSMutableArray alloc] initWithCapacity:optionNum];
        NSString * groupId = [ NSString stringWithFormat: @ "group% d" ,i];
        [ _observerList setObject:_observer forKey:groupId];
        [ _statusList setObject:_status forKey:groupId];
        for (int j =0; j < optionNum; j + + )
        {
            UIButton * button = [ UIButton buttonWithType:UIButtonTypeCustom];
            button. frame = CGRectMake(i * 320 +40, 140 +45 * j,22, 22);
            UILabel * label = [ [ UILabel alloc] init];
            label. text = [ [ [ _questions objectAtIndex:i] optionDetail] objectAtIndex:j];
            label. frame = CGRectMake(i * 320 +80, 140 +45 * j, 100, 22);
            label. backgroundColor = [ [ UIColor lightGrayColor] colorWithAlphaComponent:0];
            [ self addSubview:label];
            [ self addSubview:button];
            //[ button addGroupId:[ NSString stringWithFormat:@ "% d" ,i] Index:j];
             [ button   setImage: [ UIImage   imageNamed: @ " RadioButton-Unselected" ]  forState:
UIControlStateNormal];
              [ button   setImage: [ UIImage   imageNamed: @ " RadioButton-Selected" ]  forState:
UIControlStateSelected];
                [ button   addTarget: self   action: @ selector ( clickButton: )  forControlEvents:
UIControlEventTouchUpInside];
            NSMutableString * groupAndIndex = [ [ NSMutableString alloc] init];
            [ groupAndIndex appendFormat:@ "% d" ,i +1];
            [ groupAndIndex appendFormat:@ "/% d" ,j +1];
            button. titleLabel. text = groupAndIndex;
```

```
            [_buttonIndex addObject:button];
            //NSLog(@"%@", groupId);
            [_buttons setObject:groupId forKey:groupAndIndex];
            //[_buttons setValue:button forKey:groupAndIndex];
        }
        [_list setObject:_buttonIndex forKey:groupId];
    }
```

3 Data Interaction Between Client and Server

After the user logs on the server, the client sends a request to the server to return Json format packaged evaluation data.

```
$result = mysql_query("SELECT * FROM user WHERE userName ='$userName'");
    if(! $result) {
        die('Connect Error: '. mysql_error());
    }
    $arr = array();
    $i = 0;
    while( $row = mysql_fetch_assoc( $result)) {
        $arr[ $i++] = $row;
    }
    $user = array("user" => $arr);
    $jsonencode = json_encode( $user);
    echo $jsonencode;
```

Moreover, new evaluations can be added to the server for users.

4 Conclusion

This paper is a preliminary exploration of the online science education evaluation system. Comparing with web, evaluation system implanted in mobile platforms such as iPhone, becomes more convenient to use. In addition, objective-C, which combines the advantages of the popular, portable C language and Smalltalk language, is already a mainstream programming language. [2]

Previous teaching evaluation as formative assessment tools include papers, oral questioning, evaluation inventory. With the development of computers and the Internet and multimedia technology, many evaluations can be conducted online. Today, online education evaluation mainly concentrated in the PC platform, for example, using remote online library to conduct Science Education evaluations. If the evaluations of science education are implanted to the mobile platform, especially IOS devices, taking advantage of their touch screen, mobility and minimalist design as well as its visibility and accessibility, science education evaluation will provide services for users more easily and quickly, and it will also provide efficient access to massive information of the evaluations.

References

[1] lvaro Fernández-López, María José Rodríguez-Fórtiz b, María Luisa Rodríguez-Almendros b, et al. Mobile learning technology based on iOS devices to support students with special education needs. Computers & Education, 2013, 61: 77-90.

[2] Dalrymple M, Knaster S. Learn Objective-C on the Mac For OS X and iOS. Beijing: The People's Posts and Telecommunications Press, 2009.

Histidine in Saliva of Child Response to Stress Task and Impact of Age

Xiaoxiao Wu[1,a], Xuejun Kang[1,b,*], Lei Ma[1,c], Yu Wang[1,d], Zhao Zhang[1,e], Shibing Yu[1,f]

[1] Key Laboratory of Child Development and Learning Science of Ministry of Education, Research Center for Learning Science, Southeast University, Nanjing, 210096, China

[c]wxx2010xiaoxiao@139.com, [b]xjkang64@163.com, [c]mlmyhero@163.com, [d]w.yuer@163.com, [e]zhzhzz@qq.com, [f]yushibing88@126.com

[*] Corresponding author

Keywords: Histidine; Child; Stress; Age

Abstract: Histidine is important for the growth of infants and children, but studies on its response to stress have been limited. In this research, eighty healthy children were presented with a control condition and an exercise stress. We intended to verify the feasibility of histidine in saliva of child as a stress marker and explore the impact of age on histidine level and its response to stress task.

There was a significant difference in salivary histidine baseline levels between children aged 6 and 10 years ($t = 3.02$, $p = 0.005$). The histidine had significant increase ($t = 4.65$, $p = 0.000$) and decrease ($t = -4.80$, $p = 0.000$) during the stress experiment, while it had almost no changes in the control group. No significant difference was found in histidine response to stress at different ages, which suggested that histidine was a stable stress marker not affected by age.

In conclusion, histidine in saliva of child could be a physiological parameter indicator for the study of early childhood development. Further research should be designed to replicate these findings, explore the reasons for the individual differences and elucidate the mechanisms of the changes.

1 Introduction

Histidine (His), an essential amino acid, is important for the growth of infants and children, which is also conducive to the repair of tissues[1]. It widely exists in meat, bananas, grapes, milk and dairy products. Histidine participates in various processes, such as enzyme catalysis, metal binding and phosphorylation, because its imidazole side chain is a common coordinating ligand[2]. In addition, human histidine can be used as a clinical indicator or pharmaceutical for the diagnosis and treatment of relevant diseases[3]. Due to the noninvasive and convenient sampling, human saliva has gotten major league attention in the academia, especially when the study involved children.

In recent years, human response to stress has been widely paid attention to in the academia, and gradually become a hotspot, whose activation to a threatening negative or unexpected experience evokes a chain of neuroendocrine and nervous system reactions[4]. Therefore, reliable biological markers for stress responses are valuable in both psychophysiological research and clinical practice. Cortisol (CORT), salivary alpha-amylase (SAA) and catecholamine, as the traditional stress markers, have been found[5,6] to effectively indicate the reactivity of physiological stress systems, such as the hypothalamic-pituitary-adrenal (HPA) axis and the sympathetic-adrenal- medullary (SAM) system. However, it is well-known that stress is a complicated phenomenon that requires a multidimensional measurement approach. Thus, despite the wide array of parameters used in stress research, a widening of the methodological canon is desired[7]. Moreover, the concentrations of cortisol and catecholamine in human saliva are too low to quantify.

Studies suggest that histidine, as the histaminergic precursor, plays a significant role in the central nervous system (CNS)[8]. The histaminegic system in the brain is a phylogenetically old group of neurons that project to most of CNS[9], which is involved in different physiological, behavior and stress-related processes such as learning, memory, emotion, wakefulness and sleep-wake cycle[10]. A recent research showed histidine enhanced learning and modulates stress responses in zebrafish[11]. Furthermore, histaminergic neurons also play a key role in maintaining the brain in an awake faced with behavioral challenges. Nakamura et al. found that during the university examination period, salivary histidine of undergraduate students was slightly elevated[12]. Using these results as support, we hypothesize that histidine can be used as a new biological indicator for stress response, which were studied tentatively in our previous work[13].

The present research was designed to verify the feasibility of histidine in saliva of child as a stress marker and explore the specific changes. Besides that, we intended to explore the impact of age on the salivary histidine level and its response to stress task.

2 Methods

2.1 Participants

The participants were 80 healthy children, with an even split between 6 and 10 years old. All the children's parents signed an informed consent, which had been accepted by the Guideline of the Intramural Ethics Committee. Participants were asked to complete a questionnaire that contained some basic information and exclusion criteria in order to reduce confounding factors affecting physiological dependent measures. They were instructed not to undergo excessive physical activity the day before the study. In addition, subjects were required to refrain from brushing their teeth, eating or drinking for at least 30 min before the experiment.

2.2 Procedure

The experiment started at two o'clock in the afternoon. The participants were randomized into an experimental group and a control group, with even age and balanced gender ratio. The experimental group was under exercise stress, running for 5 min. The control group was under the condition of rest during the whole experiment.

2.3 Sample collection and analyses

During the experiment, salivary samples were obtained at three points, baseline before the study started, post task and 20 minutes recovery. Saliva was collected with 4 mL salivette and stored at −20 ℃ in the refrigerator after collection before analysis. After thawing at low temperature, saliva samples were centrifuged ($12\,000\ r \cdot min^{-1}$) for 5 min. Salivary histidine was analyzed using High Performance Liquid Chromatography with fluorescence detection after o-phthaldialdehyde derivatization. Inter and intra assay coefficients of variation were below 10%.

2.4 Statistical analysis

Basic data processing and analysis were realized in Excel, including histidine levels at different time points. Changes of His levels before and after the experiment were examined by the method of Paired-sample T test. Independent-Sample T test was used to analyze the difference of His levels and its response to exercise stress in saliva of children between two age groups. The results were meaningful and reported if they achieved the level of significance at least $p<0.05$.

3 Results and discussion

3.1 Demographic characteristics

Eighty participants were healthy children, 46 girls and 34 boys. They had no history of psychiatric illness, and they were no medicines and stimulant recently.

3.2 Histidine in saliva of child response to stress

Previous researches revealed that CORT and SAA levels had responses to stress with significantly rising[14]. In this research, we found that histidine in saliva of child had different response to stress. His levels had almost no changes in the control condition.

Twenty children were found increased distinctly ($t = 4.65$, $p = 0.000$) in histidine levels and twenty declined ($t = -4.80$, $p = 0.000$) obviously during exercise stress (Figure 1). According to the results, we suppose there are obvious individual differences in histidine response to stress, and we will explore the reasons for the differences in our subsequent work. Furthermore, the salivary histidine levels presented dramatic recoveries both in the increased group ($t = -3.79$, $p = 0.001$) and decreased group ($t = 4.99$, $p = 0.000$) after a 20 minutes rest.

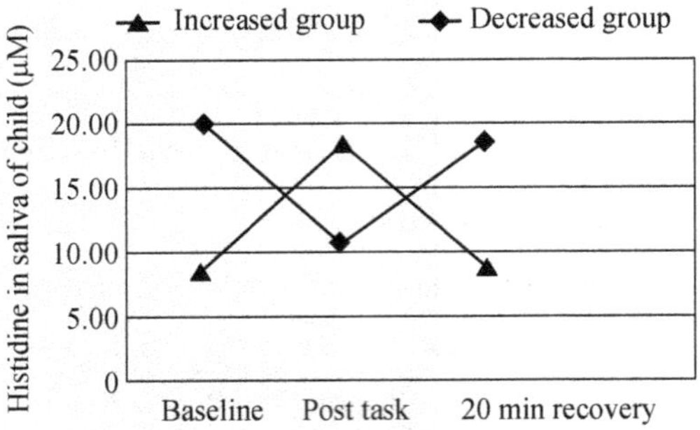

Figure 1　The mean histidine levels in saliva of children in the experimental group at different time points

3.3　Impact of Age

3.3.1　Impact of age on the histidine baseline levels

It was reported[15] that salivary histidine had no significant correlation with age in a recent study. However, in our research, histidine baseline levels in saliva of child had significant difference ($t = 3.02$, $p = 0.005$) with age (Figure 2). One possible reason of the different results was that there were less than three participants at every age in the previous research. Besides that, most of the subjects were adults with only two children aged 5 in the previous research.

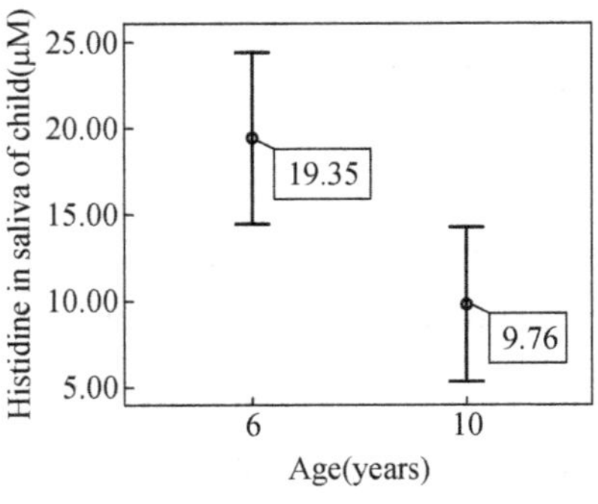

Figure 2　The mean histidine baseline levels at different ages for all subjects ($t = 3.02$, $p = 0.005$)

3.3.2 Impact of age on the salivary histidine response to stress

In order to explore the impact of age on histidine response to stress, we defined a parameter called rate of change, which referred to (B - A) /A. The A represented the baseline level of histidine, and the B represented the histidine level in post task. There was no significant difference in rate of change between children aged 6 and 10 years old (Figure 3). The result suggest that histidine in saliva of child is a stable stress marker not affected by age.

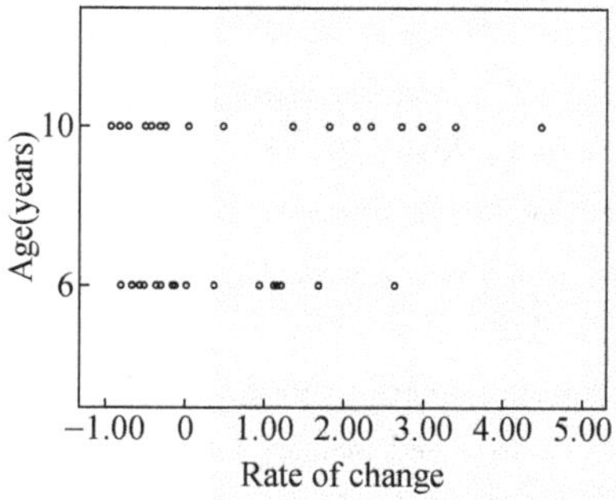

Figure 3 The rate of changes at different ages in the experiment group

4 Conclusion

In summary, our research showed that histidine in saliva of child changed obviously and was not affected by age during the stress experiment. In addition, the His baseline levels had significant difference between children aged 6 and 10 years. These findings supported our previous hypothesis histidine could be a physiological parameter indicator for the study of early childhood development.

Certainly, the evident defects existed in our research were the small sample size and the limited stress task. Therefore, further studies are recommended on a larger group of subjects with multiple stress stimulations to replicate these findings, explore the reasons for the individual differences and elucidate the mechanisms of the changes.

Acknowledgement

This work was supported by the National Natural Science Foundation of China (No. 81172720, and No. 21307086) and Colleges and Universities in Jiangsu Province plans to graduate research and innovation projects (CXLX12_0121).

References

[1] Y Hu, Q Wang, C Zheng, et al. Recyclable decoration of amine-functionalized magnetic nanoparticles with Ni(2+) for determination of histidine by photochemical vapor generation atomic spectrometry. Analytical Chemistry, 2014, 86: 842-848.

[2] A A Sehgal, L Duma, G Bodenhausen, et al. Fast proton exchange in histidine: Measurement of rate constants through indirect detection by NMR spectroscopy. Chemistry-a European Journal, 2014, 20: 6332-6338.

[3] S Shintani, H Hamakawa, Y Ueyama, et al. Identification of a truncated cystatin SA-I as a saliva biomarker for oral squamous cell carcinoma using the SELDI ProteinChip platform. International Journal of Oral and Maxillofacial Surgery, 2010, 39: 68-74.

[4] H K Laurent, S M Laurent, D A Granger. Salivary nerve growth factor reactivity to acute psychosocial stress: A new frontier for stress research. Psychosomatic Medicine, 2013, 75: 744-750.

[5] A R Tyrka, L M Wier, L H Price, et al. Cortisol and ACTH responses to the Dex/CRH test: Influence of temperament. Hormones and Behavior, 2008, 53: 518-525.

[6] S Kuhlmann, O T Wolf. Cortisol and memory retrieval in women: Influence of menstrual cycle and oral contraceptives. Psychopharmacology, 2005, 183: 65-71.

[7] U M Nater, R La Marca, L Florin, et al. Stress-induced changes in human salivary alpha-amylase activity—associations with adrenergic activity. Psychoneuroendocrinology, 2006, 31: 49-58.

[8] Z Chen, C Kamei. Facilitating effects of histamine on spatial memory deficit induced by scopolamine in rats. Acta Pharmacologica Sinica, 2000, 21: 814-818.

[9] H Haas, P Panula. The role of histamine and the tuberomamillary nucleus in the nervous system. Nature Review Neuroscience, 2003, 4: 121-130.

[10] N Peitsaro, J Kaslin, O V Anichtchik, et al. Modulation of the histaminergic system and behaviour by alpha-fluoromethylhistidine in zebrafish. Journal of Neurochemistry, 2003, 86: 432-441.

[11] L P V Cofiel, R Mattioli. L-histidine enhances learning in stressed zebrafish. Brazilian Journal of Medical and Biological Research, 2009, 42: 28-134.

[12] Y Nakamura, H Kodama, T Satoh, et al. Diurnal changes in salivary amino acid concentrations. Vivo, 2010, 24: 837-842.

[13] J Sun, X J Kang, Y Q Ma, et al. A Potential Quick Determination Used for Monitor Biological Response of Human under Stress. International Society for the Study of Behavioural Development, 2009.

[14] T W Buchanan, D Tranel, R Adolphs. Impaired memory retrieval correlates with individual differences in cortisol response but not autonomic response. Learning & Memory, 2006, 13: 382-387.

[15] T Shoji, M Mamoru, A Sayoko, et al. Changes in salivary amino acid composition during aging. Vivo, 2010, 24: 853-856.

Gender and Age Differences of Steroids in Human Hair

Shifei Li[1], Jing Zhang[1], Youyun Xu[1], Yijiang Chen[1], Zheng Chen[1], Wei Gao[1], Huihua Deng[1,a,*]

[1]Key Laboratory of Child Development and Learning Science of Ministry of Education, Southeast University, Research Center for Learning Science, Southeast University, Nanjing 210096, China

[a]dengrcls@seu.edu.cn

[*]Corresponding author

Keywords: Gender; Age; Hair steroids; Adolescents

Abstract: This study investigated the effect of gender and age on hair levels of cortisol, cortisone, testosterone, and progesterone, dehydroepiandrosterone (DHEA) in adolescents and early adults. Hair hormones were extracted with methanol and measured by high performance liquid chromatography-tandem mass spectrometry. Results showed significantly higher levels of hair cortisone and testosterone in male adolescents than females. Early male adults showed significantly higher testosterone levels and lower cortisone levels than male adolescents.

1 Introduction

Adrenal steroid hormones play important roles in physiological and psychological functions. For example, glucocorticoids (e. g., cortisol and its inactive metabolite cortisone) have anti-inflammatory, anti-allergic and immunosuppressive functions. Gonadal hormones, such as the androgen dehydroepiandrosterone (DHEA) and its sulphated form (DHEAS), play crucial roles in the maintenance and development of sexual function. DHEA(S) also acts as a neurosteroid to antagonize the cortisol's function. Progesterone and DHEA are androgen precursors of male and female sex hormones. Testosterone is bioactive androgen responsible for development of male specific characteristics. These hormones were associated with several clinical syndromes or psychological diseases[1-4].

Gender and age have disparate effect on levels of adrenal steroid hormones. Laughlin et al. found that there was the age-related decline of DHEA and age-related increase of cortisol in older population exhibiting gender difference[5]. Genazzani et al. found that progesterone and DHEA levels showed gender- and age-differences in adults older 19 years old[6]. Salivary cortisol and DHEA levels were related to gender and puberty development in children and adolescents[7,8]. Netherton et al. demonstrated that mean morning salivary cortisol in mid-post pubertal girls was greater than that in boys and mean salivary DHEA in mid-post pubertal boys and girls was greater than those in pre-early pubertal[8]. Unfortunately, in the previous, limited studies separately reported several hormone levels related to gender and age, especially for adolescents and early adults.

Previous studies focused on hormone levels in blood, salivary or urine which just reflect relatively short time concentration in few hours (blood, salivary) or 24 hours (urine)[9]. Recently, increasing researchers have paid their attention to hormone levels in human hair. The hair-based hormone levels reflected the cumulative hormone levels during several months which are more suitable for psychological investigation[9]. The biomarkers were independent of the diurnal rhythm of hormone secretion. Because early adolescence is the key period responsible for the appearance and development of emotion, psychological and behavior problems[10], the alternation of these hormones may result in potential psychological dysfunction. This paper aimed to explore the age and gender difference in cortisol, cortisone, progesterone, DHEA, and testosterone levels in hair between adolescent and early adults.

2 Materials and methods

2.1 Participants

In order to investigate the effect of gender and age on the levels of the five steroids, two cohorts of participants were recruited. Cohort A consisted of 324 adolescents [male/female: 133/191; age: 14—18 years, mean age: (15.61 ±0.45) years] recruited from a senior high school in Nanjing, China. Cohort B was composed of 229 male early adults [age: 16—22 years, mean age: (19.60 ± 0.82) years] from a technical university in Nanjing, China. There was no age difference between male and female adolescents, $t(322) = -0.266$, $p = 0.790$. Male participants in Cohort A were significantly younger than those in Cohort B, $t(242.80) = -55.794$, $p < 0.001$.

2.2 Hair collection and analysis of hair steroids

Collection of hair samples was performed in the participants' school and university. Hair strands in the posterior vertex region were cut with iron scissors as close as possible to the scalp. The hair strands were stored at −20 degree Centigrade and were cut into 1 cm segments prior to use. The 1 cm segment closest to the scalp was used in the following cortisol assay.

The procedures for measuring hair cortisol were described elsewhere in detail[11].

Briefly, the hair samples were washed twice with 2 mL methanol at room temperature. This procedure aimed to remove contaminations coated at the hair shaft from atmosphere and hair-care products which contain the analytes. The 30 mg clean hair samples were finely cut into pieces and incubated in 1.5 mL methanol for 1 day at 25 degree Centigrade. The 1 day incubated solution was centrifuged at 10 000 r/min for 1 min. A 1 mL of supernatant was took out and dried with nitrogen at 50 degree Centigrade. The dry residue was redissolved with 1 mL deionized water and 50 μL methanol and then transferred to the SPE column activated by 3 mL methanol and followed by 3 mL deionized water. After rinsing with 3 mL deionized water, eluted with 80 μL methanol then dried and redissolved in 50 μL mobile phase. Internal standards, cortisol-d4, cortisone-d7, testosterone-d5, progesterone-d9 and DHEA-d4, were added in the incubation. The SPE procedure was used to minimize the matrix effect.

The analyses were performed in a 3 200 QTRAP liquid chromatography tandem mass spectrometer (ABI, USA). The five analytes were ionized with an atmospheric pressure chemical ionization (APCI) and identified in positive ion mode using multiple reaction monitoring mode, and quantified by internal standard method[12]. The assay method showed limits of detection and quantitation at 0.25 and 0.5 pg/mg for hair cortisol, cortisone and testosterone, and at 0.5 and 1.0 pg/mg for hair progesterone, and at 1.25 and 2.50 pg/mg for hair DHEA. Intra-day and inter-day coefficients of variation were less than 10% and accuracy ranged 97%—103%.

2.3 Statistical methods

t-test for two independent samples was done for comparison of age, hair cortisol, cortisone, testosterone, DHEA and progesterone between different age and gender groups.

3 Results and discussion

The current LC-ESI-MS/MS method gave the detectable contents of all 553 participants for the five analytes, which were higher than their corresponding LOD. It gave the reliable contents of 551 participants for cortisol, of all 553 participants for cortisone and testosterone contents, and of 546 participants for progesterone and DHEA, which were higher than their corresponding LOQ. The measured contents ranged 0.25—105.84 pg/mg for cortisol, 1.76—267.26 pg/mg for cortisone, 0.86—172.22 pg/mg for testosterone, 0.78—348.81 pg/mg for progesterone and 1.25—1191.02 pg/mg for DHEA. Table 1 gave the mean contents of the five hair steroids in male and female adolescents and early male adults.

Table 1 The mean contents of hair cortisol, cortisone, DHEA, testosterone and progesterone in female and male adolescents and male adults

MSD (pg/mg)	Female adolescents ($n = 191$)	Male adolescents ($n = 133$)	Adults ($n = 229$)
Cortisol	8.76 ± 10.32	8.08 ± 6.46	7.96 ± 7.69
Cortisone	36.02 ± 21.60	42.48 ± 25.18	26.72 ± 30.69
Testosterone	6.31 ± 1.23	6.74 ± 1.79	8.69 ± 14.49
Progesterone	6.24 ± 25.03	4.10 ± 2.26	4.48 ± 5.95
DHEA	30.99 ± 48.26	34.42 ± 103.10	25.99 ± 34.35

As shown in Figure 1(a), there was no significant difference between male and female adolescents in hair cortisol, progesterone and DHEA contents ($p > 0.327$), but male adolescents showed significantly higher cortisone and testosterone contents than females ($t_{322} = 2.474$, $t_{217.65} = -2.441$, $p < 0.05$). As shown in Figure 1(b), there was no significant difference between male adolescents and adults in hair cortisol, progesterone and DHEA contents ($p > 0.257$), but adolescents showed significantly higher cortisone content and lower testosterone content than adults ($t_{360} = 5.021$, $p < 0.001$; $t_{239.85} = -2.009$, $p < 0.05$).

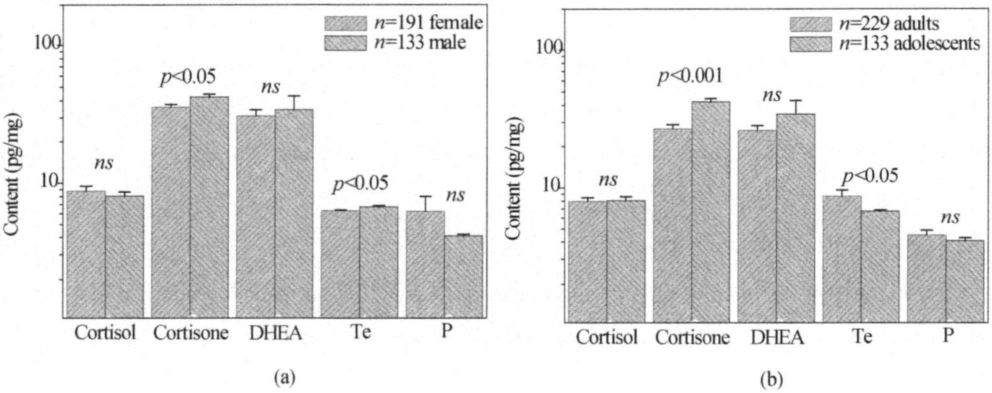

Figure 1 Comparison of the five hair steroids between (a) female and male adolescents and (b) male adolescents and early adults. *T*-test for two independent samples was done for the comparison. Te and P in the figure were testosterone and progesterone in hair, respectively. The error bar in the figure was standard error of mean (SEM)

This study found that male adolescents showed higher hair testosterone than females (Figure 1). The gender difference in hair testosterone was consistent with that measured by on-line SPE LC-MS/MS analysis Gao et al. developed for whole, nonpulverized hair from adults[12]. The result was an additional proof-of-concept for the feasibility of the current LC-APCI-MS/MS method. This study also found the effect of age on hair testosterone, which was consistent with that in serum[13].

This study found no effect of gender on hair cortisol in adolescents. The result was in line with that in the study of Dettenborn et al. who found no gender difference in adolescents aged 10—17 years[14]. Previous studies using a small sample demonstrated no effect of gender on hair cortisol levels among adults aged 18—90 years[15-19]. But a study using a large sample found the effect of gender in children aged 19 years and adults 18—49 years[14]. This study also found no significant difference in hair cortisol between adolescents and early adults. Previous studies demonstrated no effect of age on hair cortisol levels among adults aged 18—90 years[15-18]. But a study using a large sample found a linear increase of hair cortisol level with age ranged 1—91 years[14]. For example, young children aged ranged 19 years showed higher hair cortisol than adults ranged 18—39 years.

This study found that male adolescents showed higher hair cortisone than females. Previous studies using a small sample demonstrated that male adults had higher hair cortisone levels than females, but the difference was not statistically significant[15,18]. This study found significantly higher hair cortisone in male adolescents than adults, which was in agreement with the result of Raul et al. showing significantly higher hair cortisone in the group with age < 20-year-old than older adults[18]. But there was no effect of age in adults[15,18].

This study found that there were no effects of gender and age on hair progesterone and DHEA. In the previous, progesterone level in morning serum showed a age-related decrease among adults elder than 19 years old and was significantly higher in women than in men[6]. Salivary progesterone level showed no gender difference and was increased with age among pubertal adolescents[7,8]. DHEA(S) level in serum showed a age-related decrease[6]. Compared to men, DHEA(S) levels in women were significantly higher among adults elder than 19 years old[6]. In addition, a study using a small sample showed higher hair DHEAS in male adults than females[15], but did not show the age difference among adults[15]. The difference between this study and the literature might be attributed to the differences in population and biomarkers. The current participants were in the transition stage from puberty to adults, showing a complicated gender- and age-dependent development which is characterized by the beginning of endocrine activation of gonadal hormones[13]. The current hair-based biomarkers reflected integrated levels of long-term accumulative exposure, while the serum- and saliva-based biomarkers represented short-term levels within short time intervals or acute levels at specific time points[9]. The current findings may have implications for the changes in hypothalamic-pituitary-adrenal axis and hypothalamic-pituitary-gonadal axis function among adolescents.

Acknowledgements

This research was supported by Humanities and Social Science Foundation (11YJAZH019) and Program for New Century Excellent Talents in University (NCET-08-0122), Ministry of Education, China.

References

[1] Burke H M, Davis M C, Otte C, et al. Depression and cortisol responses to psychological stress: A meta-analysis. Psychoneuroendocrinology, 2005, 30: 846 - 856.

[2] Kurita H, Maeshima H, Kida S, et al. Serum dehydroepiandrosterone (DHEA) and DHEA-sulfate (S) levels in medicated patients with major depressive disorder compared with controls. Journal of Affective Disorders, 2013, 146: 205 - 212.

[3] Mason J W, Giller E L, Kosten T R, et al. Serum testosterone levels in post - traumatic stress disorder inpatients. Journal of Traumatic Stress, 1990, 3: 449 - 457.

[4] Wirth M M, Meier E A, Fredrickson B L, et al. Relationship between salivary cortisol and progesterone levels in humans. Biological Psychology, 2007, 74: 104 - 107.

[5] Laughlin G A, Barrett-Connor E. Sexual dimorphism in the influence of advanced aging in adrenal hormone levels: The Rancho Bernardo study. Clinical Endocrinology Metabolism, 2000, 85: 3561 - 3568.

[6] Genazzani A R, Petraglia F, Bernardi F, et al. Circulating levels of allopregnanolone in humans: Gnder, age, and endocrine influences. Clinical Endocrinology Metabolism, 1998, 83: 2099 - 2103.

[7] Gröschl M, Rauh M, Dörr H-G. Circadian rhythm of salivary cortisol, 17α-hydroxyprogesterone, and progesterone in healthy children. Clinical Chemistry, 2003, 49: 1688 - 1691.

[8] Netherton, C Goodyer I, Tamplin A, et al. Salivary cortisol and dehydroepiandrosterone in relation to puberty and gender. Psychoneuroendocrinology, 2004, 29: 125 - 140.

[9] Russell E, Koren G, Rieder M, et al. Hair cortisol as a biological marker of chronic stress: Current status, future directions and unanswered questions. Psychoneuroendocrinology, 2012, 37: 589 - 601.

[10] McGee R, Feehan M, Williams S, et al. DSM-Ⅲ disorders from age 11 to age 15 years. Journal of the American Academy of Child & Adolescent Psychiatry, 1992, 31: 50 - 59.

[11] Qi X, Zhang J, Liu Y, et al. Relationship between effort-reward imbalance and hair cortisol concentration in female kindergarten teachers. Journal of Psychosomatic Research, 2014, 76: 329 - 332.

[12] Gao W, Stalder T, Foley P, et al. Quantitative analysis of steroid hormones in human hair using a column-switching LC-APCI-MS/MS assay. Journal of Chromatography, 2013, 928: 1 - 8.

[13] Kushnir M M, Blamires T, Rockwood A L, et al. Liquid chromatography-tandem mass

spectrometry assay for androstenedione, dehydroepiandrosterone, and testosterone with pediatric and adult reference intervals. Clin Chem, 2010, 56: 1138 - 1147.

[14] Dettenborn L, Tietze A, Kirschbaum C, et al. The assessment of cortisol in human hair: Associations with sociodemographic variables and potential confounders. Stress, 2012, 15: 578 - 588.

[15] Chen Z, Li J, Zhang J, et al. Simultaneous determination of hair cortisol, cortisone and DHEAS with liquid chromatography-electrospray ionization-tandem mass spectrometry in negative mode. Journal of Chromatography, 2013, 929: 187 - 194.

[16] Gao W, Xie Q, Jin J, et al. HPLC-FLU detection of cortisol distribution in human hair. Clinical Biochemistry, 2010, 43: 677 - 682.

[17] Manenschijn L, Koper J W, Lamberts S W, et al. Evaluation of a method to measure long term cortisol levels. Steroids, 2011, 76: 1032 - 1036.

[18] Raul J S, Cirimele V, Ludes B, et al. Detection of physiological concentrations of cortisol and cortisone in human hair. Clinical Biochemistry, 2004, 37: 1105 - 1111.

[19] Thomson S, Koren G, Fraser L-A, et al. Hair analysis provides a historical record of cortisol levels in Cushing's syndrome. Experimental and Clinical Endocrinology & Diabete, 2010, 118: 133.

The Development of Chinese Early Childhood Environment Rating Scale (CECERS) and Its Initial Validation

Kejian Li[1,a], Biying Hu[2], Jiayi Chen[1], Xuejiao Qin[1], Jinliang Qin[1,b,*]

[1]Hangzhou Preschool Teachers College, Zhejiang Normal University, China

[2]Faculty of Education, University of Macau, China

[a]likj@zjnu.cn, [b]qjlzjnu@126.com

[*]Corresponding author

Keywords: early childhood education; quality measurement; reliability; validity

Abstract: Since 2010, The Central Government of China has significantly increased the investments on early childhood education (ECE), aiming to provide each age-qualifying child aged 3—6 a basic but quality early education by the year of 2020. Then, the development of a culturally appropriate and psychometrically sound measure of ECE program quality has become a task of high importance. In response to this, the Chinese Early Childhood Environment Rating Scale (trial) (CECERS) thus comes into being. The CECERS is developed by a multi-disciplinary team from Zhejiang Normal University of China in close collaboration with several oversea scholars from UMAC and UNC at Chapel Hill. Inspired by the renowned Early Childhood Environment Rating Scale-Revised Edition (ECERS-R) which was developed in the context of the US but has been widely used cross-culturally, the CECERS aims to become an effective new instrument for measuring early childhood program quality in the Chinese socio-cultural contexts. The CECERS has 51 items organized in eight subscales, using a 7-point Likert scale as its scoring method. The development and validation process of the CECERS is presented below.

Empirical data were collected from a stratified random sample 178 classrooms, from which a random sample of 1,012 children (roughly six children from each participant classroom) was measured for child development outcomes (including language, early math, social cognition, and motor skills). Guided by the framework of broad conceptualization of validity and validation as advocated by Messick (1989), evidence in a variety of forms is presented and discussed, including content validity considerations (e. g., measuring socially and culturally relevant domains), measurement reliability considerations (e. g., internal consistency reliability, inter-rater reliability), and measurement validity considerations (concurrent validity, criterion-related validity, internal structure based on exploratory factor analysis). The empirical findings for CECERS compare very favorably with the validation outcomes of ECERS-R. The body of evidence accumulated in the initial validation process supports the use and interpretation of CECERS scores as quality indicators of early childhood education program in the Chinese social and cultural contexts. Limitations and future directions are also discussed.

《中国托幼机构教育质量评价量表》的研发及其效度的初步验证

李克建[1,a]，胡碧颖[2]，陈佳艺[1]，秦雪娇[1]，秦金亮[1,b,*]

[1]浙江师范大学杭州幼儿师范学院,杭州,中国

[2]澳门大学教育学院,澳门,中国

[a]likj@zjnu.cn, [b]qjlzjnu@126.com

[*]通讯作者

关键词:学前教育;质量测量;信度;效度

中文摘要:自2010年以来,中国政府不断加大对学前教育领域的投资,致力于实现到2020年"有质量地普及学前三年教育"的目标。因此,建构适宜中国国情、具有良好测量学特性的托幼机构教育质量评价工具,变得尤为重要而迫切。

基于当代人类发展生态学"环境即人与物质、社会、文化的交互作用过程"的思想观念,美国研制了《幼儿学习环境评价量表》(ECERS)及其修订版(ECERS-R)。我们在借鉴其过程质量观念的基础上,依据我国托幼机构教育倚重集体教学的特征,编制了区别于美国ECERS-R的《中国托幼机构教育质量评价量表(试用版)》(简称《量表》,英文缩写为CECERS)。该量表由浙江师范大学为主进行研发,组建了包括澳门大学、北卡大学多名研究者在内的多学科国际合作团队,历时3年进行项目筛选、标准化。该量表构建了适应中国社会文化背景的托幼机构教育质量评价的概念框架,萃取了中国幼儿园教育有证据支持的优质实践,经过了严谨的研发程序,成为一个包含8个子量表51个评分项目的7点评分量表,致力于成为能够全面衡量中国托幼机构教育质量的有效评价工具。本报告描述了该量表的研发及其初步信效度验证过程与结果。

《量表》的观察性实证研究数据来自分层随机抽样的178个幼儿园班级样本,并从中随机抽取1 012名儿童进行一对一测试(每个样本班级约6名儿童),获取其语言、早期数学、社会认知和动作技能发展结果数据。基于Messick关于效度验证的宽泛的理论框架,本报告呈现和讨论了《量表》多种形式的信效度证据,包括内容效度(例如,衡量文化背景和教育情境适宜性)、测量信度(例如,评分者间一致性、内部一致性)、测量效度(例如,同时效度、效标关联效度、基于因子分析的内部结构效度)等。本研究发现,《量表》信效度的初步实证研究结果总体上优于ECERS-R已有研究中报告的结果。这些信效度研究证据支持在中国社会文化背景下使用该《量表》的测量得分来作为托幼机构的教育质量指标。报告最后讨论了本研究的局限性以及未来的研究方向。

1 研究背景

2010年,《国家中长期改革和发展规划纲要2010—2020》(2010)提出,95%的幼儿应接受学前一年教育,75%的幼儿到2020年应获得为期三年的学前教育。《国务院关于当前发展学前教育的若干意见》中指出,"加大财政投入","建立幼儿园保教质量评估体系",以"保障适龄儿童接受基本的有质量的学前教育"。[1]为了实现这些国家目标,就需要有一个良好的学前教育质量测量工具和测量结果为财政措施和政策的制定提供依据。从20世纪80年代末以来,各地教育行政部门陆续建立了一些地方性的幼儿园评估体系。这些评估体系主要是基于国家颁布的学前教育法规和政策性文件(如1996年的《幼儿园工作规程》、2001年的《幼儿园教育指导纲要(试行)》)来制定评价标准。许多研究者指出,这些地方性幼儿园评估标准一般强调结构性质量(如办园条件和管理),而相对忽视过程性质量,如各类课程教学活动的过程以及人际互动。[2-5]此外,这些地方性幼儿园评估体系在测量学属性(如测量信度和效度)上是未知的,因为它们没有经过任何效度验证的过程。[3,6]因此,研发文化上适宜且测量学属性良好的托幼机构教育质量测量工具已成为一项十分重要的任务。本研究正是致力于这一目标的努力。在本文中,我们描述了《中国托幼机构教育评价量表(试用版)》的研发过程,并呈现了该量表初步的测量学特性的证据。

1.1 《量表》的研发过程

1.1.1 ECERS-R在中国的试用研究

基于当代人类发展生态学"环境即人与物质、社会、文化的交互作用过程"[7]的思想观念,美国北卡大学的FPG儿童发展研究所研制了《幼儿学习环境评价量表》(Early Childhood Environment Rating Scale, ECERS)[8]及其修订版(ECERS-R)[8,9]。到目前为止,ECERS-R是美国也是国际上研究最充分、使用最广泛的托幼机构教育质量测量工具。[10]不同版本的ECERS-R已应用于20多个不同国家和社会情境中[11]。但在不同社会文化背景中,研究者在使用ECERS/ECERS-R时做了各种改编和修订,如智利[12]和韩国[13]删除了一些特定的质量要素;瑞典在使用ECERS时减少了项目的数量[14,15];在孟加拉国使用时删除了与社会文化无关的项目并添加了一些新的文化关联度更高的项目[16];另外,印度在使用ECERS时,做了很多实质性的修订[17]。以上研究印证了一个普遍的共识:必须要对ECERS/ECERS-R进行必要的改变和修订,以提高其在不同社会文化背景下的文化适宜性。

为了了解ECERS-R中代表的托幼机构教育质量的概念适合中国社会文化背景的程度,2011年,ECERS-R被用来测量中国105个幼儿园的教育质量[18]。研究结果表明,ECERS-R的多项测量学指标存在不同程度的问题(如活动、语言推理、作息结构和互动等多个子量表内部一致性信度不足)。这些发现加上实践者和评分员的反馈表明,ECERS-R缺乏对于中国社会文化和教育情境的适宜性,不经任何修改,无法直接用来测量中国的托幼机构教育质量[19]。ECERS-R在中国情境中缺乏文化适宜性的原因很多,其中一个主要的原因是,ECERS-R是在美国的社会文化背景中研发的,在早期教育领域崇尚自由游戏和个别化互动;而在中国文化中集体主义受到高度重视,倚重集体活动和集体教学是中国幼儿园教育中最鲜明的特征[3,20,21]。因而,蕴含在ECERS-R中的一些学前教育质量观念(如以自由游戏为主的课程模式,舒适区域和隐私空间,接纳多元文化等)并没有被中国学前教育实践工作者普遍认可。另一方面,一些在中国社会文化和教育情境中具有重要价值的质量观念(如集体主义文化与集体教学)在ECERS-R中没有体现。因此,我们致力于在借鉴ECERS-R过程质量观的基础上,研发更加符合中国社会文化情境和教育实际、信效度更高的测量工具,以更好地服务于我国的托幼机构教育质量评价实践。

1.1.2 《中国托幼机构教育质量评价量表(试用版)》的编制

《中国托幼机构教育质量评价量表(试用版)》由浙江师范大学(ZJNU)为主进行研发,组建了包括澳门大学(UMAC)、北卡大学(UNC at Chapel Hill)多名学者在内的多学科国际合作团队,历时3年进行项目筛选、标准化。在借鉴了ECERS-R过程质量观的基础上,该量表构建了适应中国社会文化背景的托幼机构教育质量评价的概念框架,萃取了中国幼儿园教育有证据支持的优质实践,经过了严谨的研发步骤,致力于使该量表成为能够全面衡量中国托幼机构教育质量的有效评价工具。

在内容结构(子量表—项目构成)上,《量表》与ECERS-R基本一致。不同的是,基于集体教学在我国托幼机构教育中的重要地位,我们增设了一个新的子量表"集体教学"。研究者首先对国内有关集体教学评价以及集体教学有效性的相关文献[22,23]进行了系统的梳理和总结,以确立集体教学子量表的项目框架。美国的《班级评定计分系统》[24]也为我们提供了有益的借鉴(比如,CLASS从情感支持、课堂组织和教学支持三个维度对班级中的人际互动进行测量,这些维度对于集体教学的评价同样重要)。经过充分的研讨和审慎考虑,新创建的"集体教学"子量表包含以下7个评价项目,主要评价内容如下:(1) 教学目标与内容:内容的适宜性,清晰的教学目标,目标和内容符合儿童的兴趣和经验;(2) 情感支持:课堂情绪情感氛围,老师对儿童情绪需求的回应能力,学生和老师之间的相互尊重;(3) 教学设计与组织:教学准备的充分性,组织教学活动、空间、设备和材料的运用;(4) 教学过程:课堂管理(行为、时间)、效率;(5) 教学支持:教学方法、促进幼儿语言和思维/技能的发展,对幼儿学习的反馈;(6) 幼儿表现:幼儿的参与、专注、态度、社会情感行为;(7) 课堂文化:集体教学中平等和公平的问题(如教师接受个体差异)。该子量表的增设,是对ECERS-R修订中最为重大的改变,是评价中国托幼机构教育质量必需的重要内容,也是我们重要的理论创新。

相对于ECERS-R而言,《量表》的另一个重大改变是为每个项目建构了评价的维度——在量表中称为“子项目”。这一做法受到了《中国幼儿园教育环境评价量表(试用版)》[25]的启发。“子项目”是对特定项目的不同角度或不同层面的评价。比如,子量表一的第1个项目“班级室内空间”由以下三个子项目组成:空间面积与结构、基础设施、安全与维护。每一个子项目,均由1分(不适当)、3分(合格)、5分(良好)、7分(优良)四个等级的具体指标来进行界定。子项目的增设加强了评价项目内容的逻辑性,同时也引起了每个项目评价内容的重组和指标的大量增加(ECERS-R是基于项目而非子项目建构,子项目的不同等级指标未必能够全部从ECERS-R中找到,因而需要为子项目创编和补充新的等级指标)。因此,即使许多项目保留了原来的名称和内容,其结构和内容也因为子项目的增设而作了一些或者较大的调整。这样,对于每个子项目而言,四个相应的等级指标实际上构成了一个特定方面质量水平变化的连续体,可能的分数为1、3、5或7。《量表》的这一新特性使得评分过程比ECERS-R更加容易,同时实现“对所有指标评分”的目的,防止由ECERS-R中所采用的“终止评分程序”所造成的“质量信息丢失”和“指标等级混乱”问题[26]。因此,使用《量表》,不仅能够得到项目分数(ECERS-R目前主要就是获得项目分),还能得到更多的子项目分(1,3,5或7)和所有指标的评分结果(“是”或“否”)。这为进一步深入分析《量表》的内容和测量学特性提供了良好的基础性架构。

除了“集体教学”子量表的增设和为每个项目创设若干子项目(评价维度),对ECERS-R的修订还包括:(1)对于反应灵敏但文化适宜性不足的指标,修订其解释及举例以体现文化适宜性;(2)对于反应不够灵敏的指标,调整(适当提高或降低)其评分尺度以适应我国国情(如重新界定了儿童自由游戏各个项目中“最低要求”、“良好”和“优秀”指标中对于时间的要求),提升其反应的灵敏性;(3)去除与中国文化和教育情境无关或暂不适用的指标(比如,鉴于融合教育在我国尚未普遍开展的国情,我们去除了分散在ECERS-R各个评价项目中关于支持特殊需求儿童的许多指标)。

1.1.3 专家实践者对《量表》内容和编制质量的评价

2011年下半年,研究者邀请了176位来自全国的专家型实践者(园长或骨干教师)对《量表》进行评价,主要是审视其能否作为中国幼儿园教育质量适宜的评价工具[27]。评价者被要求评价整个量表和每个子量表的内容适宜性和编制质量,与ECERS-R相比主要的变化[28],并对每个子量表的修订提出建议。总体来说,绝大多数(90.5%以上)评价者认为,《量表》比ECERS-R更适宜于中国文化和教育情境,是迄今为止最适宜的、最好的一个幼儿园教育质量评价工具;评价者们肯定了《量表》对ECERS-R的改变和修订,尤其对“集体教学”子量表的增设和子项目(评价维度)的建构持高度肯定态度[27]。这些证据表明了《量表》具有良好的内容效度。同时,一些评价者也对《量表》的一些具体指标表示了疑问或提出了具体的建议。这些疑问和建议的合理成分被吸收进后续的量表内容和指标的修订中。

1.1.4 《量表》与ECERS-R的内容比较

最终用于本研究的试用版《量表》包含8个子量表(见表1)51个评价项目177个子项目,采用了与ECERS-R同样的7点评分方式。为理清《量表》与ECERS-R的关系与异同,研究者在指标层面上对两个评价工具进行了内容分析。内容分析由熟悉两个评价工具的两位经验丰富的评分员各自独立进行;然后,《量表》首席研究者(本文第一作者)参与进来,与两位评分员就其间存在的分歧进行讨论,直到三个人消除分歧、达成一致意见。内容分析表明,《中国托幼机构教育质量评价量表(试用版)》中共包含685个具体评分指标,其中53.4%的指标是基于ECERS-R中的相应指标修订而来(修订的方式包括翻译、解释与举例的改编以及评分标准的调整),而其余46.6%的指标是《量表》独特的、自主研发的。

1.2 本研究的目的

基于Messick[29]的有关理论,我们将《量表》的效度验证看作一个宽泛的概念和持续的过程,各种形式的证据都可以用来支持《量表》使用的合理性和解释测量的分数。本次大规模研究就是为了检验《中国托幼机构教育质量评价量表(试用版)》的测量学属性;所获得的证据都有助于检视该《量表》在测量中国托幼机构教育质量方面的有效性。本研究是在地方教育行政部门、样本幼儿园、样本儿童家长知情同意的基础上开展的。

本研究旨在获得广泛的实证性证据来检验《量表》多个方面的测量学特性,包括(但不限于)评分者间一致性信度,《量表》内部一致性信度,《量表》和儿童发展结果(效标效度)之间的关系,《量表》和幼儿园等级评价标准(同时效度)之间的关系,以及《量表》的潜在结构的证据。

2 研究方法

2.1 样本

本研究在浙江省内根据不同的性质对幼儿园进行分层随机抽样:(1)根据浙江省政府经济发展水平(高、中、低)划分的地区;(2)根据当前浙江省幼儿园等级评价标准(优秀、良好、合格)的幼儿园;(3)根据不同的地理位置(城市、县、乡、村);(4)根据不同的资金来源(公立和私立)。最终,本研究共涵盖了91所幼儿园178个班级(每个幼儿园约抽取2个班级)。根据年龄划分,样本班级情况如下:小班45个,中班53个,大班74个,混龄班6个。每个班级随机抽取6名儿童进行儿童发展评价测试,测试主要包括语言、早期数学、社会认知和动作技能等领域,从而获得儿童发展的结果。

2.2 工具

2.2.1 《中国托幼机构质量评价量表(试用版)》

这是一个为中国的托幼机构教育质量评价而研发的班级观察量表,包含8个子量表、51个评价项目和177个子项目。如前所述,该量表借鉴了ECERS-R的过程质量观和基本的逻辑架构,但研发了许多独特的内容和指标,并对量表的测量学特性进行了优化,从而具有了许多不同于ECERS-R的新特性。但它同样运用了7点评分的里克特式量表,每个项目下有若干个子项目,每个子项目分为四个等级:1分(不适宜),3分(最低要求),5分(良好),7分(优秀)。项目得分的计算方法与ECERS-R相同,依据该项目下等级指标的评分结果进行由低到高的推算。子量表得分是该子量表下所有项目的均分。量表总分即所有被评项目的均分,用以代表托幼机构(班级)的整体质量。

2.2.2 浙江省幼儿园等级评价体系

该评价体系为当前浙江省教育行政部门运用的幼儿园评价工具,它将通过评估的幼儿园分成三个等级:省一级(优秀)、省二级(良好)、省三级(合格)。幼儿园等级评定主要采用查阅档案、园长报告和调查报告等方式;在评价指标上主要关注园所层面的结构性质量,但无法反映班级层面的过程性质量[30]。

2.2.3 《中国儿童发展量表(3—6岁)》

该量表是一套用于评价3—6岁儿童发展的常模测验工具,包含语言、早期数学、社会认知和动作技能四个子量表[31]。该工具被证明有良好的测量学属性[32]。

2.3 数据收集

2012年上半年,《量表》的第一作者培训了28名学前教育专业的硕士研究生成为合格的评分员,带领该团队运用《量表》对浙江省内6个地市91所幼儿园的178个班级进行了测试。每所幼儿园由评分员到达现场后随机选择2个左右不同年龄组的班级。每个班级安排3名评分员,其中2名评分员各自独立进行观察和评分。各自的评分结束后,再进行小组合议,对评分不一致的子项目和项目进行讨论,直至达成一致意见,给出小组评分。每个班级的观察时间一般为8个小时(从早晨幼儿入园到下午离园),包含中午大约30分钟对班级教室的访谈。同时,另一名评分员运用《中国儿童发展量表(3—6岁)》从班级中随机抽取6名左右儿童进行发展水平测查(内容包括语言、早期数学、社会认知、动作技能),共获取了1 012名幼儿的发展结果数据。

3 研究结果

3.1 测量信度

本研究中的测量信度包括评分者间一致性信度及量表的内部一致性信度,结果如下。

3.1.1　评分者间一致性

研究采用同组的两位评分员的原始评分(合议之前各自的评分),在子项目、项目、子量表和总量表水平上分别计算了量表的评分者间一致性。纳入统计的173个子项目中,两位评分者评分完全一致的比例为75%;51个项目中,两位评分者评分完全一致的比例为64%,1分以内一致性的比例为91%。项目水平上两位评分者原始评分的相关系数上,仅1个项目低于0.60(子量表五第36个项目"音像设备和电脑的使用",该项目仅适用于18%的班级),4个项目得分在0.60—0.70之间;其余46个项目的评分者间一致性信度估计值在0.70—0.90(总体均值为0.77)。考虑到类似量表单个项目的测量误差通常较大,因此本研究中项目水平上的评分者间一致性信度估计值已相当不错。8个子量表的评分者间一致性信度估计值处于0.85—0.94,均值为0.89。在《量表》总分水平上,评分者间一致性信度是0.94。对于这样的等级评分量表而言,这些数值显示了较高的评分者间一致性信度。与ECERS-R的评分者间一致性信度结果相比,本量表的结果更令人满意。

3.1.2　内部一致性

由表1可见,整个量表的Cronbach'α为0.98,显示了出色的内部一致性。8个子量表的α系数均大于0.83(处于0.83—0.93之间),均具有较好的内部一致性。这些数据表明,不仅《量表》总体上可以用于托幼机构的测量,每个子量表也可相对独立使用,服务于托幼机构特定方面的质量评价。

表1　《量表》内部一致性系数

子量表	内部一致性系数(Cronbach'α)
(一)空间与设施	0.93
(二)保育	0.89
(三)课程计划与实施	0.90
(四)集体教学	0.93
(五)游戏与活动	0.90
(六)语言与推理	0.83
(七)监护与互动	0.90
(八)家长和教师	0.89
总量表	0.98

3.2　测量效度

3.2.1　同时效度

本研究中的91所幼儿园,其中81所通过了浙江省幼儿园等级评定(17所省一级园,32所省二级园,32所省三级园)。其余10所幼儿园有办学许可证但没有通过等级评定,这10所无等级幼儿园的数据没有被采用。目前,浙江省幼儿园等级评定标准对于这些幼儿园来说是唯一有效的质量指标。这个质量分类是独立于本研究的，样本幼儿园的等级信息也没有透露给评分者。本研究分析了《量表》得分与幼儿园等级的相关性，以作为同时效度证据的一个来源。

运用多元方差方法分析幼儿园三个等级是否与《量表》得分有显著差异。由图1可知，浙江省幼儿园等级评定的结果与《量表》的评价结果一致。幼儿园的三个等级在该量表8个子量表上的得分明显不同，并且等级高低（一级——优秀、二级——良好、三级——合格）与8个子量表的得分趋势完全一致。另外，多元方差分析结果表明，三个等级的幼儿园在8个子量表上的得分具有显著性差异（Wilk's $\lambda = 0.415$，$F_{(df1=16,\ df2=302)} = 10.43$，$p < 0.001$）。此外，幼儿园的三个等级在每个子量表得分上的两两比较也具有显著性差异（$p < 0.001$）。

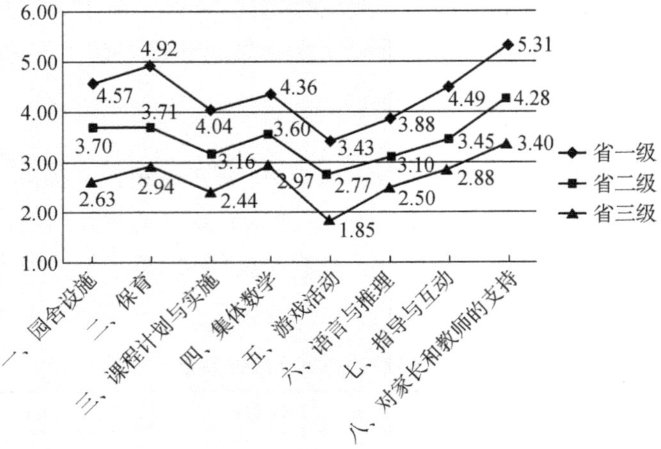

图1　中国托幼机构教育质量评价量表在幼儿园等级上的得分

在效应量方面，多元 R^2（见公式（1））接近0.585，表明幼儿园的三个等级在《量表》的8个子量表上的得分解释了将近59%的变量。在教育研究中，这是一个相当大的效应量[33-35]。单因素方差分析模型下的效应量（比较幼儿园的三个等级在每个子量表上的得分）也是非常大的，对于这8个子量表而言，R^2 的范围从0.28—0.50 。毫无疑问，幼儿园的三个等级在《量表》总分上也具有显著性差异（$p < 0.001$），同时也得到了一个相当大的效应量（$R^2 = 0.48$）。这些分析结果显示了两个独立的质量评价体系的结果具有良好的聚合性。因此，这些研究结果为《量表》的同时效度提供了一个强有力的证据。

$$R^2 \approx 1 - \text{wilk's } \lambda \tag{1}$$

3.2.2　效标关联效度

本研究还使用了《中国儿童发展量表（3—6岁）》[31]对儿童进行测试。研究者从每个班级随机抽取5—6名儿童，总共从178个班级中抽取了1 012名儿童。对数据进行筛选后,排除了在园时长少于6个月的儿童,因为时间过短,很难观测到托幼机构的环境和教育对儿童发展的影响。因此,我们排除了77个样本,最终的样本量为来自163个班级中的935名幼儿。

表2的上半部分为《量表》得分与样本儿童发展结果的二元相关。直接的零阶相关分析结果表明,除了动作技能与《量表》的质量指标关系较弱,其他3个子量表得分(语言、早期数学、社会认知)与《量表》的质量指标具有显著的相关性(-0.20—0.30)。由于儿童的年龄及其家庭社会经济背景可能在《量表》得分和儿童发展结果之间产生一定的作用,进而,我们采用了偏二元相关的分析方法,目的是控制儿童的年龄及其父母的受教育背景(父母的平均受教育年限,这是研究者能够获取的唯一一个与家庭社会经济水平相关的变量)对这两组变量的影响。由表2的下半部分可见,在控制儿童的年龄以及父母的受教育背景后,相比之前零阶二元相关的结果,儿童语言、早期数学以及社会认知的得分与《量表》各项得分的相关系数略有降低(-0.10—0.20)。但总体来说,《量表》效标关联效度的结果同样优于ECERS[35]和ECERS-R[36]的研究结果。同时,值得指出的是,尽管儿童的动作技能与《量表》得分呈现较弱的关系,但与《量表》总分以及"集体教学"、"语言与推理"、"指导与互动"三个子量表得分显著相关。

表2 中国托幼机构教育质量评价量表与儿童发展结果的关系

(N=935,来自于178个班级)

儿童发展量表	子量表和量表总分								
	1. 空间与设施	2. 保育	3. 课程计划与实施	4. 集体教学	5. 游戏与活动	6. 语言与推理	7. 指导与互动	8. 家长与教师	总分
零阶相关									
语言	0.23**	0.22**	0.21**	0.26**	0.19**	0.26**	0.22**	0.27**	0.26**
早期数学	0.23**	0.23**	0.19**	0.26**	0.18**	0.27**	0.24**	0.26**	0.26**
社会认知	0.24**	0.24**	0.19**	0.25**	0.22**	0.25**	0.22**	0.30**	0.26**
动作技能	0.02	0.04	0.02	0.07*	0.00	0.08*	0.08*	0.05	0.05
偏相关(控制幼儿年龄、父母教育背景)[a]									
语言	0.13**	0.15**	0.08**	0.15**	0.14**	0.14**	0.14**	0.16**	0.15**
早期数学	0.14**	0.17**	0.11**	0.13**	0.13*	0.15**	0.17**	0.18**	0.17**
社会认知	0.13**	0.14**	0.08**	0.10**	0.10**	0.13**	0.13**	0.18**	0.14**
动作技能	0.01	0.02	0.02	0.09**	0.03	0.09**	0.10**	0.03	0.11**

注:a. 偏相关控制了幼儿年龄、父母的教育水平(受教育年限)。**:$p<0.01$;*:$p<0.05$

3.2.3 结构效度

为了探明本量表的结构效度,我们运用本次测量数据进行了探索性因素分析。最后一个子量表"家长与教师"被去除,因为该子量表的项目内容与幼儿发展不直接相关;同时也去除了缺失值较多的项目,因为部分班级在部分项目上被评为"不适用",这些项目分别是安抚和独处的空间、课堂文化、音像设备和电脑以及尊重和欣赏差异。因此,最终纳入因素分析的项目共有41个。

在因素分析中,基于传统特征根值大于1的办法,共可以提取四个因子[37,39]。然而,特征根值碎石图的拐点效应却表明只可以提取两个因子。平行分析法[40,41],即把真实的数据特征根值与随机抽样的数据特征根值做比较[42],表明应该只保留前两个因子(如图2)。基于以上分析,本研究共提取了两个因子,这两个因子的方差贡献率为61%。斜交旋转呈现了一个清晰的量表因子结构,两个因子之间的相关系数是0.76(表3)。同时,这两个因子的成分相当明确(详见表3):组成因子Ⅰ的项目主要来自子量表一(空间与设施)和子量表五(游戏与活动);组成因子Ⅱ的项目主要来自子量表四(集体教学)、子量表六(语言与推理)、子量表七(指导与互动)。通过进一步的分析发现,这个因子结构具有实质性意义,同时,与Sakai等人[43]的关于ECERS-R的两因子结构有很大的相似性。类似于Sakai等人[43]的解释,我们把因子Ⅰ暂命名为"学习条件",即为幼儿的学习所提供的条件,涉及各类空间、设施、材料及其使用,以及对各类游戏活动的安排(包括空间、材料、机会与时间、设计与指导等);把因子Ⅱ暂命名为"教学与互动",主要指与早期儿童教育相关的集体教学、人际互动与活动指导。这说明《量表》既保持了与ECERS-R结构上的延续性,同时又能抓住中国托幼机构教育质量的核心要素,具有良好的结构效度和本土文化适宜性。但需要注意的是,子量表二"保育"、子量表三"课程计划与实施"中多个项目出现了交叉负载的现象,归属于哪个因子并不明确。这些项目在未来的量表修订中,有必要对其内容和指标进行深入的检视。

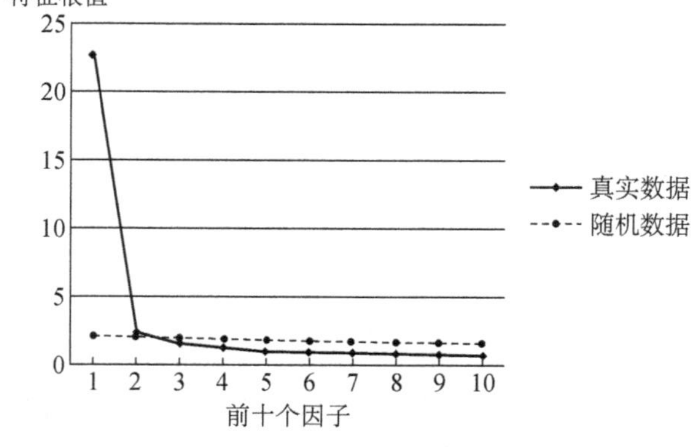

图2 真实数据和随机数据的前十个特征根值

表3　两因子结构（$N=178$）

子量表	项目	因子（$r=0.76$）	
		Ⅰ	Ⅱ
（一）空间与设施（9）（项目6排除）	1.1　班级室内空间	0.841	
	1.2　家具/教学设备	0.769	
	1.3　卫生间	0.571	
	1.4　午睡的空间与设施	0.447	
	1.5　活动区角	0.812	
	1.7　环境装饰和幼儿作品展示	0.664	
	1.8　户外/体育活动场地与设施	0.870	
	1.9　满足教师需求的空间与设施	0.904	
（二）保育（6）	2.10　入园/离园		0.450
	2.11　如厕/盥洗/饮水	0.426	0.450
	2.12　进餐	0.402	0.393
	2.13　午睡/休息	0.557	
	2.14　健康	0.497	0.359
	2.15　安全	0.649	
（三）课程计划与实施（5）	3.16　一周课程计划	0.424	0.374
	3.17　一日活动安排与组织	0.467	0.414
	3.18　自由游戏	0.558	
	3.19　集体活动	0.355	0.494
	3.20　户外/体育活动	0.589	
（四）集体教学（7）（项目27排除）	4.21　目标与内容		0.832
	4.22　情感支持		0.912
	4.23　教学设计与组织		0.803
	4.24　教学过程		0.977
	4.25　教学支持		0.816
	4.26　幼儿表现		0.766

续表 3

子量表	项目	因子($r=0.76$)	
		Ⅰ	Ⅱ
(五) 游戏与活动(9)(项目 36 排除)	5.28　角色/戏剧游戏	0.762	
	5.29　建构游戏	0.707	
	5.30　精细操作活动	0.662	
	5.31　数学	0.813	
	5.32　自然/科学	0.761	
	5.33　音乐/律动	0.393	
	5.34　美术	0.709	
	5.35　沙/水	0.851	
(六) 语言与推理(4)	6.37　图书和阅读	0.586	
	6.38　鼓励幼儿沟通	0.405	0.461
	6.39　日常交流		0.773
	6.40　概念与推理		0.558
(七) 指导与互动(5)(项目 45 排除)	7.41　指导和监护		0.724
	7.42　常规和纪律		0.735
	7.43　师幼互动		0.721
	7.44　同伴互动		0.865
(八) 家长和教师(6)	6 个项目都被排除;这些项目是通过访谈得到,而不是根据班级观察		

4　讨论

在中国社会文化和教育情境中,迫切需要对托幼机构教育质量进行有效的评价,以便把改进托幼机构教育质量的努力建立在科学实证的基础上——而不仅仅是依据行政命令或政策文件。然而,对于早期教育实践工作者和研究者而言,缺乏具有良好测量学特性的评价工具,是托幼机构发展和质量改进的主要障碍之一。《中国托幼机构教育质量评价量表》(CECERS) 的研发正是为了填补这一空缺,致力于成为中国托幼机构质量评价的有效工具。基于 Messick[27] 关于测量工具效度验证的整合性理论,本文呈现并讨论了多角度的证据以表明《量表》具有足够的适应力按照设计的目标正常发挥功能。

4.1　关于《量表》的测量信度

在测量信度方面,本研究考虑和计算了多种形式的信度指标,包括量表的内部一致性(比如,Cronbach's α),以及在多种测量水平上的评分者间一致性(比如,项目得分水平、子量表得分水平和总量表得分水平)。在另一项研究中,研究者运用概化理论对本次测量进行了信度估计[43]。以上多种实证性分析结果表明,《量表》具有相当不错的测量信度;同时,这些结果总体上优于类似的测量工具(比如ECERS或ECERS-R)[9,45]。当然,《量表》的内部一致性很高,也提示研究者在将来的修订中进一步检视量表各个项目中的评价指标和内容,把项目间可能的交叉重复降至最低程度。

4.2 关于《量表》的测量效度

在测量效度方面,研究者努力获取了多种形式的证据并运用了多种分析路径,以验证这些不同形式的证据是否共同支持该量表的有效性。在传统意义上的同时效度方面,研究者采用了多元方差分析与判别分析方法,检验了样本班级的量表得分与所在幼儿园的政府评级结果之间的相互关系。分析结果显示,量表得分与幼儿园的办园等级之间具有良好的聚合性,表明《量表》较好地体现了设计意图,能够发挥测量和区分中国托幼机构教育质量的功能。

在效标关联效度上,研究者运用了多种分析方法检验了量表得分与儿童发展结果(语言、早期数学、社会认知以及动作技能)之间的相互关系模型。零阶二元相关以及偏相关(控制了儿童年龄、作为家庭社会经济地位代表性指标的父母亲受教育水平)的结果显示了与预期一致的清晰的相互关系结果模型。二元相关分析(零阶相关和偏相关)的结果为《量表》的效度提供了有力的证据,表明该量表得分能够作为中国托幼机构教育质量的指标,理论上,高质量的托幼机构教育更有利于儿童的发展。同时,两者相关性的程度优于本领域的一些权威测量工具所报告的结果,比如ECERS[36]、ECERS-R[37]。

从结果数据上看,量表得分与儿童发展结果之间的相关性程度并不高(比如,零阶相关系数为0.20—0.30,偏相关系数为0.10—0.20),但在同类研究中,这种大小的效应量作为效度的证据已经非常充分了。从儿童发展的生态学视角来看,儿童的发展实际上受到一系列复杂因素的影响[7];在这一错综复杂的环境系统中,托幼机构教育仅仅是其中的一小部分,因而,与儿童发展结果相关性不高是合理的。同时,本研究中所揭示的托幼机构教育质量与儿童发展结果之间的相关性程度优于类似的工具。

值得注意的是,“集体教学”子量表与儿童发展结果的每一个方面(包括语言、早期数学、社会认知和动作技能)均展现出一致的稳定关联。这些证据让我们相信“集体教学”这一子量表在中国社会文化背景中能够敏感地反映和评价托幼机构的教育质量。

另一方面,研究结果显示量表得分与儿童动作技能的发展关系微弱。多种社会和文化上的原因可能会导致这一结果。在中国目前的社会环境中,教育竞争高度激烈,家长和教育工作者大都把知识获得和学业成绩看得比任何其他事情都重要[20,46]。进而,就连在幼儿园中,可供幼儿进行户外/体育活动的有效时间也被牺牲了。自从1980年初的“独生子女政策”以来,中国家庭中的育儿环境逐渐演变成“6:1”的模式(即6位成人高度关切1个孩子)。家长的“安全焦虑”自然会传递给幼儿园教师,给教师带来了巨大的心理压力，为自我保护而不得不采取“过度保护”式的教育方式，尽可能减少户外/体育活动的自由程度和挑战性，甚至少组织“危险的”户外体育活动[47]。另外一些情境因素也有可能会削弱托幼机构教育经验与儿童运动能力之间的关联性，比如，户外活动场地和设施的有限性，过多的集体化的组织方式而缺乏幼儿的自由体育活动，导致了个体儿童运动机会和时间的有限性和运动量的严重不足[48]。

为探索《量表》的内部结构，研究者进行了探索性因素分析（EFA），并采用了“最佳策略”（即“平行分析”）以决定因子数目的保留。探索性因素分析揭示了一个两因子的结构模型——这一结构在很大程度上与 ECERS 以及 ECERS-R 的一些研究结果相近[43]，并同样把这两个因子分别称为“学习条件”和“教学与互动”。但鉴于类似评价工具（即 ECERS 与 ECERS-R）因子分析的相关研究结果（即所探索出的因子数量以及各个因子所包含的项目）往往并不一致[43,49-51]，我们把本研究中的因子分析的结果也看作试探性的。这一因子结构的稳定性和可推论性有待于未来新的样本数据的检验。

综上所述，我们以宽宏的视角从多个维度检验了《中国托幼机构教育质量评价量表（试用版）》的测量信度和效度。本研究所呈现和讨论的这些结果与 ECERS 和 ECERS-R 相比更加可取。这一系列的证据支持我们得出结论：《量表》显示了良好的测量学属性；正如 ECERS 和 ECERS-R 在美国教育情境中所发挥的功能与作用，《量表》也能在中国教育情境中为托幼机构教育质量提供有价值的评价指标。

4.3 局限与展望

当然，本研究也存在一些局限性，这些局限性也预示了未来的研究方向。比如，本研究的样本量尽管已经不小，但难以同时支持探索性和验证性因素分析（如将样本分成两半，一半用于探索性因素分析，一半用于验证性因素分析）。将来需要收集更大、更具代表性的样本，以检验本研究探索出来的因子结构的普遍性和稳定性。将来，可以同时使用本量表和其他权威的托幼机构质量测量工具（如 ECERS-R 或 CLASS）进行数据采集，以进一步检验《量表》的同时效度，也是非常重要的。同时，使用纵向研究设计更好的儿童发展评价工具，多次收集儿童发展结果数据，也是十分必要的（以检验《量表》的预测效度）。另外，也需要运用新的数据分析技术（如项目反应理论），从不同角度更深入、更具体地（比如在子项目或指标水平上）分析《量表》的心理测量学特性。在本研究结果的基础上，通过不断的研究努力，《中国托幼机构教育质量评价量表》有潜力成为中国社会和文化背景下有效的托幼机构质量测量工具。该量表对引领和提高中国托幼机构的教育质量有望发挥重要作用。

致谢

本文为全国教科规划国家社科基金青年项目“基于多维整合观的中国托幼机构教育质量评价研究”（主持人：李克建；项目编号：CHA110131），全国教科规划国家社科基金重点项目“保障适龄儿童接受基本而有质量的学前教育政策和机制研究”（主持人：秦金亮；项目编号：AHA110004）的阶段性成果之一。

References

[1] Central People's Government of the People's Republic of China. Compendium for China's mid-and long-term education development. www. gov. cn/jrzg/2010-07/29/content_1667143. htm, 2011.

[2] Dai S X, Liu X. Current evaluation tools for preschool quality rating in China. Studies in Early Childhood Education, 2003, 7: 39 - 41.

[3] Li K, Hu B. On quality assessment of early childhood programs in the international contexts and reconstructing related conceptions in China. Comparative Education Review, 2012, 7: 15 - 20.

[4] Liu Y. Several issues regarding preschool program quality evaluation. Studies in Preschool Education, 1998, 3: 14 - 17.

[5] Pan Y, Liu Y, Lau E. Evaluation of the kindergarten quality rating system in Beijing. Early Education and Development, 2010, 2: 186 - 204.

[6] Li K, Hu B. The Quality rating system of Chinese preschool education: Prospects and challenges. Childhood Education, 2012, 1: 14 - 22.

[7] Bronfenbrenner U. The Ecology of Human Development: Experiments by Nature and Design. Cambridge, MA: Harvard University Press, 1979.

[8] Harms T, Clifford R M. Early Childhood Environment Rating Scale. New York: Teachers College Press, 1980.

[9] Harms T, Clifford R M, Cryer D. Early Childhood Environment Rating Scale (Rev. ed.). New York: Teachers College Press, 2005.

[10] Gol-Guven M. Evaluation of the quality of early childhood class- rooms in Turkey. Early Child Development and Care, 2009, 4: 437 - 451.

[11] Myers R G. In search of quality programmes of early child- hood care and education. Background paper for Education for All, Global Monitoring Report 2005. Paris, France: UNESCO, 2004.

[12] Villalon M, Suzuki E, Herrera M O, et al. Quality of chilean early childhood education from an international perspective. International Journal of Early Years Education, 2002, 1: 49 - 59.

[13] Lim J T. A preliminary study on validation of ECERS. Journal of Education, 1983, 10: 107 - 143.

[14] Kärrby G. A Swedish Research Version of the Early Childhood Environment Rating Scale (ECERS). Goïeborg, Sweden: University of Gothenburg, Department of Education, 1989.

[15] Kärrby G, Giota J. Dimensions of quality in Swedish day care centers: Ananlysis of early childhood environment rating scale. Early Child Development and Care, 1994, 104: 1 - 22.

[16] Aboud F E. Evaluation of an early childhood preschool program in rural Bangladesh. Early Childhood Research Quarterly, 2006, 1: 46 - 60.

[17] Isley B J. Tamil Nadu Early Childhood Environment Rating Scale (TECERS). Madras, India:

M. S. Swaminathan Research Foundation, 2000.

[18] Li K J, Hu B Y, Pan Y, et al. Chinese Early Childhood Environment Rating Scale (trial) (CECERS): A Validity Study. Early Childhood Research Quarterly, available online 21 March 2014. http://dx. doi. org/10. 1016/j. ecresq. 2014. 02. 007.

[19] Li K, Hu B, Pan Y, et al. Exploring the ECERS- R's cultural adaptability for early childhood education in China. (submitted for publication),2013.

[20] Tobin J, Hsueh Y, Karasawa M. Preschool in Three Cultures Revisited: China, Japan, and the United States. Chicago, IL: University of Chicago Press, 2009.

[21] Ng S S N, Rao N. Teaching mathematics in Hong Kong: A comparison between the pre-primary and early primary years. Hong Kong Journal of Early Childhood, 2005, 1: 30 - 36.

[22] Yu Y P. Evaluating group teaching activities in kindergartens. Early Education, 2005, 3: 8 - 9.

[23] Yang J, Wang C. A reflection on the effectiveness of kindergarten group teaching activities. Early Childhood Education, 2013, 4: 17 - 20.

[24] Pianta R C, La Paro K M, Hamre B K. Classroom Assessment Scoring System (CLASS) Manual, Pre-k. Baltimore, MD: Paul H. Brookes, 2007.

[25] Liu Y, Pan Y (unpublished). Kindergarten Environment Rating Scale (KERS). Unpublished instrument.

[26] Gordon R A, Fujimoto K, Kaestner R, et al. An assess- ment of the validity of the ECERS-R with implications for measures of child care quality and relations to child development. Developmental Psychology, 2013, 49: 146 - 160.

[27] Hu B, Zhou Y, Li K, et al. Examining program quality disparities between urban and rural Kindergartens in China: Evidence from Zhejiang. Journal of Research in Childhood Education (in press), 2014.

[28] Guo-Li Z W, Chen S F. Early Childhood Environment Rating Scale Revised Edition (ECERS-R). Taipei: Psychology Press, 2006.

[29] Messick S. Validity//R L Linn. Educational Measurement. 3rd ed. New York: Macmillan, 1989.

[30] Li K J. Quality rating system for kindergarten under the scientific concept of development: Experiences from Zhejiang province. Early Childhood Education, 2010, 4: 1 - 5.

[31] Zhang H C, Zhou R, Chen G M, et al. Children's Developmental Scale of China (age 3—6). Beijing: Child Development Center of China, 1992.

[32] Zhou R, Zhang H C. The development of Children's Developmental Scale (age 3 to 6). The Science of Psychology, 1994, 3: 137 - 192.

[33] Cohen J. Statistical Power Analysis for the Behavioral Sciences. 2nd ed. Hillsdale, NJ: Erlbaum, 1988.

[34] Fan X. Statistical significance and effect size: Two sides of a coin. Journal of Educational Research, 2001, 5: 275 - 282.

[35] Stevens J. Applied multivariate statistics for the social sciences. 5th ed. New York: Routledge, 2009.

[36] Peisner-Feinberg E S, Burchinal M R, Clifford R M, et al. The relation of preschool child-care quality to children's cognitive and social developmental trajectories through second grade. Child Development, 2001, 72: 1534 - 1553.

[37] Burchinal M, Howes C, Pianta R, et al. Predicting child outcomes at the end of kindergarten from the quality of pre-kindergarten teacher - child interactions and instruction. Applied Developmental Science, 2008, 12: 140 - 153.

[38] Guttman L. Some necessary conditions for common-factor analysis. Psychometrika, 1954, 19: 149 - 161.

[39] Kaiser H. The application of electronic computers to factor analysis. Educational and Psychological Measurement, 1960, 1: 141 - 151.

[40] Horn J L. A rationale and test for the number of factors in factor analysis. Psychometrika, 1965, 2: 179 - 185.

[41] Thompson B. Exploratory and Confirmatory Factor Analysis: Understanding Concepts and Applications. Washington, DC: American Psychological Association, 2004.

[42] Widaman K F. Exploratory factor analysis and confirmatory factor analysis//H Cooper, P M Camic, D L Long, et al. APA handbook of research methods in psychology. Washington, DC: American Psychological Association, 2012.

[43] Sakai L M, Whitebook M, Wishard A, et al. Evaluating the Early Childhood Environment Rating Scale (ECERS): Assessing differences between the first and revised editions. Early Childhood Research Quality, 2003, 4: 427 - 445.

[44] Chen D, Hu B, Fan X, et al. Measurement quality of the Chinese Early Childhood Program Rating Scale (CECPRS): An investigation using multivariate generalizability theory. Journal of Psychoeducational Assessment, 2014, 32: 236 - 248.

[45] Clifford R M, Reszka S S, Rossbach H-G. Reliability and validity of the Early Childhood Environment Rating Scale. Unpublished manuscript, 2010, 4: 25 - 32.

[46] Li H, Rao N. Influences on literacy attainment: Evidence from Beijing, Hong Kong and Singapore. International Journal of Early Years Education, 2005, 3: 235 - 253.

[47] Hu B, Li K, De Marco A, et al. Examining the quality of outdoor play in Chinese kindergartens. (Manuscript accepted by International Journal of Early Childhood, IJEC), 2014.

[48] Chen Y W, Hu B Y, Li K J. The relationship between outdoor play's quality and children's motor development. Studies in Preschool Education, 2013, 4: 25 - 32.

[49] Gordon R A, Fujimoto K, Kaestner R, et al. An assess- ment of the validity of the ECERS-R with implications for measures of child care quality and relations to child development. Developmental Psychology, 2013, 49: 146 - 160.

[50] Holloway S D, Kagan S, Fuller B, et al. Assessing child-care quality with a telephone interview. Early Childhood Research Quarterly, 2001, 2: 165 - 189.

[51] Perlman M, Zellman G L, Le V. Examining the psychometric properties of the early childhood environment rating scale-revised (ECERS-R). Early Childhood Research Quarterly, 2004, 3: 398 - 412.

后 记

2014年5月,在韦钰院士的积极倡导和支持下,东南大学学习科学研究中心(简称中心)在南京紫金山庄召开了"儿童早期发展前沿研究国际会议",此时正值中心成立10周年之际,这无疑是对中心10年工作的最好总结。

学习科学研究中心暨儿童发展与学习科学教育部重点实验室创建于2002年,是在国际前沿的神经教育学研究领域中,围绕儿童发展和学习科学开展多学科交叉的转换研究,建立了一个从基因、神经递质、生理心理、脑功能到行为的多层次的儿童发展与学习科学的转化研究平台,我们的目的在于为我国儿童发展和基础教育改革及创新能力的培养提供实证性的研究支持。在韦钰院士的长期领导下,实验室吸引了一批国内外的优秀人才,凝聚成了一支富有创新性的研究队伍,包括有中国工程院院士、长江学者特聘教授、青年专家、科研贡献奖获得者以及学科带头人,同时还培养了大批专业人才。中心承担了"985"二期和三期建设项目,同时承担了"973"、"863"和国家自然科学基金,以及教育部人文社科类基金等一批国家和省部级科研项目,科研经费总额超过2 500万元。到目前为止,中心获得全国基础教育课程改革成果一等奖一项、教育部自然科学奖二等奖一项、江苏省科技进步二等奖三等奖各一项;中心申请国家发明专利41项,其中已授权发明专利22项,在国内外核心期刊发表论文314篇,其中被SCI和SSCI收录的论文158篇;中心与国内外知名大学及研究院所开展了广泛的合作,有国际合作项目4项,承办国际学术会议6次;学习中心的目标就是希望对中国儿童的养育和教育产生积极和深远的影响,并将不断努力为我国教育政策的制定和选择提供科学依据。

会议论文集的编写得到了国内外专家学者和教育领导者的关心、指导和支持。韦钰院士特地为此论文集撰写了序言，在此表示衷心的感谢！

参与本论文集整理工作的还有学习科学研究中心朱艳梅博士、金怡老师，还有来自中心科学教育与技术应用研究室的研究生张叶欣、刘佳、徐燕、刘枳杉等，在此一并表示衷心的感谢！还要感谢东南大学出版社领导江建中社长、李涛书记，以及戴丽副社长、张新建总编辑和唐允编辑，正是他们的共同努力才使得此论文集得以顺利出版。

东南大学学习科学研究中心　柏毅于李文正楼

儿童发展与学习科学教育部重点实验室

http://rcls.seu.edu.cn

by.rcls@seu.edu.cn

2014 年 12 月 31 日